Principles of

DATABASE SYSTEMS

with Internet
and Java Applications

Principles of

DATABASE SYSTEMS

with Internet and Java Applications

Greg Riccardi
Florida State University

Addison
Wesley

Boston San Francisco New York
London Toronto Sydney Tokyo Singapore Madrid
Mexico City Munich Paris Cape Town Hong Kong Montreal

Senior Acquisitions Editor	Maite Suarez-Rivas
Project Editor	Katherine Harutunian
Production Services	Diane Freed
Executive Marketing Manager	Michael Hirsch
Senior Prepress Supervisor and Manufacturing	Caroline Fell
Cover Design	Leslie Haimes
Interior Design	Geri Davis for the Davis Group
Design Manager	Gina Hagen
Composition	Rob Mauhar
Technical Art	George Nichols

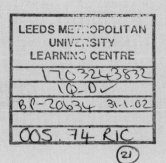
Access the latest information about Addison-Wesley titles from our World Wide Web site at `http://www.awl.com/cs`

The programs and applications presented in this book have been included for their instructional value. They have been tested with care but are not guaranteed for any purpose. The publisher does not offer any warranties or representations, not does it accept any liabilities with respect to the programs or applications.

All Java code, sample databases in Microsoft Access, and sample databases in SQL are available to the readers from the ftp site `ftp.aw.com` in the directory `cseng/authors/riccardi/database`.

Library of Congress Cataloging-In-Publication Data

Riccardi, Greg.
   Principles of database systems with Internet and Java applications / Greg Riccardi.
     p. cm.
  ISBN 0-201-61247-X
     1. Database management. 2. Internet (Computer network) 3. Java (Computer program language) I. Title.
   QA76.9.D3 R52 2001
   005.75'8—dc21

00-029314

2 3 4 5 6 7 8 9 0 DOH 03020100

To my wife, Ann,
and my daughters,
Mary, Christina, and Elizabeth

Contents

Advanced Data Models   55

3

The Relational Data Model   71

4

Improving the Quality of Database Designs   95

5

All Java code, sample databases in Microsoft Access, and sample databases in SQL are available to the readers from the ftp site `ftp.aw.com` in the directory `cseng/ authors/riccardi/database`.

Preface

*P*rinciples of Database Systems with Internet and Java Applications provides a concise and modern treatment of introductory database topics that is suitable for use in undergraduate database courses, applications-oriented courses on database interaction with the World Wide Web, and professional development. As part of this effort, it enlists Java and the Internet to add an applications perspective to the core DBMS theory.

This book covers the basic material related to information management, database systems, Java programming, and interaction with databases on the World Wide Web. It assumes that readers have a background in programming and helps them to improve their skills in the design and implementation of complex information systems.

Information management is the central theme of *Principles of Database Systems*. It motivates the development of data models and the representation of information in relational database systems. Readers learn how to define information content with Entity–Relationship models as well as how to represent that content in relational database systems. Along the way, they become thoroughly familiar with SQL, the Structured Query Language, plus the advanced features of relational database systems. They learn exactly what is required to build high-quality, information-rich applications. In addition, they see how the Web and Java can work together to help them publish and collect information in the widest possible context.

Database and information systems material is covered extensively in this book. Topics include analyzing information requirements, developing conceptual data models, translating conceptual models into relational models, normalizing and improving relational schemas, writing queries in SQL, and developing database applications. Interesting examples are used to show students how to apply this material. Additional topics include object-oriented modeling and databases, database performance and optimization, constraints and triggers, transactions, backup and recovery, file structures, indexing, and distributed object technology.

The thorough treatment of relational database systems includes the use of readily available database tools, such as Microsoft Access, SQL databases, and object-oriented design tools. Microsoft Access is used to illustrate the role of relational models in developing information applications. We demonstrate the use of SQL databases with ODBC interaction and with JDBC and Java. Instructors will be able to use the programming projects in Oracle or adapt them to other relational database systems as desired.

Java provides the basis for discussing how information is represented in an object-oriented language. The presentation of this programming language begins with a description of how it interacts with relational database systems. In addition, Java is employed in creating Web interactions, representing file structures and indexes, creating distributed applications, and designing object-oriented data models. A student who is familiar with an object-oriented language will be able to readily understand this material. In contrast, one who is not already a Java programmer will benefit by perusing the appendix on Java and may need to consult a language supplement.

The interaction between applications and databases is discussed and illustrated in the context of Web sites. The JDBC classes of Java provide a database- and platform-independent method of creating database applications. The book includes a thorough discussion of these classes, puncuated with abundant examples. After learning the fundamentals of HTML and CGI programming, students are asked to create their own Web sites using Java programs to service CGI requests and generate HTML responses. Additional topics include the use of Java servlets to replace CGI programs and the development of simple Java applets as database user interfaces.

The important principles of file structures are presented in a way that emphasizes software development. Students are shown an object-oriented style of representing information in files. The book includes class definitions for direct-access file I/O, buffer packing and unpacking, indexing, and B+ trees. The file structures section ends by discussing methods of implementing relational database systems.

Database Applications and Examples

Among the unique features of this book are its emphasis on software development, its use of the Java programming language, and its presentation of the World Wide Web as a tool for database interaction. Java is used to first introduce object-oriented methods and then apply those methods to produce database applications. Its support for database interaction is the key to success in providing access to information on the Internet. Detailed discussions of the interaction between Java and the Web make it clear just what is required to create useful applications. As a consequence, this book will prove particularly appealing to instructors who want to make their database courses relevant to Internet activities.

Complex information applications are introduced early in the book and used throughout to illustrate the concepts and the details. *BigHit Video Company*, a (fictional) chain of video rental and sales stores, provides our major example. The information and application needs of this company are sufficient to construct applications that range from simple to complex. Each new topic is fully illustrated by showing how it can be used to satisfy the needs of specific information applications.

Supplementary materials that are available online include the database, SQL, and programming examples that are included in the book. In addition, full implementations of the Microsoft Access database examples are available to the instructors. These databases are carefully constructed to allow students to extend and enhance them for course projects. The SQL examples are suitable for use in Access or any other standard SQL database system. We have taken care to ensure that the SQL code used both in this book and in the supplements comes from a subset of standard SQL that is universally applicable.

A Book for Teaching Database Systems

The upper-division course in database systems for computer science is one of the most important courses in the curriculum, because it combines the needs of users, developers, and maintainers of software systems. Instructors must present a blend of topics that allows students to understand what is required to satisfy these diverse needs. Although students taking this course may already have a significant amount of expertise in computer programming, they still need to learn how to combine analysis, design, and programming skills to produce useful and effective software.

A database course for computer science majors must include the basics of information systems design and implementation, relational database systems, and SQL. It must improve the general skills and maturity of the students as they seek to become software professionals. Finally, it must motivate students to work hard—a goal easily accomplished by a particularly interesting course.

The premise of this book is that combining databases, Java, and the World Wide Web will produce a course that is extremely effective in meeting these challenges. It will be particularly appealing to students because of its presentation of up-to-date and interesting material.

The most appealing and exciting part of a database course may be the development of database applications that support Web sites. In *Principles of Database Systems,* the object-oriented programming theme is extended to show how application programs can interact with databases using SQL. The book covers the basics of HTML, HTML forms, and CGI programming. It even includes the use of Java servlets as an alternative to CGI.

Students do not need extensive experience with Java before using this book. Here, the coverage of Java starts from very basic classes and progressively includes more complex structures as required. Students who know any object-oriented language will understand the programming examples and exercises.

Possible Course Outlines

At least three approaches to teaching database systems can benefit from this book: a traditional database systems course, an object-oriented database applications course, and an applications-oriented database course. All courses will cover the introduction and the chapters on data modeling, Entity–Relationship modeling and its extensions, relational schemas, manipulation of relational information, and SQL. My experience is that these common topics take approximately one-half semester. This material is covered in the following chapters:

- Chapter 1: Information Management and Database Systems;
- Part 1: Chapters 2–5, Information Models and Relational Databases; and
- Part 2: Chapters 6–7, Manipulating Relational Data.

In a traditional database systems course, the greatest emphasis in the remainder of the course is placed on ways that relational database systems contribute to information systems. The major emphasis focuses on how relational database systems are built on a foundation of file structures and indexing, how queries are executed and optimized, and how concurrency, transactions, security, and backup and recovery are supported. This material is covered in the following chapters:

- Part 4: Chapters 11–12, Physical Characteristics of Databases; and
- Part 5: Chapters 13–15, Achieving Performance and Reliability with Relational Database Systems.

In contrast, an object-oriented database applications course will place the greatest emphasis in the remainder of the course on the development of information-rich applications using Java as the primary programming language. The focus in this case is on the interactions between applications and relational database systems, database applications' support for Web sites, distributed information systems, and object-oriented and object-relational database systems. This material is covered in the following chapters:

- Part 3: Chapters 8–10, Database Applications and the World Wide Web; and
- Part 6: Chapters 16–17, Object-Oriented and Distributed Information Systems.

I prefer to teach an applications-oriented database course that combines these two approaches. In the first half of the course, we cover the standard material and the students complete a sophisticated application and user interface using Microsoft Access. We begin the second half of the course by considering relational database applications in Java (Chapter 8) and database–Web interaction (Chapter 9). At that point, the students begin working on creating a Web site using Java and an SQL database. The course continues with a brief treatment of physical databases (Part 4) and query processing (Chapter 13) and finishes with a detailed treatment of transactions, security, and backup and recovery (Chapters 14 and 15).

Database Applications Programming in Java

The applications developed in this book rely heavily on the Java programming language. For readers who are unfamiliar with Java, an introduction to Java is included as an appendix. I have been teaching Java in undergraduate database classes at Florida State University for several years. Most of the students are competent C++ programmers, but have had no previous experience with Java. I always assure them that the Java programming required to create database applications and Web sites is very straightforward. They are often worried, but always successful in the end. Indeed, they are pleased to find that our programming projects use almost none of the features of Java that people find most difficult. In particular, no graphical user interface programming is required!

Many people think of Java as a language for creating lively Web pages. It's true that it is a reasonable tool for creating user interfaces that run in Web browsers. But Java is also the best available programming tool for developing the kinds of database applications found in this book.

The true strength of Java derives from its ability to work behind the Web server and between applications. Its ability to interact with any database server on any platform is crucial to the quality development of dynamic Web sites, and its distributed object capabilities are truly amazing.

The code examples in the book provide a roadmap for developing Java applications and for becoming a skilled Java database programmer. For most of the projects, students can adapt one or more included Java classes to create a solution. A few changes here and there, and a completely different application emerges. My students find that they can readily understand the Java code because they already know C++. As they complete one assignment after another, they begin to understand the capabilities of the language and become increasingly more competent. After graduating, they often find that Java and database programming are their most marketable skills.

Understanding the code examples of this book requires careful reading and access to the complete implementations that are found on the book's Web site. The code samples in the book are often fragmentary and have limited explanatory comments. In contrast, the code found on the Web site is complete and includes more extensive documentation.

Supplementary Materials

Instructors and students have a variety of supplementary materials available online. All Java code, sample databases in Microsoft Access, and sample databases in SQL are available to the readers from the ftp site `ftp.aw.com` in the directory `cseng/ authors/riccardi/database`. Although much of the material is freely available, the instructor's manual, sample tests, answers to exercises, and some extensive applications are available only to instructors through contact with their Addison-Wesley local sales representatives.

All of the database schemas, SQL statements, and applications programs that appear in the book are available online. This material includes Microsoft Access databases, the SQL code required to create and populate tables, the complete Java code required to produce applications and Web sites, and the code required to integrate applications with the Web for both Unix and Windows systems.

Java packages that support the interaction between Web browsers, Web servers, and database applications are provided at the Web site in two versions. One version supports Microsoft Windows platforms using Microsoft Access, ODBC, and the personal Web server that is freely distributed by Microsoft. With this version, the Web site examples are fully implemented in a way that makes it easy for students and instructors to install them on any Windows platform. The other version of Web support uses a Unix platform with the Apache Web server and an SQL database with JDBC support. All examples have been tested using the freely available MySql database system and the Oracle8 database system. Java database application programs can be run on either Unix or Windows systems.

An online instructor's manual contains course lecture notes, answers to exercises, and sample tests. This material is available exclusively to instructors who are teaching with this text. One way that the book will be kept up-to-date is by the occasional addition of new exercises and extensive projects to the Web site. It is available through your Addison-Wesley sales representative.

Please feel free to contact me by e-mail (riccardi@acm.org) to report or ask about errors and to get the latest supplements.

Acknowledgments

I would like to thank the editorial and production teams at the Computer Science Group of Addison-Wesley for their support and encouragement. Acquisitions editor Maite Suarez-Rivas insisted that it was possible for me to write an excellent book, and that she could get me to do it. Katherine Harutunian, the project editor, has now worked with me on two books, and I could not ask for a more helpful and pleasant editor. The production process greatly benefited from the work of Pat Mahtani and Diane Freed.

This book was extensively and thoroughly reviewed by Professors Munindar P. Singh of North Carolina State University, Henry A. Etlinger of Rochester Institute of Technology, Salih Yurttas of Texas A&M University, Arijit Sengupta of Georgia State University, and Le Gruenwald of the University of Oklahoma. Their suggestions were invaluable. Professors Suzanne Dietrich of Arizona State University, Bill Grosky of Wayne State University, and Junping Sun of Nova Southeastern University also contributed with their reviews of selected chapters.

My experiences teaching database systems and working with both students and faculty at Florida State University have been most helpful to me. I am particularly thankful to Lawrence Dennis, Bryon Ehlmann, Charles W. Ford, Jr., Lois Wright Hawkes,

Samuel J. Eaves II, Dmitriy Blaginin, Troy Cochran, and Shanmaguraja Ramaswamy. Students in COP 4710 Databases, at Florida State University consented to use preliminary versions of this book as their textbook. My thanks go out to all of those students, and especially to Shang-Wen Cheng, Ahmed Moussa, Gabrielle Reed, Tilak Madan, Andres Naranjo, Huey Ling Toh, Ronie Robinson, William Maher, Ron Steedman, and Solomon Williams.

My greatest debts are owed to my wife Ann and daughters Mary, Christina, and Elizabeth. They have put up with my many absences, both physical and mental, as I struggled with this project. I owe all of my successes to their support and encouragement.

ABOUT THE AUTHOR

Greg Riccardi is a professor in the Department of Computer Science at Florida State University, a faculty associate of the Florida State University School of Computational Sciences and Information Technology, and a member of the Hall B Collaboration at the Thomas Jefferson National Accelerator Facility in Newport News, Virginia. Professor Riccardi's research interests include scientific databases, scientific computation, and distributed object computing. He received the President's Award for Excellence in Undergraduate Teaching in 1997 from Florida State University.

1
Information Management and Database Systems

CHAPTER OBJECTIVES

In this chapter, you will learn:

- The purposes and advantages of information management systems
- The major ideas that support the management of information systems
- The basic architecture of database management systems
- The ways in which database systems are used in businesses and on the Web
- The advantages of the independence of data storage, data representation, and applications
- The major events in the history of database systems

Computers are information-processing machines. The management of that information is one of the most challenging aspects of software development. The development of a significant software application includes determining the information content of the application, defining a model of that information, representing that model with specific computer data structures, and providing the software mechanisms for creating, maintaining, and protecting the information content.

Databases are at the center of computing. Today's database management systems (DBMS) are the result of decades of research and development. The use of a commercial DBMS can lead to the creation of systems that are accurate, efficient, reliable, and secure. Indeed, the professional people who work with databases are responsible for much of the positive effects that computer systems have had on industry. In today's computer-intensive economy, database systems and database applications are increasing in importance to commerce around the world. Businesses rely on database systems to store crucial business information, to maintain its accuracy, and to make it readily available.

Database systems form the primary means for representing information that is needed by people and computers. A thorough understanding of the capabilities of database systems is therefore crucial for the personal and professional development of computer software developers.

It is the capabilities of database systems and database professionals that make it possible for many companies and industries to be so successful. Advances in database systems can have significant benefits for many organizations. Consequently, people who hope to participate in the organization's future must be dedicated to keeping up with those advances. In addition, people who know how to design and implement database systems and database applications are extremely valuable to those organizations and are in great demand.

This book focuses on the role of information management in computing and the database management technology that supports it. It is particularly concerned with information in Internet applications, and especially information that supports sites on the World Wide Web. Web sites use information to provide content, searching, electronic commerce, and user management. Much of the software development for Web sites is concerned with the interaction between Web servers and databases. In this book, we emphasize the use of the Java programming language for supporting Web sites with information stored in databases.

The Importance of Databases to the Economy

1.1

The importance of databases to commerce can be illustrated by two examples from the retail sales industry: the Wal-Mart Company, the world's largest retail sales business, and L. L. Bean, a major mail-order catalog retailer.

Both of these companies make extensive use of *database systems* to record details about sales. That information is used to make operational and strategic decisions. Although both companies share common activities and uses, there also are significant differences in the goals and benefits of their systems.

Wal-Mart, like many retail businesses, uses electronic cash registers connected to database systems to record every item purchased in every store. Each time a customer makes a purchase, a record is made of the identity, quantity, and price for each item, the total purchase, and the means of payment. This information can be analyzed to determine information about the individual store and about the entire corporation. Recording the details of each purchase allows the following types of analysis:

- Sales of items
    - Comparisons between daily totals of items sold and items in inventory
    - Seasonal variations in sales of specific and similar items
    - Relative sales of similar items with different features

- Market-basket collections (all items in a single purchase)
  - Average and variation in total purchase amount
  - Average and variation in number and price of items
  - Correlation between sales of items in a single purchase
- Customer analysis
  - Behavior of average customer
  - Preferences of individual customers

Analysis of sales of items allows the company to determine what it needs to purchase on a *just-in-time* basis to keep the stores stocked with items that are likely to be purchased. Analysis may determine that light-colored bathing suits sell better in mid-summer than in the spring, or that people purchase more charcoal on Thursday than Monday. Using this information, a retail store can make better use of its inventory and its capital.

Market-basket analysis can find combinations of items that are typically purchased at the same time. This information can be used in organizing the sales floor. For example, if it is determined that there is a correlation between milk and bread purchases, then putting the bread in the front of the store and the milk in the back may encourage customers to go to the back of the store. They might see and select bread and then look for milk.

It is unlikely that Wal-Mart is interested in tracking the individual behavior of its customers, because the company has so many millions of them. Whenever a purchase is made by check or credit card, however, that information is recorded and can be used to identify the purchaser. Multiple purchases with the same credit card are assumed to be from the same person or household.

L. L. Bean differs from Wal-Mart in the total number of customers (many fewer) and the amount of information stored for each customer (much more). L. L. Bean records the name and address of each customer and can directly associate that information with each purchased item. This matching allows the company to customize the distribution of its catalogs. Someone who buys camping equipment will receive the outdoors catalog, for example. The system also allows the company to interact with customers based on their likely purchases. "That polo shirt that you like is on sale," is what a sales clerk might say to a phone customer who is known to have purchased several similar shirts over a period of years. L. L. Bean offers additional value to its customers by responding to their individual profiles.

Wal-Mart is limited in how much information it can extract from sales data because of the sheer size of its databases. Multiple terabytes of sales data are collected in a single year. Managing those data, making sure the information is accurate, protecting it from access by competitors, and developing applications to analyze it and distribute the results are all difficult and expensive activities.

Overall, the field of database systems is experiencing phenomenal growth. Microsoft sells more than 1 million licenses for its Access database system each month. Oracle Corporation has become the second largest software company in the world by specializing in database systems. Every day in major newspapers or news sites on the Web, one can find stories about the effects of database systems on our lives.

How Databases Represent Information

| 1.2 |

Database professionals draw a distinction between data and information. By *data*, we mean an organized collection of bits. By *information*, we mean data that have a specific interpretation or meaning. A value stored in some specific bytes of a file on a computer is data. Associating information content with the value requires its type (integer, string, float, and so on), a name that describes it, and a context in which the name has meaning. If we know that bytes 1003–1022 of a file have a specific hexadecimal value, then we have the bytes' data content. If we know the bytes hold a 20-character string that represents the last name of a customer of a business, we have their information content.

The important first step in building an information-rich application is to produce a specification of its information content. Database systems provide means for transforming such specifications into databases that can maintain the information content.

A *database management system (DBMS)* is a combination of software and data:

- **The physical database:** a collection of files that contain the data content;
- **The schema:** a specification of the information content of the physical database;
- **The database engine:** software that supports access to and modification of the contents of the database; and
- **The data definition and manipulation languages:** programming languages that support schema definition and database access.

A *relational database management system (RDBMS)* is a DBMS that incorporates the relational model, in which all data are stored in tables. A row of a table represents a database object, and a column of a table represents the values of a single attribute or characteristic of the objects in the table.

For example, Fig. 1.1 includes a sample table that might be part of a database for the BigHit Video Company, a fictitious chain of video rental stores that is the major database example in the book. It also shows a logical definition of the structure, or *schema*, for the table and a table creation statement that can be used to create the table in a DBMS. The table schema consists of a name (Customer) and a list of column names. The table creation statement goes even further, specifying type information about each column. The table itself contains the definition of the columns and a set of rows. Each row in the table represents information about a single customer and has a value for each column.

The schema of a database system is stored inside the system. That is, a database system is self-describing. When the table creation statement of Fig. 1.1 is executed in the database, the table schema is stored inside the database. The contents of the database are accessed by this schema information, rather than by any physical characteristics.

Customer table

accountId	lastName	firstName
101	Block	Jane
102	Hamilton	Cherry
103	Harrison	Kate
104	Breaux	Carroll

Logical description (schema)

```
Customer (accountId, lastName, firstName)
```

Table creation statement

```
create table Customer (accountId integer,
lastName char(20), firstName char(20))
```

FIGURE 1.1 _____

Customer table for BigHit Video, including a logical description and a database table definition

An application program typically interacts with a database system through a client-server interface, as illustrated in Fig. 1.2. In a *client-server system*, the application runs on a computer and stores information in its memory as objects. The server executes on another computer and stores information in its memory and its disks as relational tables.

The application issues requests for access to information in the database. The requests are made based on the database schema. In response to the requests, the database server extracts the requested information from its tables and sends it to the client in a standard format. The client knows what information to expect, although it may not know the exact format.

In its role as database client, the application can submit requests to modify the database contents and the database schema. The database server processes these requests only if they are consistent with that user's access privileges.

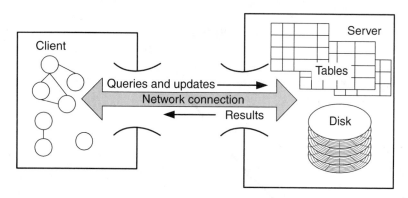

FIGURE 1.2 _____

Client-server interaction

Thus the DBMS is a combination of the data, its structure, and the complex software system that supports access to the contents, modification of the structure, and interaction with database client applications.

People in Database Systems

1.3

People who work with database systems have a variety of skills, knowledge, and tasks. The division of database development and use into interrelated activities has allowed people to become specialists. Roles that people play may include the following:

- End users
- Database designers
- Applications developers
- Database administrators

The *end users* of a database system are the people whose jobs require them to have access to the information content of a database system. *Casual users* make occasional use of the system but have little or no training. They access the system through simple user interfaces and are typically not allowed to directly modify database content in any significant way. *Sophisticated users* are people who thoroughly familiarize themselves with database systems so that they can satisfy their needs for information.

Database designers are software professionals who specify information content and create database systems. They begin by consulting with users to determine what needs to be done. Then they gather documents and other evidence of the information content of the system to be built. Next, they produce a specification of information content that forms the basis of an agreement between the developers and the users. This document is eventually translated into the data definition language of some database system and used to create the database.

Applications developers design and develop applications that extend the functionality of the database system. These applications interact with the database to accomplish specific tasks. Typical applications include user interfaces, data analysis programs, and a variety of business services.

Database administrators are people who administer databases. They are responsible for controlling access to the database system, maintaining data accuracy and integrity, and monitoring and improving database performance.

Management of Information

1.4

A major advantage of the database system approach to application development is that it divides development into several well-defined activities. The development of software is a very complex process. It is impossible to be an efficient and effective software developer without having a methodology that reduces the complexity in this way.

The division of the development process into smaller steps greatly reduces its overall complexity. The individual development phases and the resulting software systems can be specialized in order to limit their complexity. The division also provides a major advantage to the developers. The people who develop systems do not have to know everything required to build complete systems. Instead, they can have specialized knowledge that is applicable to only parts of the process. In this way, the complexity of the software is reduced and learning the technology becomes less difficult.

1.4.1 Independence of Programs and Data

The most important step in managing complexity is to make a clear division between programs and data. Early data-processing programs included explicit physical data formatting. That is, a program was dependent on the format of the data, and any change in that format required a corresponding change in the program. The year 2000 (Y2K) program errors were a direct result of such a rigid coupling of programs and data. The expense and difficulty of program and data maintenance are greatly decreased by making a clean separation between programs and data.

A database system stores information that can be made available to any program. The programs access data in a logical fashion that is independent of the physical storage representation of the data. This approach leads to *program–data independence*.

A database application requests access to data based on the *logical* structure of the data. The database system maps the logical structure into a physical representation. That is, the database system interprets the request, fetches the data, puts it into a standard format, and delivers it to the application. The application program loads the data into its variables without ever knowing how the information was stored. The physical layout of data can be modified without requiring any changes in the application.

Another aspect of program–data independence is having different models or views of the data for different users. Designers of database systems work with a conceptual model for the users of the system. This model emphasizes the information content and does not determine the physical or logical representation. A logical model of the data is used to define the database system; it must be consistent with the conceptual model. A physical model of the data places performance requirements on the data. Each of these models has its own strengths and is used for specific purposes.

A key to the success of database systems is their ability to handle multiple concurrent users. Once again, the independence of applications from physical data representation makes this concurrency possible. It would be much too difficult to build applications like airline reservation systems if each application had to make sure that it interacted with multiple users correctly. Concurrency control systems take the burden off the applications developers and place it on the database administrators. With such systems, the applications developers produce the application functionality, and the database administrators make sure that multiple users can interact correctly.

A NOTE ON HOW DATABASES COULD HAVE PREVENTED YEAR 2000 ERRORS

The year 2000 (Y2K) problems resulted from software errors and cost governments and businesses hundreds of billions of dollars. The predicted disasters never happened, but only because of the vast amounts of money and effort spent to avert them.

It is precisely the interdependence of programs and data that made January 1, 2000, a problem date. Most Y2K errors occurred because a year value was represented as a two-digit number and the age of an object was calculated by subtracting year values. A typical application would contain code like the following somewhere in it:

```
startYear: digit(2);
endYear: digit(2);
read (startYear, endYear) from file;
age = endYear - startYear;
```

When the start and end years are in different centuries,* the age calculation is wrong.

In the context of Y2K problems, a database application that calculates an age by subtracting year values would naturally treat the year value as an integer, as in the following code:

```
startYear: integer;
endYear: integer;
fetch (startYear, endYear) from database;
age = endYear - startYear;
```

If the database fetches four-digit values (for example, 1999 and 2000 for `startYear` and `endYear`) instead of two-digit values (99 and 00) for year values, the age calculation would be Y2K correct. Hence, we could simply modify the physical data representation of the year fields in the database to make them four digits and modify all existing years to have either "19" or "20" at the beginning to solve the Y2K problem! Clearly, applications with Y2K errors do not have program–data independence.

1.4.2   Management of Access, Security, and Reliability

The information stored in databases is a valuable resource of the organization that owns it. The protection of that information is a primary responsibility of the database system and the database administrator. Commercial database management systems provide a variety of mechanisms to support protection of the systems. Chapter 15 looks in detail at what is provided in the Oracle 8 DBMS and how developers and database administrators use these capabilities.

User identification and passwords are required to interact with database servers. Each user has a specific collection of operations that he or she is allowed to carry out. Limitations can be placed on any particular user's ability to access data

---

*In the context of Y2K errors, two years are considered to be in the same century if all but the last two digits of the date are the same. Hence, the year 2000 and 2001 are in the same century, even though many people consider January 1, 2001, to be the first day of the twenty-first century.

and to modify both schema and content. This assignment of rights is crucial in restricting unauthorized access and allowing authorized access.

Database systems also provide capabilities to protect the integrity of the database. A variety of content restrictions are enforced by the DBMS servers. Considerable effort is placed on the management of concurrent users through the use of transactions and transaction management software, as described in Chapter 14.

Finally, reliability would not be complete without paying close attention to backup and recovery systems. Computer hardware and software failures are a fact of life. Although DBMS vendors and database administrators go to considerable lengths to provide systems in which all of the information that is stored in a database will survive failures of any type, no system is entirely safe from failure. Consequently, no administrator or developer can afford to ignore the recovery from these failures.

Databases and the World Wide Web

1.5

It is easy to see that Web sites are dependent on information management. Statically created Web pages have largely been replaced by dynamically generated content. Every day, organizations like the New York Times Company and CNN publish large volumes of information on the Web. Almost all of it is created by Web page generation software from information stored in databases. Likewise, electronic commerce depends on the collection of information from customers and the accurate management of inventories and other records using databases. Anyone who wants a future in Web site development or management must have a working knowledge of database systems.

Databases support Web sites in several ways:

- By maintaining information that is published in the site
- By tracking usage information
- By tracking users and customers of the site
- By storing information collected from input forms
- By storing the structure and content of Web pages

Figure 1.3 shows a Netscape Navigator window that is displaying a Web page from the BigHit Video Web site. This figure is a very simple example from a database-enabled Web site. The displayed page was generated by a Java program that interacts with a BigHit Video database. This database contains information about customers, videos, rentals, and much more. This page displays information about a specific customer (Jane Block) who has entered the Web site to reserve a videotape. The page displays her account number, name, and address as well as a link to a page where that information may be updated. It also lists two movies that are available for rent. The customer has selected one of the two. When she clicks the Submit button, the displayed information is sent to the Web server for processing. The request for account number 101 to reserve a copy of the movie *Animal House* is then recorded in the BigHit Video database.

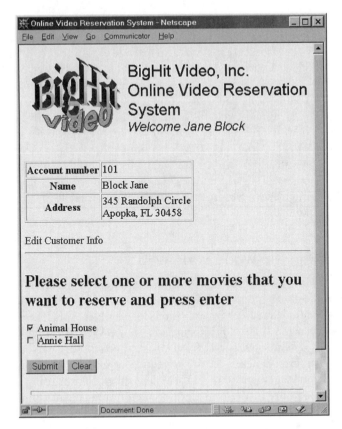

FIGURE 1.3 ——————————————————————————————————
Videotape reservation form for BigHit Video Web site

The contents, purpose, and implementation of this Web site are described in Chapter 8. It is typical of a commercial site that uses a database to maintain its information.

Database Concepts and Architecture

1.6   Many concepts and technical terms must be mastered to truly understand database systems. Most of these terms are English-language phrases that have a more specific—or even completely different—meaning within the field of database systems. We'll begin with the definitions and examples of some of the most important terms. You can be sure that many additional terms will be defined in subsequent chapters. A list of key terms and their definitions appears at the end of each chapter.

1.6.1 Data Models

A *data model* is a set of concepts that can be used to describe the structure of a collection of information. A data model is a specification of the information content of a database. Different people have different requirements for their data models. For example, users need very high-level models that describe the information that is available for their use. Database designers and applications developers need models that specify the exact structure of the data. Database administrators need models that support specifying the physical structure of databases so that performance optimization becomes possible.

A *conceptual data model* describes a system in terms that the users of the system will understand. Conceptual models are used for the initial specification of a database and for communication with users. In fact, the conceptual model provides the contract between the users and the developers of a system. Once agreement is reached regarding the content of the conceptual model, the developers build a system that correctly implements this model. The users can be confident that the significant development effort will yield a useful system. Chapter 2 is primarily concerned with conceptual modeling.

A *logical data model* specifies the structure of a database system. For a relational database, the logical model is a collection of table definitions. Once this model has been written in a suitable form, it can be used to create a database. The logical model is used as the definition of the database by the database server in constructing and maintaining the database and by the database client applications in requesting access to the database.

An *object-oriented data model* is a logical data model that is represented as a collection of class definitions in an object-oriented language. In this book, we use the Java programming language for object-oriented models. Chapter 17 considers how these models can be used as application models and how the objects can be stored in files and databases. Chapter 16 takes a more detailed look at how these models are used in distributed object-oriented applications.

A *physical data model* describes the way in which a logical data model will be represented in storage. The basic physical model of a relational database is generated automatically from the logical data model. As we will see in Chapter 12, database designers and administrators can modify the physical data model by specifying where certain database objects are stored, how they are stored, and what access methods are supported.

A *representational* (or *implementation) model* gives the details of how data are represented in files. Applications can use representational models to store data without support from database systems. Chapters 11 and 12 describe how Java can be used as a representational model for applications that want direct access to files. To use a representational model, the applications developer must specify exactly how each field of each object is stored. From this information, input/output operations can be automatically generated.

1.6.2   Schemas and Instances

Understanding database systems requires making a clear distinction between the database's structure (the schema) and its contents (the *state* or *instances*). Figure 1.1 showed the schema and four instances of the customer table. The schema of the customer table specifies that each customer has an account ID, a last name, and a first name. The instances represent facts about objects that exist outside of the database. For example, the first row of the table in Fig. 1.1 represents the fact that the customer with account ID 101 is named Jane Block.

As noted earlier, both the schema and the instances are stored in the database. The creation of the database adds the schema information. At this point, no instances exist. Once the database is used, instances are added to represent facts about real objects. The state of the database changes in response to update requests.

The database schema characterizes the facts in the database by their data types. It also specifies a variety of limitations, or *constraints*, on the state. A typical constraint is that some value must be unique within a table. For example, the schema for BigHit Video's customer table specifies that the account ID field must be a unique key for the table. That is, no two rows of the table are allowed to have the same value for the account ID. An attempt to modify the state will not be allowed if it violates this constraint.

Relationships between objects are represented as facts in the database. For instance, once Jane Block has reserved a copy of the movie *Animal House*, there will be an instance in a reservation table to record the relationship between the customer and the movie, as illustrated in Fig. 1.4. The third row of the table contains this relationship fact. If Jane Block cancels the reservation, the relationship instance must be deleted from the reservation table. We'll see the details of how to represent relationships in Chapter 4.

1.6.3   Levels of Database Schemas

Databases present different views to different users. These views are often divided into three levels: the external level, the logical level, and the internal level (see Fig. 1.5). Database users interact at the external level. They are presented with special

```
table Reservation (accountId, movieTitle)
```

accountId	movieTitle
101	Annie Hall
165	The Thirty-Nine Steps
101	Animal House
453	Annie Hall

FIGURE 1.4
Reservation table showing relationships between customers and movies

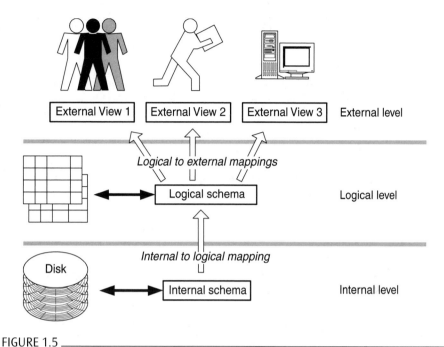

FIGURE 1.5 _____
The three levels of database schemas

views that are tailored to their specific needs. As illustrated in Fig. 1.5, general users get one external view, other interactive users get a second view, and yet a third view is used for the interaction of a specific application program.

The logical level includes the logical schema, which sees the database as a collection of tables. This level includes mappings from the logical schema to each of the *external schemas*. Changes at the logical level can be made without having any effect on the external level. These changes must be accompanied by changes in the logical-to-external mappings so that the external views remain unchanged.

The internal level and its *internal schema* see the database as a collection of files and software. The internal-to-logical mapping supports the logical view of the data. Operations performed at the logical level are translated into modifications of the contents and structure of the files. Changes in the internal or logical schemas must be accompanied by changes in the internal-to-logical mapping. Either schema can be changed without changing the other schema if the mapping is suitably modified. This consideration is particularly important because the internal level is often modified to improve the performance or reliability of the system.

The division of the database system environment into these levels allows both developers and users to work within their own levels without having to know the details of the other levels, and without having to respond to changes in the other levels.

1.6.4   Database Languages

The interaction between applications and database systems is specified using a variety of languages. A *data definition language (DDL)* is used to specify *conceptual schemas*. It supports the specification of database objects as well as their types and constraints. A *data manipulation language (DML)* is used by applications to query and modify the information stored in database servers. A *view definition language (VDL)* and a *storage definition language (SDL)* are also often used in database systems.

SQL *(Structured Query Language)* is the standard database language for DDL, DML, VDL, and SDL for relational database systems. It was based on the Sequel language of System R and originally standardized in 1986 by the American National Standards Institute (ANSI) and the International Standards Organization (ISO). The second standard, *SQL2* or *SQL-92*, appeared in 1992. In recent years, significant effort and progress has been made on SQL3, which adds object-oriented concepts and other extensions. SQL2 is covered in detail in Chapter 7 and again in Chapters 14 and 15.

SQL2 is a multipurpose programming language. It encompasses DDL statements that are used to describe the conceptual schema of a relational database, including statements to create, modify, and remove tables and attributes. The DML components of SQL include select statements that specify queries, and update, insert, and delete statements that specify the modification of table contents. Views can be defined and included in the database with VDL statements. Even the storage structure of relational databases can be modified by SDL statements.

The conceptual-to-external and internal-to-conceptual mappings of an SQL database are completely determined by the database system. SQL is used to specify the conceptual schema, external views, and some characteristics of the internal schemas. All of the mappings between these schemas are implemented automatically by the system.

Interaction between application programs and the database server must be supported by the programming language. That is, some way must be provided for sending SQL statements to the server and processing the results. Chapter 8 discusses two techniques in some detail. The first is the support provided in the Microsoft Visual Basic language, which is the programming language of the Microsoft Access database development system. The more important tool for database application development is the Java programming language. Chapters 8 and 10 provide significant details on Java's support for relational databases. Chapters 16 and 17 contain many examples of the use of object-oriented data models in application programs.

1.6.5   Database Query Operations

Access to information in databases is supported by a specific collection of operations, including queries to fetch information, updates to modify the state, and schema modifications to create, modify, and delete tables.

Queries are presented to the database as logical requests for information. Often, the query puts together information from multiple database tables. For example, we might want to ask what movies Jane Block has reserved. The request must fetch the account ID for Jane Block from the customer table, and then all of the rows of the reservation table that have that account ID. This query is formulated as a *join* operation on the two tables. In SQL, it is represented as

```
select movieTitle from Customer join Reservation on accountId
    where lastName='Block' and firstName='Jane'
```

The database server might process the query by searching for all customers with the given first and last names, then searching for the rows of the reservation table that have the same account ID.

Phases of an Information System Life Cycle

1.7

An *information system* is a combination of software, hardware, and data. Like any computer system, an information system has a lifetime—it is born, lives for some time, and dies. Many systems follow the same basic pattern, or *life cycle*. The usual phases of the life cycle of an information system are described in the chapters of this book. Here, we consider the life cycle of an information system like the one that supports the Web site of Fig. 1.3.

The first phase in such an information system occurred because some person identified a specific need for the management of information. This first phase involves an investigation of the information and processing requirements of the system. This phase is described in Section 2.1. The result of this phase is a collection of documents and other resources that describe the need for information and the context in which it exists.

The next phase—data modeling—produces a formal presentation of the information content of the system, as described in Chapters 2 and 3. Data models are prepared to describe the information content. They must be reviewed and approved by the users and the developers of the system. The data models provide an agreement with the users that the developers can use as their system requirements.

Once the data models have been finalized, the system enters the logical modeling phase, which produces a database specification. Chapters 4 and 5 describe tools for database specification and techniques for translating data models into them.

The application, or program, development phase uses the techniques of Chapters 6–10 to create database manipulations and application programs. These applications can provide direct manipulation of databases, as in Chapters 6 and 7, and database access from traditional programming languages, as in Chapters 8 and 10. Chapter 9 describes methods that support publishing and collecting information in Web sites.

The preceding phases create an information system that satisfies the information and processing needs of the users. The system then enters its deployment and improvement phase. Although it can be released to users at this point, it still requires improvements to its reliability and performance.

Achieving optimal performance of databases and applications requires some fine-tuning of the physical characteristics of databases. Chapters 11 and 12 are detailed presentations of the support that file systems provide to database systems and some of the ways that physical characteristics can be specified. Chapter 13 presents techniques that are used for the optimization of database queries.

Chapters 14 and 15 describe techniques that are used to improve the ability of the system to handle multiple concurrent users. These techniques are applied to the system early in its deployment and as needed during the rest of its lifetime. The security, backup, and recovery techniques of Chapter 15 are particularly crucial to the reliability of the system.

History of Database Systems

1.8

In the earliest days of computers, data were stored on sequential devices—that is, on media such as paper tape, punched cards, and magnetic tape that could be accessed only in storage order. The earliest efforts in managing information therefore centered on file structures and sorting algorithms.

In the early 1960s, the first general-purpose database management systems were introduced with great success. The Integrated Data Store (IDS), developed by Bachman at GE, was a major impetus for the development of the first standard data models by the Conference on Data Systems Languages (CODASYL). Bachman also introduced methods for precise specification of data models. The development of larger and less expensive disk drives and memories made it possible to store vast quantities of data and to optimize the access to that information.

In the middle to late 1960s, IBM introduced a product called the Information Management System (IMS) that added data communication capabilities to large-scale databases. Its collaboration with American Airlines led to the development of the SABRE airline reservation system, the first database system to support large numbers of concurrent users and networks for database access.

All of the major computer manufacturers produced significant and successful database systems in the early 1970s. The study of database systems also became a major academic and research area. E. F. Codd introduced the relational model, which formed the foundations of database theory. C. J. Date published his first book [Date75] on relational databases in 1975. Peter Chen showed how diagrams could be used for describing data with his Entity–Relationship model.

The relational model was the subject of significant commercial and academic research activity. By the late 1970s, it was challenging the large commercial database systems for primacy in the market. The work of the System R group at IBM showed that relational databases could provide the flexibility that was required by applications without sacrificing performance. In particular, this group demonstrated that client-server models were effective, that databases could handle large numbers of concurrent users and vast amounts of data, and that effective query optimization could produce greatly improved performance.

The early 1980s saw the emergence of several software companies that developed and sold relational database systems. Prior to this time, computer manufacturers had developed all of the database systems. Now Oracle, Ingres, Sybase, Informix, and others showed that it was possible to develop database systems that were hardware-independent with no sacrifice in performance. These companies were largely responsible for the emergence of a large independent software business in commercial markets. The 1980s also saw the emergence of the PC and the PC database systems Dbase, Paradox, and others.

The first standard for the SQL language was published in 1985. The standardization of the data definition and data manipulation languages boosted the credibility of the fledgling database software industry. Data managers could afford to buy relational database systems software for their companies, knowing that their efforts were unlikely to be sabotaged by the failure of the software vendor.

The past 10 years have seen the dominance of relational database systems. Oracle has become the second largest software company in the world, and IBM's DB2 product has driven the company's own nonrelational database software out of the market. Vast amounts of research—both industrial and academic—have pushed the quality and applicability of the relational model far beyond anyone's expectations.

Current hot topics in database systems include object-oriented databases, distributed databases, and databases to store spatial and temporal information. Many emerging problems are primarily related to the growth in the Internet and the World Wide Web and the presence of a variety of movable and wireless computing devices.

Chapter Summary

This chapter has presented an overview of the field of information systems, including how information systems and databases contribute to the economy, how databases represent information, what roles people fulfill in information systems, and how database systems enhance applications.

Businesses rely on database systems to store crucial business information, to maintain its accuracy, and to make it readily available. This information is analyzed and used to make operational and strategic decisions. The growth in revenues of database software companies is a testament to the economic importance of information systems.

Database systems developers make a clear distinction between how information is used and how it is stored. This program–data independence results in database systems that are easy to maintain and applications that are robust and flexible. The client-server architecture provides an additional layer of independence between the database systems that store the information and the applications that use it. A database management system (DBMS) is a combination of the data, its structure, and the complex software system that supports access to the contents, modification of the structure, protection and security for the system, and interaction with database client applications.

People who work with information systems are specialists. They may be users, database designers, applications developers, or database administrators. No one person needs to know everything about a system, and each can contribute in his or her own way.

Database systems are having an enormous impact on the World Wide Web. A large fraction of Web content is stored in database systems, and Web servers act as database clients. The development of software that supports Web–database interaction is a major component of this book.

A data model specifies the information content of a system. Many different types of models exist, each with its own purpose. A conceptual model provides the specification of a system that is the basis of understanding between users and developers. A logical model specifies the structure of the database system and is used to create the database. Physical models and representational models give a more detailed specification of how information is stored in computer systems.

A relational database system (RDBMS) represents information as a collection of tables. A row of a table represents a single object of a specific type and the contents of a table are the set of all objects of that type.

Database languages support interactions with database systems. Data definition languages (DDL) describe the structure of a database, and data manipulation languages (DML) describe queries and updates to its content. The Structured Query Language (SQL) is the standard language used in relational database systems as both DDL and DML.

Current strategies for designing and developing information systems are the result of many years of industrial and academic research and development. The relational model dominates the database industry and is expected to be the dominant model for years to come.

Key Terms

Applications developer. A person who designs and develops applications that extend the functionality of a database system.

Client-server system. A system made up of two or more components with an asymmetric interaction. The client makes requests, and the server listens and responds. The client-server interaction typically takes place across a communications network.

Conceptual data model. A description of a system in terms that the users of the system will understand.

Conceptual schema. A database schema that describes the database for the entire user and developer community as a collection of tables.

Data. A collection of bits that represent some value or collection of values.

Data definition language (DDL). A language for specifying the conceptual schema of a database.

Data manipulation language (DML). A language for manipulating the contents of a database.

Data model. A description of the organization and meaning of the information content of a system.

Database. That part of a database system that is concerned with creating and maintaining information content.

Database administrator. A person who is responsible for controlling access to the database system, maintaining data accuracy and integrity, and monitoring and improving database performance.

Database designer. A software professional who specifies information content and creates database systems.

Database management system (DBMS). A combination of software and data storage that is capable of creating and maintaining database systems.

Database system. A combination of software, data, and computer hardware that implements a collection of data models and applications. A database system uses a DBMS together with application programs to create an information system for a specific purpose.

End user. A person whose job requires access to the information content of a database system.

External schema. A description of part of the information content of a database for use by a particular collection of users. A database system typically supports multiple external views.

Implementation model. See *Representational model.*

Information. Data that have a specific interpretation or meaning.

Information system. A collection of software applications that store and manipulate information.

Instance. An object, or collection of values, in a database system.

Internal schema. A description of the physical representation of the data of a system.

Logical data model. A specification of the structure of a database system.

Object-oriented data model. A logical data model that is represented as class definitions in an object-oriented language.

Physical data model. A description of the way in which a logical data model will be represented in storage.

Program–data independence. The separation of the details of the storage representation of data from the use of those data by applications.

Query. A request for some of the information content of a database.

Relational database management system (RDBMS). A DBMS that implements the relational data model. RDBMSs typically use SQL as their interaction language.

Representational model. The details of how data are represented in files.

Schema. A precise description of the structure of some collection of similar objects.

SQL (Structured Query Language). The standard language for interaction with relational database management systems.

SQL2/SQL-92. The second version of SQL, standardized in 1992.

Storage definition language (SDL). A language that supports the definition of the internal schema of a database.

Transaction. A sequence of database operations from a database application. A transaction manager helps to allow multiple database applications to execute concurrently.

View. See *External schema.*

View definition language (VDL). A language that supports the definition of external views of a database.

Exercises

1. Describe three different aspects of a typical retail business that require collecting and maintaining information. Describe the basic content of the information that must be maintained.

2. Explain the difference between data and information.

3. Choose a retail sales Web site. Give general descriptions of four major categories of information that are used by the site. For each information category:

    a. Make a list of the kinds of data items stored in the site.

    b. Describe the actions of the casual users of this information. Who are they?

    c. Give an example of what a sophisticated user might do with this information.

4. Give examples of the different responsibilities of database administrators, database designers, and database applications developers.

5. Consider a database system that maintains information about student registrations for a college.

    a. Give an example of the difference between the view of the data provided to a student, the view provided to a teacher, and the view provided to an administrator in the registration office.

    b. Give an example of a problem with student registration that might occur when several students are registering simultaneously.

    c. Give three examples of potential security violations in this database.

6. Describe information that is appropriate to be stored in a database for BigHit Video, as introduced in Section 1.5. Suppose that the first analysis of its business needs has concluded that the company needs to keep information about its employees, customers, rentals, stores, and suppliers, as well as about its collection of video and music. Prepare a list of attributes of one of these sources of information.

    Your assignment is to analyze the information requirements for storing information related to a particular topic. Prepare a list of attributes of your topic that should be kept in a database. For each attribute list the topic, your user ID, the attribute name, the attribute type, and a comment that describes the attribute.

    a. Employees

    b. Customers

    c. Stores

    d. Inventory of Videos

    e. Rentals of Videos

    f. Sales of Videos

7. Describe typical updates and queries that will be applied to the information that you described in Exercise 6. Give an example of each update or query,

and describe its effect on the contents of the database (for an update) or what information in the database it uses (for a query).

8. As in Exercise 7, describe typical updates and queries that will be applied to the registration database system of Exercise 5.

Further Readings

Most of the material in this chapter is covered in more detail in later chapters. More information on the history of database systems is available from a variety of sources. The early development of databases is described in Fry and Sibley's 1976 *Computing Surveys* article [FrSi76]. Bachman's original work on data models [Bac69] appeared in the *Journal of ACM SGIBDP*. Codd's original description of the relational model is [Codd70]. His 1982 Turing award lecture [Codd82] is of particular interest for his explanations of the applicability of the relational model. The SQL standards documents are [ANSI86] and [ANSI92].

PART ONE

Information Models and Relational Databases

*T*his part contains a roadmap for the development of information systems, from the initial evaluation of system requirements through the creation of databases. An information system is meant to satisfy the need to manage and manipulate specific information. The development of such a system begins with an investigation into the information and processing requirements. It proceeds with the creation of a precise specification of those requirements. The next step is to evaluate those specifications and modify them as necessary. From the specification of information requirements, a data model can be built. This data model is then used to define the structure of a database.

This part introduces the information system needed for the BigHit Video Company, a fictional chain of video rental stores. The development of this information system begins with sample documents and business activities. It proceeds through the specification of information requirements and the creation of a relational database system to manage the information of the business. This information system forms the basis for applying the principles of information system development in this and subsequent sections.

In Chapter 2, you will investigate the information managed by an organization and produce a precise specification of the structure of that information. This specification, called a *conceptual model*, is typically represented as a diagram. The diagram identifies the types of objects (called *entity classes*) that are to be managed by the system, the characteristics (*attributes*) of the objects, and the relationships that are possible between objects of the classes. Chapter 2 focuses on the use of *Entity–Relationship (ER)* models and diagrams. In the chapter, you will find many examples of information modeling and the details regarding how a conceptual model is developed and what it means.

Chapter 3 describes how the ER model is enhanced to model inheritance and how object-oriented methods can be used for conceptual models. You will see examples of situations that require inheritance. The examples are then turned into conceptual models. The BigHit Video information system is represented by both an enhanced ER diagram and an object-oriented model.

The principal strategies of information systems development continue to be discussed in Chapter 4, which introduces the relational approach to database systems. A relational system is one in which the data are represented as tables. Each object in the database is a row of a table. Each table has a specific list of columns, each with its own name and type. The relational model allows us to represent a conceptual model in a form that can be directly translated into a relational database. Chapter 4 includes all of the details of how to transform an ER diagram into a specification of a relational database. It concludes with a description of how to turn a relational model into a database using the Microsoft Access database system.

Chapter 5 will help you to learn how to improve the quality of your relational models so that they more accurately represent the information and reduce the problems of maintaining the accuracy of the data. In particular, *normalization* techniques are used to modify relational models so as to reduce data redundancy and to make it easier to enforce a variety of important constraints. The theoretical basis for normalization is thoroughly explained and illustrated with examples.

2
Representing
Information with
Data Models

CHAPTER OBJECTIVES

In this chapter, you will learn:

- The basic principles and requirements for creating information systems
- Strategies for discovering information requirements
- How to specify information requirements with conceptual data models
- The purposes and practices of Entity–Relationship (ER) modeling
- Definitions of standard conceptual modeling terms, including entity, entity class, attribute value, attribute, relationship, and relationship type
- How to distinguish between entity classes, attributes, and relationship types
- How to draw and read Entity–Relationship diagrams
- How to use Entity–Relationship diagrams in conceptual modeling
- The meaning and use of cardinality and other constraints on relationships

*D*atabases are used to represent facts in an organized manner. The facts of interest are some of those that are part of the enterprise under consideration. Thus the contents of any database represent facts about real objects that are of interest to someone. The first step in building a system to represent information involves determining the meaning and organization of the information that is part of the enterprise. This chapter discusses tools and techniques that are used to describe the organization and meaning of data in the form of a *data model*.

The importance of data modeling cannot be overstated. Limitations on the ability to represent facts are often created in this stage. These limitations can cause serious problems much later in the development process. Fixing such errors at a later stage can be extremely costly and time-consuming.

The process of producing a data model allows us to see the options provided by possible representations and to predict the effects of our decisions.

Consider our example of the BigHit Video enterprise. To conduct its business, BigHit Video must keep track of its videotapes, rentals, customers, orders, employees, purchases, and stores. Clearly, the success of this enterprise depends on the quality of its information management. The most obvious crucial activity is the management of rentals: knowing which customer has which video, how much each customer owes, and when the videos are due. Nevertheless, many other activities, and associated information resources, are just as important to the overall success of the enterprise.

To develop an effective information management application for BigHit Video, we must understand what information must be stored and how that information is likely to be used.

Discovering and Specifying Requirements

2.1

No software development is successful unless the resulting product is useful. For an information system to be useful, it must record and manipulate information that is important to its users. The information must be accurate and complete. A developer must convert the ideas and opinions of the users into the working information system. Unfortunately, the requirements for success are almost never clear at the beginning of the development efforts. For this reason, the process of determining the requirements is often termed "discovery."

Discovery of application requirements usually involves interviews with members of the organization and the collection and analysis of current documents and computer systems. From this information, developers will describe the objects and operations that must be included in the final system. An important part of discovery is determining the vocabulary that is used to describe the objects and operations. This terminology must be incorporated into the design by the developers. Adopting the user's vocabulary shows a respect for the enterprise that often makes it much easier to persuade users to adopt the final system. In addition, it facilitates the communication between users and developers—a crucial factor in the system's ultimate success.

For BigHit Video, documents might include customer applications, rental receipts, employee time cards, store schedules, and video purchase orders. From these information sources, we can discover the major data objects and many of their attributes. Interviews with employees will be needed to add detail and description to the objects and their attributes. In addition, interviews will reveal many of the activities of the enterprise. We also learn what terms are used within the organization to denote the objects, attributes, and activities.

Because BigHit Video is a fictional company, there are no employees to interview, no documents to peruse, and no previous operation to use as a model. We hope that the familiar nature of the video rental enterprise will allow each reader to supply the details of the appropriate information and behavior. Throughout the book, discussions will focus on the information and behavior that ought to be present in an enterprise of this type. Several sample documents for our fictional enterprise are included in the book to help in the process of information modeling.

The BigHit Video enterprise was chosen as the primary example for this book because it is a rich application domain that is familiar to most readers. The presentation of the applications will follow an incremental development strategy, rather than the complete design that is preferred by software professionals. The basic structure will be discovered and specified in this chapter. Later chapters will add to the software applications and extend the data and behavior models.

Organizing Information

2.2

Before we can specify the information content of a database, we must have the tools and vocabulary that will allow us to organize the specification. A *schema* is the precise description of one or more aspects of a database system. Many different kinds of schemas are used in database systems, each with its own purpose. The high-level or *conceptual schemas* are used to specify the organizational structure and information content of a system. A conceptual schema provides a means of communication between users and designers of information systems. Ideally, it should use the vocabulary of the enterprise in a precise way. Users can read it and understand what information will be stored in the system. Developers can read it and understand the requirements for system development. Once users and developers have written and agreed on the conceptual schema, each group can be confident that they are working toward the common goal of producing a useful system.

In later chapters, we will encounter *logical schemas* that define the information content in a manner that can be used to create a database, *external schemas* that organize the information in order to improve access for users and applications, and *physical schemas* that specify the representation of information in physical terms.

A database system provides for the representation of the characteristics of objects that occur in the enterprise. We call these objects *entities* and their characteristics *attributes*. For simplicity and clarity, we divide the entities into distinct classes (*entity classes*). The entities in a class share common attributes. Each entity has a value for each attribute of its class. In BigHit Video, we know that there is a `Customer` entity class with attributes `lastName`, `firstName`, and `address`, among others.

The objects of an enterprise have associations or *relationships* with other objects. A relationship between a customer and a videotape occurs when the customer rents the videotape. That relationship ends when the customer returns the videotape. A relationship represents a fact about the entities of the system. A *relationship type* represents the possibility that an entity of one class may have a relationship with an entity of another class. By defining a `Rents` relationship type as part of the schema, for example, we allow the system to record the rental relationships as they occur.

Each object in a relationship plays a specific *role* in it. The customer is the renter of the videotape, and the videotape is the object rented by the customer. Roles are particularly important in situations where two entity classes are linked by more than one relationship type and where a relationship type links an entity class to itself. For example, the `WorksAt` and `Manages` relationship types link the `Employee` and `Store` classes. An employee may have the role of manager or the role of worker. Likewise, the marriage relationship associates one person with another person.

We can use these concepts to organize our specification of the information content of a system. We can analyze the enterprise and identify its specific entities and entity classes. We can determine the attributes of each entity class and the types of relationships that may exist between entities. All of these information details must be specified in a conceptual schema.

In this chapter, we investigate two strategies for specifying information structure. The traditional approach was first described by Peter Chen in his 1976 paper "Entity–Relationship Model: Toward a Unified View of Data" [Chen76] that appeared in the *ACM Transactions on Database Systems*. A more recent strategy is to integrate data and behavior in an object-oriented model, as described in Section 3.2.

Entity–Relationship Modeling

2.3

An *Entity–Relationship (ER) model* is a high-level, conceptual model that describes data as entities, attributes, and relationships. It constrains the representation of data but does not specify it. In this model, particular attention is paid to the relationships because they represent the interactions between entities and require special treatment in database and application development. An ER model specifies the data requirements of an application and is usually accompanied by a behavioral model that specifies the functional requirements. The development of these two models proceeds in a coordinated fashion.

ER modeling concentrates on specifying the properties of the data rather than the storage requirements. It includes a detailed description of the names and types of all data that are part of the proposed database system.

2.3.1   Entity Classes and Attributes

The discovery process that was described in Section 2.1 identifies specific objects that must be stored and managed in the enterprise. The first step in ER modeling is to name and describe the classes of those objects. Table 2.1 gives our first list of the names and brief descriptions of important entity classes for BigHit Video.

> ### A NOTE ABOUT NAMES
>
> The convention used for names in this book is consistent with the naming convention adopted in the Java language (see Section 6.8.3 of the Java Language Specification). The name of a class or attribute consists of a descriptive noun or noun phrase. The first letter of the name is capitalized if it is the name of a class; it is not capitalized if it is the name of an attribute (a *field* in Java terminology). The first letter of each subsequent word is always capitalized. No underscores are used in names. Whenever the name of a class or attribute is used in the text, it will appear in a fixed-width (monospace) font.

Each entity class has specific attributes or properties that describe its characteristics. These attributes are used to further describe the entity classes. The attributes themselves exist somewhat independently of the entities. In particular, it is not unusual for an attribute to appear in more than one entity class. A `lastName`

TABLE 2.1

Names and descriptions of entity classes for BigHit Video

Entity Class	Description
Customer	A customer of the business
Videotape	An item in the rental inventory
Employee	A person who works in one or more stores
PayStatement	A record of the wages paid to an employee
TimeCard	A record of a block of time worked by an employee at a store
Store	One of the retail outlets of BigHit Video
Rental	The rental of a videotape by a customer for a specific period and cost
PurchaseOrder	A request to purchase an item
Supplier	A company that sells items to BigHit Video

attribute, for example, is likely to represent a characteristic of both the `Customer` class and the `Employee` class. Table 2.2 lists some (but not all) attributes that represent characteristics of the entity classes of Table 2.1. Each attribute is characterized by a name, a type, a *domain* of values, and a description.

TABLE 2.2

Names and descriptions of some attributes for BigHit Video

	Attribute	Type	Domain of Values	Description
1	title	String	Unbounded	The title of an item
2	lastName	String	30 characters	The last name of a person
3	firstName	String	30 characters	The first name of a person
4	rating	String	5 characters	The rating of a movie
5	ssn	String	10 digits	A Social Security number
6	accountId	Number	4-byte integer	The identifier of a customer account
7	numberRentals	Number	4-byte integer	Number of rentals for a customer
8	otherUsers	Set	Set of strings of 30 characters	Names of other people authorized to use this account
9	dateAcquired	Date	Month, day, year	Date that a videotape was acquired
10	address	Composite	2 strings of 30 characters, one string of 2 characters, and one string of 9 digits	An address that consists of a street, city, state, and ZIP code

---

A NOTE ABOUT STORING INFORMATION IN TABLES

Tables 2.1 and 2.2 are just the first of many uses in this book of two-dimensional structures to store information. Each table has a fixed number of columns, and each column has a name. Each row has a value for each column, and the meaning of these values comes from the meaning of the column. The values in a row go together to provide information about a single idea or entity. This structure is exactly the same one that is used by relational databases to store information.

Each of the attributes in lines 1–7 of Table 2.2 is *single-valued*. The first five attributes have character strings as their values. Each has its own form, however, as described in the Domain of Values column. This column specifies *domain constraints*, which are restrictions on the allowable values of the attributes. The `title` attribute (line 1) has no restriction on its length or form, but both `lastName` and `firstName` (lines 2 and 3) are limited to no more than 30 characters and the `rating` (line 4) to no more than 5 characters. The `ssn` attribute (line 5) is constrained in length to 10 characters and also constrained to contain only the digits 1–9. Attributes `accountId` and `numberRentals` (lines 6 and 7) are integer-valued.

Each of the attributes in lines 8–10 of Table 2.2 is *multivalued*. The `otherUsers` attribute (line 8) has a set of strings as its value. The value of this attribute is a set of the names of the other people who are allowed to use this customer account. This attribute has multiple values in the sense that each name is a value of the attribute. The values of `dateAcquired` and `address` (lines 9 and 10) are *composites* (or *records*). A `dateAcquired` value is composed of three fields: month, day, and year. The `address` attribute is composed of a `street` and `city` (30-character strings), a 2-character `state`, and a 9-digit `zipcode`. These attributes have multiple values in the sense that each field of the record is a value of the attribute.

A more complete description of an entity class includes its name, its description, and its list of attributes. Table 2.3 gives the attributes of some entity classes for BigHit Video. The attributes were defined in Table 2.2. The constraints on the attributes limit their values for a specific entity or among all of the entities of the class. The attributes are variously described as *key*, *not null*, and *derived*. The constraint *not null* requires that the attribute have a value other than the null value. *Derived* means that the attribute is not stored, but rather is derived—or calculated—from some other information.

Most entity classes have one or more attributes that form a *key* of the class. The key of an entity uniquely identifies it among all entities of the class. Each entity of the class must have a unique value for its key. In other words, the values of the key attributes are constrained in that no two different entities may have the same values for the key attributes. For example, the `ssn` attribute of the `Employee` class is a single attribute key. No two employees may have the same value for the `ssn` attribute. This limitation reflects the uniqueness of Social Security numbers. Because two employee entities represent different people, and different people have different Social Security numbers, the `ssn` attribute is an appropriate key for the `Employee` class.

TABLE 2.3

Some entity classes and their attributes and constraints

Class	Attribute	Constraints or Further Description
Customer	accountId	Key
	lastName	Not null
	firstName	
	address	
	balance	Currency
	otherUsers	
	numberRentals	Derived
Videotape	videotapeId	Key
	title	Not null
	genre	
	dateAcquired	
	rating	
PayStatement	datePaid	
	hoursWorked	
	amountPaid	

In the case of the `Customer` class, the `accountId` attribute is an artificial attribute that was created for the purpose of being a key. No other attribute of a customer is guaranteed to be unique. The declaration of the *key constraint* for the attribute specifies that the information system must guarantee the uniqueness of the attribute values among the entities of the class. An attempt to add a new customer with the same `accountId` value as another customer must be disallowed.

In some cases, it is most appropriate to have a key that consists of multiple attributes. In this situation, it is the combination of values of the key attributes that is unique. For class `Customer`, for instance, we might find that the combination of `lastName`, `firstName`, and `address` forms a key. The `accountId` attribute was added to the class `Customer` as its key for several reasons. It is easier to enforce uniqueness with a single attribute key. As we will see in Chapter 4, it is much easier to represent relationships with single attribute keys. Finally, declaring that the three attributes form a key restricts the entities that we can store in the database. If two people have the same first and last names and the same address, this restriction will require that they be considered the same customer. In this situation, the data model may limit the applicability of the resulting information system. There will be no way to represent the real situation in the database.

An entity class that has no key and cannot exist by itself is called a *weak entity class*. Weak entities are discussed in more detail in Section 2.4.

A NOTE ABOUT ATTRIBUTES AND ENTITY CLASSES

The data modeling process may identify attributes that could be entity classes themselves. It is the designer's responsibility to distinguish between attributes and entity classes. For example, the address attribute of a customer is a composite attribute with several attributes of its own. We might decide that an address is an attribute of a customer entity or an independent entity. We could argue that an address represents a lodging or place of business and hence is a real object that is independent of the people who live or work there. Alternatively, we could argue that the address is simply an attribute of a person used to communicate with the person. The lodging or place of business is of no interest to our information system. The design in this book treats addresses as attributes.

Unfortunately, there is no simple rule to use in making these distinctions. A designer must decide whether an attribute should be an entity on the basis of whether it is sufficiently important to the users or is independent of other entities.

2.3.2   Entity Instances and Attribute Values

An entity is an instance of an entity class. Each entity is distinguished by the values of its attributes. Tables 2.4 and 2.5 show four entities of class `Customer` and five entities of class `Videotape`, respectively.

Each entity has a value for each of its attributes, but that value may be the special value *null*, which is represented here as an empty field. For example, the values of the `otherUsers` attribute of the middle two rows of Table 2.4 are null. It is not always easy to know what null means. In this case, because the attribute is a set of values, null refers to the empty set value. That is, there are no other users for this customer. In other cases, a null may mean

Not applicable: the attribute is not applicable to this entity and hence should not have a value;

Missing: a value of the attribute exists but is not recorded; or

Unknown: the value of the attribute may be either missing or not applicable.

For example, the spouse's name attribute of an unmarried person must be null because the attribute is not applicable to the person. A null value of a height attribute for a person means that the value is missing, because every person has a height. A null value for a phone number, however, may mean that the person has no phone (not applicable) or that the person has a phone but the value is not recorded (missing). The null value may mean that the person refuses to give the phone number, or that the number that was originally given was wrong or changed and was replaced by null. In the latter case, it may be appropriate to try to determine the customer's phone number. Is it appropriate to ask the customer for a phone number the next time he or she is in the store? The null value does not give enough information for us to determine how to interpret the attribute.

A three-valued logic can be used to make the distinction between missing and unknown. Consider an attribute `hasPhone` of a person. A true value means the person has a phone and a false value means the person has no phone. A null value

TABLE 2.4

Entities of class Customer

account Id	last Name	first Name	street	address city	state	zipcode	otherUsers	Rentals	number balance
101	Block	Jane	1010 Main St.	Apopka	FL	30458	Joe Block, Greg Jones	3	0.00
102	Hamilton	Cherry	3230 Dade St.	Dade City	FL	30555		1	3.47
103	Harrison	Kate	103 Dodd Hall	Apopka	FL	30457		0	30.57
104	Breaux	Carroll	76 Main St.	Apopka	FL	30458	Judy Breaux, Cyrus Lambeaux, Jean Deaux	2	34.58

TABLE 2.5

Entities of class Videotape

videoId	dateAcquired	title	genre	length	rating
101	1/25/98	The Thirty-Nine Steps	mystery	101	PG
145	5/12/95	Lady and the Tramp	animated comedy	93	G
90987	3/25/99	Elizabeth	costume drama	123	PG-13
99787	10/10/97	Animal House	comedy	87	PG-13
123	3/25/86	Annie Hall	romantic comedy	110	PG-13

means that it is unknown whether the person has a phone. It has even been suggested that a four-valued logic is appropriate: true, false, missing, and not applicable.

There is a great deal of controversy about the appropriate meaning and usage of nulls in information systems. C. J. Date devotes an entire chapter of his *Introduction to Database Systems* [Date99] to "missing information."

2.3.3   Relationship Types and Relationship Instances

A relationship between two objects represents some association between them. In ER modeling, relationships are characterized by type (or class). For instance, two people can be associated as parent and child (a parent–child relationship) or as husband and wife (a marriage relationship). The *relationship* occurs between two specific objects and is an instance of a *relationship type* between the classes of the objects.

Each object plays a specific *role* in the relationship. If two people are associated by marriage, one person is the wife and one is the husband. That is, the relationship is "marriage," and the roles of the individuals are "wife" and "husband." The name of a role expresses the function of a particular entity in a relationship.

A relationship type represents the possibility that one entity may have an association with another entity. A relationship instance represents the fact that a specific entity does have this particular association with another specific entity. For example, the marriage relationship type is defined between entity class `Person` and entity class `Person`. It does not, however, guarantee that any specific person is married to any other specific person or even that anyone is married to anyone else.

The name of a relationship is a verb phrase that can be used in a sentence. We say, "Jane Block rents *Annie Hall*," to represent an instance of the `Rents` relationship type. Similarly, "A customer may rent a videotape" expresses the `Rents` relationship type. We also use the roles, as in "Jane Block is the wife of Joe Block" or "Joe Block is the husband of Jane Block."

Constructing such expressions may help in the discovery process because this kind of sentence reveals the presence of the relationship type. When someone uses such a sentence to describe facts about the enterprise, that person is expressing the existence of the relationship type.

Relationships often have their own attributes. A marriage relationship has a wedding date attribute, for instance. The `Rents` relationship type has attributes `dateDue`, `dateRented`, `amountPaid`, and `amountDue`.

2.3.4   Relationships Are Not Attributes

A major goal of conceptual modeling is to identify the relationships between entities. Relationships are singled out for special treatment. As we will see in Chapter 4, we can use many strategies to represent relationships in database systems. The conceptual model identifies the relationships, but does not determine an exact representation. To maintain flexibility, we must ensure that no relationship is specified as an attribute. Unfortunately, the discovery process will often identify fields that appear to be attributes, but should actually be relationships.

BigHit Video
Rental Receipt

Account ID: 101   Video ID: 90987   Date: January 9, 1999   Cost: $2.99

Jane Block   Elizabeth   Date due: January 11, 1999

1010 Main St.

Apopka, FL 30458

FIGURE 2.1 _____

Rental receipt

Consider the example of a rental receipt from BigHit Video that appears as Fig. 2.1. It includes information about the rental, the customer, and the videotape. The account ID field that appears in the receipt is the identifier of a specific customer. As we have already determined that a customer is a separate entity, the field actually serves as an indication of a relationship. The name and address of the customer are attributes of the `Customer` entity class, not of the `Rental` class. Similarly, the video ID and title are attributes of a related `Videotape` entity. Analysis of this receipt yields the information that a `Rental` has attributes `dateRented`, `dateDue`, and `cost`, and relationships to a `Customer` and to a `Videotape`. The other fields that appear on the receipt are not attributes of `Rental`.

A NOTE ABOUT ATTRIBUTES AND RELATIONSHIPS

A simple analysis of an entity class may identify attributes that represent relationships. For example, the Social Security number (`ssn`) and name of the employee appear on a pay statement. This fact leads us to add those attributes to entity class `PayStatement`. We also know these attributes apply to the `Employee` entity class and `ssn` is its key attribute.

The modeling process is incomplete because attributes of one entity class (`Employee`) are attached to another class (`PayStatement`). We must recognize that the `ssn` attribute of `PayStatement` is an indication that class `PayStatement` is related to class `Employee`, delete these attributes from `PayStatement`, and add a relationship between the classes.

2.3.5   Constraints on Relationships

Relationship constraints limit the application of relationship types. A *cardinality constraint* on a relationship type puts restrictions on the number of relationships that may exist at any one time. When we say that a relationship type is "to-one," we mean that one entity may be related to at most one other entity through this type. For instance, the marriage relationship type is one-to-one because each person may be married to at most one other person. Making a relationship type to-one places a cardinality constraint on instances of the relationship.

As we have already seen, each relationship has two roles. Each cardinality constraint is applied to a single role of a relationship. The one-to-one constraint on the marriage relationship is actually two constraints. The role of wife and the role of husband are each constrained to have cardinality no more than one. For a particular person, the set of people for whom she is the wife has cardinality no more than one. Together, these constraints form a *cardinality ratio constraint* on the marriage relationship type. In the mathematical sense, the set of relationships that exist at any one time forms a one-to-one relationship.

Four basic types of cardinality ratios exist:

- **One-to-one.** An entity in either role may participate in at most one relationship, and hence have at most one related object.
- **One-to-many.** An entity in one role may have any number of relationships, but an entity in the other role may have at most one.
- **Many-to-one.** The same as one-to-many, but reversed.
- **Many-to-many.** An entity in either role may participate in any number of relationships.

Figure 2.2 illustrates entities related by the `Rents` relationship type. The oval on the left lists the `accountId` attributes of some `Customer` entities. The oval on the right lists the `videoId` attributes of some `Videotape` entities. The rectangle in the center contains a square for each relationship between a customer and a videotape. As the figure illustrates, each relationship connects exactly two entities—one from each class. The first relationship associates customer 101 (Jane Block) with videotape 90987 (*Elizabeth*). This relationship represents the fact that Jane Block has rented *Elizabeth* and not yet returned it.

`Rents` is one-to-many, because each customer may rent many videotapes, but each videotape can be rented at most once. Each customer may have many

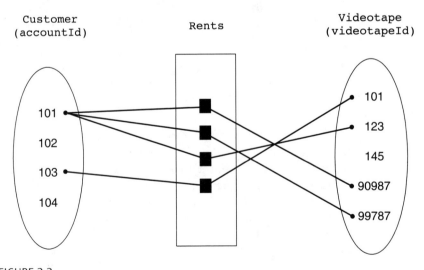

FIGURE 2.2 _____

Entities related by the one-to-many relationship type `Rents`

relationships, but each videotape has at most one relationship. The customers and videotapes that have no relationships illustrate the lack of minimum cardinality. Customer 102 (Cherry Hamilton) has no current rentals. Videotape 145 (*Lady and the Tramp*) has no current rentals, and so is available for rental.

Figure 2.3 illustrates a collection of `PreviouslyRented` relationships that record the history of rentals. The first relationship records the fact that customer 101 (Jane Block) rented and returned videotape 123 (*Annie Hall*).

The `PreviouslyRented` relationship type is many-to-many, because each videotape may be checked out many times by many different customers. This change in cardinality ratio does not affect the relationship object. Each such object still connects exactly two entities. The videotapes that have more than one relationship illustrate the change in cardinality. One fact that can be seen by reviewing Fig. 2.3 is that customer 102 (Cherry Hamilton) rented and returned videotape 101 (*The Thirty-Nine Steps*) twice, as illustrated by the fourth and fifth relationships.

A *maximum cardinality constraint* restricts the number of relationships of a particular type that an entity may have. If we want to ensure that no customer can rent more than 10 videotapes at a time, we must specify the cardinality of the renter role to be no more than 10.

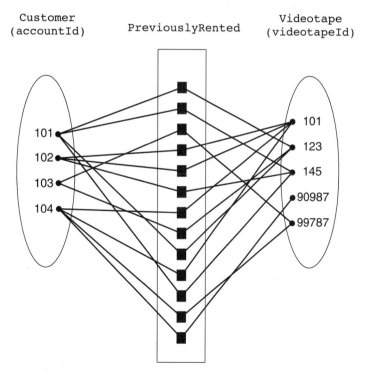

FIGURE 2.3 _____

Entities related by the many-to-many relationship type `PreviouslyRented`

Constraints may also specify a minimum number of relationships for a particular entity. A constraint that specifies whether at least one relationship must exist for each entity is often called a *participation constraint*. That is, if the cardinality is "at least one," then each entity must participate in the relationship type by being related to at least one other entity.

2.3.6 Relationships of Higher Degree

To this point, the discussion has assumed that a relationship is binary. That is, each relationship type connects two entity classes. It is not unusual to have multiparty relationships in an enterprise. For instance, a store may purchase videotapes from a supplier. This purchase represents a three-way (ternary) relationship. The relationship type connects three entity classes. The number of entity classes that are linked by a relationship type is called the *degree* of the relationship type.

Entity–Relationship Diagrams

2.4

An important aspect of ER modeling is the representation of a model by a diagram. The diagrams make ER models easier to understand and to explain. Figure 2.4 shows an ER model that includes classes `Customer` and `Videotape` and relationship type `Rents`. Entity classes are represented by rectangles, attributes by ovals, and relationships by diamonds and lines. Note that this diagram merely shows entity classes and relationship types—it does not describe any particular instances of them. The shaded boxes are comments and are not part of the ER diagram.

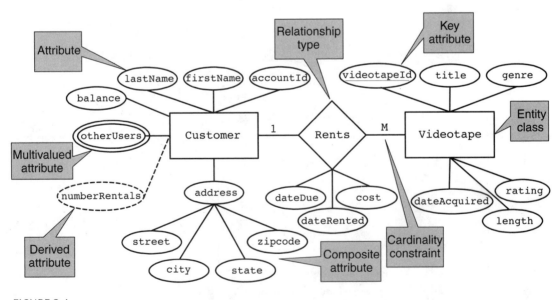

FIGURE 2.4 _____

Entity classes `Customer` *and* `Videotape` *and relationship type* `Rents`

The attributes whose names are underlined are the keys of their entity classes. The border on `numberRentals` is dashed to show that it is derived. The multivalued attribute `otherUsers` has a double border to indicate that it consists of a set of values. The fields of the composite attribute `address` are shown as its attributes.

Much of the detail that is needed to specify the information content, given in Tables 2.1 through 2.4, has been omitted from the diagram in Fig. 2.4. The descriptions of the classes and the types, descriptions, and constraints on the attributes are not shown here. Instead, this information must be maintained in text form as part of a specification of the system, as it is in Tables 2.1 and 2.2. This information is collected in a table called a *data dictionary*.

Cardinality constraints are represented in Fig. 2.4 by the symbols `1` and `M` that appear on the lines and by having single and double lines, as we will see in Fig. 2.5. The symbol `1` on the diagram means that a videotape can be rented by no more than one customer. The symbol `M` means that a customer may rent many (zero or more) videotapes; that is, it is a one-to-many relationship type. The marks tell us how many entities of the *related* class (class near the cardinality mark) can be associated with one entity of the *subject* class (class on the other side of the diamond).

We can best understand the position of the cardinality symbol by creating sentences to represent the relationship roles. Each sentence is created by listing one entity, then the relationship, then the cardinality, and finally the other entity. The following two sentences were created by reading the diagram from left to right and right to left, respectively:

- A customer may rent many videotapes.
- A videotape may be rented by one customer.

This relationship allows for customers who have no videotapes rented and for videotapes that are not rented by any customer. It allows customers to rent any number of videotapes, but does not allow a videotape to be rented by more than one customer. From these facts, we can conclude that the `Rents` relationship represents current rentals and does not represent a history of rentals, as a videotape may be rented many times during its shelf life.

You might have noticed that the original list of entity classes (Table 2.1) gave `Rental` as an entity class, but the discussion in Section 2.3 and the diagram of Fig. 2.4 considered it as a relationship type. It is perfectly appropriate to represent that relationship as class `Rental`, as in Fig. 2.5. Class `Rental` has the attributes of relationship type `Rents`. A many-to-one relationship type and a one-to-one relationship type have replaced the relationship type between `Customer` and `Videotape`.

The double lines linking `Rental` to its two relationship types specify a *participation constraint*. These double lines denote that a `Rental` entity must participate in both relationships. That is, each rental entity must be related to a customer and a videotape. We can represent the relationship types with the following sentences:

- A customer *may* have many rentals.
- A rental *must* have one customer.
- A videotape *may* have one rental.
- A rental *must* have one videotape.

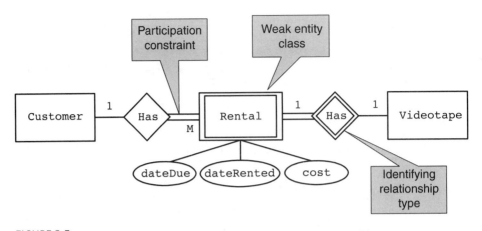

FIGURE 2.5 _____

Representation of entity class `Rental` *and its relationship types*

The sentence uses "may" before the verb if the entity is not required to participate in the relationship and "must" before the verb if it is required to participate.

A `Rental` object cannot exist without being related to a `Customer` and a `Videotape`, and no combination of attributes of class `Rental` is unique. Hence the attributes do not form a key for the class, and `Rental` must be an example of a *weak entity class*, denoted by the double border.

The double border on the diamond that relates `Rental` to `Videotape` marks this relationship type as an *identifying relationship type* for class `Rental`, and it marks `Videotape` as the *owner entity class*. From this notation, we know that a rental is identified by its relationship to a videotape. The related videotape is considered the *owner* of the rental. Without that relationship, the rental cannot exist. The key for a `Rental` entity is the `videoId` attribute, which is the key of the owner videotape.

As another example of how we draw diagrams for relationship types, consider the marriage relationship type that was described in Section 2.3.3. It relates one person to another, as shown in the ER diagram of Fig. 2.6. This diagram shows the entity class `Person` with its key attribute `ssn` and the relationship types `MarriedTo` and `IsChildOf` with their lines. The names of the roles `wife`, `husband`, `child`, and `parent` are shown on the diagram next to the lines of the relationship types. As shown in Fig. 2.6, for each pair of people related by parentage, one is the child and one is the parent.

Additional information contained in Fig. 2.6 is expressed by the following sentences:

- A person is the child of one or two parents.
- A person is the parent of zero or more children.

Reading along the relationship lines creates these sentences. Read in the order of the entity class, the relationship, the cardinality of the role, and the other role. The

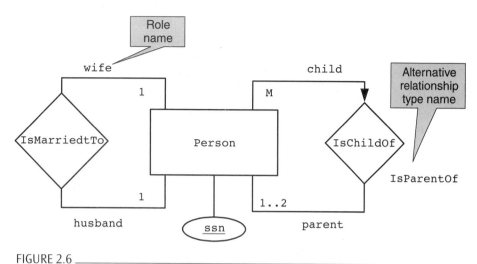

FIGURE 2.6 _____

Relationship types IsMarriedTo *and* IsChildOf *with role names*

cardinality symbol `1..2` on the `parent` line means that the child may have between one and two parents. Figure 2.6 also shows the two names for the parent–
child relationship. From the child's point of view, the relationship is called
`IsChildOf`; this phrase appears inside the diamond. Outside the diamond is the
name of the relationship from the parents' perspective: `IsParentOf`. The arrow
on the child's relationship line points toward the diamond. This depiction indicates
that the name of the relationship inside the diamond refers to this role's relationship name.

A NOTE ABOUT OVERSPECIFYING CARDINALITIES

Perhaps you've seen a flaw in the cardinalities of the diagram given in Fig. 2.6. If every person
must have one or two parents, either there are infinitely many persons or some people are
their own descendants. This problem is a common error created by overspecifying the cardinality of a relationship type. In this case, we must recognize that this relationship type will
represent parent–child relationships between people who are part of the system. Some people
in the system will have parents who are not part of the system. Consequently, the child must
be allowed to have no parent.

   Always keep in mind that we are not attempting to represent the entire world, but only
a small part of it. The cardinality of a role should represent the number of related entities
within the system of interest.

   Although ER diagrams include declarations of cardinality constraints, many
other constraints cannot be represented. The ER diagram for the `IsChildOf`
relationship type restricts the cardinality of the child so that a child has no more
than two parents. It does not, however, place any restrictions on which individuals
are the parents. It is possible for Joe to be a child of Jane and Jane to be a child of

Joe at the same time. The diagram also allows Joe to be a child of Joe! Such nonfactual relationships should not be allowed, but cannot be excluded in an ER diagram. Instead, constraints on individual membership in relationships must be written down as part of the ER modeling process. These limitations will be considered for enforcement later in the development process, either as part of specifying the database or when developing applications.

Figure 2.7 gives examples of the basic symbols that we use to draw ER diagrams. Almost as many styles of ER diagramming exist as organizations that draw them. The style presented here is used by many developers, but is not necessarily the best one. Each designer must draw diagrams that conform to the style used by his or her organization. These diagrams serve as the primary means of communication between users and developers. The particular style chosen is more important to users than to developers. It must convey a precise specification to developers, but must be easily understood by trained users. Once system designers adopt a specific ER style, it is their responsibility to teach their users to understand it.

An ER Model for BigHit Video

2.5

Figure 2.8 is an ER diagram for the BigHit Video information system. It represents all of the entity classes from Table 2.1 and their relationship types. The diagram is not complete because it omits the attributes of most of the classes. You will be asked to finish the attribute and entity class definitions as part of the exercises.

In this section, we will look at what information this conceptual schema can represent and what it cannot represent. Careful study of this diagram will expose many of the issues that are raised in the discovery and specification stages. It will also illustrate how much detail can be specified by an ER model and how that detail constrains the resulting information system.

2.5.1   Recording the History of Rentals

Entity classes `Customer`, `Rental`, and `Videotape` are related as given in Fig. 2.5. As noted earlier, `Rental` entities represent the current state of video rentals. When a videotape is returned, the corresponding `Rental` entity is removed from the database. Certainly, most businesses need to record historical information. For example, BigHit Video wants to be able to determine which videotapes are being rented and what types of videotapes a particular customer tends to rent. Class `Rental` does not provide the information required for these analyses.

Class `PreviousRental` has been added to record the history of customer and videotape rentals. The difference between `Rental` and `PreviousRental` lies in the cardinality constraints of the relationship with `Videotape`. Class `Rental` has a one-to-one relationship with `Videotape`, whereas `PreviousRental` has a many-to-one relationship. This relationship allows many rentals of each videotape to be recorded. We also want to allow a `PreviousRental` entity to have no associated customer. That is, we will place a single line between `PreviousRental` and its relationship with a `Customer`. With this cardinality, we are free to delete

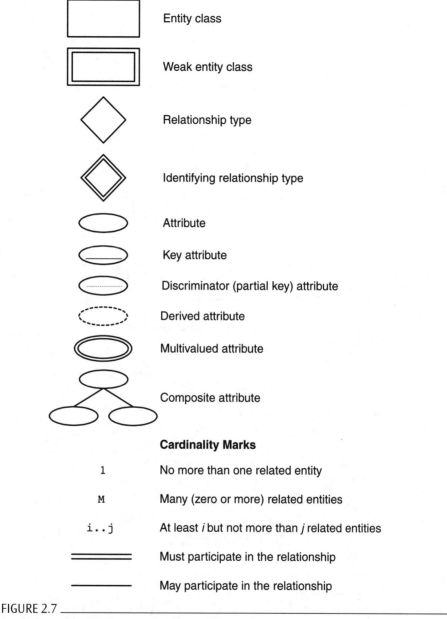

FIGURE 2.7 _____

Symbols used in ER diagrams

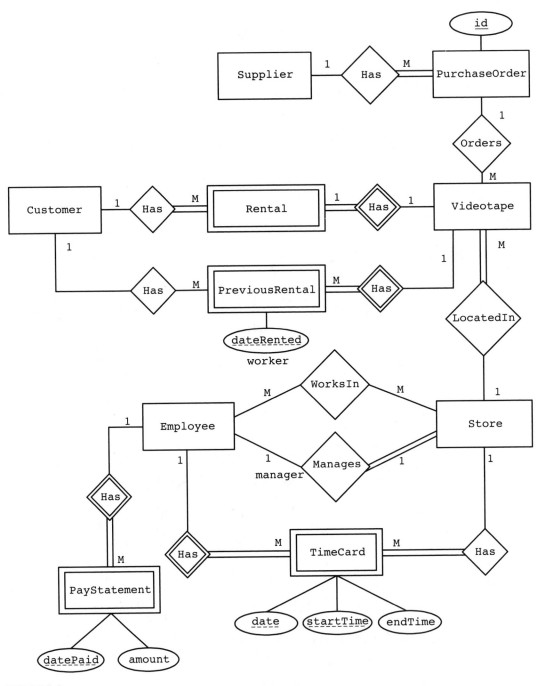

FIGURE 2.8
ER diagram for BigHit Video

inactive customers and the records of their previous rentals without compromising our ability to analyze rental activity.

Class `PreviousRental` is a weak entity with a single identifying relationship. The related videotape does not uniquely identify the `PreviousRental`, however. This property is another difference between `Rental` and `PreviousRental`. Because a videotape can participate in at most one rental at a time, the rental is uniquely determined by its relationship to the videotape.

To uniquely identify a previous rental, we must add another attribute to the key. This attribute, called a *discriminator* or *partial key*, should uniquely identify the entity among all those related to a specific identifying entity. In this case, the `dateRented` attribute and the key of the related videotape together form a unique identification. The `dateRented` attribute *discriminates* among all of the previous rentals for a particular videotape. The partial key is shown with a dashed underline in the ER diagram in Fig. 2.8.

This definition of the key of entity class `PreviousRental` may create some problems for BigHit Video stores. In particular, under this definition, a videotape cannot be rented twice on the same day. The easiest way to eliminate this problem is to change `dateRented` into `dateTimeRented`, an attribute that includes both date and time. If this modification is not appropriate, we can create an artificial key, `rentalId`, to serve as the key of the entity class.

This strategy for handling rentals and previous rentals exposes some limitations of ER models. We have defined the relationship type between `Rental` and `Customer` as to-one so that a videotape can have at most one current rental. When a videotape is checked in, however, the `Rental` entity is deleted and a similar `PreviousRental` must be created. In some sense, the `Rental` is transformed into a `PreviousRental`. Unfortunately, the ER diagram has no way to represent this required transformation.

An alternative design is to have a single rental entity class with a to-many relationship type with `Customer`. In this strategy, the current rentals comprise all of the rentals with a null return date. In this design, however, the ER diagram cannot depict the requirement that there be at most one current rental. As designers, we must decide which is most important: ensuring that there is at most one current rental or ensuring that the previous rentals are reliably handled. The model of Fig. 2.8 is a compromise.

A NOTE ABOUT ETHICAL ISSUES AND PRIVACY

An important issue in recording previous rentals relates to the privacy of the customers. Some people may find it a violation of their privacy for a company like BigHit Video to keep track of all of the videotapes they have rented. Employees of BigHit Video could search the database to find out private information about its customers. Public libraries, for instance, are very careful to keep this kind of information private. U.S. courts have supported public libraries' right to maintain the privacy of their circulation records. BigHit Video is not under the same constitutional constraints, but may not want to record a history of individual rentals.

Removal of the relationship type between `Customer` and `PreviousRental` would make it impossible for BigHit Video to record information about which customers rented which videotapes.

2.5.2 Employee Roles and Cardinalities

Two relationships exist between `Employee` and `Store`. An employee can be associated with a store as manager or as worker. These roles for the employee are shown next to the lines that connect `Employee` and its relationship types. The specification allows an employee to be both manager and worker. It also allows an employee to be a worker for more than one store—a usual occurrence in a business that has multiple outlets in an area.

According to the diagram, an employee can be the manager of no more than one store and each store has exactly one manager. This setup could be a problem if the business needs one person to manage more than one store. If the business fires a store manager, there will likely be a period of time when either there is no manager or some other manager will be asked to fill the vacancy temporarily. The database will be unable to represent this situation. As a result, it will be necessary to add a fictional employee to the `Employee` class and associate that employee with the store as manager. An alternative approach is to modify the cardinalities of the `manages` relationship type so that a store can have no manager and an employee can manage more than one store.

The precise specification of the cardinalities exposes this question about real business practices. It is the users' responsibility to determine whether the representation of their enterprise is correct. It is the developers' responsibility to find and expose the questions that always arise as part of the discovery and specification of information systems.

2.5.3 Purchase Orders and the True Meaning of Videotape

Class `PurchaseOrder` is a class that could be defined as weak. The cardinalities of its relationships require that a purchase order have a single supplier and at least one videotape; hence a purchase order cannot exist unless it is related to other entities. This structure is one characteristic of a weak class. Its natural key is some combination of date, supplier ID, and items. In this case, it is much more straightforward to create an artificial key (`id`) and to define `PurchaseOrder` as a strong entity, as is done in Fig. 2.8.

A weak entity has no key of its own. An example from BigHit Video is class `PayStatement`. This class has no key, because many employees may be paid on the same day. The relationship type `PaidTo`, however, is a many-to-one relationship that links each pay statement to a single employee.

The relationship between a purchase order and a videotape indicates that the specific videotape is being ordered as part of the purchase order. A purchase order can be related to many videotapes—many tapes are included in a single order. In contrast, a videotape can be related to only one order, because it is purchased only once. To create a purchase order, an entity must be added to the `Videotape` class for each item in the order. Each of these videotape entities is associated with a specific store. When the order is received, the information in the database can be used to determine where the tapes go.

This strategy is not the usual approach to purchasing. Typically, a purchase order contains a list of items to be purchased. Each item has some identifying information (for example, a catalog number) and a quantity. In this case, the intention may be to purchase 25 copies of *Lady and the Tramp*. Figure 2.4 would require that 25 entities be created, each with title "Lady and the Tramp," genre "animated comedy," and its own unique value for `videoId`. In turn, each entity would be individually linked with the purchase order. The effect would be an order for 25 items, rather than an order for one item with quantity 25.

This approach is a clear mistake in the diagram. To be correct, the conceptual schema should have a close correspondence to the real objects that it represents. As it now stands, a `PurchaseOrder` entity is not an accurate representation of a real purchase order.

We might be tempted to place a quantity attribute on the `Orders` relationship type, as shown in Fig. 2.9. Now the purchase order is a set of items, each with a quantity. In this model, however, the meaning of `Videotape` has changed. In Fig. 2.8, a `Videotape` entity represents a specific tape that may be rented. In Fig 2.9, a `Videotape` entity represents a specific title but not a specific physical tape. A tape can now be purchased multiple times and may represent more than one physical tape.

The problem that is exposed by this analysis is actually more than a problem with the correspondence between an entity class and its real counterpart. It is an error in the understanding of the nature of a videotape. Two different entity classes have been confused as a single class. One class represents the physical videotape—an object that can be rented, is taken away by a customer, and must be returned before its next rental. The other class represents a more conceptual object—the movie or the catalog item. Each physical videotape is a copy of a specific movie. The movie must be represented by another entity class. It is this object that is purchased and this object that a customer wants to find. After all, a customer will ask, "Do you have a copy of *Lady and the Tramp*?", not "Do you have videotape number 112376?"

Figure 2.10 gives a more appropriate ER diagram for videotapes, movies, purchases, and sales. In this diagram, a videotape is a copy of a movie. The title, genre, and other attributes that are common to all copies of a single movie are attached to the movie class. A purchase order consists of many detail lines, each representing the purchase of some quantity of a single movie. The application that

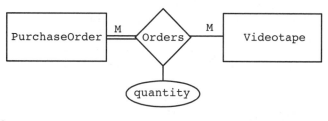

FIGURE 2.9

Representing a purchase order as many items, each with a quantity

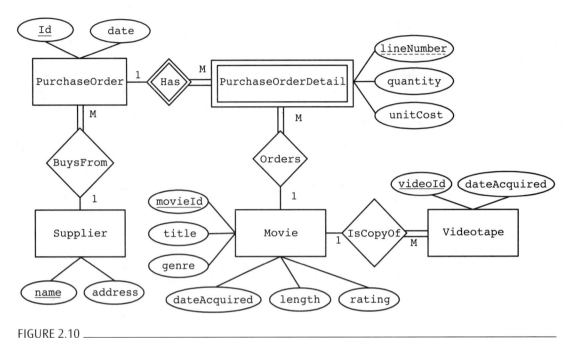

FIGURE 2.10 _____

ER diagram for suppliers, purchases, movies, and videotapes

handles the receipt of movie shipments will have to create `Videotape` entities for each videotape so that the tapes can be entered into the rental inventory.

2.5.4   Employees, Time Cards, and Pay Statements

The weak entity classes `TimeCard` and `PayStatement` record when employees work and what they are paid. In both cases, the entities are not uniquely determined by their identifying relationships. For instance, a pay statement is identified by its related employee, but is not unique for that employee. It is the combination of employee's `ssn` and `datePaid` that is unique. The attribute `datePaid` is called a *discriminator* (or *partial key*) because it identifies the entity among all of those that depend on the same strong entity.

Each time card is associated with an employee and a store. It records the date and the starting and ending times of a single period of work for one employee at one store. It is not possible to represent a situation in which an employee works in two stores with a single time card. Instead, a work period for an employee who begins work in one store, then changes to a different store, must be represented by two time cards.

Chapter Summary

An information system is an organized repository of facts about an enterprise that includes application software to manipulate and create those facts. The development of an information system must begin with data modeling. The goal of data modeling is to produce a conceptual schema for the information system. The data modeling process exposes design options and alternatives so that designers and users can consider their effects. However, faulty or incomplete data modeling often creates limitations on the ability of an information system to represent facts. Later phases of system development include the translation of the conceptual schema into a logical schema that can be used to create a relational database.

Discovery of application requirements—both information and processing—involves an investigation of the enterprise and its current information and processing methods. Developers must translate this information into precise data models using one of a variety of methods.

Entity–relationship modeling divides the information world into entities, attribute values, and relationships. An *entity class* represents the common properties of a collection of similar entities. An *attribute* is a property that describes a characteristic of an entity class. An *attribute value* is the value of that attribute for a specific entity in the class. An *entity* is an instance of an entity class. Each entity has a value for each attribute of its class.

A *relationship type* represents a particular association between entity classes. A *relationship* is an instance of a relationship type; it consists of two (or more) entities that are associated by the relationship type. A relationship type represents the possibility that two entities may be related. Each entity that participates in a relationship has a specific role.

A *cardinality ratio* is associated with each relationship type. This ratio limits the number of times that an individual entity may participate in the relationship type. In a one-to-one relationship type, an entity in either role may participate in at most one relationship. In a one-to-many relationship type, an entity in one role may have many related entities. In a many-to-many relationship type, an entity in either role may be related to many entities.

A *strong entity class* is one that has a *key*—that is, a set of attributes that uniquely determine an entity. A *weak entity class* has no key. The identity of a weak entity is determined by its identifying relationships along with zero or more attributes, or *discriminators*, of the entity.

An Entity–Relationship diagram (ER diagram) is a graphical representation of an ER model. In such a diagram, entity classes are represented as rectangles, attributes as ovals, and relationship types as diamonds and lines. ER diagrams depict the classes and interconnections, but do not show the individual entities and their properties.

Key Terms

Attribute value. The values of a specific attribute for one entity.

Attributes (properties). The characteristics that describe an entity.

Cardinality constraint. A restriction on the cardinality of a role of a relationship. Typical constraints are *to-one*, in which an entity may be related to no more than one entity of the related type, and *to-many*, in which an entity may be related to an unlimited number of entities of the related class. A cardinality constraint may specify a minimum or maximum number of related entities.

Cardinality ratio constraint. A combination of two cardinality constraints, one on each role of a relationship. The four basic types of cardinality ratios are *one-to-one*, *one-to-many*, *many-to-one*, and *many-to-many*.

Composite attribute. An attribute whose value is composed of a collection of individual fields.

Conceptual schema. A precise definition of the data requirements of a system that is understandable to both users and developers of a database. This model includes detailed descriptions of data types, relationships, and constraints and is often represented as an ER model, ER diagram, or object-oriented model.

Constraint. A limitation on the contents of a database. Data models include constraints on the values of attributes and the cardinality of relationships, among others.

Data dictionary. A table that contains the descriptions of classes and the types, descriptions, and constraints on attributes of an information system.

Discriminator. An attribute of a weak entity class that identifies an entity from among all of those with the same identifying entities. A discriminator is part of the key of the weak entity class.

Domain. The set of allowable values of an attribute.

Domain constraint. A requirement that the values of an attribute must come from a specific domain.

Entity. An object in the real world that is of interest to the application.

Entity class. The common characteristics that represent a collection of entities.

Entity–Relationship (ER) model. A strategy for constructing conceptual data models using diagrams that focus on entity classes, relationship types, and attributes.

External schema. A definition of a user's or application's view of the information content of a system.

Identifying relationship type. A to-one relationship type between a weak entity class and a strong entity class that helps to uniquely identify an object of the weak class.

Key. A set of attributes of an entity class whose values uniquely identify an entity.

Key constraint. A constraint on the entities of a class such that no two different entities can have the same values for a specific set of attributes. This set of attributes acts as a key for the class.

Logical schema. The definition of the information content of a system in a manner that can be used to create a database.

Multivalued attribute. An attribute with a set of values.

Null value. A special attribute value that is different from any value in the domain of the attribute. The meaning of a null attribute value of an entity is ambiguous. It may represent a missing value, one that is unknown, or an attribute that is not applicable to the entity.

Owner entity class. The entity class that is related by an identifying relationship to a weak entity class.

Partial key. See *Discriminator*.

Participation constraint. A cardinality constraint on a role in a relationship that requires an entity to be related to at least one entity of the related class.

Physical schema. The definition of the information content of a system in physical terms.

Relationship (instance). An association between two or more entities.

Relationship type. A representation of the possibility that entities of two or more entity classes may be associated.

Role. The function of an entity in a relationship.

Schema. A precise description of one or more aspects of a database system.

Single-valued attribute. An attribute with a single, indivisible value.

Weak entity class. An entity class with no key. It must have at least one identifying relationship type.

Exercises

1. List four important characteristics that must be present for an information system to be successful.

2. Suppose that you are designing an information system for a university. What documents would you use to determine the information requirements?

3. Discuss the importance of data modeling to the success of an information system development. Be sure to describe how vocabulary can be used to improve the communication between developers and users.

4. What is meant by *discovery* in data modeling? What resources are available to developers in discovering information requirements?

5. Define the terms *conceptual model, logical model, physical model,* and *external model.*

6. Create a collection of documents for BigHit Video. Include the following items:
   a. Customer application
   b. Rental receipt
   c. Purchase order
   d. Employment application
   e. Time card
   f. Pay statement
   g. Report on rental activity

7. Characterize the difference between the following pairs of terms:
   a. Entity and entity class
   b. Relationship and relationship type
   c. Attribute value and attribute
   d. Strong entity class and weak entity class
   e. Conceptual schema and logical schema

8. What is a cardinality constraint? What is a participation constraint? Give an example of relationship types that are one-to-one, one-to-many, and many-to-many. What are the participation constraints on these relationship types?

9. Why are weak entity classes important to conceptual modeling? Give an example (not from BigHit Video) of a weak entity class. What are its identifying relationship(s), its owner entity class(es) and its discriminators, if any?

10. Give an example of a relationship type of degree higher than 2. Show how a weak entity class can represent this relationship type.

11. Augment the ER diagrams given in this chapter with attributes as follows:

    a. Augment Fig. 2.4 by including attributes for information about customer preferences, credit cards, and forms of identification. You may use the customer application from Exercise 6(a) as the model.

    b. Augment Fig. 2.4 by including attributes for information about videotapes, including length, rating, studio, and so on.

    c. Augment Fig. 2.8 by including attributes for employee information, as described in the employee application form of Exercise 6(d).

12. Consider the ER diagram shown in Fig. 2.10.

    a. Write a sentence (in English) that expresses the role of a supplier in the diagram.

    b. Write sentences that express the roles of a purchase order in the diagram.

    c. Write sentences that express the roles of a movie in the diagram.

    d. Can a movie be purchased from more than one supplier?

    e. Can a purchase order include more than one detail line for a single movie?

    f. Write three more questions like (d) and (e) that ask questions about cardinalities and participation that can be answered from the diagram.

13. Create an ER model to maintain information about a university's course offerings, students, faculty, student registrations, and student transcripts.

14. Create an ER model for the following enterprise:

    Each building in an organization has a different building name and address. The meeting rooms in each building have their own room numbers and seating capacities. Rooms may be reserved for meetings, and each meeting must start on the hour. The hour and length of use are recorded. Each reservation is made by a group in the company. Each group has a group number and a contact phone.

15. Create an ER model for the following enterprise:

    The Lafayette Park Tennis Club teaches tennis and offers both private and group lessons. The Club charges $45 per hour per student (or couple) for private lessons and $6 per hour for group lessons. Students must preregister for private and group lessons. Each individual lesson has an instructor. Each group lesson must have two instructors. The Club also has weekly tournaments that can be attended by any member of the club at a cost of $5 per person. The Club would like to have an information system to keep track of lessons, students, and the schedules of lessons and instructors. It would also like to record the number of attendees in the tournaments and the amount collected; it is not interested in recording who plays, however.

16. Consider the following ER diagram and attributes:

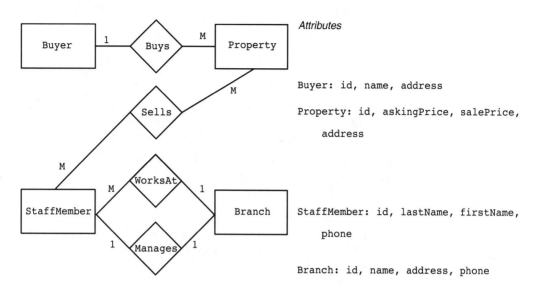

Attributes

Buyer: id, name, address

Property: id, askingPrice, salePrice,
address

StaffMember: id, lastName, firstName,
phone

Branch: id, name, address, phone

a. Write sentences (in English) to describe the roles of staff members in the diagram.
b. Write sentences to describe the roles of property in the diagram.
c. Can the amount of sales for a branch be calculated?
d. Can a property have more than one buyer?
e. Can a property be sold more than once?

17. Consider the following ER diagram:

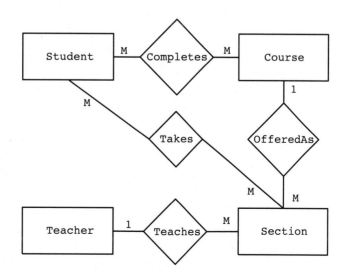

    a. Add attributes to complete the conceptual model. Include keys.

    b. Write sentences to describe the roles of sections in the diagram.

    c. Does every student have to take a section to complete the corresponding course?

    d. Can a teacher teach more than one section of the same course?

    e. Does the `Section` class need a unique key? Why or why not?

18. Develop a full ER diagram for one of the aspects of the BigHit Video information system, as listed below. Include all appropriate attributes of the primary entity classes and relevant attributes of all related classes.

    a. Employees, their time cards and pay statements, and the stores in which they work

    b. Customers, rentals, history of rentals, videotapes, and movies

    c. Suppliers, purchase orders, movies, and videotapes

19. Develop a full ER diagram for an information system that records student records. Include the registration of students for courses, the list of class offerings, the students, and their grades.

Further Readings

Discovery and modeling of information systems are described in Herbst [Her97] and Teorey [Teo94]. The original paper on ER modeling is [Chen76]. Several books have extensive discussions of ER modeling, including Elmasri and Navathe [ElNa99]; Date [Date99]; Batini, Ceri, and Navathe [BCN92]; Benyon [Ben90]; and Howe [Howe89].

3
Advanced Data Models

CHAPTER OBJECTIVES

In this chapter, you will learn:

- Why the object-oriented principles of inheritance and class hierarchies are needed in data modeling
- Techniques for creating enhanced Entity–Relationship models and inheritance
- How to use object-oriented data models to specify information content and behavior
- The principles of specifying entity classes, attributes, relationship types, and inheritance in object-oriented models

*I*nformation systems typically include entities that belong in more than one entity class or that share properties with entities from different classes. These concepts correspond to the object-oriented notions of inheritance and class hierarchies. It is crucial for the conceptual model of the information content to accurately represent the real objects. So far, we have not seen any way to faithfully represent this structure in ER models.

This chapter presents of an extension to ER modeling called the *Enhanced Entity–Relationship (EER) model* and introduces object-oriented data modeling using the *Object Definition Language (ODL)*.

Enhanced ER Modeling

3.1

The enhanced ER model (EER model) has direct and natural support for these object-oriented concepts. It adds new symbols to ER diagramming, as we describe next.

3.1.1   Inheritance and Class Hierarchies

In certain situations, some objects in a class have properties that are not shared by all objects in the class. In such a case, we might consider that groups of objects with shared properties form subclasses of the whole class. For instance, BigHit Video has some employees who are paid hourly and others who are paid a weekly salary. The hourly employees have an hourly pay rate, whereas the salaried employees have a weekly pay rate. In addition, salaried employees earn vacation and sick leave, unlike hourly employees.

It is natural to define an entity class `HourlyEmployee` as a subclass of `Employee`. That is, an `HourlyEmployee` entity is an `Employee` and has all of its characteristics. An `HourlyEmployee` entity has additional characteristics, such as hourly pay rate. These additional characteristics are shared with other hourly employees but not with employees who are not paid on an hourly basis. Similarly, salaried employees are employees who are different from hourly employees.

Figure 3.1 is an EER diagram that depicts subclass–superclass relationship types. These inheritance relationship types are often called *is-a* types because a member of the subclass *is a* member of the superclass. The subclasses `HourlyEmployee` and `SalariedEmployee` are connected to the superclass `Employee` with lines connected through a circle. The *inheritance* (cup) symbols have their open sides facing the superclass. Entity class `HourlyEmployee` has six attributes: five from `Employee` and one of its own. Similarly, `SalariedEmployee` has eight attributes, including three of its own.

The superclass–subclass relationship type in an EER diagram takes the general form of a specialization circle with a single connection to a superclass and multiple connections to subclasses. Each subclass connection has an inheritance symbol that points in the direction of the circle and thence to the superclass. As we will see in Section 3.1.2, there are several constraints that can be imposed on these diagrams.

Class hierarchies are discovered in two ways: by recognizing that a class has subclasses, called *specialization*, and by recognizing that two or more classes have a common superclass, called *generalization*.

The earlier discussion of the subclasses of `Employee` began with the statement that some members of the `Employee` entity class have special properties. This recognition led to the creation of specialized subclasses. The process of finding and specifying differences among objects of a single class is called specialization. A single class is divided into one or more specialized subclasses.

When discovery leads to the realization that two or more separate classes have common properties, we can generalize those classes to create a superclass with the common properties. This process is called generalization.

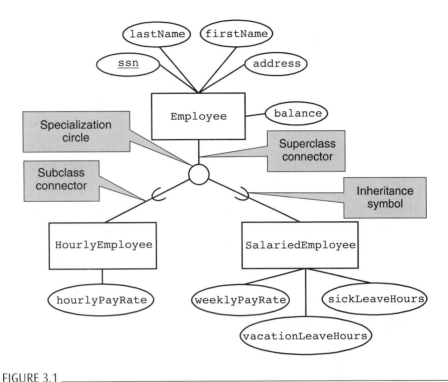

FIGURE 3.1 _____

EER diagram for superclass `Employee` *and its two subclasses*

An entity class can belong to more than one *specialization hierarchy*. Suppose that we want to further characterize employees by the jobs that they perform. Employees can work as a cashier, secretary, purchaser, or stock clerk. The specialization of employees according to their jobs is independent of their specialization by wage type. A design that records this second specialization type is shown in Fig. 3.2. A single employee may be a salaried secretary, an hourly shipping clerk, and so on.

An entity class can also belong to more than one generalization. That is, it can have more than one superclass. In object-oriented designs, this structure is called *multiple inheritance*. For instance, consider a model of the people who are part of a university. It is natural to classify these people as either employees or students. The employees are further specialized as staff or faculty. The new twist here is that a student may be employed as a teaching assistant and be both student and faculty. Figure 3.3 shows an EER diagram that depicts this inheritance structure. Entity class `TeachingAssistant` has two superclasses: `Faculty` and `Student`. You will also notice that the specialization circle has been omitted in the specializations that have only a single subclass.

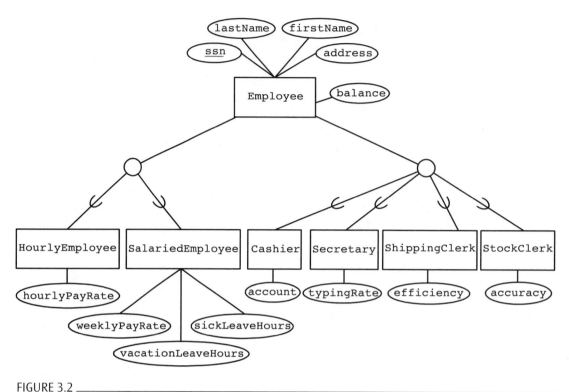

FIGURE 3.2

EER diagram for superclass Employee *with two specialization hierarchies*

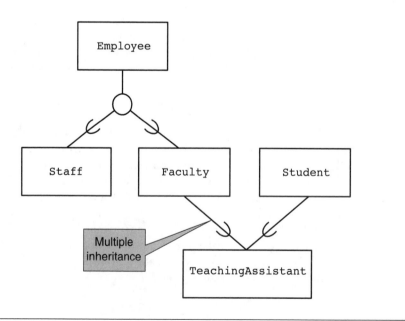

FIGURE 3.3

EER diagram showing multiple inheritance of entity class Instructor

3.1.2   Constraints and Characteristics of Specialization Hierarchies

It is important to put as much information as possible into the EER diagram and to constrain the classes and entities that conform to it. Several options are available for these particular classes. For instance,

1. Is it possible for someone to be both an hourly employee and a salaried employee, or both a cashier and a stock clerk?
2. Are there employees who are neither salaried nor hourly?
3. Is there an attribute or expression whose value determines whether an employee is hourly or salaried?

The diagram of Fig. 3.2 does not give the answers to these questions.

The first question addresses *disjointness*, the property stating that an entity belongs to a single subclass. One can imagine that a manager of one store (a salaried employee) might work overtime at another store as a clerk and be paid on an hourly basis. This employee therefore has two roles and belongs to both subclasses.

The second question addresses *completeness*, the property stating that an entity must belong to at least one subclass. In this case, because we can pay employees only in one of these two ways, and every employee must be paid, it is appropriate to impose a completeness constraint.

The third question indicates whether the specialization is *attribute defined*. An attribute-defined specialization is one in which the value of a particular attribute (the *defining attribute*) determines subclass membership. In this case, an attribute `wageType` could be used as the basis for discrimination. A value of "hourly" or "salaried" is appropriate.

Figure 3.4 shows the diagram of Fig 3.2 augmented to depict the completeness and disjointness constraints of each specialization hierarchy and to indicate that the wage type specialization is attribute defined. A double line from the circle to the superclass represents the completeness constraint. On the right side, the job type specialization is partial, as indicated by a single line.

The disjointness constraint is shown with a "d" in the specialization circle. An "o" in the circle indicates overlap, as in the job type specialization.

The defining attribute for the wage type specialization is indicated by the name `wageType`. Its two possible values, "hourly" and "salaried," are positioned near the subclass connectors. The diagram of Fig. 3.2 has no defining attribute and hence represents a specialization that is not attribute defined.

3.1.3   Modeling Unions with Categories

A final enhancement to our data model is to allow an entity class to be a subset of a union of superclasses. This situation can happen when an entity is a member of a subclass and one of a set of superclasses. In the BigHit Video system, this case can arise when we extend the business to include sales of items as well as rentals. In a single transaction, a customer might rent several videotapes and purchase other items. The sales receipt for this customer transaction includes sales details that

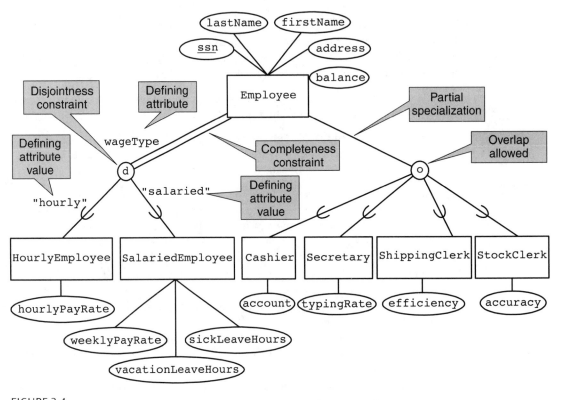

FIGURE 3.4 _____

Constrained EER diagram for `Employee`

come from either rentals or purchases. Figure 3.5 shows an EER diagram for this situation.

The inheritance symbol (pointing down) in Fig. 3.5 is attached to a double line that connects the subclass `TransactionItem` to the specialization circle, which has a "u" inside to show that it is a union. As in Fig. 3.3, the double line represents a completeness constraint. In this case, each transaction item must be either a rental or a sale.

The two superclasses, `Rental` and `Sale`, are also connected to the specialization circle. The `Rental` class is the same as in Fig. 2.8 and represents the rental of a videotape by a customer. The `Sale` entity class represents the sale of some quantity of a particular inventory item.

The entity class `TransactionItem` is called a *union type* or *category*. A transaction item must be a member of exactly one superclass. The category is different from an entity class, in particular because the entities in the category do not all have the same key attributes. A `Rental` entity gets its key from the `videoId` of the related `Videotape` entity. A `Sale` entity gets its key from the `itemId` of its related `InventoryItem` entity.

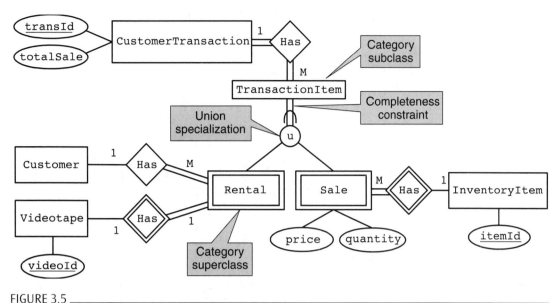

FIGURE 3.5 _____
EER diagram for customer rentals and sales

Object-Oriented Data Modeling

3.2

An *object-oriented (OO) model* is a description of the information content and the behavior of a system. It differs from an ER model primarily in that it includes definitions of the functions (or methods) that are used to manipulate objects. In the ER approach, the information content is specified in ER diagrams and the behavior is specified using independent systems-analysis techniques. This section focuses on the use of OO models for specifying information content.

An OO model differs from an ER model in both form and content. The form of OO models used in this book comes from the Object Definition Language (ODL) developed by the Object Database Management Group (ODMG). ODL is a standard language for defining conceptual schemas as collections of object classes.

An ODL schema consists of a collection of *interface* definitions. An interface definition differs from a class definition in a programming language such as Java in that it lacks an explicit definition of the storage representation for objects. This omission is consistent with the ER model definitions of conceptual schemas. In later chapters, we will translate our ER models and ODL models into relational database schemas and other storage representations. The ODMG standard defines mappings from ODL to various object-oriented programming languages. These mappings are used to create database representations for ODL schemas. Although this book uses the Java mapping in later chapters, ODMG has also defined mappings to C++ and Smalltalk.

The content of an OO model combines a data model and a behavior model into a single schema. Like any other OO language, ODL supports the definition of methods on class objects. An interface definition therefore includes the attributes and relationship types of the ER model and adds definitions of methods or operations on the data members.

3.2.1   Representing Entity Classes as Interfaces

Each entity class of the ER model is represented by an interface declaration in ODL. An interface looks very much like a C++ class definition, consisting of the keyword `interface,` the name, and a set of property specifications surrounded by set braces. Each property of an interface is an attribute, a relationship, or a method.

Figure 3.6 gives a preliminary definition of entity class `Customer`. Each line beginning with the keyword `attribute` defines a single attribute by listing its type and name. The three attributes of Table 2.2 that required special attention in the ER model are the last three properties listed in Fig. 3.6. Attribute `address` is a composite, `otherUsers` is a set, and `numberRentals` is derived. Attribute `address` is defined as a `Struct` called `Addr` with four fields. This code is an example of the use of an ODL composite type definition. Attribute `otherUsers` has type `Set<string>` and its value is a set of string values. The derived attribute `numberRentals` is specified as a method with no parameters that returns an integer value.

3.2.2   Specifying Relationship Types

A binary relationship type is specified in ODL as two properties, one in each of the related entity classes. Relationship types of higher degree cannot be directly represented in ODL, but must first be converted to binary relationship types, as discussed in Chapter 4.

```
interface Customer {
   attribute integer accountId;
   attribute string lastName;
   attribute string firstName;
   attribute struct Addr
       {string street, string city, string state, string zipcode}
     address;
   attribute double balance;
   attribute Set<string> otherUsers;
   method integer numberRentals();
    . . .
   }
```

FIGURE 3.6 _____

Preliminary ODL definition of entity class `Customer`

Relationship types are represented as properties and named with their role names. Figure 3.7 gives partial definitions of classes `Customer` and `Rental`, showing the two properties that represent their association. `Customer` has property `rents` as its role in the relationship type. The property definition includes the type `Set<Rental>`, a multivalued type that specifies the `rents` role as to-many. The definition of `rents` also explicitly lists the inverse role as `Rental::renter`—the role that `Rental` plays in the same relationship type. The `renter` property of `Rental` has the single-valued type `Customer`, which specifies the `renter` property as to-one. Hence the relationship type between `Customer` and `Rental` is one-to-many.

The representation of relationship types as properties is based on each object's unique *object identity* (OID). In an object-oriented data model, an object has an identity that is independent of its property values. This approach is different from that of ER models, where an object is simply a collection of values. In ODL, a relationship property has as its value a unique OID for each related object. No change in values of related objects—not even a change in key attribute values—has any effect on relationships.

ODL does not offer an opportunity to name the relationship type. This point is a disadvantage when compared with an ER model, where the relationship type as well as the roles may be named. You might have noticed in the example ER diagrams that not every relationship type has a distinguishing name. A few relationship types are named `Has` in Fig. 2.8, for instance. These relationship types are relatively anonymous and are primarily distinguished by the classes that they associate.

3.2.3   Subclasses and Inheritance

The object-oriented model supports the definition of class hierarchies. Each class has zero or more superclasses and zero or more subclasses. A subclass inherits (shares) all of the properties of its superclass and may have additional properties that are not shared with the parent class. Figure 3.8 gives parts of the ODL definitions of class `Employee` and its two subclasses, `HourlyEmployee` and `SalariedEmployee`, as described in Section 3.1.1.

```
interface Customer {
  relationship Set<Rental> rents
    inverse Rental::renter;
}
interface Rental {
  relationship Customer renter
    inverse Customer::rents;
}
```

FIGURE 3.7 _____

`Customer` *and* `Rental` *classes and their relationship properties*

```
interface Employee {
   attribute string ssn;
   attribute string lastName;
   attribute string firstName;
   attribute struct Addr
       {string street, string city, string state, string zipcode}
     address;
   attribute double balance;
   relationship Set<Store> worksIn
     inverse Store::staff;
   relationship Store managerOf
     inverse Store::manager;
}
interface HourlyEmployee: Employee {
   attribute float hourlyPayRate;
}
interface SalariedEmployee: Employee {
   attribute float weeklyPayRate;
   attribute integer vacationLeaveHours;
   attribute integer sickLeaveHours;
}
```

FIGURE 3.8 _____

ODL definitions for `Employee,` `HourlyEmployee,` *and* `SalariedEmployee`

Each entity of class `HourlyEmployee` and `SalariedEmployee` is also an entity of class `Employee` and has all of the properties of that class. Every employee, including hourly and salaried employees, has attribute properties `ssn`, `lastName`, `firstName`, and `address` as well as relationship properties `worksIn` and `managerOf`. Only hourly employees have attribute `hourlyPayRate`, however.

In the general form, as described in Section 3.1, inheritance allows many different combinations that are not included in this diagram or in the object model of ODL.

An OO Model for BigHit Video

3.3   Figure 3.9 shows a part of an object-oriented model for BigHit Video.

```
interface Customer {
  attribute integer accountId;
  attribute string lastName;
  attribute string firstName;
  attribute struct Addr
      {string street, string city, string state, string zipcode}
    address;
  attribute double balance;
  attribute Set<string> otherUsers;
  method integer numberRentals();
  relationship Set<Rental> rents
    inverse Rental::renter;
  relationship Set<PreviousRental> rented
    inverse PreviousRental::customer;
};
interface Rental {
  attribute Date dateDue;
  attribute Date dateRented;
  attribute integer cost;
  relationship Customer renter
    inverse Customer::rents;
  relationship Videotape tapeRented
    inverse Videotape::rentedBy;
}
interface Videotape {
  attribute integer videoId;
  attribute date dateAcquired;
  attribute string title;
  attribute string genre;
  relationship Rental rentedBy
    inverse Rental::tapeRented;
  relationship Set<PreviousRental> previouslyRentedBy
    inverse PreviousRental::tapeRented;
  relationship Store location
    inverse Store::videotape;
  relationship Set <PurchaseOrder> orderedBy
    inverse PurchaseOrder::videotape;
};
```

FIGURE 3.9 _____

ODL specification for some classes of BigHit Video

Chapter Summary

Inheritance is included in the Enhanced ER (EER) model to allow different classes that share common properties to be placed into a class hierarchy. The common properties are encapsulated into a superclass, and the properties that are unique to the different classes are encapsulated into subclasses. An entity of a subclass inherits all of the properties of its superclass and usually has its own properties that are not shared with the superclass or other subclasses.

An object-oriented (OO) model defines the structure of the data of a system and includes descriptions of the operations on the data. The Object Definition Language (ODL) is a standard language for defining conceptual schemas as collections of object classes. Each class is represented by an interface definition that defines the properties of objects of the class. No explicit storage representation is implied by the ODL specification.

Attributes are defined as properties within an interface. Each attribute definition includes its name and type. A composite attribute is defined by a `struct` definition that gives a name and type to each field of the attribute. A multivalued attribute is defined using an aggregate type constructor, such as `Set`, that is constrained to a specific type.

A relationship type is included in an ODL specification by defining a property in each related class that represents the role of that class in the relationship. A single-valued attribute is represented as a property whose type is the related class. A multivalued attribute is defined with an aggregate constructor (`Set`) whose elements come from the related class.

Object-oriented data models and the ODL offer an alternative to ER models for conceptual modeling. The main advantage of OO models is that they are familiar to OO developers and are easily translated into OO class definitions. Their two main disadvantages are that the standard ODL model is a text model and is not based on diagrams, and that the ODL view of inheritance is considerably restricted. The issues are discussed in much more detail in Chapter 17.

Key Terms

Attribute-defined specialization. A specialization in which a value of an attribute determines the subclass to which an entity belongs.

Category. A subclass that is a subset of the union of several superclasses. A category differs from an entity class in that it has no key of its own.

Completeness constraint. A constraint of a specialization hierarchy such that each entity of the superclass must be a member of one of the subclasses.

Defining attribute. An attribute whose value determines the subclass to which an entity belongs.

Disjointness constraint. A constraint on a specialization hierarchy such that each entity is a member of no more than one subclass.

Enhanced Entity–Relationship (EER) model. An extension to the ER model that supports specialization and generalization for class inheritance.

Generalization. The creation of a superclass from the common attributes of a collection of subclasses.

Inheritance. A one-to-one relationship type between two entity classes (a subclass and a superclass) in which two related entities represent the same real-world object. The properties of the subclass include all of the properties of the superclass.

Interface. An ODL definition of the name and properties of a class of objects.

Is-a relationship. An inheritance relationship between a superclass and subclass.

Multiple inheritance. A situation in which an entity class is part of more than one specialization hierarchy and hence has more than one superclass.

Object Definition Language (ODL). A standard language for defining object-oriented conceptual schemas. ODL was developed by the Object Database Management Group (ODMG).

Object-oriented (OO) model. A tool for conceptual modeling that describes information as a set of classes. Each class has a set of properties, and each property is either an attribute, a method, or a relationship.

Specialization. The creation of one or more subclasses of a class with their own individual attributes.

Specialization hierarchy. A superclass and its related subclasses. A class may be the superclass of more than one specialization hierarchy.

Union type. See *Category*.

Exercises

1. Define specialization and generalization. Give an example from your experience in which multiple classes are seen to have common characteristics and objects of a single class can be divided into subclasses.

2. Explain and give examples of the use of participation constraints in EER models.

3. Explain and give examples of the differences between overlapping and disjoint specialization and between attribute-defined and non-attribute-defined specialization.

4. What is the difference between a superclass and a category? Give a new example of each.

5. Consider an information system that will represent information about vehicles. Create an EER diagram that records information about cars, trucks, and motorcycles. Add attributes to the classes to represent information that is common to all vehicles and that is specific to particular subclasses.

6. Consider an information system for course registration, as in Exercise 13 in Chapter 2. Use the principles of specialization and generalization to create an EER model in which students and faculty are all members of a `Person` class, students can be either graduate students or undergraduate students,

and course instructors can be either faculty or graduate students. (This situation is similar to, but not the same as, the EER diagram of Fig. 3.3.)

7. Extend the object-oriented model of Fig. 3.6 to represent the content of the ER model of Fig. 2.8.

   a. Define the `Store` interface.

   b. Define the `TimeCard` interface.

   c. Define the `PayStatement` interface.

8. Modify the object-oriented model of Fig. 3.6 to represent the content of the ER model of Fig. 2.10.

   a. Define the `Movie` interface.

   b. Define the `PurchaseOrderDetail` interface.

   c. Define the `PurchaseOrder` interface.

9. The products in the following ER diagram come in three types: Videotapes, Audio CDs, and Playstation CDs. Videotapes have length, genre, and rating. Audio CDs have an artist and a genre. Playstation CDs have a game type and a rating. Modify the EER diagram to reflect these facts.

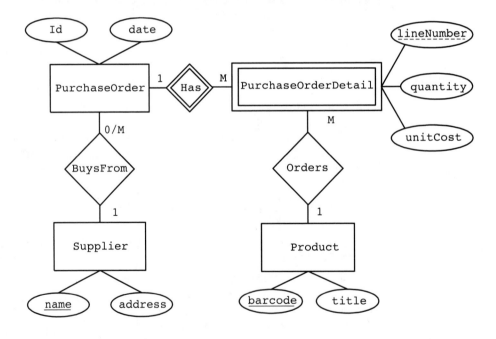

10. Draw an EER diagram for the information system described below:

    The Aquarium Modeling Society wants to keep track of all of the major aquaria in the world. Each aquarium has many tanks and each tank has many creatures in it. Each aquarium has a name and location, and each tank has a name and location. The creatures are divided into fish, mammals, and other species. The creatures are also divided into carnivores (that eat other creatures) and herbivores (that don't). Some creatures are both carnivores and herbivores. Each creature has food that it eats. The society also wants to keep track of which creatures are eaten by which carnivores.

Please identify classes A (aquarium), C (creature), F (fish), M (mammal), T (tank), X (carnivore), H (herbivore), Y (food). Add attributes to these classes as appropriate.

Further Readings

Descriptions and examples of EER models are covered in Elmasri and Navathe [ElNa99]. The standard for ODL is published in Cattell et al. [CBB97]. Object-oriented design and development are well covered in many books and articles. They range from basic introductions, as in Irvine [Irv96], to the presentation of examples of solving business problems with object-oriented methodology, as in Yourdon and Argilla [YoAr96]. Booch [Boo94] is a comprehensive study of the use of object-oriented design methods. Issues in the use of object-oriented methods in database systems are the subject of Bertino and Martino [BeMa93].

4
The Relational
Data Model

CHAPTER OBJECTIVES

In this chapter, you will learn:

- The characteristics of the relational model
- How to define a database structure with relation schemas and database schemas
- How to store database content in tables
- How to represent entity classes as relation schemas
- How to represent attributes and relationships in the relational model
- Various methods for representing specialization and generalization in the relational model
- Specific rules for the translation from ER diagrams to relational models
- How to build databases in Microsoft Access

*T*he *relational model* is used to define logical schemas for information systems. It provides a method for defining a database's structure so that it can be directly implemented in a relational database system. This chapter describes the relational model and details specific methods for translating an ER model into a relational model. Once this translation has been performed, the relational model can be used to define a relational database that is capable of storing the entities and relationships that are specified by the ER model.

The relational model provides the *relation* as the single data structure for representing entities. A relation is a two-dimensional table. The columns of the table represent attributes, and the rows represent entities. The relational data model offers two great advantages: It is supported by an algebra of operations, and it is directly representable by relational database systems.

We must be careful to distinguish between *relations* and *relationships*. Both are based on the mathematical notion of relation—a subset of a Cartesian product of specific sets—but the two terms have very different meanings in database nomenclature. As noted earlier, a relation is a two-dimensional table of values that represent a set of entities from a specific entity class. A relationship, as we saw in Chapter 2, is an association between two entities. An important part of relational modeling is the translation of relationship types. The relationships between entities of an ER model are represented by attributes of the relations of the corresponding relational model.

Introduction to the Relational Model

4.1

A relational model of an information system consists of a set of relation definitions, called *relation schemas*. A relation schema represents an entity class. A relational database system defines a relation, or table, for each relation schema. In turn, the contents of a particular relation represent a specific set of entities. A relation schema provides the structure for a table that can be used to represent entities. We use the term *intension* to describe the structure or schema of a relation and *extension* to indicate its contents or state.

The relational model is supported by a *relational algebra* that provides operations to support the creation and manipulation of relations. The capabilities of this algebra give flexibility and expressive power to relational models and relational database systems. The discussion of the manipulation of relations is contained in Chapter 6. In this chapter, we concentrate on the representation of conceptual data models by relational models.

A relational table is a set of *tuples*. Each tuple represents the values of a specific collection of attributes of a single entity. Because a table is a set, each row must be unique. Thus the relational model requires that every entity be different from every other entity in its values. An entity is completely determined by its values, because any two entities whose property values are identical are considered the same entity. As a consequence, an attempt to add a new row to a relational table will fail if its values are identical to those of an existing row of the table.

This structure is one way in which the relational model differs from an object-oriented approach, in which an object's identity is independent of its value, as discussed in Section 3.2.2. An object-oriented approach allows two distinct objects to have identical values for all properties.

Relation Schemas

4.2

The specification of a relation—the relation schema—consists of the specification of the name and type of each attribute and the constraints on the values of attributes. A relational model, also called a *database schema*, is a collection of relation schemas.

As noted earlier, a relation is a table that contains information about entities of a specific class. A database is a collection of tables. Hence, a database is a collection of sets of entities. Each entity in a database is part of a specific table and belongs to the class associated with the table.

The specification of a relation schema must include the *declaration* of at least one key. As described in Chapter 2, a *key* is a set of attributes whose values uniquely determine a single entity. For a relational table, each row must have a distinct value for its set of key attributes.

Keys are declared, which means that the designer of a schema specifies that the contents of the key attributes will be unique. The declaration of a key creates a *constraint* on the values that are allowed to be in the table. As a result, no two rows will be allowed to have the same value for the key.

For example, if `videoId` is declared to be the key for the `Videotape` schema, then no two rows in the `Videotape` table will have the same `videoId` value. An attempt to add a videotape will not be allowed if the new `videoId` value is the same as that of an existing videotape. An attempt to change the `videoId` of a videotape will not be allowed if it violates this key constraint.

Because a relational table is a set of tuples (rows), a designer could simply declare that the key of a schema is the set of all attributes. In most cases, a better key could be found. Nevertheless, some schemas will have a multiattribute key that consists of all attributes of the schema. (A more complete and formal treatment of keys is found in Section 5.1.)

The process of translating an ER model into a relational model is complex and requires the designer to make several decisions. Those decisions must be made with the goal of improving the quality and especially the effectiveness of the resulting relational database system. They require the designer to have significant experience in order to choose well.

The translation process first creates a relation schema that is a faithful representation of the ER model. Once a correct schema has been created, the process of schema improvement begins. We apply a variety of transformations to the relation schema to make the database more efficient, easier to maintain, and easier to modify.

Don't worry if the original schema is unwieldy, has redundant information, or appears inefficient. The quality improvement processes described in Chapter 5 will be used to create a schema that meets all of the information system requirements.

4.2.1 Representing Entity Classes as Relation Schemas

For each entity class in a conceptual model, there is a relation schema in the corresponding relational model. The attributes of the relation schema are the attributes of the entity class. A relational model for BigHit Video will contain a relation schema for each entity class in the ER model. Hence, there will be a relation schema for customers, one for rentals, one for videotapes, and so on.

There will usually be more relation schemas than entity classes. Schemas will be created to represent both relationships and multivalued attributes. They will also be created to increase the quality of the database with respect to ease of maintenance, redundancy, and consistency.

The translation of an ER model into a relational model begins with the creation of a relation schema for each entity class of the ER model. We then proceed to add attributes to these schemas, identify their key attributes, and choose representations for all of the relationships of the ER model. In the simplest cases, this translation is very simple. Unfortunately, many complex situations will require more explanation.

Figure 4.1 gives the schema and a sample table for class `Movie`. The key of the schema is the single attribute `movieId`, which is underlined in the schema and in the table. Each row of the table represents a single movie.

4.2.2   Atomic Attribute Domains

As noted earlier, a relation is a two-dimensional table of attribute values. The values for an attribute are stored in one column of the table, and all values for an attribute come from a specific domain. This idea corresponds exactly to the definition of attributes in conceptual modeling. The relational model, however, places some restrictions on the domains of attributes that are not present in conceptual modeling.

The domains that are available in the relational model are restricted to indivisible, or *atomic*, values. That is, each domain must be based on some type that cannot be divided into simpler values. Numbers, strings, and dates are considered atomic. It is true that a string is composed of characters and a date is composed of a year, month, and day. Nevertheless, strings and dates are considered atomic because their components cannot be directly referenced within the model. In relational modeling, we are free to designate any set of values as atomic. Once a domain is designated as atomic, however, its components will be difficult to manipulate within the database system.

The attributes `address` and `otherUsers` of entity class `Customer` (Table 2.2) should not be considered atomic. We want to be able to search for customers

Schema: Movie (<u>movieId</u>, title, genre, length, rating)

Table:

movieId	title	genre	length	rating
101	The Thirty-Nine Steps	mystery	101	PG
145	Lady and the Tramp	animated comedy	93	G
90987	Elizabeth	costume drama	123	PG-13
99787	Animal House	comedy	87	PG-13
123	Annie Hall	romantic comedy	110	PG-13

FIGURE 4.1 _____

Schema definition and sample table for class Movie

from a specific city or ZIP code, and to be able to ask whether a specific individual appears in the list of other users for a customer account. Treating these attributes as atomic means that these operations cannot be directly represented as database system operations; some additional programming is required to implement them. For example, suppose that `otherUsers` is specified as an atomic string attribute. The individual names would be stored within the string and separated by commas. An attempt to determine whether a specific person appears on the list would be a complex pattern-matching operation. An attempt to modify the value would be even more complicated.

A composite attribute like `address` violates atomicity because it is composed of several attributes, each with its own name and type. We want the database system to represent each component as a separate attribute in order to support searching for entities with specific values for the components and modifying the components of one or more entities. Figure 4.2 shows entity `Customer` with `address` decomposed into its four fields, each listed as a separate attribute. Notice that "address" does not appear in the schema. Instead, the correspondence between attribute `address` and its four components must be maintained in the data dictionary mentioned in Section 2.4.

A multivalued attribute like `otherUsers` violates atomicity because the value of the attribute for a single entity comprises a set of component values. Each value comes from the same domain, but the attribute has many values. The value of `otherUsers` can be decomposed as a set of attributes, but such a set is not directly representable in the relational model. The only sets are sets of entities—that is, tables.

One approach is to add a single `otherUser` attribute and make a new entity for each other user. For instance, in Table 2.4, customer Carroll Breaux had three other users. Figure 4.3 shows what this strategy would produce. There are now three rows for a single customer. The only difference between these rows is the

Schema: `Customer (`<u>`accountId`</u>`, lastName, firstName, street, city, state,`
         `zipcode, balance)`

Table:

account <u>Id</u>	last Name	first Name	street	city	state	zipcode	balance
101	Block	Jane	1010 Main St.	Apopka	FL	30458	0.00
102	Hamilton	Cherry	3230 Dade St.	Dade City	FL	30555	4.47
103	Harrison	Kate	103 Dodd Hall	Apopka	FL	30457	30.57
104	Breaux	Carroll	76 Main St.	Apopka	FL	30458	34.58

FIGURE 4.2

Schema definition and sample table for class `Customer` *with attribute* `address` *represented by four attributes*

Schema: `Customer (accountId, `<u>`lastName`</u>`, firstName, street, city, state,`
`         zipcode, `<u>`otherUser`</u>`)`

Table:

account Id	last Name	first Name	street	city	state	zipcode	otherUser
104	Breaux	Carroll	76 Main St.	Apopka	FL	30458	Judy Breaux
104	Breaux	Carroll	76 Main St.	Apopka	FL	30458	Cyrus Lambeaux
104	Breaux	Carroll	76 Main St.	Apopka	FL	30458	Jean Deaux

FIGURE 4.3 _____

Schema definition and sample table for class `Customer` *with attribute* `otherUser`*; all other attribute values are duplicated*

value of the last attribute. The key of the schema is the set {`accountId`, `otherUser`}.

It is easy to see that searching and updating the customer table will be very difficult with this schema, which violates two basic principles of information systems. The first principle is that all data models should have a close correspondence with the real situations that they represent. In this case, three entities represent a single real customer. The second principle is that duplication of values should be minimized. Clearly, almost all of the information is duplicated. If Carroll Breaux moves to a new address, every customer entry for him must be changed. This schema is not a good one.

> ## A NOTE ON USING A FIXED NUMBER OF VALUES FOR MULTIVALUED ATTRIBUTES
>
> Another strategy that might work for representing multivalued attributes is adding a particular number of attributes to represent some of the values. For instance, we could have three attributes: `otherUser1`, `otherUser2`, and `otherUser3`. This approach would limit the maximum number of other users to three and make searching difficult. To determine whether someone is allowed to use an account, we would have to look in all three other user attributes. In some cases, this strategy works well; in most cases, however, it is unacceptable.

If multivalued attributes cannot be represented as attributes of the containing schema, they must be put in a separate schema. We'll look at this modification first as a change in the conceptual schema, and then as a relational model. In the ER model, create an `OtherUser` entity class and make it related to class `Customer`, as shown in Fig. 4.4. Class `OtherUser` has a single attribute, `otherUser`. The relationship ratio is one-to-many between `Customer` and `OtherUser`. A single customer may have many other users, but another user of an account must have exactly one customer. `OtherUser` is a weak entity because it has no key of its own. Thus the multivalued attribute has become a multivalued relationship.

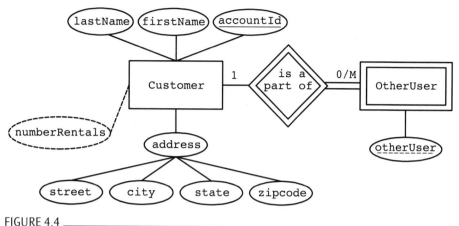

FIGURE 4.4 _____

ER diagram showing `otherUsers` *represented as a separate weak entity class*

The best representation of the `otherUsers` attribute as a separate relation in the relational model is as a schema with two attributes: `accountId` and `otherUser`. Attribute `accountId` represents the relationship between the other user and the customer account. The full reasons for this choice will be covered in the discussions of one-to-many relationships and weak entities later in this chapter. Figure 4.5 gives the schema and a sample table for `OtherUser`.

4.2.3   Representing Relationships as Attributes

The relational model does not support a special data structure to represent relationships; it has only tables and attributes. Hence, each relationship type in a conceptual model must be represented in the relational model either by tables, attributes, or some combination of the two.

In Chapter 2, we saw that each strong entity class has a key that uniquely identifies its entities. The relational model requires that every relation schema have a key that consists of one or more attributes of the schema. The relational model uses these keys to represent relationships.

Schema: `OtherUser` (`accountId`, `otherUser`)

Table:

accountId	otherUser
104	Judy Breaux
104	Cyrus Lambeaux
104	Jean Deaux

FIGURE 4.5 _____

Schema definition and sample table for Class `OtherUser`

Schema: Videotape (<u>videoId</u>, dateAcquired, movieId, storeId)

Table:

videoId	dateAcquired	movieId	storeId
101	1/25/98	101	3
111	2/5/97	123	3
112	12/31/95	123	5
113	4/5/98	123	5
114	4/5/98	189	5
123	3/25/86	123	3
145	5/12/95	145	5
77564	4/29/91	189	3
90987	3/25/99	450	3
99787	10/10/97	987	5

FIGURE 4.6

Schema definition and sample table for class Videotape

For example, consider the Videotape schema of Fig. 4.6. The attributes of Videotape include the simple attributes videoId and dateAcquired of the entity class. In addition, the movieId that is the key of entity class Movie and the storeId attribute that is the key of entity class Store have been added to Videotape. These attributes represent the IsCopyOf and LocatedIn relationship types, respectively. The value of the movieId attribute identifies the movie of which the tape is a copy. The value of the storeId attribute of a Videotape entity identifies the store where the tape is located.

The storeId attribute of schema Videotape is called a *foreign key* attribute because its values are keys of another (foreign) schema. The foreign key value of attribute storeId of a videotape identifies a single store where the videotape is located.

Because LocatedIn is a many-to-one relationship between Videotape and Store, each videotape is located in a single store, and a store has many videotapes located in it. We could not add a videoId attribute to schema Store to represent the LocatedIn relationship type because that attribute would have to be multivalued.

We can always represent a one-to-many relationship by adding a foreign key attribute to the schema that is "to-one" in the relationship.

For a one-to-one relationship type, a foreign key attribute can be added to either related schema. The designer must choose one of the schemas in which to include the foreign key. In some cases, one choice is better than the other.

Figure 4.7 shows two alternative representations of the one-to-one Manages relationship type between classes Store and Employee. Schema Store includes foreign key attribute manager. Schema Employee includes foreign key attribute managed.

(a) Schema: `Store (storeId, street, city, state, zipcode, manager)`

Table:

storeId	street	city	state	zipcode	manager
3	2010 Liberty Rd.	Apopka	FL	34505	145-09-0967
5	1004 N. Monroe St.	Apopka	FL	34506	588-99-0093

(b) Schema: `Employee (ssn, lastName, firstName, managed)`

Table:

ssn	lastName	firstName	managed
145-09-0967	Uno	Jane	3
245-11-4554	Toulouse	Jennifer	
376-77-0099	Threat	Ayisha	
479-98-0098	Fortune	Bruce	
588-99-0093	Fivozinsky	Bruce	5

FIGURE 4.7 _____

Schema definitions and sample tables for classes `Store` *and* `Employee`

We know that there are more employees than stores. In Fig. 4.7, there are two stores and five employees. Every store has a manager, but many employees are not managers. Suppose foreign key `manager` is included in the `Store` schema, as in Fig. 4.7a. The value of `manager` is then the key of the employee who manages the store. Each row of the `Store` table will contain a non-null value for `manager`. If foreign key `manager` is included in the `Employee` schema, as in Fig. 4.7b, its value is the key of the store that the employee manages. Most rows of the `Employee` table will have null as the value for `manager`. As noted in Section 2.3.2, the presence of many nulls in a table is confusing and should be avoided.

> **A NOTE ON NAMES OF FOREIGN KEY ATTRIBUTES |**
>
> We have two obvious choices for the name of a foreign key attribute. We can name it with the name of the key attribute of the related class (`storeId` in schema `Videotape`) or with the role name of the related class (`manager` in schema `Store`). The role name is the best choice, but the attribute name is acceptable in many cases.

4.2.4 Representing Relationships as Tables

Many-to-many relationship types cannot be represented using the method described in the preceding section. A foreign key added to one of the related schemas could not be single-valued. Instead, the foreign key of an entity would have to have a

Schema: `IsChildOf` (`child`, `parent`)

Table:

child	parent
358-44-7865	269-02-8765
579-98-8778	479-98-0098
358-44-7865	579-98-8778

FIGURE 4.8 _____

Schema definition and sample table for relationship type `IsChildOf`

value for each related entity. A set of (many) related entities would exist and would be a corresponding set of values for the foreign key.

A many-to-many relationship must be represented as a separate relation schema whose attributes are the keys of the associated entity types. For instance, the `IsChildOf` relationship type of Fig. 2.6 can be represented by a relation schema whose attributes are `child` and `parent`. The value of each of these attributes is the Social Security number (`ssn`) of the related person. Figure 4.8 shows the schema definition and a sample table for this relationship type. There are four people in the table (their Social Security numbers begin with 2, 3, 4, and 5). Person 3 is the child of person 2 and person 4. Person 5 is the child of person 4.

It is possible—but not necessary—to represent a one-to-one or one-to-many relationship type as a table. In essence, using this structure elevates the relationship type to the status of an entity and hence may be inconsistent with the ER model. It may be appropriate to create a table for a very sparse relationship type, but otherwise it is better to use foreign keys.

4.2.5   Representing Relationships by Merging Entities

A final alternative for representing one-to-one relationships is illustrated in Fig. 4.9. In this case, the two related entity classes `Employee` and `Store` have been merged into a single relation `EmployeeStore` using the `Manages` relationship.

The main reasons that this table is a poor representation are that it removes the distinction between the two entity classes and it fails to explicitly represent the relationship. The conceptual model identifies two separate entity classes and a relationship type, but the relational model has just one table. A clear distinction is no longer drawn between employees and stores, even though they are very different entities. It is also not clear which relationship the merger represents. Nowhere in this schema does "manager" appear!

4.2.6   Representing Weak Entity Classes

Weak entity classes cause difficulties because they lack unique key attributes. In the entity class `TimeCard`, for instance, the attributes are `date`, `startTime`, `endTime`, and `paid`. If two employees start and end work at the same time on the same day,

Schema: EmployeeStore (<u>ssn</u>, lastName, firstName, storeId, storeStreet,
                             storeCity, storeState, storeZipcode)

Table:

<u>ssn</u>	last Name	first Name	store Id	store Street	store City	store State	store Zipcode
145-09-0967	Uno	Jane	3	2010 Liberty Rd.	Apopka	FL	34505
245-11-4554	Toulouse	Jennifer					
376-77-0099	Threat	Ayisha					
479-98-0098	Fortune	Bruce					
588-99-0093	Fivozinsky	Bruce	5	1004 N. Monroe St.	Apopka	FL	34506

FIGURE 4.9 _____

Schema EmployeeStore *that is the combination of* Employee *and* Store

their time card records will be identical. A relation schema with only those three attributes would consider these two time cards to be a single entity. The schema for a weak entity class must have additional attributes that are part of its key. For example, the time card would add an ssn attribute whose value is the key (ssn) of the identifying entity class.

Figure 4.10 shows a schema and a sample table for weak entity TimeCard. Notice that the key of the schema is {ssn, date, startTime}. Attributes date and startTime are the partial keys of the weak entity class. From the attribute values, we can see that no combination of two attributes is unique. The first two rows have identical date, startTime, and endTime values. The last two rows have identical ssn and date values.

Because the relationship between TimeCard and Employee is many-to-one, attribute ssn cannot be the key of TimeCard. The two attributes of entity class TimeCard that combine with ssn to form the key of the schema are called *discriminators*.

Schema: TimeCard (<u>ssn</u>, <u>date</u>, <u>startTime</u>, endTime, storeID, paid)

Table:

ssn	date	startTime	endTime	storeId	paid
145-09-0967	01/14/99	8:15	12:00	3	yes
245-11-4554	01/14/99	8:15	12:00	3	yes
376-77-0099	02/23/99	14:00	22:00	5	yes
145-09-0967	01/16/99	8:15	12:00	3	yes
376-77-0099	01/03/99	10:00	14:00	5	yes
376-77-0099	01/03/99	15:00	19:00	5	yes

FIGURE 4.10 _____

Schema definition and sample table for entity class TimeCard

4.2.7   Representing a Simple Specialization Hierarchy as Tables

Let's first consider the simplest case of a single superclass and multiple subclasses. Figure 4.11 lists the three basic strategies for representing a specialization hierarchy as tables.

Consider the example of hourly and salaried employee specialization that is part of Fig. 3.4, repeated here as Fig. 4.12. This specialization has a single superclass, a defining attribute, and two subclasses.

1. Create a table for the superclass with its attributes and a table for each subclass with its attributes.
2. Create a table for the superclass with all of the subclass attributes.
3. Create a table for each subclass that includes both subclass and superclass attributes.

FIGURE 4.11 _____

Three strategies for representing specialization as tables

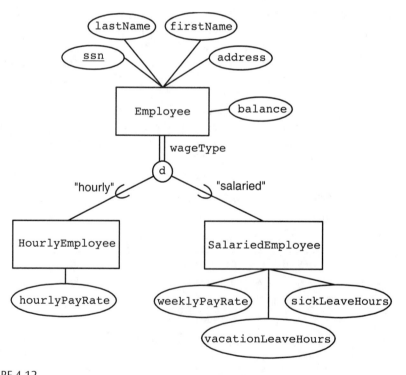

FIGURE 4.12 _____

EER diagram for a specialization with one superclass and two subclasses

```
Employee:(ssn, lastName, firstName, address, balance, wageType)
HourlyEmployee:(ssn, hourlyRate)
SalariedEmployee:(ssn, weeklyPayRate, vacationLeaveHours, sickLeaveHours)
```

FIGURE 4.13 _____

Representing specialization as one table for the superclass and one for each subclass

The first strategy for representing specialization as tables is to create three tables, as shown in Fig. 4.13. The key of the superclass (`Employee.ssn`) is added to each subclass table as a key and foreign key. The defining attribute is added to the superclass table. For each hourly employee, an entry appears in the `Employee` table and the `HourlyEmployee` table. Similarly, a salaried employee has an entry in `Employee` and `SalariedEmployee`. Accessing all of the attributes of a single object requires accessing a row from the superclass table and a row from each relevant subclass table.

In this strategy, a subclass is essentially treated as a weak entity class whose identifying relationship type is its specialization, as with tables `HourlyEmployee` and `SalariedEmployee` in Fig. 4.13. Attribute `ssn` is a foreign key to `Employee` and forms the key of each of these classes. Because the specialization is always one-to-one, no discriminator is required to form the key of a subclass. The BigHit Video database includes tables for both hourly and salaried employees.

The second strategy, as illustrated in Fig. 4.14, creates a single class with all of the attributes, including the defining attribute. Accessing all of the attributes of a single object requires accessing a row from the table and ignoring the irrelevant attributes.

An attribute of an object is non-null only when it is an attribute of the actual type of the object. The hourly employee attribute (`hourlyRate`) will be non-null only when `wageType` is "hourly." The salaried employee attributer ∂?eeklyPayRate, `vacationLeaveHours`, and `sickLeaveHours`) will be non-null only when `wageType` is "salaried."

This strategy has some problems, primarily because it relies heavily on null values and leaves subclass membership somewhat vague. The example of Fig. 4.14 uses attribute `wageType` to define subclass membership. Suppose we omit this attribute. We know that an employee is paid on an hourly basis if the `hourlyRate` attribute is not null, but what does it mean if `hourlyRate` is null? Perhaps the hourly rate has not been entered or is not known. Hence, we can't always determine subclass membership simply by looking for null (or non-null) values.

The third strategy for representing specialization as tables is most similar to the way that object-oriented languages represent inheritance. As we see in Fig. 4.15,

```
Employee:(ssn, lastName, firstName, wageType, hourlyRate, weeklyPayRate,
          vacationLeaveHours, sickLeaveHours)
```

FIGURE 4.14 _____

Representing specialization as a single table with attributes from the superclass and subclasses

```
HourlyEmployee:(ssn, lastName, firstName, address, balance, wageType,
                hourlyRate)
SalariedEmployee:(ssn, lastName, firstName, address, balance, wageType
                weeklyPayRate, vacationLeaveHours, sickLeaveHours)
```

FIGURE 4.15 _____

Representing specialization as one table for each subclass

there is no superclass table. Instead, the superclass attributes appear in each subclass table. Each object belongs in a single subclass and has all of its attributes in that table. Accessing all of the superclass (`Employee`) objects requires accessing the employee attributes in both tables.

4.2.8   Representing More Complex Specializations and Generalizations as Tables

The example of hourly and salaried employees represents single, disjoint, attribute-defined, total specialization. The strategies described earlier are generally applicable, but the details change for multiple generalizations, partial and overlapping specializations, and multiple specializations.

The adaptation to multiple generalizations (multiple inheritance) is straightforward. For strategy 1 of Fig. 4.11, for instance, we add a foreign key to a subclass table for *each* superclass and use the combination of foreign keys as the key of the subclass table.

Strategy 2 of Fig. 4.11 is not appropriate for multiple inheritance. It would call on us to merge the multiple superclass tables in violation of the separation of these entity classes in the conceptual model.

To use the third strategy of Fig. 4.11 (include superclass attributes in the subclass tables), we add all of the attributes of all superclasses to each subclass. As with strategy 1, the key of the subclass table is the combination of the superclass keys.

The first two strategies can be directly applied to nontotal inheritance (no participation constraint). For the third strategy, we must add a superclass table to hold information for all objects that belong to the superclass but to none of the subclasses.

Likewise, overlapping specialization does not create any problem for strategies 1 or 2. Strategy 3 is inappropriate for overlapping specialization.

Multiple specializations, as in the wage type and job type specializations of Fig. 3.2, are obviously very similar to overlapping specializations. Objects belong to multiple subclasses of a superclass. Hence, strategies 1 and 2 are appropriate, but strategy 3 is not.

The bottom line is that strategy 1—creating a table for each superclass and each subclass—is always applicable and is often the best choice. The second strategy—a single table that includes all superclass and subclass attributes—is often dominated by null values and does not always clearly identify subclass membership. The third strategy is not universally applicable, but is often appropriate in the context of object-oriented applications.

None of these strategies is sufficient to enforce all of the constraints of a specialization graph. Additional rules must be implemented to enforce totality, disjointness, values of defining attributes, and subclass and superclass membership.

4.2.9   Representing Category Relationship Types

A category, as described in Section 3.1.3, is defined to allow a relationship type to have a union of classes as its target. The `Has` relationship type shown in Fig. 4.16a, for example, connects a `CustomerTransaction` with either a `Rental` or a `Sale` through category `TransactionItem`. This figure is a simplification of Fig. 3.5. A correct representation for the category relationship type is to treat it as though it were two individual relationship types, as shown in Fig. 4.16b.

Two important aspects of Fig 4.16b make it a flawed representation. First, the category `TransactionItem` has disappeared. It is not explicitly represented in the diagram. Second, the participation constraint on the category relationship has been weakened. A `CustomerTransaction` is required by Fig. 4.16a to have at least one `TransactionItem`, but this requirement doesn't mean that it must have at least one `Sale` and at least one `Rental`. Hence, the participation of a `CustomerTransaction` in the `Has` relationship types of Fig 4.16b must not be required. Enforcement of the original participation constraint will not be automatic with this diagram.

The representation of the category relationship type can now be created from the revised EER diagram. Simply translate the relationship types in the normal manner for one-to-many types. The result is the schemas of Fig. 4.17. To access all of the transaction items associated with a customer transaction will require accessing both the `Sale` and `Rental` tables.

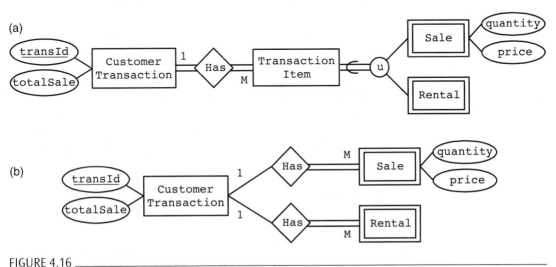

FIGURE 4.16 _____

EER diagrams with category `TransactionItem`

```
CustomerTransaction (transId, totalSale. ...)
Sale (transId, quantity, price, ...)
Rental (transId, ...)
```

FIGURE 4.17 _____

Partial schemas to represent the category relationship type of Fig. 4.16a

It is also possible to treat a category relationship as though it were an entity class. In this case, the class `TransactionItem` would have a relationship type with target `Sale` and a relationship type with target `Rental` instead of the union superclass relationship type. As in the earlier treatment, a simple transformation of the EER diagram would allow the category to be treated as normal entity classes and relationship types.

Translation from ER Model to Relation Schemas

4.3

This section lists the rules that guide us in creating a set of relation schemas to represent an ER model. Examples of the application of these rules were given in Section 4.2.

As with most aspects of information system development, the application of these rules does not necessarily create an ideal representation. It is always important to make sure that the representation is faithful to the objects being represented. It is very appropriate to apply these rules in an informal manner.

4.3.1   Strong Entity Classes

The first three rules of translating ER diagrams to relation schemas tell us how to manage strong entities and their simple attributes.

Rule 1: For each strong entity class of the ER model, create a relation schema by the same name.

Rule 2: For each simple attribute of a strong entity class, create an attribute by the same name in the relation schema.

Rule 3: Choose one of the keys of the strong entity class to be the key of the relation schema. If the chosen key consists of multiple simple attributes, the key of the relation schema will be a set of attributes.

4.3.2   Composite Attributes

Because a relational model attribute cannot have multiple component values, we must represent a component attribute by its constituent fields.

Rule 4: For each composite attribute of a strong entity class, create an attribute in the relation schema for each simple field of the composite attribute.

The name of the component attribute is often lost in this translation. Using it as a prefix to the field names can preserve the name within the relation schema. For example, we could call the attributes created for the `address` attribute `addressStreet`, `addressCity`, `addressState`, and `addressZipcode`.

4.3.3   One-to-Many Relationship Types

For a one-to-many relationship type, we add the key attributes of one entity class to the other entity class. We add attributes to the class whose cardinality is 1. The attributes that represent the relationship type are single-valued because no more than one related entity exists.

Rule 5:   For each one-to-many relationship type R between subject class S and target class T, add the key attributes of class S to class T as foreign keys. Name the attributes using the role that S plays in relationship type R.

Rule 6:   Add the attributes of the relationship type R to target class T.

4.3.4   One-to-One Relationship Types

A one-to-one relationship can be represented as a foreign key in either related schema. The choice of where to put the foreign key is often based on a careful analysis of the expected number of entities in each related class and the expected number of instances of the relationship type. It is appropriate to put the foreign key into the schema where it will have the fewest null values.

Rule 7:   For each one-to-one relationship type R between classes S and T, choose one class to be the subject and one to be the target. Add the key attributes of the subject class to the target schema as foreign key attributes, just as in Rule 4. Add the attributes of the relationship type to the target class, as in Rule 6.

4.3.5   Many-to-Many Relationship Types

A many-to-many relationship type cannot be represented by single-valued attributes in either of the related classes, because an entity of either class can have many related entities. The solution to this dilemma is to represent the relationship as a separate relation schema. An example of adding a schema to represent a relationship appears in Fig. 4.4.

Rule 8:   For each many-to-many relationship type R between classes S and T, create a new relation schema R and add attributes to represent the key of S and the key of T as foreign key attributes. The key of schema R is the combination of those attributes. Add the relationship attributes to schema R, as in Rule 6.

In designing representations for relationship types, we are free to use Rule 8 no matter what the cardinality ratio of the relationship type is. A new schema may be employed to represent one-to-many and one-to-one relationship types. This approach may be used when the relationship type is so important that it deserves to be treated as an entity class. In addition, it might be used when there are many fewer relationships than there are entities in the related classes. A further discussion of the efficiency of relational representations appears in Chapters 6 and 13.

4.3.6   Weak Entity Classes

A weak entity class cannot be directly represented as a relation schema because it has no key. Translation of a weak entity class to a relation schema begins with the creation of a new schema and the addition of the class attributes to the schema. More attributes must be added to the schema for the identifying relationships. The key of the schema is those attributes plus the partial key attributes, if any. Rule 9 formalizes this translation.

> **Rule 9:**   For each weak entity class W, create a new relation schema. For each strong entity class that is related by an identifying relationship, add the key attributes of that class to the new schema as foreign key attributes. Declare the key of the schema to be the combination of the foreign key attributes and the partial key attributes of the weak entity class. Add the simple and composite attributes of class W to the schema, as in Rules 2 and 4.

4.3.7   Specialization and Generalization

The translation from specialization graph to relation schemas must be coordinated among the entity classes in the collection. Usually, the same rule should be used for all classes in the collection. These entity classes may be represented as separate relations, each with its own attributes (Rule 10), as a single relation C with all attributes (Rule 11), or as separate relations, each of which has all of the superclass attributes and its individual subclass attributes (Rule 12).

> **Rule 10:**   Create a relation for each superclass C using the appropriate rules. For each specialization of C that has a defining attribute, add that attribute to the schema for C. For each subclass S, create a new relation schema. Add the simple and composite attributes of class S to the schema, as in Rules 2 and 4. For each superclass C of S, add the key of C as a foreign key referencing relation C. Declare the key of the subclass relation for S to be the composite of these foreign keys.

> **Rule 11:**   For each superclass C, create a new relation schema using the appropriate rules. For each specialization of C that has a defining attribute, add that attribute to the schema for C. For each subclass S of C, add the simple and composite attributes of S to the schema for C.

> **Rule 12:**   For each subclass S, create a new relation schema. For each superclass C of S, add the simple and composite attributes of C

and S to the new schema, as in Rules 2 and 4. Declare the key of the schema to be the combination of the key attributes from the superclasses. For each superclass C that has a partial specialization, create a new relation schema and add all of the attributes of C.

Rule 10 is applicable to every specialization class. Rule 11 should not be used for multiple generalizations (multiple inheritance), and Rule 12 should not be used for overlapping specialization and multiple specializations.

For Rules 10 and 11, the superclass schemas may have already been created by the application of Rule 1 or 8.

4.3.8   Category Relationship Types

Each category relationship type should be translated into relationship types—one between the related type and each superclass of the category.

Rule 13:   For each category C with related class P and superclass B, create a relationship type between P and B of the same cardinality as the relationship type between P and C in the original diagram. Translate this new relationship type into the relational model using Rule 5, 6, 7, or 8, as appropriate.

4.3.9   Multivalued Attributes

A multivalued attribute cannot be represented as a single attribute, but rather must be treated as a separate entity. In essence, the multivalued attribute is treated as if it were a weak entity class in a many-to-one relationship with its containing class.

Rule 14:   For each multivalued attribute M of an entity class C, define a new relation schema M. Add the fields of attribute M to the new schema. Add the key attributes of the schema that contains the other attributes of C to M as a foreign key. Define the key of the new schema to be the combination of all of its attributes.

Building Databases in Microsoft Access

4.4

A database is a collection of tables, each defined by a relation schema. In Chapter 7, we will see how databases can be built using the data definition language of the Standard Query Language (SQL). For now, we will consider how databases can be created using the graphical user interface of Microsoft Access. Once a new database has been created, we simply manipulate the user interface to create the tables one by one.

A database in Microsoft Access is contained in a single file with an ".mdb" extension. Once the Access program has been started, the user is allowed to create a new database. Its name is specified as a file name within the file system of the computer. In this case, a file called "BigHitVideo.mdb" has been created in some local directory. After creating a new database, the designer must enter the metadata using the various tools of the system.

The schemas of the BigHit Video database are implemented in Access using the table design view. Each relation schema is represented as a table. The attributes are specified by name and type, and Access includes a comment field for each attribute. Figure 4.18 shows an example of the design of the `Customer` table. Here the `accountId` field is the key, as indicated by the key symbol to the left of the field name. This designation was entered by selecting the field and clicking on the key toolbar entry, which is shown indented in Fig 4.18. The field's type is `Number` and the `Field Size` entry in the lower half of the screen shows that it is a long integer. It is also a required field and is indexed with no duplicates allowed.

Each table in the database is defined with this tool. It is also possible to create default values, default captions for use in forms, validation rules, and formats. In addition, you can specify a default representation for use in forms.

Once the tables have been designed, it is appropriate to use the Access relationship tools to define the relationships between tables. Selecting Relationship on the Tools menu causes a window to pop up. Figure 4.19 shows the Relationship window for the BigHit Video database.

The lines that connect the tables in Fig. 4.19 represent the relationship types that are defined by key and foreign key correspondence. The line between `Customer`

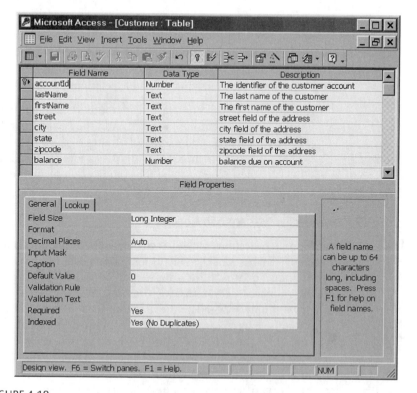

FIGURE 4.18 _____

Design view of `Customer` *table*

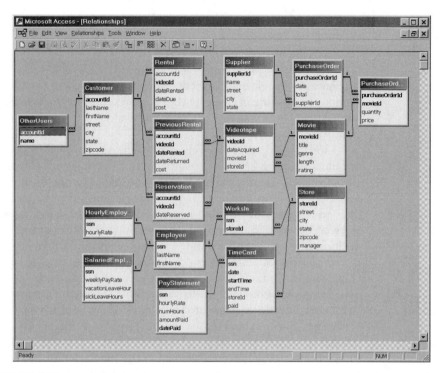

FIGURE 4.19
Relationships in the BigHit Video Database

and `Rental`, for instance, shows that a one-to-many correspondence exists between the `accountId` field of `Customer` and the `accountId` field of `Rental`. The line between `Rental` and `Videotape` shows that a one-to-one relationship type exists between these tables. These connections are created using the capabilities of the Relationship window.

Chapter Summary

The *relational data model* is used to define logical schemas for information systems. It has a single data structure, the *relation*, that is used to store the contents of the database. The conceptual data model defined using the techniques of Chapter 2 can be directly translated into a relational data model. In turn, the relational data model is supported by a *relational algebra* that provides operations to support the creation and manipulation of relations.

A relation is a two-dimensional table of *atomic* values. It consists of a set of tuples (rows), each with the same number of fields (columns). Each tuple represents an entity. Each row of a relation is unique, and each relation has a key set of attributes. There is no ordering of the rows. The structure of a relation is defined by a *relation schema* that defines the name of the relation and the name and type of each of its attributes. A *database schema* is the set of the relation schemas for the tables of the database.

A relation schema is created to represent an entity class in a conceptual model. The attributes of the schema include the attributes of the class. The single-valued attributes of the class are directly represented by schema attributes. In contrast, a composite attribute of an entity class is represented by one attribute for each single-valued field of the composite type. A multivalued attribute is usually represented by a separate relation schema.

Relationship types are represented in the relational model by foreign key attributes. A foreign key is a set of attributes in one relation schema that refer to a key of the related schema. Such a key may be added to one of the related schemas to represent a one-to-one or many-to-one relationship type. A new schema must be created to represent a many-to-many relationship type with foreign key attributes to reference each of the related schemas. As part of this effort, the attributes of the relationship type are placed in the schema with the foreign key attributes.

A relation schema is created for each weak entity class in the conceptual model. This schema contains all of the attributes of the weak entity class plus foreign key attributes for each owner entity class. This key of the schema is the foreign key attributes plus the discriminator attributes of the weak class.

Specialization graphs are translated into relational schemas either by creating a schema for the superclass and each subclass, by creating a single schema with attributes from the superclass and all of the subclasses, or by creating a schema for each subclass that includes the superclass attributes.

Each multivalued attribute of an entity class is represented as a weak entity class related to the containing class.

This chapter also presented 14 rules that describe a strategy for transforming a conceptual model into a relational model.

Key Terms

Atomic attribute. An attribute that cannot be decomposed into simpler values.

Constraint. A restriction on the state (or contents) of a table.

Database schema. The collection of relation schemas that define a database.

Foreign key. A set of attributes of a relation schema that reference the key of another schema.

Key. A minimal set of attributes that are unique in a table. More formally, a superkey for which no subset of attributes is a superkey.

Relation. A set of tuples that come from the domain of a relation schema.

Relation schema. The definition of a domain of values.

Relational algebra. A collection of operations on relations and a set of equivalence rules that together determine a language for relational expressions.

Relational model. A data model that describes all data as relations made from the Cartesian products of specific attribute domains.

Tuple. An ordered list of values, one for each attribute of a relation schema.

Exercises

1. Describe the difference between a conceptual model and a logical model.

2. What are the differences between an ER model and a relational model of an information system?

3. Define the terms *relation, relation schema, database schema, atomic domain, tuple, key,* and *foreign key.*

4. Why must keys be declared? Why is it not always possible to infer a key constraint from the contents of a table?

5. Why is there no such thing as a weak relation schema?

6. How do the attributes in an ER diagram differ from the attributes in the relational model? What restrictions are placed on attributes in the relational model?

7. What are the disadvantages of representing a multivalued attribute of an entity class as a single-valued attribute of the corresponding schema?

8. Describe the difference between a relation and a relationship. How are relationships represented in the relational model? Illustrate your answer with examples.

9. What information can be used to help decide on a representation for a one-to-one relationship type in the relational model?

10. Give three circumstances in which a relation is created that does not directly represent an entity class.

11. Give three examples in which a relation that represents an entity class contains attributes that are not attributes of the entity class.

12. Translate the ER diagram of Fig. 4.4 into a database schema.

13. Create a database schema for the ER diagram of Exercise 16 of Chapter 2.

14. Create a database schema for the ER diagram of Exercise 17 of Chapter 2.

15. Give a database schema for the EER diagram on the following page.

16. Create a database in Microsoft Access. Create and populate tables for the BigHit Video schema.

17. Create a database in Microsoft Access. Create and populate tables for the schema developed in Exercise 13.

18. Create a database in Microsoft Access. Create and populate tables for the schema developed in Exercise 14.

19. Create a database in Microsoft Access. Create and populate tables for the schema developed in Exercise 15.

20. Continue the information system development for BigHit Video by transforming the ER model you created for Exercise 18 in Chapter 2 into a relational database schema.

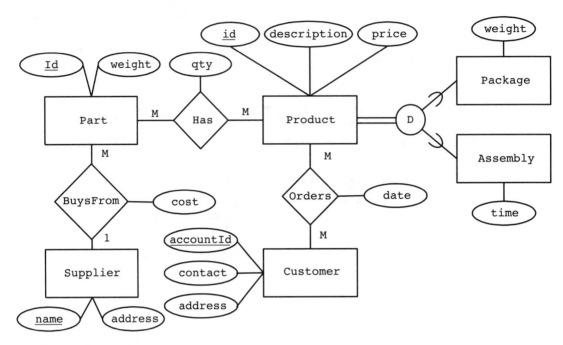

EER diagram for Exercise 15

21. Create a Microsoft Access database for the schema of Exercise 20 and populate it with sample data.

22. Continue the information system development for student records by transforming the ER model you created Exercise 19 in Chapter 2 into a relational database schema.

23. Create a Microsoft Access database for the schema of Exercise 22 and populate it with sample data.

Further Readings

E. F. Codd introduced the relational model in his 1970 paper in the *Communications of the ACM* [Codd70]. He received the ACM Turing award in 1981 and described his efforts in his award lecture [Codd82].

Many excellent books present significantly more detail on this subject than is given in this text. Codd's 1990 book [Codd90] is his restatement of the relational model 20 years later. Date's book [Date99], now in its seventh edition, is recognized as one of the most comprehensive treatments of the relational model.

5
Improving <u>the</u> Quality
<u>of</u> Database Designs

CHAPTER OBJECTIVES

In this chapter, you will learn:
- General strategies for improving database schemas
- The roles of keys, foreign keys, and functional dependencies in defining the quality of schemas
- The definitions of various normal forms
- How to decompose relations to achieve normal form
- How to define and enforce constraints on database content

*W*e are now ready to consider the quality of the database design. The careful application of the rules given in Section 4.3 results in a database schema that is an accurate representation of the ER model. A database built from the schema will be able to represent all of the information that was described by the ER model.

Unfortunately, sometimes a correct and faithful schema may lead to a database that is difficult to use, inefficient to query and update, and hard to understand. This chapter presents some ideas that have been developed to measure the quality of schemas and some techniques that can be used to improve that quality.

The general criteria for quality are that each attribute and schema should have a simple meaning; redundant values in tables should be minimized; the presence of null values in tables should be minimized; and spurious, or meaningless, tuples should not be allowed. The translation from the ER model produces a database schema that has meaningful attributes and schemas but no meaningless tuples.

Redundancy is a particular problem with relation schemas for several reasons. Most obviously, redundant values waste space. A more serious issue is that modification of tuples with redundant values is quite complex. Several anomalous things happen as a result of modifications of redundant values.

An *update anomaly* is a situation in which an update to one value affects another value. To illustrate this circumstance, Fig. 5.1 shows a schema and its contents based on the definition of entity class `Videotape` from Table 2.5. The redundancy in this schema is that multiple copies of the same movie will have the same value for `title` and will have the same values for `genre`, `length`, and `rating`. It is important to the consistency of the database that every copy of *Elizabeth*, for instance, has the same genre, length, and rating. We saw in Section 2.5.3 that these attributes are more properly considered part of `Movie` and not of `Videotape`.

Consider what happens if the length of video 90987 is changed to 107. One copy of *Elizabeth* now has a different length than the other two copies—an *anomalous* situation. To preserve the consistency of the database, any attempt to change the length of a videotape must change the length of every other videotape with the same title. This situation is called a *modification anomaly*.

Two other types of update anomalies are possible: *insertion anomalies* and *deletion anomalies*. An insertion anomaly occurs when adding a tuple results in an inconsistency. For instance, adding tuple (102, 1/1/99, Elizabeth, costume drama, 110, PG-13) creates an inconsistency in the length of the copies of *Elizabeth*. The attempt to add a new tuple to `Videotape` must not be allowed if it will create an inconsistency. In essence, finding the appropriate values for each redundant attribute must precede every insertion. A deletion anomaly may be the most insidious anomaly. Notice that if we delete videotape 123 (the last row of Fig. 5.1), we delete not only the `videoId` and `dateAcquired` of videotape 123 but also all of the information about *Annie Hall*. Deleting the last videotape for a movie will result in the loss of information about the movie.

Videotape:(<u>videoId</u>, dateAcquired, title, genre, length, rating)

videoId	dateAcquired	title	genre	length	rating
101	1/25/98	The Thirty-Nine Steps	mystery	120	R
90987	2/5/97	Elizabeth	costume drama	105	PG-13
145	12/31/95	Lady and the Tramp	animated drama	93	PG
8034	4/5/98	Lady and the Tramp	animated drama	93	PG
90988	4/5/98	Elizabeth	costume drama	105	PG-13
90989	3/25/86	Elizabeth	costume drama	105	PG-13
543	5/12/95	The Thirty-Nine Steps	mystery	120	R
123	4/29/91	Annie Hall	romantic comedy	120	R

FIGURE 5.1

Schema and Contents of `Videotape`

These anomalous situations arise because of the redundancy of the attributes. The schema of Fig. 4.6 that is derived from the revised ER diagram of Fig. 2.10 does not exhibit these redundancies, because the title, genre, and other attributes that are common to the movie have been moved to the `Movie` schema.

Entity class `Videotape` was modified in Section 2.5.3. That is, it was decomposed into two classes, `Videotape` and `Movie`. The result was a reduction in the amount of redundancy in the classes. Such decompositions will allow us to improve schemas by eliminating redundancy.

Functional Dependencies between Attributes

5.1

An attribute B is *functionally dependent* on an attribute A in a relational table if the value of A uniquely determines the value of B. Any two rows that have the same value for A will also have the same value for B. We also say that A *functionally determines* B. We express this idea as

$$A \rightarrow B$$

If B is functionally dependent on A, then the state of the table determines a function from A to B. It does not have to be a function in the sense that some formula or expression allows the value of B to be calculated from A. Instead, a dependency function is determined by the rows of the table. It is calculated as follows. For value a of attribute A:

1. Find any row in the table whose value for attribute A is a.

2. Return the value of B for that row.

If the state of the table changes, the function that determines B from A may also change.

Consider the `Customer` schema of Fig. 5.2. Included in a `Customer` table is a set of postal addresses in the United States. The `state` attribute is functionally dependent on the `zipcode` attribute. That is, every address with a particular ZIP code is in the same state. The arrow pointing from `zipcode` to `state` illustrates the functional dependency.

At any particular time, the ZIP code column of the table does not include every five-digit number. Hence, the function determined by the table is undefined for some numbers in the domain of the `zipcode` attribute. When an address is added whose ZIP code is not already in the table, the function changes to include that ZIP code–state pair. Even if the table includes all of the postal addresses in the

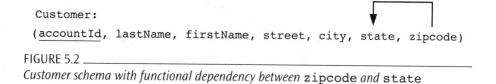

Customer:

(<u>accountId</u>, lastName, firstName, street, city, state, zipcode)

FIGURE 5.2 _____

Customer schema with functional dependency between `zipcode` *and* `state`

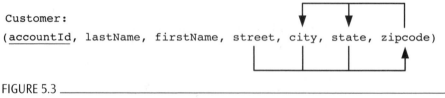

```
Customer:
(accountId, lastName, firstName, street, city, state, zipcode)
```

FIGURE 5.3 _____

`Customer` *schema with functional dependencies*

country, when the U.S. Postal Service assigns a new ZIP code, the function defined by the table will change.

Functional dependencies are also used with sets of attributes. Figure 5.3 shows a more complete set of functional dependencies for the `Customer` schema. Here `zipcode` determines `state` and `city`, and the combination of `street`, `city`, and `state` determines `zipcode`. We write these dependencies as follows:

```
zipcode → {city, state}
{street, city, state} → zipcode
```

A functional dependency is a declared constraint on the contents of a table, much as a key declaration is a constraint. In fact, a key constraint *is* a functional dependency. In the `Videotape` schema, for instance, attribute `videoId` is the key. Every other attribute is functionally dependent on the `videoId`, as illustrated in Fig. 5.4. The definition of functional dependency applies very easily, as two different rows in the table never have the same value for `videoId`. The key of a relation schema functionally determines the set of non-key attributes of the schema.

The enforcement of the `zipcode` → {`city`, `state`} dependency requires that every update to a `city`, `state`, or `zipcode` field be checked for consistency. A change in a customer's `city`, `state`, or `zipcode` cannot be allowed unless it is consistent with all other customers who share the `zipcode`. Checking these constraints can be very expensive. You might also notice that the `Customer` table contains significant redundancy: The `city` and `state` are repeated for every row with a particular `zipcode`.

A NOTE ON MAINTAINING FUNCTIONAL DEPENDENCIES

Once the functional dependencies in a database schema have been specified, the database designers and implementers must ensure that those dependencies are not violated. Users of database systems want to be sure that all data in the database are consistent with the functional dependencies. Any attempt to modify the data in the database must be denied if the modification will create an inconsistent state. In the ZIP code example, every new address must be checked for consistency with addresses that are already in the table. If the table contains a row that shows that ZIP code 32306 is in Florida, no new row can associate ZIP code 32306 with some other state.

A major issue with database design is the need to find ways to reduce the cost of maintaining functional dependency constraints.

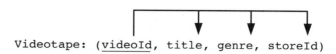

Videotape: (videoId, title, genre, storeId)

FIGURE 5.4 _____

`Videotape` *schema with functional dependency between key and non-key attributes*

5.1.1   Superkeys and Keys

A *superkey* of a relation schema is a set of attributes that functionally determine all other attributes of the table. A key of a schema is a superkey. It is trivially true that the set of all attributes of a schema is a superkey.

We can now give a formal definition of "key" based on the definition of functional dependency. A set of attributes A is a *key* of a relation schema if A is a superkey and any proper subset of A is not a superkey. Removing any attribute from a key produces a set of attributes that does not functionally determine the rest of the attributes of the schema. A key is therefore a minimal superkey.

The great advantage of key constraints over other functional dependencies is that database systems support the enforcement of key constraints. In contrast, they do not support the enforcement of other functional dependencies. In the next section, we will see how arbitrary functional dependencies can be transformed into key constraints. This transformation greatly improves the quality of relation schemas.

The next section describes methods for substituting key constraints for other functional dependencies. Several rules identify tables with functional dependencies that are not key constraints. Those tables can be decomposed into smaller tables in which all functional dependencies are key constraints.

5.1.2   Inferring Functional Dependencies

Database designers have the obligation to specify functional dependencies that arise from the meaning of the data. In addition, many other dependencies are less obvious but can be inferred from the ones provided by the designers. Improvements in the quality of database schemas must be based on all of the functional dependencies. This section investigates the inference rules that are used to discover all of the dependencies of a schema.

You should already be familiar with logical inference of logical expressions. This inference process involves the application of inference rules. That is, from a set of true statements, we can infer other statements that are true.

Six rules of inference for functional dependencies are typically used in schema development. Suppose that W, X, Y, and Z are sets of functional dependencies and that XY is the union of X and Y.

Rule 1:   Reflexivity: If $X \supseteq Y$, then $X \rightarrow Y$.

Rule 2:   Augmentation: If $X \rightarrow Y$, then $XZ \rightarrow YZ$.

Rule 3:   Transitivity: If $X \rightarrow Y$ and $Y \rightarrow Z$, then $X \rightarrow Z$.

Rule 4: Decomposition: If X → YZ, then X → Y.

Rule 5: Union: If X → Y and X → Z, then X → YZ.

Rule 6: Pseudo-transitivity: If X → Y and WY → Z, then WX → Z.

The first three rules are called Armstrong's axioms and were introduced in Armstrong's 1974 paper [Arm74]. Armstrong showed that this set of rules can be used to derive Rules 4 and 5.

These rules will be explained using the example of the following schema and functional dependencies of Fig. 5.5. Schema `PurchaseInfo` records information about purchase orders for items.

Figure 5.6 shows six functional dependencies that can be inferred from the set in Fig. 5.5 by using the inference rules. The reflexivity rule means that a set of attributes X functionally determines any subset Y of X; FD9 is an application of reflexivity that removes the attribute `supplierId` from the left set. The augmentation rule means that attributes may be added to both sides of a functional dependency; attribute `dateOrdered` was added to FD4 to produce FD10. The transitivity rule can be used to infer FD11 because `supplierId` is functionally dependent on `purchaseOrderId` and `supplierName` is functionally dependent on `supplierId`.

`PurchaseInfo:(`<u>`purchaseOrderId`</u>`, supplierId, supplierName, street, city, state, zipcode, `<u>`movieId`</u>`, title, quantity, dateOrdered)`

FD1. `purchaseOrderId`→`{supplierId, dateOrdered}`

FD2. `supplierId`→`supplierName`

FD5. `supplierId`→`{street, zipcode}`

FD4. `zipcode`→`{city,state}`

FD5. `{street,city,state}`→`zipcode`

FD6. `movieId`→`title`

FD7. `{title,dateOrdered}`→`quantity`

FD8. `title`→`movieId`

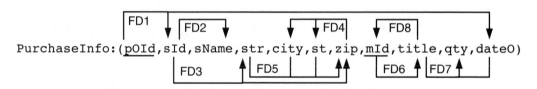

FIGURE 5.5
Schema, functional dependencies, and functional dependency diagram for schema `PurchaseInfo`

FD9. {`purchaseOrderId, supplierId, street`} → {`supplierId, street`} (reflexivity)

FD10. {`zipcode, dateOrdered`} → {`city, state, dateOrdered`} (augmentation)

FD11. `purchaseOrderId` → `supplierName` (transitivity)

FD12. `zipcode` → `state` (decomposition)

FD13. `supplierId` → {`supplierName, street, zipcode`} (union)

FD14. {`movieId, dateOrdered`} → `quantity` (pseudo-transitivity)

FIGURE 5.6 _____

Functional dependencies discovered by the application of inference rules

The decomposition rule allows attributes to be removed from the right side of a functional dependency; FD12 of Fig. 5.6 was inferred by removing attribute `city` from FD4. The union rule allows two rules with the same left side to be combined; application of this rule to FD2 and FD3 produced FD13. The pseudo-transitivity rule is a combination of the augmentation and transitivity rule; $WX \to WY$ from $X \to Y$ by augmentation and $WX \to Z$ by transitivity. FD6 and FD7 were combined in a single step by pseudo-transitivity to produce FD14.

The *closure* of a set of functional dependencies is the largest set of dependencies that can be produced by repeated application of the inference rules to the original set. The closure of a set of dependencies describes every dependency that can be inferred from the dependencies that are declared as part of the schema. It is used to evaluate a schema for opportunities to improve its quality, especially with respect to redundancy and ease of maintenance.

5.1.3 Determining Keys from Functional Dependencies

The normal forms that are included here are all based on the keys of schemas. We know that keys are declared as part of the specification of a schema. In addition, we know that key constraints are functional dependencies. Hence, an alternative approach to determining keys is to specify all of the functional dependencies and then to use them to discover the keys. The following is a formal definition of the keys of a schema:

Suppose S is a schema that is specified as a set of attributes A and a set of functional dependencies F. Let F^+ be the closure of the functional dependencies defined for S. A set of attributes X is a key of S if and only if $X \to A - X$ is in F^+ and for each $Y \subset X$, $Y \to X$ is not in F^+.

Another way of stating this definition is that if a functional dependency $X \to Z$ includes all of the attributes of the schema, then X is a superkey.

Figure 5.7 shows the inference of the key {`purchaseOrderId, movieId`} of the schema shown in Fig. 5.5. A similar inference yields the key {`purchaseOrderId,`

`supplierId` → {`supplierName, street, city, state,` `zipcode`}	union and transitivity
`purchaseOrderId` → {`supplierId, dateOrdered,` `supplierName, street, city, state, zipcode` }	union and transitivity
{`movieId, dateOrdered`} → `quantity`	pseudo-transitivity
{`movieId, dateOrdered`} → {`title, quantity`}	augmentation and union

{`purchaseOrderId, movieId`} → {`supplierId,`
    `supplierName, street, city, state, zipcode, title,`
    `quantity, dateOrdered`}
	pseudo-transitivity

FIGURE 5.7 _____

Inference of a key for schema `PurchaseInfo`

`title`}, because `movieId` is dependent on `title`. The meaning of our key analysis is that the combination of purchase order ID and video ID (or title) is unique. Each purchase order (single purchase order ID) includes any number of videotapes, but no single movie ID may appear twice on a purchase order.

The discovery of keys by analysis of functional dependencies supports the division of the attributes of the schema into two sets. An attribute that is part of any key of the schema is called a *prime attribute*. An attribute that is not part of any key is called a *non-prime attribute*.

Normal Forms

5.2

Normalization is the process of transforming some objects into a structural form that satisfies some collection of rules. Relation schema *normal form* rules are designed so that any schema that is in normal form is guaranteed to have certain quality characteristics. A tremendous amount of research and experimentation has been invested in defining normal form rules. This section covers those rules that are concerned with turning functional dependencies into key dependencies. These rules provide the greatest benefits to fledgling database designers. As database schemas grow more complex, other rules become important. For details on the literature on normal forms, please see the further readings at the end of the chapter.

Four normal form rules are covered in this chapter: first normal form (1NF), second normal form (2NF), third normal form (3NF), and Boyce-Codd normal form (BCNF). Each of these rules extends the previous rule. As a result, a BCNF database schema is usually in proper form to be used to build a relational database system.

Each normal form has a rule that describes what kinds of functional dependencies the normal form allows. Normalization is the process of transforming schemas in order to remove violations of the normal form rules. It is applied independently to each relation schema in a database schema. Thus a database schema is said to be *in normal form* if each of its relation schemas is in the normal form.

Not every functional dependency should be considered a potential normal form violation. The general rule of thumb is to consider only those dependencies

A NOTE ON SCHEMA DECOMPOSITION |

Normal form violations can be removed from a schema by *decomposing* it into two schemas. Suppose the schema

S: (<u>A</u>, <u>B</u>, <u>C</u>, D, E, F) with key {A, B, C} has a functional dependency {A, B} → {E, F}.

The decomposition process removes the right attributes (E, F) of the dependency from the original schema to create a new base schema

S: (<u>A</u>, <u>B</u>, <u>C</u>, D).

All of the attributes of the dependency are combined to create a new related schema

R: (<u>A</u>, <u>B</u>, E, F).

The left attributes of the dependency form the key of the new schema. Those attributes remain in the base schema as a foreign key to the new schema. Examples are given in the following sections.

that have a minimal set of left-side attributes, a maximal set of right-side attributes, and no attributes that are part of both sides. We can say precisely what this means after introducing some notation.

A dependency X → Y is a *full dependency* if Y is not dependent on any subset of X. That is, for all A in X, not X − {A} → Y. Of course, if X has only one attribute, then X → Y is a full functional dependency. A full functional dependency has a minimal left side.

A dependency X → Y is a *maximal dependency* if there is no attribute A not in X or Y such that X → Y ∪ {A}. That is, no additional attribute can be added to the right side of the dependency.

A dependency X → Y is a *trivial dependency* if at least one attribute is part of both sides; that is, where X ∩ Y is not empty.

The following restriction can be made with no loss of generality. Only full, maximal, non-trival functional dependencies should be considered as normal form violations.

5.2.1   First Normal Form: Atomic Attributes

The *first normal form (1NF)* is primarily of interest from a historical perspective. It specifies that every attribute of a schema must take its values from an atomic domain. At some point in the development of the relational model, 1NF was incorporated into the basic definition. Every relation schema that follows the rules of the relational model as defined in Section 4.2 is 1NF.

5.2.2   Second Normal Form: No Partial Key Dependencies

The second normal form is designed to eliminate functional dependencies that have part of a key on the left side.

A relation schema is in *second normal form (2NF)* if no non-prime attributes are partially dependent on any key of the schema. In other words, a functional dependency violates 2NF if its left-side attributes form a proper subset of some key and its right-side attributes are all non-prime.

More formally, a functional dependency $X \rightarrow Y$ is a *partial key dependency* of schema R if there is a set of attributes $W \supset X$ such that W is a key of R. A schema is in 2NF if there are no partial key dependencies.

Schema `PurchaseInfo` is not in 2NF because of the partial key dependencies of several non-prime attributes on `purchaseOrderId`:

purchaseOrderId → {supplierId, dateOrdered, supplierName,
    street, city, state, zipcode }

This dependency states that the name and address of the supplier and the order date are functionally determined by the purchase order ID. Thus each purchase order is given to a single supplier on a single day. Because the purchase order ID is not the key, each ID is associated with many videotapes, each having its own ID, title, and quantity.

To put `PurchaseInfo` into 2NF, we must remove these partial key dependencies by decomposing this schema into smaller schemas. We can remove all of the dependencies in a single step. We split the table into two tables: one that contains all of the attributes of the schema that are not on the right side of the dependency (the independent attributes), and one that has all of the attributes in the partial key dependency. The result is the following two schemas:

S1: (<u>purchaseOrderId</u>, <u>movieId</u>, title, quantity)
        (original schema with the right side of the dependency removed)

S2: (<u>purchaseOrderId</u>, supplierId, dateOrdered,
    supplierName, street, city, state, zipcode)
        (attributes in the functional dependency)

The keys of the first schema (`S1`) are the same two that were keys of the original schema, as no prime attributes have been removed. The key of the second schema (`S2`) is the left side of the functional dependency. The key of `S2`—attribute `purchaseOrderId`—has become a foreign key in schema `S1`. Notice that the non-key dependency in `PurchaseInfo` has been turned into a key dependency in `S2`, just as was promised.

Another partial key dependency, `movieId` → `title`, is not a 2NF violation. That is, `title` is a prime attribute and is not covered by the 2NF rule. In essence, `movieId` and `title` are synonyms. Both identify the videotape. It is important that the normal forms do not forbid synonyms and other multiple key situations.

Now that we have removed the 2NF violation, is the process finished? Only if both of the resulting schemas are in 2NF. To determine whether they are requires another key analysis. The keys of `S1` are {`purchaseOrderId`, `movieId`} and {`purchaseOrderId`, `title`}. The only non-prime attribute, `quantity`, is fully dependent on both keys. Hence, this schema is in 2NF. `S2` has a single key with only one attribute, so there can be no partial dependence on the key. Thus the two new schemas are in 2NF.

In general, the process of testing for 2NF violations and decomposing to remove them continues until every schema is in 2NF.

5.2.3   Third Normal Form: No Transitive Dependencies

The transformation of `PurchaseInfo` did not remove all of the non-key dependencies. Schema `S2` has the following non-key dependencies:

supplierId → {supplierName, street, city, state, zipcode}

zipcode → {city, state}

{street, city, state} → zipcode

These dependencies are all violations of third normal form . Each is a non-key dependency—one in which non-prime attributes are dependent on attributes that do not include a key. Each is transitive because the key of the schema determines a non-key set of attributes that, in turn, determines a set of non-prime attributes.

Functional dependency $X \to Y$ is a *transitive dependency* if there is a set of attributes Z that is not a subset of any key and both $X \to Z$ and $Z \to Y$.

A schema is *in third normal form (3NF)* if it is in 2NF and has no transitive dependencies. We resolve a violation of 3NF by using the same decomposition rule as for 2NF violations.

Schema `S1` is in 3NF, but `S2`'s dependencies are violations of 3NF. We must therefore decompose schema `S2` to remove the violation. Multiple violations are handled one at a time. First, we can remove the first violation by decomposing schema `S2` into two new schemas:

S3: (purchaseOrderId, supplierId, dateOrdered)
                    (S2 with right side of the dependency removed)

S4: (supplierId, supplierName, street, city, state,
zipcode)   (attributes in the functional dependency)

Schema `S3` is in 3NF because no dependencies exist between non-key attributes. The ZIP code dependencies have been moved to schema `S4`.

In schema `S4`, two dependencies violate 3NF. Removing either of them will remove the other because they are interrelated. At this time, a decision must be made. Removing the dependency of `city` and `state` on `zipcode` yields the following schemas:

S5: (supplierId, supplierName, street, zipcode)

S6: (zipcode, city, state)

Removing the dependency of `zipcode` on address, city, and state results in the following schemas:

S7: (supplierId, supplierName, street, city, state)

S8: (street, city, state, zipcode)

It seems clear that it is better to choose the decomposition into `S5` and `S6` instead of that into `S7` and `S8`. First, there are more attributes duplicated in `S7` and `S8`. Second, the three attributes `street`, `city`, and `state` are a foreign key in `S7`. Because foreign keys will be used to find an entity in schema `S8` from one in

```
PurchaseOrder: (purchaseOrderId, supplierId, dateOrdered)
PurchaseOrderDetail: (purchaseOrderId, movieId, title, quantity)
Supplier: (supplierId, supplierName, street, zipcode)
Zipcode: (zipcode, city, state)
```

FIGURE 5.8 _____

3NF Schemas formed from the normalization of `PurchaseInfo`

S7, a multiattribute foreign key will cause significant trouble in terms of efficiency and maintenance.

The original schema `PurchaseInfo` has now been transformed into four new 3NF schemas: S1, S3, S5, and S6. The normalization process is not finished, however, because the names of the schemas are unsuitable. An analysis of the information content (and some knowledge of the usual naming of such objects) yields the completed relation schemas of Fig. 5.8. The purchase order contains the ID, the supplier ID, and the date ordered. This information is common to every item ordered with this purchase order. The detail schema contains the items to be purchased and their quantities. The final schemas contain information about the supplier.

A NOTE ON LOSSLESS DECOMPOSITIONS |

During the early development of normalization methods, a great concern arose that all decompositions should preserve the meaning of the data. It was noted that unconstrained decomposition can create relationships between unrelated objects. In essence, joining the tables produced by decomposition should reproduce the original table. If any tuples appear in the join that were not in the original table, then the decomposition was incorrect. The notion of *lossless decomposition* was developed to characterize those decompositions that do not create such false tuples. The decomposition of a relation into two relations is lossless as long as one of the decomposed relations includes the key of the original relation.

Fortunately, as long as all of our decompositions are based on functional dependencies, we always leave the primary key in the base relation. Hence, we are guaranteed that these decompositions are lossless.

5.2.4   Boyce-Codd Normal Form: No Non-Key Dependencies

Boyce-Codd normal form (BCNF) is the easiest normal form rule to specify. A schema is BCNF if it has no non-key dependencies. BCNF strengthens 3NF so that prime attributes cannot be dependent on non-keys. It was intended to address the dependencies that exist when a schema has two (or more) composite keys that share at least one attribute.

As an example, consider the `Supplier` schema of Fig 5.8. Suppose that `supplierId` and `supplierName` determine one another and that the combination of `supplierId` and `zipcode` is a key. This example models the situation in which a company has offices in different places and each office is considered a different supplier. The following diagram shows the dependencies:

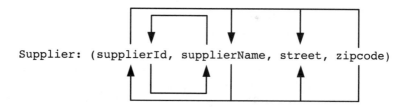

Supplier: (supplierId, supplierName, street, zipcode)

There are two candidate keys: {supplierId, zipcode} and {supplierName, zipcode}. The dependencies between supplierId and supplierName are non-key dependencies, as neither is a key. Although these dependencies are BCNF violations, they are not 3NF violations because the attributes are prime.

Our goal of turning all functional dependencies into key dependencies is not satisfied by this schema. The following table satisfies the two key constraints, because every row has a unique value for each key.

<u>supplierId</u>	supplierName	street	<u>zipcode</u>
101101	Acme Video	312 South St.	44444
101101	Acme Video	45 Park Ave.	01455
101101	Not Acme Video	12370 12th St.	32306

The dependency supplierId → supplierName is not satisfied, however. The key constraints are not sufficient to enforce the dependencies.

The violation of BCNF is resolved in the usual fashion: by splitting the table to remove the dependency. The following BCNF schemas result:

```
Supplier: (supplierId, street, zipcode)
SupplierName: (supplierId, supplierName)
```

In the preceding example, the dependency of supplierId on supplierName is not enforced in the new schema. We must identify supplierName as a secondary key of schema SupplierName to ensure that all dependencies are enforced.

Unfortunately, sometimes we cannot achieve BCNF without removing functional dependencies. As an example, consider a reservation schema that supports the reservation of videotapes by customers for specific days:

```
FutureReservation: (accountId, movieId, date)
```

The functional dependencies for this schema require that a person cannot reserve the same movie more than once and that only one videotape can be reserved on a particular day.*

---

* This example is certainly not realistic, but it allows us to see potential problems with BCNF.

(1) {accountId, videoId} → date
(2) date → videoId

From the functional dependencies, we can determine that the schema has two keys: {accountId, videoId} and {accountId, date}. The functional dependencies allow a videotape to have multiple reservations on different days and a customer to reserve multiple videotapes. That is, the following are not functional dependencies:

(3) not (accountId → videoId)
(4) not (videoId → date)

Functional dependency 2 violates BCNF, but there is no satisfactory decomposition to BCNF relations. The decomposition to remove the violation produces the following two relations:

FR1: (<u>accountId</u>, date)
FR2: (<u>date</u>, videoId)

Functional dependency 1 is not preserved. That is, we can have tuples (a, d1) and (a, d2) in FR1 and (d1, v), and (d2, v) in FR2 where d1 ≠ d2.

From this discussion, we can see that BCNF is beneficial in some cases, but not in others. In addition, it is clear that normalization cannot solve all problems in schema design. Instead, it is merely one tool to help designers achieve useful and effective database schemas. In later chapters, we will even see some reasons why unnormalized relations may be used to improve performance of database operations.

5.2.5   Additional Dependencies and Normal Forms

BCNF is the ultimate normal form based on functional dependencies, but not the last of the normal forms. Researchers and practitioners have identified several normal forms based on other types of dependencies. In particular, there is a fourth normal form (4NF) based on multivalued dependencies and a fifth normal form (5NF) based on join dependencies. These dependencies and normal forms are beyond the scope of this book. The further readings listed at the end of the chapter give sources in which you can learn about these and other normal forms.

A NOTE ON THE AUTOMATIC GENERATION OF NORMAL FORM DATABASE SCHEMAS

A variety of algorithms and even software tools are available to normalize database schemas. The basic strategy follows that described in Section 5.2: Begin with a set of schemas and a set of dependencies; calculate the closure of the set of dependencies; identify a violation of a normal form; eliminate the violation by decomposition; and continue to identify and eliminate violations until none is left. The Further Readings listings provide sources of detailed descriptions of automatic normalization.

Normalization Examples

5.3

5.3.1   Car Registration Example

In this example, we will develop a relation schema without going through the data modeling described in Chapter 2. As has been emphasized, it is not good practice to skip data modeling. Nevertheless, the power of functional dependency analysis and normalization is clearly shown by this example.

Let's consider the record of automobile registrations that is maintained by a state's Department of Motor Vehicles. This agency issues car titles and keeps track of license plates. Figure 5.9 shows a sample of the form that is issued by the State of Florida when a new owner first registers a car. The form also has the fees paid to register the car and to transfer the title. It has information about the car, the title, the owners, the registration, and the license plate. Attributes for these entities are all mixed together on the form.

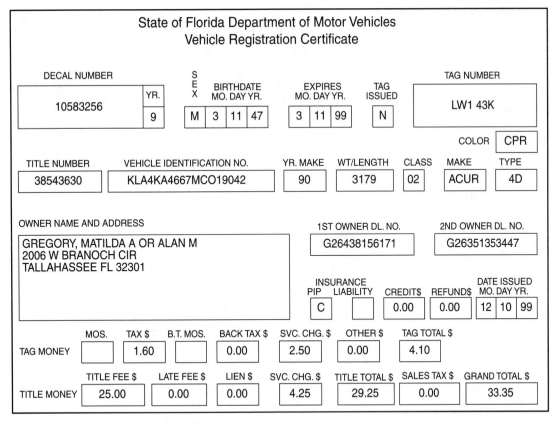

FIGURE 5.9
Sample car registration form

Our goal is to create a database schema in BCNF to store the information in the form. We do so by listing the attributes of a single relation containing this entity. Next, we determine an appropriate set of functional dependencies. We then go through the normalization process.

The first step in creating a schema is to list the attributes. From Fig. 5.9, we find the following attributes:

```
decalNumber, year, sex, birthDate, expiresDate, tagIssued,
    tagNumber, titleNumber, vehicleIdNumber, yearMake, wtLength,
    class, make, type, color, ownerNameAddress, ownerDL1, ownerDL2,
    pip, liability, creditAmt, refundAmt, issuedDate, taxMonths,
    taxAmt, btMonths, btAmt, tagSvcChargeAmt, otherAmt, tagTotalAmt,
    titleFeeAmt, titleLateFeeAmt, lienAmt, titleSvcChargeAmt,
    titleTotalAmt, salesTaxAmt, grandTotalAmt
```

The functional dependencies among these attributes come primarily from their organization into entities. From what we know of car registration, we expect to find that the entities represented by these attributes are the car, the title, the owners, and the registration. Functional dependencies should be defined that represent likely keys for these various entities. The car, owners, and title have obvious keys. The key for the registration is more difficult to analyze and requires some specific knowledge. In Florida, a new registration is issued for each car each year. A decal with the year is issued to the owners and must be attached to the license plate. The number on the decal is unique for the registration. Hence, we can use decalNumber as the key for the registration.

The following rules include each attribute. You will notice that some duplication of attributes occurs. This redundancy could have been avoided by more careful analysis, but it is a normal situation and makes the normalization more interesting.

(d1) VehicleIdNumber → {yearMake, wtLength, class, make, type, color}

(d2) TitleNumber → {yearMake, wtLength, titleFeeAmt, titleLateFeeAmt, lienAmt, titleSvcChargeAmt, titleTotalAmt, salesTaxAmt}

(d3) {ownerDL1, ownerDL2} → {sex, birthDate, ownerNameAddress}

(d4) decalNumber → {year, sex, birthMonth, birthDay, birthYear, expiresDate, tagIssued, tagNumber, pip, liability, creditAmt, refundAmt, issuedDate, taxMonths, taxAmt, btMonths, btAmt, tagSvcChargeAmt, otherAmt, tagTotalAmt, grandTotalAmt}

There are also dependencies between the entities. The registration has a single title, a single car, and one or two owners. The car has one or two owners. These rules can be represented by the following functional dependencies:

(d5) decalNumber → {TitleNumber, VehicleIdNumber, ownerDL1, ownerDL2}

(d6) TitleNumber → {VehicleIdNumber, ownerDL1, ownerDL2}

The normalization could be done informally or formally. As an illustration of the process, it's better to proceed formally. To do so, we begin with a simple renaming of the attributes, as described in the next section.

5.3.2 Working from Dependencies

So far, all of our examples of functional dependency and normalization have begun with an analysis of the meaning of relations and attributes. From these meanings, we infer functional dependencies, and normalization proceeds in the context of our understanding of those meanings.

Not surprisingly, the intuition of a designer may interfere with the normalization of schemas. For this reason, normalization is best seen as a formal process that applies specific syntactic rules to sets of attributes and functional dependencies. It is better that the attributes have names that are not meaningful, because attribute names may distract us from the process of normalization.

Figure 5.10 provides a renaming of the attributes and a restatement of the functional dependencies in terms of the new names. The relation that includes all of the attributes is called R.

Attributes of relation R

New	Old	New	Old	New	Old
A	decalNumber	N	class	AA	btAmt
B	year	O	color	BB	tagSvcChargeAmt
C	sex	P	ownerNameAddr	CC	otherAmt
D	birthDate	Q	ownerDL1	DD	tagTotalAmt
E	expiresDate	R	ownerDL2	EE	titleFeeAmt
F	tagIssued	S	pip	FF	titleLateFeeAmt
G	tagNumber	T	liability	GG	lienAmt
H	titleNumber	U	creditAmt	HH	titleSvcChargeAmt
I	vehicleIdNumber	V	refundAmt	II	titleTotalAmt
J	yearMake	W	issuedDate	JJ	salesTaxAmt
K	wtLength	X	taxMonths	KK	grandTotalAmt
L	make	Y	taxAmt		
M	type	Z	btMonths		

(d1) I → {J, K, L, M, N, O}
(d2) H → {J, K, EE, FF, GG, HH, II, JJ}
(d3) {Q, R} → {C, D, P}
(d4) A → {B, C, D, E, F, G, S, T, U, V, W, X, Y, Z, AA, BB, CC, DD, KK}
(d5) A → {H, I, Q, R}
(d6) H → {I, Q, R}

FIGURE 5.10 _____

Renaming of registration attributes and list of functional dependencies

Analysis for normalization begins with finding the closure of the set of functional dependencies. Some inferred dependencies follow:

(d7) A → {B, C, D, E, F, G, H, I, J, K, L, M, N, O, P, Q, R, S,
          T, U, V, W, X, Y, Z, AA, BB, CC, DD, EE, FF, GG, HH, II,
          JJ, KK}

(d8) H → {C, D, I, J, K, L, M, N, O, P, Q, R, EE, FF, GG, HH, II,
          JJ}

Dependency d7 is a superkey dependency, as every attribute is included. Because the left side is a single attribute, it is a key. Nothing determines A, so A is the only key of the relation R. There are no 2NF violations, because the key has a single attribute.

The other functional dependencies (except d4, a subset of d7) represent 3NF violations. The first decomposition is made from dependency d8, the largest violation. Decomposition using d8 yields two relations:

```
R1: (A, B, E, F, G, H, S, T, U, V, W, X, Y, Z, AA, BB, CC,
     DD, KK)
R2: (H, C, D, I, J, K, L, M, N, O, P, Q, R, EE, FF, GG, HH,
     II, JJ)
```

Dependencies d1 and d3 are 3NF violations in R2. Decomposing R2 according to dependency d1 yields relations R3 and R4:

```
R3: (H, C, D, I, P, Q, R, EE, FF, GG, HH, II, JJ)
R4: (I, J, K, L, M, N, O)
```

Dependency d3 is now a violation in R5. Decomposition of R3 by dependency d3 yields relations R5 and R6:

```
R5: (H, I, Q, R, EE, FF, GG, HH, II, JJ)
R6: (Q, R, C, D, P)
```

The database schema {R1, R4, R5, R6} is in BCNF. Figure 5.11 shows the database schema with the original attribute names and reasonable schema names. You may notice that the duplication of non-key attributes has been eliminated and the attributes are in the correct relations.

A NOTE ABOUT HAVING NO SECOND OWNER

The key for the `Owners` relation in Fig. 5.11 is the combination of the driver's license numbers of the two owners. In many cases, however, there will be no second owner. This situation causes a problem because database systems often require that key attributes must be non-null. Hence, for this schema, we must have a non-null value that means that there is no second owner.

A solution to this problem is to designate a specific driver's license number, such as 11111111111, to stand for the null second owner. The database applications must recognize this designation and react appropriately.

```
Registration (R1): (decalNumber, year, expiresDate,
        tagIssued, tagNumber, titleNumber, pip, liability,
        creditAmt, refundAmt, issuedDate, taxMonths, taxAmt,
        btMonths, btAmt, tagSvcChargAmt, otherAmt,
        tagTotalAmt, grandTotalAmt}
    foreign key: titleNumber to relation Title


Vehicle (R4): (vehicleIdNumber, yearMake, wtLength, class,
        make, type, color)


Title (R5): (titleNumber, vehicleIdNumber, ownerDL1,
        ownerDL2, titleFeeAmt, titleLateFeeAmt, lienAmt,
        titleSvcChargeAmt, titleTotalAmt, salesTaxAmt)
    foreign keys: vehicleIdNumber to relation Vehicle,
        {ownerDL1, ownerDL2} to relation Owners


Owners (R6): (ownerDL1, ownerDL2, sex, birthDate,
        ownerNameAddress)
```

FIGURE 5.11 _____
BCNF database schema for car registration

5.3.3   Formal Example

This section takes us through the normalization of relations with no meaning, only functional dependencies. Consider the relation R and its functional dependencies d1, d2, d3, and d4. The dependencies are represented in text and with dependency arrows as follows:

R: (A, B, C, D, E, F, G, H)

(d1) A →{B, C, D}

(d2) B → C

(d3) E →{F, G, H}

(d4) G →{H, E}

We can infer functional dependencies d5, d6, and d7, as shown below:

(d5) {A, E} →{B, C, D, F, G, H}

(d6) G →{E, F, H}

(d7) {A, G} →{B, C, D, E, F, H}

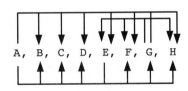

From these dependencies, we conclude that there are two keys: {A, E} and {A, G}. Arbitrarily, we let {A, E} be the primary key. The dependencies on A, E, and G (dependencies d1, d3, d4, and d6) all contain 2NF violations, although the dependencies E → G and G → E are not violations because E and G are prime attributes. We can remove the G and E from the right sides of d3, d4, and d6. After this action, the following dependencies are 2NF violations:

(d1) A → {B, C, D}

(d3') E → {F, H}

(d4') G → H

(d6') G → {F, H}

We are free to choose any violating dependency for the first decomposition. Decomposing by d1 yields

```
R1:(A, E, F, G, H)
R2:(A, B, C, D)
```

Dependencies d3' and d6' are 2NF violations in R1. Decomposing by d3' yields

```
R3:(A, E, G)
R4:(E, F, H)
```

There are no 2NF violations in R2, R3, or R4. The decomposition by d3' has also removed the violations of d4' and d6' because G (left side) is not in the same relation as F or H.

Dependency d2 is a 3NF violation in R2. Decomposing R2 by d2 yields the final BCNF database schema.

```
R3:(A, E, G)
R4:(E, F, H)
R5:(A, B, D)
R6:(B, C)
```

Referential Integrity and Other Constraints

5.4

By now, declaring and enforcing constraints should be second nature to you. We have seen domain constraints, key constraints, and functional dependency constraints. This section attempts to clarify some additional important constraints that are specified as part of a database schema. The general term *integrity constraint* refers to a restriction on the contents of a database.

The normalization process transforms relations to remove non-key dependencies. The dependencies don't disappear, however. Instead, they are transformed into key dependencies and foreign key constraints. Key dependencies have been discussed in detail in previous sections, but foreign keys have not been considered fully.

Consider the PurchaseOrder (PO) and PurchaseOrderDetail (POD) schemas of Fig. 5.7. Schema POD has an attribute purchaseOrderId that is a foreign key. Each POD entity has a value of `purchaseOrderId` that identifies an element of the PO table. This foreign key is in the POD table precisely to designate the purchase order of which the detail entity is a part. It would be a mistake if a detail entity referenced a nonexistent PO entity—that is, a POD whose `purchaseOrderId` value did not appear in the PO table.

A *foreign key constraint*, also called a *referential integrity constraint*, is used to ensure that each value of a foreign key attribute refers to an entity that appears in the foreign table. As with other constraints, any attempt to modify the database contents that would cause a foreign key constraint violation must be disallowed.

Fortunately, relational database systems provide enforcement of referential integrity constraints. The constraint is specified in the database schema, and the database system enforces it.

The normalization process identifies the functional dependency constraints that are difficult and expensive to enforce and replaces them with key constraints and foreign key constraints. The database system can enforce these constraints efficiently because the algorithms are built into the systems and because the only modifications that must be checked are modifications in key values. Any attribute that is neither a key nor a foreign key may be freely modified. On the other hand, those few attributes that are part of keys or foreign keys must be carefully monitored. The benefits in the integrity of the database contents are well worth the cost of constraint enforcement.

Chapter Summary

Once a relational model has been created, it must be subjected to analysis and modification to ensure that the final model is of an appropriate quality. The general criteria for quality are that each attribute and schema should have a simple meaning, redundant values in tables should be minimized, the presence of null values in tables should be minimized, and spurious or meaningless tuples should be disallowed. More formal measures of quality are based on functional dependencies and normal forms. Overall, the goal of normalization is to represent functional dependencies as key and foreign key dependencies, thereby reducing redundancy and making the functional dependency constraints easier to enforce.

A functional dependency is a constraint on a table that specifies that a certain set of attributes functionally determines another set. That is, any two tuples that have the same values for their first set of attributes also have the same values for their dependent set of attributes. Inference rules can be used to find all of the dependencies that can be derived from a set of dependencies. The keys of a schema can be determined from the functional dependencies. A key declaration, in turn, defines a functional dependency.

Each normal form places a restriction on functional dependencies. If a relation schema contains a violation of the normal form, it must be decomposed into two schemas. The result of the decomposition is to transform a non-key dependency into a key dependency.

Database systems support the enforcement of some constraints, including primary and secondary key constraints and foreign key (referential integrity) constraints. Other constraints must be enforced by applications or other database programs.

Key Terms

Boyce-Codd normal form (BCNF) schema. A schema in which every non-trivial functional dependency has a superkey on the left side.

Decomposition. The process of dividing a schema into two smaller schemas, often for the purpose of removing a normal form violation.

Deletion anomaly. A situation, usually caused by redundancy in the schema, in which the deletion of one row of a table results in the deletion of unintended information.

First normal form (1NF) schema. A schema whose attributes are all single-valued.

Functional dependency. The situation in which the values of one set of attributes determine the values of another set.

Insertion anomaly. A situation, usually caused by redundancy in the schema, in which the insertion of a row in a table creates an inconsistency with other rows.

Modification anomaly. A situation, usually caused by redundancy in the schema, in which the modification of a row of a table creates an inconsistency with another row.

Non-prime attribute. An attribute in a relation schema that is not part of any key of the relation schema.

Normal form. A collection of rules that describes an acceptable form of a relation schema.

Partial key dependency. A dependency whose left side is a subset of a key.

Prime attribute. An attribute in a relation schema that is part of some key of the schema.

Referential integrity. A constraint on a table that a value of a foreign key must represent an entity in the related table.

Second normal form (2NF) schema. A schema that has no non-prime attribute that is partially dependent on a key.

Superkey. A set of attributes of a relation schema that together determine the rest of the attributes of the schema. Alternatively, the left side of a functional dependency that includes all of the attributes of a schema. Every key is also a superkey.

Third normal form (3NF) schema. A schema that is in 2NF and has no non-prime attribute that is transitively dependent on a key of the schema.

Transitive dependency. The nontrivial dependency of an attribute A on some set of attributes X that are themselves nontrivially dependent on another set of attributes Y. That is, $Y \rightarrow X \rightarrow A$.

Trivial dependency. A functional dependency that has an attribute that appears on both sides.

Update anomaly. A situation, usually caused by redundancy in the schema, in which an update to one value affects another value. An update anomaly may be a deletion anomaly, an insertion anomaly, or a modification anomaly.

Exercises

1. Give three reasons why redundancy in schemas creates problems and an example of each.

2. Give an example (not from the book) of each type (deletion, insertion, modification) of anomaly for the schema and table shown in Fig. 5.1.

3. Is it necessary to *declare* functional dependencies, or is it possible to infer them from sample tables? Can any apparent functional dependencies be inferred from the table in Fig. 5.1 that are not truly functional dependencies?

4. What does it mean to violate a constraint on the contents of a database?

5. Give an informal argument that inference Rule 4 (see Section 5.1.2) can be derived from Rules 1, 2, and 3.

6. Give an informal argument that inference Rule 5 (Section 5.1.2) can be derived from Rules 1, 2, and 3.

7. Give an informal argument that inference Rule 6 (Section 5.1.2) can be derived from Rules 1, 2, and 3.

8. Use the inference rules of Section 5.1.2 and the functional dependencies of Fig. 5.5 to give a formal derivation of functional dependencies FD9, FD10, FD11, FD12, FD13, and FD14 of Fig. 5.6.

9. Suppose a student registration database has a table for student grades:

   ```
   Grades: (studentId, lastName, firstName, courseId,
       courseTitle, sectionNumber, semester, numHours,
       meetingTime, meetingRoom, grade)
   ```

   a. Give a sample table for the `Grades` schema that shows the redundancy inherent in the meaning of the information.

   b. Define appropriate functional dependencies for the `Grades` schema.

   c. List the full, maximal, nontrivial dependencies that can be inferred from the dependencies you defined in (b).

   d. Identify and remove any 2NF violations in the `Grades` schema. Show the resulting schemas and tables.

   e. Identify and remove any 3NF violations resulting from (c). Show the resulting schemas and tables.

Suppose R: (A, B, C, D, E, F, G, H) is a relation. Answer Exercises 10–16 based on the functional dependencies given in each question.

10. With no functional dependencies defined, what is the key of R?

11. Suppose {A, B} is the key of R, and A → {C, D} and B → {E, F, H}.
    a. List the full, maximal, nontrivial functional dependencies of R.
    b. Which dependencies represent 2NF violations?
    c. Eliminate the 2NF violations by decomposition.
    d. Which dependencies represent 3NF violations?
    e. Eliminate the 3NF violations.

12. Suppose A → {B, C, D, F, G}, B → {C, D}, and E → {G, H}.
    a. Which sets of attributes are the keys of R?
    b. Identify and eliminate any 2NF violations.
    c. Identify and eliminate any 3NF violations.

13. Suppose {A, B} → {C, D, E, F, G, H}, C → {B, E, F}, and G → H.
    a. Which sets of attributes are the keys of R?
    b. Identify and eliminate any 2NF violations.
    c. Identify and eliminate any 3NF violations.

14. Suppose {A, B} → {C, D, E, F, G, H} and C → {A, B, E, F}
    a. Which sets of attributes are the keys of R?
    b. Identify and eliminate any 2NF violations.
    c. Identify and eliminate any 3NF violations.

15. Suppose A → {B, C, D}, {A, E} → {G, H}, E → F, and F → E.
    a. Which sets of attributes are the keys of R?
    b. Identify and eliminate any 2NF violations.
    c. Identify and eliminate any 3NF violations.

Further Readings

Date's book [Date99], now in its seventh edition, contains a thorough treatment of how to create high-quality relational models and covers normalization in much more detail than provided in this chapter. Date includes comprehensive bibliographies of all major topics in relational modeling. Silbershatz, Korth, and Sudarshan [SKS97] and Elmasri and Navathe [ElNa99] devote several chapters to discussions of normalization and schema improvement.

PART TWO

Manipulating
Relational Data

*I*n this part we begin to look at the processing and manipulation of relational data. The primary emphasis here is on using the capabilities of the relational model to answer questions about information stored in a database. We learn how to select information based on specific criteria and how to combine information from multiple tables. In addition, we investigate both formal and practical methods of achieving these operations. The fundamental operations of the relational model use tables as input and produce tables as output.

The ability to manipulate relational data is the foundation of database application development. This part introduces methods of specifying queries and updates that will be used to create complete applications in Part Three.

Chapter 6 contains the models of relational operations that provide the basis for all database operations. The *relational algebra* is a collection of operations and associated algebraic rules that can be used to describe queries that answer questions and updates that change the contents of a database. It describes a query as an expression whose evaluation produces the query results. The *relational calculus* is a nonprocedural approach to specifying queries by describing the structure of the results. Chapter 6 ends with a brief discussion of a graphical style for describing queries using the Microsoft Access database system as the primary example.

Chapter 7 introduces SQL, the standard language for specifying relational operations. SQL is a large language that includes both data definition and data manipulation languages. Its use is illustrated with many examples, primarily from the BigHit Video system. From this chapter, you can expect to become familiar with the capabilities of SQL and learn to write SQL statements for a variety of complex queries.

6

Techniques for Manipulating Relational Data

CHAPTER OBJECTIVES

In this chapter, you will learn:

- The basic principles involved in manipulating relational databases
- The definitions of the main relational operations: selection, projection, and join
- The syntax and semantics of the relational algebra
- Ways to write database queries as relational algebra expressions
- Additional relational operations: union, intersection, assignment, division, and aggregation
- The basic principles underlying the algebraic manipulation of relational expressions
- Ways to write database updates as relational algebra expressions
- The syntax and semantics of the relational calculus
- Ways to write database queries as relational calculus expressions
- Ways to define queries with QBE and Microsoft Access

*N*ow that we understand how to design, specify, and construct relational databases, we are ready to deal with the manipulation of their information content. The *data definition language (DDL)* of a relational system is used to define the database's attributes, tables, relationships, and indexes. The *data manipulation language (DML)* is used to extract, insert, and modify the information content of the database.

The DML of most interest to us is *SQL, the Structured Query Language,* which is described in Chapter 7. This language specifies the manipulation of relations by describing the results of queries, but does not give specific strategies for executing queries.

It is of fundamental importance that queries be written so that people can understand them. Although we will not write queries so that they have fast execution, it is also important that queries execute efficiently. For this reason, we need a formal model that is sufficiently powerful to allow optimization of queries.

The formal model that is typically used to define implementations of SQL is a relational algebra, as described in Section 6.1. The details of how the relational algebra is used in query processing are presented in Chapter 13. SQL is primarily based on another formalism, the relational calculus, which is described in Section 6.2.

Manipulating Information with the Relational Algebra

6.1

From the definition of the relational model in Chapter 4, we know that a relation is a set of tuples and that each tuple in a relation has the same number and types of attributes. The relational algebra includes operators that

- Reduce the number of tuples in a set by selecting those that satisfy some criteria (selection operators),
- Reduce the size of each tuple in a set by eliminating specific attributes (projection operators),
- Manipulate two similar sets of tuples by combining or comparing (set operators), and
- Increase the size of each tuple by adding attributes (join and product operations).

The names of the relational operators come from an analogy with manipulations of mathematical tuples. We are familiar with using tuples to represent images, for instance. A two-dimensional image is represented by a set of three-tuples. Each tuple includes two coordinate values and an image value (x, y, c) where x is the horizontal coordinate, y is the vertical coordinate, and c is the color of that square of the image. Similarly, three-dimensional images are represented by four-tuples, and three-dimensional animations have five attributes (x, y, z, c, t), three spatial coordinates (x, y, z), a color value (c), and a time or frame number (t).

We can *select* the tuples in the two-dimensional image that are red or that lie on the x-axis. We can *project* the tuples into a single dimension by eliminating one

---

A NOTE ABOUT THE NAMES OF RELATIONAL OPERATORS

The names of the relational operators are inspired by operations on multidimensional mathematical relations, but the meanings of the relational operators are much simpler. For instance, many of the projections that we use for geometrical images are complex mathematical transformations. Relational operations are always very simple. No relational projection corresponds to a perspective drawing or a map of the globe. A relational projection that removes the z coordinate from a three-dimensional image (a set of four-tuples) produces a set of the (x, y, c) values. That is, the relational projection yields the set of all color values for each (x, y) coordinate. In contrast, a geometric projection from three to two dimensions is expected to produce a single color value for each (x, y) coordinate.

of the coordinates. We can overlay two images by taking the *union* of the sets of tuples, or find all of the common values with an *intersection. Join* and *product* operations can turn a two-dimensional image into a three-dimensional one by adding a z coordinate to each tuple. Alternatively, we can turn a three-dimensional image into the first frame of an animation by adding a time value of 0 to each tuple.

The operations of the relational algebra are described in the next sections using examples from the BigHit Video sample database. The contents of the tables used in the examples are shown in Fig. 6.1.

Customer

account Id	last Name	first Name	street	city	state	zipcode	balance
101	Block	Jane	345 Randolph Circle	Apopka	FL	30458-	$0.00
102	Hamilton	Cherry	3230 Dade St.	Dade City	FL	30555-	$3.00
103	Harrison	Katherine	103 Landis Hall	Bratt	FL	30457-	$31.00
104	Breaux	Carroll	76 Main St.	Apopka	FL	30458-	$35.00
106	Morehouse	Anita	9501 Lafayette St.	Houma	LA	44099-	$0.00
111	Doe	Jane	123 Main St.	Apopka	FL	30458-	$0.00
201	Greaves	Joseph	14325 N. Bankside St.	Godfrey	IL	43580-	$0.00
444	Doe	Jane	Cawthon Dorm, room 142	Tallahassee	FL	32306-	$10.55

Videotape

videoId	dateAcquired	movieId	storeId
101	1/25/98	101	3
111	2/5/97	123	3
112	12/31/95	123	5
113	4/5/98	123	5
114	4/5/98	189	5
123	3/25/86	123	3
145	5/12/95	145	5
77564	4/29/91	189	3
90987	3/25/99	450	3
99787	10/10/97	987	5

FIGURE 6.1 ⎯⎯⎯⎯⎯⎯⎯⎯⎯⎯⎯⎯⎯⎯⎯⎯⎯⎯⎯⎯⎯⎯⎯⎯⎯⎯⎯⎯

Schemas and contents of sample tables for BigHit Video (continues)

Movie

movieId	title	genre	length	rating
101	The Thirty-Nine Steps	mystery	101	R
123	Annie Hall	romantic comedy	110	R
145	Lady and the Tramp	animated comedy	93	PG
189	Animal House	comedy	87	PG-13
450	Elizabeth	costume drama	123	PG-13
553	Stagecoach	western	130	R
987	Duck Soup	comedy	99	PG-13

Rental

accountId	videoId	dateRented	dateDue	cost
103	101	1/3/99	1/4/99	$1.59
101	113	2/22/99	2/25/99	$3.00
101	114	2/22/99	2/25/99	$3.00
103	123	12/1/98	12/31/98	$10.99
101	145	2/14/99	2/16/99	$1.99
101	90987	1/1/99	1/8/99	$2.99
101	99787	1/1/99	1/4/99	$3.49

PreviousRental

accountId	videoId	dateRented	dateReturned	cost
101	101	12/9/98	12/10/98	$2.49
101	112	1/13/98	1/4/98	$1.99
101	113	1/15/99	1/15/99	$0.99
102	113	12/1/98	12/3/98	$2.49
111	101	12/4/98	12/6/98	$2.49
111	99787	1/1/99	1/4/99	$3.95
201	113	12/9/98	12/14/98	$3.99
201	77564	1/14/99	1/24/99	$3.35

FIGURE 6.1 _____

continues

Employee

ssn	lastName	firstName
145-09-0967	Uno	Jane
245-11-4554	Toulouse	Jennifer
376-77-0099	Threat	Ayisha
479-98-0098	Fortune	Bruce
588-99-0093	Fivozinsky	Bruce

TimeCard

ssn	date	startTime	endTime	storeId	paid
145-09-0967	01/14/99	8:15	12:00	3	yes
245-11-4554	01/14/99	8:15	12:00	3	yes
376-77-0099	02/23/99	14:00	22:00	5	yes
145-09-0967	01/16/99	8:15	12:00	3	yes
376-77-0099	01/03/99	10:00	14:00	5	yes
376-77-0099	01/03/99	15:00	19:00	5	yes

FIGURE 6.1
continued

6.1.1   Selection Operator

The *selection* operator selects all tuples from a relation that satisfy particular criteria. For example, we can select all customers whose last name is "Doe" with the expression *select from Customer where lastName = 'Doe'*. Table 6.1 shows the result of this operation. In an algebraic notation, using the Greek letter sigma for the selection operator, we write

$$\sigma_{lastName='Doe'}(\texttt{Customer})$$

TABLE 6.1

Result of select from Customer where lastName = 'Doe'

account Id	first Name	last Name	street	city	state	zipcode	balance
111	Jane	Doe	123 Main St.	Apopka	FL	34331	0.00
444	Jane	Doe	Cawthon Dorm, room 142	Tallahassee	FL	32306	10.55

The new relation that results from a selection has the same attributes as the input relation, but may have fewer rows.

We can build complex selection conditions from the standard relational and logical operations. For instance, we might want a list of all time cards for a specific employee and after a particular date. The selection of all tuples from `TimeCard` where `ssn` is '376-77-0099' and `startDate` is after '01-mar-1998' results in all time cards for a single employee since March 1, 1998. Table 6.2 shows the result of this operation. We write this operation as follows:

$$\sigma_{ssn='376-77-0099' \text{ and } date>'01-mar-1999'}(\texttt{TimeCard})$$

6.1.2   Projection Operator

The *projection* operator selects certain attributes from a relation and produces a new relation that has only those attributes. For instance, to get a list of the first and last names of all customers in the `Customer` table, we *project Customer onto (lastName, firstName)*. Table 6.3 shows the result of this operation. In the algebraic notation, we write

$$\pi_{\texttt{lastName,firstName}}(\texttt{Customer})$$

using the Greek letter pi for the projection operator. This expression produces a new relation with only two attributes. The tuples of the new relation are all of the

TABLE 6.2

Result of select TimeCard where ssn = '376-77-0099' and date > '01-mar-1998'

ssn	date	startTime	endTime	storeId	paid
376-77-0099	02/23/99	14:00	22:00	5	yes
376-77-0099	01/03/99	10:00	14:00	5	yes
376-77-0099	01/03/99	15:00	19:00	5	yes

TABLE 6.3

Result of project Customer onto (lastName, firstName)

lastName	firstName
Morehouse	Anita
Block	Jane
Breaux	Carroll
Hamilton	Cherry
Harrison	Catherine
Doe	Jane
Greaves	Joseph

`lastName`, `firstName` combinations that correspond to the values of those attributes from the `Customer` table.

Because the output of a projection is a set, any duplicates are eliminated. Hence, for the two customers named Jane Doe, there is only one tuple in the projected relation to represent both customers.

6.1.3   Set Operators

When two relations have the same shape, that is, when the types of the attributes are the same, we can apply the usual *set operators* to the relations: union, intersection, and difference. In the BigHit Video database, the tables `Rental` and `PreviousRental` have the same shape, even though their attribute names are not the same. The schemas for these two tables are as follows:

```
Rental (accountId, videoId, dateRented, dateDue, cost)
PreviousRental (accountId, videoId, dateRented,
    dateReturned, cost)
```

The shape of the tables is a tuple of types: (`text`, `text`, `datetime`, `datetime`, `currency`). The fourth attributes have different names in the two tables, but that difference is irrelevant to the set operators.

The union of two relations is a relation that contains the set of each tuple that is in at least one of the input relations. As with projection, the output is a set, so some output tuples may represent more than one input tuple. It is not clear what the names of the attributes of the result relation should be. As in the preceding example, the names of the attributes of the two inputs may not be consistent. A simple convention that is often adopted calls for the attribute names to be taken from the left-side operand.

Table 6.4 shows some of the rows in the result of *Rental ∪ PreviousRental*. There are actually 15 rows in the result—7 from `Rental` and 8 from `PreviousRental`. The attribute names come from `Rental`. It is impossible to tell which tuple came from which input. Table 6.4 represents the set of all rentals, current and previous. It would be useful for an analysis of rental activity that includes all rentals—even those that have not yet been returned.

TABLE 6.4

Partial result of the union expression Rental ∪ PreviousRental

accountId	videoId	dateRented	dateDue	cost
101	90987	1/1/99	1/8/99	$2.99
101	99787	1/1/99	1/4/99	$3.49
103	101	1/3/99	1/4/99	$1.59
103	123	12/1/98	12/31/98	$10.99
111	101	12/4/98	12/6/98	$2.49
201	77564	1/14/99	1/24/99	$3.35

The intersection of two relations is the set of all tuples that occur in both input relations. The intersection of the relations *Rental* ∩ *PreviousRental* is the set of all rentals that are both current and previous. We certainly expect this set to be empty. A more interesting use of intersection would be the intersection between the video IDs of the two tables. This set would be the videotapes that are currently rented as well as those that have been rented before. Creating this relational algebra expression requires first projecting the `videoId` fields of the two tables and taking the intersection of the results. The expression is

$$\pi_{\text{videoId}}(\texttt{Rental}) \cap \pi_{\text{videoId}}(\texttt{PreviousRental})$$

The difference between two relations is the set of all tuples that are in the first relation but not in the second. The difference between the videotapes that are currently checked out and those that were previously checked out is exactly those videotapes that are currently checked out for the first time. The relational algebra expression is as follows:

$$\pi_{\text{videoId}}(\texttt{Rental}) - \pi_{\text{videoId}}(\texttt{PreviousRental})$$

Similarly, the set of all videotapes that have been rented previously but are not currently rented is the commutation of the above expression:

$$\pi_{\text{videoId}}(\texttt{PreviousRental}) - \pi_{\text{videoId}}(\texttt{Rental})$$

6.1.4 Join and Product Operators

Up to this point, we have not seen any operators that create a relation with more attributes than the original relation. Combining the attributes from two different relations, however, will produce a new relation with more attributes than either of the original ones. For instance, we may want to combine the `Employee` relation and the `TimeCard` relation to produce a new relation that has an attribute for each employee attribute and for each time card attribute.

The simplest product operator is the *Cartesian product*. It produces a tuple of the new relation for each combination of one tuple from the left operand and one tuple from the right operand. For the `Employee` and `TimeCard` example, for each employee there are as many output tuples as there are `TimeCard` tuples. We write this operation as follows:

`Employee × TimeCard`

The result of this operation has 30 tuples, because there are 5 employees and 6 time cards. Each tuple has 9 attributes, 3 from `Employee` and 6 from `TimeCard`. Table 6.5 shows a few rows of this relation. The names of the attributes had to be changed to produce the new schema. Without any change, the schema would include two attributes named `ssn`. Table 6.5 shows the use of a *qualified* name for these two attributes. `Employee.ssn` is the `ssn` attribute from the `Employee` table, and `TimeCard.ssn` is the `ssn` attribute from `TimeCard`.

TABLE 6.5

Partial result of Cartesian product `Employee` × `TimeCard`

Employee.ssn	last Name	first Name	TimeCard.ssn	date	start Time	end Time	store Id	paid
145-09-0967	Uno	Jane	145-09-0967	01/14/99	8:15	12:00	3	no
245-11-4554	Toulouse	Jie	245-11-4554	01/14/99	8:15	12:00	3	no
145-09-0967	Uno	Jane	376-77-0099	02/23/99	14:00	22:00	5	no
245-11-4554	Toulouse	Jie	145-09-0967	01/14/99	8:15	12:00	3	no

The tuples of Table 6.5 are not particularly meaningful. The first row shows the combination of an employee record and a time card for employee number 145-09-0967. The third row, however, shows an employee record for employee 145-09-0967 and a time card for employee 376-77-0099. If this table were used to produce paychecks, one employee would be paid for time worked by another employee! The company would also pay more than once for the same work, because the first and fourth rows are both created from the same time card.

A more appropriate product is one that produces a tuple for each combination of employee tuple and time card tuple, where the employee numbers in the two original tuples are the same. That is, of all possible combinations of employee and time card, only those that have information about an employee and a time card for that same employee are included in the output. You can think of this product as a selection of those tuples where `Employee.ssn` equals `TimeCard.ssn`. If a particular employee worked a particular time period, we would get an output tuple with all of the information about that employee (Social Security number, last name, and first name) and all of the information about the time card (Social Security number, date, start time, and end time).

This product is expressed as the selection of those rows in the product whose `ssn` fields match, or by the relational expression

$$\sigma_{\texttt{Employee.ssn=TimeCard.ssn}}(\texttt{Employee} \times \texttt{TimeCard})$$

This type of product is called a *join*, and the specific expression is *join Employee and TimeCard on ssn*. It puts together related objects from two relations. In fact, it is often used to combine objects that are connected by the relationships that were defined in the data model used to construct the database. In this case, where the two relations are joined by attributes that have exactly the same name, we write the join as

$$\texttt{Employee} \bowtie_{\texttt{ssn}} \texttt{TimeCard}$$

This combination is often called a *natural join* and is defined so that the shared attribute appears only once in the output table. Table 6.6 shows the result of this operation.

TABLE 6.6

Result of the natural join of Employees and TimeCard on ssn

ssn	last Name	first Name	date	start Time	end Time	store Id	paid
145-09-0967	Uno	Jane	01/14/99	8:15	12:00	3	no
145-09-0967	Uno	Jane	01/16/99	8:15	12:00	3	no
245-11-4554	Toulouse	Jie	01/14/99	8:15	12:00	3	no
376-77-0099	Threat	Ayisha	02/23/99	14:00	22:00	5	no
376-77-0099	Threat	Ayisha	01/03/99	10:00	14:00	5	no
376-77-0099	Threat	Ayisha	01/03/99	15:00	19:00	5	no

The information in Table 6.6 is appropriate for use in creating paychecks. Each time card is associated with the correct employee and appears only once. This join operation puts together entities that are associated by instances of the relationship type between entity classes `Employee` and `TimeCard`. The relations are joined on the key field of `Employee` and the foreign key field of `TimeCard`. These attributes were used to represent this relationship type in the relational model. The relationship type was represented by the foreign key attribute exactly so that this join operation could be used to associate related objects.

The number of rows in the table is the same number as in the `TimeCard` table. This correspondence is no coincidence. The relationship type between `Employee` and `TimeCard` is one-to-many. Thus, there is exactly one employee for each time card, but there may be many time cards per employee. A natural join of a one-to-many relationship always produces as many tuples in the output as there are tuples in the relation on the to-many side of the relationship type.

An employee does not appear in the join result unless at least one time card exists for that employee. Notice that Julian Fortune, employee 479-98-0098, and Bruce Fivozinsky, employee 588-99-0093, are not represented in Table 6.6.

The more general case of the join operation allows an arbitrary expression for the join condition. The join expression that most closely matches the one of Table 6.6 is *join Employee and TimeCard where Employee.ssn = TimeCard.ssn*. A join expression whose join condition is an equality operation is often called an *equi-join*. We write this expression as

$$\text{Employee} \bowtie_{\text{Employee.ssn=TimeCard.ssn}} \text{TimeCard}$$

Table 6.7 shows the result of this operation, which is the same as the result of the natural join of Table 6.6 except that the `ssn` attribute appears twice, once for each input table. The name given in the result table for the attribute from `Employee` is `Employee.ssn` and the name for the attribute from `TimeCard` is `TimeCard.ssn`.

TABLE 6.7

Result of join Employee and TimeCard where Employee.ssn = TimeCard.ssn

Employee.ssn	last Name	first Name	TimeCard.ssn	date	start Time	store Id	paid	end Time
145-09-0967	Uno	Jane	145-09-0967	01/14/99	8:15	3	no	12:00
145-09-0967	Uno	Jane	145-09-0967	01/16/99	8:15	3	no	12:00
245-11-4554	Toulouse	Jie	245-11-4554	01/14/99	8:15	3	no	12:00
376-77-0099	Threat	Ayisha	376-77-0099	02/23/99	14:00	5	no	22:00
376-77-0099	Threat	Ayisha	376-77-0099	01/03/99	10:00	5	no	14:00
376-77-0099	Threat	Ayisha	376-77-0099	01/03/99	15:00	5	no	19:00

A join operation has three arguments: the left and right relation operands and the join condition, which is similar to the selection condition of a selection operator.

6.1.5   Combining Relational Operators

The relational operators can be combined to produce *relational algebra expressions*. The combination of selection and projection, for instance, produces a restriction on both rows and columns of a table. To find out which videotapes a particular customer has rented and when those videotapes are due requires selecting the Rental rows for the customer and projecting the videoId and dateDue fields:

$$\pi_{\text{videoId, dateDue}}(\sigma_{\text{accountId=113}}(\text{Rental}))$$

It would be helpful, however, to include the title of the videotape. Achieving this goal requires adding a join operation between Rental and Videotape and another between Videotape and Movie:

$$\pi_{\text{videoId, title, dateDue}}((\sigma_{\text{accountId=113}}(\text{Rental})) \bowtie_{\text{videoId}} \text{Videotape} \bowtie_{\text{movieId}} \text{Movie})$$

An even more complicated example involves producing a list of previous rentals of comedy (genre) movies whose dateRented was after December 1, 1998. This expression should return the customer name, video title, and date rented. To produce this information, we must perform join, selection, and projection operations on the Customer, Videotape, Movie, and PreviousRental relations. We want to perform the following steps:

1. Select the comedy movies.

2. Join the results of step 1 and Videotape on movieId.

3. Select the previous rentals with a date rented that is after December 1, 1998.

4. Join the results of steps 2 and 3 on videoId.

5. Join the results of step 4 and Customer on accountId.

6. Project the first name, last name, title, and date rented from step 5.

A relational expression for these steps is as follows:

$\pi_{\text{firstName, lastName, title, dateRented}}($ Step 6

$((\sigma_{\text{genre='comedy'}}(\texttt{Movie})$ Step 1

$\bowtie_{\text{movieId}} \texttt{Videotape})$ Step 2

$\bowtie_{\text{videoId}}$ Step 4

$\sigma_{\text{dateRented>'01-Dec-1998'}}(\texttt{PreviousRental}))$ Step 3

$\bowtie_{\text{accountId}} \texttt{Customer})$ Step 5

Table 6.8 has the result of this expression.

6.1.6   Assignment and Renaming in the Relational Algebra

An assignment operator is included in the relational algebra. It allows us to create names for intermediate results, rename tables, and modify tables. For example, the following sequence of expressions changes the balance of customer 101 to 2.00:

```
1 c101    ← σ_accountId=101(Customer);      // customer 101
2 cRest   ← σ_accountId≠101(Customer);      // all other customers
3 c101Part ← π_accountId,lastName,firstName,street,city,state,zipcode(c101);
4 c101New  ← c101Part × {(2.00)};  // create table with
                                    // one tuple
5 Customer ← c101Rest ∪ c101New;   // replace Customer
```

This sequence of operations creates a table with a single tuple for account 101 (line 1) and a table with all of the rest of the tuples from `Customer` (line 2). Line 3 creates a table with a single tuple for account 101 with all of the attributes of `Customer` except the `balance` attribute. Line 4 combines the result of line 3 (`c101Part`) with a new `balance` attribute value of 2.00. Finally, line 5 replaces the `Customer` table with the union of the new tuple for account 101 and the rest of the tuples from the previous `Customer` table.

The assignment operator transforms relational expressions into a more powerful language for representing a collection (database) of relational tables. Chapter

TABLE 6.8

List of previous rentals of comedy movies since December 1, 1998

firstName	lastName	title	dateRented
Jane	Doe	Duck Soup	1998-12-04
Joseph	Greaves	Animal House	1999-01-14

13 includes details on how the relational algebra is used to support the execution of relational queries.

6.1.7   Additional Relational Operators

Several other types of relational operators add important functionality to the relational algebra. Two of the most useful categories are the division operators and the aggregation and grouping operators.

A division operator is used to find objects that match every element of another set of objects. For instance, we can use division to find all customers who have rented a particular set of movies. First, we create a set consisting of all of the movies previously rented by each customer:

$$\texttt{MoviesRented} \leftarrow \pi_{\text{accountId, movieId}} (\texttt{PreviousRental} \bowtie_{\text{videoId}} \texttt{Videotape})$$

`MoviesRented` is a set of pairs (`accountId`, `movieId`) where there is a previous rental by the customer of some videotape of the movie. Table 6.9a shows an example of such a table.

Given a set of movies `Movies`, as in Table 6.9b, we can divide `MoviesRented` by `Movies` as in the following expression:

$$\texttt{RentsAll} \leftarrow \texttt{MoviesRented} \div \texttt{Movies}$$

This expression yields the set of each `accountId` that has a row in `MoviesRented` for each `movieId` in `Movies`, as shown in Table 6.9c. Accounts 101 and 111 are the only two that have rented both movies from the table `Movies`. It doesn't matter that account 101 has rented another movie. It is also irrelevant that accounts 102 and 201 have each rented one of the movies.

TABLE 6.9

Tables illustrating the use of the division operator

a. MoviesRented		b. Movies	c. RentsAll ← MoviesRented ÷ Movies
accountId	movieId	moviedId	accountId
101	656	656	101
101	723	723	111
101	789		
102	723		
111	656		
111	723		
201	656		
201	789		

The division operator can be defined using projection, difference, and Cartesian product:

```
1 Accounts ← π_accountId (MoviesRented)
2 PossibleRentals ← Accounts × Movies
3 NonRentals ← PossibleRentals – MoviesRented
4 NonRenters ← π_accountId (NonRentals)
5 RentsAll ← Accounts – NonRenters
```

Relation `Accounts` (line 1) is the set of all accounts of interest. `PossibleRentals` (line 2) is the set of all possible movie rentals for the accounts and movies of interest. `NonRentals` (line 3) is the set of all customer–movie pairs that do not represent rentals. It is created by removing all of the actual rentals (`MoviesRented`) from `PossibleRentals`. If an account has rented every movie, then `NonRentals` does not contain a row for that account. After projecting on `accountId` (line 4), we are left with `NonRenters`, the set of all accounts that have not rented at least one movie in the set. Hence `RentsAll` (line 5) contains all of the accounts that have rented every movie in `Movies`.

Aggregation operators are used to apply arithmetic (count, sum, average) or comparison (maximum, minimum) operators to the elements of a set. Section 7.1.6 has a detailed explanation and examples of the use of these operators in SQL. For the relational algebra, examples include

$\text{Average}_{hourlyWage}(\texttt{HourlyEmployee})$ Average hourly wage

$\text{Count}_{accountId}(\texttt{Customer})$ The number of customers

As we will see in Section 7.1.6, we can group objects into sets and apply aggregate operators to those sets. For instance, we can group all videotapes by `movieId`, creating a group of videotapes for each movie. Counting how many videotapes are in each group yields a relation in which each row has a `moviedId` and the number of videotapes for that movie.

6.1.8   Algebraic Manipulation of Relational Expressions

The essence of algebra is the availability of a variety of rules of equivalence for expressions. The standard numeric algebra includes commutative, associative, and distributive rules, among others. These rules allow for the creation of a wide variety of different representations for a single expression. An optimizing compiler, for instance, can search many possible representations of an expression to find the one that has the optimal performance for a particular computer system.

The relational algebra has its own equivalence rules, which database optimizers can exploit. A brief examination of the rules and how they are used in optimization is included in Chapter 13. More detailed presentations can be found in many advanced database textbooks. For now, it is sufficient to understand that the relational algebra makes it possible for a database system to find efficient methods of executing various expressions. Whereas optimizing compilers are able to find modest improvements, database *query optimizers* may be able to reduce the expense of executing a query by factors of 1,000 or more. The effectiveness of database optimizations is dependent on the capabilities of the relational algebra.

Many execution strategies are available for the example relational expression of Section 6.1.5. The expression is specified as two selections, three joins, and a projection. After the joins are executed, there will be 20 attributes: 5 from `Movie`, 3 from `Videotape`, 5 from `PreviousRental`, and 7 from `Customer`. Only 4 of the attributes are required for the final relation. Hence, we may want to put the projection operations earlier in the execution sequence so that fewer bytes of data will be processed. Care must be taken not to remove any attributes that are needed. The removal of the `dateReturned` and `cost` attributes from `PreviousRental` and the address attributes from `Customer` can be accomplished before the joins. The `genre` attribute can be removed from `Movie` as soon as the selection of the comedy movies is complete. The choice of the best execution strategy must be made on the basis of the way the database tables are represented, the speed of various operations on the computer systems, and other performance factors. We address these issues in much more detail in Chapter 13.

Describing Queries with Relational Calculus

6.2

A relational calculus describes queries in terms of the results to be created. This approach is in contrast to that carried out by the relational algebra, which describes queries in terms of the operations to be performed. In this sense, relational calculus is nonprocedural. The expressive power of the relational algebra and calculus are equivalent.

Several forms of relational calculus exist. This section provides a brief introduction to the *tuple relational calculus*, which uses quantifiers and Boolean expressions to define sets of tuples. Figure 6.2 shows relational calculus expressions that define the same relations as the relational algebra expressions of Tables 6.1 through 6.8.

Expression 1 of Fig. 6.2 describes the set of all customer tuples whose last name is "Doe," just as in Table 6.1. Variable c ranges over all tuples, and condition `Customer(c)` is true if c is an element of the set of customers. Table 6.2 is produced by expression 2, with variable t representing all of the `TimeCard` tuples. The first and last names of customers are defined by expression 3 of Fig. 6.2. The union of `Rental` and `PreviousRental` is defined by expression 4.

The Cartesian product and join of `Employee` and `TimeCard` are defined by expressions 5 and 6, respectively, of Fig. 6.2. There are two tuple variables: e (an employee) and t (a time card). The natural join of Table 6.7 appears in line 7. Both expressions 6 and 7 include the join condition `e.ssn=t.ssn`.

The final, more complex, query of Section 6.1.5 that produces Table 6.8 is given in expression 8 of Fig. 6.2. It has the three join conditions linking the four tuple variables, and the selection condition in a single large condition.

As we will see in Section 7.1, the tuple relational algebra provides a theoretical foundation for SQL.

```
1 {c | Customer(c) and c.lastName = 'Doe'}                              Table 6.1
2 {t | TimeCard(t) and t.ssn='376-77-0099' and
      t.date>'01-mar-1998'}                                            Table 6.2
3 {c.firstName, c.lastName | Customer(c)}                              Table 6.3
4 {r | Rental(r) or PreviousRental(r)}                                 Table 6.4
5 {e.ssn,e.lastName,e.firstName,t.ssn,t.date,t.startTime,
      t.endTime,t.storeId,t.paid | Employee(e) and TimeCard(t)}        Table 6.5
6 {e.ssn,e.lastName,e.firstName,t.ssn,t.date,t.startTime,
      t.endTime,t.storeId,t.paid | Employee(e) and TimeCard(t)
      and e.ssn = t.ssn}                                               Table 6.6
7 {e.ssn,e.lastName,e.firstName,t.date,t.startTime,t.endTime,
      t.storeId,t.paid | Employee(e) and TimeCard(t)
      and e.ssn = t.ssn}                                               Table 6.7
8 {e.ssn, c.firstName,c.lastName,m.title,r.dateRented |
      Customer(c)and Rental(r) and Videotape(v) and Movie(m)
      and c.accountId=r.accountId and r.videoId=v.videoId and
      v.movieId=m.movieId and m.genre='comedy' and
      r.dateRented>'01-Dec-1998'}                                      Table 6.8
```

FIGURE 6.2 _____

Relational calculus expressions for the queries of Tables 6.1–6.8

Defining Queries with QBE and Microsoft Access

6.3

Microsoft Access uses a variation on the technique called *Query by Example (QBE)* [Zlo77] to define queries with a graphical user interface. The user interface is used to specify the input tables, the selection criteria, the join criteria, and the output attributes. A single query can represent a complex relational algebra or relational calculus expression. Figure 6.3 shows a Microsoft Access screen with the designs of the queries that produce Tables 6.1, 6.2, 6.3, and 6.7. Each query design window has two major divisions. The upper area is a canvas that shows the input tables of the query. All but the last of these queries has a single input table. The lower area shows a list of the fields that are either included in the result query or part of a selection criteria, or both. These queries were created by selecting New from the query window, selecting the input tables from the Show Tables dialog, and dragging fields into the lower section of the query design window.

The upper-left area of Fig. 6.3 shows a simple selection query that produces Table 6.1. Its input table is `Customer`, and its output includes all fields of that table. The first entry in the list of output fields is `Customer.*`, which means that all fields are part of the result table. The second entry in the field list is `lastName`. The Show box is unchecked, meaning that this entry is not used as part of the output table. The Criteria box contains the literal `"Doe"`, which is the selection condition of the query. Thus an input tuple is used to produce an output tuple only if the `lastName` field has value `"Doe"`.

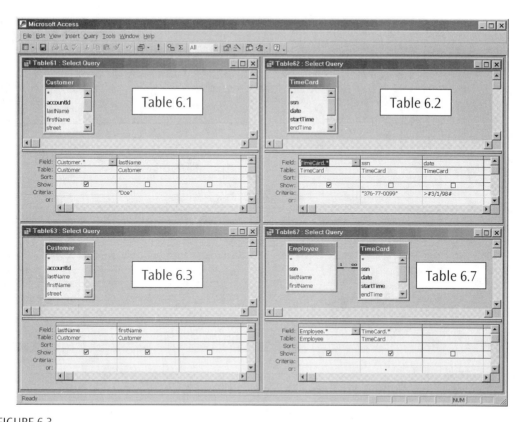

FIGURE 6.3 _____

Microsoft Access screen showing queries that produce Tables 6.1, 6.2, 6.3, and 6.7

The query in the upper-right area of Fig. 6.3 implements the selection query of Table 6.2. It has two selection conditions. Neither of these fields is part of the output table.

The query in the lower-left area of Fig. 6.3 shows a query that produces Table 6.3. It lists the two fields of the input table that are to be shown in the output table. All other fields are omitted. This query shows how Microsoft Access represents the projection operator.

The query in the lower-right area of Fig. 6.3 shows a join query that produces Table 6.7. Two input tables are linked by a line that shows the relationship between the two tables, as was described in Chapters 2 and 4. In this context, the line represents a join operation on the table. It is an equijoin on the attributes that are connected by the line. This query gives the complete specification of a join operation in Microsoft Access. The output fields are `Employee.*` and `TimeCard.*`, and there are no selection criteria. The query has no selection or projection operations.

The union and difference queries of Section 6.1.3 and Table 6.4 cannot be defined using QBE in Access, but must be written in SQL. The Query menu has an SQL Specific entry that lists Union as an option. Selecting this menu item results

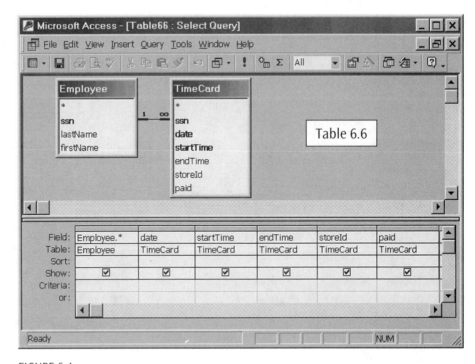

FIGURE 6.4 _____

Microsoft Access selection query that produces Table 6.6

in the presentation of a blank SQL entry screen. In other words, Access supports these queries, but you must write the proper SQL by yourself. The use of set operations in SQL is covered in Section 7.1.8.

The production of the natural join of Table 6.6 is a little more complex in Access and is shown in Fig. 6.4. The output fields are all of the fields of `Employee` and all of the fields of `TimeCard` except for `TimeCard.ssn`. The fields of `TimeCard` are listed one by one.

Figure 6.5 shows the more complex query that produces Table 6.8. Here, we have used four input tables. These tables are linked by lines and hence are joined in the query. These three join operations are part of the query. The four fields specify the projection operation. Each of these has the Show box checked. The Criteria field of the `dateRented` field shows that we are selecting only those rows whose date rented is after December 1, 1998.

As can be seen in the figure, Microsoft Access provides a very flexible interface that is simple to use for both experienced and inexperienced database programmers.

Chapter Summary

This chapter presented different methods of manipulating relational database tables. The relational algebra is a language for writing expressions that produce new relations

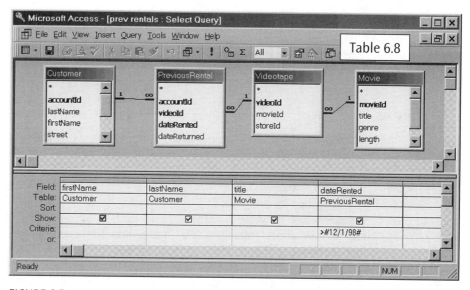

FIGURE 6.5 _____

Microsoft Access query that produces Table 6.8

from existing ones. Query by Example (QBE) is a graphical style of writing table manipulations. SQL (Structured Query Language) is a textual style of writing the same manipulations. All three of these styles are useful, each in its own way.

The fundamental benefit of the relational model comes from its ability to create new tables through the execution of queries. Database designers do not have to describe all of the ways that data can be extracted from the database. Instead, they create tables and define the primary relationships, and users of a relational system are free to construct new tables in a variety of ways.

The relational algebra is a collection of operations that transform input tables into result tables. The major operations are selection, projection, and join. The selection operator selects rows from a table according to a selection condition. The projection operator produces a new table with fewer columns than the original table. The join operator combines the attributes of one table with the attributes of another table to produce a new table that is wider than its input tables. The rows of the result are constructed by combining a row of one table with a row of the other table. The join condition determines which combinations of input rows appear in the result table. A natural join is the join operator that combines tables having a common attribute. Set operators support the combining of tables that are the same shape. These operators include union, intersection, and difference.

The relational algebra is most useful as a tool for specifying and implementing query optimization. Relational operators can be combined to form complex expressions. The algebraic characteristics of the operators include rules of equivalence. Using these rules, relational expressions can be transformed into equivalent expressions that may have significantly different execution behavior. Query optimizers take advantage of these algebraic characteristics to improve query performance.

QBE is the technique that has been adapted for use in Microsoft Access and other graphical database tools to define queries. It allows a designer to select input tables and specify projections and the join and selection conditions. QBE is a very useful tool for displaying the structure of a query.

Key Terms

Cartesian product. A relational product operation that produces a table that includes one row for each combination of a row from its left operand and a row from its right operand. The number of output table rows is the product of the number of rows in the left operand and the number of rows in the right operand.

Data definition language (DDL). A language for specifying the structure of the components of a database system.

Data manipulation language (DML). A language for specifying operations that extract, insert, and update the contents of a database system.

Equi-join. A relational join operation whose join condition is an equality expression.

Join. The relational product operation that combines tables based on a join condition. The result table has a row for each pair of rows of the input tables for which the join condition is true.

Natural join. The relational join operation that combines two tables with a common attribute. The result of a natural join is a table with a row for each pair of rows in the input tables in which the common attribute has an equal value. The common attributes appear only once in the output table.

Product. The relational algebra operation that combines two tables to produce a new table whose attributes are the attributes of the input tables. Join and Cartesian products are both product operations.

Projection. The relational algebra operation that produces an output table consisting of selected columns from its input table. The number of rows in the result table may be less than the number of rows in the input table as a result of the removal of duplicate rows.

Query by Example (QBE). A style of designing queries using a graphical user interface. QBE was developed at IBM and has been incorporated into a variety of database tools, including Microsoft Access.

Query optimization. A strategy for improving the execution performance of queries by exploiting the algebraic characteristics of relational operators.

Relational algebra. A collection of operations on relations including selection, projection, union, and join. The operations support a variety of equivalence rules for expressions. These rules, in turn, support the optimization of the algebraic expressions that represent database queries.

Relational algebra expression. An expression that consists of the application of relational operations to tables.

Relational calculus. A nonprocedural approach to specifying queries by describing the structure of the results.

Selection. The relational algebra operation that selects all rows from a table that satisfy a selection condition.

Set operation. The relational algebra operations that combine tables of the same shape. The set operations include union, intersection, and difference.

SQL (Structured Query Language). The ANSI standard language for the definition and manipulation of relational databases. SQL includes both a data definition language and a data manipulation language.

Exercises

1. Explain the difference between a data manipulation language and a data definition language.

2. Why is it important to have a relational algebra to support the relational model?

3. Which relational operators provide the following capabilities?

   a. Transform a relation into a new relation with fewer attributes.

   b. Transform a relation into a new relation with fewer rows and the same attributes.

   c. Combine two relations of the same shape into a new relation with the same attributes.

   d. Combine two relations into a new relation that has attributes from both input relations.

4. How does relational projection differ from geometric projection?

5. Under what conditions does a projection operation produce fewer rows in its output table than are present in its input table? Give an example from the database of Figs. 6.1 and 6.6.

HourlyEmployee

ssn	hourlyRate
145-09-0967	$6.05
245-11-4554	$5.50
376-77-0099	$10.75
479-98-0098	$9.50
579-98-8778	$5.50

SalariedEmployee

ssn	weekly PayRate	vacation LeaveHours	sickLeave Hours
145-09-0967	$0.00	0	0

FIGURE 6.6 _____

Additional tables of the BigHit Video database (continues)

PayStatement

ssn	hourlyRate	numHours	amountPaid	datePaid
145-09-0967	$6.05	8	$45.38	5/17/99
245-11-4554	$5.50	4	$20.63	5/17/99
376-77-0099	$10.75	16	$172.00	5/17/99

WorksIn

ssn	storeId
145-09-0967	3
145-09-0967	5
245-11-4554	3
245-11-4554	5
376-77-0099	5

Store

storeId	street	city	state	zipcode
3	2010 Liberty Rd.	Apopka	FL	34505
5	1004 N. Monroe St.	Apopka	FL	34506

PurchaseOrder

purchase OrderId	supplierId	date	total
99001	101101	1/15/99	$100.00

PurchaseOrderDetail

purchase OrderId	movieId	quantity	price
99001	450	3	$25.00
99001	987	1	$25.00

Supplier

supplierId	name	street	city	state
101101	Acme Video	101 Main	Smithfield	LA

FIGURE 6.6
continued

6. What rules govern the application of set operators to relations? Define the notion of the shape of a table and describe how it relates to the application of set operators.

7. Suppose that table R ($\underline{a}$, b, c, d, e) has n rows and table S ($\underline{f}$, g, h, i, j, k) has m rows, and S.h is a foreign key referencing R.a.

   a. Write a relational algebra expression for the Cartesian product of R and S. How many rows does this expression produce? How many columns does this expression produce?

   b. Write a relational algebra expression for the join of R and S on R.a = S.h. What are the minimum and maximum number of rows that the expression produces? Under what circumstances does it produce the minimum and the maximum number of rows? How many columns does this expression produce?

   c. Write a relational algebra expression for the join of R and S on R.b = S.k. What are the minimum and maximum number of rows that the expression produces? Under what circumstances does it produce the minimum and the maximum number of rows?

8. Show the relations that result from executing the following queries on the BigHit Video database of Figs. 6.1 and 6.6.

   a. All customers who live in California.

   b. All employees who work at store number 3.

   c. The names of all movies whose genre is comedy.

   d. The names of all customers who have rented a movie since January 1, 1999.

   e. The employee name, date worked, and hours worked for each time card that has more than eight hours worked.

   f. All videotapes currently rented by customers who live in Florida.

   g. All hourly employees who work at store number 3.

   h. All customers whose last names are also the last name of an employee.

   i. All employees who work in all stores (use division).

9. Write relational algebra expressions to represent the queries of Exercise 8.

10. Using the relations of the BigHit Video database of Figs. 6.1 and 6.6, for each relational expression below, give an English description of the expression and the relations that result when it is executed.

    a. $\pi_{\text{title,genre}}(\sigma_{\text{length} > 110}(\text{Movie}))$

    b. $\pi_{\text{firstName,lastName}}(\sigma_{\text{ssn='376-77-0099'}}(\text{Employee}))$

    c. $\pi_{\text{firstName,lastName,date}}(\sigma_{\text{ssn='376-77-0099'}}(\text{Employee} \bowtie_{\text{ssn}} \text{TimeCard}))$

    d. $\pi_{\text{id,price,quantity,movieId}}(\sigma_{\text{date>'01/01/99'}}$
       $(\text{PurchaseOrder} \bowtie_{\text{ssn}} \text{PurchaseOrderDetail}))$

11. Write relational calculus expressions for the queries of Exercise 8.

12. Write tuple relational calculus expressions for the queries of Exercise 10.
13. Define queries in the Microsoft Access BigHit Video database for the queries of Exercise 8.
14. Define queries in the Microsoft Access BigHit Video database for the queries of Exercise 10.
15. Consider the following relational tables. Show the results of each query.

Book

Id	Title	Publisher
Key		
PH10	Database Systems	Prentice-Hall
AW12	Database Systems	Addison-Wesley
AW14	File Structures	Addison-Wesley
MH123	First Course in Database Systems	McGraw Hill

BookCopies

BookId	BranchId	NumCopies
Key(FK)	*Key(FK)*	
PH10	NW	3
PH10	Main	1
AW12	DSL	4
AW14	Main	3
AW14	NW	5

Branch

BranchId	BranchName	Address
key		
NW	Northwest	US 319
Main	Strozier	Palmetto St.
DSL	Dirac Library	Woodward Ave.

```
Author
```

BookId	Name
Key(FK)	*Key*
PH10	Jeff Ullman
AW12	CJ Date
AW14	Greg Riccardi
PH10	J Widom
MH123	Silberschatz
AW14	M Folk
MH123	Korth
MH123	Sudarshan

   a. List the title of each book published by Addison-Wesley.

   b. List the name of each book that has at least two copies in the NW branch.

   c. How many books are in the Main library? (Use aggregation).

   d. List the author's name for each book that has copies in the NW library.

   e. What are the names of the branches that have copies of books published by Addison-Wesley?

   f. For each book and branch, list the name of the book, the name of the branch, and the number of copies of the book in the branch.

16. Write relational algebra expressions for each query of Exercise 15.

17. Write tuple relational calculus expressions for each query of Exercise 15.

Further Readings

The relational algebra was introduced by Codd [Codd70] in his original presentation of the relational model. Extensive presentations of the relational algebra, including proofs of its completeness, are presented in several database books, including [Date99, ElNa99, SKS97].

An alternative formal model of relational operations is the relational calculus, which represents operations as declarative statements, rather than as the expressions of relational algebra. In 1971, Codd introduced the Alpha language [Codd71] for expressing a relational calculus. Ullman [Ull88] presents an extensive evaluation of relational calculus, including a sketch of a proof of its equivalence to the relational algebra.

7

SQL, <u>the</u> Structured Query Language

CHAPTER OBJECTIVES

In this chapter, you will learn:

- The syntax and semantics of SQL
- Ways to write and execute SQL statements
- Ways to represent relational algebra expressions with SQL statements
- Ways to use SQL select statements for projection, selection, and join queries
- Ways to write set operations in SQL
- Ways to use the aggregation and group by capabilities of SQL
- Ways to modify database content with SQL
- Ways to create and manipulate schemas with SQL

*S*QL (Structured Query Language) is a comprehensive database language that was originally standardized by the American National Standards Institute (ANSI) and the International Standards Organization in 1986 [ANSI86]. It includes statements that specify and modify database schemas (DDL statements) as well as statements that manipulate database content (DML). After much revision and expansion, SQL was standardized as SQL-2 (or SQL-92) in 1992 [ANSI92]. Work is ongoing on the development of SQL-3. The term *SQL* is usually pronounced "S-Q-L," but it can also be pronounced as the word "sequel."*

We begin our study of SQL by considering query statements. These statements extract information from the database. Subsequent sections discuss statements that modify database content and that define database schemas.

---

* The Sequel language (Standard English Query Language) was a predecessor of SQL. It was developed as the query language of the System R project at IBM.

The query language of SQL is based on the relational calculus that was described in Section 6.2. An SQL query includes references to tuple variables and the attributes of those variables. It specifies the attributes to be returned, the tables from which the base tuples come, and the conditions that determine the selection.

A NOTE ON SQL SYNTAX

Many syntactic and stylistic rules pertain to writing SQL. In almost all cases, SQL is case insensitive. That is, the keywords, the names of tables and attributes, and the values of string constants are case insensitive. It doesn't matter to SQL if we write "SELECT" or "select" or call a table "Customer" or "customer." This book uses the naming conventions of Java (explained in Chapter 2), which is a case-sensitive language. SQL keywords are shown in boldface.

As we will see in more detail in later chapters, a table is most like a class and an attribute of a table is most like a member of a class. For that reason, tables are given names that are capitalized and attributes are given names that do not begin with an initial capital. Many SQL references choose to write keywords with all capital letters, but this book writes them with all lowercase and uses boldface to distinguish them from other identifiers.

Using SQL Select Statements for Queries

7.1

7.1.1   The Simplest Select Statements

The main statement that is used to extract information from a relational database is the select statement. Its standard form incorporates selection, projection, and join operations in a single statement. As with those relational algebra operations, the select statement produces a relation as its result. The basic select statement includes three clauses: a **select** *clause*, a **from** *clause*, and a **where** *clause*. Its syntax is

```
select <attribute names> from <tables> where <condition>
```

The **select** clause specifies the attributes that are part of the resulting relation. The **from** clause specifies the tables that serve as the input to the statement. The **where** clause specifies the selection conditions, including the join condition. By way of illustration, we will look at statements that are equivalent to the relational expressions of Section 6.1.

The SQL statements of Fig. 7.1 produce Tables 6.1 through 6.3.

Lines a and b of Fig. 7.1 show select statements, each of which represents a single selection operation. The asterisk (*) in the **select** clause denotes that every attribute of the input table is to be selected. String literals in SQL are written with single quotes. A single quote inside a string literal is indicated by two consecutive single quotes.

Lines c and d of Fig. 7.1 also show select statements, each of which represents a single projection operation. The **select** clause is used to list the names and

```
a) select * from Customer where lastName = 'Doe'          Table 6.1
b) select * from TimeCard                                  Table 6.2
      where ssn = '376-77-0099' and date > '01-mar-1998'
c) select lastName, firstName from Customer
d) select distinct lastName, firstName from Customer      Table 6.3
```

FIGURE 7.1 _____

Simple select statements that produce Tables 6.1–6.3

order of the attributes of the output relation. The difference between lines c and d lies in the use of the keyword **distinct**. Its use emphasizes one difference between the relational algebra and SQL. The presence of **distinct** is necessary to produce Table 6.3, which has only one row to represent the two customers named Jane Doe. Without this keyword, eight rows would be produced: one for each Jane Doe, and one for each of the other six customers.

A NOTE ON THE RESULT OF SELECT STATEMENTS |

Select statements in SQL do not produce a set of values, but rather a list of values. The lack of order and the guarantee of uniqueness of the relational model are not part of SQL. Like many other SQL features, uniqueness is not guaranteed because it is expensive. If a query is known to yield unique results, it doesn't need to be checked. If it doesn't matter whether the rows are unique, it also doesn't need to be checked. Checking for uniqueness requires that the rows be sorted by some value and then compared. The cost of executing this operation is quite high for large tables. SQL leaves it to the developer to decide whether uniqueness is important. Adding the keyword **distinct** after **select** forces the SQL processor to produce a table with unique rows.

7.1.2   Simple Join Queries

Figure 7.2 shows select statements, each of which represents a single join operation. The join is specified in the **from** clause, which lists the two input relations, and the **where** clause, which lists the join condition. Line a of Fig. 7.2 is the standard SQL form of the join operation of Table 6.7. All of the columns are selected (**select ***), the two input tables are Employee and TimeCard, and the join condition is Employee.ssn = TimeCard.ssn.

Some versions of SQL, including that used in Microsoft Access, support an explicit join operator. In those versions, the query of line a of Fig. 7.2 can be written

```
a) select * from Employee, TimeCard
      where Employee.ssn = TimeCard.ssn
b) select * from Employee join TimeCard
      on Employee.ssn = TimeCard.ssn
```

FIGURE 7.2 _____

SQL queries for the simple join operation of Table 6.7

as in line b by using the **join** verb. In this case, the join condition has been moved from the **where** clause to the **on** clause.

Four different versions of the join operator are supported by some SQL systems: **inner join**, **outer join**, **left join**, and **right join**. Without a modifier, the join operator is an inner join, which produces an output tuple for each match between two input tuples. This case is the join operator of the relational algebra. A left join produces all of the output of the inner join and adds a tuple for each row of its left operand that does not match any row of the right operand. The output fields that are attributes of the right operand are given null values. For instance, the following select statement produces Table 7.1:

```
select * from Employee left join TimeCard
    on Employee.ssn = TimeCard.ssn
```

Two more rows have been added to those of Table 6.7 to hold information about employees 479-98-0098 and 579-98-8778, who have no time cards.

A right join is like a left join, but it contains the inner join plus a row for each row of the right operand that does not match any row of the left operand. An outer join is the union of the left and right joins. It has a row for each match, plus a row for each unmatched row of the left input table and one for each unmatched row of the right input table.

In Access, a left join can be expressed by selecting the line connecting the two tables, clicking the right mouse button, and selecting Join Properties. The Join Properties dialog allows the selection of an inner, left, or right join. Figure 7.3 shows the left join query of Table 6.7 and the Join Properties dialog with left join selected. An arrowhead on the connecting line points to the `TimeCard` table.

7.1.3 Queries with Multiple Relational Operators

Figure 7.4 gives the select statement that produces Table 6.8. This statement contains three join operations, one selection operation, and one projection operation.

TABLE 7.1

Left join of `Employee` *and* `TimeCard`

Employee.ssn	last Name	first Name	TimeCard.ssn	date	start Time	store Id	paid	end Time
145-09-0967	Uno	Jane	145-09-0967	01/14/99	8:15	3	no	12:00
145-09-0967	Uno	Jane	145-09-0967	01/16/99	8:15	3	no	12:00
245-11-4554	Toulouse	Jie	245-11-4554	01/14/99	8:15	3	no	12:00
376-77-0099	Threat	Ayisha	376-77-0099	02/23/99	14:00	5	no	22:00
376-77-0099	Threat	Ayisha	376-77-0099	01/03/99	10:00	5	no	14:00
376-77-0099	Threat	Ayisha	376-77-0099	01/03/99	15:00	5	no	19:00
479-98-0098	Fortune	Julian						
579-98-8778	Fivozinsky	Bruce						

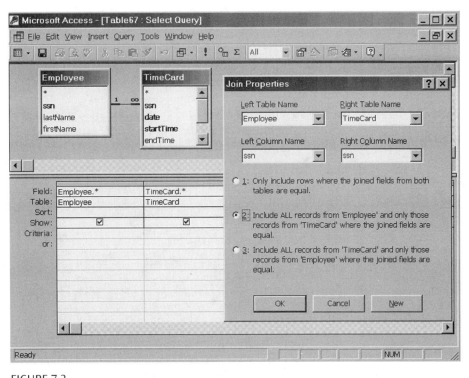

FIGURE 7.3 _____

Access query for left join of `Employee` *and* `TimeCard`

It is difficult to see exactly where these operations occur in the select statement. It is even appropriate to think that more (or fewer) relational operations might be present.

The select statement describes the output relation more clearly than it describes the relational operations that produce the output. That is, SQL is used to describe *what* has to be done, not *how* to do it. We rely on query processing to translate an SQL query into a relational algebra expression, and we count on query optimization to find an efficient strategy for executing the expression.

```
select lastName, firstName, title, dateRented            Projection
  from Movie, Videotape, PreviousRental, Customer         Source tables
  where Movie.movieId = Videotape.movieId                 Join condition
    and Customer.accountId = Rental.accountId             Join condition
    and Videotape.videoId = Rental.videoId                Join condition
    and dateRented > '1998-dec-1'                         Selection condition
```

FIGURE 7.4 _____

Select statement that produces Table 6.8

```
select Customer.firstName, Customer.lastName, Movie.title,
    PreviousRental.dateRented
  from (Movie inner join Videotape
    on Movie.movieId = Videotape.movieId)
    inner join (Customer
      inner join PreviousRental
      on Customer.accountId = PreviousRental.accountId)
    on Videotape.videoId = PreviousRental.videoId
  where (((PreviousRental.dateRented)>#12/1/98#));
```

FIGURE 7.5 _____

Microsoft Access select statement that produces Table 6.8

A NOTE ON THE CONFUSION BETWEEN SQL AND RELATIONAL ALGEBRA TERMS

You may have noticed that the names of the relational operations and the clauses of the select statement are not consistent. The *selection* operation is included in the **where** clause, and the *projection* operation is specified by the **select** clause.

Selecting the SQL window option for the Microsoft Access query depicted in Fig. 6.4 produces the select statement of Fig. 7.5. The primary difference between Figs. 7.4 and 7.5 relates to the use of the **join** verb in the Access version. This syntax makes the join operations more obvious and puts the selection condition in the **where** clause by itself. You will also notice that Access is also more verbose with attribute names. It always includes the table name, even when it is not required. The attribute names in Fig. 7.4 are qualified with table names only where the names are required to resolve ambiguities.

7.1.4   Substrings and Ordering

SQL supports pattern matching in selection criteria with the **like** operator and a simple pattern alphabet. In a **like** expression, the percent symbol matches an arbitrary string and the underscore matches any single character. For example, the first select statement below returns all movies whose genre attribute includes "comedy." The second select statement returns all movies whose title does not start with "the." Pattern matching in SQL is case insensitive, so `'the %'` matches movie titles even if they begin with a capital T.

```
select * from Movie where genre like '%comedy%'
select * from Movie where title not like 'the %'
select * from Employee where ssn like '___-44-____'
```

The third select statement selects employees whose Social Security numbers have "44" in the middle. It is difficult to read these underscore characters on the printed page, but the pattern has three underscores, minus, 44, minus, and four underscores. Because each Social Security number consists of three digits, two digits, then four digits, separated by minus signs, this pattern matches Social Security numbers with "44" as the center two digits.

A NOTE ABOUT ORDERING THE RESULTS OF SELECT QUERIES

As noted in the box on page 149, each select statement returns a list of rows, in a specific order. If a select statement does not specify the desired order, the SQL processor is free to produce the result table in any order. In many cases, the order is significant to the application that issues the select statement. An **order by** clause requires that the output table be produced in a specific order. The first select statement below produces a list of customers ordered by last name and then by first name. The second select statement adds the **desc** keyword to produce a list in descending order by account ID. The keyword **asc** can be used to produce a list in ascending order. These keywords can be mixed within a single **order by** clause, as in the third select statement

```
select * from Customer order by lastName, firstName
select * from Customer order by accountId desc
select * from Customer order by lastName desc, zipcode, asc
```

7.1.5   Expressions, Literals, and Aggregates

So far, we have seen select statements that return values that occur as attribute values in the input tables. We also need to be able to create new values to include in the output. For instance, we may wish to report the number of hours worked in a time card report. The number of hours worked is the difference between the ending time and the starting time on a time card. In SQL, time calculations return numeric values represented as fractions of days. Hence we must multiply the difference in ending and starting times by 24 to obtain the number of hours worked. We can include the expression `(endTime-startTime)*24` as a selected attribute as in the following statement:

```
select lastName, firstName, Employee.ssn, date,
    (endTime-startTime)*24
  from Employee, TimeCard
  where Employee.ssn = TimeCard.ssn
```

The preceding statement produces a single row of output for each row in its input, which is the join of `Employee` and `TimeCard`. The value of the expression for an output row is calculated from the values of the attributes `endTime` and `startTime` of the joined input row. Table 7.2 shows the results of executing this SQL.

One difference between selecting an expression and selecting an attribute of a source table is that we have no obvious name for the selected attribute that represents the value of the expression. What would you call `(endTime-startTime)*24`? Every attribute of every relation has a name, but the SQL standard does not specify what the name should be in these cases. One SQL database system calls this attribute `column5`. Microsoft Access, which was used to generate Table 7.2, calls the attribute `Expr1`. We can use the **as** clause to give a name to the attribute. For

TABLE 7.2

Time card report with number of hours worked represented as attribute `Expr1`

lastName	firstName	ssn	date	Expr1
Uno	Jane	145-09-0967	1/14/99	3.75
Uno	Jane	145-09-0967	1/16/99	3.75
Toulouse	Jie	245-11-4554	1/14/99	3.75
Threat	Ayisha	376-77-0099	2/23/99	8
Threat	Ayisha	376-77-0099	1/3/99	4
Threat	Ayisha	376-77-0099	2/23/99	4

example, the following select statement calls the calculated attribute `hoursWorked`. The result table has five attributes; the last one is `hoursWorked`, a floating-point value.

```
select lastName, firstName, Employee.ssn, date,
    (endTime-startTime)*24 as hoursWorked
  from Employee, TimeCard
  where Employee.ssn = TimeCard.ssn
```

Expressions in a select clause can include string and numeric literals (for example, 100), values of attributes (for example, `lastName`), standard numeric operators (for example, /), and function calls.

SQL offers a wide variety of functions, including numeric functions, string manipulation functions, and date formatting functions. The usual syntax, rules of precedence, associativity, and numeric type conversion apply to SQL expressions. An SQL reference manual is the best source of information on exactly which types, operators, and functions are available.

The next issue to address is the collection of information that is extracted from more than one row of a table. For instance, in Chapter 2 we defined a derived attribute `numberRented` of `Customer` that represents the number of videotapes that are currently rented by the customer. It requires the use of an aggregate operator, one that puts together values from multiple rows of the `Rental` table. Select statements can include aggregate functions in the **select** clause. The following select statement returns the number of videotapes rented for the customer with account number 101:

```
select count(*) from Rental where accountId = 101
```

The **count** function returns the number of values of the attribute in the table. In this case, we use **count(*)** to indicate that the number of rows should be counted. To find the number of different last names of customers, we would write:

```
select count(distinct lastName) from Customer
```

Each of the preceding queries returns a single row in its result table.

SQL includes aggregate functions to calculate average, minimum, maximum, and sum of numeric attributes. We can calculate the average number of hours worked on the time cards of employees as follows:

```
select avg((endTime-startTime)*24) as hoursWorked from
    TimeCard
```

Whenever an aggregate appears in the **select** clause, all values in the **select** clause must be either aggregates or constants. Other functions that can be used in an aggregating select statement include **min**, **max**, and **sum**.

7.1.6   group by and having Clauses

In many circumstances, an aggregating query should return more than one row—for instance, selecting the average cost and the number of previous rentals for each videotape. We want to divide the tuples into groups and return an aggregate for each group. The ***group by*** *clause* provides this functionality. The following query returns one row for each videotape ID. Each row contains the videotape ID, the average cost for that videotape, and the number of previous rentals for that videotape. Table 7.3 shows the result of the execution of this query.

```
select videoId, avg(cost) as averageCost,
    count(*) as numRentals
    from PreviousRental group by videoId
```

With a **group by** clause, one row is returned for each group of input rows. In the previous query, the tuples of the `PreviousRental` table are grouped by `videoId`. Within each group, all of the tuples have the same value for `videoId`; every other group has a different value for `videoId`.

The derived attribute `numberRented` of `Customer` can be created for all customers by joining the `Customer` and `Rental` tables, grouping by `accountId`, and counting the number of rows. The following select statement accomplishes this task:

```
select Customer.accountId, count(*) as numberRented
    from Customer, Rental
    where Customer.accountId = Rental.accountId
    group by Customer.accountId
```

TABLE 7.3

Videotape report of average cost and number of previous rentals

videoId	averageCost	numRentals
101	$2.49	2
112	$1.99	1
113	$2.49	3
77564	$3.65	2

The fields that can be selected in a **group by** query are restricted to the attributes that appear in the **group by** clause, aggregate expressions, and literals. No attribute that does not appear in the **group by** clause can be listed in the select clause. This restriction applies because those attributes are not guaranteed to have constant value within a group. Hence, it is not possible to uniquely determine the value of the attribute that correctly represents the group. To select the customer name in the preceding query, this name must be included in the **group by** clause, as shown below:

```
select Customer.accountId, lastName, firstName,
    count(*) as numberRented
  from Customer, Rental
  where Customer.accountId = Rental.accountId
  group by Customer.accountId, lastName, firstName
```

The final piece of this feature is the **having** *clause*, which is a selection clause applied to groups. Any group that does not satisfy the **having** clause does not contribute a tuple to the result table. The values that can appear in the **having** clause are the same as those that can appear in the **select** clause. Consequently, we can restrict groups by size or other aggregate, or by the values of **group by** attributes. Figure 7.6 shows a query that selects the movie title and genre, the number of rentals, the average rental cost, and the total cost for all movies that have at least two rentals. Table 7.4. gives the result of this query. As you can see in the table, only two movies satisfy the **having** clause.

```
select title, genre, count(*) as numRentals,
    avg(cost) as average, sum(cost) as sum
  from Movie, Videotape, PreviousRental
  where Movie.movieId = Videotape.movieId
    and Videotape.videoId = PreviousRental.videoId
  group by Movie.movieId, title, genre
  having count(*)>=2
```

FIGURE 7.6 _____

Group by *and* **having** *clauses in a query to select movies*

TABLE 7.4 _____

Result of query of Fig. 7.6

title	genre	numRentals	average	sum
Annie Hall	comedy	4	$2.37	$9.46
The Thirty-Nine Steps	mystery	2	$2.49	$4.98

To select the title and genre, we had to include them in the **group by** clause. Their inclusion does not change the grouping, because `movieId` is a key of `Movie`. That is, each movie has a single title and a single genre. These attributes appear to be superfluous in the **group by** clause, and perhaps they are. Nevertheless, SQL requires their inclusion.

The **having** clause and the **where** clause both restrict the query. The **where** clause restricts the tuples that become members of groups. Only tuples that satisfy the **where** clause are used in forming the groups. Once the groups have been formed, the **having** clause determines which groups produce output tuples. Only groups that satisfy the **having** clause produce output tuples.

Figure 7.7 shows a Microsoft Access representation of the query depicted in Fig. 7.6 and Table 7.4. A new row appears in the list of fields to hold a Total. Right-clicking on a field and clicking the Σ Totals button makes this row appear. This row has values Group By, Sum, and Expression for different fields. The list of **group by** fields matches those given in Fig. 7.6. The **having** clause is represented by the third field. The Criteria row shows >= 2—that is, at least two rentals for this movie. The last field specifies **group by** `movieId`.

The SQL view of this query will show the joins using the **inner join** verb and thus is different from Fig. 7.6. If the SQL statement of Fig 7.6 is pasted into the SQL view of a new query in Access, the resulting design view will not include the join lines shown in Fig. 7.7. Instead, the join conditions, which are expressed in the **where** clause of the query, appear in the Criteria row of the Field list. This

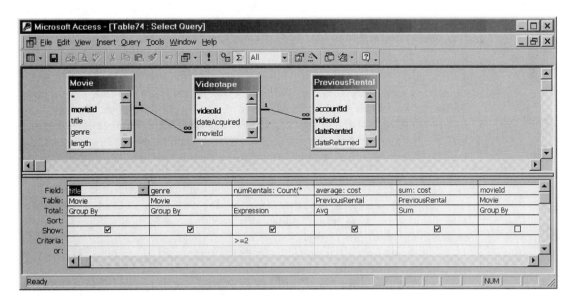

FIGURE 7.7

Microsoft Access representation of the query of Fig. 7.6

placement indicates that Access does not fully understand SQL or at least has a very primitive query optimizer.* The query shown in Fig. 7.7 was created from QBE, not directly from the SQL statement.

7.1.7   Nested Select Statements

It is not unusual for a query to be so complex that it cannot easily fit into the form of a single select statement. SQL allows a select statement to be used inside the **where** clause of another select statement. Such *nested select statements* can make complex queries easier to write and easier to read. To select all of the customers who rented some videotape in December 1998, for example, we use the following query.

```
select * from Customer where accountId in
  (select accountId from PreviousRental
    where dateRented >='dec/1/1998' and dateRented<'1/1/99')
```

Reading from inside out, this query selects all previous rentals from December 1998, then selects all customers for those rentals. It is equivalent to a join of the two tables with a selection of rentals from December 1998. A good query optimizer recognizes the equivalence of the nested select query and the join query and can produce the same execution strategy for both.

The nested select statement can include references to fields of the containing statement. The following is a selection of all customers who have not rented any videotape:

```
select * from Customer C where not exists
  (select * from PreviousRental P
    where C.accountId = P.accountId)
```

The operator **not exists** is true when its operand is an empty table. The use of C and P is a way of simplifying the query text by introducing local names for tables. C stands for `Customer`, and P stands for `PreviousRental`. One acceptable execution of this select statement is to iterate through the rows of table C. For each row in C, the nested query is executed with the account number of the current row of C as the value for `C.accountId`. If the nested query returns no rows, the main query produces an output row. If the nested query returns any rows, the main query does not produce an output row.

The operators and keywords that can be used in nested select statements include **in**, **all**, **exists**, **unique**, **contains**, **union**, **not**, and **intersect**. The meaning of these terms is fairly obvious. A good SQL reference book will contain many examples of their use.

Microsoft Access has no facility for building nested queries in QBE. Pasting the preceding query into an Access query window and switching to design view yields the configuration shown in Fig. 7.8. The nested select statement is shown in

---

* A *query optimizer* is a program that reformulates SQL statements to improve their execution efficiency. Query optimization is discussed in detail in Chapter 13.

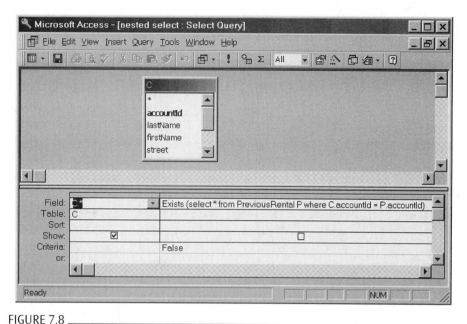

FIGURE 7.8 _____
Microsoft Access representation of a nested select statement

text form as the argument of the `Exists` function in the second field. The negation of the **exists** operation is represented by the `False` in the Criteria field.

7.1.8   Set Operations

SQL can perform union, intersection, and difference operations on select statements. The example of combining `Rental` and `PreviousRental` of Section 6.1.3 and Fig. 7.4 can be produced by using the following expression:

```
(select * from Rental) union (select * from PreviousRental)
```

The discussion in Section 6.1.3 noted that it is impossible to determine the source of a row in the table produced by this union. The following query uses string literals to mark the source of the rows:

```
    (select *, 'Rental' as sourceTable from Rental)
union
    (select *, 'PreviousRental' as sourceTable from
       PreviousRental)
```

The result table has an extra column whose value is the name of the source table. Table 7.5 gives the result of this union statement.

The intersection operation is called **intersect** in SQL. The difference operator is called **except**. The following queries (from Section 6.1.3) produce the

TABLE 7.5

Result of union query

accountId	videoId	dateRented	dateDue	cost	sourceTable
101	101	12/9/98	12/10/98	$2.49	PreviousRental
101	112	1/13/98	1/4/98	$1.99	PreviousRental
101	113	1/15/99	1/15/99	$0.99	PreviousRental
102	113	12/1/98	12/3/98	$2.49	PreviousRental
111	101	12/4/98	12/6/98	$2.49	PreviousRental
111	77564	1/1/99	1/4/99	$3.95	PreviousRental
201	113	12/9/98	12/14/98	$3.99	PreviousRental
201	77564	1/14/99	1/24/99	$3.35	PreviousRental
101	90987	1/1/99	1/8/99	$2.99	Rental
101	99787	1/1/99	1/4/99	$3.49	Rental
103	101	1/3/99	1/4/99	$1.59	Rental
103	123	12/1/98	12/31/98	$10.99	Rental

list of the `videoId` values for the videotapes that are currently rented and have been rented before:

```
(select videoId from Rental)
intersect
(select videoId from PreviousRental)
```

those that are currently being rented for the first time:

```
(select videoId from Rental)
except
(select videoId from PreviousRental)
```

and those that have been rented but are not currently rented:

```
(select videoId from PreviousRental)
except
(select videoId from Rental)
```

Modifying Database Content with SQL

7.2   SQL includes insert, update, and delete statements to support the modification of the contents of tables. An *insert statement* adds new rows to a table. An *update statement* modifies one or more attributes of specified rows of a table. A *delete statement* deletes one or more rows from a table.

7.2.1   Insert Statements

To insert a row into a table, it is necessary to have a value for each attribute. The insert query below gives a literal value for each attribute of one new row of table `Customer`. The new customer, Jia Yu, has account number "555," street "540 Magnolia Hall," city "Tallahassee," state "FL," and ZIP code "32306." The **values** in the statement appear in the same order as the attributes of the table.

```
insert into Customer values (555, 'Yu', 'Jia',
    '540 Magnolia Hall', 'Tallahassee', 'FL', '32306', 0.00)
```

The order and even the presence of attributes can be specified by listing them, in parentheses, after the table name. In the following query, the order of attributes is different, and no value is given for the address attributes:

```
insert into Customer (firstName, lastName, accountId)
    values ('Jia', 'Yu', 555)
```

Each of the missing attributes will take on its default value. If this value is not specified as part of the table definition, the attribute takes the value **null**. If the **address** attribute was specified as non-null with no default value, this insert statement would fail.

An insert statement can contain a select statement to add multiple rows to a table. The form of this query is as follows:

```
insert into <table> <select statement>
```

Consider the process of creating pay statements. At the end of a pay period, all of the time cards from that pay period are collected and the number of hours is calculated for each employee. Next, the hourly pay rate for each employee is multiplied by the number of hours worked. Finally, a new entity is created in the `PayStatement` table to record the amount to be paid.

We must write a select statement that produces a table that is the same shape as the `PayStatement` table. The schema for `PayStatement` is as follows:

```
PayStatement (ssn, hourlyRate, numHours, amountPaid, datePaid)
```

The select statement must provide a value for every field, in the proper order. We develop this select statement in a series of steps.

The following select statement will select every pay statement that has not yet been paid (paid attribute = false) and perform the total hours worked calculation:[*]

```
select TimeCard.ssn, sum((endTime-startTime)*24) as hoursWorked
    from TimeCard where paid=false group by ssn
```

---

[*] The date calculations in this section are based on the data types and operations of Microsoft Access. The result of subtracting dates is represented as a number of days. Hence, the number of hours is calculated by multiplying by 24.

The calculation of the amount to be paid must use the `hourlyRate` field from the `HourlyEmployee` table. You will recall that some employees are hourly employees. Only those employees will be paid by time card. We can add the pay calculation to the preceding SQL statement. In addition, we must include fields for the hourly rate and the pay date. We use the SQL constant **today** to represent the day that the statement is executed.

```
select TimeCard.ssn, hourlyRate,
    sum((endTime-startTime)*24) as hoursWorked,
    sum((endTime-startTime)*24*hourlyRate) as amountPaid,
    today
  from TimeCard, HourlyEmployee
  where TimeCard.ssn = HourlyEmployee.ssn and paid = false
  group by TimeCard.ssn, hourlyRate
```

The preceding statement will create a table that has the same attribute types as `PayStatement` and hence can be used in the insert statement of Fig. 7.9.

7.2.2   Update Statements

The update statement in SQL changes one or more rows of a table. An update statement has three clauses.

```
update <table> set <attribute>=<value> ...
  where <selection condition>
```

The **update** clause specifies which table to update, the **set** clause contains one or more assignments that specify which attributes to change and what their new values are, and the **where** clause specifies which rows to change.

For instance, the following statement finishes the pay statement application of Fig. 7.9 by marking all of the time cards as paid:

```
update TimeCard set paid = true
  where paid = false
```

```
insert into PayStatement
    (ssn, hourlyRate, numHours, amountPaid, datePaid)
  select TimeCard.ssn, hourlyRate,
      sum((endTime-startTime)*24) as hoursWorked,
      sum((endTime-startTime)*24*hourlyRate) as amountPaid,
      today
    from TimeCard, HourlyEmployee
    where TimeCard.ssn=HourlyEmployee.ssn and paid = false
    group by TimeCard.ssn, hourlyRate
```

FIGURE 7.9 _____

Insert statement that calculates the amount to pay employees from the time cards

An assignment in an update statement can refer to attributes of the update table. For instance, the following query gives a specific hourly employee a 10% raise:

```
update HourlyEmployee set hourlyRate = hourlyRate *1.1
   where ssn = '145-09-0967'
```

Care must be taken with update statements to ensure that they affect the correct rows. If we leave out the **where** clause in the preceding statement, it will change every hourly employee's pay rate.

The expression on the right side of an assignment can be very complex and may include nested select statements, much like the expressions discussed in Section 7.1.7.

7.2.3   Delete Statements

A delete statement specifies a table and a selection condition. Each row of the table that satisfies the condition is deleted when the statement executes. For instance, the following statement deletes every row of the `TimeCard` table where the employee is not an hourly employee:

```
delete from Timecard
    where not exists
       (select * from HourlyEmployee
          where TimeCard.ssn = HourlyEmployee.ssn)
```

Creating and Manipulating Schemas with SQL

7.3

In Chapter 4, we saw what relation schemas contain and how to implement them in Microsoft Access. In this section, we see how to implement relation schemas in SQL database systems. The DDL of SQL is centered around the create table statement. It includes statements to specify the physical characteristics of databases, such as indexing, clustering, and distribution. The DDL may be the part of SQL that has the most variation in practice, as each database system includes its own extensions.

7.3.1   Specifying Attributes and Their Types

A *create table statement* gives a name and a list of attributes for a table. Each attribute must have a name and a type. Figure 7.10 shows an SQL statement that creates the `Customer` table. The name attributes are listed as variable-length text fields with a maximum of 32 characters in each one (**varchar(32)**). The `street` field is expected to be longer, so it has a maximum of 100 characters. The `accountId` field is an **int**, which is a four-byte integer.

SQL supports a specific collection of attribute types, listed in Table 7.6. There are integer and floating-point types of various lengths. There are three date types that are used for a date and a time (**datetime**), a date with no time (**date**), and a time with no date (**time**). In the student records database, we might use a **datetime**

```
Create table Customer (
   accountId int,
   lastName varchar(32),
   firstName varchar(32),
   street varchar(100),
   city varchar(32),
   state char(2),
   zipcode varchar(9),
   balance real
)
```

FIGURE 7.10 _____

SQL statement to create the Customer *table*

TABLE 7.6 _____

Some attribute types of SQL

Type Category	Type	SQL Types
Numeric types	Integer	integer, int, smallint, long
	Floating point	float, real, double precision
	Formatted	decimal(i,j), dec(i,j)
Character-string types	Fixed length	char(n), character(n)
	Varying length	varchar(n), char varying(n), character varying(n)
Bit-string types	Fixed length	bit(n)
	Varying length	bit varying(n)
Date and time types		date, time, datetime, timestamp, time with time zone, interval
Large types	Character	long varchar(n), clob, text
	Binary	blob

for the dateDue and dateRented of a rental, a **date** for the date of a time card, and a **time** for its startTime and endTime.

The text types are extensive and include both fixed- and variable-length types. These types have a limit on their length, often 256 characters. Longer string attributes must be defined as type **longvarchar** or **text**. Attributes of these types may be unlimited in length. Many recent implementations of SQL include **blob** (binary long object) and even **clob** (character long object) types. These types are typically used for values that do not need to support searching. For example, a video clip or a block of numeric data can be stored in an SQL database as a **blob**.

7.3.2   Key and Foreign Key Constraint Specifications

Attributes have characteristics other than simply a name and a type. This section and Section 7.3.3 illustrate some of the characteristics that can be declared in SQL. In Chapter 4, we saw that some attributes represent primary and secondary keys of relations. Other attributes represent foreign keys—relationships with other relations. These key characteristics of attributes are constraints on the tuples that can be part of the relationships. Figure 7.11 shows three create table statements that declare key and foreign key constraints.

The SQL phrase **primary key** declares an attribute or set of attributes to be the primary key of a relationship. A single-attribute key can be declared by adding the phrase to the attribute declaration, as in the declarations of tables `Store` (line 2) and `Movie` (line 10). A multiple attribute key must be declared in a separate constraint clause, as in the declaration of table `Rental` (line 22). A constraint clause can also be used to declare a single attribute to be a primary key.

```
 1 create table Store (
 2    storeId int primary key,
 3    street varchar(100),
 4    city varchar(32),
 5    state char(2),
 6    zipcode varchar(9),
 7    manager int references Employee
 8 )
 9 create table Movie (
10    movieId varchar(10) primary key,
11    title varchar(100) unique,
12    genre varchar(32),
13    rating varchar(5),
14    accountId int
15 )
16 create table Rental (
17    accountId int,
18    videoId varchar(10),
19    dateRented datetime,
20    dateRented datetime,
21    cost real,
22    primary key (accountId, videoId),
23    foreign key (accountId)references Customer(accountId),
24    foreign key (videoId)references Videotape(videoId)
25 )
```

FIGURE 7.11 _____

SQL statements to create `Store`, `Movie`, *and* `Rental` *tables*

Secondary keys are declared by including a **unique** constraint for the attribute or set of attributes. The `title` attribute of `Movie` (line 11) is a secondary key, as specified by the **unique** constraint.

For both primary and secondary keys, the relational database system will enforce the constraints and ensure that no violation occurs. Any attempt to insert or update a row that results in a constraint violation will not be allowed.

Foreign kW! constraints are specified with a ***references*** *clause*, as shown in its two forms in Fig. 7.11. The attribute `manager` of table `Store` (line 7) is a foreign key that references the primary key of the `Employee` table. The constraint clauses for `accountId` and `videoId` of the `Rental` table (lines 23 and 24) show the general form of a ***references*** clause. The foreign key attributes are listed in the first pair of parentheses, and the primary key of the referenced table is listed in the second set of parentheses. This form allows the foreign key to consist of more than one attribute and to refer to attributes other than the primary key of the referenced table.

As with key constraints, foreign key constraints are enforced by relational database systems.

7.3.3   Default Values, Nulls, and Constraints

Earlier, we saw that it is often convenient to have default values for attributes. Their use can often simplify the insert statements employed to add rows to those tables.

It is not unusual to have attributes whose values must be supplied; the **not null** characteristic is given to such attributes. Likewise, it is not unusual for a foreign key to be declared not null. The `movieId` attribute of `Videotape` is not null to enforce the participation constraint—that each videotape be represented by a corresponding entity in the `Movie` table. This condition is specified in the create table statement for the class.

```
create table Videotape (
  videoId varchar(10) primary key,
  movieId varchar(10) not null references Movie,
  storeId int references Store
)
```

7.3.4   Schemas and Catalogs

Tables and other definitions in a relational database are collected into *schemas*. The SQL use of *schema* is analogous to what was called a *database schema* in Chapter 4. It includes all of the definitions related to a particular database. Typically, each SQL connection to a database occurs in the context of a particular schema. Once a client program is connected to an SQL server, an element of the schema can be referred to as `schemaName.tableName` or simply as `tableName`. Each schema has a name and an owner.

A schema is created by the execution of a create schema statement. All of the tables of our BigHit Video database are part of a single schema that was created with the following statement:

```
create schema BigHitVideo
```

7.3.5   Drop Statements

The drop table statement is used to remove a table from a database. There are two *drop behavior* options: **cascade** and **restrict**. The **cascade** option specifies that any foreign key constraint violations that are caused by dropping the table will cause the corresponding rows of the related table to be deleted. The **restrict** option blocks the deletion of the table if any foreign key constraint violations would be created.

The drop schema statement is used to remove a schema from a database. The **restrict** option blocks deletion of the schema unless it has no elements. The **cascade** option causes all of the elements of the schema to be deleted.

7.3.6   Additional SQL Statements

This chapter has presented a "tip of the iceberg" discussion of SQL. Chapters 12–15 describe some of the additional aspects of SQL, including the specification of physical database properties. Our coverage here has also been a "rule of 90/10" discussion. A rule of thumb for computer science is that 90% of the functionality of a system is produced by 10% of the work. The other side of that coin is that the last 10% of the functionality requires 90% of the work. This consideration explains why computer programmers are such optimists and why it is easy to imagine that a project might be completed in a short time. We typically see how 90% of the functionality can be produced. The last 10% may never get done!

The SQL topics covered in Chapter 7 represent the 10% of SQL that produces 90% of the utility of the language. Most of what is required to implement database systems in SQL was mentioned. Unfortunately, that last 10% is the most difficult and often the most crucial part of database system development.

True mastery of SQL will require additional study, lots of practice, and a shelf full of database books and SQL reference manuals. A sad fact of database systems is that, despite the standardization of SQL, every database system has its own extensions and dialects. It is often necessary to use the nonstandard parts of the database to achieve acceptable results.

Chapter Summary

SQL is a standard language for describing database definition, manipulation, and applications. The data manipulation language (DML) of SQL supports queries that extract data from databases (select statements), add new rows to tables (insert statements), and modify attribute values of existing rows (update statements). SQL is not an exact implementation of the relational algebra, as it does not guarantee the uniqueness of rows in a table and does impose an order on the rows.

The select statement combines selection, projection, and join operators into a single statement. The **select** clause contains the projection, the **from** clause lists the input tables, and the **where** clause contains the join conditions and the selection conditions. Additional clauses can be used to specify grouping of rows.

Update, insert, and delete statements are used to describe modifications to the content of a database.

The data definition language (DDL) of SQL supports the definition of both the logical and physical structures of databases. The create table statement specifies a relation schema. It describes the attributes, their types, default values, and constraints. It can be used to define key and foreign key constraints. In addition, it supports the definition of physical characteristics of databases, as will be described in Chapter 12.

Key Terms

Aggregate operator. A function that produces a single value from multiple rows of a table. SQL supports aggregate operators **avg**, **count**, **max**, **min**, and **sum**.

Create table statement. An SQL statement that specifies the creation of a new table with specific attributes and constraints.

Delete statement. An SQL statement that specifies the deletion of rows from a table.

from clause. A clause in an SQL select statement that specifies the source tables of the statement. Multiple source tables in a from clause represent product operations on those tables. Join conditions are specified in the where clause or in the on clause of a join verb.

group by clause. A clause in an SQL select statement that specifies how select rows will be grouped. One output row is produced for each group of selected rows.

having clause. A clause in an SQL select statement that specifies a selection condition on the groups. A **having** clause always appears in combination with a group by clause.

Insert statement. An SQL statement that specifies a set of rows to be added to a table.

Nested select statement. An SQL select statement that includes a subselect statement in the **from** or **where** clause.

references clause. A clause in an SQL create table statement that declares a set of attributes to be a foreign key that references a particular table.

select clause. A clause in an SQL select statement that specifies the projection operation of the statement. The **select** clause lists those attributes that are included in the result table.

Update statement. An SQL statement that specifies a modification of particular attributes in particular rows of a table.

where clause. A clause in an SQL select statement that specifies a condition that determines whether particular rows will be included in the output table. The **where** clause includes the selection operation of the query and often includes the join condition.

Exercises

1. What are the major differences between the relational data model and the SQL data model?

2. Which clause of the select statement is used to specify the following?

   a. Projection operation

   b. Selection operation

   c. Join operation

3. Write SQL statements to represent the queries of Exercise 8 in Chapter 6.

4. Write SQL statements to represent the queries of Exercise 10 in Chapter 6.

5. Write SQL queries to represent the following:

   a. Which customers have an "x" in their names?

   b. Which customers live in Florida (FL) or New Jersey (NJ)?

   c. Which customers currently have more than three videotapes rented?

   d. How many copies of *Elizabeth* have been ordered?

   e. Which salaried employees work in store 5?

6. Using the relations of the BigHit Video database, for each of the following SQL statements, give an English description of the statement and the relations that result when it is executed.

   a. **select * from** Customer **where exists select**
      accountId **from** Rental

   b. **select** title, genre **from** Movie, PreviousRental
         where Movie.movieId = PreviousRental.movieId **and**
         accountId = 101

   c. **select** movieId, title **from** Movie m,
         PurchaseOrderDetail p, PurchaseOrder d, Supplier s
         where m.movieId=d.movieId **and** d.id = p.id **and**
         p.supplierId = s.supplierId **and** s.state='LA'

7. Write relational expressions to represent the SQL statements in Exercise 6.

8. Write an SQL statement to select all hourly employees who worked in (had a time card for) store number 3 during the week of Monday, February 22, 1999.

9. Write an SQL statement to select the title of every videotape that was previously rented by a customer whose last name is the same as the last name of an employee.

10. Write SQL statements for the following database update operations:

    a. Create a new hourly employee with your own attribute values.

    b. Record that you work in store 3.

    c. Add a new store.

    d. Record a purchase order for five copies of *Elizabeth* and three copies of *Annie Hall* from Acme Video.

    e. Delete all previous rental records that are more than one year old.

    f. Delete all movies that have no rental copies.

    g. Give a 10% raise to all salaried employees.

    h. Delete all purchase order records that are more than one year old. Don't forget the purchase order detail records.

11. Write the SQL statements that create (insert) pay statements for salaried employees.

12. Use the property sales database schema created in Exercise 13 of Chapter 4 to do the following:

    a. Create SQL DDL statements to create the tables of the property sales database.

    b. Use those statements to create tables in an SQL database.

    c. Write insert statements to add entities to the BigHit Video database.

    d. Populate the database by executing the insert statements.

13. Using the database for BigHit Video shown in Figs. 6.1 and 6.6, do the following:

    a. Create SQL DDL statements to create the tables of the student records database.

    b. Use those statements to create tables in an SQL database.

    c. Write insert statements to add entities to the student records database.

    d. Populate the database by executing the insert statements.

14. Using the student records database schema created in Exercise 22 of Chapter 4, do the following:

    a. Create SQL DDL statements to create the tables of the student records database.

    b. Use those statements to create tables in an SQL database.

    c. Write insert statements to add entities to the student records database.

    d. Populate the database by executing the insert statements.

    e. Write SQL statements that produce a list of all grades for a particular student.

Further Readings

The standard for SQL-92 is published in [ANSI92]. Previous versions of SQL are Sequel 2, as described in Chamberlin et al. [Cha76], and the standard SQL-89 [ANSI89]. The next version of the SQL standard, tentatively called SQL-3, is now under development. Texts on SQL include Cannan and Otten [CaOt93] and Date and Darwen [DaDa93]. SQL-3 is discussed in Melton [Mel96].

PART THREE
Database Applications
and the World Wide Web

*I*n this part, we become deeply involved in applying programming tools, together with SQL, to create applications. We are particularly concerned with developing applications that support Web sites with database information. The Java programming language is the vehicle we use to create these applications.

Chapter 8 begins with an explanation of the client-server model that is used by database applications. We will see how to use the standard Java client library, JDBC, in a systematic way. We will not try to understand the details of how JDBC is implemented, but rather will focus on making this library work in our applications. Several Java classes are provided to facilitate performing standard database interactions. In addition, we will see many examples of the use of Java for executing SQL select and update statements.

The World Wide Web is the subject of Chapter 9. This chapter includes a brief introduction to HTML and an extensive discussion of the creation and processing of forms. You will learn how to use Java to create Web pages. The primary way in which Java is used in dynamic Web sites is through *servlet* classes. A servlet is a Java object that a Web server uses to service requests from browsers. In the exercises provided in Chapter 9, you will be asked to implement a complex Web site for the BigHit Video information system.

Chapter 10 includes discussions of many additional features of JDBC and examples of how to use them. The major application in this chapter is a servlet that keeps track of the interactions of multiple users. Each user is presented with a form that supports browsing and editing a collection of database objects. We will see how to track the individual users and maintain a separate state and database connection for each one.

8
Applications Programming for Relational Databases

*T*he role of an application program is to extract and update the information in the database. Some application programs provide user interfaces that allow people to interact with the database; others perform noninteractive processes. In either case, each application program is a client of a database server.

Every application program that modifies the database must be constructed so that it preserves the integrity of the database and the quality of the information. All of the constraints that have been defined as part of the database must be respected by the applications.

Applications that extract information must be constructed so that the information that they deliver is consistent with the contents of the database. The application shares this responsibility with the database system. Nevertheless, relational databases are designed to be flexible. For example, an application can issue queries that were not designed by the database designers. In all cases, the application developers have a serious responsibility to be faithful to the structure and meaning of the database.

This chapter addresses how application programs interact with database servers and what application developers must do to ensure that their applications are well behaved.

Overview of Database Applications Programming

8.1

Database application programs are written in many different programming languages. User interfaces are often built with development tools like Microsoft Access, Powersoft Power Builder, and Oracle Developer 2000. Although the traditional programming languages—COBOL, C, C++, Java, and others—are used for user interfaces, they also provide for the more complex applications that are needed for many situations.

8.1.1   Client-Server Architectures for Information Systems

A *database client* is either an application that connects to a database server during its execution or a software package that is used by the application to create and manage that connection. The application behaves as a client to the database by incorporating the client software package, initializing it, and calling methods that support the connection to a server and the manipulation of the database. The *client software* provides capabilities that are common to all database systems and possibly capabilities that are specific to the system. Consequently, the Oracle client software is different from the SQL Server or Sybase client software. That is, each package has its own specific methods and its own protocols for interaction with the server.

Figure 8.1 shows a variety of *client-server architectures* that are based on two or three tiers (also called layers). User interfaces and application programs appear in the top layer; they access information by acting as clients to servers that are located in the middle or lower layer. The lowest layer contains *database servers*, which provide a data manipulation language interface that is used by the higher layers to access and update the contents of the database. The *middleware*, or *application services*, layer contains programs that act as servers to the user layer and clients of the database layer.

Programs in the user and application layer include user interfaces, report generators, and other user tools. These programs can access information resources by connecting directly to a database server, as the left and right programs in Fig. 8.1 do. In addition, they can connect to a middleware server that acts as a broker for the database server, as the middle two programs in the figure do. Requests issued by programs in the top layer can consist of direct data manipulation commands written in SQL or in some other database client interface. Alternatively, they can be requests for method invocation by the servers. Both middleware and database servers support the execution of methods or functions that interact with the database. A user layer program may interact with more than one middleware or database server during its execution.

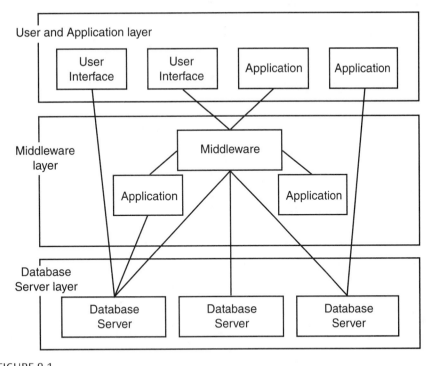

FIGURE 8.1 _____

A variety of client-server architectures for information systems

Much of the discussion of database applications in this book centers on the middleware layer. Middleware servers generally provide a reliable and secure interface between the unprotected and largely unreliable user layer programs and the highly controlled and protected database servers.

A middleware product is subject to more careful control than a user application. For this reason, it can be relied upon to properly enforce the constraints and business rules of the information system.

A Web site that is supported by a database is often implemented with a *three-tiered architecture*, as shown in Fig. 8.2. The user tier contains the Web browsers that display the Web pages and forms and collect information for processing. The middle tier contains the *Web server* and the database client programs that access the database. The lowest tier contains the database servers.

A Web interaction begins when a browser sends a request to the Web server in the form of a *uniform resource locator (URL)*.* The server analyzes the URL to see what processing is required to respond to the request. If the URL designates a file, that file is retrieved from the file system and sent back to the browser. If the URL

_____

* HTML 4.0 uses the term uniform resource identifier (URI) as a more general form of the uniform resource locator (URL) that was defined in HTML 2.0.

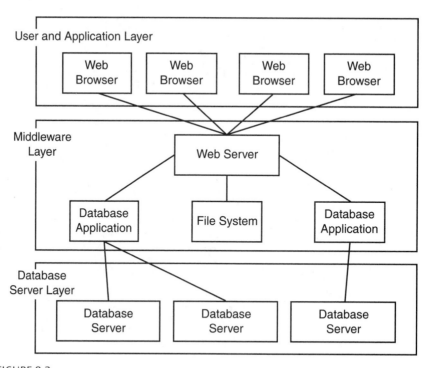

FIGURE 8.2 _____
Architecture of a Web site supported by databases

designates an executable program, that program is executed and its output is returned to the browser. Browser–server interaction is discussed in detail in Chapter 9.

8.1.2 Database Interaction in Microsoft Access

Microsoft Access is a system for directly interacting with databases and for implementing database applications. It is not intended primarily for professional information system designers, but rather is marketed as a desktop tool for database interaction. Each new release of Access extends the system's capabilities and makes it a more appropriate tool for application development. Microsoft offers a developer's version of Access that has a broader range of tools and supports the delivery of stand-alone applications. Any database application built using the Microsoft Office version of Access can be used only on a system that has Access installed.

An Access application is constructed using the graphical user interface (GUI) builder that supports a drag-and-drop style of interface construction. Code modules that are written in Visual Basic for Applications (VBA) specify the behavior of the application. Access applications are event-based—that is, their primary activity is performed in response to events that occur as a result of user interaction.

Most forms (windows) in Access use a specific table or query as a source of data. The `record source` property of the form identifies this source. A field within a form can be bound to an attribute of the data source through its `control source` property. This binding is specified independently of the database to which the application is connected. When a form is open, it displays the data associated with one or more entities. Typically, forms have navigation buttons that allow a user to move among the entities of the data source.

Microsoft Access offers two strategies for connecting to databases. First, you can use the Microsoft Jet database engine, which supports SQL access to databases stored in a variety of file formats, including Access database files. Second, you can use the *Other Database Connectivity (ODBC)* standard that is part of the Microsoft Windows operating system family. ODBC supports interaction with SQL databases.

ODBC lies at the heart of Access's ability to interact with a variety of data sources. It provides a database-independent manipulation facility. Using the ODBC programming package, an application is free to issue SQL statements and process their results without depending on a specific database server.

The ODBC standard specifies a collection of object types and methods that must be provided by each ODBC package. The implementation of these types and methods is called a *driver*. Each database system has its own driver. The *driver package* allows a program to become a client of the database system.

Several steps are required to make a data source available to an ODBC application, as illustrated in Fig. 8.3. First, the ODBC *driver manager* must be installed on the computer that will execute the application. The driver manager is a part of the operating system that allows an application to find the appropriate driver for a particular data source. Next, a driver for the particular database system must be installed. All major vendors of database systems provide ODBC drivers. Figure 8.3 shows two ODBC drivers, one for Oracle databases and one for Access databases. Finally, the particular database must be registered as a data source to the driver manager.

The application program contacts the driver manager in order to request access to a specific data source. The driver manager then determines which driver to use and establishes a connection to the driver for use by the application. Once the connection has been established, the application interacts with the driver by using the ODBC client library.

A developer using Microsoft Access can create links to databases statically, using the Get External Data/Link Tables item on the File menu. Selecting this item causes a dialog to pop up. In the dialog, the developer can select database connections to a variety of file types, including Access, Excel, FoxPro, Dbase, and text. The dialog also supports SQL databases through the ODBC Databases option.

Alternatively, links to tables can be created dynamically using the *Data Access Objects (DAO)* object types. Object types include `Database`, `TableDef`, `Recordset`, and `Field`. An object of type `RecordSet` is implicitly associated with a form through its `record source` property. A `Field` object is associated with a field of a form through its `control source` property. VBA modules can explicitly create DAO objects, link them to data sources, and manipulate those data sources. Section 8.10 provides examples of the use of ODBC in Access.

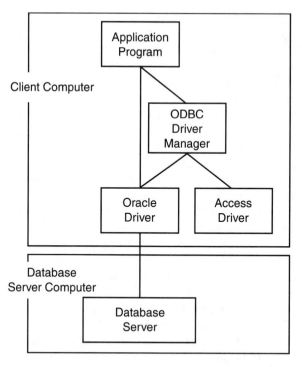

FIGURE 8.3
The ODBC architecture for database access

8.1.3 Database Interaction in Java

The Java standard packages include the `java.sql` package, which supports the *JDBC** strategy for accessing SQL databases. JDBC makes Java unique among general-purpose programming languages in that Java incorporates a database-independent strategy for database interaction. JDBC is very similar to ODBC. It runs in a client-server environment, with the client software being supplied as an implementation of the `java.sql` interfaces. Each JDBC client consists of a collection of Java classes. A major difference between JDBC and ODBC is that the JDBC driver manager is a part of the Java application. This driver manager does not require any installation on the client machine.

Interaction with an SQL database in Java is accomplished by first connecting to the database, then creating and executing SQL statements. For a select statement, the result table is returned as a Java object, which can be manipulated to

---

* We can think of JDBC as an abbreviation for *Java Database Connectivity*, although Sun Microsystems, which owns the JDBC trademark, claims that it is not.

access its rows and columns as Java values. Other SQL statements return simple integer results that may represent the number of affected rows.

The details of database interaction in Java are the subject of Sections 8.2 through 8.9, which include extensive examples and explanations.

8.1.4   Database Interaction with Embedded SQL

Database system vendors often provide a strategy for embedding SQL processing into one or more programming languages. The C programming language, for instance, is supported as a host language for embedding SQL by most vendors. The language is extended with new keywords or new syntax to allow SQL statements to appear in the program. The exact syntax depends on the language and the database system. The C function `addEmployee`, given below, uses a typical syntax. When called, `addEmployee` executes an SQL statement that inserts an employee into the database.

```
void addEmployee (char * ssn, char * lastName, char *
firstName) {
  EXEC SQL
    insert into Customer (ssn, lastName, firstName)
      values (:ssn, :lastName, :firstName);
}
```

The `EXEC SQL <sql statement>;` block substitutes the values of the variables `ssn`, `lastName`, and `firstName` into the insert statement before this statement is executed. The colon before a variable name is interpreted as a reference to the value of the variable. Hence, a call to the function `addEmployee` that provides values for its parameters will result in the creation of a new entity in the `Employee` table.

The preceding function is clearly not legal in C. Compilation of the function must be preceded by a translation from the embedded SQL form into legal C code. A preprocessor that is supplied by the database system vendor performs this translation. A runtime library that includes the database client software and embedded SQL enhancements completes the system.

Database applications are often developed in a host language with embedded SQL extensions. Embedded SQL offers many advantages—indeed, it is the preferred approach of many database application developers. Its disadvantages are primarily that the resulting applications are not completely portable between database systems and are written in a special-purpose language, not directly in the host language. It is not unusual for it to be difficult to use host language debugging tools with embedded SQL, for instance.

In this book, we concentrate on application development using tools that are a normal part of the host programming language. Both ODBC and JDBC have this distinct advantage over embedded SQL implementations.

JDBC Packages and Database Connections

| 8.2

The `java.sql` package defines a collection of interfaces and classes that allow programs to interact with databases.* The following interfaces provide the primary SQL execution:

- `Driver`: supports the creation of a data connection
- `Connection`: represents the connection between a Java client and an SQL database server
- `DatabaseMetaData`: contains information about the database server
- `Statement`: includes methods for executing text queries
- `PreparedStatement`: represents a precompiled and stored query
- `CallableStatement`: used to execute SQL stored procedures
- `ResultSet`: contains the results of the execution of a select query
- `ResultSetMetaData`: contains information about a `ResultSet`, including the attribute names and types

Each *JDBC package* implements these interfaces in order to provide a connection to a specific collection of database servers. A variety of implementation strategies exist. A Java program that uses JDBC is independent of the particular JDBC package and of its implementation. Although you may find it interesting to learn about the costs and benefits of different JDBC packages and their implementations, this information does not affect the code that must be written to access databases from Java.

Figure 8.4 illustrates three strategies that a Java program may use to connect to a database: JDBC–ODBC bridge, the JDBC database client, and the JDBC middleware client. Three different database systems have been chosen as examples; there is no particular significance attached to the choice of these three.

All three methods begin with the `java.sql` package. The Java program uses the classes, interfaces, and methods of `java.sql` to initiate a connection using a specific JDBC driver. Each box labeled "JDBC package" represents a collection of Java classes and other software. Each package includes server-specific software that provides the database client functionality. In the JDBC–ODBC bridge driver, the server software is the ODBC client package. In the middleware case, it is the middleware client package.

In the first strategy, a *JDBC–ODBC bridge* implements the JDBC package through a collection of native methods that use the ODBC application programming interface. The JDBC methods' implementation relies on native ODBC methods. Database connections are made by using ODBC drivers installed on the computer that executes the Java program. For this approach to work, the executing computer must have an ODBC system installed and possess an ODBC driver for

---

* The features of JDBC that are discussed in this chapter and Chapter 9 are part of JDBC, version 1.0, which is part of Java 1.1. JDBC, version 2.0, is included in Java 1.2 and has additional features that are described in Chapter 10.

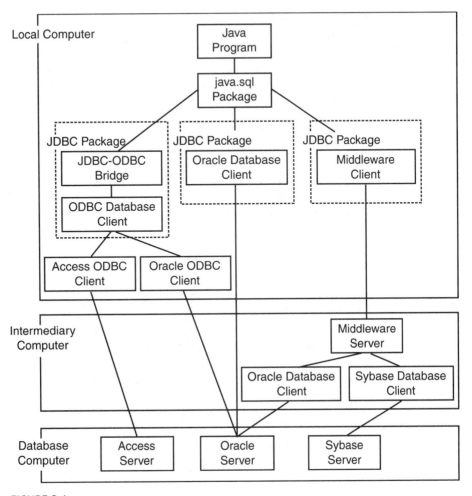

FIGURE 8.4

Strategies for implementing JDBC packages

the particular database of interest. In this case, drivers are available for Microsoft Access and Oracle databases.

A major advantage of the JDBC–ODBC bridge package is that it can be used on particular computers to connect to databases provided by any vendor. The major disadvantage is that ODBC software must be installed on each computer that will execute the application. This implementation can prove very difficult to use in applet programming, for instance.

In the second strategy, a JDBC database client implements the database client library in the JDBC package. All JDBC methods are implemented using vendor-specific communication with a database server that may reside on another computer. Figure 8.4 shows a connection using an Oracle JDBC package. Most database vendors provide JDBC database clients. This very attractive approach is implemented on both commercial and public domain database systems. Its major disadvantage is that each JDBC database client is specific to some vendor's database server. Although a Java program can use more than one JDBC package during a single session, each package must be available on the local machine.

The third implementation strategy employs an intermediary computer between the Java application and the database server. Two good reasons explain why one might adopt this strategy. First, a single JDBC package serves all databases. This setup is particularly helpful because many JDBC packages add nonstandard features to the `java.sql` interfaces. We can take advantage of the features supplied by the middleware vendor and still maintain database independence. Second, the Java application does not need to connect directly to the database server computer. This characteristic is an advantage for an applet running in a Web browser, because it is allowed to establish connections only with the computer that served the applet.* A middleware approach supports the connection of applets to databases even when the database server is not on the same computer as the Web server.

Connecting to Databases with JDBC

8.3

A database connection is created from two pieces of information: the name of the JDBC package driver class and the URL that specifies which server and database to use. The URL includes the JDBC package designator, the name of the computer on which the database server resides, and some database designator. As described later, the URL, or an associated `Properties` object, can also include a user ID, password, and other information as required.

8.3.1   JDBC Drivers and Driver Managers

A JDBC driver is a Java object that provides the connection between a Java application and a database.

Class `DriverManager` provides methods that manage a set of available drivers. The driver manager is able to determine which driver to use for a particular database connection. In Java, it is possible for a program to connect to multiple databases. The `DriverManager.Connect` method accepts a URL and searches for a driver that can use the URL to connect to a database. If no suitable driver is found, an exception is thrown.

Each JDBC package implements at least one driver class, which is able to establish connections to database servers. Before a driver can be used to establish a connection, it must be registered with the JDBC driver manager. Once the driver is loaded and available, we can use it to create a database connection.

Making a driver available for connections is accomplished with the `Class.forName` method. This method causes the system to find, open, and load

---

* This restriction on network connections is part of the applet security mechanism and is enforced by all Java-enabled Web browsers.

the `.class` file associated with the class. Each JDBC driver has a static constructor that executes when the class file is loaded. This constructor informs the JDBC `DriverManager` that the driver is available for use.

The name of the `Driver` class is specific to the package. A few examples follow:

```
Class.forName("sun.jdbc.odbc.JdbcOdbcDriver");
  // driver for JDBC-ODBC Bridge
Class.forName("oracle.thin.Driver"); // driver for Oracle
Class.forName("gwe.sql.gweMySqlDriver");
  // driver for MySql
Class.forName("symantec.dbanywhere.Driver");
  // dbAnywhere middleware driver
```

8.3.2 Connections

Each `Driver` class supports the `connect` method, which establishes a connection with a database server. This method accepts a URL and a `Properties` object as arguments and returns a `Connection` object. A single program can have multiple connections to a single database or connections to more than one database. Each connection provides a facility for creating statements that are used to execute SQL statements.

Every URL begins with a protocol. You are undoubtedly used to seeing the protocols http (Hypertext Transfer Protocol), ftp (File Transfer Protocol), file, and mailto, as in the following examples:

- http://www.cs.fsu.edu/cop4540/
- ftp://ftp.javasoft.com/docs/jdk1.2
- file:/usr/local/java/docs/api/packages.html
- mailto:riccardi@cs.fsu.edu

A database connection URL has the form

```
jdbc:<subprotocol>:<subname>
```

The protocol of the URL includes a main protocol (`jdbc`) and a subprotocol, which identifies the driver or the database connectivity protocol. The subname identifies the particular data source and is specific to the JDBC driver. For example, the following URL refers to an ODBC data source called mydatabase, using the JDBC–ODBC bridge protocol:

```
jdbc:odbc:mydatabase
```

Connections to databases that reside on remote machines are made by using URLs whose subname is of the form

```
//hostname:port/subsubname
```

Each JDBC package supports a variety of other parameters that may be specified as part of the URL or with an associated `Properties` object.

```
Class.forName("oracle.thin.driver");
String protocol = "jdbc.oracle.thin:";
String subname = "//oracle.cs.fsu.edu/bighit:";
String user = "user=bighit,password=incharge";
Connection con;
Statement stmt;
try {
  con = DriverManager.connect(protocol+subname+user);
  stmt = con.createStatement();
} catch (SQLException e) {
  System.err.println(e.getMessage());
}
```

FIGURE 8.5 ───
Java code to connect to an Oracle database

Once a connection has been established, it can be used to create any number of statements. Three types of statements exist, defined by the interfaces `Statement`, `PreparedStatement`, and `CallableStatement`. For now, we'll concentrate on `Statement`, which is used to execute text SQL statements. In some cases, the number of statements that can be active at once may be limited by the particular JDBC package.

A `Statement` is created by the method `Connection.createStatement`.

8.3.3 Statements

A `Statement` object is used to send your SQL statements to the database server for execution. The methods `executeQuery`, `executeUpdate`, and `execute` are the means by which SQL statements are executed.

Figure 8.5 contains the Java code needed to connect to an Oracle database called BigHit using the Oracle thin JDBC package, the user ID `bighit`, and the password `incharge`.

8.3.4 Database Meta-Data

Interface `DatabaseMetaData` gives a program access to a considerable amount of information about the connected database (meta-data). For example, methods whose names start with `get`, `supports`, `stores`, or `uses` return information about capabilities of the database and the JDBC package. The following are some of these useful methods:

- `getTimeDateFunctions`: returns a list of all time and date functions
- `getUserName`: returns the user name as known to the database
- `storesLowerCaseIdentifiers`: returns true if SQL identifiers are case insensitive and stored as lowercase in the meta-data tables

```
DatabaseMetaData meta = theConnection.getMetaData();
System.out.println("time date: "+ meta.getTimeDateFunctions());
System.out.println("user: "+ meta.getUserName());
System.out.println("lowercase: "+ meta.storesLowerCaseIdentifiers());
System.out.println("transactions: "+ meta.supportsTransactions());
```

Results
```
time date: CURDATE,CURTIME,DAYOFMONTH,DAYOFWEEK,DAYOFYEAR,HOUR,
   MINUTE,MONTH,NOW,SECOND,WEEK,YEAR
user: admin
lowercase: false
transactions: true
```

FIGURE 8.6 _____

Code and results of execution for `DatabaseMetaData` *methods*

- `supportsTransactions`: returns false if the database does not support transactions

Figure 8.6 shows a section of Java code and the results of its execution. The results are the response to this code that is returned by the JDBC–ODBC bridge when connected to a Microsoft Access database.

Connecting to Databases with Class DBConnect

8.4

The details of connecting to a database and creating a statement to use in processing SQL statements can be encapsulated into class `dbjava.database.DBConnect`. This class, which is part of the software developed for this book, has members whose values are the name of the driver class and URL to use for the connection, a `Connection` object, and a `Statement` object. Figure 8.7 shows a part of the definition of this class and a subclass that extends it. The full class definitions can be found on the Addison-Wesley Web site.

The following code uses class `DBConnect` to initiate a JDBC database connection:

```
1  DBConnect myDB = new DBConnect("sun.jdbc.odbc.JdbcOdbcDriver",
2       "jdbc:odbc:","BigHit");
3  Connection conn = myDB.makeConnection();
4  if (conn==null) {// connection failed
5    // insert code to respond to connection failure
6  }
7  Statement stmt= myDB.getStatement();
```

```
 1 public class DBConnect {
 2   public DBConnect(String driverName, String protocol,
 3       String subname){
 4     this.theDriver=driverName;
 5     this.protocol = protocol;
 6     this. subname = subname;
 7   }
 8   public Connection makeConnection();//implementation omitted
 9   protected String theDriver; // driver package name
10   protected String protocol; // server and protocol
11   protected String subname; // name of database
12   protected Statement theStatement = null;
13   public Statement getStatement() {return stmt;}
14   protected Connection theConnection = null;
15   public Connection getConnection() {return connect;}
16 }
17 public class BigHitDBConnect extends DBConnect {
18   BigHitDBConnect() {
19     theDriver = "sun.jdbc.odbc.JdbcOdbcDriver";
20     protocol = "jdbc:odbc:";
21     subname = "BigHit";
22   }
23 }
```

FIGURE 8.7 _____

Partial implementations of classes DBConnect *and* BigHitDBConnect

Lines 1 and 2 create an object by using the name of the driver class, the protocol, and the subname as arguments to the constructor. Line 3 calls method makeConnection. The DBConnect object handles the details of loading the driver, establishing the connection, creating a Statement, and catching exceptions. Method makeConnection simply returns the Connection object that was created or null if the connection could not be established.

   Class DBConnect can be extended so that the driver name, protocol, and subname are set for this particular database connection. Class BigHitDBConnect in Fig. 8.7 (lines 17–22) makes this extension. An object of this class is created with the simpler form given below, instead of lines 1 and 2 in the preceding code:

```
DBConnect myDB = new BigHitDBConnect();
```

The object myDB is still of type DBConnect, as that class has all of the operations needed to create the connection and use the database.

Executing Select Statements

8.5

Method `Statement.executeQuery` supports execution of any query that returns a table as its result. The result is returned as a `ResultSet` object that has a collection of rows and a related `ResultSetMetadata` object. To get information about all customers in the BigHit database, we execute the following Java statement:

```
ResultSet result = stmt.executeQuery("select * from Customer");
```

The result of this query contains a row for each customer. Each row, in turn, contains a value for `accountId`, `lastName`, `firstName`, `street`, `city`, `state`, and `zipcode`. To access these values, we use methods of the `ResultSet` interface. The rows of the result can be accessed one at a time in the order delivered by the database. The `ResultSet` has a cursor that is initially positioned before the first row of the result; this cursor is advanced by calling method `ResultSet.next`.

Method `ResultSet.next` advances the `ResultSet` cursor to the next row. The first call to `next` positions the cursor on the first row. Method `next` returns true if another row is available to access and false if all rows have been processed. It is not possible to process the rows in any other order or to return to a previous row. The details of processing the `ResultSet` are given in Section 8.5.2.

If the SQL statement has any errors, method `executeQuery` will throw an `SQLException`. The exception's message will consist of the SQL error message. The catch block given in Fig. 8.5 shows an example of how to print the error message to standard error.

All of the execute methods of a `Statement` class close the previous `ResultSet` before they execute. As a consequence, a program must finish processing one result set before it executes the next query. A program that needs to process multiple queries concurrently must therefore create multiple statements, one for each concurrent query. It is possible to have multiple `Statement` objects using a single connection to a database and to have multiple `Connection` objects, each connected to a different database.

8.5.1   Extracting and Manipulating Result Set Meta-Data

Each `ResultSet` object has an associated `ResultSetMetaData` object that contains information about the types and properties of the columns in the `ResultSet`. Method `getMetaData` returns this meta-data object:

```
ResultSetMetaData meta = result.getMetaData();
```

From `meta`, we can get the number of columns (method `numColumns`) and the name (method `getColumnName`) and type (methods `getColumnType` and `getColumnTypeName`). Figure 8.8 prints the names and types of each column of the result.

Executing the code of Fig. 8.8 for query `Select * from TimeCard` with the Access database for BigHit Video yields the following:

```
Column ssn is JDBC type 12 which is called TEXT
Column date is JDBC type 93 which is called DATETIME
```

```
for (int col=1; col<=meta.getColumnCount(); col++) {
  int type = meta.getColumnType(col);
  String typeName = meta.getColumnTypeName(col);
  String name = meta.getColumnName(col);
  System.out.println("Column "+name+" is JDBC type "+type+
    " which is called "+typeName);
}
```

FIGURE 8.8 _____

Java code that prints the names and types of all columns of a `ResultSet`

```
Column startTime is JDBC type 93 which is called DATETIME
Column endTime is JDBC type 93 which is called DATETIME
Column storeId is JDBC type 4 which is called LONG
Column paid is JDBC type -7 which is called BIT
```

A variety of other information is available about each column, including the suggested column label, display size, precision, scale, table name, and schema name.

8.5.2   Processing the Results of Select Statements

Each row of a result set contains a value for each column, and each value in turn has a specific type. These values can be accessed by column number (starting with 1) or by column name. A variety of methods are available that fetch values from result sets; these methods differ in the type of the value returned. To clarify this relationship, we will begin by assuming that a program needs a `String` representation for each value. We will start with the methods that return the value as a `String`. As with all of the `get` methods, two versions of `getString` exist: one with a column number (`int`) parameter and one with a column name (`String`) parameter.

Figure 8.9 contains Java code that prints the values of all information about all customers in the database, using the `ResultSet` returned by `executeQuery` given in Section 8.4. The code goes through the rows by using a while loop and through the columns by using a for loop. For each column, the value is fetched as a `String` and printed to the standard output file (`System.out`). Method `getString`

```
while (result.next()) {
  for (int col = 1; col <= meta.getColumnCount(); col++)
    System.out.print(result.getString(col));
    System.out.print("&");
  }
  System.out.println();
}
```

FIGURE 8.9 _____

Java code to print all rows and columns of a `ResultSet`

first gets the object, then calls its `toString` method. This operation yields the default `String` representation for each value. Using `getString` eliminates the need for a program to consider the type of a value. It explicitly converts the value, allowing the programmer to easily use the default format of the field.

A NOTE ON JDBC DATA TYPES

Nineteen JDBC types are defined in the JDBC standard. There are methods defined for each type to return an object of a specific type for each JDBC type. These methods are called `getXXX`, where `XXX` comes from `Byte`, `Short`, `Int`, `Long`, `Float`, `Double`, `BigDecimal`, `String`, `Bytes`, `Date`, `Time`, `Timestamp`, `AsciiStream`, `UnicodeStream`, `BinaryObject`, or `Object`. The methods `getString` and `getObject` can be used for all JDBC types, and all methods except `getBytes` and `getBinaryStream` can be used with JDBC types `CHAR`, `VARCHAR`, and `LONGVARCHAR`. Of course, if a value cannot be converted to a number, then calling `getInt` on the value, for instance, will result in an exception. You should consult the JDBC documentation to see which methods can be used for each JDBC type.

A special case is when a query expects to return a table with one row and one column. Class `DBConnect` includes method `getField`, which handles this operation. It accepts an SQL statement as its parameter and returns a single string as the result. If the query fails or no data are returned, the method returns `null`. Any error message from the query execution is placed in the `message` member of the `DBConnect` object. The `getMessage` method can be used to access the error message.

A Simple Java SQL Application

8.6 An SQL filter is a simple and useful application that accepts an SQL statement, executes it, and then formats the results in a simple style. A *filter* reads from the standard input file without prompting and writes to the standard output file. This kind of program can be embedded in a shell script program or used interactively. The SQL filter reads a line of text and executes it as an SQL statement. The result of the SQL statement's execution is formatted with the number of columns and the column names on the first line, with ampersand (&) delimiters, and the output tuples on the following lines. The last line contains the text END SQL.

First line: column count & column 1 name & column 2 name & ... &
Second line: row 1 column 1 value & row 1 column 2 value & ... &
k + first line: row k column 1 value & ... &
Last line: END SQL

Class `dbjava.samples.SQLFilter`, whose complete implementation is shown in Fig. 8.10, puts together the Java code from the previous sections. Lines 11–15 connect to the database (as in Section 8.4). Method `ExecSqlToString`, (lines 33–64) executes an SQL statement, extracts the `ResultSet` meta-data (as in Fig. 8.8), and fetches the results as strings (as in Fig. 8.9). The `main` method for class `SQLFilter` (lines 5–8) simply creates an `SQLFilter` object and calls its run method, which does all of the work.

```
1 public class SQLFilter {
2   public DBConnect db = null;
3   public Statement stmt = null;
4   public String ErrMsg;
5   static public void main (String[] args) {
6     SQLFilter sqlFilter = new SQLFilter();
7     sqlFilter.run();
8   }
9   public void run() {
10  // run the SQL filter: read and process a sequence of lines
11    db = new BigHitDBConnect();
12    Connection conn = db.makeConnection();
13    if (conn==null) {ErrMsg += db.messages.toString();
14      System.out.println(" Can't connect: "+ErrMsg); return;}
15    stmt=db.getStatement();
16    BufferedReader input = // create from system.in
17      new BufferedReader(new InputStreamReader(System.in));
18    // read an SQL statement, execute it,
19    // and output the result set
20    while (true) {
21      try {
22        String line = input.readLine();
23        if (line == null) break;// finished on empty line
24        if (line.equals("")) break;// finished on empty line
25        String out = ExecSqlToString(line);
26        System.out.print(out);
27        System.out.println("End Sql");
28      } catch(IOException e) {
30          e.printStackTrace();
31          System.exit(-1);
32  } } }

33   public String ExecSqlToString(String sqlStmt) {
34  // execute sqlStmt, return result formatted in String
35    // buffer to hold output
36    StringBuffer outString = new StringBuffer();
37    try {
```

FIGURE 8.10 ⎯⎯⎯⎯⎯⎯⎯⎯⎯⎯⎯⎯⎯⎯⎯⎯⎯⎯⎯⎯⎯⎯⎯⎯⎯⎯⎯⎯

Complete implementation of class `dbjava.samples.SQLFilter` *(continues)*

```
38        ResultSet result;
39        result = stmt.executeQuery(sqlStmt);
40        ResultSetMetaData meta = result.getMetaData();
41        char fieldDelim = '&'; // delimiter between fields
42        char rowDelim = '\n'; // delimiter between lines
43        int colCount = meta.getColumnCount();

44        // add column count and column names to outString
45        outString.append(colCount).append(fieldDelim);
46        for (int i = 1; i <= colCount; i++) {
47          outString.append(meta.getColumnName(i)+fieldDelim);
48        }
49        outString.append(rowDelim);

50        while (result.next()) {// append rows to outString
51          for (int j = 1; j <= colCount; j++) {
52            String value = result.getString(j);
53            outString.append(value);
54            outString.append(fieldDelim) ;
55          }
56          outString.append(rowDelim);
57        }
58        result.close();
59      } catch (SQLException e) {
60        // on SQL exception, return the SQL error message
61        outString.append(e.getMessage());
62      }
63      return outString.toString();
64    }
65 }// end of class SqlFilter
```

FIGURE 8.10 _____

continued

Method `run` creates a `BigHitDBConnect` object and calls its `makeConnection` method to establish the database connection. It then creates a `BufferedReader` from the standard input file (`System.in`). It reads a line and calls `ExecSqlToString` to execute the statement, extract the meta-data and the results, and format the output string. The resulting string is printed to the standard output file.

The small size and clear meaning of class `SQLFilter` demonstrates the ease with which Java can be used as a database application language. A comparable program in some other language or one that uses a proprietary embedded SQL system is much more complicated to write and much more difficult to understand.

A NOTE ON ENHANCEMENTS TO SQLFilter |

Class SQLFilter has a few problems that need to be fixed to create a usable filter. These corrections are left as exercises for the reader (see Exercises 16–18 at the end of this chapter). The main problem is that this class is written to process only select statements, but doesn't check the input for validity. The processing of other SQL statements is described in Sections 8.7 and 8.8. The class must be modified so that it either requires that the statement begin with **select** or correctly processes other SQL statements.

A less important, but still significant, problem with class SQLFilter relates to the field and row delimiters. If a field (&) or row (\n) delimiter is contained in any attribute value in the table produced by the SQL statement, the output will be formatted incorrectly. Method ExecSqlToString must be modified to check for the presence of a delimiter in the output. Any delimiter in the output text must be modified to use some other symbol.

Executing Insert and Update Statements

8.7

Many statements in SQL do not return a single table and hence are unsuitable for execution by executeQuery. Method executeUpdate should be used to execute any statement that returns a row count, as insert, update, and delete statements do. It is also useful for SQL DDL statements or other statements that return no result. Method executeUpdate returns a single integer that is the number of rows affected by an insert, update, or delete statement; this value is always 0 for statements that return no result.

The following is an insert to the customer table to add new customer Mary Brown:

```
int rowcount = stmt.executeUpdate("insert into Customer "
    + "(accountId,lastName,firstName) " +
    + " values (1239,'Brown','Mary')");
if (rowcount == 0) // insert failed
```

If the row count that is returned by executeUpdate is not 1, then this insert did not work properly. If the count is 0, the insert failed, possibly because of an access violation or because of a primary key conflict. For this statement, the row count will never be larger than 1, because only a single row is described by the SQL statement.

Method executeUpdate is used to execute any SQL statement that is not a select statement, which includes the insert, update, and delete statements that modify table contents. It also includes the DDL statements that modify the database schema definition. Method executeUpdate allows a program to create and drop tables, modify the physical database by adding and removing indexes, and make any other modifications to the schema. Execution of a DDL statement returns 0 as its value. An error in a DDL statement will cause an exception to be raised. Hence, if the execution of a DDL statement returns without exception, the statement succeeded.

Executing Other Statements

8.8

A single execution of an SQL statement could potentially lead to multiple results. In this case, method `execute` should be used to execute the statement. It is also useful for situations in which it is not known whether the statement returns a table (`ResultSet`).

Method `execute` allows a statement to return multiple values. Each value returned is either a `ResultSet` or a row count. Figure 8.11 gives an example of a proper way to use `execute`. The call to `execute` (line 1) returns a `boolean` value that indicates whether the first returned value is a `ResultSet`. Line 2 begins the loop that extracts all of the results, one at a time. At the end of the loop (line 14), method `getMoreResults` is called to determine whether the next result is a `ResultSet`.

Within the loop, if `isResultSet` is true, `getResultSet` is called to fetch the `ResultSet` (line 7). If `isResultSet` is false, `getUpdateCount` is called to fetch the row count (line 10). If the row count is –1 (line 11), then there are no more results and the loop is finished. These alternate calls to `getResultSet` and `getUpdateCount` continue until `getResultSet` returns false and `getUpdateCount` returns –1, as in line 11.

A Sample BigHit Video Application in Java

8.9

The processing of time cards and pay statements for hourly employees was described in Section 7.2.2 to illustrate the use of update statements in SQL. A more comprehensive package for pay statements should include some consistency checks.

```
1 boolean isResultSet; // true if current result is a ResultSet
2 resultSet result; // current ResultSet
3 int rowcount; // current row count

4 isResultSet = stmt.execute(sqlStatement);
5 while (true) {// loop through all results
6    if (isResultSet){// result set returned
7       result = stmt.getResultSet();
8       // insert code here to process result set
9    } else {// this result is not a ResultSet
10      rowcount = stmt.getUpdateCount();
11      if (rowcount == -1) break; // no more results
12      // insert code here to process row count
13   }
14   isResultSet = stmt.getMoreResults()); // get next result
15 }
```

FIGURE 8.11 _____

Java code to process an SQL statement with multiple results

In Java, our application will execute the SQL update statements, then check the resulting pay statements to ensure that no employees are being paid for too many hours or at too high a rate. We will also create pay statements for the salaried employees. Finally, we'll create a report of the new pay statements.

Figure 8.12 gives the class definition and methods `main` and `createPayStatements` for class `ProcessPayStatements`. The `main` method makes an object of the class, creates the pay statements, checks them, and prints a report. Method `createPayStatements` defines the SQL statements and executes them. The variable `insertSQL` contains the SQL statement of Fig. 7.9, modified so that the `datePaid` attribute of the inserted rows is the date provided in the constructor and stored in the `datePaid` variable. This value is surrounded by single quotes in the select statement.*

Checking the pay statements is accomplished by method `checkPayStatements`. It begins by selecting the new pay statements from the database. It then goes through them, checking each to verify that the number of hours is less than 80 and the total pay is less than $1,000. Checking these values requires extracting the values of the fields as `float` and `int`, respectively. The following code accomplishes this task:

```
String selectSQL = "select * from PayStatement "
   + "where datePaid = '" + datePaid + "'";
try {
   ResultSet result = stmt.executeQuery(selectSQL);
   while (result.next()) { // check each pay statement
      float amount = result.getFloat("amountPaid");
      int numHours = result.getInt("numHours");
      if (amount > 1000.00) return false;
      if (numHours > 80) return false;
   }
}
```

User Interfaces in Microsoft Access

8.10   Microsoft Access is an excellent tool for developing database interfaces. This section will demonstrate a few of its features as part of an application to be used by clerks to record rentals of videotapes. Applications in Access consist of a combination of forms and form elements, often called *controls*, and Visual Basic functions that respond to user input. Developing an application in Access also means relying on the extensive wizards that perform initial form layouts and are capable of generating much of the code required for responding to user input.

---

* In Microsoft Access, date constants are surrounded by pound signs (#). This convention is an indication of the lack of consistency between different SQL systems, but specifically shows that Access does not support standard SQL.

```
public class ProcessPayStatements {
  protected DBConnect bighitDB = new BigHitDBConnect ();
  protected String datePaid; //date for new pay statements
  protected int numPayStatements; // number of pay statements created
  protected int numTimeCards; // number of time cards marked as paid

  public ProcessPayStatements(String datePaid) {// constructor
    bighitDB.makeConnection();
    stmt = bighitDB.getStatement();
    this.datePaid = datePaid;
  }
  public static void main (String[] args) {//args[0] is datePaid
    ProcessPayStatements process
      = new ProcessPayStatements(args[0]);
    process.createPayStatements();
    process.checkPayStatements();
    process.printReport(System.out);
  }
  public boolean createPayStatements () {
    String insertSQL =
      "insert into PayStatement "
      + "  (ssn, hourlyRate, numHours, amountPaid, datePaid)"
      + "  select TimeCard.ssn, hourlyRate,"
      + "  sum((endTime-startTime)*24) as hoursWorked,"
      + "  sum((endTime-startTime)*24*hourlyRate) as amountPaid,"
      + "' " + datePaid + "'"
      + " from TimeCard, HourlyEmployee "
      + " where TimeCard.ssn=HourlyEmployee.ssn and paid=false "
      + " group by TimeCard.ssn, hourlyRate";
    String updateTimeCardSQL =
      "update TimeCard set paid = true where paid = false";

    try {
      numPayStatements = stmt.executeUpdate(insertSQL);
      numTimeCards = stmt.executeUpdate(updateTimeCardSQL);
    } catch (SQLException e) {
      e.printStackTrace(System.out);
      return false;
    }
    return true;
  }}
```

FIGURE 8.12 _____

Partial definition of class ProcessPayStatements

In Fig. 2.1, we saw a typical rental receipt. It contained the name and address of the customer, the customer's `accountId`, and a list of videotapes that were rented together. Each videotape was specified in terms of its ID, its name, and its due date. This information is contained in the `Customer`, `Rental`, `Videotape`, and `Movie` tables. Joining all of these tables together would result in a table with the customer information repeated for every rental by that customer. This approach does not match the presentation in the rental receipt.

Microsoft Access provides the capability of representing the customer information in one form and the videotape information in a subform, as shown in Fig. 8.13. The customer information and the date of the rental are shown in the upper part of the form; the videotape information is shown in the lower part, which is a subform. The two forms are presented within a single window and are linked together. The records shown in the subform include only those that match the main form in the `accountId` and `dateRented` fields. The main form includes a subform object called `RentalSubform` that can be seen in the design view of the form in Fig. 8.14. The `LinkChildFields` and `LinkMasterFields` properties of the subform are set so that both the `accountId` and the `dateRented` fields determine which records are shown when the subform is open, as in Fig. 8.13.

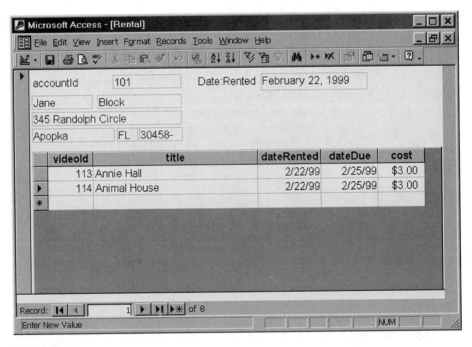

FIGURE 8.13

Simple version of a rental form in Access

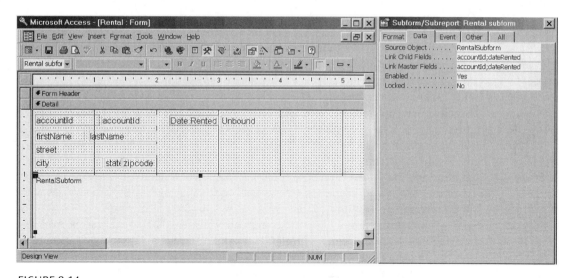

FIGURE 8.14 _____

Design view of the rental form showing the data properties of `RentalSubform`

The data for the rental subform come from a query that joins `Rental`, `Videotape`, and `Movie` and shows only selected fields.

Access allows new `Rental` entities to be added through the subform. Selecting the last row (labeled with `*`) of the subform in Fig. 8.13 will prepare a new record to be added to `Rental`. As soon as a `videoId` is entered, the `dateRented` will be set to the value in the linked field of the master form and the title will be displayed. When the row of the form loses focus, the new row is added to `Rental`.

The date rented in the main form is set by the Visual Basic code when the form loads. The method `Form_Open` is the event-handling method that is executed when the form first opens. Its code is shown below:

```
Private Sub Form_Open(Cancel As Integer)
    dateRented.SetFocus
    dateRented.Text = Format(Now(), "mmmm dd, yyyy")
End Sub
```

The `Text` property of the `dateRented` control is set to the result found by calling the `Format` function with arguments `Now()`, the current time, and the format string `"mmmm dd, yyyy"`, which formats the date as the full month name, day of the month, comma, space, and four-digit year.

To make a complete form, the sum of the costs of the videotapes should be calculated. A tax field should allow for data input and calculate the total from those figures. It would also be appropriate for the cost and date due to be retrieved from information stored in the database and entered automatically. These modifications comprise a combination of controls added to the forms and Visual Basic code added to the code modules.

Chapter Summary

An application interacts with a database server to provide user interaction, report generation, database updates, or data analysis. It is a database client and relies on the client-server architecture for its database interaction.

Client-server systems are constructed in two or more layers. In a two-layer architecture, applications connect directly to database servers. In a three-layer (three-tiered) architecture, a middleware server acts as a server to the applications and as a client to the database servers. A Web server is an example of a middleware server.

Microsoft Access database interaction is based on the Microsoft Jet Database Engine and the ODBC database client package. Access databases are able to access data that are stored in files as well as data that are stored in SQL databases with their own server programs.

Interaction between Java programs and relational database servers is provided through the JDBC system, as implemented in the `java.sql` package. JDBC supports a variety of classes and interfaces that allow Java programs to connect to database servers, execute SQL statements, and process the results.

The `java.sql` package has a variety of implementations. Each major database system has its own JDBC package. In addition, myriad middleware packages support one or more database systems. The JDBC–ODBC bridge is a freely available JDBC package that allows a Java program to connect to any ODBC data source that is registered on the local computer. The data sources can themselves be connected to SQL database servers on remote machines.

The JDBC driver manager creates the connection between a Java program and a database or middleware server. This connection can be used to create a `Statement` object whose `executeQuery`, `executeUpdate`, and `execute` methods provide for SQL statement execution. Any error encountered by the database server in executing an SQL statement results in a thrown `SQLException`.

The result of an `executeQuery` call is a `ResultSet` object. The `ResultSet` contains a cursor that can be used to navigate through the rows returned for the query. The fields of the `ResultSet` can be extracted by name or location and as `String` values or specifically typed values.

JDBC driver packages support access to a significant amount of database meta-data. The JDBC client program can also extract meta-data from the results of queries.

The `SQLFilter` class demonstrates the ease with which SQL applications can be written in Java. A comparable program in some other language constructed using embedded SQL would be very complex.

The `executeUpdate` method is used to execute any SQL statement that does not return a table as its result. For insert, update, and delete statements, `executeUpdate` returns an integer that represents the number of rows affected by the statement. For other SQL statements, including those that modify the schema, `executeUpdate` returns 0.

The code in this chapter demonstrated some of the techniques used to write database client applications in Java. The SQL statements were represented by `String` values, either included as constants or generated by the program. These statements were processed by `executeQuery` and `executeUpdate` methods, and the results of the queries were processed as appropriate.

In Chapter 9, we will focus on the use of Java and databases to support a Web site that allows users to interact with databases. Further examples of Java client programs can be found there.

Key Terms

Client-server architecture. A software architecture in which independent programs communicate in an asymmetrical fashion. The client program sends requests to the server program. The server program performs the activities required and sends a response to the client.

Client software. A software package that allows a program to act as a client to a particular server. Database vendors provide client software that supports interaction with their database servers.

Data Access Objects (DAO). A package of object types provided by Microsoft for use by programs written in Visual Basic. Microsoft Access uses DAO objects for its database interaction.

Database client. A program that interacts with a database through a client-server software architecture.

Database server. A program that provides database services to clients.

Driver manager. A software package that is able to select the proper driver for a client connection to a server.

Driver package. A software package that supports a client connection to a particular server. See also *Client software*.

Filter. A program that reads from standard input and writes to standard output. It filters its input to produce its output. Filters typically execute quietly—that is, without prompting for input—and are often used in shell script programs.

JDBC (Java Database Connectivity). A Java software library, contained in package `java.sql`, that allows a Java program to acts as a database client and interact with a database server through the SQL language. The `java.sql` package defines a collection of interfaces that are implemented by a variety of JDBC packages.

JDBC package. A Java package that supports interaction with a specific type of database server. It includes a driver package and implementations of the `java.sql` interfaces that support SQL access to a database server.

JDBC–ODBC bridge. A JDBC package that supports database interaction through a local connection to ODBC. To use the JDBC–ODBC bridge, a local computer must have ODBC installed and the particular data source registered with the ODBC driver manager.

Meta-Data. Information about the structure of a database or its components.

Middleware. A program that provides an interface between a client and a server. The middleware program is a server to the client program and a client to the server program.

Other Database Connectivity (ODBC). A Microsoft standard for database client-server interaction. A program using the ODBC access operates independently of the particular database server and can be easily used with any ODBC data source. ODBC is a standard feature of Microsoft operating systems and is also available on many other operating systems. Most database system vendors provide ODBC drivers that allow ODBC access to their database servers.

Three-tiered architecture. A client-server architecture that has three tiers (layers): the client layer, the middleware layer, and the server layer.

Uniform resource locator (URL). The unique address of an Internet document or resource. A URL consists of a protocol, an Internet domain name, and a document identifier. URLs are used by JDBC to establish connections with database servers.

Web server. A middleware server that provides access to resources through HTTP and other protocols. A Web server frequently provides database middleware services to Web sites whose content is partially or fully dependent on database contents.

Exercises

1. Why is client-server architecture important to data independence?
2. Give three advantages of a three-tiered architecture.
3. What is the difference between a database client and a database server? Which program executes the SQL statements?
4. Define middleware. List three disadvantages of incorporating a middleware server in an information system.
5. Using the Internet, find a company that sells a middleware database product.
   a. What platforms (operating systems and computers) are able to execute client programs?
   b. What platforms are able to execute the middleware server program?
   c. What database systems can be servers for the middleware program?
   d. What programming languages are available for client software development?
   e. How much does the middleware server cost? What are the conditions and restrictions on its use? How many clients are allowed to connect?
6. Using the Internet, find a Web server that supports database access.
   a. How do Web site developers use the database in their Web pages?
   b. What extensions to HTML, if any, does the system support?
   c. What database systems does the server support?

7. For a Windows computer that supports ODBC:

    a. Determine what types of data sources are supported.

    b. Add a new data source to the ODBC system.

    c. Connect a Microsoft Access database to tables in the new data source.

8. Access the Web site of a major database system vendor.

    a. Does the vendor provide a JDBC package?

    b. Is there any restriction on which computers can execute the JDBC package?

    c. Does the vendor provide a middleware package to support JDBC access?

    d. What Web site development tools does the vendor provide that support access to its database servers? Is a Web server part of the package?

9. For some SQL database to which you have access, determine the programming languages that are available for application development. For each language, what tools does the database system vendor provide?

10. Investigate the embedded SQL tools that are available with your SQL database. What host languages are supported? What is the syntax of the embedded SQL? How are dynamic SQL statements processed?

11. Investigate the user interface development tools that are available with your SQL database. On what client systems are they supported? Are they available for Microsoft Windows? For Unix? For Macintosh?

12. Answer the following questions for a JDBC package that you have available.

    a. What is the name of the `Driver` class?

    b. What is the name of the `Connection` class?

    c. What is the name of the `Statement` class?

    d. Are there any extensions to package `java.sql` included in the JDBC package?

    e. What client-server architecture does it use?

    f. What is the form of the database connection URL? What is the subprotocol? What is the subname? How are the user and password specified?

13. Extend class `DBConnect` to support connection to your SQL database server. Test this new class using class `SQLFilter`.

14. Write a simple Java program to extract database meta-data from your database server. Use the code from Fig. 8.9.

15. Determine the data types supported by JDBC. What are their JDBC type numbers and type names?

16. Modify class `SQLFilter` so that it prompts the user for input and accepts multiline select statements. Use a semicolon (;) to mark the end of a statement.

17. Modify class `SQLFilter` so that it can properly process all SQL statements. In particular, modify it so that it uses `execute` instead of `executeQuery`. Be sure to modify the output so that it gives the number of rows affected by a nonselect statement.

18. Modify class `SQLFilter` so that it properly handlles the presence of a delimiter character inside an attribute value.

19. Develop a BigHit Video application in Microsoft Access. Suggested topics are as follows:

    a. Videotape rental and return

    b. Purchase order creation and processing of the receipt of ordered movies

    c. Employee time card creation and payroll processing

    d. Scheduling of employee work at stores and entry of time cards

    e. Reporting on rental activity

20. Develop a student records database application in Microsoft Access. Suggested topics are as follows:

    a. Student registration and drop/add procedures

    b. Recording grades and producing student transcripts

    c. Class rosters and attendance records

21. Develop a payroll application in Java that creates pay statements and updates the database as described in Section 8.9.

Further Readings

A general overview of client-server architectures can be found in Heinckiens and Loomis [HeLo97]

Many excellent books cover programming in Microsoft Access and Visual Basic for Applications. Books by Sams and Que publishing are generally excellent. The *Learn Access in XX Days* books are geared for new users and offer many just what they need. Individual skills and needs are sufficiently diverse that it is impossible to recommend any one book.

Information about Java and JDBC is available online at Microsystems' Java Web site, http://java.sun.com. An excellent book about JDBC that explains both client and server aspects is Hamilton, Cattell, and Fisher [HCF97]. The second edition [HCF99] covers JDBC for Java 2. Additional information can be found in Taylor [Tay99] and Reese [Ree97].

9
Supporting Database Interaction on the World Wide Web

CHAPTER OBJECTIVES

In this chapter, you will learn:
- The basic features of Web page development using HTML
- Ways to create and process HTML forms
- Techniques for CGI programming with Java
- Simple ways to use Java to generate HTML
- Ways to generate HTML from database queries
- Ways to design and use Java servlets for processing CGI requests
- A strategy for creating the BigHit Video reservation Web application from Chapter 1
- Techniques for creating BigHit Video Web applications

*T*his chapter demonstrates how to create and maintain database-supported Web sites using Java as the database interaction language. From Chapter 8, we know how to use Java to interact with SQL databases. In this chapter, we learn about HTML, forms, and CGI programming. We also reinforce the use of Java as a database programming language and emphasize the advantages of the object-oriented programming style.

The interaction between Web browsers and Web servers is first described as simple CGI interaction, which can be executed with any Web server. Next, we introduce and demonstrate the use of Java servlets, which are much more powerful but require additional support from the server.

Introduction to HTML

9.1

The World Wide Web was originally proposed in 1989 at CERN, the European Laboratory for Particle Physics, for use in creating and sharing multimedia, integrated electronic documents over the Internet. *HTML (Hypertext Markup Language)* was first described in a 1992 document; it has been standardized and modified extensively since then. HTML 2.0 was standardized by the Internet Engineering Task Force in 1999. The current proposal of the World Wide Web Consortium (W3C), called HTML 4, forms the basis for the documents described in this book.

An HTML document consists of text with embedded *markup tags* that specify formatting and links to other documents. The collection of HTML documents distributed over many sites on the Internet became known as the World Wide Web.

In 1993, students, faculty, and staff of the National Center for Supercomputing Applications (NCSA) at the University of Illinois recognized the potential of HTML and began the development of the Mosaic Web browser and the http Web server. The ready availability and high quality of these systems made it possible for the World Wide Web to expand beyond anyone's expectations. Later development of browsers, servers, and search engines brought financial success to many companies, both large and small.

An HTML document contains text, formatting instructions, references to other documents, and other information. A Web *browser* formats the document and displays it. In addition, the browser supports interaction between HTML documents and a variety of information servers. Clicking on a document reference causes the browser to issue a request to some server. Whatever the server returns is displayed by the browser.

In HTML, a markup tag, or simply *tag*, is a string that begins with "<" and ends with ">". The contents of the tag consist of a name and a list of attributes and attribute–value pairs. The tag names are case insensitive. The following is an example of a *table data* `<td>` tag:

```
<td align=left colspan=3 rowspan=2 nowrap>
```

Here the tag name is `td`. The tag has four attributes: three attributes with values, and one, `nowrap`, with no value.

Each tag is the beginning of a delimited section of the document that terminates with an *end tag*, which is a tag with the same name that starts with "</". The end tag for `<td>` is `</td>`. Although HTML requires that each tag be paired with an end tag, most Web browsers allow some end tags to be omitted.

9.1.1 Example of an HTML Document

Consider the document being displayed by the Netscape Navigator browser in Fig. 9.1, which is a welcome page for BigHit Video members. The upper part of the page (above the dotted line) is the header information. It consists of the title, which appears in the Navigator title bar as "Online Reservation System," and a picture and text. The middle of the page contains the working portion, or body—in this case, a single (underlined) link to the videotape reservation system. The bottom of

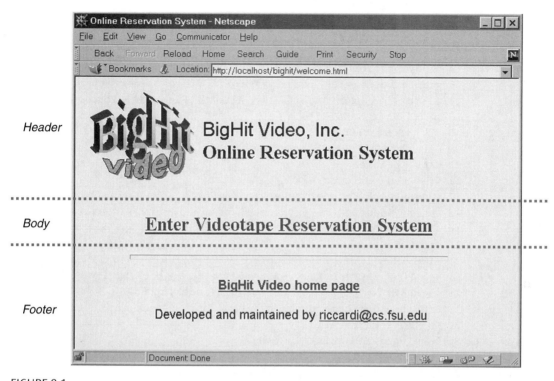

Header

Body

Footer

FIGURE 9.1 _____
Browser displaying the BigHit Video welcome page

the page (below the second dotted line) contains the footer, which is a horizontal line, a link to the home page, and a link to the person responsible for the Web site.

This page serves as the style guide for the entire collection of pages that make up this Web site. To maintain a common look and feel, every page contains the BigHit logo graphic on the upper left, a title next to it, and a footer at the bottom.

The HTML source for the page, with line numbers, is given in Fig. 9.2. The header of the page appears in lines 1–10. The body section consists of lines 11–13. The footer is in lines 14–23. Lines 11 and 14 consist of comment tags. The document begins with an HTML start tag `<html>` and ends with an HTML end tag `</html>`. These tags are required for every HTML document, although many browsers do not require an end tag. The beginning and ending head tags surround a section with document information. The title is displayed in the browser's title bar.

The BigHit Video graphic and title are contained in an HTML table, one of the constructs that are available to guide document formatting. This example (lines 5–10) is a table with no visible border and a single row. The information to be displayed in the row begins with the tag `<tr>` (line 5), which stands for *table row*. The first table data element (line 6) begins with `<td>` (*table data*) and consists of an image tag that is a relative reference to the document `Bighit.jpg`. The second

```
 1 <html><head>
 2 <title>BigHit Video Online Reservation System</title>
 3 </head>
 4 <body bgcolor="#FFFFFF">
 5 <table border="0" summary="BigHit Video header"><tr>
 6   <td><img src="Bighit.jpg" alt="BigHit Video logo"></td>
 7   <TD VALIGN="middle">
 8     <FONT FACE="Arial" SIZE=5>BigHit Video, Inc.</FONT>
 9     <br><h1><em>Online Reservation System</em></h1></td>
10 </tr></table>
11 <!-- body of page -->
12 <center><h2><a href=reservation.html>
13 Enter Videotape Reservation System </a></h2></center>
14 <!-- footer of page -->
15 <center><p>
16 <IMG SRC="line.gif" HEIGHT=8 WIDTH=513 alt="3-d line">
17 <p><FONT FACE="Arial" SIZE=+0><b>
18 <A HREF="http://localhost/bighit/index.html">
19 BigHit Video home page</A></b></font>
20 <p><FONT FACE="Arial">
21 Developed and maintained by
22 <A HREF="mailto:riccardi@cs.fsu.edu">riccardi@cs.fsu.edu</A>
23 </FONT></center></body></html>
```

FIGURE 9.2 _____

HTML source (with line numbers) for the BigHit Video welcome page

element in the first table row (line 7) is the title with a break tag `<br>` in the middle (line 9) to force a line break.

The body of the table contains a phrase delimited by beginning and ending *anchor* tags. A tag with name A is an anchor, or *hyperlink*, tag. The `href` attribute of an anchor is a reference to another document, or another place in the same document. The value of the `href` is a URL (universal resource locator). We first encountered URLs in the context of database connections in Section 8.3.2.

Each URL consists of the naming scheme of the mechanism used to access the resource, the host machine of the resource, and the name of the resource, given as a path. For instance, the following URL is a reference to the HTML 4.0 specification:

```
http://www.w3.org/TR/REC-html40/
```

The mechanism used to fetch the resource is `http` (*HTTP* stands for *Hypertext Transfer Protocol*), the hosting computer is `www.w3.org`, and the document name is `/TR/REC-html40/`. This URL is the address of a good place to look for information about HTML version 4.0.

The URL on line 12 is `reservation.html`. It is a *relative URL*, as the naming schemes for the mechanism and the host computer are omitted. A relative URL is resolved to a full URL by appending it to the base URL of the page. In this page, the base URL is the URL of the directory that includes the page. That is, the base URL is the URL with the part of the name that follows the last slash (/) removed. This URL refers to a page named `reservation.html` on the same machine in the same directory as the page that contains the tag. From the location field of the Navigator page, we know that the URL of the page is

```
http://localhost/bighit/index.html
```

The mechanism is `http`, and the host computer is `localhost`, the name that many computers use for a reference to the machine itself. The base URL is

```
http://localhost/bighit/
```

Therefore, the absolute URLs of the relative URLs in lines 6, 12, and 16 are

```
http://localhost/bighit/bighit.jpg
http://localhost/bighit/reservation.html
http://localhost/bighit/line.gif
```

The footer of the page has an image tag that produces the separating line, a hyperlink to the home page of the Web site, and a `mailto` hyperlink. The `href` of the anchor tag in line 22 uses the `mailto` mechanism. Clicking this link causes an e-mail form to pop up to send mail to the specified address.

9.1.2 Extending HTML with New Tags

HTML defines a set of standard tag names, but does not exclude other tag names. Most browsers ignore any tag whose name is foreign to them. In this sense, HTML is extensible. That is, an author is free to add new tag names with meanings that may be unknown to browsers. Indeed, many developers of software for generating and processing HTML documents have defined new tags that describe actions that should take place when a Web server selects the page.

An excellent example of enhancing HTML with tags is the Cold Fusion software system from Allaire Corporation. Cold Fusion consists of an extension to HTML called CFML (Cold Fusion Markup Language) and software support for translating CFML to HTML. The tags of a CFML document specify database connections, queries, and the transformation of query results into HTML. For a Web site that is supported by Cold Fusion, an HTTP or CGI request for a CFML document is handed off to the Cold Fusion server. The server reads the CFML document, executes all of the queries, and performs the other operations of the document. The result is an HTML file that is sent back to the browser.

Another popular extension to HTML is Active Server Pages (ASP), a Microsoft product that is supported by Microsoft Web servers. ASP combines HTML and a scripting language for Windows. An HTTP or CGI request for an ASP document results in the execution of the document by the ASP scripting engine. As with Cold Fusion, the resulting HTML document is delivered as the result of the request.

Finally, the Java Server Pages (JSP) system is an evolving standard for server scripting that uses HTML tags to specify interaction with Java programs, using the servlet model that is described in Sections 9.5 and 9.6. Each JSP page is translated from an HTML page into a Java program that generates the page. The JSP tags typically contain Java code and references to Java method calls. They can be used to direct interaction with databases.

Active URLs and Forms in HTML

9.2

Web servers accept certain URLs as representing a request for the execution of a specific program. The output of the program is returned to the browser to be displayed just like any Web page.

The interaction between browser and server includes a transfer of information from browser to server. The *Common Gateway Interface (CGI)* is a specification of one strategy for transmitting information between browser and server. It allows a browser to initiate a request to a Web server. The server, in turn, executes an application, provides user-specific information to the application, and passes its results back to the browser.

9.2.1 Analysis of a Sample HTML Form

An *HTML form* can be used to collect data from users for transmission to a Web server. Consider the very simple form shown in Fig. 9.3. It has the same header and footer style as the page shown in Fig. 9.1. The header has a different title and subtitle, but the same graphic and the same basic format. The HTML source for the body of the form is shown in Fig. 9.4. Line 3 begins the form with a `form` tag. The `action` attribute specifies the URL of the program that processes the information collected by the form. The URL is a relative reference to a program called `reservation.cgi` in directory `/cgi-bin`. Because the relative URL begins with `/`, it is relative to the root directory of the Web server and not to the directory of the page.

Clicking the Submit button on the form causes the browser to collect all of the information in the input fields, encode and format it in a specific style, and transmit it to the Web server, as specified in the `action` attribute of the `form` tag in line 3. The Web server, in turn, initiates the execution of the specified *CGI application* and makes the input information available to that program.

Each input field is specified by its name and value. The encoded format of the input information is described in Section 9.2.2.

The information made available to the CGI program includes much more than just the inputs. The *CGI request* has quite a few attributes, including the browser type, the URL of the request, the name of the Web server, and the request action, as represented by the `action` attribute of the `form` tag.

The `method` attribute of the `form` tag in line 3 of Fig. 9.4 has value `GET`. In the CGI specification, a *GET method* is translated into a URL that includes the

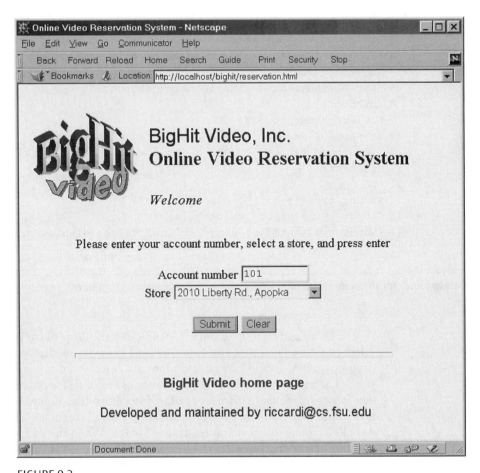

FIGURE 9.3 _____
BigHit Video reservation system page with simple form

input information from the form. A GET method transmits the program name and the information in a single step. The alternative method is a *POST method*, in which the program name is part of the URL and the input information is transmitted separately.

Five inputs are listed in the body of this form. The first, on line 5, is named `accountId` and is a single-line text box with room to display 10 characters. The `input` tag of line 5 produces the text box in Fig 9.3 that contains the value "101". The value 101 is not part of the page specification, but has been typed into the text box by the user.

```
 1 <center>
 2 Please enter your account number, select a store, and press enter
 3 <form action="/cgi-bin/reservation.cgi" method="GET">
 4 Account number
 5 <input type="text" size=10 name="accountId">
 6 <br>Store
 7 <select name=storeId>
 8    <option value="3">2010 Liberty Rd., Apopka
 9    <option value="5">1004 N. Monroe St., Apopka
10 </select>
11 <p>
12 <input type="submit" value="Submit">
13 <input type="reset" value="Clear">
14 <input type="hidden" name="action" value="displayForm">
15 </form></center>
```

FIGURE 9.4 _____

HTML source for the body of the page of Fig. 9.3 with line numbers (continues)

The `select` group of lines 7–10 specifies the drop-down box that is used to select the store. The `select` tags surround the options that are included in the drop-down box. In this case, two options are listed in lines 8 and 9, one for each store. The `value` attribute of the tag contains the value for the `storeId`, and the text following the tag is displayed in the drop-down box. Figure 9.3 shows a selection of the first store, number 3, as the drop-down box shows "2010 Liberty Rd., Apopka". The other store information is hidden. When the user clicks the Submit button, parameter `storeId` will have value 3.

The inputs on lines 12 and 13 represent the two buttons on the form. The `submit` input type is the special input that represents submission of the form information to the Web server. The `clear` input type represents clearing the values in the form fields.

The final input, on line 14, does not appear on the form because its type is `hidden`. This input contains information that is put into the form when it is created. It is transmitted to the Web server as a name and a value, just like any other input. This input, named `action`, is used in the CGI processing style of this book to specify which action the `reservation.cgi` program takes when the server invokes it. In this case, the program will be asked to display the reservation form. The use of this parameter will be explained in Section 9.4.

9.2.2   CGI, the Common Gateway Interface Specification

CGI describes two methods of transmitting information from a browser to a server. The GET method appends the form contents to the URL given in the `action` attribute and sends the result to the server. The POST method sends the information in two steps. First, the browser contacts the server specified in the `action` attribute. Once contact is made, it sends the form contents.

The form contents are formatted as a sequence of name–value pairs, with each pair separated from the next by an ampersand (`&`). This format is the Internet Media Type `application/x-www-form-urlencoded`. For the form of Section 9.2.1, the contents are represented as follows:

```
accountId=101&storeId=3&action=displayForm
```

When this form is submitted, the actual URL is put together as the base URL, the relative URL from the `action` attribute, a question mark (`?`) that separates the program locator from the data, and the form contents, encoded as above. The result is the following URL:

```
http://localhost/cgi-bin/
reservation.cgi?accountId=101&storeId=3&action=displayForm
```

The `GET` method can be used directly as a hyperlink by making it the value of the `href` attribute of an anchor tag. It can also be typed into the location field of a browser. Pasting the preceding URL into Netscape Navigator will have the same effect as clicking the Submit button on this form.

A `POST` method cannot be created without help from the browser. The major advantages of this method are that it hides the *CGI query string* from the user and that it simplifies the URL that is displayed in the browser, especially when there are many variables or long values. Because the query string is not part of the URL, the `POST` method also bypasses any restriction that servers or browsers may have on the length of a URL.

It is possible in an HTML form to have multiple values for the same variable. The query string represents this situation by having the same variable represented in multiple name–value pairs, one for each value of the variable.

9.2.3   Encoding CGI Form Data

The data that are transmitted from the browser to the server are encoded in a simple style—one that relies on a collection of delimiters, including `?`, `=`, and `&`. URL encoding also requires that all information be represented as printable characters that can be part of a URL. These two constraints demand that CGI information be encoded. An encoding strategy must be used to represent delimiters and nonprintable characters. This encoding is included in the Internet Media Type `application/x-www-form-urlencoded`. Spaces are replaced by plus signs (`+`). Each delimiter or nonalphanumeric character is replaced by the three-character sequence `%XX`, where `XX` is the hexadecimal representation of the ASCII code for the character.

The following table shows a string and its encoding.

					Character-by-Character Encoding					
String	104 x+& </.	1	0	4	x	+	&	<	/	.
Encoding	104+x%2B%26+%3C%2F.	1	0	4	+	x	&2B	&26	+	&3c	&2F	.

The digits, letters, and period (.) are not modified. The spaces are encoded by pluses (+), and the symbols +, &, <, and / are encoded as the hexadecimal values %2B, %26, %3C, and %2F, respectively.

Fortunately, we don't have to worry about explicitly encoding or decoding CGI strings. The browser extracts the information and encodes and formats it. All of the standard CGI programming languages have modules that perform encoding and decoding. In the next sections, we will see how to use the Java packages that support encoding and decoding.

9.2.4   CGI Input

For a Unix Web server, CGI data are passed to the CGI program through a combination of environment variables and the standard input file. The method type is passed as an uppercase value in the REQUEST_METHOD environment variable.

For a GET method CGI interaction, the input data are provided as the value of the QUERY_STRING environment variable. The following C shell (csh) statement passes the query string as the first argument to the main program of Java class dbjava.website.CustomerCGI:

```
java dbjava.website.CustomerCGI $QUERY_STRING
```

For a POST method CGI interaction, the query string is passed to the CGI program in its standard input file. The environment variable CONTENT_LENGTH contains the number of characters in the input file. In csh, the standard input file is called $<. The following line passes the POST query string to the Java program:

```
java dbjava.website.CustomerCGI $<
```

One difficulty in CGI execution in Unix is that the script must execute as a special HTTP user, often the "nobody" user. As we developers like to say, "Nobody ain't got no CLASSPATH!" That is, the CLASSPATH and PATH variables of the "nobody" user may not be set properly for Java execution. The following csh script takes this consideration into account, correctly processing both GET and POST requests. The CLASSPATH is set to include the classes directory of faculty user riccardi. The path of the Java execution program is included explicitly as /usr/local/java/bin/java. Each Web site developer must change this script so that the CLASSPATH includes all directories that are needed by the Java program. In addition, the developer must ensure that the protections on files and directories are appropriate for the "nobody" user.

```
#!/bin/csh
setenv CLASSPATH=/home/faculty/riccardi/classes
if ("$REQUEST_METHOD" == "GET") then
    /usr/local/java/bin/java dbjava.website.CustomerCGI
      "$QUERY_STRING"
else
    /usr/local/java/bin/java dbjava.website.CustomerCGI $<
endif
```

Web servers for Microsoft Windows NT and Windows 98 systems also rely on scripting languages for CGI interaction. Unfortunately, these operating systems have no standard scripting languages. Many Web servers, including Apache, require that system administrators or users provide an executable for a scripting language. The primary method of processing CGI for the Microsoft Internet Information Server is to use Active Server Pages.

9.2.5   CGI Results

The Web server returns the standard output file of a CGI program to the browser. The output file must be *MIME (Multipurpose Internet Mail Extension)* encoded. MIME is a strategy for representing objects within e-mail that is also used by Web servers and browsers. The first line of the output must be a MIME content-type descriptor. If the application returns an HTML document, the first line is

```
Content-type: text/html
```

The second line must be completely empty. It is also possible for a CGI program to return some other MIME type. A GIF image is type `image/gif`. A text file that is not to be interpreted as HTML has type `text/plain`. Any MIME content type is acceptable, as long as the proper type is specified and as long as the second line is empty!

The two most common errors that are made by CGI programmers are to place improper permissions on the CGI applications and the directories in which they reside, and to create an improper header for the output page.

Using Java to Generate HTML

9.3

This section describes a collection of Java classes that encapsulate many aspects of the generation of HTML documents. Section 9.4 describes how HTML forms can be processed by Java classes.

A program that generates HTML consists mainly of print statements. An object-oriented approach to generating HTML seeks to encapsulate common document features to make it as easy as possible to create new pages and to maintain existing pages.

The main class that is used to generate HTML using the methods of this book is `dbjava.html.HtmlWriter`, which extends `java.io.PrintWriter`. This class inherits the print methods of `PrintWriter` and adds a variety of HTML-specific print methods. It also adds methods that are used to convert the results of database queries into HTML. The code for `HtmlWriter` is available at the Web site for this book.

Figure 9.5 shows part of the definition of class `HtmlWriter`. It includes the standard constructors expected for a subclass of `PrintWriter` and abstract methods for printing page headers and footers. To use the class, one must first define a subclass that establishes the style of the page by defining the `printHeader` and `printFooter` methods. Class `BigHitHtmlWriter` defines the methods that produce the headers and footers of the pages shown in Figs. 9.1 and 9.3.

```
1 package dbjava.html;
2 abstract public class HtmlWriter extends PrintWriter {
3 // Constructors
4    public HtmlWriter(Writer out) {super(out); }
5    public HtmlWriter(Writer out, boolean autoFlush) {
6      super(out,autoFlush); }
7    public HtmlWriter(OutputStream out) {super(out);}
8    public HtmlWriter(OutputStream out, boolean autoFlush) {
9      super(out,autoFlush);}
10   // abstract methods to print header and footer
11   abstract public void printHeader(String title, String subtitle);
12   abstract public void printFooter();
13   ...}
14 public class BigHitHtmlWriter extends HtmlWriter {
15   public void printHeader (...
16   public void printFooter (...
```

FIGURE 9.5 _____

Partial definitions of classes HtmlWriter *and* BigHitHtmlWriter

9.3.1   Methods That Produce Standard HTML Elements

Class HtmlWriter includes methods to produce simple anchor tags and other HTML elements, as shown in Fig. 9.6. These methods can be overridden in a subclass to change the style of presentation for these elements. For example, the horizontal rule that is used in BigHit Video's Web site is an indented three-dimensional image. To enforce this style, class BigHitHtmlWriter redefines method printHRule so that it prints an image tag instead of using the standard horizontal rule tag <hr> that is printed by HtmlWriter.printHRule.

```
1 public void printHRule() {println("<hr>");}
2 public void printContentType(String type) {
3   println("Content-type: "+type); println("");}
4 public void printMailto(String email, String label) {
5   println("<A HREF=\"mailto:"+email+"\">"+label+"</A>");
6 }
7 public void printMailto(String email) {printMailto(email,email);}
8 public void printLink(String URL, String label) {
9   println("<A HREF=\"" + URL + "\">" + label + "</A>");}
10 public void printLink(String URL) {printLink(URL,URL);}
```

FIGURE 9.6 _____

Methods of class HtmlWriter *that print simple HTML elements*

An important feature of `HtmlWriter` is its support for printing plain text in HTML. Many characters cannot be safely added to HTML text or don't print properly in it. The obvious character that gives us problems is the less than symbol (<). A phrase like `b<a and b>c` will be interpreted by a browser as including the anchor tag `<a and b>`. The less than character must be encoded as `&lt;` so that it will be displayed correctly in the browser. The form `&name;` is used for certain special symbols, including `&gt;`, `&quot;`, and `&amp;`. Any character can be represented as `&#nnn;`, where *nnn* is the decimal representation of the ASCII code of the character. Another problem with plain text in HTML is the embedded end-of-line mark, which browsers ignore. Proper display of this symbol requires translation to a `<br>` or `<p>` tag.

Class `HtmlWriter` includes the methods of Fig 9.7, which support the correct display of text in browsers. The main method, `convertChar`, replaces every occurrence of the character `from` in the string `inStr` with the string `to`. In turn, the other conversion methods use this method. For instance, `convertEOL` simply replaces every end-of-line character by the string `<br>`.

```
public static String convertEOL(String inStr) {
        return convertChar(inStr, '\n', "<br>");}
```

The print methods are all implemented by calls to the conversion methods.

The method `htmlStr` converts a null or empty string into ` ` (a nonbreaking space), a string that is not ignored by browsers. For a nonempty string, the result has each <, >, or & replaced by its named equivalent and each end-of-line character replaced by a break tag. In addition, if `htmlStr` is called with a nonzero second argument, the string is trimmed to a maximum length before being converted.

The page shown in Fig. 9.1 is produced by method `main` of class `WelcomePage` given in Fig. 9.8. It simply prints a header with title and no subtitle, format specification for the body, a link, and a footer. That's it!

```
1 // methods to convert a string to an HTML-safe version
2 public static String htmlStr (String inStr);
3 public static String htmlStr (String inStr, int maxWidth);
4 public static String convertEOL(String inStr);
5 public static String convertChar(String inStr,char from,String to);
6 // methods to print an HTML-safe version of a string
7 public void printHtmlStr (String inStr);
8 public void printHtmlStr (String inStr, int maxWidth);
9 public void printConvertEOL(String inStr);
```

FIGURE 9.7 _____

Methods of class `HtmlWriter` *that convert text for accurate display by a Web browser*

```
 1 package dbjava.website;
 2 import dbjava.html.*;
 3 public class WelcomePage {
 4   public static void main (String args[]) {
 5     HtmlWriter out = new BigHitHtmlWriter(System.out, true);
 6     out.printHeader("Online Reservation System", null);
 7     out.println("<center><h2>");
 8     out.printLink("reservation.html",
 9       "Enter Videotape Reservation System");
10     out.println("</h2></center>");
11     out.printFooter();
12   }
13 }
```

FIGURE 9.8 _____

Java code to produce the page of Figs. 9.1 and 9.2

9.3.2   Methods That Produce Forms and Form Elements

Class `HtmlWriter` also supports a systematic style of producing forms. Figure 9.9 lists the basic methods for writing form elements. As with the other methods of `HtmlWriter`, a subclass can impose its own style by redefining these methods.

Three form inputs represent sets of alternative choices: drop-down combo boxes, radio buttons, and check boxes. Each of these inputs is characterized by a table of value–label pairs. Class `HtmlWriter` includes methods that produce the form inputs from a table produced as the result of a query. Figure 9.10 gives the code for the `addOption` method. It simply prints the `select` tag to begin the option list, then prints an `option` tag and a label for each row of the `ResultSet`.

Now we are ready to show how the HTML page of Fig. 9.3 is produced. Method `makeEntryPage`, shown in Fig. 9.11, generates the complete page. The area for entering the `accountId` is produced by a call to `addTextarea` (line 10). The drop-down box is produced by first issuing a query to the database for the store names and addresses (lines 12–15), and then calling `addOption` (line 16) to

```
1 public void openForm(String action, String method);
2 public void endForm();
3 public void addTextarea (String name, int size, String value);
4 public void addTextarea (String name, int size);
5 public void addButton(String type, String value, String name);
6 public void addButtons();// add submit and clear buttons
```

FIGURE 9.9 _____

Methods of class `HtmlWriter` *that produce form elements*

```
 1 public void addOption(String name, ResultSet options) {
 2     // add an option set for options
 3     //   options must have at least 2 columns,
 4     //   the first for values, the second for labels.
 5   try {
 6     println("<select name="+name+">");
 7     while (options.next()) {
 8       print("    <option value=\""+options.getString(1)+"\">");
 9       println(options.getString(2));
10     }
11     println("</select>");
12   } catch (SQLException e) {
13     println("</select>");
14   }
15 }
```

FIGURE 9.10 _____

Method addOption *of class* HtmlWriter

```
 1 public void makeEntryPage(HtmlWriter htmlOut) {
 2   // make the page for customer registration
 3   htmlOut.printHeader("Online Video Reservation System",
 4     "<i>Welcome</i>");
 5   htmlOut.println("<center>");
 6   htmlOut.println("Please enter your account number, "
 7     +"select a store, and press enter");
 8   htmlOut.openForm("/cgi-bin/reservation","GET");
 9   htmlOut.println("Account number ");
10   htmlOut.addTextarea("accountId",10);
11   htmlOut.println("<br>Store ");
12   String storeSQL =
13     "select storeId,street&','&city as addr from Store";
14   try {
15     ResultSet stores = stmt.executeQuery(storeSQL);
16     htmlOut.addOption("storeId",stores);
17   } catch (SQLException e) {
18     htmlOut.println("<p>error in sql<br>");
19     htmlOut.println(storeSQL+"<br>");
20     htmlOut.println(e.getMessage());
21   }
```

FIGURE 9.11 _____

Method makeEntryPage *that produces the HTML page of Figs. 9.3 and 9.4 (continues)*

```
22   htmlOut.println(
23      "<input name=action value=\"displayEntry\" type=hidden>");
24   htmlOut.addButtons();
25   htmlOut.endForm();
26   htmlOut.printFooter();
```

FIGURE 9.11 _____
continued

turn the results into a drop-down box. The SQL statement that produces the list of stores is

```
select storeId, street&','&city as addr from Store
```

The second attribute of the **select** clause is the concatenation of the **street** and **city**, with a comma and space in between. After the drop-down box is added, **addButtons** is called (line 24) to add the Submit and Clear buttons, and the form is closed with calls to **endForm** (line 25) and **printFooter** (line 26).

Figure 9.12 shows the reservation selection page that is produced by **reservation.cgi** from the query string

```
accountId=101&storeId=3&action=displayForm
```

The **accountId** is used to select the customer information that is displayed as a table. The Edit Customer Info hyperlink is part of the customer area on the page. The link is declared as follows:

```
<A HREF=
   "/cgi-bin/customer?action=displayForm&accountId=101">
Edit Customer Info</A>
```

It is what we might call an *active link*—that is, a link that is part of a page and that is a CGI request.

Clicking on the Edit Customer Info hyperlink results in the page shown in Fig. 9.13. This page is produced by executing a select statement for the specified customer. Each field of the **Customer** table is represented by a text area on the page. Class **Customer** was created to handle the details of processing customers. It includes a constructor that makes a **Customer** from a **ResultSet** and another constructor that makes one from a query string. The following code in **Customer.printForm** produces the header and first row of the table:

```
out.println("<table border>");
out.println("<tr><th colspan=2>Customer account
id:"+accountId);
out.println("</th></tr>");
out.println("<tr><th>Last Name</th><td>");
out.addTextarea("lastName",40,lastName);
```

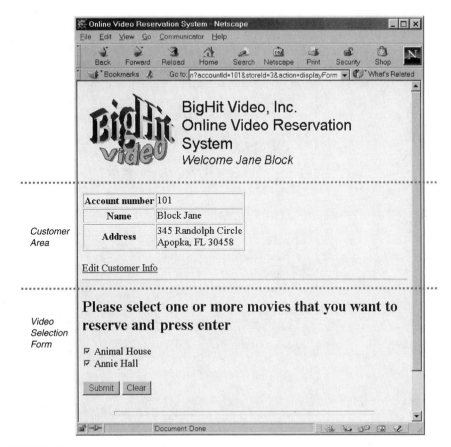

FIGURE 9.12

Video reservation form produced by `reservation.cgi` *with two movies selected*

Processing the customer information form requires constructing an SQL update statement from the CGI input. The update statement is created by method `Customer.updateSQL`, as shown in Fig. 9.14. It is sent to the database with a call to `statement.executeUpdate`.

The second form in Fig. 9.12 has two check boxes, both with the same name. The following HTML code defines the check boxes:

```
<input type=checkbox name="movieId" value="90987">Animal
    House</input><br>
<input type=checkbox name="movieId" value="123">Annie
    Hall</input><br>
```

The CGI program produced this HTML by issuing a query to select the `movieId` and `title` of each movie with unreserved videotapes at store 3 and passing the result to `HtmlWriter.addCheckBoxes`.

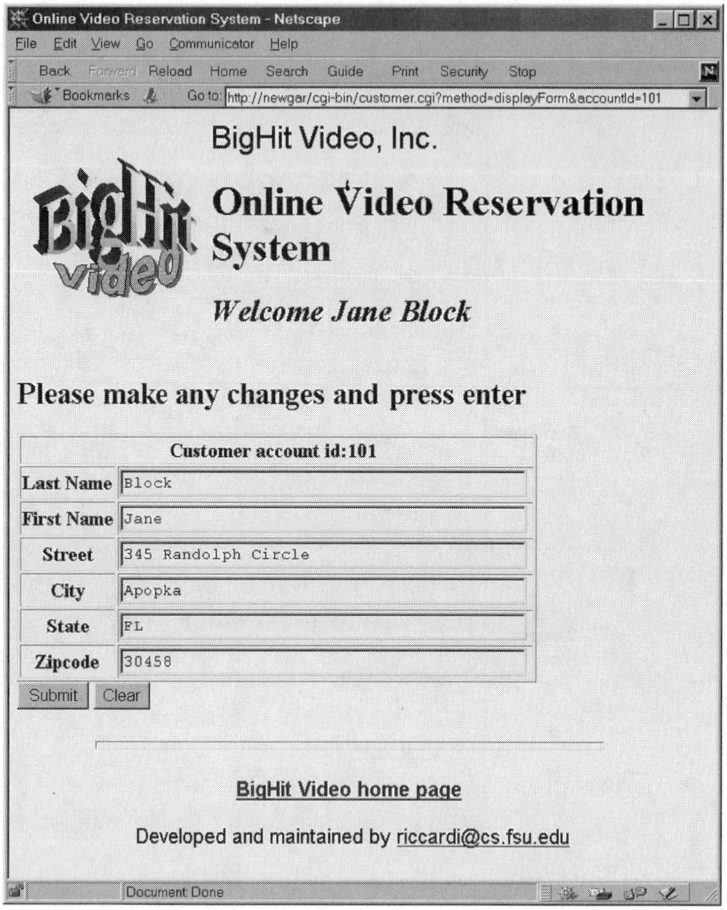

FIGURE 9.13 _____
Customer information edit form

Clicking the Submit button results in a CGI request to the same program, `reservation.cgi`, with the query string

```
action=processForm&accountId=101&storeId=3&movieId=
    90987&movieId=123
```

The `movieId` variable occurs twice, once for each movie selected.

The processing of the query string proceeds in two steps: (1) create and process update queries to make the reservations, and (2) create a report of all reservations for this customer. Figure 9.15 shows the page that is generated in response to this CGI request. The details of the processing of the request and the production of this page are given in Section 9.3.3.

```
 1 public String updateSql() {
 2    StringBuffer sql = new StringBuffer();
 3    sql.append("update Customer set ");
 4    sql.append("lastName='").append(lastName);
 5    sql.append("', firstName='").append(firstName);
 6    sql.append("', street='").append(street);
 7    sql.append("', city='").append(city);
 8    sql.append("', zipcode='").append(zipcode);
 9    sql.append("' where accountId =");
10    sql.append(accountId);
11    return sql.toString();
12 }
```

FIGURE 9.14 _____

Method updateSQL *of class* Customer

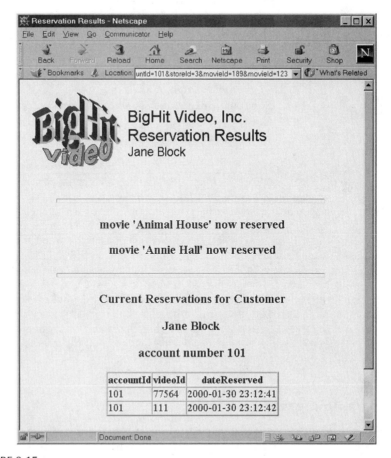

FIGURE 9.15 _____

Result of reserving two videotapes

9.3.3   Methods That Produce HTML Tables from Result Sets

Class `HtmlWriter` includes two methods to print HTML tables from query results: `printTableByRows` and `printTableByCols`. The `printTableByRows` method prints a table in the normal order. Each row of the HTML table displays a row of the query. In many instances, however, the number of attributes is so large that a row will not easily fit across the browser page. In these cases, the `printTableByCols` method can be used to display one row of the HTML table for each column of the query result. It is particularly useful when the result has few rows.

The code for these methods is long, but not too complicated. Method `printTableByRows` simply extracts the column names from `ResultSetMetadata`, displays those names in a single row as table headers, then iterates through the rows of the `ResultSet`, making a table row for each row of the query result. To ensure that the table structure is preserved, all table elements are transformed by the `htmlStr` method of `HtmlWriter` before printing.

The table in the lower part of the body of the page of Fig. 9.15 is produced by executing a select statement and calling `printTableByRows`.

```
1 String reservationSql = "select * from Reservation where"
2     + " accountId=" + customer.accountId;
3 ResultSet reservations = stmt.executeQuery(reservationSql);
4 if (reservations.next()) {
5   htmlOut.printTableByRows(reservations);
6 } else {
7   htmlOut.println("<p><h3>No Current Reservations</h3>");
```

A NOTE ABOUT TESTING FOR EMPTY RESULT SETS

A major problem with the JDBC 1.0 result sets is that an initial call to **next** is required to determine whether a result set has any rows. The cursor is initially positioned before the first row, and a call to **next** positions it on the first row. In JDBC 1.0, there is no way to return the cursor to its initial position. This problem makes it difficult to design reliable and simple methods to use result sets.

For example, the code given in Section 9.3.3 includes a call to **next** in line 4 that is used to determine whether the **reservations ResultSet** includes any rows . After the test, the code calls **printTableByRows** to print the rows of the **ResultSet**. If **printTableByRows** begins by calling **next**, it will skip the first row. Hence, each call to **printTableByRows** must call **next** to position the cursor on the first row. Failure to do so will cause an error in the print method.

CGI Programming with Java

9.4

Because Java was created to support the Web, it is not surprising to find that it supports CGI programming as well. Unfortunately, this support does not include direct access to the environment variables that contain the CGI method type and query string. Some additional help from the Web server or intermediate operating system scripts are required to produce the connection between a Web server and a Java program. In this section, we investigate the direct support for encoding and decoding query strings that makes it easy for us to use Java programs as CGI programs.

9.4.1 Encoding Query Strings and URLs

Package `java.net` includes class `URLEncoder` for encoding strings with the Internet Media Type `application/x-www-form-urlencoded`, as described in Section 9.2.2. Method `encode` of the class transforms a string into one that is suitable for inclusion in a URL. This step is particularly important for generating links that use `GET` methods for CGI programs.

The active URL of Section 9.3.2 is produced by the following code:

```
out.print("<A HREF=\"/cgi-bin/"
    +"customer?action=displayForm&accountId=");
out.print(java.net.URLEncoder.encode(accountId));
out.println(">");
```

9.4.2 Decoding Query Strings

Package `javax.servlet.http` includes class `HttpUtils` and its method `parseQueryString` that translates an encoded query string into a `Hashtable`, which is a mapping from keys to values. The `Hashtable` produced has keys that are strings and values that are string arrays. That is, each CGI variable is mapped to an array of `String` values. The method also decodes the names and values and restores the original string values.

Packages `javax.servlet` and `javax.servlet.http` are part of the Java Servlet Development Kit (JSDK). Servlets, which represent an alternative to CGI programs, are discussed in detail in Section 9.5.

Once the query string has been parsed, we can query the `Hashtable` for the values of specific CGI variables or iterate through all variables in the query string.

Method `processReservationForm` processes the reservation request of the page shown in Fig. 9.12. It includes the code given in Fig. 9.16, which iterates through the requested movies, queries for a videotape at the specified store, and issues an insert into the `Reservation` table.

Considerable error checking is required to make the videotape reservations work. In Fig. 9.16, the first query finds all of the available videotapes that match the movie and store. We expect that at least one match will exist, as the reservation page includes only movies that are available. Between the production of the reservation page and the processing of the request, however, some other customers may have rented or reserved all of the videotapes for a particular movie. Hence, there may be no entities in the query for videotapes. Method `DBConnect.getField` is called to process the query. It takes a select statement as its argument, executes the select statement, and returns the value in the first column of the first row of the result table. The result of this call will be `null` if no rows are selected. Thus the

```
 1 Hashtable request = parse QueryString(queryString);
 2 String movies[] = (String[])request.get("movieId");
 3 for (int i = 0; i < movies.length; i++) { //find unrented copy
 4    String findSql = "select videoId from UnrentedVideo where "
 5    +"movieId=movies[i]+" and storeId="+storeId;
 6    String movieTitleSql = "select title from Movie where movieId="
 7       +movies[i];
 8    String videoId = db.getField(findSql);// get the first videoId
 9    String movieTitle = db.getField(movieTitleSql);// get title
10    if (videoId==null) {// no videotape available for movie and store
11       htmlOut.println("<h3> movie '"+movieTitle
12          +"' not available</h3>");
13    } else {//reserve videotape
14       String reserveSql="insert into Reservation values("
15          +customer.accountId+","+videoId+",now)";
16       try{ // insert into reservation
17          int count = stmt.executeUpdate(reserveSql);
18          if (count!=1) {// did insert succeed?
19             htmlOut.println("<h3> movie "+movieTitle
20                +" not available</h3>");
21          } else {
22             htmlOut.println("<h3> movie '"+movieTitle
23                +"' now reserved</h3>");
```

FIGURE 9.16 _____

Partial code for processing a movie reservation request

test for `videoId==null` tells whether at least one tape is available. If `videoId` is `null`, we report that the movie is not available.

If there is an available videotape, an insert statement is created and sent to the database. Another possibility of error arises here. A "race" condition may make this tape unavailable. For example, imagine that two customers are attempting to reserve the same movie at the same store concurrently. Both CGI requests receive the same `videoId`, and both insert it into the `Reservation` table. One of those insert operations will not succeed, because `videoId` is the key of `Reservation`. Thus it is necessary to check how many rows are affected by the insert (variable `count`). If `count` is not 1, the insert did not succeed.

This problem can be resolved by performing the query to select a `videoId` and the insert into `Reservation` as a single database transaction. The details of transaction management are in Chapter 14, and some examples of transaction management in Java are in Section 10.1.

A real application to reserve videotapes must necessarily have a manual component. That is, a clerk must take the videotape from the rental area and place it in the reserved area. It is likely that the reservation request would be followed by the manual procedure and transmittal of a confirmation by e-mail. When designing applications, we must be careful to make them as accurate and reliable as possible and to consider the human activities that accompany the automated processes.

Java Servlets

9.5

The previously outlined strategy, which uses Unix shell scripts as a pass-through to transport CGI request strings to Java applications, leaves much to be desired. In particular, it limits the interaction between the browser and the application. Only the query string passes from browser to application, and only the resulting document passes back to the browser. Nevertheless, the CGI standard provides for considerably more information to be transferred from the browser to the application and even supports an extended interaction between them. Execution of an intermediary script is also undesirable because of the relatively high cost of starting the Java runtime environment for each CGI request.

Both Java and Perl can be used to construct *servlets*, or small servers dedicated to specific CGI requests. A servlet is a program that waits for a request, executes the appropriate application, and waits for the next request. Its execution begins when the Web server starts its execution and does not have to be restarted for each request. When a servlet request reaches the Web server, it is turned over to the servlet for processing.

Servlets are supported by a strategy that treats each CGI request as a lightweight interaction with a running system. This strategy allows the database connection to persist between CGI requests and permits direct connection between the browser and the application.

The Java Servlet Development Kit (JSDK) is a part of the Java system that contains packages `javax.servlet` and `javax.servlet.http`. These packages contain the classes and interfaces necessary to develop servlets for CGI processing. Of course, servlets must also be supported by enhancements to the Web server. The Apache Server Project, for instance, has a related project, the Java Apache Project, that has produced a server add-on called *Apache Jserve* that manages servlet executions.

Java servlets are merely a small part of a larger trend toward developing methods of integrating applications and servers using the Java language. Chapter 16 includes more detail on how these Java application services are defined and used.

A *Java servlet* is a Java object that responds to CGI requests. The object is created by a servlet execution engine, such as the JServe plug-in for the Apache HTTP server. The servlet execution engine creates a thread for each servlet. The servlet object in the thread is initialized (`init` method) and waits for service requests. When the engine receives a request for service by a specific servlet, it calls an action method (`doGet` or `doPost`) of the servlet.

Figure 9.17 shows a partial implementation of class `ReservationServlet`. The full implementation of this class is included in the code available at the Web site for this book. The basic structure of a servlet includes an `init` method and the service methods `doGet` and `doPost`. When a servlet is created, its default constructor and its `init` method are called. It then waits for service requests. The values of the members of a servlet object persist across multiple requests.

```
1 package dbjava.website;
2 import javax.servlet.*; import javax.servlet.http.*;
3 public class ReservationServlet extends HttpServlet {
4    public void init(ServletConfig config)
5       throws UnavailableException, ServletException {
6      super.init(config);
7      init();
8    }
9    public void init() {
10     db = new BigHitDBConnect();
11     db.makeConnection();
12     stmt = db.getStatement();
13   }
14   public void doGet(HttpServletRequest req,
15       HttpServletResponse res)
16       throws IOException , ServletException {
17     doPost(req, res);
18   }
19   public void doPost(HttpServletRequest req,
20       HttpServletResponse res)
21       throws IOException , ServletException {
22     request=req;
23     response=res;
24     PrintWriter out = response.getWriter();
25     htmlOut = new BigHitHtmlWriter(out);
26     response.setContentType("text/html");
27     String action[] = request.getParameterValues("action");
28     if (action==null) {// no action, create error page
```

FIGURE 9.17 ——

Partial implementation of class `ReservationServlet` *that processes the CGI requests for the Web page shown in Fig. 9.12*

Methods `doPost` and `doGet` respond to CGI requests. In this implementation, we don't care whether a request is a `POST` or a `GET`, so `doGet` (lines 14–18 of Fig. 9.17) simply calls `doPost`. Method `doPost` (lines 19–28) begins by initializing the response. First, it calls `getWriter` (line 24) to get the output stream that will be sent back to the Web server. Next, it wraps that stream with an `HtmlWriter` (line 25). Finally, `doPost` calls `setContentType` (line 26) to create the output header of the response.

Method `doPost` uses the `action` parameter to indicate what response is requested. This parameter is the same CGI parameter that we used for CGI requests in Section 9.4. Method `getParameterValues` (line 27) of class `HttpServletRequest` returns a `String` array with the values of the named

CGI parameter. If the named variable does not appear in the list of CGI variables, `getParameterValues` returns `null`. If the variable appears without a value, `getParameterValues` returns an array with no elements. This strategy is very similar to the CGI approach in which the query string is parsed and turned into a `Hashtable`, as was described in Section 9.4.2 and Fig. 9.16.

Servlet Applications for BigHit Video

9.6

Many of the pieces of the CGI applications for the BigHit Video reservation system have already been presented. In this section, we pull those pieces together by showing the class definitions and main methods that drive the applications.

The four dynamically generated Web pages presented in this chapter are produced by five different CGI actions. Two servlet classes contain the five actions. First, `ReservationServlet` includes methods to generate the registration page, the reservation page, and the reservation results page and to process their CGI requests. Second, `CustomerServlet` includes methods to generate the customer edit page and to process the customer edit CGI request.

9.6.1   Strategy for Processing Requests

Each of the HTML forms includes a hidden `action` parameter that the classes use to determine which action should be executed for a particular request. The values for `action` have been standardized with the following values:

- `displayForm`: display the main form page of the class
- `processForm`: process the CGI request from the main form and produce the response page
- `displayEntry`: display the entry page for the class

The BigHit Video servlet classes are configured with `doPost` methods that expect an `action` CGI parameter that determines the action to be taken. They produce an HTML document on the output file that is provided as part of the servlet response argument. The `doPost` method for `CustomerServlet` is shown in Fig. 9.18.

Method `doPost` extracts the `action` parameter (line 8) and responds by calling the appropriate method that implements the specific action. Method `printSimplePage` (lines 10 and 16) produces the error page. Method `processCustomerEditForm` (line 21) contains the code to update the customer record from information in the form. Method `makeCustomerEditPage` (line 25) generates the HTML page shown in Fig. 9.13.

Method `processRequest`, also included in Fig. 9.18, decodes the query string, gets the `action` and `accountId` parameters, then calls the appropriate method to process the request. Some error checking has been omitted from Fig 9.18. The real code would check whether the `action` and `accountId` parameters are part of the request.

The full code for these applications can be found in the Web site for the book.

```
 1 public void doPost(HttpServletRequest req, HttpServletResponse res)
 2     throws IOException , ServletException {
 3   request = req;
 4   response = res;
 5   PrintWriter out = response.getWriter();
 6   res.setContentType("text/html");
 7   htmlOut = new BigHitHtmlWriter(out);
 8   String actions[] = request.getParameterValues("action");
 9   if (actions==null) {// must have actions
10     htmlOut.printSimplePage("No action supplied","");
11     htmlOut.close();
12     return;
13   }
14   String customers[] = request.getParameterValues("accountId");
15   if (customers==null) {// must have accountId
16     htmlOut.printSimplePage("No customer argument supplied","");
17     htmlOut.close();
18     return;
19   }
20   if (actions[0].equals("processForm")) {// process edit form
21     processCustomerEditForm();
22   }
23   if (actions[0].equals("displayForm")){// form to edit customer
24     // all parameters available
25     makeCustomerEditPage(customers[0]);
26   }
27 }
```

FIGURE 9.18

Method doPost *of class* CustomerServlet

Chapter Summary

HTML is a simple language for representing documents, their format, hyperlinks, and data entry forms. Browsers format and display HTML and allow users to create interactions with a variety of Web servers and resources.

Java can be adapted to generating HTML through classes like HtmlWriter and BigHitHtmlWriter. A class for generating HTML should include print methods that make it easy to generate standard HTML objects, such as tags. Such a class should also make it easy for a Web designer to create and enforce styles that are used by many pages.

CGI (Common Gateway Interface) supports active interactions between browsers and Web servers. The browser can collect user input, encode it according the URL encoding standard, and create CGI requests for the Web server. The CGI program can accept a request, process it, and write an HTML document to its standard output file. The Web server sends the output file back to the browser. Java has been adapted to CGI service by the development of packages and classes for encoding and decoding query strings.

Class `HtmlWriter` includes methods that support the generation of HTML forms. The connection between databases and forms is supported by methods that generate form elements from the results of select queries. Methods `printTableByRows` and `printTableByColumns` of class `HtmlWriter` generate HTML tables from the query results.

A servlet is a program that is installed in a Web server that has been enhanced by the addition of a servlet execution engine. The Web server executes the servlet in response to specific requests. The `doGet` and `doPost` methods of a Java servlet class are responsible for responding to CGI requests. Parameters to these methods supply the CGI parameters and the output stream used to return results to the browser. Java servlets provide a more direct interaction with Web browsers than is usual for CGI programs. The servlet mechanism is the preferred method of supporting Web sites with Java. Support for Java servlets is provided by the packages `javax.servlet` and `javax.servlet.http` and by servlet plug-ins for a variety of Web servers.

Key Terms

Anchor tag. An HTML tag that references another document; also called a *hyperlink*.

Browser. A graphical user interface that displays HTML documents and facilitates access to Web documents.

CGI application. A program that is executed by a Web server in response to a CGI request.

CGI query string. The URL-encoded string that contains the arguments and values of a CGI request.

CGI request. A request initiated by a browser for service by a Web server application.

Common Gateway Interface (CGI). A standard interface for supporting interaction between browsers and Web servers.

GET method. A CGI request that uses the URL to transmit the CGI query string.

HTML (Hypertext Markup Language). A standard language for representing text, formatting specifications, and hyperlinks.

HTML form. A part of an HTML document that contains input areas. Clicking on a submit button on a form initiates a CGI request.

HTTP (Hypertext Transfer Protocol). The standard for requesting and transmitting information between a browser and a Web server.

Hyperlink. A reference in an HTML document to another document or other object, possibly on another server.

Java servlet. A Java object that is embedded in a Web server and responds to CGI requests through its `doGet` and `doPost` methods.

MIME (Multipurpose Internet Mail Extension). A strategy for representing objects within e-mail that is also used by Web servers and browsers.

POST method. A CGI request that uses a two-step process to transmit the CGI query string and other information. In Unix, the query string is available in the standard input file of the CGI application.

Servlet. A CGI application that has continuous execution. It waits for a CGI request to arrive, processes it, then waits for the next request.

Tag. A markup notation within an HTML document. Each tag begins with a less than symbol (<), has a name and a sequence of attributes, and ends with a greater than symbol (>).

URL encoding. The translation of CGI query strings to replace characters with special meaning with their hexadecimal codes.

Web server. A program that listens for and services http requests, including CGI requests.

Exercises

1. Consult an HTML reference. For each type of tag below, list each attribute that can be included and give its purpose.

   a. Anchor tag

   b. Base tag

   c. Title tag

   d. Paragraph tag

   e. Meta tag

   f. Table tag

   g. Table row tag

   h. Table header tag

2. Search the Web for an HTML page that utilizes forms. Determine the method and action. List all variables appearing on the form and the values that are produced by clicking the Submit button.

3. What is a hidden input in an HTML form? Why might a designer designate an input as hidden? Give an example of an appropriate use of a hidden input in an HTML document.

4. Consult a reference on CGI programming. List all of the variables that are available to a CGI application.

5. What is the difference between a GET method and a POST method in an HTML form? Give two advantages of each method.

6. Write a CGI script that echoes the CGI query string so that it is displayed in the browser. Create an active URL in a Web page that references your CGI script.

7. What is MIME type `application/x-www-form-urlencoded`? How does it encode text strings? What special characters must be encoded in this type?

8. Create a simple text entry form using the `GET` method whose action is the CGI script of Exercise 6. Use this form to translate the following strings to MIME type `application/x-www-form-urlencoded`:

   a. `I've fallen! and "I can't get ^^"`

   b. `103 S. Main St.`

   c. `You & Bobbie need $2.00.`

9. Investigate the use of scripting languages for CGI programming on Windows NT or Windows 98. Find a public domain scripting tool, install it on a Web server, and write a script to echo form input, as in Exercise 6.

10. Design a new HTML page style for your own BigHit Video Web site. Create a new class derived from `HtmlWriter` that has `printHeader`, `printFooter`, and other methods to enforce your new style. Test this style by writing a simple program to generate a new version of the welcome page shown in Fig. 9.1.

11. Create a simple BigHit Video Web site using a Web server to which you have access. Modify the `bighit/index.html` page so that its base tag, entry link, and `mailto` link are correct for the site. Similarly modify `reservation.html`.

12. Modify the classes of package `dbjava.website` so that they correctly access the BigHit Video database on your local system. Install the Web site on that system.

13. Create a Web site to manage one of the applications for BigHit Video listed in Exercise 19 of Chapter 8. Using the classes of package `dbjava.website` as your guide, design pages and applications that present and collect the information required by the site.

14. Design a Web site for one of the student records database applications of Exercise 20 of Chapter 8. Using the classes of package `dbjava.website` as your guide, design pages and applications that present and collect the information required by the site.

Further Readings

The Web is the best source for information on HTML. The World Wide Web Consortium (W3C) has a variety of documents online at its Web site, http://www.w3.org. The proposal for HTML 4 can be found at http://www.w3.org/TR/REC-html40/. Some historical information is available from CERN at http://www.cern.ch.

Many good HTML books are available, including Musciano and Kennedy [MuKe98], which covers HTML 4. CGI programming details can be found in Guelich, Gundavaram, and Birznieks [GGB96] and in a variety of trade publications.

The emerging standard for Web content is XML, the Extended Markup Language. Significant efforts to use XML as a method of describing Web content and Web sites are ongoing in commercial and academic settings. The proceedings of the Very Large Database Conference [VLDB99] include several papers on XML, and the proceedings of the Workshop on the Web and Databases [ClMi99] are available on the Web.

The best references for extended HTML tag languages are found on the Web. Cold Fusion is described at Allaire's Web site at http://www.allaire.com, Active Server Pages (ASP) at the Microsoft developer site at http://developer.microsoft.com, and Java Server Pages at Sun Microsystems' Java site at http://java.sun.com.

In addition, many excellent books describe these techniques. Extensions to HTML for Cold Fusion are given in several books by Ben Forta, including [For98]. Active Server Pages are the subject of many books, including Federov et al [Fed98], Walther [Wal99], and Weissinger's Nutshell book [Wei99]. Java Server Pages (JSP) is a quickly emerging standard and is covered in books by Patzer et al [Pat99] and Fields and Kolb [FiKo00].

The use of Java to support Web sites is discussed in books on servlets, such as those by Hunter and Crawford [HuCR98], Callaway [Cal99], and Asbury and Weiner [AsWe99].

10

Enhancing Object-Oriented Applications with JDBC

CHAPTER OBJECTIVES

In this chapter, you will learn:

- Some of the advanced features of JDBC 2.0
- Java's strategies for managing transactions, including distributed transactions
- Ways to interact with databases using prepared statements in Java
- The basic operations needed to support user interfaces
- The purposes and capabilities of updatable cursors in JDBC
- Ways to create Web-based user interfaces with Java servlets
- Ways to handle multiple user interactions with a single servlet

*T*his chapter details how information-rich, object-oriented applications should be designed and how they may be packaged and deployed. The object-oriented model focuses on the development of class libraries. An application program is a thin layer built on top of these libraries, either as a user interface or as a simple manipulation of objects. The proper packaging of class libraries must make it easy to create, maintain, and execute the application programs. In this environment, an application program represents the integration of multiple components, often spread across multiple computers.

The Java language and its packages and class libraries have standardized more of the application environment than any other language has. There are standard methods of accessing databases, of sharing objects and their methods in a distributed execution environment, and of deploying objects and methods in a client-server environment. This chapter, together with Chapter 16, describes some of the capabilities of this rapidly evolving system as they existed at the time of publication.

Transactions in JDBC

10.1

A *transaction* in a database is a collection of queries and updates that execute as a single unit. In particular, either all of the updates succeed fully or none of them does. Transactions are covered in detail in Chapter 14. For the purposes of this section, it is sufficient to understand that one or more updates to a database are made within a single transaction. When a database client is finished with a collection of updates, it requests that the transaction be *committed* and the updates made permanent. Alternatively, the client can request that the transaction be *rolled back* and all updated entities returned to the values they had before the transaction began.

JDBC provides two modes of executing transactions, just as SQL does. In the *autocommit mode*, each SQL statement is executed as a single transaction. In the *explicit commit mode*, commit and rollback methods can be used with a collection of SQL statements.

In the autocommit mode, a transaction starts when a statement is executed. The transaction is committed when all of its result sets and update counts have been retrieved, or when the statement is explicitly closed. In most cases, all of the result sets and update counts are retrieved by the JDBC package and the transaction is committed immediately after the statement's execution. It is possible, however, that a JDBC package may defer committing the transaction until the results have been retrieved by the application.

To allow multiple SQL statements to execute as a single transaction, the autocommit mode can be turned off by calling method `Connection. setAutoCommit(false)`. A new transaction is started with the execution of the next SQL statement. This transaction is not committed until the `commit` method is called or the JDBC `Connection` object is closed.

Once a program enters a non-autocommit transaction, two results are possible: the transaction may be committed or it may be aborted. Calling the `commit` method makes all changes permanent and releases any locks currently held by the `Connection`. Calling the `rollback` method aborts the transaction; all changes are then dropped and database locks released.

In the `createPayStatements` example of Fig. 8.12, we would like to make sure that the time cards that are used to create the pay statements are the same ones that are marked as paid. When this operation is executed as autocommit transactions, a new time card could potentially be entered between the execution of the insert and update statements. If so, the new time card will be marked as paid, even though it was not used to create the pay statement. The proper way to avoid this error is to process the insert and the update statements as a single transaction. Figure 10.1 shows the modified body of `createPayStatements`, which now guarantees that the time cards that are used to create the pay statements are exactly the ones marked as paid.

The effect of putting the insert and update statements into a transaction can be seen by running a Java program, such as `dbjava.samples. ProcessPayStatements`, that connects to an Access database. Try using a Java

```
 1 try {
 2   bigHitDB.Connection.setAutoCommit(false);
 3   numPayStatements = stmt.executeUpdate(insertSQL);
 4   numTimeCards = stmt.executeUpdate(updateTimeCardSQL);
 5   System.out.println("numstmts "+numPayStatements
 6       +" time cards "+numTimeCards);
 7   bigHitDB.Connection.commit();
 8 } catch (SQLException e) {
 9   bigHitDB.Connection.rollback();
10   return false;
11 }
```

FIGURE 10.1 _____

Using a transaction to ensure the correctness of the pay statements and time cards

debugger to stop the program inside the transaction. If you open the same database in Access, you will see no change in the tables during the transaction. The tables can be opened, but the database server will block an attempt to modify either table. After the commit operation, you can see the changes by opening the tables in Access. You may, however, see some anomalous behavior when using Microsoft Access.

JDBC also supports management of transaction conflicts through the method `setIsolationLevel`. Five levels of isolation exist. The lowest level has no support for transactions, and hence no checking for conflicts between concurrent processes. The restrictions placed on interactions between transactions increase at each higher level. The highest level supports no interactions between transactions. Typically, the higher the isolation level, the slower the execution of the transaction. The transaction isolation levels for JDBC are as follows:

1. `TRANSACTION_NONE`. There is no support for transactions at all.
2. `TRANSACTION_READ_UNCOMMITTED`. Dirty, nonrepeatable, and phantom reads can occur.
3. `TRANSACTION_READ_COMMITTED`. Dirty reads are prevented, but nonrepeatable and phantom reads can occur.
4. `TRANSACTION_REPEATABLE_READ`. Dirty and nonrepeatable reads are prevented, but phantom reads can occur.
5. `TRANSACTION_SERIALIZABLE`. Dirty, nonrepeatable, and phantom reads are prevented.

When a new connection is created, its isolation level depends on the driver, which normally sets the default for the database. To change the isolation level for a transaction, `setIsolationLevel` must be called before the execution of the first statement of the transaction. It should be reset after the transaction is committed or aborted.

Prepared Statements and Callable Statements

10.2 Interface `PreparedStatement` allows Java programmers to take advantage of the ability of many databases to precompile (prepare) parameterized SQL statements. These prepared statements can then be executed many times with different parameter substitutions. The result is both more efficient to execute (because it is compiled only once) and easier to use (because it contains parameters).

Consider, for example, an application that needs to update the grades of several students for different assignments. The following code creates a statement to be used for the update queries:

```
PreparedStatement pstmt = connection.prepareStatement(
    "update grades set points=? where id=? and assignmentId=?");
```

To use `pstmt` for an update, it is necessary to specify the values of the three parameters, identified in the query by the question marks (**?**). The following code will change the points to 75 for student 12345 on assignment 1:

```
pstmt.setInt(1,75);// first parameter is number of points
pstmt.setInt(2,12345); // second parameter is student ID
pstmt.setInt(3,1); // third parameter is assignment ID
rowcount = pstmt.executeUpdate();
```

The parameters are identified by position: first, second, and third. You may have noticed that the SQL statement parameter to `executeUpdate` has disappeared. The SQL statement is specified when the `PreparedStatement` object is constructed and cannot be changed. Once a parameter has been set, it can be used for multiple statements. Hence changing the points for another student on the same assignment will require replacing only parameters 1 and 2.

Interface `PreparedStatement` extends `Statement` and adds new versions of methods `executeQuery`, `executeUpdate`, and `execute` that have no parameters. Calls to `Statement` execute methods for a `PreparedStatement` object result in an `SQLException`.

Interface `CallableStatement` extends `PreparedStatement` to support calls to SQL procedures. It allows parameters to be specified for the inputs and outputs of stored procedures. The use of `CallableStatement` is much like that of `PreparedStatement`, with `setXXX` methods being used to set the parameters. A major difference is its support for output and input/output parameters. Parameters to a `PreparedStatement` can consist of only inputs.

Advanced Features of JDBC

10.3 The capabilities of JDBC 1.0, as described in Chapters 8 and 9, are very limited compared with those of a fully featured database language like Oracle PL/SQL. The second release of the JDBC API, JDBC 2.0, is a significant extension that makes it comparable to other fully featured database languages. JDBC 2.0 is a part of the Java 1.2 (or Java 2) release that is now the accepted version of Java.

A major improvement of JDBC relates to the result sets. A JDBC 1.0 `ResultSet` object allows a user to iterate through its rows one at a time. In JDBC 2.0, result sets support forward and backward iteration. In addition, a JDBC 2.0 result set can be used to modify database tables.

JDBC now offers enhanced support for SQL3 data types, including BLOB (binary large object), CLOB (character large object), arrays, and structured types. Likewise, it now supports storing serialized Java objects in a database, and batch execution of update statements.

Several Java APIs are important for JDBC, including the Java Transaction Service (JTS), the Java Naming and Directory Interface (JNDI), JavaBeans, and Enterprise JavaBeans (EJB).

A new package, `javax.sql`, includes a set of standard extensions that can be implemented by particular JDBC packages. These extensions include support for sharing database connections and treating connections as JavaBeans.

Interface `javax.sql.RowSet` is an extension to `ResultSet` that encapsulates a set of rows. It may or may not maintain an open database connection. The `RowSet` interface can accommodate a variety of implementations, including class `CachedRowSet`, which loads the data from a `ResultSet` into a local cache that is independent of the database connection and statement that were used to fetch the data. Once a `CachedRowSet` object has been created and loaded with data, it can be used independently of the result set that was used to fill it.

Result Sets in JDBC 2.0

10.4

The result of the execution of a select query in the Oracle PL/SQL database language can be returned as a *cursor* with operations to iterate forward or backward, to move to the first or last row, to update fields of the associated row, and to insert and delete rows. This option is particularly useful when implementing user interfaces. A user interface typically allows a user to perform the actions listed in Table 10.1.

In this section, we discuss how all of these operations can be implemented in JDBC 2.0 using an example interface from the BigHit Video application. Effective

TABLE 10.1

Actions typically performed with user interface

1. Specify a list of objects using some type of filter and ordering
2. Extract the values of the fields of one or more objects for display in the interface
3. Move forward and backward in the list of objects
4. Move directly to an object by its index in the list
5. Change the displayed values and update the corresponding object in the database
6. Delete an object from the database
7. Insert a new object into the database

implementations of the operations of Table 10.1 require objects that can do the following:

1. Execute a select statement and maintain an active list, or cursor, of the selected objects

2. Maintain a position in the cursor that selects a single object and fetch the field values of that object

3. Move the cursor position forward and backward by a single object

4. Move the cursor position to a specific object identified by its index in the list

5. Update the database object at the current cursor position

6. Delete the selected object from the database and from the cursor

7. Use the cursor to create a new object in the database and in the cursor

The following sections describe, with examples, how JDBC result sets can be used to accomplish all of these requirements. The user interface shown in Fig. 10.2 has all of the capabilities of Table 10.1. The labels identify which operations are associated with each user interface component.

The set of operations listed in Table 10.1 can be encapsulated in class `dbjava.website.CustomerEditor`, as shown in Fig. 10.3. The implementations of the operations are given in the next sections. The state of the edit form is maintained in the JDBC `Connection`, `Statement`, and `ResultSet` objects.

10.4.1   Types and Concurrency for Result Sets

Three new types of result sets are distinguished by their *scrolling* capabilities and update sensitivity: forward-only, scroll-sensitive, and scroll-insensitive. A forward-only result set allows scrolling in the forward direction only. The other two types support arbitrary scrolling, including absolute and relative positioning, as described in Section 10.4.3. Scrollable result sets differ in whether the values in the result set are sensitive to updates made while the result set is open.

A *scroll-insensitive result set* provides a static view of the underlying data. The membership, order, and column values of rows are fixed when the select statement is executed. Updates made by other users while the result set is open are not visible to the result set.

A *scroll-sensitive result set* provides a view of the underlying data that changes dynamically. Updates to fields of rows by other users that are part of the result set are visible while the result is open. The membership and the ordering of the rows may or may not change, depending on the implementation of the JDBC package.

Two concurrency types are possible with result sets: read-only and updatable. The level of concurrency allowed for *updatable result sets* depends on the transaction mode of the `Statement`, as described in Section 10.1.

The operations of Table 10.1 require a result set that is scroll-sensitive and updatable, so that updates can be made and their results will be visible to the user interface.

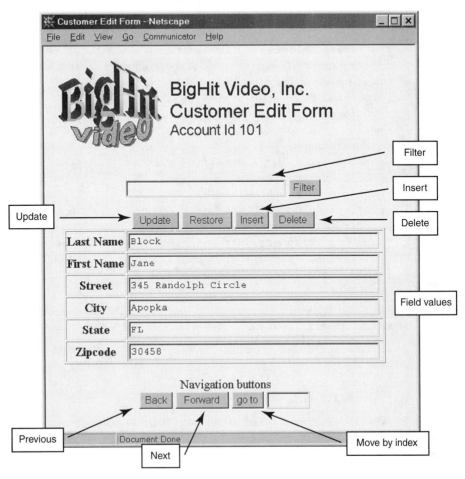

FIGURE 10.2 _____
User interface for editing the `Customer` *table labeled to show the operations associated with interface components*

10.4.2   Creating Result Sets with Special Properties

A `ResultSet` object is strongly associated with the `Statement` that was used to construct it. As we saw in Chapter 8, each time a `Statement` is used in the execution of an SQL statement, the `ResultSet` from the previous execution is closed and its values are no longer available. It is in the creation of the `Statement` that special properties are specified.

A `Statement` with default properties is created in JDBC 2.0 exactly as it was in JDBC 1.0. The `ResultSet` object that is returned from `executeQuery` using the `Statement` acts just like a JDBC 1.0 `ResultSet`. The following code

```
 1 public class CustomerEditor { // members and method headers
only
 2 // services for editing customers
 3   // members to maintain database connection and result set
 4   protected Connection conn = null;
 5   protected Statement stmt = null;
 6   protected ResultSet result = null;
 7   public CustomerEditor ();
 8   // operations
 9   public void selectRows(String filter);    // operation 1
10   public Customer getCustomer ();           // operation 2
11   public void moveForward();                // operation 3
12   public void moveBackward();               // operation 3
13   public void moveAbsolute(int index);      // operation 4
14   public void update(Customer customer);    // operation 5
15   public void delete(int accountId);        // operation 6
16   public void insert(Customer customer);    // operation 7
17 }
```

FIGURE 10.3 _____

A sketch of class CustomerEditor *with methods to implement the operations of Table 10.1*

creates a Statement object from a database connection and uses it to create a ResultSet object:

```
Statement stmt = connection.createStatement();
ResultSet result = stmt.executeQuery(selectStatement);
```

JDBC 2.0 adds additional createStatement methods with parameters that specify how the result sets can be scrolled and updated. The following code creates a scroll-sensitive, updatable result set for use in the application given in Fig 10.2. The first two lines are part of the constructor of class CustomerEditor.

```
Statement stmt = connection.createStatement(
    ResultSet.TYPE_SCROLL_SENSITIVE,
ResultSet.CONCUR_UPDATABLE);
ResultSet result = stmt.executeQuery(selectStatement);
```

The parameters for createStatement have values that are defined in class ResultSet:

```
ResultSet.TYPE_FORWARD_ONLY
ResultSet.TYPE_SCROLL_INSENSITIVE
ResultSet.TYPE_SCROLL_SENSITIVE
ResultSet.CONCUR_READ_ONLY
ResultSet.CONCUR_UPDATABLE
```

The result set with the filter shown in the Fig. 10.2 and ordered by the
`accountId` field (operation 1 of Table 10.1) is created by adding the filter expression
as the **where** clause of a select statement:

select * from Customer **where** state = 'FL' **order by** accountId

Of course, a result set can be created from any select statement. This example here
is a very simple case.

When the user enters a new filter value and clicks the Filter button, the application
must call `CustomerEditor.selectRows`, as shown in lines 2–10 of Fig.
10.4, to create a new select statement and a new result set. The previous result set
is closed (line 7) and the `Statement` is used to create a new result set (line 8).
Notice that all of the methods of class `CustomerEditor` are declared as throwing
an `SQLException`, a detail that was omitted from Fig. 10.3 for the sake of
brevity.

Extracting values from the result set for display in the form (operation 2 of
Table 10.1) is the same in JDBC 2.0 as it was in JDBC 1.0. Figure 10.5 includes a
constructor for class `Customer` that initializes the fields from a result set. Method
`getCustomer` can construct a `Customer` from the current position in the result
set.

```
1 public class CustomerEditor { // some of the methods
2    public void selectRows(String filter) throws SQLException {
3       // create a new result set and position it on the first row
4       selectStatement = "select * from Customer";
5       if (filter!=null) selectStatement += (" where "+filter);
6       selectStatement += " order by accountId";
7       result.close(); // close the previous result set
8       result = stmt.executeQuery(selectStatement);
9       result.first();
10   }
11   public Customer getCustomer () throws SQLException {
12      return new Customer(result); // load from cursor
13   }
14   public void moveForward() throws SQLException {
15      if (!result.next()) result.last();
16   }
17   public void moveAbsolute(int index) throws SQLException {
18      if (!result.absolute(index)) result.last();
19   }
20 }
```

FIGURE 10.4 ───

Partial definition of class `CustomerEditor` *with methods* `selectRows`, `getCustomer`,
`moveForward`, *and* `moveAbsolute`

```
 1 class Customer { // some of the methods
 2   public Customer(ResultSet result) {
 3     try {
 4       accountId = result.getString("accountId");
 5       lastName = result.getString("lastName");
 6       firstName = result.getString("firstName");
 7       street = result.getString("street");
 8       city = result.getString("city");
 9       state = result.getString("state");
10       zipcode = result.getString("zipcode");
11     } catch (SQLException e) {// not able to get all fields
12       accountId = null;
13     }
14   }
15   public void update (ResultSet result)
16     // transfer field values from customer to result
17       throws SQLException {
18     result.updateString("accountId", accountId);
19     result.updateString("lastName", lastName);
20     result.updateString("firstName", firstName);
21     result.updateString("street", street);
22     result.updateString("city", city);
23     result.updateString("state", state);
24     result.updateString("zipcode", zipcode);
25   }
26 }
```

FIGURE 10.5 _____

Partial implementation of class Customer *including a constructor with a*
ResultSet *parameter and an* update *method*

The first method of the ResultSet moves the cursor position to the first row. To create a Customer object representing the first row of the cursor, we simply write the following code:

```
result.first();
Customer customer = getCustomer();
```

You may have noticed in the code of Fig. 10.5 that once the cursor position has been established, values are extracted from the result set with no reference to the position. The Customer constructor simply gets the values from the fields at the current position of the result set.

In Section 9.3, we saw that a major problem with the JDBC 1.0 result sets is that an initial call to next is required to determine whether a result set has any rows. This problem makes it difficult to design reliable and simple methods to use result sets. The cursor is initially positioned before the first row, and a call to next positions it on the first row. In JDBC 1.0, there is no way to return the cursor to its initial position. In contrast, JDBC 2.0 includes methods `beforeFirst` to put the cursor back and `afterLast` to position it after the last row, just the same as if `next` was called with the cursor on the last row. Methods `isFirst`, `isLast`, `isBeforeFirst`, and `isAfterLast` test for the cursor positions.

10.4.3   Scrolling with Result Sets

The `ResultSet` interface includes methods `next`, `previous`, `first`, and `last` to control the cursor position within the result set. The implementation of the move-forward operation (operation 3 of Table 10.1) appears in lines 14–16 of Fig. 10.4. This code moves the cursor to the last row if the cursor cannot be advanced by the `next` method. The move-backward operation (operation 4 of Table 10.1) is implemented similarly using the `previous` and `first` methods.

Moving to a specific row by index (operation 5 of Table 10.1) is accomplished with method `absolute`, as shown in lines 17–19 of Fig. 10.4.

JDBC also includes method `relative`, which moves a specified number of rows forward with a positive argument and backward with a negative argument.

10.4.4   Modifying the Database with Result Sets

A variety of update methods are used to modify the values of fields in a result set. For instance, we can change the `lastName` field of the current customer to "Jones" with method `updateString`:

```
result.updateString("lastName","Jones");
```

The `update` method of class `Customer` (lines 15–25 of Fig. 10.5) uses calls on `updateString` to transfer the fields of a `Customer` into the fields of a `ResultSet`.

Updating the result set does not modify the database record associated with the cursor position (operation 5 of Table 10.1). Method `updateRow` must be called to update the database with the new contents of the current row. The full implementation of the `update` method of class `CustomerEditor` is given in lines 2–8 of Fig. 10.6. Its parameter contains the values of all fields, whether they've been changed or not. The method first checks (lines 3–5) to make sure the `accountId` field of the parameter is the same as that of the current row of the result set. The method does not allow a user to change the `accountId` of a customer, thereby protecting the primary key of the table. The fields of the result set are modified and the row updated by lines 6 and 7.

To delete an object associated with the result set (operation 6 of Table 10.1), simply position the cursor and call `deleteRow`. The full implementation of the `delete` method of class `CustomerEditor` is given in lines 9–15 of Fig. 10.6.

Inserting a new row (operation 7 of Table 10.1) is only a little more complicated. Each updatable result set has a special *insert row* that is used to create a new row. The first step in insertion is moving the cursor to the insert row. Calls to the update methods then initialize the fields of the insert row. Finally, the `insertRow` method is called to add a new row to the database with those values. The `insert`

```
 1 public class CustomerEditor { // some of the methods
 2   public void update(Customer customer) throws SQLException {
 3       if (customer.accountId!=result.getInt("accountId")) {
 4         return; // no update allowed if accountIds don't match
 5       }
 6     customer.update(result);
 7     result.updateRow();
 8   }
 9 public void delete(int accountId) throws SQLException {
10       if (accountId!=result.getInt("accountId")) {
11         // cannot delete if accountIds don't match
12         throw new SQLException("accountId does not match delete ");
13       }
14     result.deleteRow();
15   }
16   public void insert(Customer customer) throws SQLException
17     result.moveToInsertRow(); //exception if not updatable
18     customer.update(result);
19     result.insertRow(); // exception if insert fails
20   }
21 }
```

FIGURE 10.6 _____

Methods update, delete, *and* insert *and the private method* updateResultSet *of class* CustomerEditor

method of class `CustomerService` (lines 16–20 of Fig. 10.6) inserts a new row into the `Customer` table of the database. An exception will be thrown if the result set is not updatable, if any of the named fields are not in the result set, or if the insert fails. Method `moveToRememberedRow` can be called to move the cursor back to the row it was on before the call to `moveToInsertRow`.

An insert, update, or delete operation on a result set always affects the database. Whether the result set is affected by updates from other sessions depends on the type of its statement. If the statement was created with `TYPE_SCROLL_INSENSITIVE`, it will not be affected by database modifications that are not applied directly to the result set. In this case, inconsistencies may arise between the result set and the database that can be resolved only by closing and recreating the result set.

Integrating Result Sets and HTML Forms

10.5 The user interface of Fig. 10.2 is an HTML form displayed in a browser. In Chapter 9, we saw that HTML forms interact with servers through the CGI protocol. Each CGI request is sent to a Web server and processed by some CGI program.

The strategy for forms processing discussed in Chapter 9 is a stateless approach. That is, the program that handles a CGI request does not maintain any state information between one request and the next. Consequently, the CGI program starts over from scratch with each new request.

The strategy for processing form actions described in Section 10.4 must be implemented by a program that maintains significant state information between requests. The result set is created when the form is displayed and its value (the *state* of the result set) is maintained for use in servicing user actions. The servlet approach to processing CGI requests, as discussed in Section 9.5, uses a continuously running program to service multiple requests. This approach can be used to create the servlet program needed to service the application.

10.5.1   A Servlet to Process Customer Edits

Figure 10.7 shows a partial implementation of class `CustomerServlet` that manages the form of Fig. 10.2. It creates a `CustomerEditor` object, `customerEditor`, when it is initialized (line 8) and uses that same object for every CGI request. The `doPost` method (lines 16–45) sets up the output stream (lines 20–22) and fetches the `action` parameter (lines 25–29). Lines 31–40 call methods of the `CustomerEditor` object to carry out the actions required to service the form.

```
1 public class CustomerServlet extends HttpServlet {
2     // members that persist between service requests
3     CustomerEditor customerEditor = null;
4     // methods
5     public void init(ServletConfig config)
6         throws UnavailableException, ServletException {
7       super.init(config);
8       customerEditor = new CustomerEditor ();
9     // initialize members here!
10    }
11    public void doGet(HttpServletRequest req,
12        HttpServletResponse res)
13        throws IOException , ServletException {
14      doPost(req, res);
15    }
16    public void doPost(HttpServletRequest request,
17        HttpServletResponse response)
18        throws IOException, ServletException {
19      // initialize response with header and make HtmlWriter
20      response.setContentType("text/html");
21      PrintWriter out = response.getWriter();
```

FIGURE 10.7 ⎯⎯⎯⎯⎯⎯⎯⎯⎯⎯⎯⎯⎯⎯⎯⎯⎯⎯⎯⎯⎯⎯⎯⎯⎯⎯⎯⎯⎯⎯⎯⎯⎯⎯⎯⎯

Partial implementation of class `CustomerServlet` *with the* `doPost` *method (continues)*

```
22      HtmlWriter htmlOut = new BigHitHtmlWriter(out, true);
23      // get action parameter
24      String action = request.getParameter("action");
25      if (action==null) {// no value for action parameter
26        htmlOut.printErrorPage("No action given");
27        out.close();
28        return;
29      }
30      try {
31        if (action.equals("Forward")) {
32          customerEditor.moveForward();
33        } else if (action.equals("Update")) {
34          customerEditor.update(new Customer(req));
35        } else if (action.equals("Backward")) {
36          customerEditor.moveBackward();
37        } else { // other actions follow
38        }
39        // return new page after action is complete
40        refreshPage(htmlOut);
41      } catch (SQLException e) {
42        htmlOut.printSimplePage("failure of action "+action,null);
43      }
44      out.close();
45    }
46    // other methods shown without implementation
47    public void refreshPage(HtmlWriter out) {
48    public void printEditPage(Customer customer, HtmlWriter out) {
49 }
```

FIGURE 10.7 _____
continued

The doPost method responds to the Forward request (lines 31–32) by calling customerEditor.moveForward to select a new row and refreshPage (line 40) to regenerate the HTML form. The other actions are similar to those described in Section 10.2.

This development gives us a start on maintaining the *context* for the application. To create a robust application, we must provide a way to handle the case when more than one user is interacting with the same Web server, and hence the same servlet object. Each user should interact in the context of his or her own individual information. The implementation of Fig. 10.7 uses a single context—that is, a single CustomerEditor object—for all users, however. Section 10.5.2 demonstrates how to keep track of multiple contexts—one for each user.

10.5.2   Context Tracking with Servlet Sessions

Fortunately, class `HttpServlet` has the capability of maintaining context through its *session-tracking* methods. The servlet manager allows the servlet to create an `HttpSession` object for each user session. The servlet manager keeps track of the session objects. Each session object maintains a list of named objects. Methods `putValue` and `getValue` are used to save and restore objects from this list. Figure 10.8 shows how session tracking can be used to maintain the contexts of multiple users. The changes from Fig. 10.7 are the addition of method `restoreContext` (lines 6–17), the removal of the initialization of `customerEditor` in `init` (lines 3–5), and the call to `restoreContext` in `doPost` (line 21).

Method `restoreContext` (lines 6–17) is responsible for restoring the values of the context variable (`CustomerEditor`) from a previous session. If there was no previous session, `restoreContext` creates a session object, creates a new context object, and stores the context object in the session object. The call to

```
1 class MultiCustomerServlet extends javax.servlet.http.HttpServlet {
2    CustomerEditor customerEditor = null;
3    public void init (ServletConfig conf) throws ServletException {
4       super.init();
5    }
6    public Boolean restoreContext (HttpServletRequest request) {
7       HttpSession session = request.getSession(true);
8       if (session.isNew()) { // new session for this user
9          customerEditor = new CustomerEditor();
10         // store context objects in new session
11            session.putValue("customerEditor", customerEditor);
12      } else { // create new context
13         // restore context objects from session
14            customerEditor=
15               (customerEditor) session.getValue("customerEditor");
16      }
17   }
18   public void doPost(HttpServletRequest request,
19         HttpServletResponse response)
20         throws IOException , ServletException {
21      restoreContext(request);
22      // rest of method as in Fig. 10.7
23   }
24 }
```

FIGURE 10.8 _____

Partial implementation of class `MultiCustomerServlet` *showing the use of session tracking to maintain context*

`getSession` (line 7) returns the stored session object associated with the request, if one has been created; otherwise, it creates a new session. A call with `false` as its argument returns `null` if no session has been created for this user.

If the session returned in line 7 is a new session, a new context must be created and stored in the session. Line 9 creates a new `CustomerEditor` object, to be used as the context of this new session. Because a new session has been created, we need only store the new object in the session (line 11).

If the call on line 7 returns a previously created session object, this user has an existing context that we can use. The servlet gets the stored object from the session object and stores it in the context variable (lines 14 and 15). Now the context object has been restored.

The new version of method `doPost` (lines 18–23) differs from that of Fig. 10.7 only in line 21, where it calls `restoreContext`. Once the value of member `customerEditor` has been restored, the code proceeds exactly as it did when there was only one value. No further change is required!

The preceding discussion and example have prepared us for implementing database applications, but the presentation is not truly complete. A professional application must be constructed to emphasize reliability and error management. It must use a specific security model that incorporates login security and encryption. It must manage session inactivity and time-out situations. A major issue in our example application is how to deal with the inherent limitations of HTML as a user interface. It is likely that some use of Java applets, JavaScript, or dynamic HTML will be required to create an interface that is thoroughly reliable from the user's perspective.

As mentioned earlier, the rule of 90/10 applies to software development. It states that 90% of the functionality is accomplished with 10% of the code or, alternatively, that 10% of the behavior requires 90% of the work. Error processing is part of this recalcitrant 10%. To modify an application that works correctly with correct input so that it works accurately and reliably all of the time often takes 10 times longer than the original development.

Chapter Summary

Database applications can be expected to involve multiple databases, multiple computers, and multiple software packages. The Java language has a large collection of tools to make object-oriented database applications easier to write and maintain.

JDBC supports a transaction mechanism to provide the ability to execute a sequence of SQL statements as a single unit. JDBC defines several levels of transaction isolation. Not all database systems support all of these levels. Transactions are covered in detail in Chapter 14.

JDBC 2.0 is a part of Java 2 and offers many extensions that make database programming more straightforward. These extensions include support for SQL3 data types, batch updates, and storage of Java objects in relational databases. The standard extensions, found in package `javax.sql`, include support for caching result sets and sharing database connections.

The result sets created with JDBC 2.0 have scrolling and update capabilities that were missing from those available in JDBC 1.0. These features are crucial to implementing user interfaces and other applications that need database cursors. The scrolling and update capabilities of a result set are specified in the creation of the `Statement` object that produces the result set.

Java servlets provide for a close integration of database applications and Web servers. Each servlet class can have a session object associated with each Web user. The session object can be used to store context (state) information associated with the user's interaction.

Key Terms

Autocommit mode. A mode of transaction processing in which each SQL statement is executed as a single transaction.

Context. Information that is maintained by a server to keep track of the interaction of a single client.

Cursor. A reference to a specific collection of rows in a database that includes a pointer to one row. The pointer can be moved to any row. A cursor can be used to update or delete the current row or to insert a new row in the collection.

Explicit commit mode. A mode of transaction processing in which a transaction is created by the execution of an SQL statement and terminated by an explicit commit or rollback operation.

RowSet. A JDBC extension to `ResultSet` that allows values to be stored in the Java client without requiring the maintenance of a database connection.

Scroll-insensitive result set. A JDBC cursor that provides a static view of the contents of its collection of rows. The values seen by the cursor change only as a result of changes that are applied directly to the cursor.

Scroll-sensitive result set. A JDBC cursor whose collection of rows is sensitive to updates by other users.

Scrolling. Moving the pointer of a cursor or result set so that it points to a different row.

Session tracking. The process of keeping track of the users of a Web site. Context information can be stored in a session object to maintain servlet information.

Transaction. A collection of database queries and updates that execute as a single unit. In particular, either all of the updates succeed fully or none of them does.

Updatable result set. A JDBC cursor that can be used to update its collection of rows in the database.

Exercises

1. What is the difference between the autocommit and explicit commit modes of transaction processing?

2. What is the symbol used to represent input parameters in a Java `PreparedStatement`? What methods can be used to set the values of these parameters?

3. Which methods in JDBC 2.0 perform the following actions?

    a. Position the cursor at the first row of a result set

    b. Create a scroll-sensitive result set

    c. Move the cursor to the insert row

    d. Update the database from the cursor

    e. Set the value of a field of the current row

    f. Delete a row of the database using a result set

4. What is meant by context tracking for servlets? What kind of objects can be stored in a servlet context? What method is used to access the context of a CGI request? What method is used to store an object in the context?

5. Using the classes `CustomerEditor` and `CustomerServlet` as a guide, create a Web site that supports the editing of the Movie table of the BigHit Video database.

6. Using the classes `CustomerEditor` and `CustomerServlet` as a guide, create an application that supports the videotape rental process, including checkout and check-in of rentals.

7. Choose a Web search engine and try to determine how it manages continuing sessions—that is, when a user enters a search parameter and receives a list of the first few hits. Clicking on Next brings up the next few hits. How does the server keep track of the subsequent pages?

Further Readings

The features of JDBC 2.0 can be found on Sun Microsystem's Java Web site (http://java.sun.com) in the description of the Java 2 development system. Further details on servlets, session tracking, and Java's transaction-handling capabilities can be found in [Cal99] and [HuCr98]. We take up the subject of using Java in distributed environments in Chapter 16.

Physical Characteristics of Databases

*T*his part addresses the ways that information is physically represented on computers. You will learn about the hardware characteristics that support the storage of information on disks and the operating system structures that allow applications to store and retrieve data from file systems. This part takes us from the hardware and operating system primitives through all of the steps required to efficiently represent and access relational data using files. Of particular importance are the strategies that execute relational operations quickly. Efficient execution of the join and selection relational operations requires efficient access to information by value. This efficiency is achieved through the indexing structures presented in Chapter 12.

Chapter 11 begins by presenting computer hardware, with an emphasis on those characteristics that slow access to data stored on disk drives. The description of methods of storing information in files takes us from the most primitive representation of primitive values as bit strings, through reading and writing individual values and records of values. We see how the performance of disk drives and input/output software must be exploited to create structures that achieve high performance in terms of data access. This information is covered in great detail to remove any mystery from the file performance issues. By the end of the chapter, you will know what is required to create efficient file structures that support reading, writing, and updating of information in relational database tables. The file structure definitions are accompanied by full implementations using the input/output capabilities of Java.

The main purpose of Chapter 12 is to demonstrate how we can improve the performance of value-based access to file structures. This consideration is particularly important for implementing databases, because value-based access is the basis for the selection and join operations. An example of accessing information by value is finding all rows of a table that have a specific value or a specific range of values for a field. You will learn the principles underlying the creation of index structures that provide a secondary organization to files. The focus is on the B+ tree index structure and hashing indexes.

11
Managing Information in Files

CHAPTER OBJECTIVES

In this chapter, you will learn:

- The importance of file structures to applications
- The hardware characteristics of secondary storage
- The ways that operating systems organize file systems
- The fundamentals of input and output in Java
- Several techniques for representing attribute values in files
- Ways to store and retrieve attribute values from files
- Strategies for manipulating files in Java
- Ways to use files to store and retrieve Java objects
- Ways to define and manipulate direct access files of application objects
- Ways to use files to represent relational database tables

*E*very application involves some input and output. Most rely on disk files to hold at least some of their input and output (I/O) data. The choice of data structures and algorithms to be used for I/O can be crucial to the development, maintenance, and execution cost of the application. Poor data structures lead to code that is difficult to develop and maintain as well as files that are impossible to manage. Poor algorithms can result in applications whose execution performance is dominated by the file I/O operations. The wrong algorithm can make an application 1,000 times slower than it might otherwise be. Put another way, some programs can be sped up 1,000 times by choosing the appropriate file algorithms.

This chapter introduces the notion of a *file structure*, which is a combination of data structures and algorithms used for application input and output. We will find that file structures can be systematically designed and implemented using object-oriented methods.

These methods produce file structures that are easy for application developers to use. At the same time, they support the flexibility required for performance tuning.

Hardware performance is of crucial importance to file structure design. In particular, the horribly slow performance of disks and their tremendously low cost necessitate the creation of file structures. Some applications require or generate so much data that all of the information cannot be stored in memory. Such applications must use disk files for temporary storage during their execution. Other applications may require information to persist between executions. Still other applications need to transfer information from one program to another. All of these situations require the ability to transfer information between memory and disk. Consequently, a major goal of this chapter is to understand how a DBMS can be implemented using file structures.

Another goal is to develop a detailed understanding of how to implement file systems in applications. To satisfy this goal, the book goes into great detail in presenting Java implementations of the file structure operations. This approach also serves to present a detailed example of the proper use of the Java programming language for the object-oriented modeling and implementation of complex data structures. Hence, we can accomplish three things:

- Provide a detailed understanding of the implementation of file structures.
- Ensure an understanding of the Java input/output classes.
- Develop a detailed example of object-oriented design and implementation of complex data structures.

Hardware Characteristics of File Systems

11.1

The economics and the physical limitations of computer hardware dictate that computers use a hierarchy of storage devices. The general rule is that the fastest device is both very expensive and very small. Table 11.1 provides a representation of the *storage hierarchy*.

TABLE 11.1

Storage hierarchy

Type of Storage	Capacity	Speed	Cost per Megabyte
Register	100 bytes	100 bytes per cycle	Unknown
Primary cache	10 KB	16 bytes per 4 cycles	Unknown
Secondary cache	1 MB	16 bytes per 8 cycles	$100/1 MB
Main memory	1,000 MB	64 bytes per 32 cycles	$100/50 MB
Disk drive	50 GB	1,024 bytes per 20 ms	$100/15,000 MB
Tape drive	100 GB per tape	10 megabytes per 1 s	$100/100,000 MB

The memory found within a CPU is organized as registers and cache. The registers of a CPU are very fast and have a fast interconnection to the functional units. In fact, the contents of multiple registers can be moved to multiple functional units in a single clock cycle. The *cache memory* is slower and larger, and it features a more limited interconnection. A single group of cache bytes may move to or from registers at one time.

The storage devices that are not part of the CPU are larger, less expensive, and slower, and they have a more restrictive interconnection than their CPU counterparts do. Secondary cache is typically 512 KB, and main memories are measured in the tens or hundreds of megabytes. Although prices change rapidly, 128 MB of memory cost less than $200 in 2000.

The next level in the storage hierarchy is the magnetic disk drive. Such devices have capacities in the tens of gigabytes, and many of them can be attached to a single computer. Disk drives are limited in their ability to randomly access data and are many times slower than memory. Removable devices like Zip and Jaz drives are still slower, and floppy disk drives are the slowest of all.

Magnetic tape systems have the largest capacity and lowest price per bit of all storage media. A $50 tape can hold 50 GB of data. Tape systems are often combined with automatic loading systems and have been configured with thousands of gigabytes online.

11.1.1   Disk Drives

Disks are constant-speed, rotating devices. Each *disk drive* has a rotating spindle that turns at constant speed. This spindle holds some number of platters, which contain magnetic material on both sides. Figure 11.1 shows a very simplified picture of a disk with four platters. The number of platters on a disk typically ranges from 1 to 12. Each surface is divided into some number of concentric circles, called *tracks*, that hold data. Although the disk in Fig. 11.1 has only five tracks, real disks have 15,000 or more tracks. Each surface is also divided into some number of pie-shaped pieces. The part of a track found within one pie slice is called a *sector*. A sector is the smallest unit of information on a disk that can be read or written.

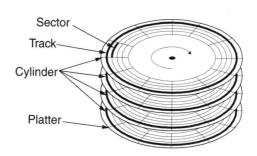

FIGURE 11.1 _____

Organization of a disk drive

Figure 11.1 shows 12 sectors in each track; a real disk may have 400 or more. Typically, a sector contains 512 bytes of data.

Reading from and writing to a disk are accomplished through the use of magnetic read/write *heads*. The usual configuration of disks includes one head per surface. The heads for the various surfaces are coordinated so that each one is the same distance from the edge of its platter. In other words, the heads for all surfaces are positioned over the same track. This collection of tracks, stacked one on top of the other, is called a *cylinder*. The disk in Fig. 11.1 has eight tracks per cylinder—two for each platter.

The performance of disk systems is determined by two factors: the *latency* and the *transfer rate*. The latency is the amount of time that elapses between the issuing of a request for a read or write operation and the arrival of the first byte of data. The transfer rate is the number of bytes per second that can be moved.

The latency of disk access also has two components. The first delay, called *seek time*, is caused by the movement of the heads to a position over the proper cylinder. The minimum seek time is the time needed to reach an adjacent track and is typically less than 1 millisecond. The maximum seek time occurs when the heads must move from one extreme position to the other extreme position on the disk surface. This time may be 20 milliseconds. After the heads are positioned, a *rotational delay* occurs as the system waits for the proper sector to be positioned under the heads. The average rotational delay is one-half rotation. Because disks rotate at 5,000 to 10,000 revolutions per minute, the average rotational delay is between 6 and 3 milliseconds.

The maximum transfer rate can be calculated from the rotational speed, the number of bytes per sector, and the number of sectors per track. That is, the complete contents of a single track can be transferred in one rotation. On modern drives, this transfer rate can be sustained by switching to another track in the same cylinder. This procedure requires changing the head that is processing the data, but not the head position.

Thus we can see that the ideal organization of data on a disk involves putting data that will be accessed together in the same cylinder and, if one cylinder is not enough, on cylinders that are close together. This organization minimizes the latency and maximizes the transfer rate for accessing those data.

Table 11.2 shows the capacity and performance characteristics of some recent disk drives.

11.1.2   Hardware Architecture of Storage Systems

The memory hierarchy is supported by a complex system architecture. Figure 11.2 shows a picture of a typical Pentium II mainboard. We will trace the movement of data from application to file through the various hardware components.

Suppose that a request to write data begins with the data in CPU registers. To be manipulated by the CPU, the data must be in a register. Results of CPU operations are written into the primary cache through the primary cache controller. As

TABLE 11.2

Capacity and performance characteristics of three disk drives

Characteristic	Seagate Cheetah 73	IBM Ultrastar 36	IBM Travelstar 6
Capacity	73,400 MB	35,400 MB	6,400 MB
Minimum (track-to-track) seek time	0.6 ms	0.3 ms	2.5 ms
Average seek time	6 ms	7.5 ms	13 ms
Spindle speed	10,000 rpm	7,200 rpm	4,200 rpm
Average rotational delay	3 ms	4 ms	7 ms
Maximum transfer rate	6 ms/track, or 24 KB/s	12 ms/track, or 2,796 bytes/ms	13.3 ms/track, or 2,419 bytes/ms
Bytes per sector	512	512	512
Sectors per track	423	381	268
Tracks per cylinder	24	20	4
Cylinders	14,100	17,494	11,648

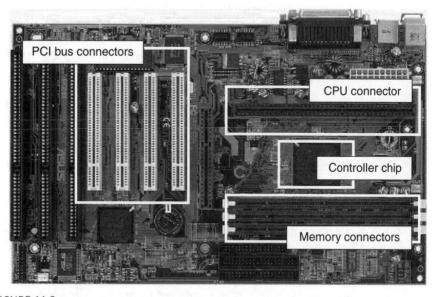

FIGURE 11.2

An ASUS P2B Pentium II mainboard

with all hardware *controllers*, a cache controller is a small, independent processor that controls the movement of data between two hardware devices. In this case, the cache controller arranges for data to move between the registers and the primary cache, and between the primary and secondary caches.

From the primary cache, the data move out through the CPU connector to the mainboard, where they arrive at the secondary cache controller. Data move from the secondary cache to *main memory* via a port of the main memory controller, which manages access to the main memory. The memory controller is also connected to the primary system bus—in this case, a PCI bus.

The data to be written are transferred from main memory to a small memory buffer in the I/O controller, which is also connected to the PCI bus. One way to connect disk drives is by plugging a SCSI (small computer system interface) controller into a PCI bus slot. A SCSI controller can control a number of peripheral devices, including disk, tape, and CD drives. It is connected via a cable to the disk drive. The data move from the SCSI controller to the cache memory of the disk controller, which is located inside the disk drive. Finally, the disk controller arranges for the data to be transferred to the appropriate location on the surface of the disk.

As you can see, the performance of a disk drive is greatly enhanced by the size of its cache memory. High-performance disks typically have 1 MB or more of cache memory.

11.1.3   Software Architecture of File Systems

The movement of data to and from disk drives is managed by a complex software architecture. Because each controller is a processor, it is supported by its own software. Each of the controller programs is quite simple and has a very restricted functionality. For instance, the controllers deal only with hardware addresses. The organization of disk storage into files is solely the responsibility of the operating system.

The file system treats each file as a sequence of bytes. The *file manager* is the component of the operating system that is responsible for creating and maintaining this view. A *file* is physically represented by a sequence of disk pages. Each *page* is a contiguous block of a particular number of disk sectors, typically two or four. In our example, we assume a sector size of 512 bytes and a page of two sectors, or 1,024 bytes.

The representation of a file includes a table that contains the hardware address of each disk page that is part of the file. Table 11.3 shows the mapping from pages to hardware address, where the hardware address is represented as the cylinder, track, and sector numbers of the first sector in the block. The first page of the file is given in the first table entry, the second page in the second entry, and so on. When an application program requests access to a particular byte of the file, the file manager calculates its page number by dividing the address by the page size. The physical address of the page containing the byte is shown in the corresponding entry in the table. As you can see, the file of Table 11.3 has its first three pages in contiguous sectors. Page 4 is close by, in another track of the same cylinder. The last two pages are close to each other but far away from the first five pages.

TABLE 11.3

A file access table for a file that contains six pages of two sectors each

Page Number	Disk Address (Cylinder, Track, Sector)	Range of Bytes
0	1200, 1, 98	0–1023
1	1200, 1, 100	1024–2047
2	1200, 1, 102	2048–3071
3	1200, 2, 56	3072–4095
4	490, 0, 0	4096–5119
5	490, 3, 8	5120–6143

A NOTE ON FRAGMENTATION OF DISK FILES

The pages of the file shown in Table 11.3 are spread out on the disk. It is possible to read the first three pages very quickly, because they are located on the same cylinder. Reading the fourth page, however, will take significantly longer. This file is considered *fragmented* because it is so spread out on the disk drive. Every operating system includes *defragmenting* software that can reorganize the physical layout of files so that the pages of a file will be close together. This software also puts the unallocated pages of the disk together. Running a defragmenter will improve sequential access to files.

To write a data item to a file, the application must first request that the operating system open the file. The open operation requires that an area of memory, often called a *file descriptor*, be allocated to the file. The file manager accesses the file and reads the file access table into the file descriptor. From this point forward, access to any page in the file can be accomplished by using the file access table to determine the physical address of the page and then issuing a single disk access to that page. The file descriptor also includes an *I/O buffer*, which is an area of memory that contains data that have been read from the file or will be written to the file.

The application requests a write operation to a file by specifying four items: the address of the file descriptor, the byte address of the location in the file, the memory address of the data item, and the number of bytes in the data item. This information is passed to the file manager for processing. For simplicity, let's assume that the data item to be written is smaller than one disk page and fits completely within a single page.

The file manager locates the disk page and checks whether its contents are already in memory. If they are not, the file manager issues a read request to get the page into memory. This read operation is required because the data item occupies only part of the page, but the disk page is the smallest amount of data that can be written. Hence, the contents of the page are loaded into the I/O buffer, and then the data item is copied into the appropriate place in the buffer.

Once the I/O buffer has been modified to contain the new disk page value, the file manager can initiate the page transfer by requesting that the I/O controller write the I/O buffer into the specific disk page. The journey of data that was described earlier causes the page contents to move to the I/O controller and then to the disk controller. Finally, the contents of the correct disk page are replaced by the new value.

In practice, the I/O buffers are usually contained within a *disk cache*—that is, an area of memory that the file manager uses to hold disk pages. This cache has the usual cache behavior. That is, pages are loaded into the cache and referenced from there. The cache pages are written back to the disk only when the cache is full and pages need to be freed. Hence, the actual contents of the disk drive are inconsistent with the operating system view of the file system while the computer is running.

Whenever the computer is shut off, all of the modified pages in the disk cache must be written (*flushed*) to the disk drive. If the system stops before the cache has been flushed, the disk drive will likely be in an inconsistent state. For this reason, most operating systems require an explicit shutdown command to halt the system properly. This effect of disk caching can usually be seen when a computer is rebooted after a crash or power failure. The disk analysis routine that runs as part of the boot process will find errors in the file system that were caused by the failure to flush the cache.

Applications reference files by name, and the file manager knows how to find the file associated with a particular name. In most file systems, files are organized in a hierarchical directory structure. Each directory is a file that contains the names and disk addresses of the files and directories that are contained within it. The name of a file includes a path that describes its location. The file manager knows how to find the root directory (named "/"). In a Microsoft Windows file system, each disk has its own root directory. The file manager uses the path to find the directory containing the file, and thus can find the file's disk address.

A NOTE ON INCREASING EFFICIENCY THROUGH BLOCK ACCESS

Most operating systems provide a mechanism for defining the *block size* of files—that is, the minimum amount of data that can be read or written in a single access. This size can often be specified for each disk drive individually. The block size can be as small as two sectors (1 KB). For applications that require high-performance access to large amounts of data, a disk might have a block size as large as one or more full tracks. On the Seagate Cheetah 73, one track is more than 20 KB. If we put eight disks together and treat them as a single file system, we might even have a block size of one track per disk—160 KB for the Seagate Cheetah.

When an application issues a request to read a particular sequence of bytes, the operating system will read the entire block that contains the bytes and store the block in an I/O buffer in memory. Subsequent requests to read bytes that are also located in the same block can be satisfied from the buffer with no access to the disk.

Manipulating Streams and Files in Java

| **11.2** | Java supports input and output through an extensive collection of classes found in package `java.io`. This collection includes classes for both formatted and unformatted I/O and for managing files. The base classes `InputStream` and `OutputStream` are extended in a variety of ways. Classes are defined for streams that are attached to files, to strings, and to byte arrays. Other classes provide buffer, filter, and pipe capabilities for streams, and one class even supports input from a sequence of streams. In addition, classes are defined to support binary I/O for Java primitive types (data streams) and sequential I/O for complex Java objects. These classes can be combined to create almost any functionality. For instance, we can create a file to support output of complex Java objects, or a stream that reads primitive Java types from a byte array. |

11.2.1   Java Classes for Input and Output

Java classifies I/O classes into those for input and those for output. The primary classes are the `Stream` classes, which support a view of files as simple *streams* of bytes. `Stream` classes support sequential input and output. Part of the definition of class `InputStream` is given in Fig. 11.3. The methods support reading a single byte or an array of bytes, and querying to see how many bytes are available to be read without blocking.

Like all other programming languages, Java supports three standard streams: standard input, standard output, and standard error. In Java, these streams are called `System.in`, `System.out`, and `System.err`, respectively. `System.in` is an `InputStream`, whereas `System.out` and `System.err` are `PrintStream`

```
public abstract class InputStream {
   public abstract int read() throws IOException;
      // read one byte
   public int read(byte b[]) throws IOException;
      // read an array of bytes, return the number read
   public long skip(long n) throws IOException;
      // skip forward n bytes
   public int available() throws IOException;
      // return number of bytes that can be read without blocking
   // other members
   };
```

FIGURE 11.3 _____

Some members of class `java.io.InputStream`

objects. Class `PrintStream` extends `OutputStream`* with a variety of methods
to output textual representations of Java data types. A `print` method and a `println`
method are defined with a parameter type of `boolean`, `int`, `char`, `long`, `float`,
`double`, `char[]`, `String`, and `Object`. In the case of printing an `Object`, the
`toString` method of the object is called to produce a textual representation of the
object.

In our first example, we will create a printed version of the contents of an
object. Figure 11.4 shows a `print` method for a simplified class `Movie` and a call
to method `Movie.print` to print an object onto standard output. For simplicity,
the class has been reduced to only three members. The `dateAcquired` and `rating`
members have been removed. The result of this call is as follows:

```
title    Animal House
movieId 189
genre    comedy
```

This representation of the `Movie` object is suitable for a person to read, but is not
the best representation for an application to read. In particular, the field names are

```java
public class Movie {
  // members
  String title; int movieId; String genre;
  // constructor
  public Movie (String t, int i, String g) {
    title = t; movieId = i; genre = g;
  }
  // print method
  public void print (PrintStream out) {
    out.println ("title    "+name);
    out.println ("movieId "+id);
    out.println ("genre    "+genre);
  }
  public static void main (String [] args) {
    // sample code to call the print method
    Movie m = new Movie (189, "Animal House", " comedy");
    m.print (System.out);
  }
};
```

FIGURE 11.4 _____

A method to print a `Movie` *object and a call on the method*

---

* Actually, `PrintStream` extends class `FilterOutputStream`, which extends
`OutputStream`. A `FilterOutputStream` object applies some filtering operations to
data before the data are inserted into the output stream. In the case of `PrintStream`, data
objects are filtered by translating them to text before they are written.

not required as long as the fields always appear in the same order. If we eliminate the headings, the output would look like

```
Animal House
189
comedy
```

We have produced a representation of the fields that can be used for output and for input. The fields are listed in a specific order, one per line. Another way to think of this representation is to say that the value of each field is delimited by an end-of-line character. If we look at this stream with the Unix od command,* we see the following:

```
0000000    416e    696d    616c    2048    6f75    7365    0a31    3839
           A  n     i  m    a  l       H    o  u    s  e    \n 1    8  9
0000010    0a63    6f6d    6564    790a
           \n c    o  m    e  d    y \n
```

The first line of each pair of lines gives the address of the first byte in hexadecimal and the hexadecimal representation of 16 bytes. The second line of each pair is the character representation. Notice the highlighted \n in the second line. It is the end-of-line character found at the end of the name field. Its hexadecimal representation, shown highlighted in the first line, is 0x0a. Also, notice that immediately after the end-of-line character the integer id field is represented as a three-character text field (highlighted) followed by another end-of-line character.

So far, we have produced a representation of Movie objects as byte streams that are suitable for reading. Although this representation has problems when a value contains an end-of-line character, we have just seen our first instance of representing objects using *delimited-text fields*. We will see other methods of representing objects later.

The memory representation of this object is different from its representation in a file. In memory, the object consists of a block of memory, as described below:

Offset	Field Name	Type	Representation
0	title	String	Reference to object
4	movieId	int	Four-byte integer
8	genre	String	Reference to object

The fields whose type is String are represented in memory as references to other objects. For our purposes, we can assume that such a reference is the address in

---

* The Unix od command and its MS-DOS equivalent debug display the binary contents of a file. This representation was created using the command od -A x -xc movie.txt. The options -xc specify that first the hexadecimal and then the character representation of the file are displayed. Each line is preceded by the address in hexadecimal (option -A x) and contains 16 bytes.

memory where the `String` object is found. In the preceding table, we assumed that this reference takes four bytes. If we copy this reference into an output stream, the value of the string will be lost. In our earlier example of a stream representation of a `Movie` object, we wrote the contents of the `String` object into the file. The information content of the `Movie` object is independent of the location in memory of the `name` and `genre` strings. Hence, we are striving to transfer the information content of the object—not its memory representation—into the output stream.

Our `read` method breaks up the stream into fields and builds a new memory representation of an object whose information content is the same as that of the one that was originally written into the stream. The exact details of the `read` method are deferred to the point where we have a few more input operations at our disposal.

11.2.2   Readers and Writers

The *Reader and Writer classes* support character input and output. The main difference between byte I/O and character I/O is the use of Unicode character encoding, which supports 16-bit characters and is suitable for internationalization of programs. With the `Reader` and `Writer` classes, text streams are made up of single-byte characters, but the I/O operations correctly handle the conversion between local encodings and the Unicode characters that are used in the Java `char` and `String` types in memory. These classes were introduced in Java 1.1 to supersede the `Stream` classes for text I/O. The `print` method given earlier, because it produces a text file, is more properly implemented using `PrintWriter` instead of `PrintStream`.

The `read` method for class `Movie` described earlier could be written more easily if we had a method that reads a line and returns it as a `String`. This method is available in class `BufferedReader`. The end-of-line character is not part of the string returned by `readLine`.

The `read` method, as given in lines 2–7 of Fig. 11.5, reads from a stream and sets the fields of the calling object to the values from the next three fields in the stream. The assignment of values to `name` and `genre` (lines 4 and 6, respectively) are reference assignments. The `readLine` method creates `String` objects, and the assignments make the `Movie` fields refer to those objects. Notice in line 5 that the string representation of the `id` field must be converted into a primitive `int` value by the method `Integer.parseInt`.

In method `Movie.read`, the memory representation of the `Movie` object must be created from the text stream representation by creating new objects in memory and converting from simple text representations to the more complex Java memory representations. This method could be used to read an object from standard input as follows:

```
BufferedReader in =
  new BufferedReader(new InputStreamReader(System.in));
Movie m = new Movie();
m.read(in);
```

```
 1 public class Movie {
 2   public void read (BufferedReader in) throws IOException {
 3   // read a Movie object into the calling object
 4     name  = in.readLine();
 5     id    = Integer.parseInt(in.readLine());
 6     genre = in.readLine();
 7   }
 8   public static Movie readInstance (BufferedReader in)
 9       throws IOException {
10   // create a new Movie object and read into it from the Reader
11     Movie newMovie = new Movie();
12     newMovie.read (in);
13     return newMovie;
14   }
15 };
```

FIGURE 11.5 _____

Two methods to read a Movie *object using the class* BufferedReader

The convoluted creation of the BufferedReader is required because its constructors require that a Reader be supplied, and only the InputStreamReader can construct a Reader from an InputStream like System.in.

An alternative to loading an existing object from the stream is to use the static method readInstance (lines 8–13 in Fig. 11.5), which creates a new object, loads it from the stream, and returns it. This method could be called as follows:

```
Movie m = Movie.readInstance (in);
```

11.2.3   File Classes

In Java, files are supported by the following classes: File, FileInputStream, FileOutputStream, FileReader, FileWriter, and RandomAccessFile. We will begin by considering files as streams of bytes using the FileInputStream and FileOutputStream classes.

To write a Movie object to a file, we can open the file as a stream, then pass it as a parameter to the print method:

```
PrintStream file =
      new PrintStream(new FileOutputStream("Movie.txt"));
m.print(file);
```

The FileOutputStream constructor throws an IOException if the file cannot be opened. This exception could be a FileNotFoundException if no file with the given name exists. Other exceptions could result from invalid permissions or other operating system restrictions on files.

The creation of a file object in Java includes its connection to an operating system file. Most other programming languages separate the creation of a file object from the connection of the object to a file. In C++, for instance, the code given earlier might look as follows:

```
ofstream & file = new ofstream;// unattached output stream object
file.open ("movie.txt");// attach stream object to the OS file
    m.print(file);
```

The first line creates the output stream object but does not attach it to an operating system file. All of the necessary space to hold the memory image of the file has been allocated. It might include space for the file table and buffers. The stream object is not attached to a real file, however, so it cannot be used for output.

The second line attaches the stream object to the operating system file. A request is sent to the operating system to find the physical address of the file, to read the file table and other information from the disk, and to initialize the stream object so that it can be used to write to the file.

Java file classes do support `close` methods that break the connection between the stream object and the operating system file. A `close` method requests that the operating system take any steps necessary to release the file from the Java application. It is called automatically when the Java object is removed from memory. This event occurs when the Java program terminates, if not earlier. Proper processing of files often requires that files be explicitly closed, which Java supports. For example, an application may write a file and then read from it. A standard way to support reading after writing is to open the file as an output stream, write to it, and close it. The same file can then be opened as an input stream for reading.

Methods for Representing Values in Streams

11.3

As we saw earlier, reading and writing objects is accomplished by designing a stream representation for the fields of the object and then using the primitive stream operations to transform objects between the memory and stream representations. The stream representation shown in Section 11.2.1 represents each member of the object as a delimited-text field (a text value followed by a delimiter) and places the members in a particular order. This section discusses several other methods for representing values in streams.

11.3.1   Length-Based Fields

An alternative method for stream representations for values is to write the length of the value (in bytes) followed by the value in exactly that number of bytes. We call this representation a *length-based field*. If we write the length as a two-byte character string, we would represent the `Movie` object of Fig. 11.4 as follows (the length values are highlighted):

```
12Animal House0318906comedy
```

The representation of the length as a two-byte character string restricts each field to at most 99 characters in length, even though two bytes in binary can represent values from –32,767 to 32,767. It would be better, therefore, to represent the length as a binary value, using two bytes. We expect the result to look as follows (the lengths are highlighted):

```
0000000   000c    416e    696d    616c    2048    6f75    7365    0003
          \0 \f   A   n   i   m   a   l       H   o   u   s   e   \0 003
0000010   3138    3900    0663    6f6d    6564    79
          1   8   9  \0 006  c   o   m   e   d   y
```

The first two bytes are the value 0x000c, or decimal 12. The next 12 bytes are the value of the `title` member. The other highlighted two bytes on the first line are the number 0x0003, decimal 3, which is the length of the text representation of the `id` member.

This representation relies on a capability to read and write binary values, which is provided by the Java data stream classes, as we discuss in Section 11.4.

11.3.2   Fixed-Length Fields

We have just seen that the length value can be stored as a *fixed-length field*, using a binary representation. This strategy can be applied to field values as well. For instance, an integer field could be stored in four bytes, allowing a range of values from -2^{31} to 2^{31}. The same four bytes, in a length-based representation, would allow values ranging from –9 to 99 only. In addition, the representation of the integer value as a text string requires a conversion from text to and from binary values as part of the I/O operation.

Representing the `id` member as a fixed-length, binary field results in the following stream value for the `Movie` object of Fig. 11.4 (the value of `id` is highlighted):

```
0000000   000c    416e    696d    616c    2048    6f75    7365    0000
          \0 \f   A   n   i   m   a   l       H   o   u   s   e   \0 \0
0000010   00bd    0006    636f    6d65    6479
          \0 275  \0 006  c   o   m   e   d   y
```

The value of the `id` member is now represented beginning at the last two bytes of the first line as 0x000000bd—the hexadecimal value of the four-byte integer 189.

Our representation of the `Movie` object now uses a combination of length-based and fixed-length fields. In Section 11.4, we will see how these different field types can be incorporated into Java classes that support field input and output.

11.3.3   Identified Fields

A variation on the delimited-text field, known as an *identified field*, allows the stream to include both the name of the field and the value. Both of these items are represented as delimited-text fields. We either maintain the stream as pairs of values or use a different delimiter to separate the name from the value. Because we are using the end-of-line character as the field delimiter, we could use the tab character to represent the name delimiter. The result can be produced using a simple modification of the `print` method of Fig. 11.4 and looks like the following (field names and name delimiters are highlighted):

```
0000000    7469    746c    6509    416e    696d    616c    2048    6f75
           t  i    t  l    e \t    A  n    i  m    a  l       H    o  u
0000010    7365    0a6d    6f76    6965    4964    0931    3839    0a67
           s  e    \n m    o  v    i  e    I  d    \t 1    8  9    \n g
0000020    656e    7265    0963    6f6d    6564    79
           e  n    r  e    \t c    o  m    e  d    y
```

Reading and Writing Binary Values with Data Streams

11.4 Java provides the capability to read and write primitive data objects as binary values through the data stream classes `DataInputStream` and `DataOutputStream`. A part of the definition of `DataOutputStream` is given in Fig. 11.6. The `write` methods for the numeric values write a value with a specific number of bytes: 1 for `writeByte`, 2 for `writeShort`, 4 for `writeInt`, and 8 for `writeLong`. Method `writeBytes` writes a character string as a sequence of bytes—exactly as many as there are characters in the `String`.

We can write a `Movie` object into a `DataOutputStream` using a binary, length-based representation as in the `write` method shown in Fig. 11.7. Reading the object is somewhat more complicated, because the length must be read to determine how many bytes to read for the value. The reading and writing of a `String` value as a length-based stream value are, of course, independent of which member is used to receive or supply the value. In Section 11.4.2, we will incorporate the length-based operations into a new Java class.

```
public class DataOutputStream extends FilterOutputStream {
    public final void writeBoolean (boolean v) throws IOException;
    public final void writeByte (int v) throws IOException;
    public final void writeShort (int v) throws IOException;
    public final void writeInt (int v) throws IOException;
    public final void writeLong (long v) throws IOException;
    public final void writeFloat (float v) throws IOException;
    public final void writeDouble (double v) throws IOException;
    public final void writeBytes (String v) throws IOException;
    . . .
};
```

FIGURE 11.6 ———————————————————————————
Part of the definition of class `DataOutputStream`

```
public class Movie { …
  public void write(DataOutputStream out)
    throws IOException {
  // write object as length-based and fixed-length fields
    out.writeShort(name.length());
    out.writeBytes(name);
    out.writeInt(id);
    out.writeShort(genre.length());
    out.writeBytes(genre);
  }
};
```

FIGURE 11.7 _____

Method to write `Movie` *objects using binary length-based and fixed-length encodings*

11.4.1   Portability of Data Streams

The data stream classes produce values that are portable to any Java runtime environment. If you are using a Microsoft Windows computer to run these I/O tests, you may have noticed a few differences between the files produced by Windows and displayed with the `debug` command and the files produced by Unix.

The first difference between Windows and Unix is evident in the streams produced using end-of-line characters. In Unix, the end-of-line character is the newline character (0x0a or `\n`). Windows, on the other hand, represents end-of-line by two characters: carriage return (0x0d or `\r`) and newline. The `println` and `readLine` methods are intended to use a *platform-dependent* line separator. Hence, execution on a Windows platform of the Java program that produced the stream shown in Section 11.2.1 produces the following with two-character line separators (the line separators are highlighted):

```
0000000    416e    696d    616c    2048    6f75    7365    0d0a    3138
           A  n    i  m    a  l       H    o  u    s  e    \r \n   1  8
0000010    390d    0a63    6f6d    6564    790d    0a
           9  \r   \n c    o  m    e  d    y  \r   \n
```

The file can be properly read only by a program running on a compatible platform.

Another difference between the platforms lies in the order of bytes for numeric values. An Intel Pentium computer and a Sun Microsystems computer represent integer values with different byte orders. For example, the two-byte hexadecimal representation for the number 189 is 0x00bd on a Sun and 0xbd00 on an Intel. This variation is often called an *-endian* difference. The two styles are called *big-endian* and *little-endian*.

If you are using Java on an Intel-based computer, the data streams generated will be identical to those described here, because data streams are platform-independent.

The read and write methods make the translation from the native memory representation of numbers to the portable stream representation. Because Java is a Sun Microsystems product, it is not surprising that the Sun representation is used for integers.

A similar situation exists for floating-point values. The representations of floating-point values vary between machines, and consequently the read and write methods must make the appropriate translation of values. Most current machines, however, have adopted the IEEE floating-point standard, which makes it less likely that any translation will be required for floating-point values. Nevertheless, we still expect the -endian differences in floating-point values on different computers. As with other Java primitive values, data streams represent floating-point values in a platform-independent fashion.

11.4.2   A Java Class with Length-Based Fields

We want to add `readLength` and `writeLength` methods to the data stream classes and have two strategies available to us. The first strategy is to define new classes that extend the data stream classes and add methods to the new classes. The second strategy is to define a class that includes static methods that read and write these new field types. Figure 11.8 defines class `FieldOps`, which includes static `readLength` and `writeLength` methods.

These methods use the `DataInput` and `DataOutput` interfaces that define the read and write methods of classes `DataInputStream` and `DataOutputStream`, respectively. The interface approach is more general, because the methods can be applied to an object of any class that implements the

```
1 class FieldOps {
2 // a class that supports static operations on length-based fields
3   public static String readLength(DataInput in)
4     throws IOException {
5   // read string from 2-byte length and bytes
6     int len = in.readShort();
7     byte [] bytes = new byte[len];
8     in.readFully(bytes);
9     return new String(bytes);
10  }
11  public static void writeLength(DataOutput out, String str)
12      throws IOException{
13    // write string as 2-byte length plus bytes
14    out.writeShort(str.length());
15    out.writeBytes(str);
16  }
17 };
```

FIGURE 11.8 _____

Classes to support input and output of fields

interface and not just the Java data stream classes. In particular, class `RandomAccessFile`, which we use later, implements both `DataInput` and `DataOutput` in a single class. It does not extend the data stream classes, but does include all of the data input and output operations. The methods of class `FieldOps` can be used with objects of type `RandomAccessFile`.

As noted earlier, the read operation is more complex than its write counterpart. It first reads the length (line 6 in Fig. 11.8), then creates an array of that many bytes (line 7). This array is used to read the stream (line 8). Finally, the byte array is converted to a `String` and returned (line 9).

The read method of class `Movie` is simply written as follows:

```
public void read(DataInput in)
   throws IOException {
   // read object as length-based and fixed-length fields
   name = FieldOps.readLength(in);
   id = in.readInt();
   genre = FieldOps.readLength(in);
}
```

You may notice that the calls to the static methods of class `FieldOps` are different than the calls to the nonstatic methods. In the static method calls, the method name is specified with the class name as its prefix. The data stream is passed as a parameter in the call to the static `readLength` method, but is the object (prefix) of the call to the nonstatic method `readInt`.

A NOTE ON DETECTING AND HANDLING I/O ERRORS

A major concern with all I/O operations is what to do about error handling. Most of the methods we've used are defined as throwing an `IOException` if errors occur, but we have not explicitly thrown exceptions in any method. How can we be sure that errors such as trying to read past the end of the file will be properly caught and signaled?

The `readLength` method of `FieldOps` is of particular concern. It first reads a length value, then reads exactly that many bytes. If an end-of-file occurs at any point, the method should throw an `EOFException`. The code of the method ignores this concern and has no explicit references to throwing exceptions. An investigation of the Java API documentation yields the following information:

- Method `DataInput.readShort` throws `EOFException` if this stream reaches the end before reading all the bytes and `IOException` if an I/O error occurs.
- Method `DataInput.readFully` throws `EOFException` if this stream reaches the end before reading all the bytes and `IOException` if an I/O error occurs.

Further analysis allows us to conclude that the methods of `FieldOps` handle the error conditions correctly. For example, consider a call to `FieldOps.readLength`, as shown in Fig. 11.8. If an end-of-file is reached in the call to method `readInt` or the call to method `readFully`, an `EOFException` will be thrown. This exception is not caught in `readLength`, so the execution of `readLength` terminates and the exception is propagated to the method that called `readLength`. Similarly, if any other I/O error occurs during execution of `readLength`, the resulting `IOException` will be thrown by `readLength`.

The `read` and `write` methods of class `Movie` implement a particular representation of the object in a data stream. The two methods agree on the order of fields and on their representation. Each one represents `name` as length-based text, `id` as a four-byte integer, and `genre` as length-based text.

Adding additional field types to class `FieldOps` is very appropriate. Exercises at the end of the chapter ask you to add delimited-text fields and identified fields to this class.

11.4.3   Reading and Writing Objects in Object Streams

Classes `ObjectInputStream` and `ObjectOutputStream` are streams that support direct input and output of Java objects. They are similar to data streams in that binary representations are used. These object streams are very powerful in their ability to store and retrieve objects. These classes are used in Section 17.3 to make objects persistent.

The `Serializable` interface is implemented by a class to indicate that its objects can be serialized and deserialized with the `writeObject` method of class `ObjectOutputStream` and the `readObject` method of class `ObjectInputStream`. This interface, which has no methods or constants, is called a *marker* interface. We can make the `Movie` class serializable simply by adding "implements serializable" to its definition. Figure 11.9 shows the contents of the file that was created by writing three `Movie` objects to an object stream using the following code:

```
Movie m1 = new Movie ("Animal House", 189, "comedy");
Movie m2 = new Movie ("Duck Soup", 987, "comedy");
Movie m3 = new Movie ("Elizabeth", 450, "costume drama");
ObjectOutputStream out = new ObjectOutputStream(System.out);
out.writeObject(m1);
out.writeObject(m2);
out.writeObject(m3);
```

Clearly, this representation of the object is much more complex than that produced by our `write` method and class `DataStream`. The following quote from the Java documentation for class `ObjectOutputStream` gives some insight into the contents of the file:

> The default serialization mechanism for an object writes the class of the object, the class signature, and the values of all non-transient and non-static fields. References to other objects (except in transient or static fields) cause those objects to be written also. Multiple references to a single object are encoded using a reference sharing mechanism so that graphs of objects can be restored to the same shape as when the original was written.

Much of the contents of the stream make no obvious sense, but some recognizable items are highlighted. For instance, the phrase `dbjava.files.Movie` (the class name) appears beginning at byte 0x08, and somewhat later we see the highlighted field names of the `Movie` class: `movieId` at byte 0x28, `genre` at byte

```
0000000    aced    0005    7372    0012    6462    6a61    7661    2e66
           254 355  \0 005   s   r  \0 022   d   b   j   a   v   a   .   f
0000010    696c    6573    2e4d    6f76    6965    c915    a49e    93ce
            i   l   e   s   .   M   o   v   i   e 311 025 244 236 223 316
0000020    8162    0200    0349    0007    6d6f    7669    6549    644c
           201   b 002  \0 003   I  \0 007   m   o   v   i   e   I   d   L
0000030    0005    6765    6e72    6574    0012    4c6a    6176    612f
           \0 005   g   e   n   r   e   t  \0 022   L   j   a   v   a   /
0000040    6c61    6e67    2f53    7472    696e    673b    4c00    0574
            l   a   n   g   /   S   t   r   i   n   g   ;   L  \0 005   t
0000050    6974    6c65    7400    124c    6a61    7661    2f6c    616e
            i   t   l   e   t  \0 022   L   j   a   v   a   /   l   a   n
0000060    672f    5374    7269    6e67    3b78    7000    0000    bd74
            g   /   S   t   r   i   n   g   ;   x   p  \0  \0  \0 275   t
0000070    0006    636f    6d65    6479    7400    0c41    6e69    6d61
           \0 006   c   o   m   e   d   y   t  \0  \f   A   n   i   m   a
0000080    6c20    486f    7573    6573    7100    7e00    0000    0003
            l       H   o   u   s   e   s   q  \0   ~  \0  \0  \0  \0 003
0000090    db71    007e    0004    7400    0944    7563    6b20    536f
           333   q  \0   ~  \0 004   t  \0  \t   D   u   c   k       S   o
00000a0    7570    7371    007e    0000    0000    01c2    7400    0d63
            u   p   s   q  \0   ~  \0  \0  \0  \0 001 302   t  \0  \r   c
00000b0    6f73    7475    6d65    2064    7261    6d61    7400    0945
            o   s   t   u   m   e       d   r   a   m   a   t  \0  \t   E
00000c0    6c69    7a61    6265    7468    7100    7e00    0800
            l   i   z   a   b   e   t   h   q  \0   ~  \0  \b
```

FIGURE 11.9 _____

Contents of a file with three serialized `Movie` *objects and some items of interest highlighted*

0x32, and `title` at byte 0x4f. The phrase `java/lang/String` appears (highlighted) at byte 0x3b after both `genre` and `title`. From this display, we can infer that the file includes a specification of class `Movie`, along with the names and types of the fields. The fields are not in the order given in the class definition.

Each field name is represented as a length-based field. Bytes 0x26 and 0x27 (highlighted) have a value of `0x0007`, the length of the following string `movieId`. We can also see two-byte length fields before other field and type names.

Looking at the highlighted text at byte 0x6b, we see the value of `movieId` represented as the four-byte integer `0x000000bd`. At byte 0x70, we see the value of `genre` represented as a length-based text field: `0x0006` at byte 0x70. The six bytes that follow are `comedy`.

From this example, we can see that the object stream contains information that is required to read the stream, create a new object of the proper type, and initialize its fields properly. In this case, the field initialization requires that two `String` objects must also be created.

Further analysis yields information suggesting that the *serialized objects* are somewhat optimized. The file includes three `Movie` objects, but the description of class `Movie` appears only once. We can conclude that the types of the objects in the file appear only once. We would expect to find additional class descriptions if objects of other classes are added to the file.

The `movieId` of the second `Movie` object in the file, `0x000003db`, appears at byte 0x8d. We can also see the `title` of the second `Movie`, Duck Soup, at address 0x99, with length `0x0009` appearing at address 0x97.

The value for the `genre` member of *Duck Soup* appears to be missing. The `Movie` objects for *Animal House* and *Duck Soup*, however, were created with the same `String` literal as the value for `genre`. An investigation of the objects in memory shows that both `genre` fields point to the same `String` object. The `String` object whose value is `comedy` is stored only once in the file. Hence, the value for the genre of the second `Movie` object apparently is represented as a reference to the first occurrence of that string—an indication of how duplicate objects are represented in object streams.

11.4.4 Advantages and Limitations of Serialized Objects

In general, Java objects are much more complicated than these simple `Movie` objects. The `writeObject` method will write objects of arbitrary complexity. Object streams give us an excellent way to allow objects to persist between executions of a program.

An application may use object streams to create persistence of objects across executions—that is, to create objects in one execution of the program that will be available to subsequent executions of the same program. To do so, the developer should first ensure that all relevant classes implement the `Serializable` interface. Then the application can create a list of all objects that should persist—for instance, using a `HashSet` object. At the end of the execution of the application, a single call to `writeObject` with that `HashSet` as its parameter will cause all of the persistent objects to be written to a file. When the application starts its next execution, a single call to `readObject` will load the `HashSet` and its list of objects into memory. In this way the program begins its execution with the same objects in memory that were there when the program last terminated.

Object streams may also be used to transport objects from one application to another. Suppose one application creates a piped object output stream, and another application links to it with a piped object input stream. Then the first application can write an object to its piped stream, and the second application can read the object from its piped stream. The object is thus transported between applications.

It may appear that object streams are the complete answer to the needs of applications for file structures. With a little effort on the programmer's part, objects can be stored and retrieved safely. Unfortunately, this view has some drawbacks. The main problem is the inefficiency of object streams when only some of their objects are required.

An application often needs access to some, but not all, of the objects stored in a file. The SQL operations described in earlier chapters, for instance, included many instances of the selection of particular records from files. Suppose that an object stream has been used to record all of the information for the BigHit Video database. To check in a videotape, we need to read the objects that represent the videotape, its movie, and its rental—only three objects from the many that are stored in the object stream.

The persistence strategy outlined previously, and described in more detail in Section 17.3, calls for an application to open the object stream, read all of the objects into memory, modify the objects as necessary, and write all of the persistent objects into a new object stream. In our current example, the application would have to read and write every videotape, movie, and rental object, even though only three are required. From our analysis of the cost of I/O, we know that this approach would make the application horribly inefficient.

Improvements in efficiency will happen only with random access object streams and some method of seeking to the beginning of particular records. Object streams do not provide these capabilities.

Representing Relational Tables as Files

11.5
Using the methods defined in previous sections, a file can be made to hold many objects. A file that contains objects all of the same type is very much like a relational table. That is, each object in the file represents one row of the table. This section considers how we can represent tables as files and what effect that representation has on the performance of relational operations.

A file can represent a relational table as follows:

1. Define an object class whose value represents a row in the table.

2. Create a file to hold the objects.

3. For each row in the table, create an object and write the object to the file.

Alternatively, we could define a single class that can hold a row of any table.

Relational operations can be represented as operations on these files. For instance, a selection operation can be executed by opening the table file for input and then creating a new file to hold the output. Next, the records of the table are read one by one. Once a particular row is loaded into an object in memory, the selection criteria can be applied to it. If the object satisfies the selection criteria, it is written to the output file. After all records have been read from the input file, the output file will contain the table that results from the selection operation. Similarly, a projection operation can be performed by reading the records and outputting only those fields of the record that are included in the projection.

Unfortunately, some relational operations will be very inefficient if executed using this sequential view of files. Suppose, for example, the selection operation specifies a specific value for the primary key of a table—`Select * from Movie where id=123`, for instance. Even though only one record satisfies the criterion, the file must be read sequentially until that record is found. The file structures that we've seen so far do not support nonsequential access to files. Even if we somehow knew exactly where a particular record was located in the file, we have no way to read it without first reading every record that precedes it.

We know that any byte in a file can be accessed in the same amount of time. Unfortunately, the file structures that we've seen so far support only sequential access. To allow direct access to particular objects in the files, we must add another level of organization. Previously, we saw how a file can be organized as fields that represent values. Now we have to organize those fields as records.

Files of Records

11.6

To support the organization of files as *records*, we need two things. First, we must be able to read and write records in a single operation. Second, we must be able to move to a specific place in the file before reading or writing. We address the first requirement by defining interfaces for record reading and writing, and the second by using class `RandomAccessFile`.

As a general rule, a file is organized as a sequence of records. The records may be uniform or non-uniform in size. A *fixed-sized record* file is one in which every data record is the same size. A *variable-sized record* file contains records of different sizes.

One advantage of a fixed-sized record file is that the address of a record can be calculated from its index. The offset of a record from the beginning of the file is found by multiplying the record index by the record size. If we know the index of a record of interest, we can go directly to that record in the file. This calculation is not possible with variable-sized record files, however. The only ways to find a particular record are to remember its address or to read every record until we find it.

Fixed-sized records do not improve the speed of access to particular records, because fast access depends on knowing a record's index. Remembering the index of a record is just as difficult as remembering its exact address. Either of these values must be stored in some data structure to be remembered.

Another apparent advantage of fixed-sized record files occurs when files are kept in sorted order. With fixed-sized records, we can perform a binary search on the file to find a record with a particular key: We can calculate the address of the middle record in the file, read that record, and continue with the records before or after it depending on its key value. This strategy carries a search cost of $\log_2(n)$ for a file containing n records. If the file has 1,000,000 records, however, the binary search requires 20 reads—too many to be effective.

Sorted, fixed-sized record files are seldom useful for three reasons: (1) a binary search is slow; (2) files can be searched only by a single key value; and (3) insertion is horribly slow. If we want to be able to search a `Movie` file by ID and by name, this file organization will not help us. To insert a new record whose key value is less than every key in the file, we must move every record in the file to accommodate the insertion. For a 1,000,000-record file, this strategy requires 1 million reads and 1 million writes.

For the rest of our treatment of files of records, we will assume that records are variable-sized and that they are stored in no particular order.

11.6.1   Organizing Variable-Sized Record Files

We can use the same approaches to variable-sized records that we employed with variable-length fields. That is, we can store the record with a delimited-text representation or with a length-based binary representation.

For a delimited text representation, we require all fields to be represented as text fields. In addition, the end-of-record delimiter we choose cannot appear within the representation of the record.

A variety of strategies ensure that delimiters and other special characters do not appear in text fields. In SQL, for instance, a single quote character inside a quoted string is represented by two single quotes together. This technique requires that each real delimiter be followed by a different character. In HTML, special characters like "<" are represented by a string beginning with "&" and ending with ";". The less than symbol is represented by "<" and the ampersand by "&".

A length-based representation of records has the advantage of allowing length-based and fixed-length, binary representations of individual fields. A record in this representation is a fixed-length, binary field whose value is the number of bytes in the record, followed by the bytes that represent the contents of the record.

The read operation for a length-based record representation begins by reading the length. Next, that specific number of bytes is read from the file and the results are placed in a byte array to be decoded into field values according to the record type.

The write operation for a length-based record representation cannot determine the length of the record until the object has been converted into its stream representation. Two techniques will work here. First, we can write a zero for the length to reserve the space, write the record, then go back and rewrite the length field. Second, we can write the record into an array of bytes, determine its length, then write the length and the array of bytes into the file. We will use the second strategy in our implementation.

11.6.2   Supporting Input and Output of `Movie` Records

The record read and write operations for class `Movie` are given in Fig. 11.10. The `read Record` method reads the length and an array of bytes containing the stream representation of the record (lines 3–5). It then uses a `ByteArrayInputStream` to allow the previously defined `Movie.read` method to read from the byte array (lines 7–9).

The byte array streams support the use of stream operations on a memory buffer.

In method `writeRecord`, the record is written into a byte array (lines 14–18) using class `ByteArrayOutputStream` and the previously defined `Movie.write` operation. The result of this call to `write` is extracted as a byte array (line 20), and the length of the array and the byte array itself are written into the output stream (lines 21 and 22).

```
 1 class Movie { …
 2   public void readRecord(DataInput in) throws IOException {
 3     int len = in.readShort();
 4     byte [] buffer = new byte[len];
 5     in.readFully(buffer);
 6     // turn the byte array buffer into an input stream
 7     DataInputStream recStream
 8       = new DataInputStream(new ByteArrayInputStream(buffer));
 9     read(recStream); // read the Movie object
10   }
11   public void writeRecord(DataOutput out)
12       throws IOException {
13     // write the record into a byte stream
14     ByteArrayOutputStream byteStream
15       = new ByteArrayOutputStream();
16     DataOutputStream recStream
17       = new DataOutputStream(byteStream);
18     write(recStream); // write the Movie object
19     // write the length and the record into the output stream
20     byte [] buffer = byteStream.toByteArray();
21     out.writeShort(buffer.length);
22     out.write(buffer);
23   }
24 };
```

FIGURE 11.10 _____

Methods of class Movie *to read and write records*

11.6.3   General Support for Input and Output of Records

This section presents a general model for reading and writing records. You can see that the methods of Fig. 11.10 depended on the Movie class only in the calls on the methods Movie.read (line 9) and Movie.write (line 18). In this section, we will encapsulate the object class read and write methods into an interface, and encapsulate the variable-sized record I/O in a new file class.

Interface InputOutputRecord, as given in Fig. 11.11, defines methods that allow reading and writing objects as single operations. Because these methods have already been defined in class Movie, we can make each Movie object into an InputOutputRecord object by including implements InputOutputRecord in the definition of the class.

These interfaces allow us to define a class dbjava.files.RecordFile that extends RandomAccessFile and has a variety of record read and write operations. Figure 11.12 shows a partial definition of this class. In this definition, you

```
1 public interface InputOutputRecord {
2    public void read(DataInput in)
3       throws IOException;
4    public void write(DataOutput out)
5       throws IOException;
6 };
```

FIGURE 11.11 _____

Java interface to support reading and writing of records

```
 1 public class RecordFile extends RandomAccessFile {
 2   public void read(InputOutputRecord rec)
 3     throws IOException {
 4     int len = readShort();
 5     byte [] buffer = new byte[len];
 6     readFully(buffer);
 7     // turn the byte array buffer into an input stream
 8     DataInputStream recStream
 9       = new DataInputStream(new ByteArrayInputStream(buffer));
10     rec.read(recStream);
11   }
12   public long write(InputOutputRecord rec)
13       throws IOException {
14     // write the record into a byte stream
15     // return the address of the record
16     long address = getFilePointer();// current address
17     ByteArrayOutputStream byteStream
18       = new ByteArrayOutputStream();
19     DataOutputStream recStream
20       = new DataOutputStream(byteStream);
21     rec.write(recStream);
22     // write the length and the record into the output stream
23     byte [] buffer = byteStream.toByteArray();
24     writeShort(buffer.length);
25     write(buffer);
26     return address;
27   }
28 };
```

FIGURE 11.12 _____

Preliminary definition of class dbjava.files.RecordFile

will see only minor changes from the methods given in Fig. 11.10 for class `Movie`. The one new component is that the `write` method returns a `long` value that gives the address of the record within the file. In the next section, we will see that this address is used to support direct access to records in files. Method `getFilePointer` of class `RandomAccessFile` returns the current position in the file, as explained in the next section.

A NOTE ON BLOCK ACCESS TO RECORD FILES |

File systems are physically organized into *blocks* that are typically larger than a single record. Operating systems read and write files in blocks, and the methods of class `RecordFile` read and write partial blocks. In essence, these methods rely on the operating system to handle the blocks. To achieve more direct control of block manipulation, we can add block read and write methods to the class. A block read method of class `RecordFile`, for example, could be defined as follows:

```
public InputOutputRecord [] readBlock () throws IOException;
```

This method reads a single operating system block, extracts and unpacks all of the records in it, and returns an array of the resulting objects.

Explicit block manipulation by a file system package is very difficult and requires detailed knowledge of the operating system. In most cases, it is better to read and write single records and allow the operating system to manage the blocks.

Direct Access to Records by Address

11.7

We are now ready to produce direct access to records in files. The Java class `RandomAccessFile` supports operations that maintain a file pointer within an open file. The file pointer indicates where the next read or write operation will occur. After each operation, the file pointer is repositioned after the last byte read or written. To support direct access, the file must allow the explicit repositioning of that pointer. Class `RandomAccessFile` includes a `seek` method for that purpose.

Method `seek` accepts a `long` parameter and moves the file pointer to that exact offset from the beginning of the file. A value of 0 moves the file pointer to the beginning of the file. The `length` method can be used to move the file pointer to the end of the file, using the call `seek(length())`.

Figure 11.13 shows the direct access read, write, and append methods. Method `append` adds a new record. Method `write` may or may not replace an existing record, but `append` is guaranteed to create a new record in the file. These methods are easy to implement because they were designed using object-oriented techniques.

Figure 11.14 is a dump of a file of `Movie` with three records written using method `RecordFile.append`. The three objects are the ones described in Section 11.4.3 and Fig. 11.9. The first object is in the file at address 0, the second is in the file at address 35 (0x23), and the third is in the file at address 75 (0x4b).

In Chapter 12, we will investigate how to use *direct access files* to support access to records by value.

```
public class RecordFile extends RandomAccessFile { …
  public void read(InputOutputRecord rec, int address)
    throws IOException {
    seek(address);
    read(rec);
  }
  public void write(InputOutputRecord rec, int address)
    throws IOException {
    seek(address);
    write(rec);
  }
  public long append(InputOutputRecord rec)
    throws IOException {
    // add record to file as new record
    // return address of record
    long address = length(); // offset of end of file
    seek(address); // move to the end of the file
    write(rec);
    return address;
  }
};
```

FIGURE 11.13 _____

Direct access read, write, _and_ append _methods of class_ RecordFile

```
0000000    0021    000c    4d65    6e20    696e    2042    6c61    636b
           \0  !   \0  \f   M   e   n       i   n       B   l   a   c   k
0000010    0000    007b    000d    6163    7469    6f6e    2063    6f6d
           \0  \0   \0  {    \0  \r   a   c   t   i   o   n       c   o   m
0000020    6564    7900    2600    1143    6f6e    7370    6972    6163
           e   d   y   \0  031 \0  005 C   o   n   s   p   i   r   a   c
0000030    7920    5468    656f    7279    0000    1e6a    000d    6163
           y       T   h   e   o   r   y   \0  \0  036 j   \0  \r   a   c
0000040    7469    6f6e    2063    6f6d    6564    7900    1900    0547
           t   i   o   n       c   o   m   e   d   y   \0  031 \0  005 G
0000050    7265    6564    0000    0022    000c    7369    6c65    6e74
           r   e   e   d   \0  \0   \0  "    \0  \f   s   i   l   e   n   t
0000060    2064    7261    6d61
               d   r   a   m   a
```

FIGURE 11.14 _____

Hexadecimal and character dump of file with three Movie _records, with the length of each record highlighted_

Updating and Deleting Records

11.8

Now that we are able to add records to files and to read and write at selective locations, we need to be concerned about what happens when we try to modify a record in the file and when we delete a record.

Modifying records is accomplished by reading an object, changing it, and then writing it back into the file. A difficulty arises when the size of the record has changed. As an example, consider the situation depicted in Fig. 11.15. The length field for each record is the distance to the next record and hence cannot be changed. Although the smaller record could be written into the file at the position of the second record, a gap would be left between the end of the second record and the beginning of the third. That is, the length field of the record would remain 20, but there would be 5 bytes unused before the next record.

Updating a record with a larger record cannot be done without moving at least one record to a new location. In this case, an attempt to write the larger record in the place of the second record would interfere with the length field of the third record. This event would destroy the integrity of the file. The most straightforward solution is to delete the second record from its current place and then append its new value to the end of the file. As long as we don't care about the order of the records, this solution will work.

This issue brings us to the problem of deleting a record. We must be able to leave the space in the file, but not the record. We cannot disturb the length field, for the same reason mentioned above. Hence, we must place some mark in the file to denote that the record is deleted. In the case of our `RecordFile`, we have stored the length as a signed short integer. Because lengths are always positive, we could use a negative value for length to denote a deleted record. The next record is located forward in the file by a number of bytes equal to the absolute value of the length.

Once we have deleted records in the file, we must modify the sequential read method to read the next undeleted record after the current position. In addition, we must change the direct read method so that it fails when trying to read a deleted record.

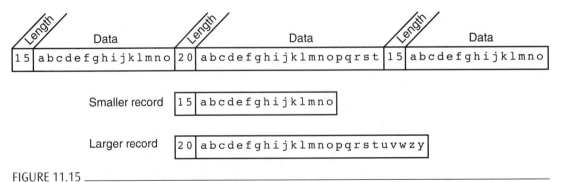

FIGURE 11.15

The difficulty with updating a record in a file

Method `write` should be renamed `update` and modified as described above so that it does not destroy the integrity of the file. This modification is left as an exercise.

Chapter Summary

Application performance is often dominated by the cost of input and output. I/O hardware is characterized by the trade-off between cost, capacity, and speed of access. For an application to have access to large amount of data, it must access disk drives and other secondary storage media. That access is necessarily very slow compared with main memory and CPU speeds.

Computer disks are rotating devices divided into cylinders, tracks, and sectors. A file system is a software system that organizes disks into sequential sequences of bytes. The mapping from the file view to the hardware view is accomplished by first organizing the disks into pages, where each page contains the same number of sectors. A file is then a list of pages that do not have to be physically contiguous. Computer operating systems provide the software to support this file system view.

The `java.io` package includes a variety of classes that support input and output of primitive values, arrays, strings, and even objects. As in C, input and output in Java are operations performed on streams. The stream classes are divided into input streams and output streams. Access to files in Java is supported by file classes in combination with the stream classes.

A file structure is a combination of data structures and algorithms used for application input and output. Careful design of file structures is necessary to achieve the appropriate application speed and to ensure that objects can be stored and retrieved without being corrupted.

Objects in memory and objects in files are necessarily different. In particular, a field of a memory object that refers to another object is represented by the memory address of that other object. The representation in a file must translate these references into file addresses or in some other way arrange for the information content of the objects to be preserved when the object is written to a file and reloaded into memory.

The representation of an object in a file consists of a sequence of field values grouped together into a record. Four field representation strategies were described in this chapter: delimited text, fixed-length binary, length-based binary, and identified text.

The records in a file can be either fixed-length or variable-length. Fixed-length records have almost no benefit to applications. In contrast, a variable-length record can be represented as delimited text, with a special record delimiter, or as length-based with a binary length value. The preferred strategy is to store variable-length records using a two-byte binary value for the length, followed by a sequence of bytes containing the record value.

Binary values are available for input and output through the data stream classes and interfaces. Interface `java.io.DataOutput` supports methods to write values of primitive types and arrays in binary. Interface `java.io.DataInput` contains the corresponding read methods.

Direct access to records by address in files is supported through class `RandomAccessFile`, which implements both `DataInput` and `DataOutput`. This class also supports operations to move the file pointer as required for direct access.

The `Serializable` interface and the object stream classes support reading and writing objects. Unfortunately, object streams support only sequential access. No direct access and no updates are allowed. This limitation makes object streams unsuitable for use as fully functional file structures.

Key Terms

Block. A collection of contiguous pages of a disk that are accessed together.

Cache memory. Memory that cannot be directly addressed, but rather is referenced as an image of a slower memory device.

Controller. A processor that controls some hardware device.

Cylinder. A collection of tracks that can be accessed without moving the disk heads.

Delimited-text field. A field in the sequential representation of a file that is stored as a text string followed by a delimiter character.

Direct access file. A file that supports access to records by their byte addresses.

Disk drive. A rotating storage device that supports a fairly uniform access time to all data. Disks are divided into cylinders, tracks, and sectors.

File. A collection of disk pages that are organized by the file system into a sequence of bytes. Also, a Java class that allows an application to determine the properties of files.

File structure. A combination of data structures and algorithms used for application input and output.

Fixed-length field. A field in the sequential representation of a file that is stored as a binary value of a specific length.

Fixed-sized record. A record that is stored in a fixed amount of space.

Identified field. A field in the sequential representation of a file that is stored as a text string consisting of the name of the field, followed by a delimiter character, followed by a text value of the field and another delimiter.

Latency. The amount of time that elapses between issuing a request for a read or write operation and the arrival of the first byte of data.

Length-based field. A field in the sequential representation of a file that is stored as a binary length value, followed by that many bytes.

Main memory. The main random access memory of a computer system. Main memory can be directly accessed by the CPU and by a variety of I/O devices.

Object stream. An input or output stream that consists of a sequence of serialized objects.

Page. A particular number of sectors that is the smallest unit that can be read or written by the file system.

Reader and Writer classes. Java classes that support text input and output that is consistent with the use of Unicode characters for the internationalization of applications.

Record. The sequential representation of an object as a sequence of fields.

Rotational delay. The portion of the latency period spent waiting for a particular sector to come under the head of a disk.

Sector. A portion of a track on a disk that is the smallest unit of storage that can be read or written. A sector is typically 512 bytes.

Seek time. The time it takes to move the heads of a disk to a position over the appropriate cylinder.

Serializable interface. The Java interface that allows objects to be transformed into a sequence of bytes that is suitable for input and output in object streams. Serializable is a marker interface with no methods. Any class that implements Serializable can be used with the readObject and writeObject methods of object streams.

Serialized object. A representation of an object as a sequence of bytes. In Java, an object that has been translated into a sequence of bytes that can be stored in a file and that has enough information to allow the object to be reloaded into memory.

Storage hierarchy. The division of computer storage into a sequence of components. Starting with storage of data in the CPU, each component is less expensive, slower, and of higher capacity than the previous component.

Stream. A sequence of bytes that can be read or written in order. Streams are the basic I/O objects in Java programs.

Track. A single concentric circle on one surface of a disk platter.

Transfer rate. The number of bytes per second that can be moved to or from a device.

Variable-sized record. A record that is stored in an amount of space that varies according to the value of the object.

Exercises

1. Consult a computer hardware supply catalog, or similar resource on the Web, to determine current costs for cache memory, main memory, disk drives, removable disk drives, and tape storage. Update Table 11.1 with this information.

2. A major improvement in Windows 98 was the FAT32 file system, in which a 32-bit value is used for disk addresses. DOS and Windows 95 use the FAT16 system, with a 16-bit address. Answer the following questions.

   a. What is the minimum page size for a 2 GB disk drive using the FAT16 file system with 2^{16} pages?

   b. Why does FAT16 impose a limit of 2 GB in a single file system (drive)?

   c. How many pages are used in FAT32 for a 2 GB disk drive with 2 KB pages?

   d. What is the maximum disk size for FAT32, using 2 KB pages?

   e. Explain how the following might happen. A system with a 1.2 GB disk using FAT16 has 200 MB free. After conversion of the drive to FAT32, 500 MB are free. All of the files are intact after the conversion.

3. Use the Web to determine the detailed characteristics of current disk drives. Replace the information in Table 11.2 with that for three different disk drives.

4. Suppose that a disk has 512-byte sectors and that a program requests that 256 bytes be written to that disk. Explain why a read operation must be performed as part of the write operation.

5. Use the Web or other reference to determine the organization of information on CD and DVD devices. Are they organized in tracks and cylinders, or in some other way? How much information can be stored on a CD? How much on a DVD? What are the latency and transfer rates of these devices?

6. Give two examples of increases in speed that can occur when the page size of a file system is increased. Give two examples of situations in which applications run faster when the page size is reduced. Explain your answers.

7. Show the sequential representation of the object of Fig. 11.4 using a fixed-length representation of `String` objects. Be sure to include a description of the fields. How can your implementation handle values that are too long?

8. Compile class `Movie`. Write and compile a class whose `main` method creates three `Movie` objects and writes them to standard output using the following `write` methods. Display the results using `od` in Unix or `debug` in Windows.

   a. Write as identified text with name delimiter "\t" and field delimiter "\n".

   b. Write as length-based binary fields.

   c. Write as delimited-text fields.

9. Add methods to class `FieldOps` to support delimited-text fields. Develop `read` and `write` methods for class `Movie` that use these new operations. Write a `main` method that demonstrates the correctness of your solution. Be sure to include a strategy for allowing the delimiter to appear as a value in the field.

10. Add methods to class `FieldOps` to support identified fields. You may be able to use the delimited-text operations of Exercise 9. Develop `read` and `write` methods for class `Movie` that use these new operations. Write a `main` method that demonstrates the correctness of your solution.

11. Implement `read` and `write` methods for the following classes of the BigHit Video application. Represent relationships with foreign key attributes. Write each object as a variable-sized record.

    a. `Customer`

    b. `Videotape`

    c. `Employee`

    d. `Rental`

12. The following is the hexadecimal dump of a file with two variable-length records. Each record consists of a two-byte length and a packed buffer of that many bytes. Each buffer has text fields packed with a two-byte length field plus value. List the values of the fields in each record.

```
0000000    003c    000a    4865    7265    2069    7420    6973    0009
            \0  <   \0  \n  H   e   r   e   2   i   t   i   s   \0  \t
0000010    6461    7461    6261    7365    7300    0d46    6c6f    7269
            d   a   t   a   b   a   s   e   s   \0  \r  F   l   o   r   i
0000020    6461    2053    7461    7465    0014    6578    6365    6c6c
            d   a       S   t   a   t   e   \0 024  e   x   c   e   l   l
0000030    656e    6365    2069    6e20    6163    7469    6f6e    0027
            e   n   c   e       i   n       a   c   t   i   o   n   \0  '
0000040    0008    5768    6174    6576    6572    0000    0000    0003
            \0  \b  W   h   a   t   e   v   e   r   \0  \0  \0  \0  \0 003
0000050    3132    3300    0c38    3520    4d61    696e    2041    7665
            1   2   3   \0  \f  8   5       M   a   i   n       A   v   e
0000060    2e00    0467    6f67    6f00    3a00    0a48    6572    6520
            .   \0 004  g   o   g   o   \0  :   \0  \n  H   e   r   e
0000070    6974    2069    7300    0000    0e6a    7573    7420    6c69
            i   t       i   s   \0  \0  \0 016  j   u   s   t       l   i
0000080    6b65    204d    696b    6500    0867    6f6f    646c    7563
            k   e       M   i   k   e   \0  \b  g   o   o   d   l   u   c
0000090    6b00    1074    6861    7427    7320    616c    6c20    666f
            k   \0 020  t   h   a   t   '   s       a   l   l       f   o
00000a0    6c6b    7300
            l   k   s
```

13. Consider the following array declaration and initialization in Java. Show the buffer that contains the field values packed as delimited text with "|" as the delimiter character. Show only the text representation.

```
String obj [] = {"COP 4710", "Midterm 2", "96", "A"};
```

14. Modify class `RecordFile` to add the methods `update` and `delete` as described in Section 11.8.

15. Use the results of Exercise 14 to develop an application to edit `Customer` records. The application must have an initialization program that creates a file with many customers. Two options exist for this system:

    a. An application that reads an update file and performs the updates. Each line of the file consists of the customer ID, the name of the field to be changed, and the new value of the field.

    b. A Web site that has a customer update form with a CGI program that updates the customer file based on the CGI request.

16. Implement an application to print a list of all customers and their rentals. Start with a file of customers and a file of rentals, both sorted by account ID. Your application should open both files, read a customer entry and print its information, read and print all rentals for that customer, then go to the next customer record.

17. Develop input/output operations for classes `Customer` and `Rental`, as in Exercise 14. In this case, however, represent relationships by record addresses. Put a field in the memory representation of each object to contain its file address. Put all records in the same file. Each time a new record is created, append it to the file and record its file address in the memory object. When relationships are changed, the files must be updated.

Further Readings

The article, "Advances in Disk Technology: Performance Issues," by Spencer Ng [Ng98], discusses developments in disk technology and evaluates the performance implications of these developments.

A much more detailed investigation of file structures in given in Folk, Zoellick, and Riccardi's *File Structures: an Object-Oriented Approach Using C++* [FZR98]. This book combines a detailed description of file structures with the full implementation of file structures in C++. The organization of the file structure implementation is significantly different from that of this book.

The operating system texts by Silberschatz and Galvin [SiGa92] and Tanenbaum and Woodhull [TaWo97] are helpful resources to learn about how operating systems use file systems. For the details of Unix file systems and how they developed, look at Ritchie and Thompson [RiTh74], Kernighan and Ritchie [KeRi88], and McKusick et al [MJLF84]. Information about I/O devices and file system services for Windows 95 and Windows NT is covered in Hart [Hart97].

Information on specific hardware systems and devices can often be found in manuals and documentation published by manufacturers and on Web sites. The information on specific disks, tapes, and CDs that is presented in this chapter comes from the Web sites for Seagate, Western Digital, and Sony, among others.

12
Techniques for Improving Access to Information by Value

CHAPTER OBJECTIVES

In this chapter, you will learn:

- The importance of accessing records by content
- The use of indexing as a method to support access to files by content
- Ways to use Java to implement simple indexes and indexed files
- The basic principles of multilevel indexing and B+ trees
- Ways to create and maintain files that are ordered by key value
- Ways to combine the ordered sequential access model with B+ trees
- The basic principles of hash tables and extendible hashing
- Ways to use SQL to create indexes
- Oracle8's ability to support optimization of physical organization

*T*he main capability needed to adapt file structure techniques to support relational databases is efficient access to records by content. Most relational operations require finding rows of tables that satisfy some condition. These conditions require that certain attributes have specific values. A select operation requires finding rows that satisfy the select condition. A join operation requires finding all rows in one table that have an attribute whose value matches some row in another table. These operations will be terribly inefficient if we must read every record of a file to find those few records that satisfy a particular condition.

The file structure techniques introduced in Chapter 11 tell us how to efficiently store and retrieve information but not how to find specific records by their content. In this chapter, we look at several ways to create secondary structures that allow us to search among records in data files. These structures are used extensively in Chapter 13 to produce efficient relational queries.

One unfortunate use of terminology in information systems relates to the way that "key" has multiple meanings depending on its context. The *search key* of a structure is the value that is used to search it. It need not be unique—indeed, often it is not. In this chapter, we use "key" to mean search key and "primary key" to mean the attribute of a relation whose values are unique.

Using Indexes to Access Records by Content

12.1

One fundamental problem in implementing a relational DBMS is executing queries efficiently. In most cases, query processing involves selecting rows that satisfy selection criteria—that is, rows whose attributes have particular values. The most usual case is the one in which a row must be selected by its primary key. Hence, we'll consider access by primary key to be our first problem.

Section 11.6 included a brief description of why files of fixed-sized records that are maintained in order by primary key will not provide efficient access. The simplest reason is that the cost of insertion is so high. A more subtle reason is that fixed-sized records waste considerable space in many applications. For string values, a fixed-sized record must include enough space for the longest possible value. In the case of family names, for instance, most people have fairly short names, containing fewer than eight letters. Some people, however, have names consisting of 20 or more letters.

No matter how the file is organized, access by content will involve searching. Our goal is to make this searching as efficient as possible. We can quantify this goal as follows:

> Given a primary key value and a 1 million-record file, it must be possible to find the record containing that key, or to determine that no such record exists, with a small number of disk accesses (for instance, no more than *three*).

Meeting this goal may seem difficult, but we'll see that the development of file structures has made it possible, and not difficult to implement. This development has two phases: the introduction of indexing methods and the subsequent extension of those methods to a dynamic, height-balanced tree index called a *B+ tree*.

12.1.1   An Index for a File of `Movie` Records

An *index* of a file resembles an index of a book in some ways—both are lists of topics and references to places where information related to those topics can be found. A book index allows us to access a book based on its content. It also allows access to the book in an order that is different from the primary order of the book. In a book index, the topics are words or phrases, and the references are page numbers. An index provides an association between a topic and the pages where that topic is covered in the book.

In a file index, the topics are search keys that consist of values that can be found in specific records. Each reference is the address in a file where further information

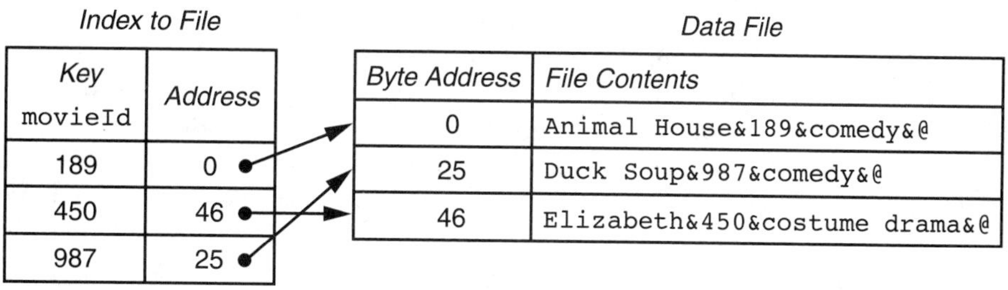

FIGURE 12.1 _____

A data file and associated index

related to the associated key can be found. Typically, the key is the value of a field in a record and the address is the location in the file where that record is stored. A single key may have many addresses.

To make this scenario simpler, let's assume that each key value is associated with a single address and that each key value appears only once in an index. Later, we can discuss more general cases. This *unique-key* index is very useful for storing keys of relational tables. Figure 12.1 shows a file with three `Movie` objects and an index to that file that is represented as a set of *key–reference* pairs. The records in the data file are represented as three text fields delimited by &, with @ as an end-of-record delimiter. This style of representing data was described in Section 11.2.

The file in Fig. 12.1 contains three records, so the index contains three pairs of values. The key values are stored in the index in increasing order. The record with the smallest key (189) is the first record in the file, at address 0. The record with key 450 is the third record in the file and is stored at address 46, and the record with key 987 is the second record and is stored at address 25.

The combination of data file and index create an *indexed file*—one in which the record read and write operations on the data file are combined with search and update operations on the index. In an indexed file, the record with key 450 can be accessed as follows:

1. Search the index for the key with value 450.
2. Extract the address, 46, associated with the key.
3. Read the record at address 46 of the data file.

Updating, inserting, or deleting a new record from an indexed file requires that both the data file and the index be modified to reflect the change. The operation to add a new record to the data file proceeds in the following way:

1. Search the index to determine that the key is not already in the file.
2. Append the record to the data file and determine the address of the new record.
3. Insert the key–reference pair into the index.

The operation to delete a record from the data file must delete the corresponding key–reference pair from the index as well. The operation to update a record must accommodate two special cases. If the key value of the record has changed, the key in the index must also be changed. If the address of the record has changed—for example, as a result of an increase in the size of the record as described in Section 11.8—the address in the index must be changed, too. If neither the key nor the address of the record has changed, no change to the index is required.

12.1.2 Java Implementation of Simple Indexes and Indexed Files

An index is a list of key–reference pairs. It has three operations: insert, search, and remove. The purpose of an index is to store an address for each key and to return the address in response to a search for the key. Figure 12.2 gives the basic definition of an index class.

These methods are not difficult to implement. (The full code is given on this book's Web site.) If we choose to keep the keys in order, we can perform a binary search on the key array to realize the optimal search speed. The insertion and deletion of key–reference pairs is fairly expensive in terms of speed. In the worst case, these operations require moving each key and each address, so that the cost growth is linear, based on the number of keys. This cost is not a serious problem as long as the number of keys is not too large. As we will see in the next section, however, as the number of keys grows, keeping them in order is much too expensive.

We use the term *simple index* to refer to the practice of keeping an entire index in a single object. We can store this object in a file to make it persistent. Class `SimpleIndexedFile`, given in Fig. 12.3, supports primary key indexing of data files. Each `SimpleIndexedFile` object includes two files: an *index file* and a data file. The `open` operation of the `SimpleIndexedFile` (lines 6–17) opens the

```
 1 public class SimpleIndex implements Serializable {
 2    //constructors
 3    public SimpleIndex(int maxSize);
 4    //insert, search and remove methods
 5    public boolean insert (int key, long address);
 6    public long getAddressOf(int key);
 7    public boolean remove(int key);
 8    public boolean remove(int key, long address);
 9    //members
10    protected int maxKeys;
11    protected int numKeys;
12    protected int [] keys;
13    protected lcng [] addresses;
14 };
```

FIGURE 12.2 _____

Basic definition of class `SimpleIndex`

```
 1 public class SimpleIndexedFile {
 2   protected RecordFile dataFile;
 3   protected SimpleIndex index;
 4   String fileName;
 5   public SimpleIndexedFile() {}
 6   public void open (String fileName) throws IOException {
 7   // open an existing indexed file
 8     try {
 9       this.fileName = fileName;
10       dataFile = new RecordFile(fileName+".dat","rw");
11       ObjectInputStream indexStream = new ObjectInputStream(
12           new FileInputStream(fileName+".ind"));
13       index = (SimpleIndex)indexStream.readObject();
14     } catch (ClassNotFoundException e) {
15       throw new IOException ("Index file corrupted");
16     }
17   }
18   public void create(String fileName, int maxKeys)
19     throws IOException {
20   // create a new indexed file
21       dataFile = new RecordFile(fileName+".dat","rw");
22       index = new SimpleIndex(maxKeys);
23       this.fileName=fileName;
24   }
25   public void close() throws IOException {
26     dataFile.close();
27     FileOutputStream indexOut
28         = new FileOutputStream(fileName+".ind");
29     ObjectOutputStream indexStream = new
30       ObjectOutputStream(indexOut);
31     indexStream.writeObject (index);
32     indexStream.close();
33   }
34   public void read(InputOutputRecord rec, int key)
35     throws IOException {}
36   public void update(InputOutputRecord rec, int key)
37     throws IOException {}
38   public void append(InputOutputRecord rec, int key)
39     throws IOException {}
40 };
```

FIGURE 12.3 _____

Partial implementation of class SimpleIndexedFile

data file, then opens the index file and loads its single object into memory. The `create` method (lines 18–24) makes a new indexed file. The `close` method (lines 25–33) closes the data file (line 26) and then writes the `SimpleIndex` object into the index file (lines 29–31). The methods `read`, `update`, and `append` are implemented as described in Sections 11.7 and 11.8.

The code given in Fig. 12.3 distinguishes between creating a new indexed file and opening an existing file, but it does not enforce this distinction properly. In particular, method `create` should check whether the data file and index file already exist. Unfortunately, the constructors for Java file classes that are used in Fig. 12.3 open a file if one exists and create a file otherwise. They cannot be used to check whether the file existed before it was opened.

The Java class `File` supports a platform-independent definition of file and directory names. A `File` object is constructed with a specific file name and path. This object supports the determination of the existence of a file (method `exists`) and the type of the file (methods `isFile` and `isDirectory`). Using a `File` object, we can check for the existence of the data file and index file. This action will allow us to enforce the difference between methods `create` and `open` in class `SimpleIndexedFile` and to ensure that the data file and the index file are consistent. This modification to class `SimpleIndexedFile` is left for you as an exercise.

12.1.3   Limitations of the Simple Index Strategy

Class `SimpleIndexedFile` requires that the entire index reside in memory while the indexed file is open. The index is much smaller than the data file. Nevertheless, as the number of records becomes large, keeping the index in memory will degrade application performance. To illustrate the problem with the speed of execution, suppose that an application needs to read only a small percentage of the records. The application must still read the entire index into memory before it can read the necessary records.

It would not be difficult to modify class `SimpleIndexedFile` to represent the index as a list of index objects. We could add methods to manage the records in memory and in the file. In addition, we could arrange for a limited number of *index records* to be held in memory at any time. We could even make the index records fixed-sized so that we could perform binary searching on the index file.

A sorted list of index records will not provide a very satisfactory indexing strategy. All of the problems that are inherent in sorted files crop up with this approach. We have mediocre search times for binary search, and insert and delete operations are extremely expensive. A proper solution to providing high-performance indexing requires the much more complex strategy of multilevel indexing and B+ trees, which is presented in Section 12.3.

Secondary Indexes

12.2

How can we support record access by values of fields other than the primary key? *Secondary indexes* provide that capability. An example is indexing a `Movie` file by `name` or by `genre`. The name of a movie may be a unique value, but certainly its genre is not. Hence, we need to consider non-unique key indexes.

12.2.1 Mapping Non-Key Fields to Primary Keys

The simplest way to add a secondary index to a data file is to use the primary key index strategy, where the reference fields point directly to data file records. This strategy requires any change in the address of the data record to be reflected in the reference fields of every secondary index. In this case, the cost of moving data records is quite high.

An alternative is to use the primary key value as the reference field of the secondary index. That is, the secondary index associates each non-key value with the primary key of each record that contains it. In the case of our `Movie` data file, the name "Animal House" in the secondary index will be associated with the ID (primary key) 189. Figure 12.4 shows a secondary index of the `Movie` file using primary keys for reference values.

This organization of secondary indexes minimizes the cost of maintaining the indexes in the presence of record updates. A change to a non-key field of a record requires a corresponding modification to the secondary index for that field, but no changes to any other index. Movement of the data record requires modification to the primary key index, but no changes to secondary indexes. A change to the key field of an object remains a very expensive operation, because it requires changes to all indexes, both primary and secondary.

12.2.2 Supporting Different Key Types

Class `SimpleIndex` is limited because it supports only integer keys. Because both `name` and `genre` are `String` fields, the `SimpleIndex` class cannot be used to create an index for these fields. If we were using C++ or Ada as our implementation language, we could make the class into a template (C++) or generic (Ada). These language features support polymorphic, or multitype, operations. Java does not have such a feature.

The implementation of class `SimpleIndex` requires that the key type support the following operations:

- Creation of an array of key values
- Assignment of key values
- Comparison of key values, both less-than and equal

Secondary Index			Index to file			Data file	
Secondary key title	Primary key movieId		Key movieId	Address		Byte Address	File Contents
Animal House	189		189	0		0	Animal H. . . .
Duck Soup	987		450	46		25	Duck Sou. . . .
Elizabeth	450		987	25		46	Elizabet. . . .

FIGURE 12.4 _____

Index that maps secondary keys to primary keys

We can create an index class that supports any key with those operations. Unfortunately, an inspection of class `Object` reveals that while array definition, assignment, and equality are supported, less-than operations are not. We have three options. First, we do not have to keep the keys sorted. In this case, we can build a class `ObjectIndex` whose key type is `Object`. Second, we can define an interface for comparable objects—that is, objects that support a less-than operation. Third, we can implement a `StringIndex` class and require that keys be translated into strings for indexing.

12.2.3   Supporting Non-Unique Indexes

The simplest method for using non-unique keys is to allow the insertion of a key that is already in the index. This solution will suffice in cases where the number of references per key is small. Otherwise, the duplication of key values—one copy for each reference—will result in a significant waste of space and a loss of efficiency in searching for particular key–reference pairs.

Another approach involves reference lists. For each key value in the index, a list of references will be stored. This technique eliminates the waste associated with duplicate key values and replaces it by a small overhead for the list structure. Figure 12.5 illustrates an implementation of this approach, where each reference list is represented as a linked list of records in a separate reference file. The figure shows some of the records in the secondary index and reference file. Many additional `Movie` objects have been added to the data file, including those with `movieId` values of 1135 and 276. These two new records have a `rating` of "G." There are now three records in the file with this same value for `rating`.

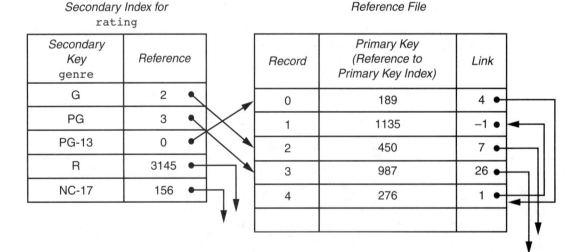

FIGURE 12.5
Representing non-unique secondary keys with a reference file

In the secondary index file of Fig. 12.5, the reference field associated with a key contains the number of the record in the reference file that contains the first reference for that key. Each record in the reference file contains a reference value for the key as well as the address of the next reference for the same key. Each linked list of primary key references is terminated by a "–1" in the link field.

A simple improvement of the organization of the reference file is to cluster the primary key values into blocks, with each block containing references to records with the same non-key value. Reading a block from the reference file yields a set of references to similar records. This organization requires fewer read operations to find all records with a common value.

Multilevel Indexes and B+ Trees

12.3

In 1964, Bayer and McCreight described a data structure called the *B-tree* that represents indexes of data files. A variation called the *B+ tree* remains the ideal indexing strategy. A B+ tree is guaranteed to be height-balanced and to have search, insert, and delete operations whose execution times are linear in the height of the tree.

The most astounding thing about B+ trees is that they can be used to guarantee very fast searching times, even for very large files. Such an index can access a data file with 1,000,000 records with no more that three disk reads. The index can be updated just as quickly.

We can think of a B+ tree as a *multilevel index* of a data file. The lowest-level index is an index of the data file, the next level is an index of the lowest level, and so on. The multiple indexes form a search tree for the data file. The explanation and specification of the B+ tree proceeds by the following steps:

1. Show how an index can be represented as an ordered list of simple index records.
2. Describe a multilevel indexing strategy.
3. Give a formal definition of a B+ tree.
4. Demonstrate the B+ tree insertion algorithm.

This depiction of B+ trees differs from many other presentations primarily in that each level of our B+ tree is an index to the next level. The Further Readings section lists references that provide more extensive treatments as well as one very similar presentation [FZR97] that includes a detailed explanation of these differences. Any difference in presentation has no significant effect on the characteristics or implementation of B+ trees.

12.3.1   Representing an Index as an Ordered List of Simple Index Records

The first step in extending the simple indexing strategy of Section 12.1.2 to support arbitrarily large data files is to break the index into multiple records in a file. We can create a list of simple index records in which each index record contains

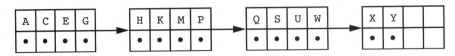

FIGURE 12.6 _____
A multirecord index of the keys `ACEGHKMPQSUWXY` *with four keys per record*

keys that are less than the keys of the next record. An index of the 14 characters `ACEGHKMPQSUWXY`, with 4 keys per record, would take 4 records, as illustrated in Fig. 12.6. In the figure, the data file references are represented with dots (•).

It's easy to see that the insertion of new keys will be expensive. Inserting B, for instance, will cause the first record to overflow. The G will have to be shifted into the second record, and so on. Consequently, every record of the index changes as a result of a single insertion. The cost of the index insertion grows linearly with the number of index records.

The solution to this problem is to treat this list of records as a linked list in the index file. That is, we will not maintain the index records in order in the file. Rather, the records will be stored at arbitrary locations. We will have to keep track of the location of each index record, however (more about that later).

The attempt to insert B in the index will cause the first record to overflow. We correct this problem by splitting the record into two records: one with three keys and one with two keys (Fig. 12.7). Now the records are no longer in sorted order in the file, and they are no longer full of keys. Our 14 keys now occupy five index records, even though they could be stored in four records. This space that appears wasted is actually the key to making the multirecord indexing strategy work. The insertion of a key now affects at most two records in the index. In addition, notice that we can insert keys D and F without any more record splitting.

We have reduced the cost of insertion to a constant that is independent of the number of keys in the index. Searching the index is very slow, however, because we must start at the beginning and look at every index record until we find the key. This approach results in reading half of the index records in the average case.

The solution to decreasing the cost of searching the index is the same one that we used in Section 12.1 for data files: Build an index for the keys of the records. This technique leads to multiple levels of indexes.

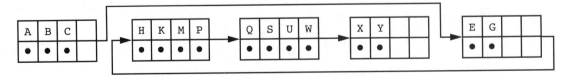

FIGURE 12.7 _____
The index of Fig. 12.6 after inserting B *and splitting the first record. The arrows show the logical order of the index records.*

12.3.2   Multilevel Indexing

To build an index to the file of index records depicted in Fig. 12.7, we need to pick a key for each record. The records are sorted, so the largest key in each index record can be used to represent the entire index record. The keys for the records will be C for the first record, G for the second record, and so on. Figure 12.8 shows a two-level index for the keys of Fig. 12.7. The records are now shown in logical order, which need not be the same as the physical order in the file.

In Fig. 12.8, the reference fields of the simple index records at the top level are denoted by arrows and are used to contain references to records in the next level of the index. The horizontal arrows show the logical order of each level of the index. The value of each reference is the address of the record in the index file that is pointed to by the arrow. The records for both levels of the index can be stored in a single file of simple index records.

We can take this process one step further by adding a third level, resulting in the tree of Fig. 12.9. Now we have a complete index—a tree whose nodes are index records. A single root node makes up the first level. This root node is an index

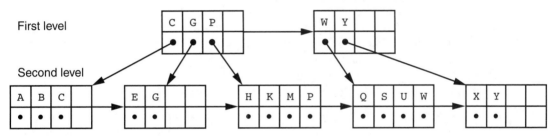

FIGURE 12.8 _____
A two-level index for the keys of Fig. 12.7. The arrows represent the reference fields associated with the keys of the first-level index.

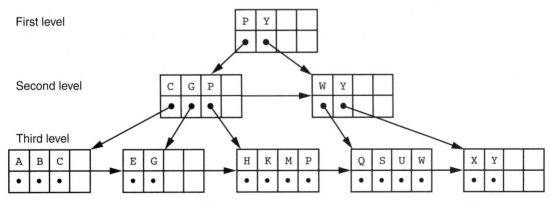

FIGURE 12.9 _____
A three-level index for the keys of Fig. 12.8

record whose references are to nodes at the second level. More nodes appear at the second level. These second-level nodes are index records whose references are to nodes at the third level. Finally, the third-level nodes are index records whose references are to records in the data file.

The search algorithm for this three-level index can best be illustrated by considering some examples. Let's search for the data record whose key value is P. We search the node at the first level and find that the first key is P. We use its reference value (arrow) to access the first node of the second level and search that node. We find P as the third key of this node and use its reference to access the third node of the third level. We find P as the fourth key, extract the data record reference (denoted by • in the figure), and use it to access the data record in the data file. Thus our search looks at three index records, one in each level.

Two more searches will complete the illustration. First, let's look for E. We do not find E in the root node. Because E is less than or equal to P and P is the largest key in its second-level node, however, we should look for E in the second-level node pointed to by P. Looking in the first node in the second level, we again do not find E, but conclude that we should look in the third-level node pointed to by key G. In this node (the second node in the third level), we find E, extract the data record address, and read the data file.

A search for F, which does not appear in the tree, follows the same path as the search for E. When we get to the bottom of the tree, we do not find F and must conclude that no data record with key F exists.

12.3.3   Definition and Performance of B+ Trees

A B+ tree is a dynamic, multilevel index with upper and lower bounds on the number of keys (and references) in each index record (or node). The maximum number of keys in a record is called the *order of the B+ tree*. The minimum number of keys per record is one-half of the maximum number of keys. The only exception to this rule relates to the root, which has no minimum number of keys. In the examples given earlier, the order is 4 and each index record must have between 2 and 4 keys. Real B+ trees typically have 100 or more keys per index record.

An important characteristic of B+ trees is that the height of the tree—that is, the number of index levels—is dynamic. As a B+ tree grows and shrinks, its height grows and shrinks as necessary. The details of the growth of a B+ tree are given in Section 12.3.4 as part of the discussion of B+ tree insertion.

For a B+ tree of order k, each node (except the root) must have between $k/2$ and k keys. The references in the interior (nonleaf) nodes refer to other B+ tree nodes. The references in leaf nodes refer to data file records. Each leaf node appears at the same height (or distance from the root) of the tree. These rules constrain the B+ tree to have the form of the multilevel indexes of Section 12.3.2.

The number of keys that may be indexed by a B+ tree is a function of the order of the tree and its height. The maximum number of keys at the leaf level of a B+ tree of order k and height h is k^h. The one root node (level 1) has k descendants, so level 2 has k^2 keys. These level-2 nodes have k descendants each, so level 3 has k^3 keys, and so on.

The minimum number of keys at level h of a B+ tree of order k is $2(k/2)^{h-1}$. This situation occurs when the root node has 2 descendants and every other node has k/2 descendants.

For a B+ tree of order 250 and height 3, the maximum number of keys in the leaf nodes is 250^3 (15,625,000), and the minimum number of keys is 31,250. The minimum number of keys at this height is less interesting than the minimum number that may cause the tree to grow in height. That is, what is the minimum number of keys in a height 4 tree? The answer is 3,906,250 keys. Thus a tree with fewer than 4 million keys will be represented by a B+ tree of order 250 and height 3.

The number of disk access operations required to read a data record using a B+ tree index is the number of access operations required to search the tree plus the one access operation of the data file. To search a data file of 1,000,000 keys, using a B+ tree of order 250, requires searching one index node in each level, for a total of 3 nodes. We routinely keep the root node of the tree in memory, so the total number of disk access operations required to search the tree is 2. Hence, we can read any record in a 1,000,000-record file with no more than 3 disk accesses.

12.3.4   B+ Tree Insertion and Deletion

The discussion of multilevel indexing so far has shown what B+ trees look like. The multilevel index of Fig. 12.9 is a B+ tree of order 4 with 15 keys. To understand how B+ trees grow, we will start with an empty tree and show how the tree of Fig. 12.9 is generated by insertion. We will insert the 15 keys in the order CSHPQAGXWYBEUMK into the tree and watch the tree grow.

The basic insertion algorithm is to search the tree for the new key and insert the new key into the leaf node that is identified by the search. Beginning with an empty tree, the first four keys are inserted into the root as shown in Fig. 12.10a. Inserting Q will cause the root node to overflow. We react to the potential overflow by splitting the node, leaving two nodes: one with keys CIO and one with keys QS. The result is not a tree, so we create a new root node and insert the keys of the two leaf nodes—namely, O and S—into the root node. The result is shown as Fig. 12.10b. The next key, A, is inserted into the first leaf node. The insertion of G will then cause the first node to overflow. Again, the overflowing node is split and the new node inserted into the root. The result is shown in Fig. 12.10c.

Inserting keys W and Y causes the third node to split, leaving four leaf nodes. Figure 12.10d shows the tree after B is inserted. The insertion of the next key, E, will cause the first leaf node to split. Figure 12.10e shows the result of inserting E. The final tree, after inserting UMK, is exactly that shown in Fig. 12.9.

Deletion of a key from a B+ tree is similar to insertion, except that insertion leads to overflow, and deletion leads to underflow. The deletion of a key begins with the deletion of the key from its leaf node. There are several additional steps:

1. If the number of keys that remain in the node is less than the minimum (an underflow condition):

   a. Move one or more keys from a sibling node (that is, an adjacent node with the same parent) so that both the original and the sibling node have at least the minimum number of keys.

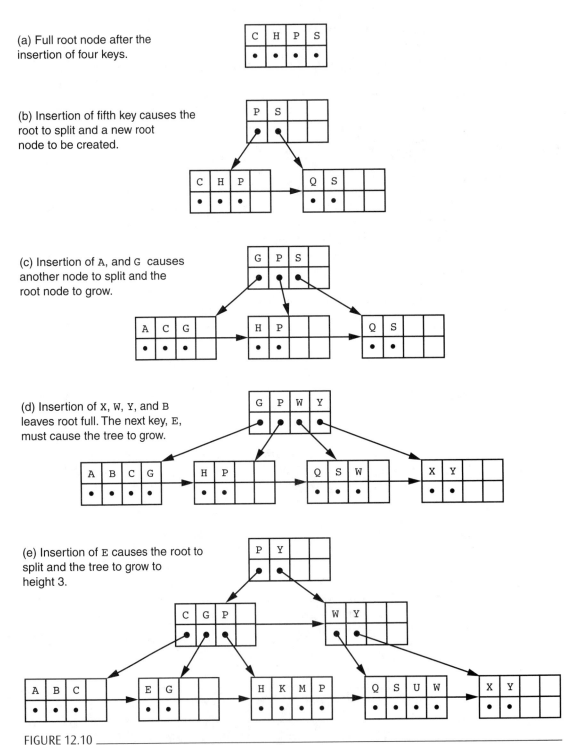

(a) Full root node after the insertion of four keys.

(b) Insertion of fifth key causes the root to split and a new root node to be created.

(c) Insertion of A, and G causes another node to split and the root node to grow.

(d) Insertion of X, W, Y, and B leaves root full. The next key, E, must cause the tree to grow.

(e) Insertion of E causes the root to split and the tree to grow to height 3.

FIGURE 12.10

The growth of a B+ tree that occurs when keys CSHPQA... *are inserted into an empty tree*

b. If the sibling nodes also have the minimum number of nodes, merge the original node and one of its siblings into a single node.

2. If the largest key in any node has changed, replace the corresponding key in the parent node with the largest key in the child node.

3. If a node was deleted as a result of step 1, delete the corresponding key in its parent node and repeat steps 1–3 for that node.

4. If the root node has only one child, delete the root node and make its child become the root. Reduce the height of the tree by 1.

As an example, consider the deletion of key G from the tree of Fig. 12.10e. Removing G from the second leaf node leaves only a single key in that node and hence creates an underflow condition. Either rule 1a or rule 1b can be used to remove the underflow.

Figure 12.11a shows the result of applying rule 1a. Key C has been moved from the first to the second leaf node, leaving two nodes in each leaf node. The largest key in the first node is B, and the largest key in the second node is E. The leftmost node in the middle level has been modified to reflect the keys in the leaf nodes.

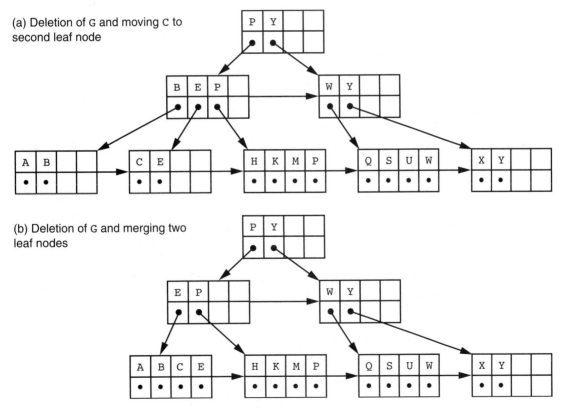

FIGURE 12.11

Two alternative results from deleting G from the tree of Fig. 12.10e

Figure 12.11b shows the result of applying rule 1b. The first two leaf nodes have been merged into a single node with four keys. One key has been deleted from the leftmost node in the middle level, leaving only two keys in that node.

A NOTE ON REPRESENTING B+ TREES IN JAVA

The details of the representation of B+ trees are not included here. Other sources cover the topic in great detail, as described in the Further Readings section. The book's Web site has a full implementation of B+ tree operations in Java.

12.3.5   Indexed Sequential Files and B+ Trees

We have seen how to make indexing very fast, but we have not looked at how much it costs to access the data file. For a single read, we must search the B+ tree to obtain a record address and read a single data file record. What happens if we want to read two data records? Suppose, for instance, that we want to read all of the records whose key value lies within a certain range of values. First, we find the record with the smallest key in the range through our normal B+ tree search. We then read the corresponding data record. The next larger key value is in an adjacent location in the B+ tree and can probably be found without reading any B+ tree records. The ideal situation would occur when the data record appears in the same block in the data file. In this case, we wouldn't need any read operations to get the next data record.

This procedure is a long way of saying that reading records by key value would be easier if the data file were in the same order as the leaf levels of the B+ tree—that is, if the data records were in key order. A file that is in order by key value and has a B+ tree for its primary key is called an *indexed sequential file*. The data structure that supports indexed sequential files is the B+ tree.

Figure 12.12 shows an indexed sequential file. It includes the B+ tree of Fig 12.10e above the gray line and the file of data records below the line. The dots in the address fields of the B+ tree nodes represent the addresses of the corresponding data records. Each data record is shown with its key value. The data record blocks are shown as a linked list to illustrate the logical order of the blocks. Nevertheless, the physical ordering of the blocks is not restricted. Each data block contains one or two data records and a pointer to the next record. Starting from any data record, we can read the records in key order by following the pointers.

The indexed sequential file organization relies on having a data file that can be efficiently read in key order and that also supports efficient insertion and deletion. We saw in Section 11.6 that a data file that is ordered by key value supports efficient sequential read, but has extremely slow insertion and deletion. We can create a better representation by allowing the data file to be a linked list of ordered blocks of records, just like the index records in a single level of a B+ tree.

An *ordered sequential file* organizes data records into blocks of fixed size that are ordered and linked. We can insert records into an ordered sequential file by

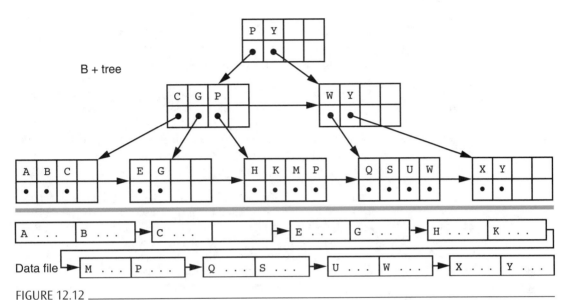

FIGURE 12.12 _____

Example of an indexed sequential file

adding the new record to an existing block and splitting on overflow. The new block created by the split can be located anywhere in the data file and is linked into position. An indexed sequential file is the combination of an index, often a B+ tree, and an ordered sequential file.

The indexed sequential file insertion algorithm controls the creation of the B+ tree index and the ordered sequential data file. To insert a record, we first search for the key in the B+ tree. The B+ tree search algorithm identifies the next largest key and its address in the data file. Then the ordered sequential file insertion algorithm is executed to insert the data record into the same block as that of this next largest key. The insertion may cause the block to split and a new block to be added to the data file. This splitting requires some modification of the B+ tree. Finally, the key–reference pair of the new data record is inserted into the B+ tree.

The indexed sequential file organization yields excellent performance for access to records by primary key. Reading all of the records whose keys fall within a range of values can be accomplished by reading a minimal number of blocks. Each block that is read contains records that are relevant to the search and are in order by primary key. No data block must be read twice to read records in key order. More detail on these advantages can be found in Chapter 13, where we discuss the use of indexed sequential files in processing select and join queries.

This organization does not preclude having additional indexes for non-key values. Finding all records with a range of values for a non-key attribute will not produce efficient usage of data blocks, however, because the records in a block will not all be relevant to the search.

A NOTE ON ENHANCEMENTS TO B+ TREE INDEXING

As noted earlier, the B+ tree presentation in this book is somewhat nonstandard. We treat a B+ tree as a multilevel index, with each level of the tree forming a complete index of the blocks in the next level. This approach is a bit of overkill. In practice, each interior node is used simply to guide the search to the next level. The keys in the interior nodes must be values that separate its children, but do not have to identify them as they do in this book.

The standard definition of B+ trees distinguishes between interior and leaf nodes. The leaf nodes are just like those in our treatment and form a complete index of the data file. Each interior node, has one fewer key than it has children, however, and the value of each key separates two subtrees. Any value less than the key searches to the left, and any value larger than the key searches to the right.

The use of separators instead of keys allows us to improve the storage utilization of interior nodes when the search keys are long strings. A *simple prefix B+ tree* uses the shortest possible value to separate each pair of subtrees. The separator is chosen to be the shortest prefix of the smallest key in the right subtree that is greater than any string in the left subtree. The diagram below shows a simple prefix B+ tree. The value R separates the two subtrees of the root node. In the second level, Cap separates the first two nodes, and so on. The search algorithm for the simple prefix tree is the same as that given for a B+ tree.

Now that the interior node values are expected to be short, we can change the rules about how many keys and subtrees are required. A reasonable rule would be to use a fixed-sized block to hold each interior node. The node would not overflow until its values and node references do not fit in the block. This approach leads to a B+ tree that is as bushy as possible for a particular physical block size.

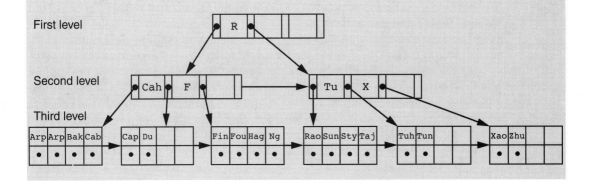

Representing Indexes with Hash Tables

12.4   *Hashing* refers to the process of converting attribute values directly into addresses. A *hash table index*, as illustrated in Fig. 12.13, stores each key–reference pair at a specific location within a *hash table*. In contrast, the indexing methods described in previous sections used searchable data structures to provide access to a collection of key–reference pairs. The address of a pair in a hash table is calculated from the key value by using a *hash function*. To search a hash table for a specific key, simply

Hash buckets

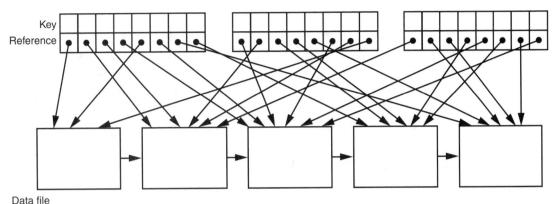

FIGURE 12.13

A hash table index

apply the hash function to the key to determine an address (a *hash value*) and then look at that location in the hash table for the key.

A hash function maps the domain of the key attribute onto a range of integer values. The range of the hash function is usually much smaller than the domain, so many key values map to the same address. Each address in a hash table index identifies a block, or *bucket*, that can contain many key–reference pairs.

Hashing yields a very fast search. At most, one disk read is needed to find an arbitrary key. What hashing does not do is order a set of keys. A hash table cannot be used to find all keys in a range or to create a list of keys in order. Hashing is most appropriate with keys that are never used for range queries.

12.4.1   Hash Functions

A hash function maps a domain of values into a range of values. A good hash function evenly distributes the values of interest among the range. If every key that we are interested in maps to the same bucket, however, the hash function is useless. It's unfortunate that a function that is good for one set of values may be terrible for another set of values. The goal of hash function design is to create a function that is very likely to work well.

Consider a function that maps 32-bit integers into 10-bit non-negative numbers—that is, into the range 0..1,023. Two obvious hash functions are to take the top 10 bits or the bottom 10 bits. If we take the top 10, all positive numbers (top bit off) map to the range 0..511 and all negative numbers (top bit on) map to the range 512..1,023. Hashing a set of positive numbers will use only half of the address space. Similarly, when using the lower 10 bits, all positive numbers map to positive values. If the key values are ASCII codes, the bit patterns are restricted and once again these simple hash functions don't work very well.

Extensive studies have found that, in many cases, a function of the following form works best:

$$h(k) = (a \times k + b) \bmod m$$

The value m determines the range of values of the hash function. The choice of a and b affects the distribution of values. In many cases, appropriate values for a and b can be found experimentally by testing the distribution of a representative sample of expected values.

We still need some way to turn an arbitrary key into a numerical value. If we start with a 10-byte string, for instance, the preceding argument suggests that we cannot start by selecting some of the bits. Instead, we need to use the entire value. We find inspiration in the dictionary definition of hash: "chop into small pieces . . . muddle or confuse." With a long key, we should chop it into small pieces and hash the pieces back together.

Specifically, we break the long key into 32-bit sections and add those sections together, taking care to avoid arithmetic overflow. The result is a 32-bit value, suitable for input into a hash function.

In this way, we can create a hash function that works on arbitrarily large key strings. We can concatenate several keys to create a long string, chop the string into 32-bit numbers, add the numbers, and hash the result to determine a bucket address. All of this arithmetic has preserved the basic principle—that identical values map to identical addresses.

12.4.2   Insertion into Hash Tables

Inserting a key–reference pair into a hash table requires several steps, including the creation of a hash value:

1. Prepare the key for hashing by transforming it into a number in the domain of the hash function.
2. Calculate the hash value of the key.
3. Determine the bucket address from the hash value.
4. Insert the pair into the bucket.
5. Handle the possible bucket overflow.

Many strategies for handling buckets exist. In-memory hash tables might consider buckets that hold a single key. Disk-resident hash tables usually have buckets whose size is one or more disk pages. A *collision* occurs when two keys in the table hash to the same address. A secondary insertion strategy is used to insert multiple keys that have the same hash address.

Small buckets are not of much interest to our efforts because we expect the bucket size to be one or more disk pages. Hence, we consider only large bucket hash tables. Insertion works easily until buckets overflow. Of course, bucket overflow is a complex subject, and a variety of complex strategies can be used to optimize search times and space requirements. In this section, we look briefly at one strategy, called *extendible hashing*. References to implementation details can be found in the Further Readings listings.

An *extendible hash table* begins with a single bucket and grows by splitting buckets. The bucket address of a key is the first few bits of its hash value. When an insertion causes a bucket to overflow, that bucket is split and its address is extended by one bit. The addresses of the two resulting buckets differ only by that bit. The keys in the bucket are all rehashed and distributed among the two buckets according to their hash values.

The hash table includes a *bucket directory* that maps hash values to buckets. The number of bits in the bucket address determines the size of the directory. Whenever a bucket splits and requires more bits than are supported by the directory, the directory doubles in size. Figure 12.14a illustrates an extendible hash table that has five buckets and a three-bit bucket address. Addresses 000 and 001 refer to the first bucket, 010 and 011 to the second, 100 to the third, 101 to the fourth, and 110 and 111 to the fifth. Buckets 1, 2, and 5 have two-bit addresses, and buckets 3 and 4 have three-bit addresses.

The rest of Fig. 12.14 illustrates what happens when buckets overflow. Figure 12.14b shows the result after bucket 5 is split. Address 110 still refers to bucket 5, but 111 now refers to the new bucket 6. The hash values for the keys that were in bucket 5 have been recalculated. Each key whose hash value begins with 111 was put in bucket 6. The keys whose hash values begin with 110 remain in bucket 5. Three bits are still sufficient for the bucket addresses.

Figure 12.14c shows the result after bucket 4 splits. Bucket 3 had a three-bit address, so the entire directory must be doubled in size. Buckets 1 and 2 still have two-bit addresses, and hence four elements refer to each of these buckets. Buckets 3, 5, and 6 have three-bit addresses and two referring elements. Bucket 4 has the four-bit address 1010, and the new bucket 7 has the four-bit address 1011.

To insert a key in an extendible hash table, we calculate the hash value, use the first bits as the index to the directory, extract the bucket address, and make the insertion into that bucket. If the bucket overflows, it must be split.

The deletion of a key from an extendible hash table is also straightforward. As with deleting from a B+ tree, deleting from a hash table may cause the table to shrink, including a reduction in the number of buckets and the number of bits in the addresses. For the details, see the implementation of these operations in the code given at the book's Web site, or consult one of the Further Readings references.

12.4.3 Searching a Hash Table

Searching a hash table begins by identifying the bucket in which the key belongs. A simple search within the bucket is next. If the key is found in the bucket, the set of all reference values for that key is returned as the search result. If the key is not found in the bucket, the secondary search strategy must be employed to continue the search. One advantage of extendible hash tables is that no secondary search strategy is required. If the search key is not in the bucket, it's not in the table at all.

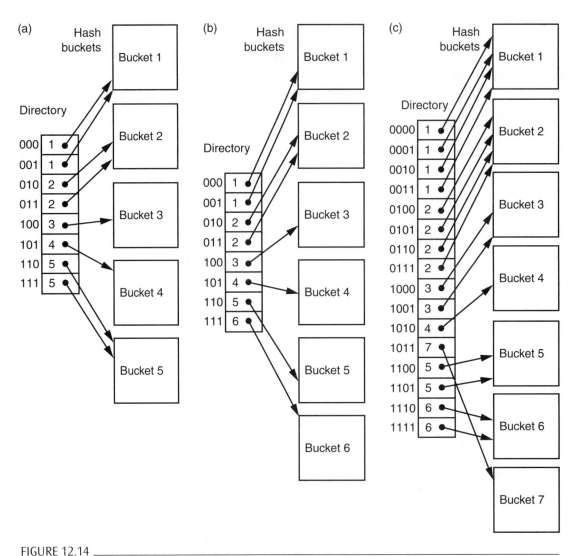

FIGURE 12.14 _____

Extendible hash table showing buckets and data record references

```
public long[] search(String key) {
    long hashValue = hash(key);
    int bucketIndex = hashValue / arraySize;
    long bucketAddress = refArray[bucketIndex];
    Bucket bucket = fetch(bucketAddress);
    return bucket.search(key);
}
```

12.4.4   Hash Tables for Partitioning

The insertion of a collection of key–reference pairs into a hash table divides them into independent sets, each in its own bucket. The buckets form a *partition* of the set of key–reference pairs—that is, if two pairs have exactly the same key, they will appear in the same bucket. Of course, having different keys does not guarantee that they will be located in different buckets.

For searching, partitioning means that if a key is in a bucket, it cannot be in any other bucket. Thus all of its references will be in the same bucket.

As we see in detail in Chapter 13, hash tables can be used to find matching values in a set. To find all duplicate rows in a set of rows, we simply create a hash table from some set of attributes, insert all rows into the hash table, and compare the values within the buckets. To perform this comparison, we must read the set of rows, create the hash table, and read the hash table. The cost is no more than three reads per block of the original set of rows.

Specifying Physical Database Characteristics

12.5

How can we improve the speed of access to information through the specification of physical database characteristics? In earlier chapters, we investigated the role of conceptual and logical models in the design and implementation of information systems. Physical models are important because of their capability to greatly improve the performance and reliability of systems.

Database administrators are responsible for the physical organization of databases. Commercial systems provide the ability to organize the database files to avoid contention and to add indexes to tables.

12.5.1   Organizing Database Files

A database is stored by a DBMS as a collection of data files, which are also called *segments* or *tablespaces*. An Oracle8 database has the following default collection of segments:

- *System*: data dictionary, including schema and table definitions
- *Data*: table contents
- *Index*: indexes for the data tables
- *RBS*: rollback segments (described in Chapter 14)
- *Temp*: temporary tables created and used during SQL processing
- *Tools*: tables for database tools
- *User*: user objects in nonproduction databases

Oracle8 allows you to specify the size and location of these segments, and to create additional segments of these basic types. It also allows the database administrator to assign certain users to specific segments.

Explicit database layout can have a significant effect on performance when the computer system has many disk drives. A DBMS is, first and foremost, a disk access manager; the speed of that access determines the speed of the system. The database server issues many requests for information stored on disks. Those requests create *contention* for disk resources. If all of the server's requests for disk access go to a single disk, the database cannot process more data than a single disk can handle. If the server's requests can be spread evenly over all of the disks, it can run as fast as the aggregate disk speed.

The contention problem has at least two facets. First, the bandwidth of a single disk drive is necessarily less than the bandwidth of two disks. Hence, when multiple requests access the same disk, the response is limited. Second, the degradation in the performance of individual disks degrades the performance of the entire system. From the descriptions of hardware and software structure in Chapter 11, we know that peak performance for a single disk is achieved through streaming data to or from a single cylinder. The lowest performance of a drive comes when each request asks for data on a cylinder far away from the previous request. Hence, if multiple unrelated requests are directed to a single disk, much of the time will be spent in moving heads between distant cylinders.

A concurrent system with severe contention for disk resources will deliver performance well below the expected performance of a single disk. Fortunately, the contention for disks can be minimized through the proper assignment of segments to disks. The *Oracle8 DBA Handbook* [Lon98] is an excellent reference on this subject, suggesting physical layouts for systems with as many as 22 disk drives. Multiple disks are also used to increase reliability by putting logs and control files on separate disks and by creating multiple copies, on different disks, of crucial system information.

A DBMS accesses the segments in predictable patterns. For instance, a complex selection query can be expected to access the index segment to find a record and then the data segment to get its contents. An update will write to the data segment and the RBS segment as well as to the redo log. These access patterns are characteristic of every database and can be used to suggest optimizations.

Specific databases and specific applications have their own patterns of access to tables. These patterns may not be obvious from the schema, but can be found using database performance analysis tools. Oracle8, for example, keeps track of the amount of I/O activity on each segment in system tables. The following select statement returns a list of the files and the amount of I/O per file:

```
select DF.name as fileName, FS.phyBlkRd+FS.phyBlkWrt as totalIO
   from V$DataFile DF, V$FileStat FS where FS.file# = DF.file#
   order by totalIO desc
```

This query uses system tables.

12.5.2   Using SQL to Create Indexes

Indexes support access to information by content. When an attribute of a table has an index, we can use that index to find the row of a table with a specific value for that attribute. An index is also used to iterate through a table in order by the value of the attribute. In addition, it can be used to find all rows for which the value of the attribute is less than a particular value.

Join operations are performed using foreign keys and the related primary keys. Hence, the performance of the join operation is directly related to the existence and quality of the primary key indexes. It is also advisable to have other fields indexed. For example, the `Customer` table of the BigHit Video database has primary key `accountId`. We certainly expect to have to find a customer by last name. Indexing the table on the `lastName` field will greatly improve the performance of this search.

The SQL-92 standard does not include any method of specifying indexes. One could conclude that this omission signals that the specification of indexes is unnecessary and that SQL database systems do not include methods of specifying indexes. Unfortunately, neither conclusion is correct.

A DBMS needs help from database administrators to know what should and should not be indexed. As we saw in detail earlier in this chapter, indexes are expensive to maintain. The cost of an update operation increases as the number of indexes increases. It is impossible to automatically determine which combinations of fields should be indexed.

Although SQL-92 lacks a statement to specify indexes, every commercial DBMS's implementation of SQL includes a create index statement. It emphasizes the need for performance-tuning capabilities in commercial systems and the status of SQL as a standard. That is, SQL has a standard, but no vendor adheres to it. Instead, each vendor makes its own extensions.

In the case of the create index statement, each vendor has a slightly different syntax and semantics. The following examples use the syntax of the Oracle8 DDL:

```
create index customerAccountIdIndex on Customer (accountId);
create index customerLastNameIndex on Customer (lastName);
drop index customerLastNameIndex;
create index prevRentalAccountIdIndex on PreviousRental
        (accountId);
create index prevRentalAcctDateIndex
        on PreviousRental (accountId,dateRented);
```

The statement gives the index a name for later reference, as in the drop index statement.

In the last example, the index covers a pair of properties in order to support fast searching by that pair of properties. For instance, consider the following query, which asks for all videos rented by a particular customer before a certain date:

```
select lastName, firstName, videoId
  from Customer c, PreviousRental p
    where dateRented < '01-may-1999' and
c.accountId=p.accountId
```

This query can be executed by iterating through all customers. For each customer, it will use `prevRentalAcctDateIndex` to select all rows of `PreviousRental` that match the customer and that satisfy the date restriction. Of course, the query optimizer has the responsibility of finding plans that take advantage of the available indexes.

Chapter Summary

Accessing records by content is a fundamental building block for processing relational queries. The primary technique is to create indexes, which are sets of key–reference pairs, as secondary file structures. An index search for a key value yields one or more reference values that can be used to access records in the data file. Effective indexes allow access to records by content with a very small number of disk reads.

An indexed file consists of a data file plus one or more associated indexes. To read a record with a specific key value in an indexed file, you search the index for the key and then use the corresponding reference as an address in the data file to read a data record. Insertion, update, and deletion of records in an indexed file require updates to the indexes.

A simple index is a list of key–reference pairs that is stored in application memory when the data file is opened and written into a file when the data file is closed. This approach works well for small files. As the size of the data file grows, however, the simple index approach becomes unwieldy. These simple indexes are used as components (nodes) of more complex indexing strategies.

A secondary index is one whose keys are not primary keys of the data file. Secondary indexes typically do not require keys to be unique. Such an index must maintain a list of references for each key. A secondary index can be designed to use primary key values as references. Finding a data record in this manner requires searching the secondary index for the expected value, searching the primary key index for the reference value from the first search, and then using the reference value from the primary key index as the address of the data file record.

A B+ tree is a multilevel, balanced tree of index nodes. Each nonleaf level of a B+ tree is an ordered, linked list of index records that serves as an index to the index records in the next lower level of the tree. The leaf level of the B+ tree is an ordered, linked index of the data file. The B+ tree insertion and deletion operations guarantee that the tree remains balanced. The large fan-out of the B+ tree nodes ensures that very few disk reads are required to find keys, even when the number of keys is very large. Because the leaf level of the B+ tree lists all keys in order, the data file can be read in key order using the leaf nodes of the B+ tree.

An indexed sequential file combines an ordered data file with a B+ tree index. The data file is an ordered list of blocks. Insertion into the data file uses block splitting to preserve order within blocks and a linked list to keep the blocks ordered without requiring a sequentially ordered file. An indexed sequential file implements an indexed and ordered sequential access mode. The records of the data file can be read in key order by following the linked list of blocks.

A hash table index represents an index as a collection of buckets, where all keys in a bucket have the same or similar hash values. Like any other index, a hashed index is a list of key–reference pairs. Hash table indexes generally offer faster search times than B+ tree indexes do, but cannot be used for inexact searching or range queries because such an index is not an ordered list of keys.

Searching a hash table index requires first turning the search key into an integer value (typically by a cut-and-add approach), applying the hash function to the integer value, determining a bucket address from the hash value, and searching that bucket for the key. A major advantage of hashing is that it can be used for arbitrarily large search keys, which may be the concatenation of multiple attributes.

Key Terms

B+ tree. A height-balanced, multilevel index structure. A B+ tree grows by splitting nodes and adding parent nodes.

Bucket. A collection of key values, or key–reference pairs, in a hash table. All of the keys in a bucket have the same or similar hash values.

Bucket directory. An array of bucket addresses in an extendible hashing scheme. The index of a directory entry is the first few bits of the hash values of the keys in the referenced bucket.

Extendible hash table. A hash table in which bucket overflow is handled by bucket splitting and a directory of bucket addresses is maintained.

Hash table. A list of key values that are placed in buckets according to their hash values.

Hash table index. An index that is organized as a hash table.

Hash value. The result of applying a hash function to a search key.

Index. A secondary access structure that consists of a list of key–reference pairs and supports access to a data file by the value of a specific attribute.

Index file. A file of index records.

Index record. A list of key–reference pairs that is stored in a single block in an index file.

Indexed file. A combination of data file and index that supports sequential access to the data file and content-based access by search key. Updating the data file requires updating the index.

Indexed sequential file. The combination of a B+ tree index and an ordered, linked-list data file. The B+ tree supports indexed access, and the ordered file supports sequential access in key order.

Key–reference pair. A pair of values consisting of the value of a search key and a reference value that can be used to find a specific record in a data file.

Multilevel index. An index that has a data file index at its lowest level, with each other level being an index of the index records at the next lowest level.

Order of a B+ tree. The maximum number of keys in a B+ tree node. The minimum number of keys is typically one-half or two-thirds of the order.

Ordered sequential file. A file that consists of a linked list of blocks that are ordered by primary key.

Partition. A division of a collection of objects into groups according to some criteria so that any two objects with the same criteria value appear in the same group. The buckets of a hash table partition the keys by hash value.

Search key. The record attribute that is used to search a particular index.

Secondary index. An index on a search key that is not the primary key of the file. A secondary index may have non-unique keys and may use primary key values for its references.

Simple index. An index that consists of a single block of key–reference pairs and is stored in memory while the data file remains open.

Exercises

1. How many records would have to be read, on average, to find a record with a specific key using a sequential search strategy in a 1,000,000-record file? What are the maximum and minimum numbers of records that would have to be read? If no record with this key existed in the file, how many records would have to be read? How would the number of read operations be affected by putting the file in key order?

2. How many records would have to be read, on average, to find a record with a specific key using a binary search strategy in a 1,000,000-record file that is in key order? What are the maximum and minimum numbers of records that would have to be read? If no record with this key existed in the file, how many records would have to be read?

3. Give an algorithm to convert an unordered data file into an indexed file (data file plus index file). Assume that methods exist to open the data file, read the next object from the file and determine its address, extract the key value from an object, create an index file, and insert key–value pairs into the index.

4. Describe the difference between representing a secondary index with data references and representing it with primary key references. Under what circumstances would each be preferable to the other?

5. Give an algorithm to list all of the primary key values whose rating has a specific value, using the secondary index strategy shown in Fig. 12.5. Begin with a definition of the operations that are available on the secondary index class and the reference list class. Your algorithm should use those operations to search the secondary key index for a given key, and traverse the reference file for all of the corresponding primary key values.

6. Suppose you have a B+ tree index of height h for an unordered file containing D blocks of data records. What are the minimum and maximum numbers of disk reads and disk writes required to:

   a. Retrieve a record from the data file?

   b. Add a record to the data file?

   c. Modify the key value of a record in the data file?

   d. Delete a record from the data file?

   e. Retrieve all records from the data file in key order?

7. Use the B+ tree insertion algorithm of Section 12.3.4 to build a B+ tree of order 4 for the following single-letter keys:

   a. YBMKC

   b. AWGXEHPQU

   c. XEHPQUMSAWG

   d. MKCYBSAWGXEHPQU

8. Show the B+ tree of order 4 that results from inserting the single-letter keys RJFTVLZD into the B+ tree of Fig. 12.10e using the algorithm of Section 12.3.4.

9. Show the B+ tree of order 4 that results from deleting key B from the tree of Fig. 12.11a.

10. Show the B+ tree of order 4 that results from deleting key X from the tree of Fig. 12.11b.

11. Use the classes of packages `dbjava.files` and `dbjava.index` (from the book's Web site) to create an indexed file of 15 `Movie` objects using a B+ tree index of order 4. Write a test class that creates the data file and index file and displays them in some symbolic form.

12. Use the classes of packages `dbjava.files` and `dbjava.index` (from the book's Web site) to produce classes that create an ordered sequential file of `Movie` objects, as described in Section 12.3.6. The new class `OrderedSequentialFile` should store a fixed number (default 4) of objects per record and support operations to read sequentially, read by address, read by key value, update, and insert. Write a test class to create an ordered sequential file of 15 `Movie` objects.

13. Using the results of Exercise 12, create a class to support indexed sequential files of `Movie` objects. Use a B+ tree for the index and an ordered sequential file for the data file. Write a test class to create an indexed sequential file of 15 `Movie` objects.

14. Consult a database administration reference to find suggestions for distributing database segments among several disk drives. List the suggested distribution for the smallest recommended number of disks. What segments are distributed in systems with more disks?

15. Using the Web or other references, describe the types of indexes and hash tables that are used in some specific database server. Give examples of the SQL statements that create each type of index.

16. Interrogate a database server and database that you have available to find three tables that have indexes. List the tables and indexes. Write SQL statements to create the tables and indexes.

17. Use the classes of packages `dbjava.files` and `dbjava.index` (from the book's Web site) to develop a program to produce grade-book information from a file of `Assignment` objects and a file of `Grade` objects, as described below. Represent the `Assignments` file as a `SimpleIndexedFile`, and the `Grade` file as a `RecordFile` with records sorted by student ID. Each assignment has an ID, name, due date, total number of points, and category. Each grade has a student ID, assignment ID, date submitted, and points assigned.

    Create output for each student as follows:

    - The first line is the student ID.
    - Subsequent lines are the grades for the student.

    The basic algorithm is as follows: for each record of the `Grade` file, read the corresponding `Assignment` record and extract the name, due date, and category. Create a line of output with this information as well as the date submitted and points assigned. When the next grade record refers to a new student ID, print a summary line that shows the total points assigned to that student.

    You will be provided with class definitions for classes `Grade` and `Assignment`, including `read` methods and a method that creates files for use in the project.

    ```
    class Grade {
        int studentId;
        int assignmentId;
        int points;
        Date dateSubmitted;
    }

    class Assignment {
        int assignmentId;
        int totalPoints;
        String name;
        Date dueDate;
        String category;
    }
    ```

Further Readings

Indexing is covered extensively in Wiederhold [Wie83]. B-trees were introduced in Bayer and McCreight [BaMc72] and described in detail in Comer's survey article

[Com79]. As it is for many data structures, the coverage in Knuth [Knu98] is careful and definitive. The author discusses many variants of B-trees beyond those covered in this text. Folk, Zoellick, and Riccardi [FZR98] has an extensive discussion of B-trees with several variants and implementations in C++. The use of hashing for indexing is covered in Enbody and Du [EnDu88] and Fagin et al. [FNPS79].

Search trees have been formulated for use in multiattribute searching. Variants called *k-d B-trees* [OuSc81, Rob81] and *R-trees* [Gut84, BKSS90, KaFa92] have been shown to be useful in some contexts. Books by Shaffer [Sha97] and Standish [Sta95] include extensive coverage of a variety of tree structures.

Achieving Performance and Reliability with Relational Database Systems

*T*his part looks at a collection of important problems that we face in the production of efficient and reliable database applications. The primary topics covered here are strategies for executing relational queries, collecting database operations into transactions, allowing concurrent transactions, providing backup and recovery, and enforcing security. The support for these operations by database systems makes them invaluable to information systems. You will learn the basics of how to enhance your applications to improve their performance and reliability. Special emphasis is placed on the ways in which Oracle database products deal with the issues of the section.

In Chapter 13, you will learn how a relational database server processes queries. The discussion first considers how the processing of simple queries takes advantage of the physical representation of database tables as file structures, as was described in Part Four. You will get a taste of what the implementers of relational database systems must consider in developing query-processing software. The chapter concludes with a discussion of how information about the contents of tables is used to create optimal query execution strategies.

Chapter 14 delves into the fascinating subject of transaction processing. A transaction is a container that surrounds a collection of database operations. The group of operations is treated as a single, atomic operation by the database server. You will learn how transactions allow an application to cancel a collection of updates through a rollback operation and how database servers typically support rollback. The most interesting aspect of this topic is in the reliable and consistent processing of multiple concurrent transactions. Here we learn how to structure operations to ensure correctness and how systems ensure correctness of multiple transactions.

Chapter 15 addresses issues of reliability, backup, recovery, and security. You will learn how database servers create truly reliable databases through the use of backups and how systems can recover from failures of almost any kind. In addition, you will see how database systems support security by restricting access to database objects. The creation of users and roles and the granting and denying of privileges are described through an extensive array of examples. The reliability of distributed information systems is addressed in the context of distributed database systems and of managing transactions that are applied to multiple databases.

13
Query Processing and Query Optimization

CHAPTER OBJECTIVES

In this chapter, you will learn:

- Basic strategies for implementing relational operations
- Specific methods for processing simple selection and projection queries
- Several methods for processing join queries
- The nature and use of query plans and relational expressions
- Strategies for evaluating the execution speed of query plans
- The goals and procedures of query optimization
- Ways to analyze databases and optimize queries in Oracle8

*I*n this chapter, we focus on how to process queries and how to optimize that processing. As we have seen in previous chapters, relational databases are stored in files. A row of a table is stored as a record in a file. A table may be stored in one or more files, or one or more tables may be stored in a single file. The primary organization is that discussed in Chapter 11. Each object (row) is turned into a sequence of bytes and then stored as a record in a file. Accessing a record requires finding its location in the file, reading the correct number of bytes, and unpacking those bytes into memory objects. Many of the issues in query processing, therefore, relate to file structures: how to represent the objects as records, how to support access to records by their content, and how to process the many sets of records that are required for complex join queries.

Query processing involves three steps. The first step is to find one or more plans for carrying out the processing. The second step is to estimate the costs and select the most efficient plan. The third step is to carry out the execution. Without the first two steps, the third step can be guaranteed to be very slow.

Our presentation will begin with basic execution strategies for selection, projection, and join queries. Next, we will consider the equivalence of execution plans and see how we can use relational algebra to create execution plans for more complex queries. We'll see how information about the data content of a database can be used to improve the cost estimates for the plans and, therefore, to find the best plans. We conclude by considering how Oracle8 collects that information and uses it in query optimization.

In this chapter, we'll assume that each file contains one table, and each record in the file represents a row of the table. This assumption is a simplification, because all of the rows of all of the tables of a database may be stored as a single file. In most cases, however, not much difference can be found between having one file and having a set of files. In those cases where this distinction does matter, dividing the database into multiple files is generally a better approach.

Processing Selection Queries

13.1   Now that we are able to read and write files and to access records by address, we are ready to consider processing select queries. Following the approach taken throughout this book, the discussion looks at general issues in terms of specific examples, working from simple to complex.

The processing of a query is illustrated in Fig. 13.1, where pentagons show the steps in the processing and gray arrows show some of the movement of information. The client sends a select statement (1) to the server to be processed. The server (2) reads the appropriate table (A in this case) and creates a temporary structure (shown

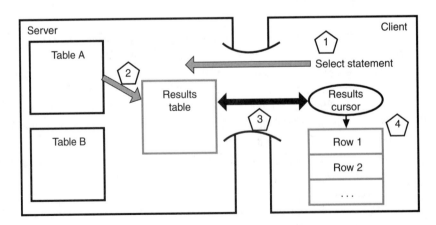

FIGURE 13.1
Query processing with a client and a server

with a gray border) to hold the select rows, either by value or by reference. The server sends a cursor (3) and some or all of the rows of the result back to the client. The black double-arrow between the results table and the cursor represents the interaction between those objects. More rows will be sent (4) as the client uses the cursor.

The results table may be a copy of all rows that satisfy the query, all addresses of the records that hold the result rows, or some kind of iterator that allows the rows to be found.

A *query plan* is a particular strategy for reading the indexes and files to process a query. The cost of a query plan is primarily determined by the number of blocks that must be read from the database files. The examples given in this section use the `Customer`, `Rental`, and `Movie` tables. Table 13.1 shows the assumptions that we use for the physical characteristics of the tables. This information will be used in estimating the cost of particular query execution plans. In general, the cost estimation is the number of block reads of indexes and data files. The number of rows that match the selection condition is another factor in the estimate. Here we ignore the cost of writing the result set in these estimates, because every plan must write the same result set.

13.1.1   Selection Based on a Single Attribute

We begin looking at query processing and cost estimation for the simple selection queries of Table 13.2. Each query selects all the attributes of rows that match a

TABLE 13.1

Physical characteristics of sample database tables

Table	Entries	Number of Entries per Block	Number of Blocks	Index Fields	Index Type	Keys per Node	Depth of B+ Tree
Customer	10,000	10	1,000	accountId	B+ tree and ordered sequential file	100	3
				lastName	B+ tree	50	3
				zipcode	hash	100	
Rental	1,000,000	100	10,000	accountId	B+ tree	100	3
				movieId	B+ tree	100	3
				date	B+ tree	100	2
Movie	10,000	20	500	movieId	B+ tree and ordered sequential file	100	3
				title	B tree	20	4
				genre	Hash	100	

TABLE 13.2

Simple queries on the `Customer` *table, their processing plans, and estimated costs*

	Query	Query Plan	Cost for k Matches	Cost for 100 Matches
1	**select** * **from** Customer **where** accountId = 101	B+ tree search and read data block	4	Not applicable
2	**select** * **from** Customer **where** accountId >= 101 **and** accountId < 300	B+ tree search and data file scan	3 + k/10	13
3	**select** * **from** Customer **where** lastName < 'D'	B+ tree search and B+ tree leaf node scan plus random read	2 + k/50 + k	104
4	**select** * **from** Customer **where** lastName = 'Jones'	B+ tree search and B+ tree leaf node scan plus random read	2 + k/50 + k	104
5	**select** * **from** Customer **where** zipcode = 32306	Hash lookup plus random read	k/100 + k	101
6	**select** * **from** Customer **where** city < 'D'	Full data file scan	1,000	1,000
7	**select** * **from** Customer **where** zipcode >= 32300 **and** zipcode < 32400	Full hash table scan plus random read	100 + k	200

selection on a single attribute. The first query returns the single row whose primary key is 101. Queries 2, 3, 6, and 7 are *range queries* that return all of the rows with an attribute value in a specific range. Queries 4 and 5 select all rows with a specific value for an attribute; they return multiple rows because the attributes `lastName` and `zipcode` are not unique. The processing strategies and estimated costs are explained next.

Query 1 of Table 13.2 can be processed by searching the `accountId` index for the value 101, then reading the corresponding block from the data file and extracting the customer information. The cost of this operation is three block reads for the index (two if the root node is in memory), and one for the data file. Figure 13.2 shows a B+ tree and indexed sequential file organization for the `Customer` table. The gray arrows show the search path; the gray nodes are the ones that must be read. As in the examples in Chapter 12, the number of keys in the B+ tree records, the number of records in the data file blocks, and the total number of records in the data file have been made artificially small to make it easier to identify the patterns.

The processing of query 2, as illustrated in Fig. 13.2, begins by searching the `accountId` index for the value 101 and reading the corresponding data file block.

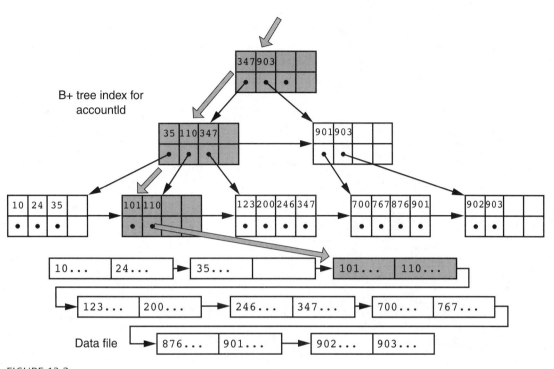

FIGURE 13.2 _____
The query plan for query 1 of Table 13.2

It must read all of the customers whose `accountId` satisfies the range criterion. The `Customer` table is stored as a B+ tree and ordered sequential file on `accountId`, its primary key. Hence, the data file is logically stored in order by `accountId` as a linked list of blocks, as was described in the B+ tree and ordered sequential file example of Fig. 12.12. The processing continues by reading through the blocks of the linked list and extracting the customer records. As shown in Fig. 13.3, three data blocks must be read before an `accountId` larger than 300 is found. The processing stops after the third data file block is read. No further access to the index is required. The cost is three for the index blocks plus the number of blocks with records in the range. If the range has k keys, k/10 blocks must be read. The total cost is 3 + k/10. If 100 records match the query, 13 blocks must be read.

The term *scan* is used in the table to refer to reading a sequence of records from a file. In the case of query 2, the data file is logically ordered by `accountId`. Once the first matching record is found (by B+ tree search), a scan is used to read the blocks in logical order until a record is found with an `accountId` that does not match. A *full scan* occurs when every block of a file is read.

Query 3 is a range query that requests all customers whose last name starts with a letter smaller than "D." This query is significantly more expensive to execute than query 2 because the data file is not ordered by the selection attribute.

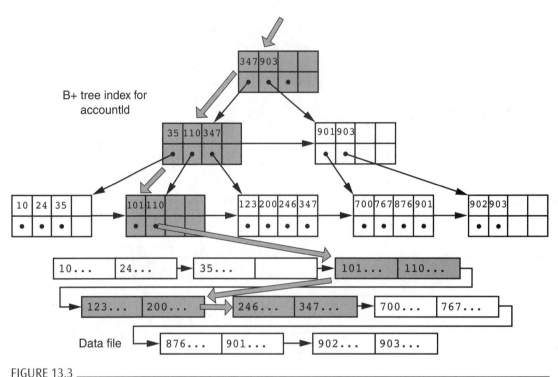

FIGURE 13.3 _____

Select with B+ tree search and ordered data file scan

Consequently, the execution must search through the B+ tree index, finding all records that satisfy the range. Then each record must be read from the data file.

As illustrated by the gray arrows in Fig. 13.4, the search must read the root and one other interior node to reach the first node in the leaf level and find the smallest value for `lastName`. The index is ordered by `lastName`, so we can scan through the leaf nodes to find all records that satisfy the condition. For the small B+ tree of Fig. 13.4, we find a `lastName` greater than or equal to "D" in the second leaf node. The gray arrows leading from the leaf nodes indicate the reading of the data file records whose last name matches the select condition. Four records that match and the corresponding four data file blocks must be read.

For k matches, the B+ tree search and scan must read k/50 leaf nodes of the B+ tree. The selected records are distributed among the blocks of the data file in no particular order. Hence, it is likely that k blocks must be read. The total cost is estimated at 2 + k/50 + k reads. If 100 records match the query, 104 blocks must be read.

Figure 13.4 is, of course, an oversimplification. Here, all of the last names consist of two or three letters, and each last name has only one customer. The proper organization for a non-unique index on `lastName` is to have a block of

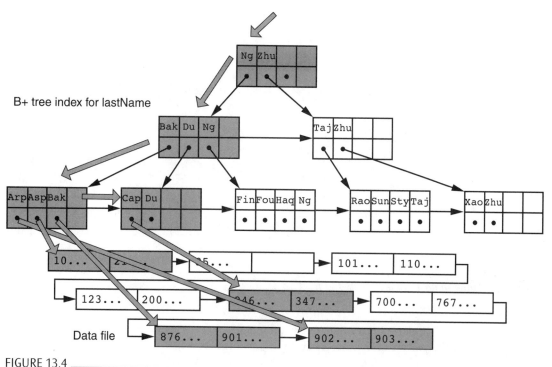

FIGURE 13.4 _____

Select with B+ tree lookup and scan, and random data file reads

references for each key in the index. A reference block organization adds another read for each matching `lastName` value.

Although query 4 is not a range query, it returns a set of rows because the `lastName` attribute is not unique. Therefore, its expected execution cost is the same as that for query 3, even though the number of matching records (k) will likely be much smaller.

Query 5 is a selection based on a hash table index. Figure 13.5 illustrates the processing of query 5, with gray arrows to show the required reads. For k matches, we must read k/100 buckets to collect the addresses for all of the matching records. As with query 3, the data records are distributed among the data file blocks, so k data blocks must be read. The total cost is estimated at k/100 + k reads. If 100 records match the query, 101 blocks must be read. The example of Fig. 13.5 shows a bucket with six references for the ZIP code 32306. After the bucket is found and read, each of the referenced data records must be read.

Query 6 is a range query on a non-indexed field. The only way to find matches to this query is to read every block in the data file. The cost is 1,000 read operations to read every block no matter how many records match. Even if only 100 records match the query, all 1,000 blocks of the data file must be read.

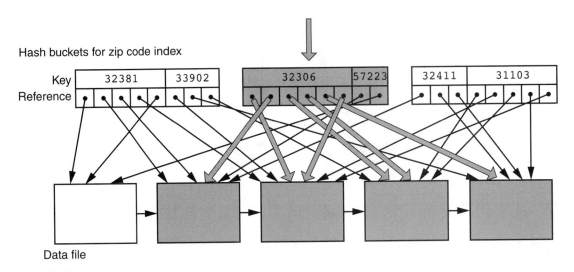

Hash buckets for zip code index

FIGURE 13.5 _____
Select operation with hash table lookup and read

Query 7 is a range query on a field with a hash table index. The matches to this query can use the hash table, but only as a list of key values—not as a true index. Hash tables are not ordered by key, so the hashing function cannot be used to find all values in a range. The query processor must read every block in the hash table to identify the matching records. Because 100 blocks are in this hash file, the cost is 100 reads of the hash file and k reads of the data file. If 100 records match the query, 200 blocks must be read.

Figure 13.6 shows a simple example of using a hash table to satisfy a range query. The horizontal gray arrows show that all buckets are read. The gray arrows that point from the hash buckets to the data file blocks represent the data file reads. In this example, finding the records requires reading all of the data file blocks. In this very simplistic case, scanning through the hash table yields no advantage.

So far, we have identified several strategies for simple select query processing. Table 13.2 shows the best strategy for each query based on the availability of B+ trees, hash table indexes, and ordered data files.

13.1.2 Selection Based on Conjunctive Conditions

Processing (and cost estimation) is much more difficult with more complex selection conditions. In this section, we look at conditions involving more than one range of values or more than one attribute. The focus is on conjunctive queries—ones that involve a sequence of conditions connected by **and** (conjunction) operators.

Equivalence rules for relational algebra are crucial to finding query plans for these queries. Each query must be represented as a relational expression, and equivalent expressions must be considered. For instance, Table 13.3 lists a sample query, four equivalent relational algebra expressions, processing plans, and estimated costs.

Hash buckets for zip code index

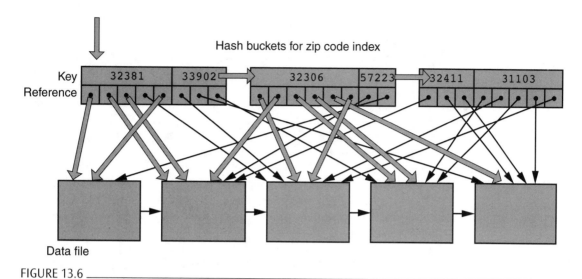

FIGURE 13.6 _____

Select operation with hash table scan and read

TABLE 13.3

A query, equivalent expressions, query plans, and estimated costs

select * from Customer where accountId < 101 and lastName < 'D'	Query Plan	Cost for k_1+k_2 Matches and k_3 Results
1 $\sigma_{accountId<101 \wedge lastName<'D'}$(Customers)	Full data file scan, check each record for match	1,000
2 $\sigma_{accountId<101}$(Customers) $\cap$ $\sigma_{lastName<'D'}$(Customers)	B+ tree searches on `accountId` and `lastName`, collect set of record addresses, compute intersection, read data file blocks	$5 + k_1/10 + k_2/50 + k_3$ if few matches
3a $\sigma_{accountId<101}$($\sigma_{lastName<'D'}$(Customers))	B+ tree search on `lastName`, read each matching record, evaluate `accountId`, output if it matches	$2 + k_2/50 + k_2$
3b	If index on last name has `accountId` as reference, B+ tree search on `lastName`, evaluate `accountId`, search `accountId` B+ tree, read only fully matching records	$2 + k_2/50 + k_3$
4 $\sigma_{lastName<'D'}$($\sigma_{accountId<101}$(Customers))	B+ tree search on `accountId`, read each matching record, evaluate `lastName`, output if it matches	$3 + k_1/10$

The costs are based on having k_1 matches to the `accountId` condition, k_2 matches to the `lastName` condition, and k_3 output rows.

Each of the expressions in Table 13.3 suggests one or more query plans. Expression 1 can be processed by directly selecting those rows that satisfy the entire condition. This approach requires a full data file scan. The query plan is to read a record and check the conditions. If both are satisfied, the record is added to the output set. This process continues until all records are read. This strategy will be cost-effective only if a very high percentage of the customers satisfy the conditions.

Expression 2 can be executed by performing the two selections separately and making sets of the record addresses for each selection, then computing the intersection of the two sets. The last step is to read the records that match both conditions. The individual selections are the same as in queries 2 and 3 of Table 13.2. Determining the record addresses takes $3 + k_1/10 + 2 + k_2/50$ block reads. Reading the matching data records takes k_3 block reads.

Computing the intersection costs nothing (in this cost model) if the number of matching records is small enough to fit in memory. The intersection is typically calculated by sorting the two sets separately and then comparing them in order.

If the number of matching records is too large to fit in memory, the plan calls for creating the set of record addresses for `accountId` matches as a searchable structure (for example, a B+ tree). As the `lastName` matches are found, the `accountId` matches are searched for the record address and marked as matching. Finally, all of the `accountId` matches that have been marked are read and written to the output file. The cost of this intersection is on the order of $k_1 + k_2$.

Expression 3 has two plans, 3a and 3b. Both are based on the selection of all customers by `lastName` and then selection among those by `accountId`. The cost of 3a is the case in which the index on `accountId` uses record addresses as references. The plan is to find all k_2 matches to `lastName`, read those k_2 records, and evaluate their `accountId` fields. The cost is the full cost of query 3 of Table 13.2: $2 + k_2/50 + k_2$ block reads.

The cost of 3b represents the case in which the index of `lastName` stores its references as primary keys. This strategy is explained in Section 12.2.1. The index selection returns the `accountId` values, which can be tested for the first condition. For each `accountId` in the range, the `accountId` B+ tree must be searched and the data record read. The cost of this selection will be the cost of searching the `lastName` ($2 + k_2/50$ blocks), searching for the `accountId` values (no more than k_3 leaf nodes), and reading only those data records whose `accountId` is in range (k_3 blocks). The total cost is therefore $2 + k_2/50 + 2k_3$ block reads.

The plan for expression 4 resembles plan 3a. All of the records that match the `accountId` condition are read, as in query 2 of Table 13.2, and then the `lastName` fields are evaluated. Only those whose last name is in the range are output. The cost is $3 + k_1/10$.

Evaluating the actual costs of the query plans to choose the best plan can be difficult. The cost of each plan depends on the contents of the database, which determines the relative number of matches of the two conditions. If k_1 is small relative to k_2, expression 4 is the best because it takes advantage of the ordering of the data file (indexed sequential). If k_2 is small, however, expression 3 is the best.

The decision to use one of these plans must be made based on estimates of the values k_1 and k_2. As we will see in Section 13.5, commercial DBMS systems provide facilities for estimating these values. Commercial query optimizers use this information to select plans for execution.

13.1.3 Selection Based on Disjunctive Conditions

Disjunctive queries involve a sequence of conditions connected by **or** (disjunction) operators. The basic strategies for evaluating these queries are the same as those given in the previous sections. The major additional problem is the elimination of duplicates.

The simplest disjunctive query is one based on multiple ranges of the primary key. An example of such a query is given in Table 13.4. The obvious processing strategy for expression 1 is to perform a full data file scan and test each row. This approach cannot be the best plan for this query, however.

TABLE 13.4

Disjunctive queries, equivalent expressions, plans, and estimated costs

	`select * from customer where accountId < 101 or accountId > 1000`	Query Plan	Cost for k_1+k_2 Matches and k_3 Results
1	$\sigma_{accountId<101 \lor accountId>1000}$(Customers)	Full data file scan, test each record for full condition	1,000
2	$\sigma_{accountId<101}$(Customers) $\cup$ $\sigma_{accountId>1000}$(Customers)	B+ tree search and data file scan, twice	$5 + k_3/10$
	`select * from customer where accountId < 101 or lastName < 'D'`		
3	$\sigma_{accountId<101 \lor lastName<'D'}$(Customers)	Full data file scan, test each record for full condition	1,000
4	$\sigma_{accountId<101}$(Customers) $\cup$ $\sigma_{lastName<'D'}$(Customers)	B+ tree search and scan, twice, union of record addresses plus read data file blocks	$6 + k_1/100 + k_2/50 + k_3$
	`select * from customer where accountId < 101 or city < 'D'`		
5	$\sigma_{accountId<101 \lor city<'D'}$(Customers)	Full data file scan, test each record for full condition	1,000
6	$\sigma_{accountId<101}$(Customers) $\cup$ $\sigma_{city<'D'}$(Customers)	B+ tree search and data file scan plus full data file scan, test each record for city condition, union results	$3 + k_1/10 + 1,000$

Expression 2 describes the query as the union of two selections. The general strategy in this case is to perform the queries independently and eliminate the duplicates in the result sets. These conditions are exclusive, however, so no record satisfies both conditions. Expression 2 can be processed with two B+ tree searches and two data file scans. The two searches read a maximum of 5 B+ tree nodes, because the root node is read only once. The two data file scans read $k_1/10$ and $k_2/10$ blocks, respectively. The total number of matches is $k_3 = k_1 + k_2$, so approximately $k_3/10$ data file blocks must be scanned. The total number of blocks to read is $5 + k_3/10$.

The second query of Table 13.4 is a disjunction of two unrelated ranges. Again, the simple translation of the query to relational expression 3 results in an inferior plan. Expression 4 is the union of two selections. It can be processed in much the same way as expression 2. Assuming that the sets of record addresses for the two queries fit in memory, the cost of finding the matching record addresses is the cost of two B+ tree search and scans $(3 + k_1/100 + 3 + k_2/50)$. After reading all of the matching records, the total cost is $6 + k_1/100 + k_2/50 + k_3$.

In a case where a field has no index, as in the third query of Table 13.4, the full data file must be scanned, as in the plan for expression 5. Using expression 6 yields no advantage.

Processing Projection Queries and Eliminating Duplicates

13.2

A projection operation eliminates columns and hence may create duplicates. No duplicates and no significant processing costs are incurred when the primary key, or any other key, is retained.

The techniques described in previous sections for eliminating duplicates in unions were based on eliminating duplicate record addresses or primary keys—that is, on ensuring that no row from the source table appeared more than once in the result set. These techniques will not work here, however. Instead, we must find duplicates by value, not by address. We will use the following simple projection query as our working example:

select distinct lastName, firstName **from** Customer

The two basic strategies for eliminating duplicates are based on sorting and on hashing. Both of the plans begin by creating an intermediate list of projected tuples. The first step is to scan the input data file and create a list by writing records with only the selected attributes. Then the plans diverge. The input to the next step for the above query is a list of records with lastName and firstName attributes. Suppose these records are smaller than the data records by a factor of t. The cost of the first step is the cost of a full scan of the data file (B blocks) plus the writing of the intermediate data file (T = B/t blocks).

Each basic strategy can work by comparing all records or by dividing them into *partitions* and comparing within each partition. A partitioning strategy would be to divide the records by last name (or by part of the last name). Within a partition, each record has the same (or similar) last name. Any duplicates in the list will appear within the same partition. Partitioning has the potential to reduce the overall cost of the operation.

13.2.1   Eliminating Duplicates with Sorting

An effective query plan is to sort the list of projected records and write out only the nonduplicates. The basic cost is on the order of $T \log T$ (where T is the number of blocks in the temporary file) for the sorting and elimination of duplicates.

The sorting algorithm can be improved by having it eliminate duplicates during the sorting and by doing the projection as part of the first sorting step. The first improvement makes the sort operation yield the actual result set, thus eliminating a full read and write of the intermediate file. The second improvement eliminates the need to write and read the intermediate file.

If the first phase in the sort is to partition by a single attribute, the cost of sorting is reduced. The plan reads the intermediate file (T reads) and writes partitions (T writes). For p partitions, the sorting cost is on the order of $p \times (T/p \log T/p)$.

Projection by sorting is particularly useful when the query has an **order by** clause, as in Section 13.3, because the sorting phase can produce the results in output order with little loss of efficiency.

13.2.2   Eliminating Duplicates with Hashing

We can hash the entire intermediate file by applying a hash function to the concatenation of all attributes. This approach partitions the file into buckets of records that have the same hash value. As in the partition sort, the result is produced by sorting and eliminating duplicates within buckets. The cost is on the order of the number of hash buckets times the average size of the buckets plus the cost of sorting the buckets. It is quite cumbersome to calculate hash functions on very large string values such as will appear in this plan.

An improvement is to partition by hashing a single attribute. Under this plan, any records in different buckets will not be duplicates. Duplicates can be eliminated within a bucket by using an in-memory hash table with one or more different attributes. As each record is inserted into a secondary bucket, it is checked against all other records in the bucket. Duplicates are eliminated at this point.

The partitioned hashing plan must scan the intermediate file (T reads) and write the hash buckets (H writes, where $H \geq B$). It must then read the hash buckets (H reads) and write the result set. The cost for this phase—$T + 2H$—is related to the number of hash buckets. With a perfect hash partitioning, the number of hash buckets is the same as the number of input blocks. It is likely, however, that some of the buckets will be much less than full and that the hash function will not produce a minimum number of buckets. This approach therefore results in a much larger number of buckets than input blocks.

Processing Join Queries

13.3

A join query combines two or more tables on matching attributes. With this type of query, the evaluation of query plans becomes more complex. In this section, the sizes of the tables will be represented symbolically instead of with specific numbers. Here we let R_c and B_c, R_r and B_r, and R_m and B_m be the number of rows and blocks of the `Customer`, `Rental`, and `Movie` tables, respectively.

Table 13.5 shows a sample join query and two query plans, represented as algorithms. The simplest and most obvious plans for the join operation are called *nested loops joins*. The code assumes that `customer` and `rental` are files that contain the input tables and that `result` is the file that will contain the output tables. This code has two versions; the only difference lies in which file is the inner loop and which is the outer one.

The number of reads in the inner loop of each plan is the product of the number of rows in the tables. Looking more carefully, we see that if the `Customer` table has R_c rows and B_c blocks and the `Rental` table has R_r rows and B_r blocks, the cost is $B_c + R_c \times B_r$ block reads for plan 1 and $B_r + R_r \times B_c$ for plan 2.

One plan is not obviously better than the other, because both appear to read the same number of data blocks. Suppose, however, that the entire `Rental` table fits into the disk cache of the system but the `Customer` table will not. Plan 1 will be much less expensive in this case.

With proper cache management, plan 1 will be able to keep the entire `Rental` table in memory during the execution of the algorithm. The first time through the

TABLE 13.5

Sample query and code for nested loops joins of Customer *and* Rental

```
select * from Customer c, Rental r          Number of Reads
where c.accountId = r.accountId
```

1. Customer outer, Rental inner $B_c + R_c \times B_r$

```
while (not customer.eof()) {
    c = customer.read();
    rental.reset();
    while (not rental.eof()) {
        r = rental.read();
        if (c.accountId==r.accountId) {
            result.write(c, r);
    }
}
}
```

2. Rental outer, Customer inner $B_r + R_r \times B_c$

```
while (not rental.eof()) {
    row2 = rental.read();
    customer.reset();
    while (not customer.eof()) {
        row1 = customer.read();
        if (c. accountId ==r.accountId) {
            result.write(c, r);
    }
}
}
```

inner loop, every block of the `Rental` table will be loaded into disk cache. In subsequent executions of the inner loop, the read operations will access blocks already in memory with no actual disk access required. Thus the cost of plan 1 in this case is $B_c + B_r$, because each file must be read only once.

In plan 2, even though the `Rental` table always stays in memory, the `Customer` table must be read once for each execution of the inner loop. The cost of this plan is $B_r + R_r \times B_c$. Each block of the `Customer` table must be read once for each row of the `Rental` table.

Of course, if `Customer` fits in memory but `Rental` does not, plan 2 offers an advantage. In any case, the plan selection should depend on the relative sizes of the tables, the number of records per block, and the amount of memory available for disk caching. An improvement of these plans is described in the next section.

13.3.2   Block Nested Loops Join

The *block nested loops join* plan takes explicit advantage of record blocking. In the code shown in Fig. 13.7, method `readBlock` reads a block of records from the file and returns an array of objects. The inner loop then reads a record from the inner file and writes an output tuple for each object in the array. We don't have to explicitly deal with blocking in the inner loop, because the I/O system takes care of it for us. The cost of this algorithm is $B_c + B_c \times B_r$. Further improvements are available by reading multiple blocks in the outer loop, instead of just one.

13.3.3   Indexed Nested Loops Join

If one of the join attributes is indexed, the plan should be adjusted to take advantage of it. Table 13.6 shows two *indexed nested loops join* plans, using the `accountId` index of the `Rental` table for plan 1 and the index of the `Customer` table for plan 2. For each customer, plan 1 retrieves all of that customer's rentals, using an indexed read. Method `readByAcctId` returns an array of all `Rental` objects for a particular `accountId` value. Plan 2 uses the `Customer` index.

The two plans have different costs because of the one-to-many cardinality of the relationship type between the tables and because of the table contents. Each

```
while (not customer.eof()) {
   Customer c[] = customer.readBlock();
   rental.reset();
   while (not rental.eof()) {
      Rental r = rental.read();
      for (int i=0; i<c.length; i++) {
         if (c[i].accountId==r.accountId) {
            result.write(c[i],r);
} } } }
```

FIGURE 13.7

Query plan for block nested loops join for the query of Table 13.5

TABLE 13.6

Indexed nested loops query plans for the query of Table 13.5

	Number of Reads
1. `rental` inner	

```
while (not customer.eof()) {                        B_c + R_r
  Customer c= customer.read();
  rental.reset();
  while (not rental.eof()) {
    Rental r[] =
      rental.readByAcctId(c.accountId);
    for (int i=0; i<r.length; i++) {
      result.write(c,r[I]);
} } }
```

2. `customer` inner	

```
while (not rental.eof()) {                          B_r + R_r
  Rental r= rental.read();
  customer.reset();
  while (not customer.eof()) {
    Customer c[] =
      customer.readByAcctId(r.accountId);
    for (int i=0; i<c.length; i++) {// length=1!
      result.write(c[i],r);
} } }
```

customer has many rentals, but each rental has only one customer. Hence, plan 1 reads every customer once and every rental once. The rentals are not ordered by `accountId`, so a rental block may be read more than once. The cost is no more than $B_c + R_r$ block reads. One read occurs for each block of the `Customer` table, and no more than one read occurs for each row of the `Rental` table. Caching and the ordering of the records in the `Rental` table may greatly reduce the actual cost.

Plan 2 reads every `Rental` block and no more than one `Customer` block for each row of the `Rental` table. The number of reads cannot exceed $B_r + R_r$. The number of blocks in the `Customer` table is not a factor in this calculation, because each rental has a customer, but not every customer has a rental. Plan 2 will not read records for customers who have no current rentals.

Plan 1 scans the `Customer` file, then reads a block of the `Rental` file for every record in result set. Plan 2 scans the `Rental` file, then reads a block of the `Customer` file for every record in the result set. Because every rental has a customer, the number of records in the result set is exactly the number of records in the `Rental` table. In essence, plan 1 reads every customer and every rental once, but plan 2 reads some customers many times and some customers no times.

The decision about which plan to use can be made simply based on the size of the two files. Plan 1 is better if the `Customer` file is smaller; otherwise, plan 2 is better. Some insight into this decision-making process can be found by looking at the blocking factors of the two files. The `Rental` records are much smaller than the `Customer` records. If the `Rental` file is larger than the `Customer` file, many rentals must exist for each customer, and hence plan 1 is superior. Otherwise, the `Rental` file is smaller, each customer has relatively few rentals, and reading the customers multiple times is not too expensive.

If `Rental` were logically ordered by `accountId`—that is, represented as an ordered sequential file on `accountId`—the cost for both plans would be $B_c + B_r$. This solution amounts to reading each data file exactly once and ignoring the indexes, as explained in the next section.

13.3.4   Sort-Merge Join

A *sort-merge join* plan first sorts both files by their join attributes, then scans both sorted files together and merges the results. The cost will depend on the cost of sorting, which is typically on the order of N log N for a file of N records. In the case of the query of Table 13.5, however, the `Customer` file is already ordered by `accountId`. Only the `Rental` file must be sorted. If the `Rental` file is already ordered by `accountId`, the plan will consist of only the merge step. The cost will be that of scanning both files.

The basic merge algorithm (shown in Fig. 13.8), is initialized by reading a record from each file (lines 1 and 2). The main loop (lines 3–12) reads through the records in both files. A record is read from one of the files each time through the main loop. Whenever the current record from one of the files has no more matches, a new record is read from that file. When a customer–rental match is found (lines 4–7), the algorithm reads from the `Rental` file (line 6), but the customer record is retained and compared to the new rental on the next iteration. If the new rental has

```
1 Customer c = customer.read();
2 Rental r = rental.read();
3 while (true) {
4    if (c.accountId == r.accountId) {match
5       result.write(c, r); // done with r
6       r = rental.read();
7       if (r == null) break;
8    } else if (c.accountId < r.accountId) {// done with c
9       c = customer.read();
10      if (c == null) // error, no more customers, but more rentals
11    } else // error, no accountId matches the rental
12 } }
```

FIGURE 13.8

Algorithm to merge two sorted files

a larger `accountId` than the current customer (line 8), the customer has no more matches and a new customer is read (line 9). The algorithm terminates when end-of-file is reached in either file. Two error conditions occur (lines 10 and 11): when records are out of order, and when a rental does not match any customer.

The merge algorithm is an example of the general technique of *cosequential file processing*. The Further Readings section gives references to detailed treatments of this type of algorithm.

13.3.5   Hash Join

As described in Section 12.4.1, a hash function divides the values of some domain into a specific number of partitions. We can use this partitioning to greatly reduce the cost of some joins. A *hash join* creates a hash table from the join attributes of each input table, then compares the corresponding hash partitions for matches. All join matches will be located in corresponding buckets.

The processing of a hash join begins with the selection of a hash function that creates a specific number of partitions. The hash function should be selected so that a partition from each file can fit in memory.

1. Scan one input file and insert the join attribute–record address pairs into a hash table.

2. Create a second hash table from the other input file.

3. Read the first partition of each hash table into memory.

4. Compare the attribute values in the partitions to find all join matches.

5. For each join match, read the two corresponding records and output the merged record.

6. Repeat steps 3–5 for each additional hash partition.

The cost of the hash join depends on the sizes of the two hash tables (H_c and H_r). The cost of the hash join is the cost of reading the two files ($B_c + B_r$ block reads), writing the hash tables ($H_c + H_r$ block writes), reading the hash tables ($H_c + H_r$ block reads), and reading the data files again ($B_c + B_r$ block reads). The total is $2(B_c + B_r + H_c + H_r)$. The size of the hash tables is considerably smaller than the size of the data files, because only the join attribute and record address values are stored in the hash table.

13.3.6   Left, Right, and Outer Joins

The only additional processing for left joins, right joins, and outer joins is to include the records that don't match. Each of these algorithms is configured to output all matching tuples. It would not be difficult for sort-merge and hash joins to add all of the unmatched tuples from the left or right input tables to the result set.

The index nested loops joins require additional work for full outer joins. In particular, the algorithms must be changed so that the tuples are marked as they are matched, and a final scan of the table can be used to put all unmatched tuples in the result set.

A NOTE ON PROCESSING AGGREGATION QUERIES

Aggregation operators in queries without **group by** clauses can be calculated by scanning the data file. Operators **min** and **max** can be calculated with the help of an index, if one is available.

An aggregation query with a **group by** clause requires the partitioning of records by the aggregation attributes. In such a case, hashing methods can be very effective for the same reasons that they are effective in hash join operations (Section 13.3.5) or projection (Section 13.2.2). A good hash function can create an initial partitioning scheme in which each group of records is clustered within a single partition. A partition may contain elements of multiple groups, but no group will span more than one partition. The grouping operations can be confined to individual partitions, thus greatly reducing the cost.

Query Plans and Query Optimization for Complex Relational Expressions

13.4

The previous sections looked at only the simplest queries. In those cases, it was usually obvious which query plans were possible and which were the best options. When multiple operations are combined into a single query, however, many query plans are possible and one may not be better than the others in all cases. This section provides a brief overview of the query optimization process, which consists of the following steps:

1. Enumerate the query plans.
2. Estimate the costs of the plans.
3. Choose the best plan for the query.

13.4.1   Creating Relational Expressions

A query plan is a relational expression that represents the query together with an evaluation strategy for each operator. The creation of a query plan begins with the translation of an SQL query into a relational algebra expression. This translation is not complicated (see the Further Readings listings at the end of the chapter for references to detailed algorithms).

Figure 13.9 shows three representations of a complex query that lists information about customer rentals. The query is represented as a select statement, a relational expression, and an expression tree.

The usual technique for producing query plans is to create equivalent expressions by applying the equivalence rules of the relational algebra. Associative, commutative, and distributive laws can be used to reorganize an expression. Figure 13.10 shows two expressions that are equivalent to the expression of Fig. 13.9. Figure 13.10a has moved the selection and projection operations lower in the tree. To do so, the selection operation was split into two selections: one by `lastName` and one by `dateDue` and `title`. The selection by `lastName` can be applied directly to the `Customer` table because it refers to an attribute that appears only in `Customer`. Similarly, the selections by `dateDue` and `title` can be applied to the

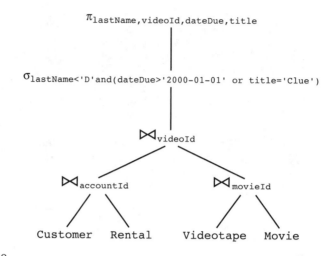

FIGURE 13.9
Example of an SQL query and its representation as an expression and a tree

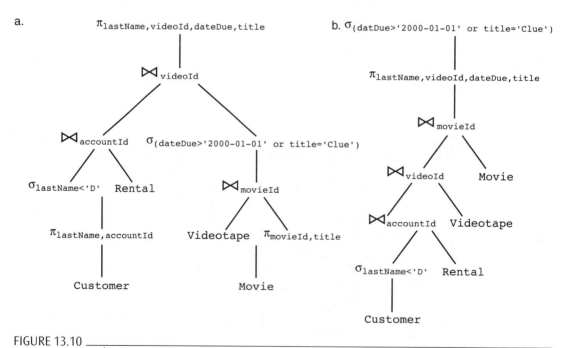

FIGURE 13.10
Expressions equivalent to those of Fig. 13.9

join of `Videotape` and `Movie` before this join is joined to the result of the join of `Customer` and `Rental`.

The projection operations cannot all be moved down the tree. In particular, `accountId` and `movieId` are required for the join operations and cannot be projected out of the data below the join operations. Instead, they must be eliminated by a projection near the top. The purpose of applying projection operations lower in the tree is to reduce the size of the records in the intermediate stages. Smaller records mean more records per block and hence fewer read and write operations.

Figure 13.10b shows an equivalent expression. The associative law of joins was used to modify the join operations so that `Customer` and `Rental` are joined, and this result is subsequently joined first to `Videotape` and finally to `Movie`. The selection and projection operations have been commuted at the top of the tree, so that now the projection is applied before the selection. Many other equivalent expressions exist as well.

Table 13.7 lists some of the basic rules of equivalence for relational expressions. The application of these rules produced the equivalent expression trees of Fig. 13.10. Similar rules exist for set operations and conditional expressions.

A query plan generator must use the equivalence rules to create expressions. A major concern of plan generators is to create all expressions that might produce efficient query plans and to not create those that won't produce such plans. Each query plan generator uses a collection of heuristics to decide which expressions to generate. As a consequence, not every expression will be generated. It is sufficient to know that it is very likely that no significant expression will be omitted. After all, if the *query optimizer* takes more time to execute than is saved by the optimal query plan, optimization has not made the execution more efficient.

TABLE 13.7

Some equivalence rules for relational algebra expressions

Equivalence Rule	Equivalent Expressions	
Cascading selections	$\sigma_{c1 \wedge c2 \wedge c3 \wedge c4}(R)$	$\sigma_{c1}(\sigma_{c2}(\sigma_{c3}(\sigma_{c4}(R))))$
Commuting selections	$\sigma_{c1}(\sigma_{c2}(R))$	$\sigma_{c2}(\sigma_{c1}(R))$
Cascading projections, for attribute sets $A1 \subseteq A2 \subseteq A3$	$\pi_{A1}(\pi_{A2}(\pi_{A3}(R)))$	$\pi_{A1}(R)$
Commuting selection and projection, when condition c uses attributes in set A	$\sigma_c(\pi_A(R))$	$\pi_A(\sigma_c(R))$
Commuting joins	$R \bowtie S$	$S \bowtie R$
Distributing selection and join, when condition c1 uses attributes in R and c2 uses attributes of S	$\sigma_{c1 \wedge c2}(R \bowtie S)$	$(\sigma_{c1}(R)) \bowtie (\sigma_{c2}(S))$
Commuting projection and join, when attribute set A1 has attributes from R and A2 has attributes from S	$\pi_{A1 \cup A2}(R \bowtie S)$	$\pi_{A1}(R)) \bowtie (\pi_{A2}(S))$
Associating joins	$R \bowtie (S \bowtie T)$	$(R \bowtie S) \bowtie T$

13.4.2   Pipelined Query Execution

The analysis of the cost of query execution for the examples of Sections 13.2 and 13.3 ignored the cost of writing the result set, because it was the same for every plan. The situation changes, however, when we consider the evaluation of multiple operations. A tremendous savings can be achieved if intermediate results are not written to files.

For instance, consider the join operations in the expression of Fig. 13.9. An indexed nested loops join can be used to join `Rental` and `Movie`. As each tuple is constructed from that join, the matching customer can be found by its `accountId` index. By *pipelining* these two joins, we avoid the expense of writing and reading the intermediate table. Similarly, the selection and projection operations can be applied to each tuple as the joins produce it. In this case, each input file is read as necessary to support the joins and the result is written with no intermediate files.

13.4.3   Constructing Query Plans from Expressions

A relational expression naturally determines an order of evaluation of the operations from bottom to top and from left to right, but does not specify how to evaluate each operation. A query plan is formed from an expression by choosing an evaluation strategy for each operation.

The processing strategy given in the example from the previous section represents a query plan that associates an indexed nested loops join with the lowest join operation, a pipelined indexed nested loops join for the join with `Customer`, and a pipelined scan, or *on-the-fly* evaluation, of the selection and projection operations.

The next step in query optimization, then, is to associate evaluation strategies with each node of each relational expression. This step usually results in more query plans than relational expressions. Exercises at the end of the chapter ask you to form query plans from the expressions of Figs. 13.9 and 13.10 and for additional queries.

13.4.4   Estimating the Cost of a Plan

Information used in cost estimation for plans includes the number of records, the size of the records in each table, the location and types of indexes, the ordering of files, the amount of memory available for disk cache and other memory structures, blocking factors, the number of levels of B+ trees, and more. The cost formulas given in Tables 13.2 through 13.6 can be used to estimate costs for those strategies. The estimates must be based on the parameters listed above.

A query optimizer needs reasonably good estimates of these parameters, but not necessarily completely up-to-date information. In the next section, we will see how the Oracle8 database supports the collection of these parameters. The database administrator or other responsible individual must decide which statistics should be collected and when they should be updated. Although the query optimizer will obviously work better with more complete information, collecting the information is also a major expense.

Once a suitable collection of query plans has been enumerated and the costs of these plans estimated, the query optimizer can choose the best one and use it to process the query. The expense of query optimization makes it important to identify queries that are processed often. These queries can be prepared for execution by running the query optimizer once and then using the selected query plan every time the query is processed.

Finally, it is crucial to realize that the treatment of query optimization in this chapter is very simplistic. A real query optimizer offers many more strategies, must use accurate estimates of I/O speed, and must account for the CPU execution costs, which we have ignored. The Further Readings section lists sources containing careful and complete explanations of these techniques.

Query Optimization and Database Analysis in Oracle8

13.5

As the previous sections have demonstrated, effective query optimization is impossible without information about the content of the database. SQL defines the *analyze statement* to allow database administrators to trigger the collection of relevant information. Oracle8 has several tables that keep information and make it available to the optimizer.

The main point of analyzing a table is to determine the size of the table and the expected cost of scanning. For columns, we need to know the likely number of rows that satisfy range queries. For indexes, we need to be able to estimate the cost of searching. The analyze statement scans a table and its indexes and creates tables of statistics as described in Table 13.8. This information is created or updated only by explicit request from a user. As a table changes, the statistics may become outdated.

Figure 13.11 contains samples of the use of the analyze statement. Line 1 computes table and index statistics, as in Table 13.8, for the `Customer` table and all of its indexes.

Column statistics include histograms of the values. A *histogram* partitions the elements of a set into cells according to their values. Each cell contains the elements of the set whose values are in a specific range. Each cell is represented as the count of the number of elements in the cell. A bar chart is often used to display a histogram. Each bar represents a cell and the height of the bar is the number of elements in the cell.

Oracle creates histograms whose cell boundaries are chosen so that all cells have approximately the same number of elements. The approximate number of elements in each cell is the total number of rows divided by the number of cells. Unless otherwise instructed, Oracle uses 75 cells for each column. Histograms are useful only if the data in the column are not uniformly distributed. In the absence of column statistics, the optimizer assumes uniform distribution. From Table 13.8, we can see that each cell is represented by its minimum and maximum values. A histogram can be used to estimate how many rows match a range condition by multiplying the number of cells touched by the range times the number of rows per cell.

TABLE 13.8

Statistics collected by the analyze statement in Oracle8

Table	Number of rows
	Number of data blocks with data
	Number of unused data blocks
	Average available free space in data blocks
	Number of chained rows[*]
	Average row length in bytes
Column	Number of distinct values in the column
	Maximum and minimum values in each histogram cell
Index	Depth of index
	Number of leaf nodes
	Number of distinct keys
	Average number of leaf blocks per key
	Average number of data blocks per key
	Clustering factor (relative ordering of data blocks as compared with index blocks)

[*] A chained row is one that occupies all or part of more than one data file block. Chained rows are more expensive to fetch because more than one data block must be read.

```
 1 analyze table Customer compute statistics;
 2 analyze table Customer compute statistics
 3     for columns zipcode size 10;
 4 analyze table Customer compute statistics for table for all
 5     indexed columns;
 6 analyze table Customer estimate statistics;
 7 analyze table Customer estimate statistics sample 35 percent;
 8 analyze table Customer estimate statistics sample 20000
 9     for columns zipcode size 100, state size 10;
10 analyze table Customer delete statistics for column firstName;
```

FIGURE 13.11 _____

Sample analyze statements for Oracle8

Lines 2 and 3 of Fig. 13.11 compute column statistics for a single column with 10 histogram cells. Lines 4 and 5 compute table and index statistics as in line 1, as well as column statistics for indexed columns using the default number of histogram cells.

The collection of statistics can be quite expensive, especially for large tables. Often, a sample of rows can be used to make accurate estimates. For example, lines 6–9 of Fig. 13.11 use the ***estimate statistics*** *option* to create estimated rather than exact statistics. The first 1,064 rows of the table are sampled to create the estimates in the default case, as in line 7. Line 8 specifies that a sample of 35% of the rows should be used, and lines 9 and 10 indicate that 20,000 rows should be used in creating statistics for specific columns.

Line 10 demonstrates the use of the analyze statement to delete statistics. This statement deletes the column statistics for a column.

Optimizers are not perfect, and they may not be able to generate an optimal plan for each query. In reality, developers may need to modify their SQL statements to improve application performance. A developer can use the *explain plan statement* to display the query plan for an SQL query. Various formulations of the same queries can then be evaluated and the most efficient SQL incorporated in the application.

Chapter Summary

This chapter described the principles and practices of query processing. We assumed that relational tables are stored as records in files. Each query then has many different strategies, or query plans, that can be used to process it. Query optimization is the process of enumerating and evaluating query plans and choosing the best one for processing.

The cost of processing a particular query plan depends on the number of objects, the number and size of blocks of the data file and the index files, and the number of rows that match the selection and join conditions.

A range query is one with a selection of rows whose values for a particular attribute lie within some range. Range queries can be processed effectively using B+ tree indexes. Hash table indexes are useful for equality conditions and joins but not particularly helpful with range queries.

Selection based on multiple conjunctive conditions is typically processed by using an index to find all rows that satisfy conditions on one attribute and then testing those records for the other conditions. The choice of which attribute to process first is based on the likely number of rows that will satisfy the condition on that attribute. Indexing should use the attribute that has the fewest number of expected matches.

Selection based on multiple disjunctive conditions typically relies on the union of the results of separate queries. Much of the expense will come from eliminating duplicate rows.

Projection queries are easy to process, unless duplicates must be removed. One strategy that helps to eliminate duplicates is using a hashing function to partition the rows and search for duplicates within hash buckets.

Several strategies for processing join queries exist. The nested loops, block nested loops, and index nested loops join strategies are all based on selecting rows from one table and searching the other table for matches. In a sort-merge join, both tables are sorted by the join attribute and then merged together. Hash joins apply the same hash function to each table separately and compare rows in corresponding buckets to identify matches.

Query optimization is the process that is used to find a reasonably good execution plan for a query. It begins by translating an SQL query into a relational expression. Next, equivalent expressions are found by applying the equivalence rules of the relational algebra. The assignment of execution strategies to each relational operator in an expression results in a query plan.

The optimizer must associate a cost estimate with each query plan and choose the plan with the lowest estimate. The estimates take into account a variety of statistics about the content and structure of the database tables.

Commercial databases include query optimizers that use all of the principles of this chapter to find good queries. The analyze statement instructs the database to collect statistics about tables, indexes, and columns for use in optimization. In addition, various query monitoring tools are available to collect and report on the performance of specific queries. The explain plan statement is used to determine which plan the optimizer chooses for a query.

Key Terms

Analyze statement. An SQL statement that directs a database server to collect statistics about tables, indexes, and columns.

Estimate statistics option. An option in the analyze statement that uses a sample of rows to estimate the information about an object.

Explain plan statement. An SQL statement that causes the query optimizer to report the query plan that it chooses for a particular select statement.

Hash join. A strategy for processing a join query in which a hash table is created from the join attributes of each table. The corresponding buckets from the two hash tables are searched for join matches.

Histogram. A partitioning of the elements of a set into cells according to their values in which each cell contains the elements of the set whose values are in a specific range. Each cell is represented as the count of the number of elements in the cell.

Nested loops join. A strategy for processing a join query in which an outer loop reads records from one file and an inner loop finds all matching records from another file. The inner loop may use indexes to improve the join performance.

Partition. The division of a collection into disjoint sets that satisfy some partitioning condition. For query processing, the typical partitioning condition is that any two records that have the same search key are placed in the same partition.

Pipelining. The process of using the output of one relational operation as input to another operation without storing that output in a file.

Query optimizer. A program that translates an SQL query into a query plan that it determines is the best plan for the query.

Query plan. A particular strategy for reading the indexes and files to process a query.

Query processing. The execution of queries in a database server.

Scan. Reading a sequence of blocks of records from a file, in linked-list or sequential order.

Sort-merge join. A strategy for processing a join in which both tables are sorted on the join attribute and then merged to create the result set.

Exercises

1. What is the difference between a relational algebra expression and a query plan? How are the two similar?

2. Describe the basic strategy for estimating the cost of execution for a query plan. What are the main cost factors in query execution? What information about the database is required to estimate the cost of query execution?

3. Give an algorithm for processing a range query for table R and attribute a for each of the following situations:

   a. Attribute a is the primary key of R, and R is stored as an indexed sequential file, sorted and indexed on attribute a.

   b. Attribute a is a non-key attribute of R, and R has a B+ tree index on attribute a.

   c. Attribute a is a non-key attribute of R, and R has a hash table index on attribute a.

   d. Attribute a is a non-key attribute of R, and R has no index on attribute a.

4. Give an algorithm for processing a projection of table R on attribute a for each of the following situations:

   a. Attribute a is the primary key of R.

   b. Attribute a is a non-unique attribute of R, and R has a B+ tree index on attribute a.

   c. Attribute a is a non-unique attribute of R, and R has a hash table index on attribute a.

   d. Attribute a is a non-unique attribute of R, and R has no index on attribute a.

5. Define and compare the performance of a block nested loops join, an indexed nested loops join, and a hash join. For each join strategy, describe a situation in which it should be used.

6. What is the purpose of converting SQL queries into relational algebra expressions before performing query optimization?

7. Define equivalence of relational expressions. Why is equivalence important to query optimization?

8. Translate each of the following SQL queries into a relational algebra expression or expression tree:

   a. **select** lastName, ssn **from** Employee

   b. **select distinct** lastName, firstName **from** Customer

   c. **select** * **from** Employee **where** firstName = 'Jane'

   d. **select** * **from** TimeCard **where** ssn = '376-77-0099' **and** date > '01-mar-1998'

   e. **select** * **from** Customer **order by** accountId **desc**

   f. **select** * **from** Employee, TimeCard **where** Employee.ssn = TimeCard.ssn

   g. **select** * **from** Customer **order by** lastName, firstName

   h. **select** title, genre **from** Movie, PreviousRental **where** Movie.movieId = PreviousRental.movieId **and** accountId = 101

   i. **select** movieId, title **from** Movie m, PurchaseOrderDetail p, PurchaseOrder d, Supplier s **where** m.movieId=d.movieId **and** d.id = p.id **and** p.supplierId = s.supplierId **and** s.state='LA'

   j. **select** * **from** Customer **where exists select** accountId **from** Rental

   k. **select** lastName, firstName, title, dateRented **from** Movie, Videotape, Rental, Customer **where** Movie.movieId = Videotape.movieId **and** Customer.accountId = Rental.accountId **and** Videotape.videoId = Rental.videoId **and** dateRented > '1998-dec-1'

   l. **select** Customer.firstName, Customer.lastName, Movie.title, PreviousRental.dateRented **from** (Movie **join** Videotape **on** Movie.movieId = Videotape.movieId) **join** (Customer **join** PreviousRental **on** Customer.accountId = PreviousRental.accountId) **on** Videotape.videoId = PreviousRental.videoId **where** (((PreviousRental.dateRented)>#12/1/98#))

9. Create a query plan for each query of Exercise 8.

10. Consider processing the query **select** * **from** R **join** S **on** R.a=S.b. The cost metric is the number of I/O pages. The cost of writing the final result should be uniformly ignored. Assume the following facts about the relations:

    - Relation R contains 10,000 tuples with 10 tuples per page.
    - Relation S contains 2,000 tuples with 10 tuples per page.
    - Attribute b of relation S is the primary key for S.
    - Both relations are stored in simple, unsorted files.
    - Neither relation has any indexes.

a. What is the cost of executing the query using a simple nested loops join? What is the minimum number of buffer pages required to achieve this cost?

b. What is the cost of executing the query using a block nested loops join using two buffer pages (one for each relation)?

c. What is the cost of executing the query using a block nested loops join with unlimited buffer pages? What is the minimum number of buffer pages required to achieve this result? Justify your answers.

d. How many tuples will the query produce, at most, and how many pages will be required to store the result on disk? Explain.

e. Which of your answers to (a)–(d) will change if R.a is a foreign key that refers to S.b?

11. Suppose that unclustered B+ tree indexes exist on R.a and S.b, with 100 keys per page and 52 buffer pages available.

a. How deep is the B+ tree index and how many leaf nodes exist?

b. What is the cost of executing the query using an indexed nested loops join? Explain.

c. How does the cost calculated in (b) change if only five buffer pages are available? Explain.

d. How would you arrange the files on disk if you had several disks available? What effect would this arrangement have on the processing?

12. Consider the following relational schema and SQL query:

```
Suppliers (sid: integer, sname: char(20), city: char(20))
Supply (did: integer, pid: integer)
Parts (pid: integer, pname: char(20), price: real)
Select s.sname, p.pname from Suppliers S, Parts P, Supply Y
where S.sid=Y.sid and Y.pid= P.pid and S.city='Madison' and
P.price<= 1000
```

a. Draw a relational algebra tree that is a direct representation of the query. Improve the tree using the equivalence rules of Table 13.7.

b. What information about these relations will the query optimizer need to select a good query execution plan for the query?

c. What indexes might be of help and why?

d. What effect would adding **distinct** to the select clause have?

e. What effect would adding **order by** sname to the query have?

13. Using a database that you can access, answer the following questions:

a. What are the system's capabilities for analyzing queries?

b. Write and execute an analyze statement for a table in the system. What are the results of the analysis?

c. What are the capabilities of the explain plan statement?

d. Write and execute an explain plan statement for a complex query of the database. What are the results?

14. Construct a query plan for the query of Fig. 13.9. Estimate the cost of your plan using the table characteristics of Table 13.1.

15. Repeat Exercise 14 for the query of Fig. 13.10a.

16. Repeat Exercise 14 for the query of Fig. 13.10b.

17. Draw two additional query trees that are equivalent to the trees of Figs. 13.9 and 13.10.

Further Readings

Graefe's survey [Gra93] of query-processing techniques contains an extensive bibliography. The developers of System R at IBM were among the first to use cost-based optimization, as discussed in Astrahan et al [Ast76]. The textbook by Ramakrishnan and Gehrke [RaGe99] has extensive discussions of implementation issues, including two chapters on query processing and query optimization. Cosequential processing for merging is explained in detail in Folk, Zoellick, and Riccardi [FZR98].

The features of Oracle8 that support query processing and optimization are described in Loney's *Oracle8 DBA Handbook* [Lon98]. It includes an extensive discussion of the effect of physical organization on query performance, as well as details about the statistics that are collected by analyze and explain plan statements.

14
Transaction Processing

CHAPTER OBJECTIVES

In this chapter, you will learn:

- The ACID characteristics of transactions: atomicity, correctness, independence, and durability
- The basic principles of transaction management for single-transaction systems
- Ways to use concurrency control and transaction management to ensure correct application processing
- The definitions and uses of tools for concurrent transaction processing
- The definition and advantages of serializable transactions
- Some details about how Oracle8 implements transaction management

*T*his chapter investigates some of the ways that a relational DBMS may enhance the performance and reliability of applications and databases, especially when many users need to access a server at the same time. Both theoretical and practical justifications apply to these enhancements. Because it is particularly important that we understand how commercial DBMS systems support these capabilities, we will look at specific examples taken from the Oracle8 DBMS. Real examples also accompany each topic.

We begin by considering the capabilities needed to produce reliable interactions with a single user. We continue by discussing the additional capabilities needed for multiple concurrent users. The capabilities of DBMS systems include support for transactions, locking, and concurrency control.

Basic Transaction Management

14.1

A *transaction*, or *atomic transaction*, is a logical unit of work that must be completed as a whole or not at all. The term *atomic* is used in the same way as it was for physicists: a unit that cannot be broken into smaller pieces.

A transaction is also a declarative unit. That is, an application designer declares a collection of database actions to be a transaction. The application will execute these actions as a unit. If any problem is encountered in completing the entire collection, all of the modifications created by the actions will be canceled and the previous state restored.

All access to databases and especially all modifications to databases must be executed as part of a transaction. An application connects to a database server and requests that a new transaction be created, or *opened*. A series of queries and updates are executed by the application within the open transaction. The application can then choose to *commit* the transaction, making all of the updates permanent, or *rollback* the transaction, canceling all of the updates and returning the database to its previous state. There is no middle ground. Either all of the updates are applied to the database, or the state of the database is not affected by the transaction at all. Once the transaction is closed as a result of a commit or rollback operation, the application must open a new transaction to continue its database access.

Database theory and practice have identified four crucial properties of transactions: the ACID (atomicity, consistency, isolation, and durability) properties.

- *Atomicity*: All of the updates of a transaction are successful, or no update takes place.
- *Consistency*: Each transaction should leave the database in a consistent state. Properties such as referential integrity must be preserved.
- *Isolation*: Each transaction, when executed concurrently with other transactions, should have the same effect as if it had been executed by itself.
- *Durability*: Once a transaction has completed successfully, its changes to the database should be permanent. Even serious failures should not affect the permanence of a transaction.

ACID transactions and the difficulties of and strategies for enforcing the ACID properties are described in subsequent sections. Atomicity and consistency can be discussed in the simple context of a single-user interaction. Isolation is related to concurrency, the subject of Section 14.2. Durability is best included in the treatment of backup and recovery in Sections 14.3 and 15.1.

Most DBMS systems support a variety of types of transactions. For example, Oracle8 identifies query, update, insert, and delete transactions.

14.1.1   The Actions of a Transaction

For the database server, the execution of a transaction involves a sequence of requests to access objects in the database. Each such request, or *action*, specifies a read operation for an object, a write operation to an object, a commit operation, or a

```
select balance from Customer where accountId = 101
update Customer set balance = 0 where accountId = 101
```

Actions of the SQL Statements

ID of the Action	Effect of the Action
A	Read the balance attribute of the `Customer` object with `accountId` = 101
B	Write the balance attribute of the `Customer` object with `accountId` = 101

FIGURE 14.1 _____

SQL statements and database actions to read and modify the balance for a customer

rollback operation. In this chapter, each transaction is characterized by its sequence of actions. Each database server contains a *transaction manager*—software that monitors the behavior of transactions and decides whether each action can be allowed to execute. In particular, the transaction manager is responsible for enforcing a variety of transaction protocols, such as those described in later sections.

Figure 14.1 shows SQL statements that read the balance for customer 101 and then set the balance to zero. It also lists the read and write actions that are made on the database when these statements execute. Each action has an identifier and an effect. For example, the first SQL statement reads the balance for a customer. Action A records the request from the perspective of the transaction manager. The first SQL statement reads a single attribute from a single row of the `Customer` table. Action B records the request to write a new value for that same attribute.

Each action in Fig. 14.1 is described as the access to an object of the database that is an attribute of a row of a table. These requests could also be considered to access an object that is the whole row or even the whole table. That is, the effect of action A could be recorded as "read the `Customer` object with `accountId` = 101" or "read the `Customer` table."

In the discussion that follows, we will be purposely vague about the size of the object of an action. What matters is that the database server, or its transaction manager, sees the action as a request to access an object, records that request, and manages the access.

14.1.2 Transaction Atomicity in a Single-Transaction System

In a single-transaction system, only one transaction is executing at any time. If a transaction is active, no other transaction can start. This situation is the same as having one application connected to the database server at a time, with that application having only a single active transaction. The application cannot start a new transaction until the previous one has ended.

To support atomicity, a database server must support operations to open a transaction, commit a transaction, and rollback a transaction. The rollback operation causes the most trouble. If a transaction makes changes and is then canceled, the state of the database must be rolled back so that it reverts to its previous state.

The default transaction mode for SQL databases is *autocommit mode*, in which each SQL statement is executed as a transaction. The execution of an SQL statement begins with an implicit request to open a transaction, followed by the processing of the statement, followed automatically by a commit request. Rollback happens only when the SQL statement fails.

An application must make explicit calls to the database transaction manager to enter *explicit-commit mode* and allow multiple SQL statements to execute as a single transaction. The application executes an open transaction statement to ask the transaction manager to create a new transaction before the next SQL statement executes. The application executes a commit transaction statement to ask the transaction manager to commit the transaction, and a rollback statement to ask the application to cancel the transaction.

A transaction may be canceled for many reasons. The simplest situation arises when the application that is executing the transaction detects some problem and issues a rollback operation. More complex scenarios involve the possibility that the execution of the application has been terminated or that the connection between the database and application has been broken. The behavior of the rollback operation is independent of the source of the rollback. For now, let's consider a simple situation in which an application voluntarily cancels the transaction.

Suppose a BigHit Video customer wants to reserve all three of the original *Star Wars* movies, but wants none to be reserved if any one is unavailable. The application proceeds by finding a copy of the first movie and inserting a row into the reservation table to hold the copy, then repeating this step for the other two movies. If a copy of *Star Wars* (first movie) is available, it is reserved. If the application then finds that no copy of *Return of the Jedi* (the second movie) is available, the reservation of *Star Wars* should be canceled. This step can be accomplished by the transaction of Fig. 14.2, which is given in pseudocode. Without the transaction operations, canceling the insert operations requires issuing delete operations, a much more complex and error-prone activity.

```
open transaction
int video1 = select id of an available copy of "Star Wars"
if (video1 == null) rollback transaction
insert row into Reservation for video1
int video2 = select id of an available copy of "Return of the Jedi"
if (video2 == null) rollback transaction
insert row into Reservation for video2
int video3 = select id of an available copy of "The Empire Strikes Back"
if (video3 == null) rollback transaction
insert row into Reservation for video3
commit transaction
```

FIGURE 14.2

Pseudocode example of a transaction to reserve three videotapes

You may be able to think of other strategies for reserving these videotapes that do not require rollback operations. The pseudocode of Fig. 14.2 merely serves to illustrate how the application can take advantage of the transaction model. You can be sure that when we add multiple concurrent transactions, all strategies for this application will require transactions.

Each time the code of Fig. 14.2 executes, a transaction is created and specific actions are applied to the database. The actions for such a transaction depend on the results of the queries. The database server sees the execution of the code as a sequence of actions, as described in Section 14.1.1. One execution may submit three select statements and three insert statements (all three movies are available); a different execution may submit only the first select, find that the movie is unavailable, and rollback.

To rollback a transaction, the system must keep track of the changes made by the transaction. As part of this effort, either the changes or the previous state must be stored in a temporary area. The mechanism that the Oracle8 server uses to support rollback is an illustrative example.

An Oracle8 database has a data area that contains a *rollback segment (RBS)* entry for each open transaction. An RBS entry is a set of images of rows that have been modified by the transaction. The images represent the values of the rows *before* the execution of the transaction. Each update operation executed by a transaction is applied to a row of a database table only after the previous value of the row is added to the RBS entry.

The transaction operations are defined in terms of the RBS entry. The open transaction operation creates a new RBS entry and associates it with the transaction. The execution of a transaction commit operation deletes the RBS entry and makes the changes permanent. The execution of a rollback operation restores all of the modified rows from the RBS entry.

Figure 14.3 illustrates the use of an RBS by a transaction. In the figure, the transaction has been opened and an RBS created. When the transaction writes new values for row r, the previous value of the row is entered into the RBS. The new

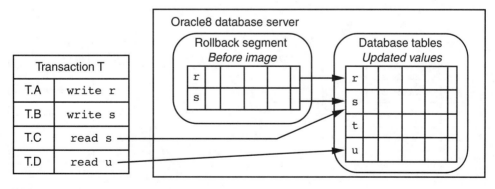

FIGURE 14.3

Database state during an Oracle8 transaction

value of row **r** is in the regular database tables segment. The figure shows the state after the transaction has modified two rows of the table. As shown by the arrows, requests by the transaction to read rows of the table ignore the RBS and go directly to the table, thus accessing the updated values.

Other DBMS systems work via a caching strategy. That is, the transaction has its own memory that acts like a cache for the modified rows. During the execution of a transaction, the database tables are not changed. Instead, the new row images are written into the memory of the transaction. All accesses to rows in database tables go first to the transaction cache. If a row is not found there, the full database tables are used. Hence the database appears to have been changed by the transaction. The commit operation flushes the cache by writing the new row values to the database tables and deleting the cache. The rollback operation simply deletes the cache, leaving the database unchanged.

Figure 14.4 illustrates update and read operations for a database table by a transaction using a server that stores updates in an *update segment* and leaves the table unchanged during the transaction. After the update of two rows, requests by the transaction to read the table go first to the cached rows and then to the unmodified database tables.

Both SQL and Oracle8 support the *savepoint operation*, which produces an intermediate rollback point. Executing a savepoint statement establishes an intermediate point in the transaction. The rollback statement can be used to restore the state that existed when the savepoint was executed. In this case, all of the updates issued after the savepoint was created are canceled, but not the updates that are part of the transaction and that occurred before the savepoint.

14.1.3   Ensuring Consistency

A database is in a consistent state if all of the constraints of the data model are satisfied. These constraints include primary and foreign key constraints, domain constraints, and additional, more complex business rules. The transaction model

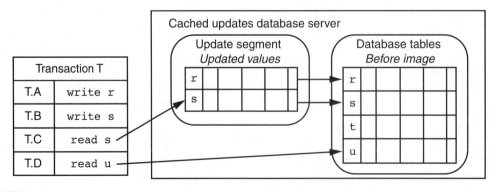

FIGURE 14.4 _____

Database state during a caching transaction

provides the option of relaxing and enforcing consistency as appropriate for the database updates.

Consider the problem of modifying the `movieId` of a movie. This step is required, for example, when the `movieId` was entered incorrectly. Suppose that we have already added a movie to the `Movie` table and copies of it to the `Videotape` table. To change the `movieId` of the movie, we must update both the `Movie` table and the `Videotape` table. Two tables must be changed, so one must be changed first. Suppose we update the `Movie` table first and then the `Videotape` table, as in the following SQL statements:

```
update Movie set movieId=101045 where movieId=101023
update Videotape set movieId=101045 where movieId=101023
```

At the end of the execution of the `Movie` update, referential integrity has been violated. A `movieId` of 101023 no longer appears in the `Movie` table, so each `Videotape` with that `movieId` no longer refers to a `Movie`. After the second update, referential integrity is reestablished.

Under the transaction model, each transaction should be designed so that if the database is in a consistent state before the execution of the transaction, then it is in a consistent state after its proper completion. The model also implies that the database may be in an inconsistent state during the execution of a transaction.

In an ideal world, the commit operation—which makes the changes permanent—would check the consistency of the resulting state. If the database were in an inconsistent state, the commit operation would fail, leaving the transaction open. The application could then either (1) rollback the transaction or (2) make changes in the state to achieve consistency and try the commit operation again. If the commit operation does not check the integrity of the modified data, the responsibility to maintain the constraints falls onto the shoulders of the application developers.

Unfortunately, most database products (including Oracle8) do not provide constraint checking as part of the commit operation. Instead, they enforce constraints that are declared in the schema, and those constraints are enforced for each update. The two update statements given earlier would not be allowed by Oracle8. Rather, we would have to change the `movieId` by creating a new `Movie` object just like the one to be changed, except that it has the new value for `movieId`, updating the `Videotape` records, and finally deleting the old `Movie`. The following SQL statements accomplish this goal:

```
insert into Movie (movieId, title, genre, length, rating)
   select 101045, title, genre, length, rating from Movie
     where movieId=101023
update Videotape set movieId=101045 where movieId=101023
delete from Movie where movieId=101023
```

The Further Readings section at the end of this chapter lists resources that describe the ways in which relational databases can support additional constraint checking by using the trigger capability.

A NOTE ON MODIFYING PRIMARY KEY VALUES |

The particular problem of maintaining primary key values is important enough that SQL has a clause in the **foreign key** constraint of the create table statement that specifies what to do when the corresponding primary key changes. In the definition of table `Videotape`, the following constraint specifies that the `movieId` be changed (**cascade** the update) when the corresponding primary key is changed and the `Videotape` is to be deleted when the corresponding `Movie` is deleted:

> **foreign key** `movieId` **references** Movie
>   **on delete cascade on update cascade**

With this constraint in place, the change in `movieId` requires only a single update statement to change the `movieId` of the `Movie`. The foreign keys will be updated appropriately. The **on delete** and **on update** clauses (**on** *clauses*) can also have value **set null** or **set default**, with the obvious meanings.

Concurrent Transaction Processing

14.2

The proper execution of ACID transactions is greatly complicated by having multiple transactions open at the same time. In information systems, we are most concerned with concurrent, rather than parallel, transactions. That is, *concurrency* arises when many applications are executing transactions at the same time. A single database server processes all operations, so only one database operation can be processed at a time. The operations of the transactions overlap, however, because independent applications are requesting service by the database server in parallel.

The isolation property comes to the fore in this context. During the execution of a transaction by an application, the isolation of the transaction relies on two general principles. First, changes made by the application that have not yet been committed must be hidden from other transactions. Second, changes made by other transactions (even committed transactions) should not be visible to the application. Although the precise meaning of these principles is included in Section 14.4, the following discussion illustrates them.

A transaction that is executing should be able to complete its execution without interference from other transactions. Figure 14.5 shows two examples of interference. Above the gray line, a write operation by transaction T2 interferes with transaction T1. At time 1 and again at time 3, transaction T1 reads the value of object r; it should see the same value both times. Changes made by other transactions should be invisible. In this case, however, transaction T2 changes the value of r at time 2. Hence, transaction T1 will read two different values for the same object r.

Below the gray line in Fig. 14.5, a change made by transaction T1 and later canceled is improperly read by transaction T2. At time 4, transaction T1 writes object u. At time 5, transaction T2 reads this value. When transaction T1 executes its rollback at time 6, the value it wrote to u is removed from the database. When transaction T2 reads the changed value (at time 5), and transaction T1 is subsequently rolled back, transaction T2 will be relying on information that is not in the database.

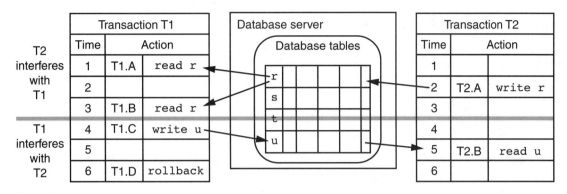

FIGURE 14.5 _____

Two examples of interference between concurrent transactions

Figure 14.5 presents a *schedule* of the execution of the two transactions. A schedule is an ordering of the actions of multiple transactions. Figure 14.5 employs the following schedule: T1.A, T2.A, T1.B, T1.C, T2.B, T1.D. Each action in the schedule happens at a specific time. In this case, the time values are simply integers that identify the sequence of actions and are not intended to represent specific units or to imply that each action takes the same amount of time.

14.2.1   Problems with Nonisolated Transactions

A variety of problems may occur when transactions are not isolated from one another. Figure 14.6 shows the actions and schedules for two nonisolated, concurrent transactions—T3 and T4—that are attempting to update the account balance of a single customer. Suppose the initial balance is $15.00. If both transactions run properly, T3 should add $5.00 to the balance and T4 should add $10.00. The final balance should be $30.00 if both transactions complete successfully. An improper sequence of operations, however, can cause two problems:

- *Lost update problem*: Schedule S₁ of Fig. 14.6 shows an execution order of T3.A, T4.A, T3.B, T4.B, and then both transactions commit. Because T3 and T4 read the same value for the balance, T3 calculates the new balance as $20.00, and T4 calculates the new balance as $25.00. Because T4 performs its update after T3, the final balance is $25. The update of the balance by T3 has been *lost*.

- *Dirty read problem*: Schedule S₂ of Fig. 14.6 shows an execution order of T3.A, T3.B, T4.A, T3.rollback, T4.B, T4.commit. T3 reads the balance and updates it as $20.00. T4 sees the balance as $20.00. T3 now rolls back, and the balance of $15.00 is correctly restored. T4 then updates the balance as $30.00. T4 has read a *dirty* value—one that was never part of the permanent database. The final balance is wrong because the action of T3 was not completed. The final balance should be $25.00.

	Actions of Transaction T3		Actions of Transaction T4
T3.A	balance1 = (select balance from Customer where accountId = 101); balance1 += 5.00;	T4.A	balance2 = (select balance from Customer where accountId = 101); balance2 += 10.00;
T3.B	update Customer set balance = ?balance1 where accountId = 101;	T4.B	update Customer set balance = ?balance1 where accountId = 101;

Schedule S₁ demonstrates the lost update problem

S_1: T3.A, T4.A, T3.B, T4.B, T3.commit, T4.commit

Time	Transaction T3	Operation	Transaction T4
1	T3.A	Read balance account 101: $15	
2		Read balance account 101: $15	T4.A
3	T3.B	Write balance account 101: $20	
4		Write balance account 101: $25	T4.B
5	T3.commit		
6			T4.commit

Schedule S₂ demonstrates the dirty read problem

S_2: T3.A, T3.B, T4.A, T3.rollback, T4.B

Time	Transaction T3	Operation	Transaction T4
1	T3.A	Read balance account 101: $15	
2	T3.B	Write balance account 101: $20	
3		Read balance account 101: $20	T4.A
4	T3.rollback	Restore balance account 101: $15	
5		Write balance account 101: $30	T4.B
6			T4.commit

Note: ? is being used in these examples to represent the substitution of the value of the variable.

FIGURE 14.6 _____

Transactions and schedules that exhibit the lost update and dirty read problems

Figure 14.7 shows two transactions that have related problems. T5 is attempting to move $10.00 from the account balance of customer 101 to the balance of customer 102, and T6 is attempting to calculate the total of the customer balances of the two customers. If the balance in each account is $15, executing T5 should result in a balance of $25 in account 101 and $5 in account 102. T6 should see a

	Actions of Transaction T5	Action of Transaction T6
T5.A	`balance1` = (select balance from `Customer` where `accountId` = 101); `balance1` += 10.00;	T6.A total = select sum=(balance) from `Customer` where `accountId` = 101 or `accountId` = 102
T5.B	update `Customer` set balance = `?balance1` where `accountId` = 101;	
T5.C	`balance1` = (select balance from `Customer` where `accountId` = 102); balance1 −= 10.00;	
T5.D	update `Customer` set balance = `?balance1` where `accountId` = 102;	

Schedule S$_3$ demonstrates the incorrect summary problem

S$_3$: T5.A, T5.B, T6.A, T6.commit, T5.C, T5.D, T5.commit

Time	Transaction T5	Operation	Transaction T6
1	T5.A	Read balance account 101: $15	
2	T5.B	Write balance account 101: $25	
3		Read balance account 101: $25	T6.A
		Read balance account 102: $15	
4			T6.commit
5	T5.C	Read balance account 102: $15	
6	T5.D	Write balance account 102: $5	
7	T5.commit		

FIGURE 14.7 _____

Transactions and a schedule that exhibit the incorrect summary problem

total of $30 in both accounts. Running T6 before T5 or after T5 gives the correct balance, because the net change by transaction T5 to the total is zero. Improper interleaving of the transactions will produce the following problem:

- *Incorrect summary problem*: Schedule S$_3$ of Fig. 14.7 shows an execution order of T5.A, T5.B, T6.A, T5.C, T5.D. This schedule yields a value to T6 of $40—$10 more than the correct sum of balances—because when T6 calculates the sum, $10.00 has been added to account 101 and has not yet been subtracted from account 102.

Now consider the transactions of Fig. 14.8. T7 reads the same value twice, and T8 updates the value. If the order of execution is T7.A, T8.A, T7.B, then the two reads of the balance by T7 will be different.

	Actions of Transaction T7	Action of Transaction T8
T7.A	`balance1` = (select balance from Customer where `accountId` = 101);	T8.A update `Customer` set balance = 0.0 where `accountId` = 101
T7.B	`balance2` = (select balance from Customer where `accountId` = 101);	

Schedule S₄ demonstrates the unrepeatable read problem

S_4: T7.A, T8.A, T8.commit, T7.B, T7.commit

Time	Transaction T7	Operation	Transaction T8
1	T7.A	Read balance account 101: $15	
2		Write balance account 101: $0	T8.A
3			T8.commit
4	T7.B	Read balance account 101: $0	
5	T7.commit		

FIGURE 14.8 _____

Transactions and a schedule that exhibit the unrepeatable read problem

- *Unrepeatable read problem*: Schedule S_4 of Fig. 14.8 shows an execution order of T7.A, T8.A, T7.B. Transaction T7 reads two different values for the balance of customer 101. This situation cannot arise except when another transaction—in this case, T8—interferes.

The final problem we consider explicitly is called the *phantom problem*. It occurs when an aggregate operation is repeated by a transaction and yields a different result because of the insertion of a row by another transaction. In the transactions of Fig. 14.9, transaction T9 calculates the total balance for all customers twice, and T10 adds a new customer. Suppose the original balance of accounts is $100. If the actions are executed in the order T9.A, T10.A, T9.B, T10.rollback, then the sum read by T9.A will be $100.00 and the sum read by T9.B will be $110. The extra $10 appears in the second sum because of the inserted row. In a sense, the new customer never appeared in the database. It was a phantom and the balance read by T9.B never was the sum of the values.

- *Phantom problem*: Schedule S_5 of Fig. 14.9 shows an execution order of T9.A, T10.A, T9.B, T10.rollback. T9 sees two different values for the total customer balance. The new row inserted by T10 was a phantom that was seen by T9 on one read but not the other. The selection of only customers with a specific ZIP code emphasizes that phantoms can occur even when only part of a table is aggregated.

	Actions of Transaction T9	Action of Transaction T10
T9.A	totalA = select sum(balance) from Customer where zipcode = 31101	T10.A insert into Customer (accountId, balance zipcode) values (105, 10.00, 31101)
T9.B	totalB = select sum(balance) from Customer where zipcode = 31101	

Schedule S_5 demonstrates the phantom problem

S_5:T9.A, T10.A, T9.B, T10.rollback, T9.commit

Time	Transaction T9	Operation	Transaction T10
1	T9.A	Read sum of account balances: $100	
2		Insert new account 105 with balance of: $10	T10.A
3	T9.B	Read sum of account balances: $110	
4		Remove account 105	T10.rollback
5	T9.commit		

FIGURE 14.9

Transactions and a schedule that exhibit the phantom problem

Even though other problems can occur, the ones listed in this section clearly illustrate the necessity for exerting some concurrency control over transactions. The solutions to this problem will involve providing a locking mechanism in the database server and carefully designing all transactions.

Any restrictions on the concurrency of transactions will have a negative effect on the number of transactions that can be executing at any time. This balancing act is a typical trade-off. The more restrictive the concurrency strategy is, the more reliable it is, and the slower it is. DBMS designers, database administrators, and application developers must all carefully consider how much concurrency can be achieved without sacrificing either speed or reliability.

14.2.2 Using Locks to Control Transactions

We can use the operating system notion of placing a *lock* on resources to avoid problems such as the ones mentioned in Section 14.2.1. For instance, in the lost update example of Fig. 14.6, if action T3.A locks the balance field for customer 101 so that no other transaction can read it, the attempt to execute T4.a will be blocked until T3 releases the lock. As long as T3 holds the lock until T3.B is finished, no lost update can occur. Resource locking can also avoid the dirty read problem. For the incorrect summary problem of Fig. 14.7, T6 needs to be able to lock the balance fields for all customers. If T6 has begun its summation, T5.A must wait for T6 to release its locks. If T5 has a lock on the balance for a customer, T6 must wait. We cannot, however, allow T5 to release the lock on customer 101 until it has finished updating both customers.

Although we need to support locks on objects, the design of any specific strategy requires answering many questions. Typically, two types of locks are used. A *read lock* is nonexclusive and can be shared among many readers. A transaction that holds a read lock on an object is not allowed to modify it. In contrast, a *write lock* is exclusive and allows a transaction to modify the object. If a transaction holds a write lock on an object, no other transaction can either read from or write to the object. For a transaction to obtain a write lock on an object, no other transaction can be holding any lock—read or write—on the object. A transaction that holds a read lock can *upgrade* the lock to a write lock only if no other transaction holds a read lock. A write lock can be *downgraded* to a read lock at any time.

A DBMS might support only exclusive locks, but then multiple reader transactions cannot execute concurrently. This constraint is a huge limitation on systems that are primarily used for searching and information retrieval. In choosing a DBMS, we should require the inclusion of both shared and exclusive locks.

The next major issue in designing a locking strategy is the granularity of the locks—that is, the size of the objects that can be locked individually. In our discussion of the lost update problem, we stated that each transaction needed a lock (a write lock) on the balance field of a single row of the `Customer` table. This need suggests a fine-grained lock that supports locking of individual fields. A larger grain would lock the entire row for the customer. Hence, when transaction T3 locks the row for customer 101, no other transaction can read any information from that row. A larger-grained lock would lock the entire table as a single object.

A smaller granularity of locks allows for higher concurrency, but at the expense of higher overhead in terms of time and space. Larger lock granularity diminishes concurrency and reduces the total number of potential locks and the amount of time spent setting and releasing locks.

From the programmer's perspective, a lock can be implicitly or explicitly obtained. Most SQL systems obtain locks as needed for the execution of a statement. The execution of a select statement, for example, requires obtaining read locks on all rows that match the query. These locks are set and released automatically. An update statement requires a write lock. Alternatively, many SQL systems support explicit lock request and release statements.

The implementation of exclusive locks in Oracle8 ensures that no writer will ever block a reader. In this system, the rollback segments mentioned earlier contain the values that existed at the beginning of a transaction. When a transaction begins executing, it is guaranteed to see the database as it was at the beginning of the transaction. All of its read operations look at the values in the rollback segments of other transactions before looking at the saved values in the database. If a row is locked for writing, the reader sees the previous value. The new value of the row is seen only by transactions that commence after the writer commits. This strategy prevents the lost update and dirty read problems, but not the unrepeatable read

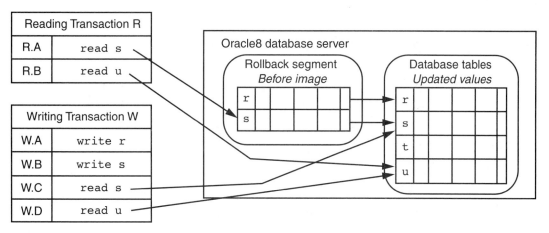

FIGURE 14.10 _____
Concurrent transactions and rollback segments

and phantom problems. A cache of modified rows does not prevent the insertion of new rows or keep those rows from being read by other transactions.

Figure 14.10 illustrates the state of an Oracle8 database after a writing transaction has updated two rows of the table. Requests to read rows of the table by the writing transaction are served from the database table that contains the updated values. Requests to read rows of the table from another transaction (the reading transaction) are serviced from either the RBS (for rows that have been modified) or the database table (for rows that have not been modified). The reading transaction sees the rows as they were before they were updated by the writing transaction.

14.2.3   Deadlocks in Transaction Processing

A major problem with locks is the possibility of *deadlock*. Consider the transactions and schedule shown in Fig. 14.11. Transaction T11 is attempting to set the balances to $0.00 for two customers, and T12 is attempting to set the balances to $10.00 for the same customers. Suppose that actions are executed in the order T11.A, T12.A, T11.B, T12.B. Transaction T11 holds an exclusive lock on the row for customer 101 and is requesting an exclusive lock on customer 102. Transaction T12 is doing just the opposite. That is, each transaction is holding a lock that is being requested by the other. This case is the standard definition of deadlock.

Because of the control that the DBMS exerts over transactions, the system can easily detect deadlock conditions. It's also very important to do so, because the deadlocked transactions hold resources and therefore block other transactions.

Servers typically respond to deadlock by aborting at least one of the deadlocked transactions and releasing its locks. The rolled back transaction can then be restarted, and other transactions may be able to obtain their locks and continue.

	Actions of Transaction T11		Actions of Transaction T12
T11.A	update `Customer` set balance = 0.0 where `accountId` = 101	T12.A	update `Customer` set balance = 10.0 where `accountId` = 102
T11.B	update `Customer` set balance = 0.0 where `accountId` = 102	T12.B	update `Customer` set balance = 10.0 where `accountId` = 101

Schedule S_6 demonstrates deadlock

S_6: T11.A, T12.A, T11.B, T12.B

Time	Transaction T11	Operation	Transaction T12
1	T11.A	Exclusive lock on account 101	
2		Exclusive lock on account 102	T12.A
3	T11.B	Request exclusive lock on account 102: block	
4		Request exclusive lock on account 101: block	T12.B

FIGURE 14.11 _____

Transactions and a deadlocked schedule

There is always the possibility that the restarted transaction will deadlock again. This abort, restart, deadlock sequence may continue indefinitely.

Detecting and breaking deadlocks are often quite expensive steps, and database administrators and application designers may institute deadlock prevention protocols to eliminate deadlocks. A *deadlock prevention protocol* establishes conventions that reduce the likelihood of deadlock. An example is to set up a priority ordering of resources and require that all locks be requested in priority order. With this approach, a transaction that holds a lock on a resource cannot request a lock on a higher-priority resource. This protocol eliminates the possibility of having two transactions that each wait for resources held by the other. Such a protocol is very difficult to enforce in SQL, however.

Recoverable Transaction Schedules

14.3

One measure of the isolation of transactions is whether a rollback in one transaction interferes with any other transaction. Consider the dirty read problem caused by schedule S_2 of Fig 14.6. Transactions T3 and T4 each attempt to add $10 to the balance of account 101. In schedule S_2 at time 2, T3.B writes a value for the account balance that reflects its addition of $10 to the account. At time 3, T4.A reads that value. At time 4, T3 is rolled back. At this point, T4 has read a value that is invalid. If T4 is allowed to continue, it will create an error in the database. To ensure database consistency, T4 must be rolled back when T3 is rolled back. Thus schedule S_2 exhibits a recoverability problem.

The worst problem with recoverability occurs when the rollback of one transaction requires the rollback of a committed transaction. For instance, Fig. 14.12 gives another schedule, S_7, for transactions T3 and T4. In this schedule, transaction T4 reads the balance written by T3 and commits leaving a balance of $30. When T3 is rolled back, its original balance of $10 is restored. In essence, T4 thinks it has added $10 to the balance of account 101, but that addition was actually lost. Transaction T4 experienced an error and must be rolled back even though it has already been committed. This rollback violates the durability property of transactions.

A schedule is said to be *recoverable* if no transaction T commits until every other transaction that writes a value that is read by T has committed. In a recoverable schedule, no transaction will ever require rollback as a result of the rollback of another transaction.

Schedule S_7 of Fig 14.12 is not a recoverable schedule because transaction T4, the reader of the dirty value, commits even though the writer, T3, has not committed. Of course, T3 will never commit because it is subsequently rolled back. The partial schedule T3.A, T3.B, T4.A, T4.B, T4.commit (schedule S_7 without T3.rollback) is not recoverable because T4 commits while T3 has not committed.

Schedule S_2 has the less serious problem of *cascading rollback*, in which a noncommitted transaction must be rolled back. It cascades in the sense that the rollback of T4 might cause the rollback of another transaction, and so on.

Finally, a *strict schedule* is one in which no transaction may read from or write to an object until any other transaction that wrote to the object has committed. In a strict schedule, no cascading rollback is required. For example, the schedule T3.A, T3.B, T3.commit, T4.A, T4.B, T4.commit is a strict schedule for transactions T3 and T4.

Not every strict schedule is a correct schedule, as we will see in the next section. Nevertheless, strict schedules support very efficient rollback, because the rollback of one transaction never requires the rollback of any other transaction. We revisit strict schedules in Section 14.4.2.

Schedule S_7 is an unrecoverable schedule for transactions T3 and T4
S_7: T3.A, T3.B, T4.A, T4.B, T4.commit, T3.rollback

Time	Transaction T3	Operation	Transaction T4
1	T3.A	Read balance account 101: $15	
2	T3.B	Write balance account 101: $20	
3		Read balance account 101: $20	T4.A
4		Write balance account 101: $30	T4.B
5			T4.commit
6	T3.rollback	Restore balance account 101: $10	

FIGURE 14.12 _____

An unrecoverable transaction schedule for transactions T3 and T4 of Fig. 14.6

Serializable Transaction Schedules

14.4

The schedule of a collection of transactions is an ordering of their actions. The explanations of the transactions in Figs. 14.6 through 14.8 included schedules of the actions. We have already seen that the behavior of transactions can be different for different schedules and that some schedules exhibit particular problems.

An action of a transaction is said to *conflict* with an action of another transaction if they both reference some data object, and one transaction updates the object. They conflict in the sense that the order of execution is significant. In Fig. 14.6 T3.A (a read of the balance of customer 101) conflicts with T4.B (an update of the balance of customer 101). A schedule that includes T3.A, T4.B and a schedule that includes T4.B, T3.A will have different results. The interleaving of actions that conflict causes the concurrency problems described earlier.

A schedule is *serial* if no interleaving of the actions of different transactions takes place. That is, all of the actions of one transaction precede the actions of the next, and so on. This schedule is exactly the single-transaction strategy described in Section 14.1.1. A serial schedule is ideal in the sense that each transaction is completely isolated from the others. No concurrency problems occur in serial schedules.

Serial schedules are far from ideal in practice, however, because they have no concurrency. In essence, when one transaction starts, the entire database is locked and no other transaction can start. Clearly, requiring serial schedules is unacceptable. In reality, serial schedules cause more problems than they fix. What we need is schedules that have concurrent execution but behave like serial schedules.

A *serializable schedule* is one that is equivalent to a serial schedule. There must be some way to reorder the actions that produces a serial schedule that has the same effect as the original schedule. Although equivalence may be interpreted in several ways, we will consider only the most common interpretation. There is a large volume of research and discussion devoted to these issues. The Further Readings section of this chapter points you to some of these resources.

Two schedules are *conflict equivalent* if the relative ordering of all pairs of conflicting actions is the same. That is, if two actions A and B conflict, and A appears before B in one schedule, it must appear before B in every equivalent schedule. It's not hard to see that if a schedule is conflict equivalent to a serial schedule, the transactions will behave the same way in both schedules. This definition of equivalence is the basis for the way serializable transaction schedules are used in practice.

As an example of the need for serializable transactions, consider the process of creating pay statements for BigHit Video that was shown in Section 7.2 and Fig. 8.12. The SQL statements of Fig. 14.13 create a transaction that inserts new pay statements from time cards and marks the time cards as paid.

A problem arises if a new time card is entered by another transaction between the execution of the insert and update statements in Fig. 14.13. The update statement (lines 11 and 12) modifies every row that is not paid, even if it was not included in the input to the insert statement (line 2–10). A time card that was entered after the insert statement will not be included in the pay statement. If it is entered before the update statement, it will be marked as paid. This sequence of actions occurs only if the two transactions have nonserializable schedules.

```
 1 begin transaction;
 2 insert into PayStatement
 3     (ssn, hourlyRate, numHours, amountPaid, datePaid)
 4   select TimeCard.ssn, hourlyRate,
 5       sum((endTime-startTime)*24) as hoursWorked,
 6       sum((endTime-startTime)*24*hourlyRate) as amountPaid,
 7       today
 8     from TimeCard, HourlyEmployee
 9     where TimeCard.ssn=HourlyEmployee.ssn and paid = false
10     group by TimeCard.ssn, hourlyRate;
11 update TimeCard set paid = true
12   where paid = false;
13 commit transaction;
```

FIGURE 14.13 _____

A transaction that creates pay statements for BigHit Video

One goal of transaction management is to execute all transactions with serializable schedules. The question is how to achieve this goal. We need to be able to detect schedules that are not serializable. In addition, we need some protocols for designing transactions that guarantee serializable schedules.

14.4.1   Detecting Nonserializable Schedules

To detect that a schedule is not serializable, a transaction management system must first determine all conflicts in the schedule. Conflicts are related to reads and writes, so they can be found by analyzing lock behavior. The system keeps track of all locks for open transactions and watches for a transaction that requests a lock on an object that was locked by another transaction. If a write lock is already in place, or if this request is for a write lock, the request comes in conflict with a previous request in the system.

The system needs to keep track of all possible serial schedules of the actions of the open transactions. When a conflicting action is attempted, the system tries to add the action to a serial schedule. If a conflict-equivalent serial schedule exists, the actual schedule is serializable. If not, the action cannot be allowed and the transaction must be rolled back.

The implementation of this testing is not difficult, but its execution is very expensive. An alternative to testing is to use a serializability protocol that each transaction must satisfy. To be effective, such a protocol must easily detect nonserializable transaction schedules. The next section describes a collection of protocols that are often used to guarantee serializable schedules. These protocols place restrictions on the behavior of transactions in order to improve system performance. Unfortunately, some serializable schedules will be rejected by the protocols.

14.4.2   Two-Phase Locking to Achieve Serializable Schedules

Early in the commercialization of relational databases, system and database developers recognized the need for a simple way to ensure serializability. A serializable schedule correctly isolates its transactions, whereas a nonserializable schedule may not. It must be possible to ensure that applications are executed with a correct schedule. For this effort to be effective, developers needed a protocol for applications to follow. It must be easy to enforce transactions' adherence to this protocol. In addition, the protocol must either enforce serializability or make it easy to detect schedules that are not serializable.

One solution is the *two-phase locking* (2PL) protocol. It simply requires each transaction to request and release locks in two phases: a growing phase and a shrinking phase. In the growing phase, a transaction is allowed to request new locks and to upgrade shared locks to exclusive locks. In the shrinking phase, a transaction is allowed to release locks and to downgrade exclusive locks to shared locks. According to the protocol, transactions must not mix the phases. Once any lock is released, the transaction cannot request any new locks.

Figure 14.14 shows two transactions that use explicit locking. Transaction T13 follows two-phase locking. Actions T13.A, T13.B, and T13.C request or upgrade locks and so are in the growing phase. Action T13.D, the first lock release, puts T13 in its shrinking phase. Actions T13.E and T13.F release the remaining locks. Transaction T14 does not follow the two-phase commit protocol. The growing phase includes actions T14.A and T14.B, which request locks. T14.C releases a lock and puts T14 in its shrinking phase. Actions T14.D and T14.E both violate the shrinking-phase requirement: T14.D requests a new read lock and T14.E requests an upgrade on a read lock it already holds.

To see how two-phase locking is a solution to our problem, we must understand that it ensures serializability and is easy to enforce. The proof that two-phase locking ensures serializability can be found in many references. To see the idea behind the proof, consider the very simple transactions of Fig. 14.6. The nonserializable schedules of Fig. 14.6 exhibited the lost update and dirty read problems. The following explains why those schedules violate the two-phase locking protocol.

We know that T3.A and T4.B conflict, as do T3.B and T4.A. If T3 and T4 are executed using two-phase locking, T3.A and T4.A will both request a read lock on customer 101. The schedule T3.A, T4.A, T3.B (or T4.B) then deadlocks, because both transactions hold a shared lock on the row and cannot obtain an exclusive lock. Suppose T3 releases its read lock; T4 can then proceed, but T3 has entered its shrinking phase and therefore will not be allowed to obtain the write lock required for T3.B. Two non-deadlocking two-phase locking schedules for these two transactions exist: T3.A, T3.B, T3.commit, T4.A, T4.B, T4.commit and T4.A, T4.B, T4.commit, T3.A, T3.B, T3.commit. Both are serial schedules. Hence, all two-phase locking schedules for T3 and T4 are serializable.

Two-phase locking is easy to enforce. The system simply keeps track of the phase of each transaction. If a transaction is in its growing phase and releases or downgrades a lock, it has entered its shrinking phase. A transaction that requests a

Transaction T13

	Lock Actions of Transaction T13	Phases
T13.A	Acquire read lock on A	*Growing phase starts*
T13.B	Acquire read lock on B	
T13.C	Upgrade lock A for writing	
T13.D	Release read lock on B	*Shrinking phase starts*
T13.E	Downgrade lock on A to read lock	
T13.F	Release read lock on A	

Transaction T14

	Lock Actions of Transaction T14	Phases
T14.A	Acquire read lock on A	*Growing phase starts*
T14.B	Acquire read lock on B	
T14.C	Release read lock on B	*Shrinking phase starts*
T14.D	Upgrade lock on A to write lock	*Violation*
T14.E	Acquire read lock on B	*Violation*

FIGURE 14.14 _____

Two-phase locking

lock or upgrade during its shrinking phase will be aborted. This strategy is called *basic two-phase locking (basic 2PL)*. The locking mechanism is used to ensure that every transaction follows the two-phase locking protocol.

Some variations of two-phase locking are even easier to enforce. In *conservative two-phase locking (conservative 2PL)*, each transaction is required to obtain all of its locks at the beginning of the transaction, before any actions take place. The growing phase occurs at the beginning, and the transaction remains in its shrinking phase during its entire execution. Conservative 2PL is conservative in the sense that once all locks are obtained, the transaction can execute to completion without any possibility of conflicts or deadlocks. It has an unfortunate problem, however: the transaction must lock all objects that it might possibly use. As a result, concurrency is severely limited because most transactions must request more locks than they really need.

The most popular version of two-phase locking is *strict two-phase locking (strict 2PL)*, in which all locks are held until the end of the transaction and released during commit or rollback. Each transaction remains in its growing phase for its entire execution. In strict 2PL, each transaction locks only what it needs. Of course, deadlock is possible. A DBMS can most easily enforce serializability by using implicit locking and unlocking and simply holding all locks while the transaction remains open. Oracle8 enforces the serializable transaction isolation mode using strict 2PL.

The pay statement transaction of Fig. 14.13 can be executed in strict 2PL by following these steps:

1. Acquire full-table read locks for `TimeCard` and `HourlyEmployee`.
2. Execute **select from** `TimeCard, HourlyEmployee`.
3. Acquire a full-table write lock on `PayStatements`.
4. Execute **insert into** `PayStatements`.
5. Upgrade the lock on `TimeCard` to a write lock.
6. Execute **update** `TimeCard`.
7. Release all locks.

Once the first step is completed, no other transaction can acquire a write lock on any row of `TimeCard`. If another transaction holds a write lock on `TimeCard`, this transaction will be blocked at step 1. Hence, the improper concurrent updates described in Section 14.4 and Fig. 14.13, cannot occur if all locks are held until the end of the transaction. Strict 2PL guarantees the proper execution of the transaction.

Strict 2PL schedules are also strict recoverable schedules, as described in Section 14.3. The definition of a strict schedule states that no object written by one uncommitted transaction can be read or written by another transaction. In strict 2PL, no lock is released before a transaction commits. Hence, in a strict 2PL schedule, no transaction can write an object that has been read by an uncommitted transaction, and no transaction can read or write an object that has been written by an uncommitted transaction.

14.4.3   Implicit Locking in SQL

Many options exist regarding when to acquire and release locks. SQL supports the specification of a transaction *isolation level* as a way of specifying when to release locks. Recall from Section 10.1 that JDBC also supports a transaction isolation level. SQL defines four levels:

1. *Read uncommitted*. Dirty, nonrepeatable, and phantom reads can occur.
2. *Read committed*. Dirty reads are prevented, but nonrepeatable and phantom reads can occur.
3. *Repeatable read*. Dirty and nonrepeatable reads are prevented, but phantom reads can occur.
4. *Serializable*. Dirty, nonrepeatable, and phantom reads are prevented.

The transaction isolation level is directly related to the time at which locks are released. If all locks are released immediately after each SQL statement, we have no isolation—that is, the *read uncommitted* level. In particular, an update statement will acquire a write lock and immediately release it. Because the transaction is not yet committed and can still be rolled back, dirty reads are possible. With the read uncommitted level, the DBMS allows arbitrary concurrency and hence does not help to isolate transactions. The SQL standard defines the read uncommitted level to be unavailable for update transactions.

The transaction isolation level *read committed* can be accomplished by holding all write locks until the transaction finishes, and releasing read locks after each SQL statement executes. This isolation level is the default for Oracle8 transactions.

Holding all locks until the termination of a transaction results in a *repeatable read* level. In this case, once a transaction reads a value, it holds the read lock. Any subsequent reads get the same value.

Phantom reads can occur unless locks are established on the access path to a query. In the transactions of Fig. 14.9, even if rows with `zipcode` 31101 are locked by the summation query, an insertion into the table (as in T10.A) or a modification to the `zipcode` of another row can create a phantom value. A solution that prevents phantoms and achieves serializable isolation is to lock the index to the `zipcode` field. If the index cannot be modified, no `zipcode` changes are allowed. We can also lock the `zipcode` column. If there is no index on `zipcode` and column locks are not supported, the entire table must be locked to prevent the phantom problem.

The SQL standard allows a DBMS to support any of these levels. It requires the serializable level to be supported as the default level, but allows a system to upgrade a transaction to a higher level. It is acceptable in SQL to support only the serializable level.

Oracle8 provides the read committed and serializable levels, but not the others. The set transaction statement is used to specify the isolation level and to indicate whether a transaction is allowed to update the database. Figure 14.15 gives examples of the Oracle8 set transaction statement.

A NOTE ON EXPLICIT LOCKING IN SQL AND ORACLE8

The SQL standard supports explicit locking of tables with the lock table statement, as shown below. Explicitly requesting locks before they are needed is one way to achieve reliable transactions. By making an explicit request, a transaction can ensure that all resources will be available and remain locked during the transaction. Of course, excessive locking also reduces concurrency.

The many options available with the lock table statement include six modes and the **nowait** attribute. Without **nowait**, a lock request will wait for the locks to be available. With **nowait**, the lock request will fail if the locks are not available and the transaction will proceed without the locks. The following are examples of explicit locking:

```
1  lock table Customer in exclusive mode;
2  lock table Rental, PreviousRental in share mode;
3  lock table Customer in share update mode nowait;
4  select * from Customer where zipcode = 31101 for update;
```

Line 4 shows how a write lock can be created and held by the execution of a select statement. When this statement executes, an exclusive lock is obtained for every row of Customer with `zipcode` 31101. This lock will remain in effect for the remainder of the transaction. The **for update** clause was originally part of the IBM DB2 database system and has since been incorporated into other systems, including Oracle8. The SQL standard allows the **for update** clause only in cursor definitions—not in other select statements. Recall that we looked at cursors in some detail in Chapter 10 as part of the discussion of JDBC 2.0.

```
set transaction read only;
set transaction read write; //default
set transaction isolation read committed; // default in Oracle8
set transaction isolation level serializable; // default in SQL
```

FIGURE 14.15 _____

Examples of the Oracle8 set transaction statement

Chapter Summary

This chapter described the capabilities that make commercial databases so valuable to businesses and developers. It focused on how the Oracle8 DBMS implements those capabilities and how database administrators take advantage of them. The main concerns are improving the reliability, consistency, availability, and performance of systems for users.

A transaction, or atomic transaction, is a logical unit of work that must be completed as a whole or not at all. All access to database information must be part of a transaction. The application programmer can take control of the stages of a transaction by explicitly executing an open operation to create and initialize the transaction and a commit or rollback operation to close the transaction. Multiple database users (or sessions) execute separate transactions concurrently.

The ideal in transaction processing is to achieve the ACID properties—atomicity, consistency, isolation, and durability. A transaction that fails to satisfy an ACID property will very likely damage a database or other transactions.

The default mode of database access is the autocommit mode, in which each SQL statement executes as a separate transaction that begins when the SQL statement processing begins and is committed when the statement successfully finishes its execution.

The atomicity of a transaction is dependent on the rollback operation, which cancels all of the updates of a transaction and restores the state as it existed before the transaction started. The Oracle8 DBMS stores information in a rollback segment (RBS) while a transaction is executing. The RBS contains the before-image of the rows modified by the transaction. The rollback operation simply writes the rows in the RBS back to the database tables. The commit operation deletes the RBS.

A transaction is considered consistent if it takes the database from one consistent state to another. In particular, the transaction key must not violate key, foreign key, and domain constraints. SQL has **on** clauses to support the modification of key values. Clauses **on delete** and **on update** may be added to foreign key field definitions to specify what to do when values in the corresponding key fields are changed.

Isolation of transactions is a problem only in the presence of multiple concurrent transactions. One transaction is not isolated from another transaction if updates of the second transaction affect the first. Interfering transactions may cause lost update, dirty read, incorrect summary, unrepeatable read, or phantom read problems.

Transaction management software uses locks to minimize or eliminate transaction interference. A read lock is a shared lock that allows reading but not writing of an object. A write lock is an exclusive lock that allows a single transaction to write to another object but blocks all other transactions from writing to it. In Oracle8, when one transaction holds a write lock on an object, other transactions are not blocked from acquiring read locks, but can only access the original image of the object. DBMS systems support a variety of lock sizes (granularities), including database, table, row, column, and field locks. They also support locking of indexes and of system resources.

SQL supports implicit locking, in which the locks are acquired and released by the SQL processor. The application can specify a transaction isolation level to force the SQL processor to guarantee a certain amount of transaction isolation. SQL supports four isolation levels, ranging from no isolation to guaranteed isolation.

As with any system in which concurrent executions request and hold locks on resources, deadlock is a major problem. Detecting and breaking deadlocks in SQL systems are possible, but can be very expensive. Deadlock prevention protocols are often used to avoid or prevent these problems.

The schedule of a collection of transactions is an ordering of their actions. A schedule is serial if no interleaving of actions of different transactions takes place. A schedule is serializable if it is equivalent to a serial schedule. Serializable schedules are ideal because each transaction remains isolated from the effects of other transactions. Each transaction sees a consistent state of the database that could have been produced by the transaction executing by itself.

The two-phase locking protocol requires that each transaction request and release locks in two phases: a growing phase and a shrinking phase. A schedule that satisfies this protocol is a serializable schedule. Although no interference between schedules is possible, transactions may deadlock. The most popular version of two-phase locking is strict 2PL, in which all locks are held until the end of the transaction and released during commit or rollback. Strict 2PL is used by commercial DBMS systems to achieve serializable schedules.

Key Terms

ACID transaction. A transaction that is atomic, consistent, isolated, and durable.

Action. A request by a transaction to read or write some database object or to commit or rollback.

Atomicity. The property that the updates of a transaction are either all successful or have no effect at all.

Autocommit mode. A mode of processing SQL statements in which each statement is a transaction that is committed when the statement processing finishes.

Cascading rollback. The situation in which the rollback of one transaction causes the rollback of other transactions, and so on.

Commit operation. The operation that brings a transaction to a successful close and makes its updates permanent.

Concurrency. A situation in which multiple independent processes are executing on one or more processors.

Concurrency control. The process of managing multiple interacting programs so that errors are minimized or reduced.

Conflict equivalence. A property of two different schedules for the same collection of transactions such that if two actions a1 and a2 conflict, and a1 occurs before a2 in one schedule, a1 occurs before a2 in the other schedule.

Conflicting actions. Two actions in different schedules that both reference some data object, with one action updating the object.

Conservative two-phase locking (conservative 2PL). A version of two-phase locking in which the growing phase takes place when the transaction is opened. Every lock needed by a transaction is requested before its first action.

Consistency. The property that if a database is in a consistent state before the execution of a transaction, it is in a consistent state afterwards.

Contention. A situation in which multiple requests for disk access interfere with one another and degrade I/O system performance.

Deadlock. A situation in which each of two or more transactions holds a lock on one object and requests a lock on an object held by the other transaction. No transaction can proceed until one of the transactions releases a lock.

Dirty read problem. A situation in which a transaction reads a value that has been written by another transaction that is subsequently rolled back.

Durability. The property that once a transaction is committed, all of its updates are permanent.

Explicit-commit mode. A mode of processing SQL statements in which a sequence of statements is executed as a transaction.

Incorrect summary problem. A situation in which a transaction reads an aggregate value—for instance, a summation—that is incorrect because it is based on at least one value that was written by a transaction that is subsequently rolled back.

Isolation. The property that a transaction is not affected by any transaction that is not committed.

Isolation level. The amount of transaction isolation that is required to execute a specific transaction. A transaction specifies an isolation level, and the database server guarantees it.

Lock. An object in a database that is held by a transaction and limits the ability of other transactions to access specific database objects.

Lost update problem. A situation in which a write action of a transaction has no effect because the value is overwritten by another transaction.

on clause. A clause in a DDL statement that specifies what to do to the value of a foreign key when the corresponding key value is modified.

Phantom problem. A situation in which a transaction reads an object that was inserted by a transaction that is subsequently rolled back.

Read lock. A shared lock that allows the holder to read but not modify the contents of specific database objects.

Recoverable schedule. A schedule in which a rollback of one transaction cannot cause the rollback of a committed transaction.

Rollback operation. A database operation that restores a database to a previous state. A transaction can be rolled back to remove its updates. A database may be rolled back to a state that existed previously.

Rollback segment (RBS). An area of storage in an Oracle8 database that contains before-images of rows that have been modified by an active transaction.

Savepoint operation. A transaction operation that produces an intermediate rollback state.

Schedule. A linear ordering of the actions of a collection of transactions.

Segment. An area of storage in a database that can contain some specific collection of tables.

Serial schedule. A schedule in which no two transactions are active at any one time.

Serializable schedule. A schedule that has the same effect as some serial schedule.

Strict schedule. A schedule in which no transaction reads or writes an object written by a noncommitted transaction.

Strict two-phase locking (strict 2PL). A version of two-phase locking in which the shrinking phase takes place as part of the commit and rollback operations. Each lock, once obtained, is held by a transaction until the transaction finishes its execution.

Transaction manager. The software within a database server that monitors the behavior of transactions and decides whether each action can be executed. The transaction manager is charged with enforcing protocols such as two-phase locking.

Two-phase locking (2PL). A transaction management protocol that requires each transaction to request and release locks in two phases: a growing phase, in which it obtains locks, and a shrinking phase, in which it releases locks.

Unrepeatable read problem. A situation in which two read actions for a single object in a transaction read different values because the object is changed in the interval between the read operations by another transaction.

Write lock. An exclusive lock that allows the holder to read and modify the contents of specific database objects.

Exercises

1. Define and give a brief justification for each of the ACID characteristics of transactions.

2. What is a transaction manager? Describe how a transaction manager might interact with a query processor in a database server.

3. How does an application enter explicit-commit mode? How does an application leave explicit-commit mode?

4. In what way does the rollback operation support atomicity of transactions? List three reasons why a rollback operation might be executed on a transaction.

5. What is a rollback segment (RBS)? How does Oracle8 use its RBS to support the rollback operation? How does Oracle8 use its RBS to support isolation of transactions? How does a caching transaction manager use its RBS to support the rollback operation? How does a caching transaction manager use its RBS to support isolation of transactions?

6. How do parallel transactions and concurrent transactions differ? Why are concurrent transactions of particular interest to information systems?

7. What is the relationship between isolation and concurrency of transactions? What techniques can be employed to ensure isolation of concurrent transactions?

8. For each problem listed below, give example transactions and schedules in the context of queries and updates to a database containing student course registrations and grades.
   a. The lost update problem
   b. The dirty read problem
   c. The incorrect summary problem
   d. The unrepeatable read problem
   e. The phantom problem

9. What does it mean to upgrade a read lock? What does it mean to downgrade a write lock? Give an example of a situation in which the absence of the upgrade request can cause problems among concurrent transactions.

10. Explain how a transaction manager can employ locks to produce recoverable transaction schedules.

11. Compare and contrast serial schedules and serializable schedules. What is conflict equivalence?

12. Explain how a transaction manager can employ locks to produce serializable transaction schedules.

13. Explain how a transaction manager can enforce the following protocols:
    a. Basic 2PL
    b. Conservative 2PL
    c. Strict 2PL

14. For each of the protocols listed in Exercise 13, give an example of a deadlocked schedule for concurrent transactions that satisfies the protocol or, if deadlock is not possible, explain why not.

15. For each of the following transaction schedules, characterize it as serial, serializable, recoverable, or strict. If it does not match any of these characteristics, list a different schedule that does.
    a. T1.read(t), T2.read(t), T2.write (t), T2.commit, T1.rollback
    b. T1.write(t), T2.read(t), T2.write (T), T2.commit, T1.rollback

16. Consider the following transaction schedule:

Time	Transaction	Action	Time	Transaction	Action
1	T1	read r	12	T3	read u
2	T2	read s	13	T5	write u
3	T1	write u	14	T4	read r
4	T4	read t	15	T4	commit
5	T5	write r	16	T5	read v
6	T2	read u	17	T3	rollback
7	T2	write u	18	T5	write r
8	T3	read v	19	T2	read u
9	T2	read v	20	T2	commit
10	T5	write r	21	T5	rollback
11	T1	commit			

a. Create a list of transactions, listing the name and the sequence of operations for each transaction in the schedule.

b. Is this schedule recoverable? If not, what is the first action in the schedule that makes it not recoverable?

c. Is this schedule strict? If not, what is the first action in the schedule that makes it not strict?

d. Create a strict schedule for these actions.

e. Identify each pair of conflicting actions.

f. Is this schedule serializable? If not, what is the first action in the schedule that makes it not serializable?

g. Create a serializable schedule for the transactions.

17. Suppose the schedule of Exercise 16 is executed using the strict 2PL protocol.

a. Show which transactions are holding read or write locks on which objects at times 5, 10, 15, and 20.

b. Show the schedule of these transactions that results if each request for a lock that cannot be granted according to strict 2PL results in a rollback of the requesting transaction.

c. Show the schedule of these transactions that results if each request for a lock that cannot be granted according to strict 2PL results in a block of the requesting transaction, and show that the lock is granted at the first later time. Does this schedule deadlock?

Further Readings

As with much of the material in this book, the relational database topics of this chapter are covered in more detail in advanced database textbooks [Date99, ElNa99,

SKS97]. Much of the material in this chapter owes a great deal to the work of Jim Gray and the other developers of System R at IBM.

One of the earliest presentations of the transaction model, including two-phase commit, is found in Gray's seminal paper [Gray78]. His book with Reuter [GrRe93] offers a comprehensive treatment of the subject. An excellent resource on the Oracle8 treatment of transactions and rollback segments, as well as other database administrator issues, is found in the *Oracle8 DBA Handbook* [Lon98]. The SQL and PL/SQL coverage of transactions and security can be found in Feuerstein and Pribyl [FePr97]. Proofs of the properties of serializable schedules can be found in Eswaran, Gray, Lorie, and Traiger [EGLT76] and in Papadimitriou [Pap86].

Constraint checking is a major research topic and has been addressed in the context of active databases. Details can be found in McCarthy and Dayal [McDa89], Widom, Cochrane, and Lindsey [WCL91], Aiken, Hellerstein, and Widom [AHW95], and Baralis, Ceri, and Parboschi [BCP96].

Locking, lock granularity, and concurrency control are the subject of more papers by Gray and his colleagues [GLP75, GLPT76]. Time-stamp locking is described in Bernstein and Goodman [BeGo80] and Reed [Reed83], intent locking in [GLP75], and other concurrency models in Kung and Robinson [KuRo81], Bayer, Heller, and Reiser [BHR80], and O'Neil [O'Ne86]. An early textbook by Papdimitriou [Pap86] presents formal models of these and other concurrency models. Operating systems approaches to locking, concurrency, and transactions can be found in operating system texts, such as [TaWo97].

15

Reliability and Security in Database Servers

CHAPTER OBJECTIVES

In this chapter, you will learn:

- Reasons why backup and recovery are of crucial importance to database servers
- Strategies for recovery from failures
- Ways in which DBMS systems define and enforce security control
- Some examples of the use of stored programs and functions
- The principles of distributed databases
- Ways in which distributed databases manage transactions

*T*his chapter investigates the role of DBMSs in creating reliable and secure systems. Minimizing the probability of failure and maximizing the probability of full recovery when failure does occur helps produce reliable systems.

Full-featured DBMSs are capable of producing backups of their database contents. These backups, together with transaction logs, provide mechanisms for recovering from even the most catastrophic failures. Controls on access to information by users and applications help to produce secure systems.

The distribution of information among multiple computers is a major source of unreliability in information systems. Modern database servers, however, are capable of reliably and efficiently distributing information. A distributed database system manages distribution of data, maintains consistency in replicated databases, provides applications with a simple view of distributed data, and even supports a reliable mechanism for managing distributed transactions.

Backup and Recovery from Failures

15.1   Possibly the most important aspect of commercial DBMSs is their support for recovering from failures. Here we must consider the broadest interpretation of failure. Imagine that you are responsible for a database that is running on a computer system located in the basement of a building in the financial district of New York City. A water main bursts, the basements fill with water,* and your computer system is destroyed! What happens to the database? This failure is catastrophic. Most failures are less severe, but still can have a significant effect on the consistency and availability of databases.

Database systems and applications must be designed for recovery after failures. Unfortunately, we cannot design systems so that failures will never occur. Instead, designers must anticipate the potential failures and create plans for reacting when these failures occur.

The goal of a *recovery* plan is to restore the database to a state that is known to be correct and put it back in service as quickly as possible. Recovery plans must include what people should do to keep their business operations functioning while the database is unavailable. If the system is unavailable for an extended period, there must be a plan for updating the database to incorporate the activities that took place during its absence.

Many potential sources of database failures exist:

1. *The database server computer crashes.* In this case, the database server will become unavailable for some time. The information content may be corrupted because of information that is stored in memory and has not been transferred to the more permanent disk storage.

2. *The database server program crashes.* This failure should never happen. An important characteristic of a commercial database server is that it never fails catastrophically without some external cause. The effect is the same as that in failure 1.

3. *A database client computer crashes.* The state of the client application will be lost and any open transactions will stop. Server operations may be degraded because of locks held by the inactive transactions.

4. *A client program crashes.* This failure is just like failure 3, except that the computer executing the client program continues running and can inform the database server that the client crashed.

5. *The network connection between client and server fails.* This failure is similar to failure 3 in that the client computer is unavailable and its transactions are stopped. The major difference is that the client may reappear at any time.

---

*Water mains break regularly in New York City. In January 1998, for example, a 48-inch water main in lower Manhattan broke. Millions of gallons of water were released and basements were flooded over a several-block area.

6. *A transaction executes a rollback operation.* The transaction has voluntarily canceled itself and its updates must be removed from the database.

7. *A transaction executes an illegal operation.* The transaction manager detects that a transaction has violated some protocol. The server must be able to abort the transaction and recover through a rollback.

8. *Two or more transactions deadlock.* If the server detects a deadlock, it must abort one or more transactions to break the deadlock. Locks held by deadlocked transactions will interfere with the execution of other transactions.

9. *One or more transactions introduce errors into the database.* This situation occurs when an application program runs incorrectly and updates the database in ways that introduce nonfactual or inconsistent information to the database. The integrity of the database is therefore compromised.

10. *Data on a disk drive is corrupted.* A hardware error causes some of the database information to become unavailable.

The primary tool for supporting recovery is redundancy. For example, in Section 14.1 we saw that an Oracle8 DBMS keeps redundant information in rollback segments during transaction processing. The database contains the new values and the rollback segment contains the old values. If the transaction fails and must be rolled back, the contents of the rollback segment are copied back to the database. This strategy accomplishes recovery from the transaction failure.

Another redundancy strategy is creating and maintaining backup copies of the database and putting those copies at a remote site. When the basements in New York flood, businesses will be either pleased to have backups stored elsewhere or distressed if their backup tapes were in the same basements.

Let's begin with catastrophic failures. In this case, something happens and the database becomes completely unavailable for some period of time. The first response must be to continue business functions in an offline or manual mode. A retail store, for instance, typically has cash registers that function as database clients. Each sale is recorded in the database as it is made. If the database is unavailable, the cash register must save the sale records. This goal can be accomplished by the paper record that the cash register creates or by the local storage of the cash register.

When the database becomes available, the cash registers must be brought back online as database clients, and the sales that were recorded during offline operations must be recorded in the database. This operation can be done immediately when the database comes up, or it may be deferred until later. If the sales were recorded on paper, there must be a capability to enter those sales at a later time.

The examples of retail sales and backups to mitigate physical problems show us that the physical and manual activities of recovery must be carefully planned in advance. No amount of computerized redundancy will be able to compensate for not having plans for physical failures.

15.1.1   Backups and Checkpoints

A *backup* is a copy of the state of a database at a specific time. It contains sufficient information to allow the restoration of the state. A database that has been restored from a backup has the same state that it had at the time the backup was created. Of course, all updates that occurred after the creation of the backup are not part of the state of the restored backup. As mentioned earlier, it is crucial to store backups in a different location than the system itself. It is not unusual for a company with more than one office to have each location keep the backups for another location. With this practice, a catastrophe in any one site will not cause the loss of information.

A *checkpoint* is an operation that forces the database on the disk to be in a state that is consistent with all of the committed transactions. It includes flushing the contents of disk caches so that the disk is up-to-date. If the DBMS crashes and the disk is not corrupted, the database on disk will contain all of the changes that were committed before the checkpoint. It is not guaranteed that changes committed after the checkpoint will be on the disk.

When a DBMS fails, recovery can take advantage of backups and checkpoints. If the disk is not corrupted, the database server can be restarted in the state it was in at the last checkpoint. If the disk was corrupted, the state can be restored to the last available backup.

Our goal, however, should be to recover to the state when the system crashed, or at least so that all updates performed by committed transactions are included. If the system crashes when transactions have been committed since the last checkpoint, we cannot be sure that all of the committed updates are in effect.

Recall that the durability property of a transaction states that once a transaction has been committed, its effects are permanent. If a database becomes corrupted and is restored from backup, the transactions that ran after the backup are not included. Thus these transactions are not durable. Durability cannot be achieved without a mechanism that goes beyond backups and checkpoints.

15.1.2   Transaction Logs

Each DBMS maintains several log files that record significant activity within the server. A *transaction log* is a file that records the actions of all transactions as they occur. An entry in a transaction log consists of the following items:

- The unique transaction ID that is automatically assigned to a transaction when it starts execution
- The name of the action performed
- The object that is referenced by the action, if any
- The effect of the action on the object, if any

Transaction logs play a crucial role in achieving durability. For example, recovery systems use these logs to recreate the state of the database after failures. The specific ways that transaction logs are used are described in the next few sections. Note, however, that a transaction cannot finish its commit operation until the transaction log has been permanently recorded. Thus the minimal condition of permanence is that the entries in the log have been force-written to the disk drive. To increase reliability, the transaction log should be copied to multiple copies of the log file. The ultimate reliability can be achieved only when a copy of the transaction log is force-written to a remote location, usually through a network connection.

15.1.3   Recovery via Reprocessing

One possibility for full recovery is to recover the database state from a backup and then reprocess all transactions that have occurred since the backup was created. For example, we might request that all clients reprocess the transactions that were committed after the backup creation time.

 Recovery via reprocessing is feasible if we are running applications that do not respond to direct user input. Even in this case, however, reprocessing does not guarantee a return to the state that existed before the failure. After all, the schedule of the transactions may change during reprocessing. Such a change is likely to affect the transactions.

 It is not possible to guarantee durability by reprocessing, except in the most limited cases.

15.1.4   Recovery via Roll Forward

A better strategy for recovery, called *recover and roll forward*, is to recover the database in a correct previous state and then reapply all of the changes of the committed transactions in the same order that they were originally committed. In this way, the database can be brought back to the state it was in just before the catastrophe.

 To support *roll forward*, the system must maintain a list of all committed changes, in order. This list is called a *redo log*. Each time an update is applied to the system, an entry is made in the log that shows the new value for the affected object.

 To recover from catastrophic failure, first we restore the database to a correct state from backup. Then we apply each change listed in the redo log, starting with the first entry that was recorded after the backup was created. After applying all of the changes, the exact state of the database will have been recovered.

 Clearly, if the redo log is recorded on the same computer as the database, a catastrophic failure is likely to corrupt both the database and the log. Thus durability will require that the log be kept physically separate from the database. In a very secure system, a transaction commit operation is not complete until the log entry has been recorded remotely. Using the Internet, we can arrange for the redo log to be recorded at a remote site. When the commit operation is executed, the log entry is sent to the remote system. When a confirmation is received, the commit operation is complete.

 Full durability of transactions can be achieved using physically remote backups and redo logs.

15.1.5   Recovery via Rollback

A *rollback* recovers a previous state by removing the effect of transactions. We have already seen how uncommitted transactions can be rolled back. However, failure 9 in the list of typical failures occurs when committed transactions have corrupted the database. Recovery from this error requires that the database be restored to a previous correct state by removing the effects of committed transactions.

Although committed transactions can be canceled using roll forward, it is often more efficient to roll back the committed transactions. The system must keep an *undo log* that includes the original image of each updated value. The rollback strategy begins with the current state and undoes each update, in reverse order, until the desired state is achieved.

Once a correct state has been recovered, it may be possible to redo some of the transactions that were committed after an erroneous transaction started. As long as a transaction does not conflict with an erroneous one, its effects can be reapplied. The roll forward of committed transactions after the rollback takes place is complex. The actions of a transaction can be applied only if they do not conflict with those of any transaction that is not applied.

15.1.6   Recovery from Disk Corruption

When a disk becomes corrupted, the information stored on it becomes faulty. It is often impossible to tell what is corrupt and what is not. In many cases, the only way to recover from hardware errors is via recovery from backup and roll forward.

If a collection of disk pages cannot be read correctly, it may be possible to recover the values from the disk cache. If not, it will be necessary to determine which database objects are stored in that area. If that goal can be realized, the transaction logs can be used to recreate these values.

15.1.7   Support for Automatic Recovery

Automatic rollback and recovery are supported by commercial DBMSs. When the server starts up, it checks the consistency of the system and corrects any faults. In particular, it removes the effects of all uncommitted transactions.

The Oracle8 system maintains a *control file* that records control information about all of the files associated with the database. It includes the names and locations of associated databases and online redo log files, the timestamp of the database creation, the current log sequence number, and checkpoint information. These data are used to maintain internal consistency and guide recovery operations. The control file is mirrored with at least one copy that is maintained automatically by the server.

When a file becomes damaged because of a disk failure, recovery from a backup and redo log is needed. The database administrator must first copy the damaged file from the best backup copy. The recover database command, when executed, prompts the database administrator for the name of each redo log that must be run. Once the redo logs have been processed, the database recovery is complete.

It is crucial that the database have regular backups. Oracle8 supports both hot (online) and cold (offline) backups. A hot backup runs while the database is open and available. The system places all files in a special backup mode and makes a copy of each file. Once this duplication step is complete, the database and the backup files are consistent. The database remains open during hot backup. In contrast, a cold backup runs when the database is unavailable to users. A typical backup schedule for an active database is to run a backup every night and, of course, to move the backup files onto removable media and place them in another location.

Oracle8 also supports a logical backup of the objects in the database. The export command accomplishes this task by extracting the schema and the contents of all tables and writing them to an export dump file. The state of the database represented by the export files can be reloaded with the import command.

Security in Relational Database Systems

15.2

Information stored in databases has enormous value, with the value being derived from the accuracy of the information and its availability. The more valuable the database becomes, the more vulnerable it is to misuse and corruption, however. The information content of a database must therefore be protected from being altered and stolen.

Database security begins with physical security for the computer systems that host the DBMS. No DBMS is safe from intrusion, corruption, or destruction by people who have physical access to the computers.

After physical security has been established, database administrators must protect the data from unauthorized users and from unauthorized access by authorized users. No DBMS can be used for valuable databases unless it has support for three types of security:

- Account security for the validation of users
- Access security for protection of database objects
- Operating system security for database and file protections

The goals of database security are to protect the integrity of the database and to prevent unauthorized use of the information. The system configuration must ensure that only authorized users and programs can access the data and the operations of the database.

15.2.1 User Authorization

A commercial DBMS stores user identifiers and passwords in system tables in the database. SQL has commands to create, alter, and drop users. In Oracle8, the user identifiers are stored in a system table. Each connection by a user or a client program must be authenticated as a valid database user.

Figure 15.1 gives a variety of statements that manipulate users. Line 1 creates a user with an initial password. In line 2, additional characteristics of a new user are specified. User `Dick` will create tables in the `USERS` segment and has a quota of 100 KB on that segment. Line 3 shows how the alter user statement can give user `Jane` an unlimited quota on the segment. The drop user statement of line 4 removes `Jane` from the database.

```
 1 create user Jane identified by crockette;
 2 create user Dick identified by go-man-go default tablespace
     USERS quota 100 K on USERS;
 3 alter user Jane quota unlimited on USERS;
 4 drop user Jane;
 5 alter user Dick account lock;
 6 alter user Dick identified by stop-please;
 7 alter user Dick password expire;
 8 create profile LimitedUser limit CONNECT_TIME 10;
 9 create user OPS$hannibal profile LimitedUser;
10 alter user OPS$hannibal identified by use-this-password;
```

FIGURE 15.1 _____
Sample SQL statements that manipulate user accounts

Using line 5 of Fig. 15.1, a database administrator can lock an account so that the user cannot log in. In line 6, the password of user `Dick` is changed. After the execution of line 7, his password has expired and he will be prompted for a new password at his next login.

A profile is a list of limitations that can be shared by many users. Line 8 shows the creation of a profile with a limit of 10 minutes on any database connection. In line 9, a new user is created using this profile to limit his connection time. The `OPS$` in front of the `hannibal` account name identifies it as an operating system account. This operating system user will be allowed to connect to the database without the use of a password; instead, we rely on the operating system to authenticate the user. Operating system users can also be identified by database passwords. The statement on line 10 allows any other operating system user to connect as `hannibal` by entering the password `use-this-password`.

15.2.2   Protection of Database Objects

SQL databases define a collection of privileges that may be granted to users, including those to read, update, append, create, and drop access to databases, schemas, tables, and views. The grant statement is used to allow and disallow privileges. *Access privileges* restrict (and allow) access by specific users to specific operations on specific objects. By default, full access to objects is granted to the creating user and no access to other users.

Figure 15.2 shows some SQL statements that affect database privileges. The privilege to insert new `Customer` objects is given to user `Jane` in line 1. After the execution of line 2, every database user (**public**) will be allowed to perform select statements on the `Customer` table. Line 3 grants all privileges on the `Employee` table to `Jane`, but line 4 denies her the privilege to delete rows. The **on** clause can refer to a variety of system resources, including databases, schemas, tables, views, and columns. Line 5 allows `Jane` to update specific columns of `Customer`, but not the other columns.

```
 1 grant insert on Customer to Jane;
 2 grant select on Customer to public;
 3 grant all on Employee to Jane;
 4 revoke delete on Employee from Jane;
 5 grant update on Customer(street, city, state, zip) to Jane;
 6 create role Clerk not identified;
 7 grant all on Rental, PreviousRental to Clerk;
 8 grant role Clerk to Dick;
 9 create role FloorManager identified by ImInCharge;
10 grant role Clerk to FloorManager;
```

FIGURE 15.2 _____

Examples of **grant** *statements*

The assigning of privileges to users may quickly become very time-consuming for database administrators. Lines 6 and 7 of Fig. 15.2 show how the *role* capability can be used to describe a collection of privileges that may be granted to many users. Line 6 creates the role and line 7 gives all clerks access to the rental tables. In line 8, a specific user is allowed to be a clerk. When `Dick` is acting as a clerk, he has all of the privileges of the `Clerk` role and can manipulate the rental tables. The database administrator can assign a collection of privileges to users according to their roles. Each user can be a member of many roles.

It is also appropriate to allow a role to be a member of another role. Line 9 of Fig. 15.2 creates a floor manager role with a password. A user who is granted the `FloorManager` role must give a password to assume that role. In line 10, the floor manager is given all of the privileges of the `Clerk` role.

Privileges in Oracle8 are stored in system tables and are accessible with a variety of views. The `DBA_TAB_PRIVS` view, for instance, contains information

---

A NOTE ON OPERATING SYSTEM SECURITY

Oracle8 is typically installed in a Unix operating system using disk drives that are not available to non-database users. The disks can be seen as raw devices to the superuser, but are not mounted as regular file systems. No user can reach the database's disks through Unix commands, and only the superuser has any access to the disks.

The Oracle8 DBMS includes all of the necessary software to access its own disk drives using its own file system. A special Unix user exists for the database servers and utilities. This user has the only access to the drives that contain the databases. All other access must take place through requests to the database server.

It is possible to install Oracle8 within the normal Unix file system, but this strategy makes the database more vulnerable to unauthorized access by Unix users.

on all users who have been granted table privileges. The following statement can be used to find all of the table privileges provided to user `Jane`:

```
select Grantee, Owner, Table_Name, Grantor, Privilege
   from DBA_TAB_PRIVS where Grantee = 'Jane';
```

The `Owner` field is the user who owns the table, the `Grantor` is the user who executed the **grant** statement, and the `Privilege` is the specific privilege that `Jane` has on the table `Table_Name`.

15.2.3   Database Audits

A commercial DBMS has the ability to keep track of all operations that are performed and to associate each operation with a specific user and a specific login. System log files are created to record this information. These log files are typically called *audit trails* because they contain the information that supports the kind of analysis of activities that is referred to as auditing.

Audit trails are particularly important for use in evaluating the source of violations of system security. Because all systems are imperfect, it is important not to assume that a DBMS is inviolable. Instead, the database administrator is responsible for putting procedures in place to detect and track security violations. Systems like Oracle8 provide tools to create reliable audit trails.

For example, Oracle8 SQL includes statements that control what information is added to audit trails. The following statements specify audit trail configuration:

```
audit option; // record each login attempt
noaudit option; // turn off recording of logins
```

Table 15.1 lists some of the options available to the database administrator to use for audit trail configuration. These operations all have some effect on either the database schema, the physical database configuration, or user privileges.

Oracle8 also supports audit trails for data manipulation operations. The options **select**, **insert**, **update**, and **delete** are used to specify auditing of those operations on specific tables. The audit command includes an **on** clause to specify which objects are to be audited.

```
audit select on TimeCard;
audit delete on Employee;
audit all on PurchaseOrder;
noaudit select on Movie;
```

In Oracle8, the audit trails are stored in a database table called `SYS.AUD$` and are available through database views. The `DBA_AUDIT_SESSION` view, for instance, contains information about logins. The information can be extracted through simple queries:

```
select OS_Username, Username, Terminal, Returncode, Timestamp,
   Logoff_time from DBA_AUDIT_SESSION;
select OS_Username, Username, Terminal, Owner, Obj_Name,
   Action_Name, Returncode, Timestamp from DBA_AUDIT_OBJECT;
```

TABLE 15.1

Some configuration options for audit trails of logins and database actions in Oracle8

Option	Operations Recorded in Audit Trail
`all`	All auditable commands
`DBA`	Commands that require DBA authority, such as **grant**, **revoke**, **audit**, **create**, or **alter tablespace**
`exists`	SQL statements that fail because an object already exists
`index`	**create**, **alter**, or **drop index**
`procedure`	**create**, **alter**, or **drop procedure**, **function**, or **package**; **create package body**
`resource`	**create** and **drop** for tables, clusters, views, indexes, tablespaces, types, and synonyms
`role`	**create**, **alter**, **drop**, or **set role**
`rollback segment`	**create**, **alter**, or **drop rollback segment**
`session`	Login attempts
`table`	**create**, **alter**, or **drop table**
`user`	**create**, **alter**, or **drop user**
`view`	**create** or **drop view**

The first select statement returns information about a user session—that is, about the connection of a client program to the database. The second statement returns the result of an attempt to modify an object.

Because audit information is stored in a database table, the reliability of the audit trails will be guaranteed by the usual database rollback and security mechanisms. Typically, you audit all user activity on the audit tables. The following statement creates audit records for any explicit modification of the audit tables, not including the inserts created by normal audit activity:

```
audit all on SYS.AUD$;
```

Stored Procedures and Functions

15.3   Commercial databases allow developers to add functionality to database servers by defining and storing complex operations. Each *stored procedure* or function has a name that can be used in SQL statements. A derived attribute can be added to a table by defining a function that returns the attribute value. In this way, complex database manipulations can be encapsulated in a single procedure.

```
create function numberRented (accId int)
    return int
as select sum(*) from Rental
    where Customer.accountId = accId;
```

FIGURE 15.3 ——————————————————————————
Stored function to calculate attribute numberRented

For example, the derived attribute numberRented of entity class Customer of the BigHit Video system is the number of videotapes currently rented by the customer. It can be represented in Oracle8 by the stored procedure definition shown in Fig. 15.3. The value can be extracted in a select statement such as the following:

```
select *, numberRented(accountId) from Customer;
```

Stored procedures and functions can be used to increase system reliability by moving an operation out of the client code and into the database code. This approach improves reliability by placing the operation inside the database, where any changes are tracked by audit trails and controlled by database security.

As an example, consider the processing required to check in a videotape. A Rental record must be deleted and a PreviousRental record must be inserted. These two operations can be encapsulated into a stored procedure, as shown in Fig. 15.4.

Oracle8 allows stored procedures and functions to have their own privileges, thereby ensuring that access to objects can be granted for specific operations. For example, it is appropriate to allow a store clerk to perform the check-in operation, but not to delete records from Rental or add records to PreviousRental. The following grant statements allow the database to enforce this security plan:

```
grant execute on checkIn to clerk;
revoke delete on Rental to clerk;
revoke insert on PreviousRental to clerk;
```

Even though the clerk role has no privilege to modify the tables, the clerk's privilege to execute the procedure allows the procedure to make those modifications.

```
create procedure checkIn (vidId int, cost double)
  as begin
    insert into PreviousRental
      select accountId, vidId, dateRented, now(), cost
        from Rental where videoId = vidId;
      delete from Rental where videoId = vidId;
    end checkIn;
```

FIGURE 15.4 ——————————————————————————
Stored procedure to check in videotapes

Distributed Databases

| 15.4 | Most businesses need to support databases at multiple sites and on multiple computers. Database client software makes this support feasible by allowing a single application to access multiple databases. In Java, for instance, multiple database connection objects can be active simultaneously. This approach brings many problems, however. The primary one is that each application must know and exploit the distribution of data. Any change in that distribution requires changes in all affected applications. Another problem is that the client programs are made responsible for any consistency that must be maintained among all of the databases.

To ensure reliability and consistency, we'd like to consider all of these databases to be part of some larger, distributed database. For example, we need some reliable way to update multiple databases similarly to the way that transactions give us reliable single-database updates.

Fortunately, commercial DBMSs support distributed databases in simple and consistent ways. A distributed database is created by allowing database servers to interact, thereby leading to a server–server system. A client connects to a single server and can issue queries that affect all databases.

15.4.1   Principles of Distributed Databases

A *distributed database* is a collection of databases that are related logically but separated physically. It is important that a client program be able to use a single database connection to access and modify all of the distributed data. A distributed database has a single logical schema whose tables are distributed over many database servers. A table of the database may be distributed in the following ways:

- *Unfragmented.* A table exists in exactly one database, with different tables in different databases.

- *Horizontally fragmented.* The rows of a table are distributed among multiple databases, and each row appears in a single database. The full table is the union of all of the distributed tables.

- *Vertically fragmented.* The columns of a table are distributed among multiple databases, with a duplication of the key columns and no other duplication. The full table is the natural join of the distributed tables.

- *Replicated.* Some or all of the rows or columns of a table are stored in more than one database. The full table is the union (without duplicates) of the distributed tables, with joins as needed.

No matter how the tables are distributed, the user must be presented with a schema that makes the distributed database look like a single database.

To this point, our evaluation and development of the BigHit Video database have assumed that the system includes a single central database server and each store has local database client applications that connect to the server using a network. A multi-database approach would use a database at each location. The client applications would then connect to the local database server, with those applications being modified to allow access to data at other locations. Any modification to the way the data are distributed among the local databases would require modification to the applications.

A distributed database approach for BigHit Video also uses a database at each location, including the central office. In this approach, however, each database has the same schema and the applications are written with no reference to the distribution of data. Each application connects to a single server. Its access to data is not based on the locality of data.

An appropriate distribution of BigHit Video data is to store data that are primarily associated with a single store in the local database and data that are primarily about the company as a whole in the central office database. Each store database therefore has the same collection of tables, but different data in the tables. Hence, these tables are horizontally fragmented.

In this distributed database, the local server must optimize query processing to take advantage of the distribution of data. For instance, suppose a clerk at store 3 issues a query to determine whether the store has a videotape for a particular movie:

```
select videoId from Videotape v where storeId=3 and movieId=12345
```

This query is sent to the local server, which analyzes it to see whether it can be processed locally. Because every row of `Videotape` with `storeId = 3` is stored locally, this query can be processed locally.

The distribution of the `Videotape` and `Rental` tables is obvious. For other tables, however, the distribution is not so obvious. Consider the `Movie` table. It contains information about all movies. Because this information is not local to a particular store, it should be stored in the central office database. Suppose a clerk wants to get the title of a videotape at the local store:

```
select title from Movie m, Videotape v where v.movieId =
    m.movieId and videoId=12345 and storeId = 3
```

The processing of this request could begin by searching the local `Videotape` table. It would then issue a request for processing to the central office server. The query could not be completed if the central server or the network connection were unavailable. Hence, the ability of the store to conduct its normal business would depend on nonlocal resources.

The best distribution for the `Movie` table is replication. That is, each store keeps a full copy of the `Movie` table. All references to movies can then be resolved locally. The major problem with replicated tables is maintaining consistency when the tables are updated. If the `Movie` table at one store is modified, all copies of the table must be modified as well. In this case, however, there is no need to perform local modifications of the `Movie` table, which is essentially a constant table for the stores. The details of managing a modification of a replicated table are discussed in Section 15.4.3.

Advantages of distributed databases include the following:

- *Autonomy and availability of local data*. Each site can access its local data, even if network connections are unavailable.

- *Independence of physical and logical layout*. No change in client programs is required when the distribution of data is modified. Changes are confined to the database servers.

- *Matching physical locality to the needs of applications*. A database application that needs only part of the whole database can access its data locally.

- *Improved performance*. A query that uses multiple servers may execute faster because the data access is distributed over multiple computers.

15.4.2   Support for Distributed Databases in Oracle8

Oracle8 supports some, but not all, of the capabilities of distributed databases. We can create multi-database schemas and manage the replication of tables.

Access to multiple databases through a single server is supported by the explicit creation of links between database servers through the create database link statement. Once the links have been created, schemas in the remote databases are referenced using the link, as in the following example:

```
create database link BigHitLink connect to BigHitSystem;
select * from Customer@BigHitLink;
```

The database developer can create synonyms and views that hide the physical details of the distribution and have the same effects as a distributed schema. For instance, the view `AllCustomers` is the union of the `Customer` tables from three store databases that are connected by database links:

```
create view AllCustomers as
   select * from Customer@Store1Link union
   select * from Customer@Store2Link union
   select * from Customer@Store3Link;
```

Triggers and snapshots support replication of tables. A trigger is a database object that executes some action in response to specific database events. Suppose the `Movie` table is replicated, as in our earlier example. Any update to the central office `Movie` table should be replicated on the `Movie` tables in each store. The following code creates the necessary trigger to respond to insertions into the table:

```
create trigger UpdateMovie after insert on Movie for each row
   begin
      insert Movie@Store1Link values (:new.movieId, :new.title,
         :new.genre, :new.rating);
   end;
```

The insert statement should be duplicated for each store. Triggers can also be used for deletions and updates. Note, however, that they are appropriate only for very simple configurations.

Fully dynamic data replication is more appropriately controlled with snapshots. In this model, a master table is stored in one database and other databases have copies (snapshots) of all or part of the master table. The master table is updatable, and each snapshot is either read-only or updatable.

A snapshot is created by the local server. Once a link with the server that contains the master table has been created, a create snapshot statement can be executed on the local server. Once the snapshot has been created, all updates are replicated. Updates to the snapshot are passed to the master table, and vice versa.

For the `Movie` table, the master copy resides in the central office database and each store has a snapshot created with the following statement:

```
create snapshot Movie as select * from Movie@CentralLink;
```

This snapshot will be updated automatically whenever the master table is updated.

One approach to managing the local tables is to keep the full database at the central site in the form of master tables. Each local site then has snapshots of the master tables. Each snapshot contains only those data relevant to the particular site. The `Videotape` table, for instance, can be created at store 3 as follows:

```
create snapshot Videotape as
    select * from Videotape@CentralLink where storeId = 3
```

This approach has two advantages: Oracle8 will manage the creation of a central repository for all data, and each local site needs a link only to the central site and not to any other site. Once the snapshots have been created, the database administrator can use database tools to manage the frequency of updates and to respond to connection and site failures.

15.4.3 Distributed Transaction Processing

A *distributed transaction* is a single unit of work that updates multiple servers of a distributed database. Such a transaction is initiated on one server of a distributed database and, in turn, initiates a transaction on each of the other servers. The atomic and durable properties of transactions require that either all of the *local transactions* commit properly or all of them abort. A major problem with distributed transactions is that no transaction can be committed unless it can be guaranteed that all transactions will commit.

Proper processing of distributed transactions requires the participation of a transaction manager to oversee the transactions on all servers. This manager must monitor the state of all transactions and abort all of them if any of the transactions aborts or if any of the servers becomes unavailable. Each commercial DBMS includes a protocol for guaranteeing the proper processing of distributed transactions.

The *two-phase commit* protocol is used to guarantee proper processing. It calls for the execution of a transaction manager on the server that initiates the distributed transaction. This manager controls the commit protocol and makes the final decision as to whether the distributed transaction will be committed or aborted.

Each local transaction must perform its commit operation in two phases. In the first phase, the *prepare phase*, the global transaction manager sends a *prepare for commit* message to each local server and waits for a response. When the local transaction executes its commit operation, the transaction's server performs whatever checking is required to determine that the commit operation can succeed. The local server must *force-write* its transaction log to permanent storage so that a permanent record of the transaction will persist. If this operation succeeds, the server sends a *ready to commit* message to the manager to report that the local transaction has successfully completed its first commit phase. At this point, the local transaction pauses to wait for the second phase.

A local transaction can abort either by executing its abort operation or by having the server determine that the commit operation cannot succeed. In either case, the local server sends a *cannot commit* message to the manager.

The second phase, the *commit phase*, begins when the manager has received responses from all of the local servers or after a time-out period has expired. The manager makes a decision and force-writes it to its permanent log. If all local servers report that they are ready to commit, the manager instructs all of the local servers to commit their transactions. The servers then commit the transactions and the distributed transaction is complete.

If any local server reports that it cannot commit or does not respond within the time-out period, the manager will rollback the distributed transaction. It then instructs all of the local servers to rollback their own transactions. The distributed transaction is then complete.

The two-phase commit protocol also includes procedures for recovering from any failure that occurs during the protocol. The permanence of the transaction logs ensures the atomicity and durability of the distributed transaction.

Chapter Summary

Commercial DBMSs offer extensive support for backup and recovery, including transaction logs, checkpoints, incremental and full backups, and database replication. It is very important that all backup and recovery information be stored away from the database computer. Checkpoints and transaction logs are used to ensure the durability of transactions. With this approach, once the actions of a transaction have been recorded in the log, the effect of the transaction can be recovered after almost any failure.

Account management and object security are important aspects of commercial systems. SQL includes statements that create user accounts and user roles. Each session between an application or user and the database server requires a login. Privileges are granted to users and roles by database administrators or other authorized users. Once a session begins, access to database objects is strictly controlled by the privileges of the user accounts and roles. Privileges can be granted (or denied) to users to control their ability to access and modify objects and schemas. Procedures can be stored in databases and access privileges granted to those procedures.

An Oracle8 database is physically organized as a collection of segments. Database administrators are granted the privilege of specifying the location of these segments. The distribution of segments among the disks of a database server can dramatically affect server performance. Oracle8 also supports the specification of indexes on fields of tables that can improve search performance.

In a distributed database, multiple database servers cooperate to represent a single schema. An application that connects to any of the servers can access all of them through the single schema. Tables in a distributed database may be unfragmented, vertically or horizontally fragmented, or replicated. Oracle8 supports distributed databases through the creation of links from one database server to another and through snapshot tables.

Transaction processing in a distributed environment can be accomplished using a two-phase commit protocol. In this protocol, a distributed transaction is initiated by one system and managed by a transaction manager on that system. The commit operation must be performed in two phases: a prepare-for-commit phase and a commit phase. If all local transactions are successful with their prepare-for-commit phases, then they can enter their commit phases and commit the transaction. An error, rollback, or time-out in any of the local transactions, however, results in a rollback of all transactions.

Key Terms

Access privileges. Rights to access database objects allocated to specific users or roles. Access privileges can be granted and denied using SQL.

Audit trail. A list of all operations of a specific type that were performed on a database. Each operation is recorded along with its user and time.

Backup. A copy of the state of a database at a specific time. Also, the process of creating such a copy.

Checkpoint. A partial backup that can be used to recover the state of the database from a full backup.

Distributed database. A collection of databases that are related logically but separated physically. A client can access all of the databases through a single schema and a single server.

Distributed transaction. A transaction in a distributed system that is initiated on one system and executed by local transactions on multiple systems.

Horizontally fragmented table. A table in a distributed database that is distributed by having different rows of the table appear on different database servers.

Local transaction. The part of a distributed transaction that is completely contained within a single system.

Recovery. The process of bringing a damaged database back to a former, consistent state.

Redo log. A transaction log in which the effect of a write action is recorded as the new value of the affected object.

Replicated table. A table in a distributed database that is distributed by having copies of the table appear on multiple database servers.

Role. A collection of database users that can have its own privileges. The privilege to be a member of a role can be granted or denied to users and other roles.

Roll forward. The recovery process that proceeds by using the redo transaction log to reprocess transactions.

Stored procedure. A complex operation that is written in a database programming language and stored in a database and can be invoked from SQL. Stored procedures can have their own privileges.

Transaction log. A file that contains a record of each transaction action. Each entry in the log identifies the transaction, the action, the object referenced by the action, and the effect of the action on the object.

Undo log. A transaction log in which the effect of a write action is recorded as the value of the affected object.

Exercises

1. How do the backup and recovery capabilities of a DBMS contribute to the atomicity of a transaction? To its durability?

2. Give four examples of failures in DBMSs. For each one, describe how recovery from this failure may be accomplished.

3. What is the difference between a backup and a checkpoint? Give a scenario in which both backups and checkpoints are required for recovery from a failure.

4. What operations are required to properly carry out each of the following actions? In particular, are any interactions with backups, RBS, locks, logs, or checkpoints required?

   a. Transaction read action

   b. Transaction write action

   c. Transaction open action

   d. Transaction commit action

   e. Transaction rollback action

5. Describe the contents and role of a redo transaction log. What entries are written in the log by read actions? What entries are written in the log by write actions? How is the redo log used in recovery from a failure?

6. Describe the contents and role of an undo transaction log. What entries are written in the log by read actions? What entries are written in the log by write actions? How is the undo log used in recovery from a failure?

7. Compare and contrast recovery via reprocessing, recovery via rollback, and recovery via roll forward. Give examples of situations in which each of these strategies would be appropriate.

8. Why is operating system security insufficient to ensure database security? At a minimum, discuss controlling access to and integrity of disk files, and the use of database-specific accounts.

9. Write SQL statements to perform the following security actions:

   a. Create a new user named "Blurge" with an initial password of "hi-ho."

   b. Give Blurge an unlimited quota on segment USER2.

   c. Set the default tablespace of Blurge to USER2.

   d. Give Blurge permission to perform all actions on the Rental table.

   e. Deny Blurge permission to insert objects into the PreviousRental table.

   f. Allow Blurge to use the Clerk role.

10. Answer the following questions about access to a database after the execution of these SQL statements:

    ```
    grant all on TimeCard to Sponge;
    revoke delete on Supplier from Eric;
    grant update on Employee(street, city, state, zip) to Sponge;
    create role Buyer not identified;
    grant all on Supplier, PurchaseOrder, PurchaseOrderDetail to
        Buyer;
    grant role Buyer to Sponge, Eric;
    ```

    a. Can the user Sponge insert a row into the Employee table?

    b. Can the table TimeCard be updated by the user Eric?

    c. Can the user Sponge assume the role of Buyer?

    d. Can Eric assume the role of Buyer?

11. What are the default permissions on a table for the owner of the table? For a user who is not the owner?

12. What is the difference between an audit log and a transaction log? What actions cause entries to be made in both logs? What actions require an entry in an audit log, but not in a transaction log? What actions require an entry in a transaction log, but not in an audit log?

13. Using a database system that you can access, list the permissions granted to your account. Describe how you were able to determine those permissions.

14. Using the syntax of Figs. 15.3 and 15.4, define a stored function or procedure that:

    a. Produces the number of overdue videotapes for a specific customer.

    b. Produces the number of time card entries for a specific employee at a specific store.

    c. Produces the title of the movie for a specific videotape.

    d. Adds a specific amount to a specific customer's balance.

15. Give a definition of a distributed database system. Name three advantages that a distributed database has relative to a distributed collection of independent database servers.

16. Describe a distribution plan for the tables of the BitHit Video database, as shown in Fig. 6.1. Describe the horizontal and vertical distribution of information and the replication of tables for the individual stores and for the database that is centrally located at the main company office. How would your distribution plan change if the main company office was divided into several regional offices, each overseeing several stores?

17. Using the Web or another reference, identify a company that claims to market a distributed database system and read the description of its system. List those features of distributed databases that are supported and those that are not supported. Is this product a true distributed database according to the definition given in this chapter? Are there obvious limitations on the ability of the system to be used in a large, worldwide organization?

Further Readings

Recovery mechanisms in the System R database are addressed in detail in Gray et al [GMB81]. The book by Bernstein, Hadzilacos, and Goodman [BHG87] is an excellent resource. More recent work on recovery systems includes the Aries system at IBM [Moh92, MoNa94] and the Exodus system [Fra92]. Strategies and mechanisms for database administrators working with Oracle8 are presented in [Lon98].

Security in System R is described in Griffiths and Wade [GrWa76]. General tutorials can be found in Denning and Denning [DeDe79] and in Denning's book [Den83].

Distributed databases are the subject of several books, including Bell and Grimson [BeGr92], Ceri and Pelagatti [CePe84], and Öszu and Valduriez [ÖzVa91]. Multidatabase transactions and recovery are discussed in [GMB81], [Reed83], and in the aforementioned books. Date [Date90] presents 12 objectives for distributed databases. A survey of parallel query processing is found in Graefe [Gra93].

Object-Oriented and Distributed Information Systems

*I*n this final part, we look at object-oriented systems and how they represent and exchange information. You will learn the foundations of this material in sufficient detail to support application development. Of course, these topics are very complex, and a complete mastery of them is beyond the scope of this book. Instead, we merely seek to understand the principles and how to apply them.

Chapter 16 is devoted to distributed applications, as supported by the Java language system. In Java, distribution of information is based on the ability to send an object from one program to another and to allow one program to invoke methods on objects that are part of another program. We look at remote method invocation (RMI), including an example of its use in creating an interactive database interface in a Web site. We divide the processing of a user's interaction with a database into four tiers: a Web browser, a servlet, a database client, and a database server. This example has a complete implementation that takes advantage of RMI and of additional capabilities of Java servlets. The notion of Enterprise JavaBeans (EJB) and enterprise transactions are introduced, with sufficient detail being provided to allow you to understand the principles.

Chapter 17 presents an overview of object-oriented data models and database systems. You will learn how to represent information and operations in an object-oriented model, with specific rules being applied to all of the features of Enhanced ER models, including entity classes, relationships, attributes, and inheritance. Both data structures and methods are covered. As elsewhere in this book, the BigHit Video information system serves as the primary example. The discussion of how to create persistent objects starts with a primitive style of saving objects in files and proceeds to the direct use of object databases. Finally, you see how relational databases can be used to support object-oriented applications through the use of an object-relational interface.

16

Developing Object-Oriented Distributed Applications

CHAPTER OBJECTIVES

In this chapter, you will learn:

- Ways that Java supports distributed objects
- Ways to use Java's remote method invocation (RMI) to create distributed applications
- Java's strategies for supporting RMI
- Ways of incorporating RMI and servlets to create four-tiered applications
- The principles of Enterprise JavaBeans (EJB) packages
- Ways that application services are packaged and deployed
- Java's strategies for managing transactions, including distributed transactions

*T*his chapter details how distributed, information-rich, object-oriented applications should be designed and how they may be packaged and deployed. The object-oriented model focuses on the development of class libraries. An application program is a thin layer built on top of these libraries, either as a user interface or as a simple manipulation of objects. The proper packaging of class libraries must make it easy to create, maintain, and execute the application programs. In this environment, an application program represents the integration of multiple components, often on multiple computers.

The Java language and its packages and class libraries have standardized more of the application environment than any other language has, including standard methods of enabling database access, sharing objects and their methods in a distributed execution environment, and deploying objects and methods in a client-server environment. Note, however, that Java is a rapidly evolving system. This chapter describes some of its capabilities at the time of this book's publication.

Creating Distributed Applications

16.1   The servlet interaction and the session management described in Chapter 10 are examples of the use of Java to create a *distributed application*—that is, an application in which the code, data, and computations are distributed among multiple computers. In this case, the browser (a client program) interacts with a servlet that is located on a remote computer. The servlet, in turn, interacts with a database server that may be located on yet another computer. The interaction between these distributed components relies on a distributed computing environment that incorporates a variety of network and communication protocols, including HTTP, CGI, JDBC, and the database client-server protocol.

In Java, distributed computing is based on the distribution of objects and their methods. The methods of an object may be *packaged* to provide remote execution and then deployed in a server to create a collection of application services. For example, the customer editor servlet described in Section 10.5.1 defines a collection of services for the browser client. The user may request display, update, insert, delete, and filter services on the data that are held in the servlet. The HTTP and CGI protocols manage the interaction, and the `action` parameter specifies which service is requested. Similarly, the database server provides data management services to the servlet through the JDBC and SQL interfaces.

The customer editor servlet is a database application, because it accesses and modifies the database in a specific manner. The servlet is also a server, because the user interacts with it to control the sequence of actions that the application performs. Thus the servlet is a hybrid—part application, part server.

An *application server* is a program that hosts application services. It provides a collection of capabilities for the services, including a standard interface for client connections. In the case of the servlet of Section 10.5.1, the application server represents a combination of the Web server and the servlet engine. We *deploy* the servlet by registering it with the servlet engine. The client makes service requests to the servlet by connecting to the Web server, calling the servlet by its name, and supplying parameters.

A very important aspect of Java application services is that they present an object-oriented view to clients. That is, all application services are based on executing methods on objects. These objects represent classes of service and the methods represent specific services. The client program uses interfaces to access objects that are located in a server.

In this section, object-oriented application services are introduced in an incremental fashion. We extend the servlet model to show how objects can be sent between a client and a server, then discuss how a client can request the execution of methods on those objects, and finally describe how these capabilities are encapsulated for deployment in an application server.

To support object-oriented client-server computing, someone must complete the following actions:

- Specification of client-server interfaces
- Development of service classes

- Development of client classes
- Deployment of application services
- Management of client sessions

16.1.1   Transmitting Objects between Java Programs

The interaction between a browser and a servlet uses a text-based interface. As we saw in Chapter 9, information is sent from the browser as encoded text formatted as name–value pairs. In turn, information is sent back to the browser from the servlet as HTML text.

A true object-oriented interaction between client and server must be based on exchanging objects. The `Serializable` capabilities of Java, as described in Section 11.4.3, make it easy to share objects. Package `java.net` includes support for creating sockets* that can be used to connect Java programs running on different machines. The process of sending an object from a server to a client, as illustrated in the diagram and code of Fig. 16.1, begins by creating a socket on each system and connecting the sockets (line 1). We will omit the details of how the sockets are connected. Each program then creates a new object stream object from the input or output stream of its socket (lines 2–5). With these object streams in place, the server can pass a reference to an object in its memory to method

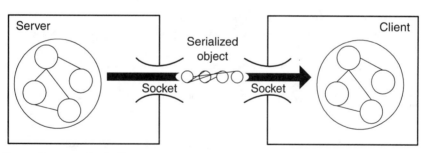

Server Program Code Fragment	Client Program Code Fragment

```
1 Socket sock = new Socket(...);        Socket sock = new Socket(...);
2 Object writeObj;                      Object readObj;
3 ObjectOutputStream out               ObjectInputStream out =
4     new ObjectOutput        (            new ObjectInputStream(
5     sock.getOutputStre   ));             sock.getInputStream());
6 out.writeObject(writeObj);           readObj = out.readObject();
```

FIGURE 16.1 _____

Strategy for sending an object from a client to a server

---

*Sockets are the basis of networking protocols in Java. A *socket* is a bidirectional network port that can be connected to or accept connections from other sockets. The details of the creation and connection of sockets are beyond the scope of this book.

`writeObject` of its output stream (line 6 of the server). The object is serialized to produce a sequence of bytes. The serialized object is sent from the server's socket to the client's socket. When the client issues a call to method `readObject` of its object input stream (line 6 of the client), the bytes of the serialized object are read and used to create an accurate copy of the server's object in the client's memory.

Objects can be sent back and forth using the bidirectional capabilities of the socket. The following code shows a code fragment that reads one object and writes another:

```
Socket sock = new Socket(...);
Object readObj, writeObj;
ObjectOutputStream out =
    new ObjectOutputStream(sock.getOutputStream());
ObjectInputStream in =
    new ObjectInputStream(sock.getInputStream());
readObj = in.readObject();
out.writeObject(writeObj);
```

16.1.2   Remote Method Invocation in Java

Now that we know how to send an object from a client to a server, we need an object-oriented way for the client to request that a specific operation be applied to an object that resides in the server. The *remote method invocation (RMI)* package `java.rmi` provides a standard way for a server to allow method invocations on its objects. This section describes the use of RMI by using class `CustomerEditor` as the main example.

An *RMI server* creates local objects and makes them available to *RMI clients* as *remote objects*. Once a client has received access to a remote object, it can request that the server execute specific methods on the object. The client supplies the arguments to the method call and receives the result object produced by the call. The RMI call is supported by automatically generated auxiliary objects called the *stub* and the *skeleton*. The details of how these objects are created and used are given later in this section.

Figure 16.2 illustrates the interaction of a client and a server through RMI. The details of this interaction are explained below. Figure 16.2 shows the objects (ovals), object references (thin lines), method interfaces (rectangles), and method call mechanisms (black arrows). The stub and skeleton objects that are created to support RMI are shown in gray. The numbered pentagons identify the steps in the RMI interaction. The gray arrows represent the creation and movement of objects in the system. The diagram in Fig. 16.2 is not intended to serve as a guide for implementing RMI services or to illustrate any particular implementation. Instead, it presents a logical view of RMI architecture as a guide to understanding enough about the meaning of this package to support the development of RMI services and clients.

The interaction shown in Fig. 16.2 proceeds as follows:

1. The server creates a *server object* in its memory and creates a remote version (stub) of the object. Both the server object and the stub object

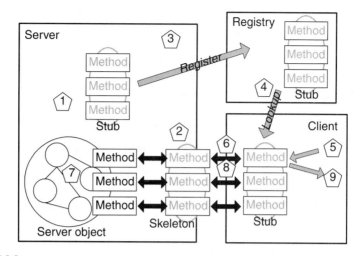

FIGURE 16.2 _____

Strategy for sending an object from a client to a server

are now in the memory of the server. The method boxes in the server object represent its ability to execute specific calls.

2. The server creates a skeleton version of the object whose purpose is to receive RMI calls. The skeleton is attached to a socket in the server. It is also attached to the server object (double-headed arrows) so that calls on its methods can be executed by calls on the server object's methods. The methods of the skeleton are exposed beyond the edge of the server box to illustrate that these methods can be called externally.

3. The server sends a copy of the stub object to the *RMI registry* service. The stub is now in the memory of the registry. The registry is a program running on the server machine that provides a naming service to RMI programs.

4. The client calls the registry and gets a copy of the stub object. A reference to the stub object is stored in a client variable. The double-headed arrows between the stub object in the client and the skeleton object in the server represent the ability of the stub to implement calls on its methods by making calls on the methods of the skeleton.

5. The client makes a call on a method of the stub with arguments.

6. The call is transferred through the network from the stub in the client to the skeleton in the server along with the arguments.

7. The skeleton method calls the corresponding method on the server object. This call executes as a local call on the server object. Its execution may modify the server object and create or modify other objects on the server.

8. The result of the method call is transferred back to the client from server object to skeleton across the network and into the stub in the client.

9. The client receives the result, which may be another remote object.

At this point, the client may call methods on the result object or create and distribute remote objects of its own.

Three classes implement the remote interface:

- The full implementation of the server object

- The stub implementation that transfers calls on its methods across a network connection to an object on the server

- The skeleton implementation that listens on the network for calls from a stub object and transfers those calls to the server object

16.1.3   Using RMI in the Servlet Application

The use of RMI in the customer editor application involves a modification to the servlet class so that it accesses the customer editor object through RMI. As part of this change, we define a new class to be the RMI object server and the servlet class to be the RMI client. This organization has several advantages. First and foremost, management of the editor objects is separated from management of the servlet. This organization may maintain a persistent database connection even if the servlet is not persistent or if simple CGI programs (not servlets) handle the CGI requests. An editor object may even be shared among multiple servlets or located on a different computer from the servlet host.

The basic architecture of the implementation, as shown in Fig. 16.3, is a four-tiered system that includes a database server, a customer editor server that is a client of the database, a Web server with a servlet that is a client of the customer editor server, and a Web browser that is a client of the servlet. Our discussion of this system begins by considering the class and method definitions that are required. The behavior of the system is illustrated with a detailed example in Section 16.4.4.

RMI uses *remote interfaces* to describe the capabilities of remote objects. Any interface can be made into a remote interface by extending `java.rmi.Remote`. The methods of a remote interface must all be defined to throw `RemoteException`. Figure 16.4 gives a remote interface for `CustomerEditor` objects.

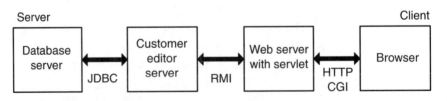

FIGURE 16.3 _____

Architecture of the customer editor application using RMI

```
 1 public interface CustomerService extends java.rmi.Remote {
 2    public void selectRows(String filter)
 3        throws RemoteException, SQLException;
 4    public Customer getCustomer()
 5        throws RemoteException, SQLException;
 6    public void moveAbsolute(int index)
 7        throws RemoteException, SQLException;
 8    public void update(Customer customer)
 9        throws RemoteException, SQLException;
10    // other methods must be added
11 }
```

FIGURE 16.4 _____

Partial definition of a remote interface for customer service

For a class to be used for remote objects, it must implement a remote interface. It also must have other characteristics that are most easily acquired by extending the base class for remote objects, `UnicastRemoteObject`. Other strategies for making a class suitable for RMI are beyond the scope of this book. See the Further Readings section at the end of the chapter for sources of more information on this topic.

We can modify the definition of class `CustomerEditor` of Section 10.4 so that it extends `UnicastRemoteObject` and implements the `CustomerService` interface; the class will then be ready for use with RMI.

```
public class CustomerEditor
    extends java.rmi.UnicastRemoteObject
    implements CustomerService {
```

> ## A NOTE ON IMPLEMENTING INTERFACES
>
> In Java, a class method that implements an interface method does not have to declare all of the exceptions that are thrown by the interface method. You may have noticed that the methods of interface `CustomerService` are declared to throw `RemoteException` but the methods of class `CustomerEditor` are not. Despite this discrepancy, no changes in the methods of class `CustomerEditor` are required for it to implement the remote interface. The class method cannot, however, throw exceptions that are not declared in the interface method.

We will create a new class, `CustomerAccess`, that creates the RMI object that is used to initiate the RMI interaction. This class must also implement a remote interface. Figure 16.5 gives the interface and class definition, including its `main` method. Interface `CustomerServer` supports a single method, `createCustomerService` (lines 2 and 3), that creates and returns a `CustomerService` object. The implementation of the method uses new to create the object. No special treatment is required to return this new object.

```
 1 public interface CustomerServer extends java.rmi.Remote {
 2    public CustomerService createCustomerService()
 3         throws java.rmi.RemoteException;
 4    public final String NAME = "//myserver/customer";
 5 }
 6 public class CustomerAccess extends java.rmi.UnicastRemoteObject
 7        implements CustomerServer {
 8    public CustomerService createCustomerService() {
 9      return new CustomerEditor();
10    }
11    public static void main(String [] args) {
12      System.setSecurityManager(new java.rmi.RMISecurityManager());
13      try {
14        CustomerServer server = new CustomerAccess() {
15        java.rmi.Naming.rebind(CustomerServer.name, server);
16        System.out.println("server bound and started");
17      } catch (Exception e) {
18        System.err.println("Server exception: +e.getMessage());
19      }
20    }
21 }
```

FIGURE 16.5 _____

Interface `CustomerServer` *and the class definition for* `CustomerAccess`

The `main` method of class `CustomerAccess` creates an object of the class using `new`. Because `CustomerAccess` extends `UnicastRemoteObject`, the stub and skeleton objects described previously are also created. The `main` method then calls `Naming.rebind` to register a copy of the stub with the RMI registry. The registry stores a copy of the stub object and makes it available, as will be explained later.

Both the stub and skeleton objects are objects of classes that implement the remote interface. The stub and skeleton class definitions are created by the RMI compiler `rmic`. The `makefile` in the code directory available from this book's Web site details how to use `rmic`. As part of the implementation of the stub and skeleton classes, each remote object is mapped to the local object on the RMI server. A method call on the stub object becomes a message that is sent to the server. The server receives the message, executes the method on its local object, and sends a result message back to the client.

The creation of a security manager in line 12 of Fig. 16.5 is required for programs that use RMI for interaction. We see the same call in the client program shown in Fig. 16.6. Such objects control the program's access to the network. In this case, the security manager object is a `java.rmi.RMISecurityManager`; any security manager that supports RMI network access is acceptable, however.

The client in our example is defined by a modification to class `CustomerServlet`, as initially given in Fig. 10.7. The modification to the class is primarily confined to the definition of member `customerEditor` and the implementation of methods `init` and `restoreContext`. These changes are shown in Fig. 16.6. The type of member `customerEditor` has been changed to use the remote interface `CustomerService` instead of the class `CustomerEditor`. With this change, the member can have a pointer to any object that implements the interface. This strategy allows `customerService` to refer to an RMI stub object. The only change to the other methods of the class is to catch the `RemoteException` that may be thrown by an RMI call.

Method `init` in lines 8 and 9 contacts the RMI registry and gains access to the remote `CustomerServer` object that is registered by the main method of `CustomerAccess`. Member `server` now contains a pointer to a stub object.

The initialization of the `customerEditor` object has been changed from creating a new object (line 8 of Fig. 10.7) to the call on method `createCustomerService`

```
1 class CustomerServlet extends javax.servlet.http.HttpServlet {
2   CustomerService customerEditor = null;
3   CustomerServer customerServer = null; // new local variable
4   public void init (ServletConfig conf) throws ServletException {
5     super.init();
6     System.setSecurityManager(new java.rmi.RMISecurityManager());
7     try{
8       customerServer = (CustomerServer)
9           java.rmi.Naming.lookup(CustomerServer.NAME);
10    } catch {Exception e) {// servlet cannot be initialized
11    }
12  }
13  public Boolean restoreContext (HttpServletRequest request) {
14    HttpSession session = request.getSession(true);
15    if (session.isNew()) { // new session for this user
16      try {
17        customerEditor = customerServer.createCustomerService();
18      // store context objects in new session
19        session.putValue("customerEditor", customerEditor);
20    } else { // create new context
21      // restore context objects from session
22        customerEditor=
23            (customerEditor) session.getValue("customerEditor");
24    }
25  }
```

FIGURE 16.6 _____

Partial definition of class `CustomerServlet` *using RMI*

(line 17 of Fig. 16.6). Instead of creating a local `CustomerEditor` object in the servlet, this version issues an RMI call to the `CustomerServer` for it to create a local `CustomerEditor` object and returns a remote stub of that object.

The rest of the use of member `customerEditor` is the same in the RMI version of the servlet as it was in the original version of Fig. 10.7. In particular, all requests to move the cursor forward or back, extract a `Customer` object from the result set, or update the `Customer` table involve calls on the local stub object. Making a call on a local object and making an RMI call are syntactically identical. The client acts as if all objects are local objects.

16.1.4   An Example of RMI Execution

Figure 16.7 illustrates the behavior of this system, using the same notation as that used in of Fig. 16.2. The figure shows the state of the system after both servlet and server have been initialized and the servlet has called methods `selectRows` and `getCustomer`. The gray arrows and numbered pentagons identify the sequence of actions that led to this state. The actions are described here:

1. The application begins by executing `CustomerAccess.main`, which creates a `CustomerAccess` object and its stub and skeleton. The skeleton is attached to a port on the server. The `main` method registers the stub with the registry.

2. The initialization of the servlet includes calling the registry and receiving a copy of the stub of the `CustomerAccess` object (lines 8 and 9 of Fig. 16.6). A reference to the stub is stored in member `customerService`. The servlet is now ready to receive requests from browsers.

3. The first request from a browser to the servlet creates a new session. The servlet in method `restoreContext` (lines 13–24 of Fig. 16.6) makes a call (line 17) to method `createCustomerService` of the stub of the `CustomerAccess` object. The call is transferred to the skeleton of the `CustomerAccess` object in the server.

4. The call is transferred to the `createCustomerService` method of the `CustomerAccess` object (lines 8–10 of Fig. 16.5), which creates a new `CustomerEditor` object (line 9). The creation of the `CustomerEditor` object includes creating its stub and skeleton objects and attaching the skeleton object to a socket. The stub of this new object is returned to the caller.

5. The skeleton object receives the stub of the `CustomerEditor` object as the return value of the call and transfers a copy of the stub to the client. The stub object is stored in the memory of the client, and a reference to it is stored in member `customerEditor` (line 17 of Fig. 16.6).

6. The servlet calls method `selectRows` of the stub of the `Customer Editor` object. The call is transferred from the stub to the method of the skeleton in the server and thence to the `CustomerEditor` object. A

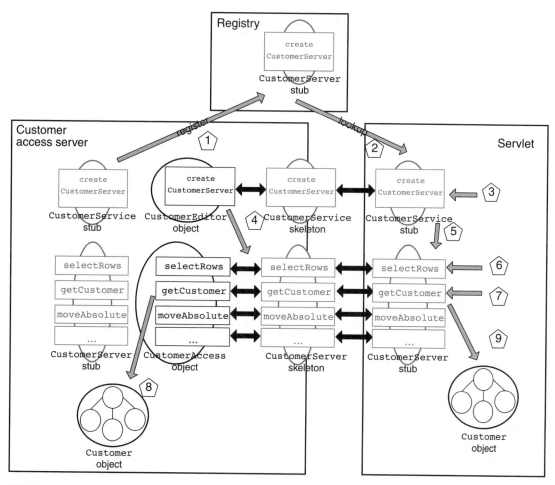

FIGURE 16.7 _____

Illustration of the RMI server and its interaction with the servlet for the BigHit Video customer editor application

new `ResultSet` is created by the `CustomerEditor` object and stored in the server. No value is returned, because the result type is `void`.

7. The servlet calls method `getCustomer` of the stub of the `Customer Editor` object. The call is transferred from the stub to the skeleton and thence to the `CustomerEditor` object.

8. The call to the `getCustomer` method of the `CustomerEditor` object results in the creation of a new `Customer` object in the server.

9. The new `Customer` object is returned to the skeleton, which in turn sends a serialized copy to the stub in the client. The `Customer` object is copied into the memory of the server.

> ## A NOTE ON PARAMETERS AND RESULTS FOR RMI CALLS
>
> The parameters and results used in RMI calls must be primitive values (as in the `int` parameter of method `moveAbsolute` of interface `CustomerService` in lines 6 and 7 of Fig. 16.4) or objects that can be passed through a network between Java programs. A class can allow objects to be passed through a network in two ways. If the class implements a remote interface, the object can be passed as a remote object. For instance, the `CustomerService` object is returned by method `createCustomerService` of the interface `CustomerServer` (lines 2 and 3 of Fig. 16.5) as a remote object.
>
> Alternatively, to pass a copy of an object (not a remote object stub) through an RMI interface, the class of the object must implement `Serializable`. For instance, method `selectRows` of interface `CustomerService` (lines 2 and 3 of Fig. 16.4) uses an object of type `String`, a `serializable` class. Method `update` (lines 8 and 9 of Fig. 16.4) has a parameter of class `Customer`. For the interface to be acceptable as an RMI interface, class `Customer` must implement `Serializable`.

Finally, we should realize that RMI is a symmetric interface. Consequently, a program can be both a client and a server. A Java program is free to create and export remote stub objects. When it does so, it becomes a server for the exported objects. It can also receive remote object stubs from other programs; thus it becomes a client for those remote objects. The description of the application given in this section as an RMI server with local objects and a client with remote stub objects is a simplification of RMI's capabilities.

Enterprise JavaBeans

16.2

The *Enterprise JavaBean (EJB)* specification builds on RMI by providing a standard organization for components of application servers. An EJB deployment of RMI services separates the roles and capabilities of servers from those of services (or components). An EJB server manages security, transactions, creation, and destruction of services, client sessions, and the interaction of service components. Packaging a collection of services as an EJB allows the developer to ignore many of the complexities involved in servers.

This section introduces the underlying concepts and some of the details of EJB, but does not include the transformation of the application given in Section 16.1. The proper packaging and deployment of services in EJB is a complex topic that is beyond the scope of this book. It is very reasonable to expect that EJB 1.0, the version described here, will be significantly expanded soon.

The primary limitations of the RMI solution to the application are that a specific computer hosts all of the customer editor objects and that the creation and destruction of these objects are under the explicit control of the RMI server. In RMI, it is difficult to have a single source of objects that are local to different computers.

EJB addresses the limitations of RMI by providing an API for packaging service components and taking advantage of server capabilities. This API allows developers of *application services* to ignore the issues of location of the services, lifetimes of the objects, registration and deployment of the services, and construction of the servers. The server, on the other hand, must take responsibility for security, maintaining the states of beans, providing client-server (and bean-to-bean) communication, and managing transactions.

EJB classes come in two flavors. *Session beans* are designed to provide particular services to clients. *Entity beans* are data objects with persistence. For example, a session bean could be defined to represent the customer editing services described in Section 16.1 and an entity bean might represent a row of a table in a database.

A class defines session beans if it implements `javax.ejb.SessionBean`. The `SessionBean` interface includes methods that are called when a bean is activated, removed, created, and made passive. It also implements the methods of some specific remote interface, although it does not declare that it implements the remote interface. Instead, the connection between a bean and a remote interface is created when the bean is placed in a container and deployed in a server.

16.2.1 Adapting Class CustomerEditor to EJB

To make class `CustomerEditor` into an EJB session bean class requires some modification. Figure 16.8 shows some of the details. We would remove `extends UnicastRemoteObject`, replace `implements CustomerService` with `implements SessionBean`, and define the methods of interface `SessionBean`. Class `CustomerAccess` would not be required, as the purpose of this class is to

```
 1 public class CustomerEditorBean implements SessionBean {
 2    public void ejbCreate() {
 3      // initialize database connection and statement
 4    }
 5    // also define ejbActivate, ejbRemove, ejbPassivate,
 6    //    setSessionContext
 7    public void void selectRows(String filter) {
 8    // rest of methods as in Figs. 16.2, 16.3, and 16.5
 9 }
10 // remote interface
11 public interface CustomerServiceBean extends EJBObject, Remote {
12    public void selectRows(String filter)
13          throws RemoteException, SQLException;
14    // the rest is just like CustomerService of Fig. 16.11
15 }
16 // home interface
17 public interface CustomerServiceBeanHome extends EJBHome {
18    public CustomerEditorBean create()
19          throws CreateException, RemoteException;
20 }
```

FIGURE 16.8 _____

Parts of the EJB specification of class CustomerEditorBean, *including the remote and home interfaces*

create the RMI server and provide a way of creating remote `CustomerEditor` objects. The application server provides the functionality of this class.

Each session bean must support two interfaces: a remote interface and a home interface. The remote interface provides client access to the services of the bean. The *home interface* provides ways to create bean objects. The remote interface for the `CustomerEditorBean` class is nearly identical to that of the RMI version shown in Fig. 16.5. The home interface defines a single method, `create`, whose purpose is to create a new `CustomerEditor` (bean) object. In general, there will be a `create` method for each constructor of the bean class. The `create` methods are not implemented by the bean class.

No further modifications are required to transform class `CustomerEditor` into class `CustomerEditorBean`, except for obvious changes in class and interface names. The rest of the RMI server activities—creating the server, registering the `CustomerAccess` object, and explicitly creating `CustomerEditor` objects— are incorporated into the standard server capabilities in EJB.

16.2.2   Deployment of EJB Objects in Servers

The first thing you should know about the deployment of EJB objects is that each object is hosted within a *container* object. The container creates and configures the bean; calls its methods upon creation and activation, and at other times; and manages its communication with clients and other beans. The container protects the bean from direct interaction with the server and its clients.

Figure 16.9 illustrates the interaction between an EJB and a client. Much of the complexity of Fig. 16.7 has been eliminated in this figure. The RMI server has been replaced by an application server that can support many EJBs of different types. Likewise, the skeleton objects have been eliminated. The server supports the `create` method of the home interface. When called, it creates a container object that in turn creates the EJB. The container serves the role of the skeleton object of

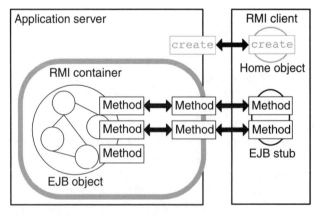

FIGURE 16.9 _____

Interaction between an EJB and a client using an RMI container in an application server

the bean. It supports the methods of the remote interface and transfers calls to the bean. This example shows a remote interface that supports only two of the three methods of the EJB object.

The EJB client closely resembles the RMI client depicted in Fig. 16.7. It has an object (the home object) that acts like a stub to the `create` method of the server. Calling the `create` method of the home object causes the application server to create, or at least allocate, an EJB object and return a stub of its remote method to the client. Calls on methods of the stub for the EJB are handled as RMI calls.

A server may provide a variety of containers for the beans it hosts. The same beans may be hosted in an RMI container (one that provides RMI client access) or a container that supports some other network communication protocol. The container takes responsibility for implementing a specific communication protocol. An EJB class does not need modification to be used for any particular protocol. Instead, we simply need a container that implements the protocol.

The information required by an EJB server to deploy an EJB class is encapsulated in an object of type `javax.ejb.deployment.DeploymentDescriptor`. The details of this object's creation are specific to the particular server involved. A typical specification method is to list the values of the fields of the object in a file. The descriptor object has values for the following fields, with each entry being followed by an appropriate name for the `CustomerServiceBean` class.

- `beanHomeName`: the name used to refer to the bean objects
    `dbjava.ejbean.CustomerService`
- `enterpriseBeanClassName`: the name of the bean class
    `dbjava.ejbean.CustomerEditorBean`
- `homeInterfaceClassName`: the name of the home interface
    `dbjava.ejbean.CustomerServiceBeanHome`
- `remoteInterfaceClassName`: the name of the remote interface
    `dbjava.ejbean.CustomerServiceBean`

Additional fields are used to specify information about the session time-out, the transaction isolation level, and the number of bean objects to be created and maintained. Application-specific fields can be included in the descriptor as well.

The bean class file is packaged in a jar file with a copy of the descriptor specification. Typically, the object is created by a tool that reads the file and creates a serialized object that can be placed in the jar file.

The jar file is passed to the server for deployment. In turn, the server must verify that the bean class faithfully implements the methods of the remote interface and that a constructor exists for each `create` method in the home interface. Once this verification has been completed successfully, the bean is ready for use.

16.2.3   Client Access to EJB Objects

Access to EJB objects in a server begins with a lookup operation. An EJB class is registered with the server by a specific name. The server takes care of making this name available to some name server using the *Java Naming and Directory Interface (JNDI)*. We first call a JNDI system to get an object of type `javax.naming.Context`. As part of creating the context object, security information must be provided to the server. The details of the creation of the JNDI context are not included here. (See the Further Readings for references.) The context object has a `lookup` method that can be used to create an object that implements the home interface of the bean class. The following code belongs in the customer editor servlet that establishes access to a remote `CustomerEditor` bean object.

```
1  javax.naming.Context ctx = // get context from JNDI service
2  CustomerServiceHome home = (CustomerServiceBeanHome)
3      ctx.lookup("dbjava.ejbean.CustomerServiceBeanHome");
4  CustomerServiceBean customerEditor = home.create();
```

The first three lines replace the security object creation and registry lookup code in the `init` method of `CustomerServlet` (lines 6–11 of Fig 16.6). Once the home object has been created, any number of `CustomerServiceBean` objects may be created. Line 4 replaces the RMI request for the creation of a new customer service in method `restoreContext` (line 17 of Fig. 16.6). No other modifications are required in class `CustomerServlet` for it to use the EJB version of the customer service objects.

16.2.4   Advantages of EJB

The advantages of EJB can be classified into four groups: partitioning of applications; protection and security for application services; improved scalability and performance; and interoperability with other systems.

EJB partitions application services with clear divisions. An EJB is a self-contained unit whose interaction with clients and with other beans is carefully controlled. This division forces applications to rely on interfaces, rather than on class definitions, for their interactions with other objects. In addition, EJB partitions the execution environment so that service developers can ignore server and deployment issues and concentrate on the basic services. As a result, much less code must be written than is required for most server applications.

Bean containers are responsible for protecting beans from interference by clients and other beans. A container surrounds the bean so that each request for bean resources must go to the container. Only those requests that satisfy strict constraints will be allowed. For instance, a socket listens to a port on a computer and hence may be subject to attack from an application that streams data to it. An EJB would be protected from such attacks by its container.

Application servers are responsible for enforcing security on access to EJB objects. As noted in Section 16.2.3, granting access to bean classes begins with providing security information. That information is used to initiate any connection to servers and bean containers. A bean class can be deployed as multiple EJBs, each with a different interface. The `CustomerEditor` class, for instance, could be deployed with an interface that did not include update, insert, and delete methods. Consequently, the bean interface in this deployment would enforce read-only access to the class. The server could be configured to grant access to the read-only interface to certain users and the full interface to other users. This security is independent of the implementation of the services and related only to its deployment in an EJB server.

Application servers are responsible for creating and destroying bean objects and for placing them on particular computers. A server can pool bean resources by using a single bean for multiple clients, or it can create a new bean for each client session. The server can also respond to computational loads by moving beans among computers to achieve optimal system, or service, performance.

Interoperability is of crucial importance to distributed systems. EJB separates the communication protocol used to link the client and server from the services themselves. The container of an EJB determines which protocols are supported. Our earlier example assumed that the client would use the RMI protocol. EJB servers allow the same EJB class to be deployed with multiple containers and hence to be used with multiple protocols.

Two environments are widely used for distributed objects. The first is the *Common Object Resource Broker Architecture (CORBA)*, a product of the Object Management Group. CORBA is supported by a variety of software systems that implement object resource brokers (ORBs) and the Internet Inter-ORB Protocol (IIOP), which is used to support interaction between brokers. The CORBA environment includes a data definition language as well as many of the capabilities of EJB application servers.

The second option is the *Distributed Component Object Model (DCOM)*, Microsoft's environment for distributed object services. It extends the Component Object Model (COM), which is used for interaction between clients and servers on a single computer.

Interaction between an EJB and the CORBA environment, for example, can be accomplished by embedding EJB services within CORBA applications and by supporting CORBA services for EJB clients. In the first case, an EJB can be deployed in a CORBA container. Replacing "RMI" in Fig. 16.9 by "CORBA" would create a picture of an EJB object interacting through the CORBA protocol with a CORBA client. The bean would look like a normal CORBA object. The symmetry of the EJB system means that this solution can be used to send objects back and forth and hence supports EJB client access to CORBA (and DCOM) objects.

CORBA is very compatible with EJB. In fact, the standard distribution of Java 2 includes full support for CORBA, including an ORB written in Java.

Transactions in Java

16.3

Transactions come in two flavors: local transactions that take place between an application and a single database server, and distributed transactions involving multiple databases and multiple distributed objects. Local transactions are handled by JDBC, as described in Section 10.1. Distributed transactions are part of the enterprise capabilities of Java in both the EJB standard and the *Java Transaction Service (JTS)*.

16.3.1   Transactions in JDBC

Transactions in JDBC are tied to connections and are controlled by methods of class `Connection`. JDBC supports two modes of executing transactions, just as SQL does (see Sections 10.1 and 14.1.2). Autocommit mode executes each SQL statement as a single transaction, whereas explicit-commit mode supports explicit commit and rollback methods for a collection of SQL statements.

Once a connection to a database server has been established, method `Connection.setAutoCommit` can be called to set the mode. Autocommit is the default mode.

In autocommit mode, a transaction starts when a statement is executed. The transaction is committed when all of its result sets have been closed and its update counts retrieved, or when the statement is explicitly closed. With a read-only `Statement` object, all of the result sets and update counts may be retrieved by the JDBC package and the transaction may be committed immediately after execution of the statement. If desired, however, a JDBC package may defer committing the transaction until the application has retrieved the results. With updatable result sets, the transaction must be kept open until the result set is closed.

The batch update facility of JDBC 2.0 allows multiple update statements to execute as a single transaction. Update statements are added to the `Statement` using method `addBatch`. The statements are executed with method `executeBatch`. This call returns an integer array of update counts. If a batch update is executed in explicit-commit mode, the program can decide whether to commit or rollback the transaction after the updates are executed.

In explicit-commit mode (autocommit off), a new transaction starts with the execution of an SQL statement. This transaction does not become complete until the `commit` or `rollback` method is called, or the JDBC `Connection` object is closed. Execution of multiple SQL statements within a transaction can involve a single `Statement` object with multiple calls to execute SQL statements, or it can involve multiple `Statement` objects, each with its own executions. The `commit` and `rollback` methods close all of the result sets and update counts of the `Statement` objects.

Class `Connection` also supports the specification of the transaction isolation level, as discussed in Sections 10.1 and 14.4.3. The JDBC isolation levels exactly match the SQL isolation levels: `TRANSACTION_READ_UNCOMMITTED`, `TRANSACTION_READ_COMMITTED`, `TRANSACTION_REPEATABLE_READ`, and `TRANSACTION_SERIALIZABLE`. The default transaction level for a database can be found by calling method `getDefaultTransactionIsolationLevel` of class `DatabaseMetadata`.

16.3.2   Enterprise Transactions in Java

The Java transaction API (`javax.transaction`) supplies a detailed transaction model that is primarily useful for developers of communication protocols, such as JDBC drivers. Fortunately, the transaction models that are part of JDBC, EJB, and the other distributed object APIs do most of the work for application and services developers. Here we briefly describe how EJB applications and beans cooperate with servers and containers to manage distributed transactions.

The basic strategy is to allow applications to do transaction management and to have all of the service requests be executed within the transaction of the application. This approach requires, for example, that a database access bean, such as the `CustomerService` bean, not do any explicit transaction management. An application can explicitly manage its own transaction states with open, commit, and rollback operations. These EJB transactions are treated as distributed transactions, as described in Section 15.4.3.

Within an open transaction, each request for service from an enterprise bean includes transaction information that is transmitted to the bean's container. When the application commits its transaction, the commit operation is sent to all affected bean containers. As with any distributed transaction, the application transaction cannot commit unless all of the bean container transactions are committed as well.

The details of the use of transactions in EJB are quite complex and worthy of a much more extensive discussion than is included here. These transactions rely on session beans that maintain client sessions and have embedded state information, and entity beans with transactional behavior.

In general, EJB is not easy to understand—and EJB transactions are no exception. Promoters of EJB argue that any systematic strategy for distributed transaction management among objects is necessarily extremely complex. EJB and JTS make distributed transactions manageable, but they remain a topic for professionals. A major benefit of EJB transactions is that they are based on and are consistent with the CORBA transaction model, which is an industry standard.

Chapter Summary

Database applications can be expected to involve multiple databases, multiple computers, and multiple software packages. The Java language includes a large collection of tools to make object-oriented distributed applications easier to write and maintain.

Communication between components in an object-oriented distributed application relies on sending objects between components. In Java, objects can be sent on sockets using object streams and serializable classes. A program can create a socket, wrap it with object input and output streams, and freely send and receive objects.

Remote method invocation (RMI) is supported by package `java.rmi`. With this technique, an object created in a server program can be sent as a remote stub to a client program. A call in the client on a method of the stub object is transmitted through the network to the server, where the call is executed on the original object. The results are then passed back to the client. A registry program is used so that remote objects can be located by name. This chapter included a detailed example of how a database application could be transformed into a remote object server. The result was a four-tiered application consisting of the database server, the remote object server, the servlet, and the Web browser.

The Enterprise JavaBean (EJB) specification builds on RMI by providing a standard organization for components of application servers. A collection of services implemented with RMI techniques can be packaged as an EJB and deployed in a standard EJB server. Much of the difficulty associated with developing application services is eliminated through the use of EJB capabilities. Each EJB is created inside a container that insulates it from clients and other beans, enforces its security rules, and manages its communication.

Java supports database transactions in JDBC and distributed application transactions through EJB and the Java Transaction Service (JTS). JDBC includes transaction methods in its `Connection` interface. The default transaction-processing mode is autocommit, with a commit operation taking place after each SQL statement. With autocommit mode turned off, the application can specify an isolation level and explicitly commit or rollback transactions.

Enterprise transactions are used to implement distributed transactions. With this strategy, most application services can ignore transaction management and allow the EJB servers and containers to take care of commit and rollback operations. An EJB that uses JDBC to connect to a database should not do its own transaction management.

Key Terms

Application server. A program that hosts application services by providing a collection of capabilities for the services, including a standard interface for client connections.

Application services. A collection of objects and their methods that provide operations relevant to a specific collection of applications.

Container. An object created in an EJB server whose job is to create, manage, and protect a session bean and to make it available for client interaction.

Common Object Resource Broker Architecture (CORBA). A standard environment for distributed object systems. CORBA is specified and promoted by the Object Management Group (OMG).

Deployment. The registration of an application service in a server to make it available for use by clients.

Distributed application. An application in which the code, the data, and the computations are distributed among multiple computers.

Distributed Component Object Model (DCOM). Microsoft's environment for distributed object services. It extends the Component Object Model (COM), which is used for interaction between clients and servers on a single computer.

Enterprise JavaBean (EJB). A Java package specification that builds on RMI by providing a standard organization for components of application servers.

Entity bean. An EJB that is a data object with persistence. Also, a class that implements `javax.ejb.EntityBean`.

Home interface. A Java interface that provides methods of creating EJB objects.

Java Naming and Directory Interface (JNDI). A standard extension to Java that provides applications with a unified interface to multiple naming and directory services.

Java Transaction Service (JTS). A standard extension to Java that provides transaction services to applications involved in distributed transactions.

Packaging. The encapsulation of a collection of application services to prepare it for deployment and use by clients.

Remote interface. A Java interface that extends `java.rmi.remote` and defines a collection of methods that can be invoked on a remote object.

Remote method invocation (RMI). An object-oriented communication mechanism that provides a standard way for a server to allow method invocations on its objects. Also, a package in the Java API.

Remote object. Any object that implements a remote interface—specifically, the server object that supports RMI calls.

RMI client. A Java program that is capable of calling methods of remote objects.

RMI registry. A Java program that maps names to remote objects. An application can use the registry to register its own remote objects and to gain access to other applications' objects.

RMI server. A Java program that allows its remote objects to be used by RMI clients.

rmic. The Java processor that reads the class file of an RMI server class and generates the stub and skeleton classes.

Server object. An implementation of a remote interface that is created as a local object in an RMI server and processes RMI requests.

Session bean. An EJB that is designed to provide particular services to clients. Also, a class that implements `javax.ejb.SessionBean`.

Skeleton object. An implementation of a remote interface that is located in the same program as the server object and listens on a socket for RMI requests. It directs the requests to the correct server object.

Socket. A bidirectional network port that can be connected to and accept connections from other sockets.

Stub object. An implementation of a remote interface whose methods execute by connecting across a network to a server object.

UnicastRemoteObject. A Java base class that can be used to define RMI classes.

Exercises

1. Remote procedure call (RPC) is a Unix standard communication strategy that allows one process to call functions that are provided by another process. Each RPC procedure is identified by its name and the name of the computer on which it resides. Compare this approach with RMI, in which a procedure is identified by its Java class. What advantages is RMI likely to have over RPC? Describe why RMI may be a more predictable and reliable protocol.

2. Define distributed object computing. Give three reasons why the strong typing of Java improves the reliability of distributed object computing.

3. List the sequence of actions that an RMI client performs to find a remote object in the RMI registry and call one of its methods.

4. List the sequence of actions that an RMI server performs to create a remote object and register it with the RMI registry.

5. Describe the purpose and structure of a remote object, a stub for a remote object, and a skeleton for a remote object.

6. Consult the reference manual for Java 1.2 at the Java Web site and describe the actions performed by the RMI compiler (`rmic`). Describe what you would have to do to transform a Java class into an RMI server using `rmic`.

7. Using the customer servlet application as an example, create a four-tiered application for videotape purchases for BigHit Video. The application should support a Web site that allows a user to select a supplier, create a filtered list of movies, and navigate through that list selecting the quantity of each movie to purchase. The user should also be able to view the purchase orders.

8. Using the customer servlet application as an example, create a student editor application for the student records database that you developed for Exercise 19 of Chapter 2 and Exercise 22 of Chapter 4. The application should be four-tiered and should support selecting and editing of student records.

9. Consider class `ProcessPayStatements` of Fig. 8.12:

   a. Define a remote interface for objects of the class.

   b. Modify the `main` method of class `ProcessPayStatements` so that it creates a remote object of the class and registers it with the RMI registry.

   c. Use `rmic` to create the stub and skeleton class files for the class.

   d. Create an RMI client class, `ProcessRemotePay`, whose main method contacts the RMI registry to access the remote object of part (b), uses it to create pay statements, and displays the resulting pay statements.

   e. Execute the programs of parts (b) and (d) to process pay statements.

10. Use the Web to locate a company that sells an application server that supports EJB. Prepare a report on the product. Describe the licensing policies and fees, the method of packaging of EJB classes, and the method of deployment. Outline the modifications to the customer editor application that would be required if the database client and servlet were to be deployed as EJBs.

Further Readings

Further details on servlets and session tracking can be found in [Cal99] and [HuCr98]. RMI is covered in Harold [Har97]. Of the many books on Enterprise JavaBeans, Asbury and Weiner [AsWe99] is a particularly well-thought-out and thorough book. Monson-Haefel [Mon99] and Valesky [Val99] also have helpful treatments of EJB and other distributed issues for Java programmers. Reese's book on JDBC [Ree97] has an extensive example of a distributed object application.

Using CORBA in enterprise applications is the subject of Slama, Garbis, and Russel [SGR99]. Issues related to the interaction between Java and CORBA are found in Orfali and Harkey [OrHa98]. Books by Grimes [Gri97] and Pinnock [Pin98] are sources for further details on DCOM.

17

Representing Information with Object-Oriented Data Models

CHAPTER OBJECTIVES

In this chapter, you will learn:

- Ways to represent data models and operations with Java
- Methods of representing relationships in object-oriented models
- Ways to use access methods to protect attributes
- Methods of representing conceptual model inheritance in Java
- Strategies for creating persistent objects
- Definitions and uses of extent sets of objects
- Specific rules to translate EER models into Java data models
- Ways to use Java for BigHit Video applications
- Approaches for representing objects in an object database system
- Some of the details of OQL, the Object Query Language
- Ways that object-relational systems represent application objects in relational databases

*W*e had a brief introduction to the use of object-oriented data models in Chapter 3 with ODL, the Object Definition Language. In that model, interface definitions represented entity classes. In Chapter 4, we saw how the relational data model is used to create useful representations of entity classes. Similarly, an object-oriented data model can be used to create useful representations of entity classes or ODL interfaces.

In this chapter, we see how Java can function as a data model and how an object-oriented data model can specify the behavior of object classes. An object-oriented data model has both advantages and disadvantages when compared with a relational data model. Java also has some advantages and disadvantages as compared with C++, especially in the context of object-oriented databases.

This chapter specifically addresses the issues of how to create persistence for application objects. Three methods are described: persistence through storing objects in files, persistence through object database systems, and persistence through object-relational database systems.

Representing Information and Operations in the Java Data Model

17.1

A Java data model consists of a collection of class definitions. Each class that is associated with an entity class (interface) of the conceptual data model contains protected members that represent the attributes and relationships of the associated entity class. It also contains *access methods* (`get` and `set`) for each protected member. Additional methods represent the methods of the conceptual model.

This section describes how to design a Java data model and discusses many of the alternative approaches that are available to designers.

17.1.1   Representing Interfaces and Attributes

The first step in translating an *object-oriented data model* into a Java representation is to define a class to represent each interface of the ODL specification. For each single-valued attribute of the ODL interface, we add a corresponding member to the class.

Consider the `Employee` and `Store` interfaces of Fig. 17.1. The Java representation, shown in Fig. 17.2, begins by defining class `Employee` and adding the member definitions for the single-valued attributes (lines 1–4).

```
1 interface Employee {
2    attribute string ssn;
3    attribute string lastName;
4    attribute string firstName;
5    attribute Struct Addr
6        {string street, string city, string state, string zipcode}
7      address;
8    attribute Set<String> positions;
9    relationship Set<Store> worksIn inverse Store::workers;
10   relationship Store managerOf inverse Store::manager;
11 }
12 interface Store {// partial definition
13   relationship Set workers inverse Employee::worksIn;
14   relationship Employee workers inverse Employee::managerOf;
15   public int numberWorkers(); // derived attribute
16 }
```

FIGURE 17.1 ———

Preliminary ODL definitions of entity classes Customer *and* Store

```
1 public class Employee {
2    protected String ssn; // attributes
3    protected String lastName;
4    protected String firstName;
5    protected Address address; // composite attribute
6    protected Collection positions; // multivalued attribute
7    protected Set worksIn; // multivalued relationship
8    protected Store managerOf; // single-valued relationship
9    public Employee () {
10      address = new Address();
11      positions = new HashSet();
12      worksIn = new HashSet();
13      managerOf = null;
14   }
15 }
16 class Address {
17    public String street, city, state, zipcode;
18 }
19 class Store {// partial definition
20    protected Set workers = new HashSet();
21    protected Employee manager = null;
22    public int numberWorkers() {//derived attribute
23      return workers.size();
24   }
25 }
```

FIGURE 17.2 _____

Preliminary Java class definitions for Employee *and* Store

Figure 17.3 shows a diagram of an Employee object and some of its related objects for the employee named "Jane Uno" who is the manager of a store. Each box represents an object whose type is listed at the top. Each of the String values is a separate object, as are the Address object and each Set. Because each field of Employee is object-valued, all of them are represented by references to other objects. Fields of primitive type have their values stored within the object.

A composite attribute, like Employee.address, is represented by a member (line 5 of Fig. 17.2) whose value is an object of a new class (lines 16–18 of Fig. 17.2). In this case, class Address must be created to contain values of the address attribute. This approach is particularly appropriate because we can use objects of the Address class to represent addresses of Employee, Store, and Supplier as well. Class Address has been defined as a very simple class with public members and no methods. We take this tack because addresses were not identified as objects in the data modeling and hence do not require any special treatment.

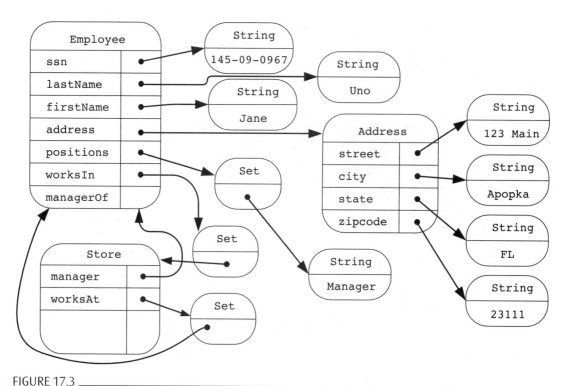

FIGURE 17.3
Diagram representing the value of an Employee *and its related objects*

In Java, a multivalued attribute is represented by a *collection* of values. Attribute positions (line 8 of Fig. 17.1) of entity class Employee is the collection of names of jobs that the employee can do. In class Employee, a Collection represents this collection of values. Note that the constraint on the types of the members of the collection has been lost in the Java code. We will recover this constraint when we add access methods in Section 17.1.3.

In Java 1.2, interface java.util.Collection is the root of the collection hierarchy. This collection hierarchy includes interfaces Set (for collections with no duplicates), List (for ordered collections), and SortedSet (for value-ordered collections with no duplicates). Defining the positions member as a Collection allows us to defer making a decision about what kind of collection to use. The initialization of positions (line 11 of Fig. 17.2) will create an object of a specific type.

A public default constructor should be defined for each class. This constructor includes code to initialize all of the object-valued fields. For class Employee, we must initialize the fields address, positions, worksIn, and managerOf. As an alternative to the default constructor, we can put initializations directly into the field declarations. Class Store is defined with an implicit default constructor. Lines 20 and 21 of Fig. 17.2 include the declaration and initialization of the two object-valued fields. These lines will execute during the construction of any object of type Store.

Package `java.util` includes collection classes that support a variety of constraints and access methods.

17.1.2   Representing Relationships

In an object-oriented model, relationships are represented by references. The ODL conceptual model uses two relationship properties to represent each binary relationship type, one in each related entity class. In the Java data model, object-valued members represent these relationship properties.

The attributes `worksIn` and `managerOf` on lines 8 and 9 and `workers` and `manager` on lines 20 and 21 of Fig. 17.2 each represent one role of a relationship type. Attributes `managerOf` and `manager` are the two roles of the one-to-one `Manages` relationship type between `Employee` and `Store`, and attributes `worksIn` and `workers` are the two roles of the many-to-many `WorksIn` relationship type.

As in the examples of `managerOf` and `manager`, each to-one role in a relationship type is represented by a field whose type is the related class. For example, the value of the `managerOf` field of an `Employee` object is a reference to the related `Store` object. The inverse role is the `manager` field in the related `Store` object, whose value is a reference to the `Employee` object. In this way, object-oriented data models represent relationships as bidirectional references.

This representation is significantly different from that of the relational model, in which shared values represent relationships. That is, in the relational model, a foreign key field contains the key value of the related object. To find the related object, one must find the record of the related table with the specific key value. In the object-oriented model, only simple dereferencing is required.

Referential integrity means that each reference from an object determines another object. In a relational model, referential integrity is satisfied when each foreign key value refers to an object in the related table. In an object model, referential integrity is satisfied when one object refers to another object, and the other object in turn refers to the first one. It is enforced in an object model by the methods that modify relationship values, as described in Section 17.1.4.

In Java, a to-many role in a relationship type is represented by a collection object. In Fig. 17.2, for example, the to-many role `worksIn` has type `Set`, thus guaranteeing that the collection will not have any duplicates. The many-to-many relationship type is represented by two fields and does not require the creation of a new class, as it does in the relational model. In the translation of the original ER diagram into a relational data model, the `WorksIn` relationship type had to be transformed into a new relation, as was shown in Fig. 4.19.

This representation of to-many roles is inadequate, however, because it does not specify a constraint on the type of the related objects. A `Set` in Java is allowed to contain values of any type. The ODL specification of the `WorksIn` relationship type includes the constraint that related objects must come from the correct classes. Unfortunately, we cannot enforce this constraint in the Java data model. Instead, we must add the constraint by requiring that all access to the role members go through access methods. As we will see in the next section, those access methods can easily enforce the type constraints.

A many-to-many relationship type with attributes cannot be represented as multivalued roles because there must be an object to contain the attributes of each relationship. The relationship type must be represented as a class of its own. The simplest approach to this situation is to modify the ER diagram to represent the relationship type as an entity class, as shown by the transformation of `Rents` in Fig. 2.4 to `Rental` in Fig. 2.5.

17.1.3   Defining Access Methods for Attributes

The member definitions of Fig. 17.2 all include the `protected` modifier. As a result, these members can be accessed only from within the declaring class and its subclasses. We must add access (`get` and `set`) methods to allow applications to access and modify the values. The Java convention, as shown in the method definitions of the standard classes, is to use the names of the form `getField` and `setField` for access methods for fields that have a single value. The following methods are the appropriate access methods for the `ssn` field of class `Employee`:

```
public String getSsn () {return ssn;}
public void setSsn (String ssn) {this.ssn = ssn;}
```

For an object variable `emp`, the following changes the value of `ssn`:

```
emp.setSsn("263-87-1123");
```

Access methods for the composite attribute address are more complex. We must make choices in our implementation. The first option is to support access methods for the individual fields. That is, class `Employee` can include methods `getAddressStreet` and `setAddressStreet`, and so on. The second option is to make `address` a public member, make the fields of class `Addr` protected, and add access methods to class `Addr`. The following two lines of code each set the `street` of employee emp. The first line uses an access method of class `Employee`. The second line uses a public `address` and an access method of class `Addr`.

```
emp.setAddressStreet("234 Main St.");
emp.address.setStreet("234 Main St.");
```

The major advantage of adding access methods to class `Addr` occurs when multiple classes have address fields. In this case, the access methods can be implemented once and used for each address field.

Access methods for multivalued attributes use a different notation. Because the attribute has many values, access to individual values requires methods like those found in `java.util.Collection`. Methods are required to select an element and to iterate through all elements. In addition, the modification of the value of the field requires methods that add and remove elements.

For member `positions` of class `Employee`, we can make the field protected and define access methods, or we can make the field public and use the methods of the `Collection` interface directly. In this case, the first option has a significant advantage: it supports constraints on the values of the field. For example, member `positions` is intended to be a list of strings. The ODL definition in line

8 of Fig. 17.1 makes this intent clear, but the Java definition of the field in line 6 of Fig. 17.2 does not require that the values be strings; a `Collection` object can have elements of arbitrary type. The following methods can be used to add an element to the collection of positions:

```
public void addPosition (String element) {
   positions.add(element);
}
```

A call to `addPosition` is thereby constrained and can provide only a `String` as its argument. Any further restrictions on the allowable values for the attribute can also be implemented in the `add` method.

For each multivalued field, additional methods must be provided to support removing an element, determining whether a value is in the collection, and iterating through the values. The following methods are a minimal set to be added:

```
public void removePosition (String element) { …
public boolean containsPosition (String element) { …
public String getFirstPosition () { …
public Iterator iterator() { …
```

17.1.4   Defining Access Methods for Relationships

Single-valued and multivalued relationship roles are implemented using the strategies outlined for attributes in Section 17.1.3. Access methods are implemented to access and modify the relationships between objects. The extra difficulty lies in maintaining both roles consistently.

The following discussion assumes that access methods have already been created for the relationship attributes following the techniques of Section 17.1.2 and 17.1.3. These methods support accessing the related objects and modifying the role values.

Creating and destroying relationships are complex operations. Any change in one role of a relationship must necessarily affect the other role. For example, suppose `emp` is an `Employee` object and `store` is a `Store` object. The call to make `emp` the manager of `store` is accomplished by either of the following method calls:

```
emp.createManagerRelationship (store);
store.createManagerRelationship (emp);
```

Several difficulties occur when defining methods for creating and destroying relationships. The first is that the code to create the relationship must set the fields of both related objects. For the `Manages` relationship type, both the `managerOf` field of the `Employee` and the `manager` field of the `Store` must be set. A preliminary implementation of the method is as follows:

```
protected void createManagesRelationship(Store store) {
   this.setManagerOf (store);
   store.setManager (this);
}
```

```
 1 public boolean createManages (Store store) {
 2 // make the change only if there are no conflicts
 3   if (getManagerOf() != null | store.getManager() != null)
 4     return false; // conflict with existing relationship
 5   this.setManagerOf(store);
 6   store.setManager(this);
 7   return true;
 8 }
 9 public void createManages (Store store) {
10 // destroy the existing relationships and then create the new
11   if (getManagerOf() != null) destroyManages ();
12   if (store.getManager() != null) store.destroyManages ();
13   this.setManagerOf(store);
14   store.setManager(this);
15 }
```

FIGURE 17.4 _____

Two implementations of `Employee.createManages`

Another difficulty with creating this new relationship is that the store may already have a manager. That is, `store.Manager` may not be null. Two meanings are possible for `emp.createManages`. First, the attempt to create the relationship may be disallowed if the store already has a manager or if the employee is a manager of another store. Second, the current manager relationship may need to be destroyed and the new relationship created. Figure 17.4 shows the implementation of the methods using these two strategies. In either case, `Store.createManages` is implemented with a call to `Employee.createManages`.

To protect the relationship roles from being set independently, the `set` methods are declared as protected. Hence, the code in Fig. 17.4 is valid only if classes `Employee` and `Store` reside in the same package. If they appear in different packages, we must make the `set` methods public.

One-to-many and many-to-many relationship access methods follow the one-to-one implementations. A to-many role is implemented just like the roles depicted in Fig. 17.3. The implementation of a `create` method for a to-many role need not check for conflicting relationships.

17.1.5 Using Inner Classes for Relationships

An alternative to adding relationship access methods to a class is to define relationship role classes with their own methods. Just as with the composite attribute methods of Section 17.1.3, access methods for relationships may be methods of the field. Creating a `Manages` relationship with role objects can be accomplished with either of these calls:

```
emp.managerOf.create(store);
store.manager.create(emp);
```

The `managerOf` and `manages` fields must be defined as objects with `create`, `destroy`, `get`, and `set` methods.

The definition of the relationship role classes is best done using *inner classes*—that is, classes that are defined inside other classes. The definition of an inner class to support the `managerOf` field of class `Employee` is shown in lines 3–20 of Fig. 17.5. This class is defined to be public so that its public methods can be called from outside the package. The `get`, `create`, and `destroy` methods (lines 7, 9, and 15, respectively) are public, and the `set` method (line 8) is protected to ensure that the relationship is bidirectional. The `managerOf` field (line 22) is declared to be a public variable of inner class `ManagerOf`.

A more complex and satisfying solution to defining role classes is to create a base class `Relationship` that includes the standard relationship operations of `create` and `destroy`. Subclasses `ToOneRelationship` and `ToManyRelationship` add operations specific to these types of roles. The inner classes for specific roles can then be defined as subclasses of the appropriate base class. In this way, all relationship role fields in all classes share common operations and can be treated in a consistent way by applications. This strategy also simplifies the implementation of

```
1 public class Employee {
2    // inner class for managerOf relationship role
3    public class ManagerOf {
4       protected Employee emp; // Employee who is manager
5       protected Store store; // Store that is managed
6       protected ManagerOf(Employee emp) {this.emp=emp;}//constructor
7       public Store get() {return store;}
8       protected void set(Store store) {this.store = store;}
9       public boolean create(Store store) {
10         if (get() != null | store.manager.get() != null)
11            return false; // conflict with existing relationship
12         store.manager.set(emp); set(store);
13         return true;
14      }
15      public boolean destroy() {
16         if (store==null) return false;// no relationship to destroy
17         store.manager.set(null); set(null);
18         return true;
19      }
20   }// end of inner class definition
21   // definition of relationship role field
22   public ManagerOf managerOf = new ManagerOf(this);
23 }
```

FIGURE 17.5 ⎯⎯⎯⎯⎯⎯⎯⎯⎯⎯⎯⎯⎯⎯⎯⎯⎯⎯⎯⎯⎯⎯⎯⎯⎯⎯⎯⎯⎯⎯

Example of a definition of an inner class for the `Manages` *relationship*

the inner classes by encapsulating a significant amount of the code for the methods. The development of these `Relationship` classes is left as an exercise.

A NOTE ON METHODS FOR DERIVED ATTRIBUTES

Each derived attribute in the conceptual model must be implemented by a method that calculates its value. The code for the method should be included in the class definition.

For example, the value of the derived attribute `numberWorkers` is the number of employees related by the `WorksIn` relationship. It is represented by a method specification in line 15 of the ODL interface `Store` in Fig. 17.1. It is simply translated into the Java method definition in lines 22–24 of Fig. 17.2.

Implementing Conceptual Model Inheritance in Java

17.2

In Chapter 3, we saw examples of the use of inheritance in conceptual data models. In both the extended ER model and ODL, inheritance is an important tool. We also saw extensive use of inheritance in Java in Chapters 8–12 and 16. Because Java provides excellent support for inheritance, the transformation of inheritance in a conceptual model into inheritance in a Java data model should be straightforward—and usually it is.

17.2.1   Single Inheritance

Java supports single inheritance, and every entity subclass with a single super class can be directly translated into Java. For example, the `SalariedEmployee` and `HourlyEmployee` classes are subclasses of `Employee` in the conceptual model and extend the Java `Employee` class in the data model. Figure 17.6 gives a partial implementation of `HourlyEmployee` and its related class `TimeCard`. The `hourlyRate` attribute and the `timeCards` relationship role of `HourlyEmployee` have been added to the inherited fields of `Employee`. Notice that a `TimeCard` must be related to an `HourlyEmployee`. An object of class `Employee` or class `SalariedEmployee` is not eligible to be related to a `TimeCard` and does not have the `timeCards` field.

The date fields of the conceptual model are represented as `long` values in this Java model, reflecting the classes that are provided by the Java API. A `Date` value in Java represents a specific instant in time, with millisecond precision. It is shown as the number of milliseconds since January 1, 1970, 00:00:00 GMT. Although the `Date` class has many capabilities for the application, the value can nevertheless be stored as a `long` value with no loss of accuracy. This representation is simpler, and the application need merely create a new `Date` value from the `long` value to use all of the class's capabilities.

An `HourlyEmployee` object exists exactly once and includes all of the fields of `Employee` plus the fields of `HourlyEmployee`. This approach is the simple and straightforward representation of single inheritance.

Figure 17.7 shows an `HourlyEmployee` object and a related `TimeCard` object. The fields of the `HourlyEmployee` include the fields of the `Employee`

```
 1 public class HourlyEmployee extends Employee {
 2    protected double hourlyRate;
 3    protected Set timeCards = new HashSet();
 4    public double getHourlyRate() {return hourlyRate;}
 5    public void setHourlyRate(double hourlyRate) {
 6       if (hourlyRate>0.0) this.hourlyRate = hourlyRate;
 7    }
 8    // additional methods must be included for access to timeCards
 9 }
10 public class TimeCard {
11    protected HourlyEmployee employee;
12    protected long startTime=0;
13    protected long endTime=0;
14    protected Store store;
15    protected boolean paid = false;
16    // access methods must be added
17 }
```

FIGURE 17.6 _____

Partial implementation of the HourlyEmployee *subclass of* Employee

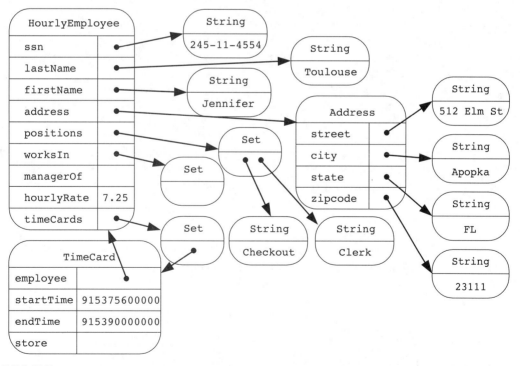

FIGURE 17.7 _____

HourlyEmployee *and* TimeCard *objects*

superclass. We can see that the values of the primitive fields `hourlyRate`, `startTime`, and `endTime` are stored inside the objects. The values of the time fields of the `TimeCard` are shown as `long` values.

17.2.2   Multiple Inheritance

A difficulty arises in designing Java data models when a class inherits from multiple superclasses, and when a single superclass object may be a member of multiple subclasses.

Recall that the relational model includes separate tables for each superclass. The key of the superclass is included in the subclass as both a key and a foreign key. We can then quite easily represent all of the possible inheritance structures. An object of the superclass is also an object of a subclass if a row in the subclass table has the same key as the superclass object. An object may be represented in multiple subclasses and in multiple superclasses in the relational model. In addition, an object may change type, in the sense that subclass objects may be inserted and deleted.

We can adopt this strategy in Java by forgoing the use of Java inheritance and instead creating a field in the subclass object that refers to the corresponding superclass object. Figure 17.8 shows a partial implementation of the `HourlyEmployee` class that does not extend `Employee`. Figure 17.9 illustrates this implementation for the same `HourlyEmployee` object shown in Fig. 17.7. The hourly employee is now represented by the combination of two objects—one of class `HourlyEmployee` and one of class `Employee`—in addition to all of the related objects.

This implementation suffers from a lack of inheritance of superclass operations. For example, subclass objects cannot be directly used as superclass objects. As a result, a method with an `Employee` parameter cannot be passed an `HourlyEmployee` as an argument.

Java gets around the restriction to single inheritance through the use of interface declarations. In this case, we could create `EmployeeInterface` and have all of the classes implement this interface. We would define class `Employee` to represent objects from the `Employee` entity class and have it implement `EmployeeInterface`. Figure 17.10 shows a partial definition of this approach.

The subclass object is implemented by an object with its fields and a reference to an object of its super class. This approach allows us to have a single superclass

```
1 public class HourlyEmployee {
2   public Employee employee;// reference to superclass object
3   public HourlyEmployee(String ssn) {
4     employee = new Employee(ssn);
5   }
6 }
```

FIGURE 17.8 _____

Nonstandard implementation of the `HourlyEmployee` *subclass of* `Employee`

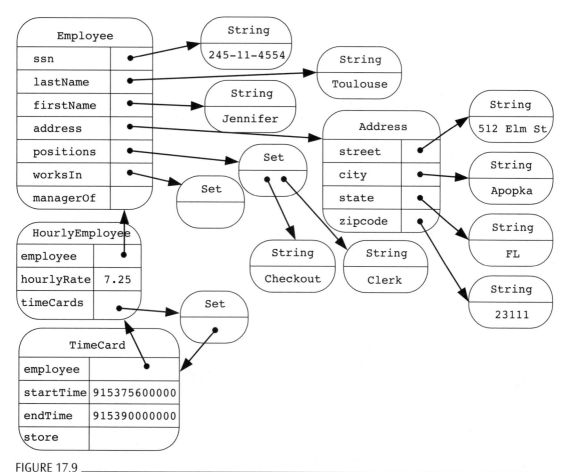

FIGURE 17.9 _____

Illustration of the nonstandard implementation of `HourlyEmployee`

object that exists in multiple subclasses. The following code uses the classes of Fig. 17.10 to create an employee who is both salaried and hourly:

```
SalariedEmployee sal = new SalariedEmployee(ssn);
HourlyEmployee hour = new HourlyEmployee(sal.employee);
```

The creation of the `SalariedEmployee` causes a new `BasicEmployee` to be created as its superclass object. That superclass object (`sal.employee`) is used as the `BasicEmployee` of the new `HourlyEmployee`. Both of the objects implement `EmployeeInterface` and share the same `BasicEmployee` object as their superclass object.

For a class that inherits from multiple superclasses, we simply implement each superclass interface and use a reference to an object of each superclass.

```
1 public interface EmployeeInterface {
2   public String getSsn ();
3   public void setSsn(String ssn);
4   // all other methods of previous class Employee
5 }
6 public class BasicEmployee implements EmployeeInterface {
7   // class body is identical to that of the previous Employee
8 }
9 public class HourlyEmployee implements EmployeeInterface {
10   protected EmployeeInterface employee;// ref to superclass object
11   public HourlyEmployee(String ssn) {
12     employee = new BasicEmployee (ssn);
13   }
14   public HourlyEmployee(EmployeeInterface employee) {
15   // make a new HourlyEmployee whose Employee already exists
16     this.employee = employee;
17   }
18   public String getSsn() {return employee.getSsn();}
19   public void setSsn(String ssn) {employee.setSsn(ssn);}
20   // rest of the methods implemented the same way
21 }
22 public class SalariedEmployee // defined like HourlyEmployee
```

FIGURE 17.10 _____

Using an interface to simulate inheritance with `HourlyEmployee` *and* `SalariedEmployee`

A further enhancement of this technique is to implement the superclass references as relationships—that is, to have a two-way connection between the subclass and superclass objects. The implementations of Figs. 17.8 and 17.10 has no way of finding a subclass object from a superclass object. Transforming the reference into a relationship allows an application to go from superclass to subclass. If the relationship between superclass and subclass is one-to-one, each superclass object can be in at most one subclass. If it is one-to-many, each superclass object can appear in many subclasses. It makes no sense for this relationship to be many-to-one or many-to-many, because this cardinality would imply that a subclass object could represent more than one object from a single superclass.

Making Objects Persistent

17.3   Now that we have created a data model, the next step is to ensure that the objects created by applications will persist between executions. Three methods of creating persistence are described in this chapter. The first, described in this section, is to create persistence by storing objects in files, either using the Java serializable interface or the file structures of Chapter 11. This second method, described in Section 17.6, is to use an object-oriented database that allows applications to directly manipulate objects in a database. The third method, described in Section 17.7, is to use software that automates the mapping from application objects to relational database objects.

An obvious strategy for creating *persistent objects* is to write objects into files at the end of the execution of a program and then to read all of the stored objects back into memory at the start of the next execution. As a result, subsequent executions of the application can pick up where the previous execution left off. For example, we can execute an application that creates a collection of BigHit Video objects and writes them into a file. Other applications can then read the file, update the objects, and rewrite the file. In many ways, the file of persistent objects behaves like a database of BigHit Video objects.

It is much more complicated to store all of the objects in files, but subsequently reload only those objects needed by the execution of an application, and to load those objects only when requested. Chapter 11 covered the file organizations that support these strategies. The same chapter also discussed the hardware and software characteristics that make file management crucial to application performance.

Writing objects to files is made very easy in Java by the `Serializable` interface. The serialization of an object involves the transformation of its memory representation into a sequence of bytes that can be stored in a file or passed to another program. A serialized object is then transformed (deserialized) into a new memory representation that preserves the object's meaning. The serialization and deserialization of an object also transform all of its referenced objects.

The details of object serialization were covered in Section 11.4.3, after a thorough treatment of file organization and the hardware characteristics of file systems. In this section, we consider the benefits that can be derived from serialization and ways to arrange for the persistence of specific objects. It suffices for us to understand that any serializable object, and all serializable objects that it references, can be written to or read from a file in a single operation. The objects read from a serialized file are identical in meaning to those that were written. The only features of the objects that are not preserved are their memory addresses.

17.3.1 Using Collections of Persistent Objects

The primary question to be addressed is, How can we arrange for specific objects to be stored and retrieved? We must either remember which objects are to be stored and retrieved, or we must create a collection of all objects of interest and store the entire collection.

Remembering which objects are in a file, in this context, amounts to having one piece of code that writes specific variables and another piece that reads those same variables in the same order. This technique works only if the list of variables can be prepared before compiling the programs. In most cases, however, we don't know which objects need to be stored before a program begins executing. For instance, an application that creates a videotape rental must add another rental object to the ones that have been created previously. In this case, it makes much more sense to create a list of all rentals than to create a variable in the program for each potential rental object.

The proper way to make information persistent in an object-oriented data model corresponds to the way in which information is stored in the relational model. A relational database contains a table, or a list, of all objects of each entity class. The list of objects of an entity class is called the *extent* of the class.

To make objects persistent, extents must be created and maintained for each object class whose objects can exist independently of their relationships with other classes. Section 17.3.2 describes how to create, save, and restore extents. Section 17.3.3 discusses the automatic maintenance of extents. Section 17.3.4 addresses the issue of which extents must be created.

We need to select an aggregate type to use for extent objects. Two requirements apply to extents: they must keep a set of object references, and they must support iteration through the elements. Iteration will often be used for searching. We are not primarily concerned with access to values by key, because relationships are implemented with references and not with the key–foreign key pairs of the relational model.

The best type for entity objects is interface `Set` of package `java.util`. `Set` is a subinterface of `Collection` that is used for collections of objects with no duplicates. Package `java.util` includes class `HashSet`—an implementation of `Set` that has constant time performance for the basic operations of `add`, `remove`, `contains`, and `size`. We can declare extent variables as `Set` variables and use class `HashSet` for the extent objects.

An alternative to using a `Collection` is to use a `Map`, which maps values to objects. Because each class in the data model comes from an entity class, it has a key that can be used to create the mapping. Because we are not primarily concerned with access to objects by key, however, the use of a `Map` would create unjustifiable overhead.

17.3.2   Creating, Saving, and Restoring Extent Collections

An *extent collection* is the set of all persistent objects of a single class. An application that uses persistent objects from a class in the data model must have a variable whose value is the extent of the class. Because only one extent variable exists for each class, its appropriate representation is as a static variable of the class. The extent collection must be a set, because duplicates are not allowed. Hence the following code is appropriate for class `Employee`:

```
public class Employee {
   static public Set extent;
```

The extent of class `Employee` can be referenced as `Employee.extent`.

The next problem to be resolved is a *chicken and egg* problem. Every application that uses persistent objects must have extent objects, but the extent objects must be created by an application that uses persistent objects. Again, the solution comes from the example of relational databases, which support a data definition language that is used to create the tables of the database. The application programs begin their executions with the existing tables. A special initialization program must create the tables so that they will be available to the applications.

We can define the `Initialize` class with a `main` method that will create all of the extent objects and make them persistent by writing them into a file. Figure 17.11 shows a partial implementation of this class. Method `createExtents` creates the extent objects. Method `saveExtents` writes them as serialized objects into a file named `BigHitVideo.obj`. Method `restoreExtent` reads the extent objects from the file and makes the extent variables reference the extent objects. The `main` method of the class simply creates the extent objects and stores them in the file.

Although storing objects from different classes in different files offers some advantages, Java's approach to serialization requires that they all be serialized in the

```
1 public class Initialize {
2 // methods to create extent objects and to save and reload using
3 // serialized object file
4    public static void createExtents () {
5       Employee.extent = new HashSet();
6       Store.extent = new HashSet();
7       // create the rest of the extent objects
8    }
9    public static void saveExtents () throws IOException {
10      FileOutputStream out=new FileOutputStream("BigHitVideo.obj");
11      ObjectOutputStream objectOut = new ObjectOutputStream(out);
12      objectOut.writeObject(Employee.extent);
13      objectOut.writeObject(Store.extent);
14      // write the rest of the extent objects
15      objectOut.close();
16    }
17    public static void restoreExtents ()
18        throws IOException, ClassNotFoundException {
19      FileInputStream in = new FileInputStream("BigHitVideo.obj");
20      ObjectInputStream objectIn = new ObjectInputStream(in);
21      Employee.extent = (Set) objectIn.readObject();
22      Store.extent = (Set) objectIn.readObject();
23      // read the rest of the extent objects
24      objectIn.close();
25    }
26    public static void main (String[] args) {
27      // create and store the extent objects
28      createExtents();
29      saveExtents();
30    }
31 }
```

FIGURE 17.11 _____

Partial implementation of class `Initialize`

same file. In particular, when `Employee.extent` is serialized and written to a file, all of the `Store` objects that are related to employees by `Manages` or `WorksAt` relationships will also be written to the same file. Because each videotape is related to a store, the videotape objects will also appear in the same file. It is likely that writing `Employee.extent` will cause all of the persistent objects to be added to the file. Similarly, reading `Employee.extent` will bring all of the `Employee` objects and all related objects back into memory.

If the different extents are written into different files, the related objects will be duplicated. When the extents are restored, the uniqueness—and hence the meaning—of the original objects will be lost.

A major problem with serialization that arises during application development is the strong binding of the objects to the class definitions. Any change in the definition of the class invalidates the serialized objects. A change as simple as adding a new method to the class will make it impossible to read old objects with the new class. We cannot use a serialized file of objects in the presence of code changes. As we will see in Section 17.6, object databases enable us to preserve objects in the presence of changes in the schema.

17.3.3 Maintaining Extent Collections

Without additional effort, the extent objects will be empty sets. To make an extent object into the set of all persistent objects of the associated class requires that each object be added to the extent when it is created—that is, when it becomes an object of the class. Similarly, when the object is destroyed, it must be removed from the extent set.

The requirement that objects must be members of the extent set can be satisfied by writing code in the object constructors, as shown in Fig. 17.12. In the simplest

```
1 public class Employee {
2   public Employee () {// default constructor
3     extent.add(this);
4     // rest of default constructor here
5   }
6   public Employee (String ssn) {
7     this(); // call default constructor
8     // rest of constructor here
9   }
10  public boolean destroy () { // make this not persistent
11    destroyWorksAt();
12    destroyManages();
13    extent.remove(this);
14  }
15 }
```

FIGURE 17.12 _____

Class `Employee` *with methods that maintain persistence*

case, the default constructor adds the object to the extent, as in line 3 of this example. The other constructors (in this case, lines 6–8) call the default constructor.

The destruction of an object occurs when the object ceases to be persistent. From the preceding discussion, we know that an object is persistent if it is in an extent or if it is related to some persistent object. To destroy an object, therefore, requires destroying its relationships to other objects and removing it from its extent. Method `destroy` of class `Employee`, as shown in lines 10–14 of Fig. 17.12, does exactly that.

Once the object has been removed from its extent and its relationships have been destroyed, the object can no longer be located, except possibly through non-persistent variables. At the end of the execution of the application that destroys the object, the file that contains the persistent objects is replaced. When the extents are reloaded from the new file, the destroyed object will be gone.

17.3.4   Deciding Which Extents to Create and Maintain

The designer of an object-oriented data model must decide which classes will have extents. Every class containing objects that can exist independently from any relationships to other objects must be supported by extents. Conversely, objects that cannot exist except when related to other objects may not require extents. Extents also support iteration through the objects of a class. In particular, searching for an object with certain characteristics from a specific class is facilitated by having an extent for the class.

Consider weak entity classes. No object of a weak class can exist without being related to an object of its defining class. Hence, an extent is not required for a Java class that corresponds to a weak entity class.

We must be careful to ensure that objects from classes with circular dependencies are included in some extent. For instance, a purchase order cannot exist without a reference to detail line, and vice versa. If no other required relationships exist in either class, there must be an extent for one of the classes.

Searching through objects of a class is necessary to support select statements and to enforce key constraints. Processing of SQL statements in an object-oriented model will be based largely on the existence of extents.

17.3.5   Extents and Inheritance

Once we've decided which classes have extents, we must then decide which objects to put in the extents. Clearly, an object of type `Employee` belongs in the `Employee` extent. But what about a `SalariedEmployee` object? Because a `SalariedEmployee` is an `Employee`, it should be in the `Employee` extent. Nevertheless, we could also arrange for an iterator for the `Employee` extent to include the extents of all subclasses.

The implementation of extents given in Section 17.3.3 relies on two principles: the default constructor for a class adds the new object to the extent of the class, and all other constructors call the default constructor.

In an object-oriented language, the creation of an object of a subclass includes a call on a constructor of each of its superclasses. Hence, with the strategy described in Section 17.3.3, an object will be placed in the extents of all of its superclasses.

To have each extent contain objects of exactly one class, the constructors must check the class of the object before adding it to the extent. The default constructor for `Employee` is as follows:

```
public Employee(){
   if (Employee.getClass() == this.getClass()) {
      extent.add(this);
   }
}
```

When inheritance is implemented with interfaces and references, as in Fig. 17.4, each object will be placed in its own extent. Hence, a subclass object will be represented in its own extent as well as the extent of its superclass object.

Translation from ER Model to the Java Object Model

17.4   This section lists the rules that guide us in creating a set of Java class definitions to represent an ER model. Examples of the application of these rules were given in previous sections.

As with most parts of information systems, the application of these rules does not necessarily create an ideal representation. Instead, it is always important to make sure that the representation is faithful to the objects being represented. It is very appropriate to apply these rules in an informal manner.

These rules differ from the rules used for translating ER models to relational models (given in Section 4.3) because object models do not require each class to have a key and allow multivalued and composite attributes to be represented directly. These rules do not distinguish between strong and weak entity classes, nor do they provide special treatment for many-to-many relationship types with no attributes.

A many-to-many relationship type with attributes is most easily represented by modifying the EER diagram to replace the relationship type with an entity class. This modification was described in Section 2.4, where the `Rents` relationship type was converted into the `Rental` weak entity class. All many-to-many relationship types with attributes must be eliminated from the EER diagram before applying the rules of this section.

17.4.1   Entity Classes

The first two rules for translating ER diagrams into Java tell us how to manage entities and their simple attributes.

Rule 1:   For each entity class of the ER model, create a Java class by the same name. This rule applies to both strong and weak entity classes and to subclasses. Add a default constructor for the class.

Rule 2:   For each simple attribute of an entity class, create an attribute by the same name in the Java class. Use primitive Java types for the attributes, when available. Use `String` for the type of text attributes, and the appropriate Java date type for date attributes.

17.4.2   Composite and Multivalued Attributes

A composite attribute is represented by an object of a new class with the fields of the composite class. A multivalued attribute is represented by a set.

Rule 3:   For each composite attribute of an entity class, create a class with the fields of the composite attribute. Create an attribute in the Java class whose type is the new class. Add an assignment statement to the entity class constructor to initialize the field to a new object of the composite class.

Rule 4:   For each multivalued attribute of an entity class, add a field of type `Set` to the class whose name is the name of the attribute. Add an assignment statement to the entity class constructor to initialize the field to a new `Set` object.

17.4.3   To-One Relationship Roles

A to-one relationship role is represented by a field whose type is the related class and whose value is a reference to the related object.

Rule 5:   For each to-one relationship role of a relationship type R between subject class S and target class T, add a protected field of type T to class S. Name the field using the role that S plays in relationship type R.

Rule 6:   Add the attributes of the relationship type R to class T as protected fields. For one-to-one relationship types, add the attributes of R to the class of only one of the to-one roles.

17.4.4   To-Many Relationship Roles

A to-many relationship role can be represented as a set of values of the related class.

Rule 7:   For each to-many relationship role of a relationship type R between classes S and T, add a protected field of type `Set` to class S. Name the field with the role S plays in R.

17.4.5   Inheritance

For an entity subclass from a single superclass, a single subclass inheritance relationship type can be represented with Java inheritance using Rule 8. Inheritance that allows multiple superclass objects for a single subclass object, or vice versa, must be represented with interfaces and references to superclass objects using Rules 9 and 10.

Rule 8:   For each entity subclass S, create a new class that extends the superclass. Add the attributes of class S to the schema as in Rules 2, 3, and 4.

Rule 9:   For each superclass S that allows multiple subclass objects for a single object of class S or has subclasses with multiple inheritance relationships, create an interface definition with all of the methods of class S. Make class S extend the new interface.

Rule 10: For each entity subclass of a class that was translated with Rule 9, define a Java class that implements each of its superclass interfaces. Add fields to the new class to reference each of the superclasses of the entity subclass. Add methods for all of the interface methods.

17.4.6   Defining Extents

Extents are not required for weak entity classes or other classes whose objects cannot exist without being related to other objects. When required, extents are created as static variables of the class and the default constructors add objects to the proper extents.

Rule 11: For each class S that has an extent, add a static member of type `Set` to class S. Add code to the default constructor of S to add the newly created object to its extent. In addition, a `destroy` method should be placed in the class so that an object can be removed from the extent.

17.4.7   Access Methods

Methods to get and set values of protected members must be added to each class. Relationship methods must be added to guarantee referential integrity.

Rule 12: For each single-valued attribute, including relationship role attributes, add `get` and `set` methods as described in Section 17.1.3.

Rule 13: For each multivalued attribute, including relationship role attributes, add methods `add`, `remove`, `contains`, `getFirst`, and `iterator`, as described in Section 17.1.3.

Rule 14: For each relationship type R between classes S and T, add `create` and `remove` attributes to both classes, as described in Section 17.1.4, to guarantee that the relationship will be bi-directional.

Using Java for the BigHit Video Case Study

17.5   As an example of an object-oriented application, we will consider the calculation of pay statements for employees. For this task, we need classes `Employee`, `SalariedEmployee`, `HourlyEmployee`, `TimeCard`, and `PayStatement`. The object model is created using the strategies given in previous sections, with extents for all classes. We will extend the preliminary definitions of the classes `HourlyEmployee` and `TimeCard` given in Fig. 17.6. Figure 17.13 shows the

```
 1 public class PayStatement implements Serializable{
 2    protected Employee employee;
 3    protected double unitsWorked;
 4    protected double amountPaid;
 5    protected long datePaid;
 6    public PayStatement(Employee employee, double unitsWorked,
 7        double amountPaid, long datePaid) {
 8      employee.createPayStatement(this);
 9      this.unitsWorked = ((long)(unitsWorked*100))/100.0;
10      this.amountPaid = ((long)(amountPaid*100))/100.0;
11      this.datePaid = datePaid;
12    }
13 }
```

FIGURE 17.13 _____

Preliminary definition of class PayStatement

definition of class PayStatement. Notice that no extent exists for the class, and the constructor initializes all of the fields and the relationship with an employee. The full code available from the this book's Web site includes the payStatements relationship role and method createPayStatement of class Employee.

The application development centers on method computePayStatement of class Employee. Because the method of calculation depends on the exact type of the employee, Employee.computePayStatement must be an abstract method, and Employee must be an abstract class. Each of the two subclasses of Employee implements its own version of this method. Figure 17.14 shows the implementation of the method for class HourlyEmployee. The method for class SalariedEmployee need merely calculate the number of weeks in the pay period and multiply by the weekly salary.

```
 1 class HourlyEmployee {
 2    public PayStatement computePayStatement
 3      (long startDate, long endDate) {
 4    // go through the time cards for this employee
 5    // for each one that is part of the time period,
 6    //   calculate the number of hours worked
 7    //create a new PayStatement with the new information
 8    Iterator cards = timeCards.iterator();
 9    double hoursWorked = 0;
10    while (cards.hasNext()) {
11      TimeCard thisCard = (TimeCard)cards.next();
```

FIGURE 17.14 _____

Method computePayStatement *of class* HourlyEmployee *(continues)*

```
12      // check whether the time card is in the range of dates
13      if (thisCard.endTime < endDate
14          & thisCard.endTime >= startDate
15          & !thisCard.paid) {
16        hoursWorked += thisCard.getHoursWorked();
17        thisCard.setPaid(true);
18      }
19    }
20    double amount = hoursWorked * hourlyRate;
21    PayStatement pay =
22        new PayStatement(this,hoursWorked,amount,endDate);
23    return pay;
24 }
```

FIGURE 17.14
continued

Creating pay statements for all employees is accomplished in method `PayStatement.computePayStatements`, shown in Fig. 17.15. This method uses the employee extent to iterate through all `Employee` objects. Method `computePayStatement` is called for each `Employee` object (line 7). Because the code uses virtual method calls, the correct processing will be performed for hourly employees and for salaried employees.

Object Databases

17.6

An object database is a collection of persistent objects that act like a database. It must be supported by an *object database system (ODB)* that provides efficient access to objects, query processing, locking of objects, security, transaction management, concurrency control, backup and recovery, and other important database features.

```
 1 public class PayStatement {
 2   public static void computePayStatements
 3       (long startDate, long endDate) {
 4     Iterator employees = Employee.extent.iterator();
 5     while (employees.hasNext()) {
 6       Employee emp = (Employee)employees.next();
 7       emp.computePayStatement(startDate, endDate);
 8     }
 9   }
10 }
```

FIGURE 17.15
The method to compute pay statements for all employees

A simple persistence strategy, such as the one described in Section 17.3, does not create an object database. In that model, a single application (no concurrency) reads a file (no locking or security) to load all of the persistent objects (inefficient), modifies the objects (no transactions), and writes a new file with the revised collection of objects (no backup and recovery). The strategy is not supported by an independent software system and cannot support interdependent objects from multiple databases. It is just too simple to be effective.

Several methods are available for converting an object model into a real database. The *object-relational database* method (covered in Section 17.7) uses a relational database to provide the required database functionality. The objects of the object model are represented by rows in a relational database; software packages transform rows into objects, and vice versa. Another strategy is to design file structures to support the object classes, as described in Chapters 11 and 12, and develop software to support the database functionality. Neither of these strategies is completely satisfactory, however.

The most effective approach to creating object databases is to have an ODB that uses the same data model as the applications use. The *Object Database Management Group (ODMG)* is an organization that has developed the object database standard called ODMG 2.0. This standard includes a programming language-independent Object Definition Language (ODL), which we first encountered in Chapter 3. It also defines bindings for ODL to C++, Smalltalk, and Java. These programming language bindings also specify a standard for object manipulation in an ODB.

According to ODMG 2.0, each ODB must support literals and objects of specific types. Each object has properties that are shared with other objects of the same type and whose values specify its state. The behavior of objects is defined by their methods. In turn, objects are collected in databases and can be shared among multiple users. Each database has a schema defined in ODL. Transactions, locking, concurrency, backup, and recovery are all supported by ODBs.

17.6.1   ODMG Object Models

The object models described in Sections 17.1–17.3 are completely compatible with the Java binding for ODL and can be used to create an object database. In addition, the translation steps described in Section 17.4 are appropriate for use with an ODMG database. The Java binding requires specific collection classes that may have to be substituted for the standard Java collections used in the previously mentioned techniques. The ODMG collection classes are consistent with the Java collection interface, and most Java databases make their own classes that implement `java.util.Collection`.

Each ODMG database system includes software that reads the Java data model and stores it in the database for use by the server and client software. The database server needs to know the internal structure of the persistent objects so that they can be moved to and from the client memory.

Whenever the Java data model changes, it must be read by the system and compared with the version of the data model that is stored in the database. Changes in the data model that do not affect the layout of the fields of the objects are incorporated into the database with no difficulty. Changes such as new or modified methods and new subclasses fall into this category. Likewise, changes that affect classes with no persistent objects are also simple to make.

Difficulties with data model changes arise when the fields of a class are changed and persistent objects of that class appear in the database. In such a case, the persistent objects will not be consistent with the new class definitions. Most database systems provide a mechanism for specifying how to modify existing objects and for carrying out the modification. For instance, if a new field is added to a class, a default value can be specified. All objects of the class can be recreated with the new field having its default value. In some cases, it may be necessary to delete all of the existing objects and recreate them with the new structure.

The support for modifications in the data model is an important feature of object databases. As described in Section 17.3.2, Java serialization has a significant deficiency in this area. Without this schema and object migration facility, it would be impossible to conduct application development with an object database.

A NOTE ON ODL AND ITS C++ BINDING

The ODL specification shown in Fig. 17.1 uses template, or parameterized, types to describe relationships and other object references. The C++ binding for ODL makes extensive use of the template features and multiple inheritance of C++. The Java binding is much less satisfying for the ODMG designers because it cannot express as many of the type constraints and does not support multiple inheritance. As we saw in Fig. 17.2, a multivalued relationship is represented in Java as a collection of references to objects of arbitrary type. We must impose the constraint on the type of the related objects through the access methods.

A word of caution regarding C++ and templates is in order. In Java, when a variable is defined to have a specific type, the value of the variable is guaranteed to be of that type. In C++, all type checking of values is performed by the compiler, and none by the runtime environment. Just because a variable is defined to be a pointer to a particular type does not mean that the value of the variable actually points to an object of that type.

To ensure that relationships and other references remain correct in C++, the system must check the object types at runtime. Because C++ does not maintain any runtime information about the types of objects, it is impossible to safely determine the types of objects. A major advantage of ODMG database systems is that they keep track of the types of all persistent objects. Each C++ database system provides methods that can be used to verify the types of objects. With the ODMG 2.0 Java binding, it is the database system's responsibility to include code that checks the types of object references as part of the relationship operations.

17.6.2   Persistence in ODMG Databases

Class `Database` is the primary structure that supports object persistence. In turn, each persistent object is associated with a `Database` object. The definition of class `Database` includes the methods shown in Fig. 17.16. An application begins its use of persistent objects by calling `Database.open`. Once a database is open, some of the persistent objects can be retrieved using method `lookup`.

The ODMG data model identifies certain classes as being *persistence-capable*. That is, each object of a persistence-capable class is either persistent or nonpersistent.

```
 1 public class Database {
 2    public static Database open(String name, int accessMode)
 3       throws ODMGException;
 4    public void close() throws ODMGException;
 5    public void bind (Object object, String name);
 6    public Object lookup(String name)
 7       throws ObjectNameNotFoundException;
 8    public void unbind (String name)
 9       throws ObjectNameNotFoundException;
10 }
```

FIGURE 17.16 _____

Partial definition of class `Database`

The exact determination of which classes are persistence-capable and which objects are persistent depends on the particular database system. In most C++ object databases, persistence can be specified when an object is created.

Object databases support assigning names to objects using method `Database.bind`. An application can then execute method `Database.lookup` to retrieve a reference to the named persistent object.

In the Java binding, an object is persistent if it is a named object in the database or if it is referenced by a persistent object. This approach is referred to as *persistence by reachability*.

The strategy of putting persistent objects into extents and making the extents persistent is supported in a Java database by binding names to each extent. This *name binding* makes the extent objects persistent; hence, all objects in the extent, and all objects reachable from those objects, are persistent.

For a Java database, we can modify class `Initialize` as in Fig. 17.17 to enforce the persistence of the extent objects. We name the `Employee` extent "Employees" (line 7) to denote that it is the set of all employees. Method `saveExtents` is no longer needed because the extents will be saved automatically by the database.

This approach opens and reads all of the extent objects. An alternative strategy is to implement access to the extent by a static method that loads the extent on its first reference. The example for class `Employee` is shown below. In this version, the extent variables are loaded only when needed.

```
public class Employee {
  static Set extent = null;
  public static getExtent(Database database)
      throws ObjectNameNotFoundException {
    if (extent==null)
      extent = (Set) database.lookup("Employees");
    return extent;
  }
}
```

```
 1 public class Initialize {
 2 // methods to create extent objects and to save and
reload
 3 // them using an ODMG Java database
 4   public static void createExtents (Database database)
 5        throws ODMGException {
 6     Employee.extent = new HashSet();
 7     database.bind(Employee.extent,"Employees");
 8     Store.extent = new HashSet();
 9     database.bind(Store.extent,"Stores");
10     // create the rest of the extent objects
11   }
12   public static void restoreExtents (Database database)
13        throws ODMGException {
14     Employee.extent = (Set) database.lookup("Employees");
15     Store.extent = (Set) database.lookup("Store");
16     // look up the rest of the extent objects
17   }
18   public static void main (String[] args) {
19     // create and name the extent objects
20     try {
21       Database database =
22         Database.open("BigHitVideo",Database.ReadWrite);
23       createExtents(database);
24       database.close();
25     } catch (ODMGException e) {
26       System.err.println("unable to load database");
27     }
28   }
29 }
```

FIGURE 17.17 _____

Partial implementation of class Initialize *using a Java database*

Once the extents have been made accessible from static variables, an application can begin to use the persistent objects. The following code assigns a reference to a store to variable store and accesses the manager of the store and the manager's name:

```
Store store = (Store) Store.extent.firstElement();
Employee manager = store.getManager();
String name = manager.getLastName();
```

The most interesting aspect of this code is that it is the same that we would use if the persistence were created by a file of objects or if the objects were not persistent at all. Once we have a reference to a persistent object, our application can treat it just like any other object. Our object model is used directly by the application. No adaptation is required to the application to make its objects persistent.

17.6.3   Managing References to Persistent Objects

The ODB system arranges for objects to move back and forth between the memory of the application and the database server. During this process, the transportation and transformation of the objects occur without the knowledge of the application or the application programmer. ODB systems are client-server systems in which part of the database system code is integrated with the application and part of it resides in a (possibly) remote server process. The reference by the application to a persistent object is interpreted by the database client software and transformed into a memory reference.

Consider the operations required to execute an access to the manager of the store. Let's assume that the `Store` object is already in the application's memory, but the `Employee` object for the manager is not. The `Store` object contains a reference to the manager, but it surely is not a memory reference. Instead, it must be a reference that the database system can interpret. This reference is processed by making a request to a database server to fetch the information content of the `Employee` object. A memory object must then be created and initialized. Finally, the application is given a memory reference to the manager object.

Based on this information, we conclude that the value stored in the `manager` field of the `Store` object is not a simple memory reference and that each dereferencing of the value requires the intervention of the database client software. In other words, the usual Java interpretation of references has been superseded by the database interpretation of references. Our analysis of this process proceeds in three steps: by examining the ODMG definition of object identity, by considering how a C++ database deals with references, and finally by assessing how a Java database manages references.

In an object database, each object has a unique identity that is independent of its value. The ODB server assigns an *object identifier (OID)* to each object when it is made persistent. This OID is stored in fields that are references to the object. Thus an extent is not a list of memory references for objects, but rather a list of OIDs. The client software supports the mapping of OIDs into memory references and the movement of objects between client and server.

Figure 17.18 illustrates how objects from an object database appear in memory. This diagram uses the same employee shown in Fig. 17.3. Previously, the fields of the `Employee` were all object-valued. In an ODB application, however, these fields have OIDs as their values. In Fig. 17.18, OID values are represented by dashed lines pointing from the fields to the OID table. The solid lines lead from the address entries to objects in memory. The ODB client software uses the table to keep track of the mapping of OIDs to memory addresses. For example, gray is used to emphasize that the reference from the `ssn` field of the `Employee` refers to an entry in the OID table, which in turn points to the `String` object that has that

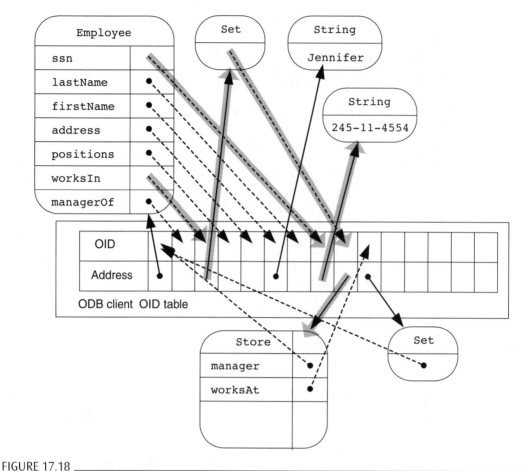

FIGURE 17.18
Object database mapping from OIDs to memory and database objects

ssn value. We can find the store in which the employee works by following the gray emphasis from the worksIn field of the Employee. The OID of the worksIn field is used to find the address of the Set object. The OID of the first element of the set is used to find the address of the Store object.

Not all of the objects related to the employee are currently in memory in Fig. 17.18. In particular, the lastName, address, and position objects are not shown, and the corresponding OID table entries have empty address values. When the application references the lastName field, the client software must arrange to bring the String object that holds the lastName value into memory, add its address to the OID table, and return the address to the application.

In C++, references to persistent objects in the data model use *template classes* d_Ref<T>, where T is the type of the referenced object. The dereferencing operators

(* and ->) for class `d_Ref<T>` are overloaded with methods that are part of the database client software. Because of the overloading, the execution of the expression `storeRef->manager` is an explicit call on the database client software. The dereferencing operator (->) takes an OID as input, checks whether the object is in memory, loads it if it is not there, and returns the memory address of the object. The template and overloading features of C++ make this approach a very natural implementation.

In Java, there are no overloading of dereferencing operators and no templates. If the Java binding for ODL specified a reference class, it would have to be typeless. The binding actually requires that persistent references use normal Java reference variables. Because the reference variable is a simple reference, the usual Java dereferencing operator must be used. This requirement leaves no opportunity for representing object references as OIDs and making database client software calls in the dereferencing operators.

The ODMG standard leaves it up to the Java database systems to choose one of two available methods for solving this problem. A database system can provide a preprocessor that translates application source code into some modified Java code, or it can provide a revised implementation of the Java runtime environment. Because a revised runtime environment would render the implementation not portable, most Java database systems rely on source code translation. This strategy is best illustrated by an example.

The database preprocessor must replace every reference to a persistent object with a reference to an object of a special reference class, and replace every dereferencing operator (.) with a call on a dereferencing method of the reference class. Figure 17.19 has some sample code for a translated `Employee` class.

In Fig. 17.19, class `Employee` has been translated into a new class called `DBEmployee`. The reference to a `Store` has become a variable of a new class, `DBRefStore`, that has the appropriate dereferencing operations. Notice that the `getManagerOf` method must take the `managerOf` field that contains the OID and translate it into a real memory reference. The code examples in the lower-left portion of Fig. 17.19 show how the translation affects declarations of variables and expressions. It is important to remember that the transformation does not alter the behavior of the objects or the code and is transparent to the application.

This implementation assumes the availability of a class `DBRefTable` with methods that translate an OID into a memory reference and a memory reference into an OID. These methods are standard parts of ODBs. The OID includes sufficient information to determine the database of which the object is part, and even to open the appropriate database, if necessary. This class maintains the client's mapping between OIDs and memory objects and loads objects from the server as necessary.

This translation makes Java databases somewhat awkward. In particular, the class files associated with the application are not based directly on the source code, which interferes with the use of debuggers and class browsing tools. On the other hand, these databases typically support language portability between database objects. We can access the same database objects from Java and from C++. We have the major advantage of support for all of the other database functionality without relying on SQL for access to objects.

Original Code	Transformed Code

```
class Employee {
    protected Store managerOf;
    public Store getManagerOf(){
        return managerOf;
    }
}
```

```
class DBEmployee {
    protected DBRefStore managerOf;
    public DBStore getManagerOf()
        return managerOf.getRef();{
    }
}

class DBRefStore {// class to support Store ref
    private OID ref;
    protected void assign(Store store) {
        ref = DBRefTable.lookupOID(store);
    }
    protected void assign (DBRefStore dbref) {
        ref = dbref.ref;
    }
    protected DBStore getRef() {
        return (DBStore) DBRefTable.lookup(this);
    }
}
class DBRefTable {// class for OID table
    static OID lookupOID (Object);
    static Object lookup (OID);
}
```

`Employee emp;`	`DBRefEmployee emp;`
`Store store;`	`DBRefStore store;`
`store = emp.getManagerOf();`	`DBStore temp = emp.getRef().getManagerOf();`
	`store = (DBStore)DBRefTable.lookup(temp);`

FIGURE 17.19

Code sketch for class `DBEmployee` *and sample application code, as generated by a Java database preprocessor*

17.6.4   OQL, the Object Query Language

ODMG databases support the *Object Query Language (OQL)*. OQL is based on the SQL query language and has many object-oriented extensions. It is a query language, not a comprehensive database language like SQL. For instance, it has no explicit update operators, but rather invokes object methods to modify the state of the database. It is possible to modify objects and to create new persistent objects through OQL statements.

OQL includes a select statement that has all of the capabilities of the SQL select statement, including **select** and **where** clauses, joins of input sets, nesting of select statements, comparison operators, aggregate functions, and **group by**, **order by**, and **having** clauses.

The **from** clause of a select statement can use any named object in the database as input. The obvious sources for select statements are the extent sets, which as we saw earlier are typically named objects. As an example, the following statement returns the set of all Social Security numbers of all employees with last name "Jones":

```
select distinct e.ssn from Employees e where e.lastName =
    'Jones'
```

`Employees` is the name assigned to the extent set of class `Employee`.

OQL is a typed language in the sense that every input and every output come from a specific class. The result of the above statement is an object of type `set<String>`. The result object is not persistent in the database.

When more than one field is included in the **select** clause, the result is cast to a particular type through the use of some object constructor. The default constructor, `struct`, creates an object of a new anonymous type. The following two statements return the identical set of objects, each containing the first and last names of an employee:

```
select distinct last:e.lastname, first:e.firstName
    from Employees e
select distinct struct(last e.lastname, first:e.firstName)
    from Employees e
```

Each object in the set returned has two fields: one named `last` that contains a last name, and one named `first` that contains a first name.

We can also create objects of a known type by using the constructors defined for the class. Because class `PayStatement`, shown in Fig. 17.13, has a constructor with four arguments, we can create a blank pay statement for every object with the following code:

```
select PayStatement(emp, 0.0, 0.0, 0) from Employees emp
```

This statement returns a set of new `PayStatement` objects, one for each employee. As each pay statement is created, the constructor is called with the given arguments. It creates a relationship between the new object and the specific employee. Because the `Employee` objects are persistent, and each new pay statement is related to an employee, the new objects are persistent.

OQL statements can also include calls on methods of their input objects. The following statement returns the average of the number of hours worked for all employees:

```
select avgHours: avg(select t.hoursWorked from emp.timeCards t)
    from Employees emp
```

The nested select statement is used to access all of the time cards for each employee. Hence, the **avg** operator is applied to all of the time cards from all employees. The syntax of OQL is flexible enough that `hoursWorked` and `hoursWorked()` both refer to a call on the method of class `TimeCard`.

OQL is a very powerful query language. It supports arbitrary nesting of method calls and attribute references. It includes sufficient type information to allow for set operations (**union**, **intersect**, **except**), quantifiers (**for all**, **exist**), and aggregation (**count**, **sum**, **min**, **max**, and **avg**). It allows objects to be selected or excluded by their subtypes, and very complex use of **group by** clauses and nested select statements.

Object-Relational Databases

17.7

In earlier chapters, we assumed that persistence of information in Java is accomplished through JDBC access to relational databases. In particular, an object must be explicitly inserted into a database to make it persistent. It must also be transformed from a Java object into a collection of rows in relational tables. To create a Java object, queries must be executed to produce result sets, and rows and fields must be extracted from the result sets to initialize the fields of the Java objects.

Section 17.6 illustrated an alternative—that Java objects can be persistent without programmer intervention. With an object database, we can directly store and fetch Java objects without translation into a relational model. We can also navigate from one persistent object to another without any direct use of database operations.

Object-oriented database applications can be created with object databases or with software tools that support more-or-less transparent access to objects that are stored in relational databases. The latter approach is called *object-relational*.

Object-relational systems have two facets: the extension of relational systems to add object-oriented features, and the direct representation of application objects in relational databases.

SQL3 is a project geared toward producing an SQL standard that incorporates many features of object-oriented data models, including support for complex types. Many commercial relational database systems already support the use of SQL3 types for attributes of tables.

JDBC supports the SQL3 data types with interfaces `Array`, `Blob`, `Clob`, `Ref`, and `Struct` in package `java.sql`. Methods `getArray`, `getBlob`, `getClob`, and `getRef` of `ResultSet` fetch values of the related types. Method `getObject` is used to retrieve `Struct` values. In addition, set methods are supplied for use in prepared statements and updatable result sets.

SQL3 also supports user-defined types. JDBC includes interfaces `SQLData`, `SQLInput`, and `SQLOutput` to manage custom mappings of these types. A developer can create a class that implements `SQLData`. Once that class is registered with the database connection, calls to `getObject` and `putObject` automatically map the Java object to the SQL object.

As noted earlier, JDBC supports a direct and easy-to-use mapping from a relational database with object extensions into Java objects. It leaves us with a use of objects that requires explicit fetch and store operations to be carried out through SQL statements.

Many software systems map Java classes into relational schemas, and vice versa, to produce a fairly seamless object persistence system. For example, JavaBlend is a commercial product from Sun Microsystems that can be used to create an object-relational mapping with any database server. It uses any standard JDBC package to move objects in and out of relational databases.

JavaBlend includes tools that can read a relational database and produce Java class definitions, and vice versa. A developer can begin with a relational database and access the objects through the generated Java classes. Alternatively, a developer can begin with Java classes and generate the SQL create table statements that define the schema. In both cases, the result is a mapping between Java objects and relational schema.

Once the Java-to-database mapping has been created, a JavaBlend application uses objects as though they were stored in an ODMG database. Methods are provided to store and fetch database objects by name. Once an object has been retrieved from the database, it can be used as a basis for navigational access to other database objects without any explicit statement to fetch objects from the database.

In addition, JavaBlend supports modification of database objects through a transaction system. Each time that the application commits a transaction, all modified objects are used to update the database.

The result is a database that can be used by the JavaBlend application, by Java programs through JDBC, and by standard relational database tools.

Chapter Summary

An object data model consists of a collection of class and interface definitions. Systematic methods exist for transforming an ER model or Object Definition Language (ODL) model into a Java object model. Of particular interest are the strategies used to represent relationships. Each relationship between two objects is typically represented by two references, with each object containing a reference to the other. To-many relationships are represented by sets of references. Many-to-many relationships and multivalued attributes can be represented in the Java object model without creating new classes, as was required for the relational model.

All fields of the object classes are best represented as protected fields. Access methods must be defined to get and set the values of these fields. Access methods for multivalued fields—both attributes and relationships—are patterned after the access methods for the Java 1.2 `Collection` interface. Access methods for relationships must enforce the type constraints specified in the conceptual model.

Java can easily represent single inheritance, but cannot directly represent the more complex forms of inheritance allowed in the extended ER model. Instead, interface definitions and references must be used for multiple inheritance and for multiple subclass objects that share the same superclass object.

The first step in making objects persistent is to create extent objects for each class of independent objects. An extent collection is a set of references to all objects of a single class. For example, a table in a relational database is an extent. The default constructor of each class is responsible for adding the new object to its extent.

The Java `Serializable` interface and object streams provide the capability of making extents persistent, thereby making all objects of the system persistent as well. The major problem with creating persistence through a single file of serialized objects is that it is impossible to load selected objects.

Object database systems support both persistence of objects and general database functionality. Applications using ODBs can reference persistent objects in exactly the same way as applications that use serialized object files. In a Java database, an object is persistent if it is a named database object or if it is reachable from a persistent object.

In an ODB, each object is associated with an object identifier (OID). A reference from one object to another in an object database application is carried out by a translation from the OID of the referenced object to its memory address. This translation may require transferring the object from the database server to the application, if it is not already in memory.

OQL, the Object Query Language, is a data access language that supports select statements. The major differences between OQL and the SQL select statements are that OQL allows queries to be based on any collection of objects, and that OQL queries can construct new objects in the result sets.

Object-relational systems have two facets: the extension of relational systems to add object-oriented features, and the direct representation of application objects in relational databases. Java supports the SQL3 object-oriented data type extensions in JDBC, which includes support for the automatic mapping of user-defined SQL3 types to Java objects. Achieving transparent access to relational objects from Java programs, without explicit use of JDBC and SQL, requires additional software support. The JavaBlend package is one tool that implements Java access in the ODMG style to objects that are stored in a relational database system.

Key Terms

Access methods. Methods of a class that support the access to and modification of protected fields.

Collection. An object that contains a collection of references to other objects. Interface `java.util.Collection` is part of Java 1.2. A collection can be a set, list, bag, or other aggregate.

Extent collection. The collection of all objects of a particular class. Extent objects are created and maintained in persistent object systems to ensure that all objects of the class remain persistent and to facilitate access to those objects.

Inner class. A Java class that is defined inside of another class definition. The scope of the inner class is inside the scope of the containing class.

Name binding. The assignment of a name to a persistent object in an ODB. Extent objects are typically named objects in ODBs.

Object Database Management Group (ODMG). An organization of individuals and companies that have collaborated to develop the Object Database Standard, ODMG 2.0.

Object database system (ODB). A database system that stores and retrieves objects. Client software can interact directly with the database by using objects in the application language. No translation to and from relational tables is required. ODBs support full database functionality, including transactions, concurrency control, security, backup and recovery, and schema evolution.

Object identifier (OID). The unique identification of an object in an ODB that is independent of the value of the object. OIDs are used to support persistent references between ODB objects.

Object-oriented data model (object model). A logical data model that is represented as class definitions in an object-oriented language.

Object Query Language (OQL). The query language of ODMG 2.0. OQL supports SQL select statements and allows for the invocation of methods during queries and the creation of new objects in the result set.

Object-relational database. The use of software tools to support more-or-less transparent access to objects that are stored in relational databases. It can involve the extension of relational systems to add object-oriented features or the direct representation of application objects in relational databases.

Persistence by reachability. A model of persistence in which every object, if it is referenced by a persistent object, is itself persistent.

Persistent object. An object whose existence lasts longer than the execution of a single application. A persistent object is stored in a file or database so that more than one application can access it.

SQL3. A proposal under development to extend SQL. Among other things, it adds object-oriented data types and type definitions to relational databases.

Template class. A parameterized class that can be instantiated by providing values for each parameter. The C++ language supports template classes. The ODMG binding to C++ makes extensive use of template classes.

Exercises

1. What is the purpose of representing relationships by a pair of attributes? How does this approach eliminate the need for indexing of key values?

2. List three ways that ODL differs from the Java data model.

3. Describe how a Java data model represents a multivalued attribute. Show how to represent the attribute `Customer.otherUsers`, from Fig. 2.4, in Java.

4. Describe how a Java data model represents a composite attribute. Show how to represent the attribute `Customer.address`, from Fig. 2.4, in Java.

5. Describe how a Java data model represents a derived attribute. Show how to represent the attribute `Customer.numRentals`, from Fig. 2.4, in Java. Include enough of the definition of class `Customer` to support the derived attribute.

6. Look up interface `java.util.Collection` in the JDK 1.2 documentation. What are the known sub-interfaces? What are the known classes that

implement the interface? How do `Collection`, `Set`, and `List` differ from one another?

7. List three things that the default constructor of a class in a data model must do.

8. Describe how a Java data model represents a one-to-one relationship type. Show how to represent the `IsMarriedTo` relationship type of Fig. 2.6 in Java.

9. Define all of the access methods required to support the Java representation of the relationship type of Exercise 8.

10. Describe how a Java data model represents a one-to-many relationship type. Show how to represent the `IsChildOf` relationship type of Fig. 2.6 in Java.

11. Define all of the access methods required to support the Java representation of the relationship type of Exercise 10.

12. Describe how a Java data model represents a to-many relationship role. Show how to represent the customer-has-rental relationship of classes `Customer` and `Rental` of Fig. 2.5.

13. Define all of the access methods required to support the Java representation of the relationship type of Exercise 12.

14. Translate the many-to-many relationship type `Rents` of Fig. 2.4 into a Java data model. Don't forget that the relationship type has attributes.

15. Define a Java model that includes the field definitions for the following BigHit Video classes:

    a. `Customer`   b. `Rental`   c. `Previous Rental`

    d. `Videotape`   e. `Movie`   f. `PurchaseOrder`

    g. `PurchaseOrderDetail`   h. `Supplier`

16. Give a full definition of the classes listed in Exercise 15, including all required access methods and constructors.

17. Draw a picture in the style of Fig. 17.3 of an object in a class from Exercise 3 as it would be created by a BigHit Video application.

18. Implement the design of classes from Exercise 15 using JDK 1.2. Design a test program to create and manipulate objects of the class.

19. What is the role of an extent object in creating persistence?

20. What is a named object in an ODMG database? Give a precise description of when an object is persistent in a Java ODMG database.

21. Use the Web to find a vendor that sells an ODMG database. Write a brief report on the Java binding for its database products. Try to determine how the mapping from OIDs to object addresses is managed. Does the database utilize a preprocessor?

22. As a major programming project, implement the application of Section 17.5 using an object database or some other Java persistence manager.

23. Use the `Relationship` base classes described in Section 17.1.5 to implement classes `Employee` and `Store` and a test program to create and manipulate objects of those classes.

Further Readings

Object-oriented design is quite well covered in many books and articles. These publications range from basic introductions using C++, as in Irvine [Irv96], to the presentation of examples of solving business problems with object-oriented methods in Yourdon and Argila [YoAr96]. Booch, Jacobson, and Rumbaugh [BJR98] is a comprehensive study of the Universal Modeling Language (UML) and its use in object-oriented design. Object-oriented methods for database design are covered in the standard advanced database books [Date99, ElNa99, SKS97].

The Object Database Standard: ODMG 2.0 [CBB97] is the reference manual for ODMG databases. Jordan's book [Jor97] about using C++ with ODMG 2.0 is an excellent source of examples of ODB applications.

Object-oriented extensions to SQL were first introduced and tested in the POSTGRES system [StRo86]. Illustra is the commercial system that is its successor. SQL standards documents have been divided into many sections for SQL3. The framework document [ANSI95] is the first volume. Beech [Bee93] gives an extensive description of the type mechanisms in SQL3.

Kim's book on modern database systems [Kim95] contains articles on some approaches to object-relational databases. Silberschatz, Korth, and Sudarshan [SKS97] have a chapter on object-relational systems.

Information on JavaBlend is available from the Java Web site, http://java.sun.com/software/javablend.

Appendix

<u>A</u> Brief Introduction <u>to</u> Java

APPENDIX OBJECTIVES

In this appendix, you will learn:

- Ways to use Java class and interface definitions to develop software tools
- Some key similarities and differences between Java and C++
- Ways to use primitive types and strings in Java
- Java's strategies for representing objects, pointers, and arrays
- The basic style and documentation guidelines of Java
- Ways to compile and execute Java classes
- Ways to use the Java package capabilities
- Ways that Java supports virtual methods and exceptions
- Some details of the software packages provided as part of the standard Java distribution

*T*he introduction to the Java programming language provided in this appendix is intended for the reader who has a basic appreciation of object-oriented programming languages. It includes coverage of those features that are relevant to the use of Java in this book. It is not a comprehensive treatment, however, and does not discuss the use of Java for user interface development.

We begin by looking at the similarities between C++ and Java, as well as their major differences. We go on to the parts of Java that make it such a useful language.

In this book, we treat the Java language in this appendix plus Chapters 8–12, 16, and 17. This coverage includes extensive discussion of its support for SQL, the input/output packages, and its support for distributed object technology.

Three major versions of the Java language have been produced: Java 1.0, Java 1.1, and Java 1.2 (also called Java 2). Java 1.0 is very different from the others and should not be used by developers. Java 1.1 and Java 1.2 are very similar and are the subject of this appendix. Most of the differences relate to new features of Java 1.2, and most Java 1.1 code can be executed in a Java 1.2 system. Some features of Java 1.2 that do not appear in Java 1.1 are discussed in Chapters 10 and 16.

Similarities and Differences between Java and C++

A.1

Like C++, the Java language takes most of its syntax from the C language. The syntax for variable and function declarations, the use of set braces `{ }` for nesting of statements, the use of `=` for assignment, and the use of `==` for equality are all the same. The primitive types `int`, `char`, `float`, `double`, `long`, and `short` are all present in Java and C++. Likewise, the major statement types—`if then else`, `while`, `switch`, `return`, and `break`—are the same in Java and C++.

The basic syntax for class definitions in Java comes from C++. A class is defined with members, methods, and constructors. The use of the `static` keyword for a member or method of a class is the same in both languages.

Many of the differences between C++ and Java are quite subtle. Figure A.1 gives the definition of three Java classes that exhibit many of these differences. We will review this code line by line.

Lines 1–11 are the definition of class `Address`, which has four member fields and one constructor method. Each member is preceded by the keyword `public`. Each class, member, and method is individually designated with its access mode. If no mode is given, the access is `private`.

A.1.1   String Objects in Java

The first major change from C++ that we see occurs in lines 2–5 of Fig. A.1. The type of these members is `String`. The objects of this predefined class represent text strings. C++, of course, has only the most primitive support for strings. A `String` value in Java is an object with a specific length—*not* an array of `char`. Class `String` supports operations for concatenation using the binary `+` operator, substring, access to the character elements, and length.

A `String` object is *immutable*. That is, once a `String` object has been created, its value cannot be changed. No operators in the `String` class modify a `String` object's value. Class `StringBuffer` is very much like class `String` and does support modification operations.

A.1.2   Objects and Object Variables in Java

Java draws a clear distinction between an object and an object variable. An object variable is represented as a reference to an object. An assignment statement, as in lines 8 and 9 of Fig. A.1, changes which object is referenced by the variable. It does not change the value of the object referenced by the variable.

Figure A.2 illustrates the effect of an assignment to the `String` variable `firstName`. The literals `"Fred"` and `"Jane"` represent `String` objects and are

```
1 public class Address {
2    public String street;
3    public String city;
4    public String state;
5    public String zipcode;
6    public Address (String street, String city, String state,
7        String zipcode) {
8      this.street = street; this.city = city;
9      this.state = state; this.zipcode = zipcode;
10   }// end of constructor
11 } // end of class Address
12 public class Employee {
13   public String ssn;
14   public String lastName;
15   public String firstName;
16   public Address address;
17   public double salary;
18   public Employee (String ssn, String lastName,
19       String firstName, Address address, double salary) {
20     this.ssn = ssn; this.lastName = lastName;
21     this.firstName = firstName; this.address = address;
22     this.salary = salary;
23   } // end of constructor
24 } // end of class Employee
25 class TestEmployee {
26   public static void main (String [] args) {
27     emp = new Employee ("145-09--967","Uno","Jane",
28         new Address("123 Main","Apopka","FL","32111"),
29         12.50);
30   } // end of method main
31   public static Employee emp;
32 } // end of class TestEmployee
```

FIGURE A.1 _____

Definitions of three simple Java classes

shown as ovals that contain the type name and the value. These two String objects exist independently of the value of firstName. When the assignment statement of Fig. A.2a is executed, the value of the variable is modified so that it refers to the "Fred" object, as indicated by the arrow that points from the variable to its value. After the execution of the second assignment statement, firstName refers to the "Jane" object. Neither assignment statement has any effect on the String objects.

The meaning of the equality operator (==) in Java is identical to that of the predefined equality operator in C and C++. The expression obj1==obj2 returns

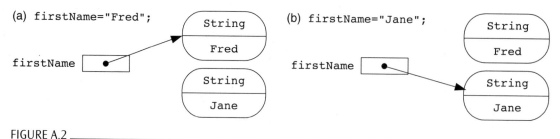

FIGURE A.2

Assignments to a `String` *variable*

true exactly if `obj1` and `obj2` refer to the same object. The equality operator tests equality of object *references*, not object values. Because no overloading of operators takes place, `==` has no other meaning.

Class `Object` includes method `equals`, which can be used to test the equality of object values. Testing to see whether two objects have equal values is accomplished with `obj1.equals(obj2)`. For this operation to work properly, the class definition for `obj1` must have an appropriate definition of `equals`. Class `String` has such a method. Its use is illustrated in Fig. A.3, which includes three `String` variables and two `String` objects. The two `String` objects are different objects, with identical values. The equality operator sees them as two separate objects, but the `equals` method recognizes that their values are equal.

This treatment of objects and object variables is in marked contrast with C++. In Java, an object variable is always represented by a single reference (or pointer) value. C++ has three types of object variables: named objects, pointers to objects, and references to objects.

```
Employee emp1;
Employee * emp2 = new Employee;
Employee & emp3 = * (new Employee);
```

This proliferation of types of variables creates many problems in C++.

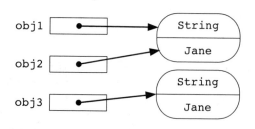

Expression	Value
`obj1 == obj2`	true
`obj1 == obj3`	false
`obj1.equals(obj3)`	true

FIGURE A.3

Illustration of object equality

The declaration and use of object variables and the creation of objects in Java is very simple:

- An object variable is a reference to an object.
- An object is created explicitly through a call to new.
- Assignment to an object variable changes the object to which the variable points.
- The equality operator (==) is true if its two operands refer to the same object.

Figure A.4 illustrates the objects created by the execution of method `TestEmployee.main`, given in lines 27–31 of Fig. A.1. In the upper-left corner is the static variable `emp`, which is declared in class `TestEmployee` in line 26. Variable `emp` refers to the object of type `Employee` that is created by the execution of the new operation in lines 28–30. The fields of the `Employee` object are three `String` variables (represented by references to `String` objects), an `Address` variable (represented by a reference to an `Address` object), and a `double` value stored directly in the `Employee` object.

A.1.3   Arrays in Java

In Java, an array is an object that contains a list of objects or values, all of the same type. The two major differences between arrays in Java and C are that Java arrays

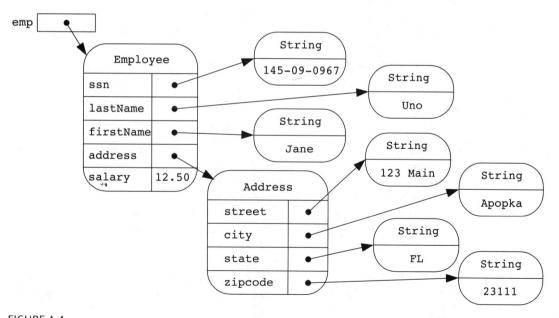

FIGURE A.4

Diagram of Java objects from the classes `Employee` *and* `Address`

must be created with a `new` operation and that an index expression must be within the bounds of the array in Java.

As with object variables, array variables are represented by references to array objects. The declaration of an array variable does not specify the bounds of the array; in fact, it does not even declare or create an array object. Figure A.5 contains a few array declaration and reference statements.

An array variable can either be `null` or point to an array object. Assignment of an array object to an array variable (line 2) changes the array object to which the variable points. Assignment to an array variable does not modify an array object, in terms of either its size or its values. Line 5, for instance, does not modify the value of the array referenced by `intArray`; it simply makes `intArray` point to a different array.

An array of `int`, or of any other primitive type, is represented by a block of memory containing space for the required number of values. An array whose elements are objects is represented by an array of object references. When an array object is created, as in line 8 of Fig. A.5, each array element is `null`. This array of `Employee` is really an array of `Employee` references, initially all `null`. The assignment of a new `Employee` object to element 0 in line 9 allows line 10 to modify a field of the referenced `Employee` object.

A reference to an array element in Java (lines 3, 6, 9, and 10) looks like a C expression, but has a different meaning. First, the array variable must point to an array object. Second, the index expression must yield an integer value that is within the bounds of the array object. If both of these conditions are met, the Java expression works just like a C expression.

An attempt to reference a nonexistent array element, as in line 6 of Fig. A.5, results in the raising of an exception. Exceptions are described in Section A.5.

A.1.4   Style Guidelines and Documentation for Java

A style guideline, called *Code Conventions for the Java Programming Language*, is available at the Java Web site [JavaCode]. This document describes naming standards

```
 1 int [] intArray = null; // declaration of array variable
 2 intArray = new int[10]; // creation of array object
 3 intArray[5];    // reference to array element
 4 intArray.length // the number of array elements
 5 intArray = new int[100]; // creation of new array
 6 int i = intArray[100]; // reference to nonexistent element
 7 Customer custArray[]; // declaration of array of objects
 8 custArray=new Customer[10];  // creation of Customer array
 9 custArray[0]=new Customer(); // initialization of element
10 custArray[0].lastName="Gray";  // modification of element
```

FIGURE A.5 _____

Example array declaration and reference statements

for files, classes, packages, and members. It also suggests code formatting and documentation styles. Conformance to style guidelines will help make your code accessible to other programmers and users.

All of the examples in this book conform to the preferred naming standards. The important details are as follows:

- Names are composed of the concatenation of words and abbreviations in mixed case, with the first letter of each internal word being capitalized, except as noted below.
- Class and interface names begin with a capital letter.
- Variable and method names begin with a lowercase letter.
- Variable names may be short and mnemonic and do not have to be concatenated words.
- Package names are all lowercase.
- Constants are all uppercase, with the underscore (_) being used as a separator.

An important aspect of Java is its documentation standards and tools. The `javadocs` processor reads Java source files and generates HTML documents like those we see in the standard Java documentation. Block comments beginning with `/**` are included in the generated documents.

A.1.5   Additional Java Features

Java has many other language features that make it superior to C and C++. The most obvious are the `boolean` primitive type and the predefined constants `true`, `false`, and `null`. Every C programmer suffers from the lack of these features.

Characters in Java come in two flavors. First, there is the usual single-byte signed integer, which in Java is represented by primitive type `byte`. Second, the primitive type `char` is a two-byte unsigned value from the Unicode character set. In most cases, developers can ignore the difference between one- and two-byte characters. Conversion of a `byte` value to `char` simply sets the upper byte to zero; conversely, conversion from `char` to `byte` deletes the upper byte. A character literal can be used as a `byte` or `char` value.

Any Java variable declaration can denote a constant value if it includes the `final` designator. A constant can be of any type. The keyword `const` from C++ is not part of Java, however.

Operators `|`, `||`, `&`, and `&&` are defined for `boolean` operands. The single-character operators are the normal Boolean operators, and the double-character operators are the conditional operators. Operator `||`, for instance, evaluates its left operand first. If its value is `true`, the operator returns `true` without evaluating the right operand. The meanings of these operators for integral operands are the same as they are in C. Java also supports the shift operators `<<`, `>>`, and `>>>` for integral operands. For example, operator `>>` performs a right shift with sign extension and operator `>>>` performs a right shift with zero extension.

Constructors in Java have been enhanced by making initializers available and by allowing one constructor to call another. The class definition shown in Fig. A.6 includes several constructor and initializer examples.

Line 3 of Fig. A.6 is the definition of a class (nonstatic) member without an initial value. Line 4 includes an initializer. The initialization of this member will be carried out whenever an object is created, just as if it had been included in the constructor.

The constructor of lines 5–8 shows a call on a constructor of its superclass (line 6). This call must be the first statement of the constructor. If a superclass constructor call does not appear as the first line, the default constructor (no parameters) of the superclass will be called. Because line 6 calls the default constructor, leaving it out would have no effect.

The constructor of lines 9–11 calls the other constructor and provides a particular value (3) for member `memberVar`. This call is an example of constructor chaining, in which one constructor calls another. The chained constructor call must be the first statement of the constructor.

The static members (lines 13 and 14) are supported by an initializer for member `staticInit` (line 14) and a static initializer method in lines 15–18. This method, which has no name, no parameters, and no return type, is called automatically by the Java execution engine when the class file is first loaded. Any complex initialization that must be performed should be included in the static initializer.

```
1 class SubClass extends SuperClass {
2   // class member section
3   int memberVar;
4   int memberInit = 7; // member initializer
5   public SubClass(int initVal) {
6     super(); // call to superclass constructor
7     memberVar = initVal;
8   }
9   public SubClass() {
10    this(3); // chained constructors
11  }
12  // static member section
13  static int staticVar;
14  static int staticInit = 5; // static variable initializer
15  static { // static initializer method
16    staticVar = 10;
17  }
18 }
```

FIGURE A.6 _____

Capabilities of Java constructors and initializers

A.1.6   Elements of C++ Missing from Java

Many features of C and C++ are missing from Java. Among them are most of the pointer operations: `sizeof`, `->`, unary `&` (address), unary `*` (dereference), pointer arithmetic, pointer types, function addresses, and reference parameters for functions. Likewise, the comma operator is omitted.

Java does not provide a delete operator or free function. All reclamation of allocated storage is done automatically in Java.

Data structures that have been removed from Java include `struct`, `union`, `enum`, `unsigned`, `typedef`, and variable-length argument lists. The language also lacks multiple inheritance, templates, and operator overloading. No user-defined conversion methods are available.

Compilation and Execution

A.2

As you probably know, Java programs can be executed on any computer without recompilation. The Java compiler, called `javac`, translates a source file into one or more class files that contain binary code that can be executed by the *Java runtime environment (RTE)*. In most cases, the source code file for class `ClassName` must be named `ClassName.java` and the compiler produces a file called `ClassName.class`.

The main method of a Java program is a static method called `main` that is defined in some class. The example of method `TestEmployee.main` in Fig. A.1 demonstrates that a main method must be `public` and `static`, must not return a value (that is, must have return type `void`), and must have a single parameter that is a `String` array.

The execution of a Java main method is initiated by the RTE. The first argument to the RTE is the name of the class whose main method is to be executed. The rest of the arguments are then passed to `main` as the elements of its parameter array. The following statement executes the program of Fig. A.1 with no arguments:

```
java TestEmployee
```

The parameter array `args` is an array of length 0 in this case.

Class files can be collected into archive files of two types. A zip file is a collection of files in directories that have been compressed using the zip format. In Java 1.1, for instance, all of the standard Java packages are contained in a zip file called `classes.zip`. A jar (Java archive) file is much like a zip file, but contains additional information that is used by Java compilers and RTEs. In Java 1.2, all of the standard Java packages appear in a jar file called `rt.jar`.

Access to class files by the compiler and RTE is controlled by the `CLASSPATH` variable. The compiler and RTE load class files as needed, with the `CLASSPATH` variable telling them where to look for those files. Every Java programmer should have a directory of Java packages and classes and the `CLASSPATH` variable should include that directory. If your package directories appear in your Java directory, the compiler and RTE will always be able to find them.

The Java language system has no preprocessor or `include` statements. Instead, all classes are compiled individually into class files. Java programs are not directly executable, and no linking/loading step is employed as in C and C++. Because Java lacks a preprocessor, there are no macros and no conditional compilation.

Packages and Names

A.3

Java classes are divided into collections called *packages*. The standard Java class libraries reside in packages `java.lang`, `java.io`, `java.util`, and so on. The class files for the classes found in a package must be located in a directory whose path follows the package name. Classes in `java.lang`, for instance, are found in a directory `java/lang`. The classes that are defined in this book are all contained in package `dbjava`, which includes packages `dbjava.database`, `dbjava.html`, and `dbjava.website`, among others.

A class is part of a package if its source code file includes a `package` statement as its first statement. The `package` statement simply lists the name of the package. For class `TestEmployee` to be part of package `dbjava.samples`, for example, the source code file for the class must start as follows:

```
package dbjava.samples;
public class TestEmployee {
```

The full name of the class is `dbjava.samples.TestEmployee`, and its execution must give the full class name:

```
java dbjava.samples.TestEmployee
```

For this command to work properly, a directory called `dbjava` must appear in the class path. This directory must have a subdirectory, `samples`, that includes a file `TestEmployee.class`.

A.3.1   Names of Classes and Methods

Like any other object-oriented language, Java defines the scope and accessibility of names within its source code. The accessibility is determined by the visibility modifier (`public`, `protected`, or `private`) applied to the member and its class as well as by the package structure. The scope of a name includes the entire unit in which it is declared. The order of member declarations does not affect the use of the names of the members.

Consider class `dbjava.samples.TestEmployee`, of Fig. A.1, a public class located in package `dbjava.samples`. Within the class, all of the members of the class are accessible. You might have noticed that member `emp` is declared on line 31 after it is referenced on line 27. This declaration is legal in Java, but not in C or C++. Outside of the package, all of the public members are accessible, and the protected members are accessible to classes that extend this class. Private members are accessible only within the defining class.

Within the package, Java offers several advantages relative to C++. All of the classes in the package have access to all of the nonprivate members of other classes in the package. Hence, the package forms a protected collection of classes that behave like C++ friend classes. A member with default visibility—that is, one that is not declared as `public`, `protected`, or `private`—is visible only within the package. The default visibility is more restrictive than `protected` visibility, because the member cannot be seen from subclasses outside of the package, but is less restrictive than `private` visibility, because the member is visible to other classes within the package.

The accessibility of the names declared in a class also depends on the availability of its class file. The compiler and RTE must be able to find the class files from the `CLASSPATH` variable. When a class is compiled, the compiler must find the class files that it references. Whenever a running Java program uses a class, the RTE must also read the class file.

Java has no global variables or global functions. Rather, every function is a method of some class. What would be a global function in C++ is represented in Java as a `public static` member of a class. Method `TestEmployee.main` is an example of this case.

A.3.2 Importing Names

Although a Java class can reference any accessible name by its fully qualified name, the use of shorter names is restricted. For instance, member `emp` of class `TestEmployee` can be called `dbjava.samples.TestEmployee.emp`.

The `import` statement allows a Java source file to use abbreviated names to refer to classes. This statement must appear after the `package` statement (if one exists) and before any other statements of the source file.

The `import` statement has two forms, as shown by the following examples:

```
import java.io.PrintWriter;
import java.io.*;
```

The first `import` statement allows the specified class to be called by its abbreviated name, `PrintWriter`. The second allows all classes in package `java.io`, including `PrintWriter` and many others, to be called by their abbreviated names.

Java compilers implicitly import all class names in package `java.lang`. This capability allows us to refer to an object of type `java.lang.String` as a `String`, as in Fig. A.1. The compiler also implicitly imports all of the classes in the source file's package. For package `dbjava.samples`, for instance, the compiler behaves as if there were two `import` statements following the `package` statement:

```
package dbjava.samples;
import java.lang.*; // implicitly included
import dbjava.samples.*; // implicitly included
```

In summary, an `import` statement in Java is not the same as an `include` statement in C++. It allows abbreviated names but does not affect which classes can be referenced.

Class and Virtual Method Hierarchies

A.4

Java supports class hierarchies through two mechanisms. First, a class can declare its immediate (or *parent*) superclass, using the `extends` clause. Second, it can belong to one or more virtual function hierarchies by implementing interfaces, using the `implements` clause.

A.4.1   Inheritance

Every Java class has exactly one parent superclass—in marked contrast to C++, in which some classes have no superclass and others have several.

The class inheritance hierarchy in Java has class `java.lang.Object` as its root. That is, `Object` is an ancestor superclass of every other Java class. The major advantage of this strategy is that methods of class `Object` are available for every class. These methods include `equals` (as described in Section A.1.2), `toString` (which gives a `String` representation for an object), and `getClass` (which returns an object of type `Class`, as discussed in Section A.4.3).

A Java class declares its position in the class inheritance hierarchy through the `extends` clause. The three classes in Fig. A.1 have no `extends` clause. By omitting this clause, they declare that they are children of `Object`.

In Java, a class that extends another class inherits the fields and methods of that superclass, just as it does in C++.

A.4.2   Virtual Methods and Interfaces

All methods in Java are virtual methods, except those declared as `final`. This approach is the opposite of that taken in C++, in which the default is nonvirtual. Each virtual method can have many implementations, each appearing in a different class. A call to a virtual method is executed by an implementation of the method. The selection of which implementation to use in Java is based on the type of the calling object, just as in any other object-oriented language.

Java diverges from C++ in its ability to define virtual method hierarchies that are independent of class inheritance. It does so by using interface definitions and `implements` clauses. Let's consider interface `java.util.Enumeration`, as shown in Fig. A.7. This interface defines two methods.

A class can implement an interface by defining all of its methods. Figure A.8 shows a class `MyEnumeration` that builds an `Enumeration` from an array of

```
1  public abstract interface Enumeration {
2     public abstract boolean hasMoreElements();
3     public abstract Object nextElement();
4  }
```

FIGURE A.7 _____

Definition of interface `Enumeration`

```
 1 public class MyEnumeration implements Enumeration {
 2    private Object [] values;
 3    private int current = 0;
 4    public MyEnumeration(Object [] values) {
 5      this.values = values;
 6    }
 7    public boolean hasMoreElements() {
 8      return current < values.length;
 9    }
10    public Object nextElement() {
11      if (hasMoreElements()) {
12        current ++;
13        return values[current-1];
14      } else return null;
15    }
16 }
17 public interface ResetEnumeration extends Enumeration {
18    public abstract void reset(); // return to beginning
19 }
```

FIGURE A.8 _____

A class and interface that extend interface Enumeration

objects. Class MyEnumeration has private fields (lines 2 and 3) that hold an array of objects and a current index. The constructor of the class (lines 4–6) has an array of Object as its parameter. The interface methods are implemented in the simplest way possible.

We can declare variables of type Enumeration and call these methods as in the following code fragment:

```
Object [] objs = new Object[10];
Enumeration enum = new MyEnumeration(objs);
if (enum.hasMoreElements()) {
  Object obj = enum.nextElement();
```

This interface acts very much like a type. A class is a member of the interface type if it implements the interface. As you can see, any class that implements the interface has the methods defined in the interface. Hence, we can call the methods for any such class.

The classes that implement an interface form a set in which all members support a particular collection of methods, but do not share the implementations of those methods.

Interfaces are used extensively in the Java packages and are particularly evident in the database package java.sql, as discussed in Chapters 8 and 10.

A.4.3   Runtime Type Information

The Java RTE maintains detailed information about the type of every object. This information is available to the programmer for a variety of uses. For example, the `instanceof` operator allows a program to determine whether an object is located in a subclass of a given class or interface. In the following code, variable b is `true` if the type of the object referenced by `obj` is `String` or a subclass of `String`:

```
Object obj;
boolean b = obj instanceof String;
```

Type information is also used to create a system of type-safe type casting. Every operation that changes the type of a reference is checked to verify that it is correct. In the following code, a variable `obj` of type `Object` refers to an object of type `Employee` (line 1):

```
1 Object obj = new Employee;
2 Employee emp = (Employee) obj; // correct type cast
3 String str = (String) obj; // erroneous type cast
```

In line 2, the value of `obj` is correctly cast to `Employee`. In line 3, the value of `obj` is incorrectly cast to `String`. Because the object is not an instance of `String`, it cannot be treated as a `String`. The execution of line 3 causes an exception, `ClassCastException`, to be thrown—exceptions are described in Section A.5— and no assignment takes place. Type casting is allowed whenever the object is an instance of the class. It is implicit from subclass to superclass, as in line 1, but must be explicit in other cases, as in line 2.

The runtime type information is also available in more detail to programmers through class `java.lang.Class`. Method `Object.getClass` returns the `Class` object associated with an object, and method `Class.forName` returns the `Class` object by its name.

```
Class empClass = emp.getClass();
Class stringClass = Class.forName("String");
```

The `Class` object for a class has methods that return the fields, methods, and constructors defined by the class. In addition, it identifies the superclass and all interfaces that it implements. The reflection package (`java.lang.reflect`) even allows a program to create objects and call methods by name.

A.5   Exceptions and Exception Handling

Many operations in a Java program can cause an error to occur—for example, an out-of-bound index on an array reference, a reference through a null object variable, and division by zero. In all of these cases, the Java RTE responds by *throwing an exception*. The Java program can *catch* the exception in an *exception handler*, respond to it in some way, and then resume normal execution.

An *exception* is a Java object that represents some sort of unusual condition. An exception object is a member of a class derived from `java.lang.Throwable`. `Throwable` has two subclasses: `java.lang.Error` and `Java.lang.Exception`. Error objects are typically related to problems with loading classes or running out of memory. Class `Exception` is of the greatest interest.

When an exceptional condition occurs, the normal execution of the Java program is interrupted and the program enters an exception-processing mode. Consider the execution of method **demo**, shown in Fig. A.9. Line 3 declares an object variable with a null initial value. Line 4 attempts to access a method through this null reference. The Java RTE detects the attempt to reference with a null pointer and throws a `NullPointerException` object. As a result, the execution of **demo** is terminated.

A.5.1   Exception Handlers: try-catch-finally Statements

The execution of a Java program cannot continue until an exception handler for the particular exception object is found. Java programmers can create exception handlers in their code to anticipate when an exception may occur. Exception handlers are built from `try` and `catch` statements, as shown in Fig. A.10, which is a revision of the **demo** method. In the figure, the null pointer reference is now contained

```
1  public class DemoException {
2    public void demo() {
3      String str = null;
4      int len;
5      len = str.length(); // null reference exception occurs
6    }
7  }
```

FIGURE A.9

Method demo, *whose execution is interrupted by an exception*

```
 1 public class DemoException {
 2   public void demo() {
 3     String str = null;
 4     int len;
 5     try { // beginning of try statement
 6     len = str.length(); // null reference exception occurs
 7     } catch (NullPointerException e) {// catch statement
 8       len = 0; // executed if exception thrown in try block
 9     }
10   }
11 }
```

FIGURE A.10

Another version of method demo, *which handles the exception*

inside a `try` statement (or `try` *block*). When the exception is thrown in line 6, the RTE jumps to the `catch` statement of line 7. The `catch` statement declares that it can handle exceptions from class `NullPointerException`. Because the exception that was thrown is a member of this class, execution resumes in line 8 and continues normally from there.

When an exception is raised in a `try` block, the RTE looks for a `catch` statement that matches the exception. Each `catch` block declares a parameter of the type of exception it can handle. It matches any exception whose class is a subclass of the declared parameter.

If a matching `catch` block is found, its statement is executed and normal execution of the program continues. If no exception handler is found for the exception, the RTE continues by throwing the exception at the end of the `try-catch` block. If no handler appears in the method, the exception is propagated to the point of call. This search-and-propagation cycle continues until a handler is found or the program reaches the end of the main method. If the program contains no handler for the exception, it terminates and the RTE prints an error message.

The exception object is available for use within the `catch` block. For debugging purposes, it may be useful to see the calling sequence. This sequence can be dumped to a file using the `printStackTrace` method. Method `getMessage` returns the message string of the exception object.

A `try-catch` block can contain many `catch` statements. Its general structure is shown in Fig. A.11. In this code, the first `catch` block that matches the exception is executed. The `finally` block is executed at the end of the code segment, regardless of what happens: if no exception is raised in the `try` block, if an exception was raised and handled by a `catch` block, or if an exception was raised and not handled.

A.5.2 Declaring Exceptions

The Java language specification requires any method whose code might generate an exception to either include an exception handler or declare that it throws the

```
try {
   statements
} catch (Type1 e) {
   statements
} catch (Type2 e) {
   statements
} // more catch statements
} finally {
   statements
}
```

FIGURE A.11 _____

General structure of a `try-catch-finally` *statement*

exception. The designer of the method may decide that a particular exception should be propagated to the caller. In this case, a `throws` clause must be added to the method definition.

In the following example, method `readIntValue` attempts to read an integer from the standard input file (`System.in`):

```
public int readIntValue( ) throws IOException {
   return System.in.readInt( ); // may throw IOException
}
```

The call to method `readInt` will result in an `IOException` if an integer value cannot be read from the standard input file. Method `readIntValue` throws the exception to its caller. The `throws IOException` clause declares that any call on this method may result in an `IOException`.

The Java compiler checks each method to see whether an exception might be thrown in it. If there is a possible exception that lacks a handler and a `throws` declaration, the compiler reports an error. If you are not sure which exceptions to declare, just compile your code and let the compiler tell you which `throws` declarations are necessary.

Many standard Java methods throw exceptions. For example, the read methods of the input classes (for example, `java.io.InputStream.readInt`) throw `java.io.IOException`, and the database access methods (for example, `java.sql.executeSQL`) throw `java.sql.SQLException`.

There is one exemption from the requirement that unhandled exceptions must be declared. Any exception derived from `Error` or from `RunTimeException` is not governed by this rule. The exceptions that don't have to be declared include `NullPointerException`, `InternalError`, and `ArrayIndexOutOfBounds`.

A.5.3   Throwing Exceptions

A Java method signals that an exceptional condition exists by creating an exception object and interrupting normal execution with a `throws` statement. Our earlier examples were based on exceptions raised by predefined Java methods. We can, however, also write code to explicitly throw exceptions. Figure A.12 gives an example of a method that converts a `String` that represents a Social Security number into a (`long`) integer.

```
1  public long convertSSNToLong (String ssn)
2      throws NumberFormatException {
3      if (ssn.length()!=9) {// ssn must be 9 characters
4          throw new NumberFormatException( );
5      }
6      return Long.parseLong(ssn); // convert to long
7  }
```

FIGURE A.12 _____

Method `convertToLong`, *which explicitly throws an exception*

The conversion of the `String` to a `long` is accomplished by calling method `java.lang.Long.parseLong`. This method throws `NumberFormatException` if it is not able to successfully parse and convert its `String` argument. We also want to require Social Security numbers to be exactly nine digits long. Lines 3–5 enforce this restriction. Line 3 checks the length of the `String` argument. If it is not exactly 9, a new exception object is created and thrown (line 4).

A.5.4 Creating Exception Classes

Designers of Java packages often need to create new exception classes so that particular exceptional conditions can be signaled. Figure A.13 gives an example—the declaration of class `IllegalSSNException` and the use of this exception in a new version of `convertSSNToLong`.

The definition of a new exception class must extend an existing exception class—in this case, `NumberFormatException`. It must also declare two constructors: one with a `String` parameter and one without. Lines 1–4 of Fig. A.13 define the exception class `IllegalSSNException`. The constructors simply call the constructor of the superclass.

Method `convertSSNToLong` given in Fig. A.13 is almost the same as that shown in Fig. A.12. The differences come in lines 6, 8, and 10–14 of Fig. A.13. The new method declares (line 6) and throws (line 8) an exception of the new `IllegalSSNException` class. Lines 10–14 configure the method to catch the anticipated `NumberFormatException` that may be thrown by the call to `parseLong` in line 11. If this exception is thrown, the method catches it and replaces it by a new `IllegalSSNException` that is thrown in line 13. In this way,

```
1 public class IllegalSSNException extends NumberFormatException {
2    public IllegalSSNException (String message){super(message);}
3    public IllegalSSNException (){super();}
4 }
5 public long convertSSNToLong (String ssn)
6      throws IllegalSSNException {
7    if (ssn.length()!=9) {// ssn must be 9 characters
8       throw new IllegalSSNException("String too long");
9    }
10   try { // prepare to catch and replace the standard exception
11      return Long.parseLong(ssn); // convert to long
12   } catch (NumberFormatException e) {
13      throw new IllegalSSNException(e.getMessage());
14   }
15 }
```

FIGURE A.13 _____

Class `IllegalSSNException` *and its use in* `convertSSNToLong`

the method in Fig. A.13 turns the general `NumberFormatException`, which can represent an arbitrary format error, into an `IllegalSSNException`, which is more specific about the cause of the format exception.

Application Programming Interfaces

A.6

Three components of Java make it the clear choice for application development: its language syntax and semantics, its machine-independent runtime environment, and the wealth of standard software packages, or *application programming interfaces (APIs)*. These packages provide reusable software components that allow applications to interoperate.

The Java 2 language contains the following packages, several of which have subpackages:

- **java.applet.** Provides the classes necessary to create an applet and the classes that an applet uses to communicate with its applet context.
- **java.awt.** The abstract windowing toolkit (AWT); contains classes for creating user interfaces and for painting graphics and images. Can be used with applets and applications.
- **java.beans.** Contains classes related to preparing classes, especially user interface components, for use in a JavaBeans environment.
- **java.io.** Provides for system input and output through data streams, serialization, and the file system. This package is described in detail in Chapter 11.
- **java.lang.** Provides classes that are fundamental to the design of the Java programming language.
- **java.math.** Provides classes for performing arbitrary-precision integer arithmetic (`BigInteger`) and arbitrary-precision decimal arithmetic (`BigDecimal`).
- **java.net.** Provides the classes for implementing networking applications.
- **java.rmi.** Provides the foundation for communication between Java programs through remote method invocation (RMI). Chapter 16 includes descriptions and examples of the use of RMI.
- **java.security.** Provides the classes and interfaces for the Java security framework. The Java 2 package is significantly different from the Java 1.1 package.
- **java.sql.** Provides the Java database access (JDBC) package that supports interaction with relational database servers. Chapters 8 and 10 include extensive discussion of this package.
- **java.text.** Provides classes and interfaces for handling text, dates, numbers, and messages in a manner independent of natural languages.

- **java.util.** Contains many utility classes that support various types of collections of objects, date and time facilities, internationalization, and miscellaneous utility classes (a string tokenizer, a random-number generator, and a bit array). Of particular interest are the `Collection`, `Set`, `List`, and `Iterator` interfaces and the `HashSet` and `Vector` classes, as discussed in Chapter 17.

In addition, the following packages are either included in the standard distribution of the Java Development Kit (JDK) or available from Sun. The `javax` packages are standard extensions of the Java language.

- **javax.accessibility.** Defines a contract between user interface components and an assistive technology that provides access to those components.
- **javax.ejb.** Supports Enterprise JavaBeans (EJB), as described in Chapter 16. EJB is used to package application services for deployment in highly robust and secure distributed applications.
- **javax.jdbc.** Includes standard extensions to the JDBC package that support row sets and connection pooling. Parts of this package are discussed in Chapter 10.
- **javax.servlet.** Provides classes to support the use of Java to enhance Web servers. Chapters 9 and 10 make extensive use of servlet classes.
- **javax.swing.** The new version of the AWT package; provides a set of "lightweight" (all-Java language) user interface components that, to the maximum degree possible, work in the same way on all platforms.
- **javax.transaction.** Supports transaction management in applications. Some details are included in Chapter 16.

Further Readings

Many excellent Java books are available. *Java in a Nutshell* is particularly useful. The second edition [Fla97a] covers Java 1.1, and the third edition [Fla99] covers Java 1.2. The books provide detailed overviews of the language and a list of most standard packages. The companion examples volume [Fla97b] has many code examples for Java 1.1. A more comprehensive treatment for novice programmers can be found in Deitel and Deitel [DeDe97] and in Budd's book on object-oriented programming [Budd00].

Many Java documents can be found at Sun's Java site (http://java.sun.com/docs). The code conventions document [JavaCode] contains suggested conventions for organizing and writing Java classes. The Java tutorial [CaWa98] has many examples and is available both online and in book form.

References

[AHW95] Aiken, A., J. Hellerstein, and J. Widom, "Static Analysis Techniques for Predicting the Behavior of Active Database Rules," *ACM Transactions on Database Systems*, **20**:1, March 1995, pp. 3–41.

[ANSI86] "The Database Language SQL," ANSI X3,135-1986, American National Standards Institute, New York, 1986.

[ANSI89] "The Database Language SQL with Integrity Enhancement," ANSI X3,135-1989, American National Standards Institute, New York, 1989. Also available as ISO/IEC Document 9075:1989.

[ANSI92] "The Database Language SQL," ANSI X3,135-1992, American National Standards Institute, New York, 1992. Also available as ISO/IEC Document 9075:1992.

[ANSI95] "The Database Language SQL: Part 1: Framework (SQL/Framework)," American National Standards Institute, New York, 1995. Also available as ISO/IEC document DIS 9075-1.

[Arm74] Armstrong, W. W., "Dependency Structures of Data Base Relationships," *Proceedings of the IFIP Congress*, Stockholm, Sweden, 1974, pp. 580–583.

[AsWe99] Asbury, S., and S. R. Weiner, *Developing Java Enterprise Applications*, New York, NY: John Wiley & Sons, 1999.

[Ast76] Astrahan, M., M. Blasgen, D. Chamberlin, K. Eswaran, J. Gray, P. Griffiths, W. King, R. Lofie, P. McJones, J. Mehl, G. Putzolu, I. Traiger, B. Wade, and V. Watson. "System R: A Relational Approach to Database Management," *ACM Transactions on Database Systems*, **1**:2, June 1976, pp. 97–137.

[Bac69] Bachman, C. W., "Data Structure Diagrams," *Journal of the ACM SIGBDP*, **1**:2, 1969, pp. 4–10.

[BCP96] Baralis, E., S. Ceri, and S. Parboschi, "Modularization Techniques for Active Rules Design," *ACM Transactions on Database Systems*, **21**:1, January 1996, pp. 1–29.

[BCN92] Batini, C., S. Ceri, and S. B. Navathe, *Conceptual Database Design: An Entity Relationship Approach*, Redwood City, CA: Benjamin/Cummings, 1992.

[BHR80] Bayer, R., M. Heller, and R. Reiser, "Parallelism and Recovery in Database Systems," *ACM Transactions on Database Systems*, **5**:2, June 1980, pp. 139–156.

[BaMc72] Bayer, R., and E. McCreight, "Organization and Maintenance of Large Ordered Indexes," *Acta Informatica*, **1**:3, February 1972, pp. 173–189.

[BKSS90] Beckman, N., H. P. Kriegel, R. Schneider, and B. Seeger, "The R Tree: An Efficient and Robust Access Method for Points and Rectangles," *Proceedings of the ACM SIGMOD International Conference on the Management of Data*, May 1990, pp. 322–331.

[Bee93] Beech, D., "Collections of Objects in SQL3," *Proceedings of the 19th International Conference on Very Large Databases*, Dublin, Ireland, 1993, pp. 244–255.

[BeGr92] Bell, D., and J. Grimson, *Distributed Database Systems*, Reading, MA: Addison-Wesley, 1992.

[Ben90] Benyon, D., *Information and Data Modelling*, Oxford, UK: Blackwell Scientific, 1990.

[BeGo80] Bernstein, P., and N. Goodman, "Timestamp-Based Algorithms for Concurrency Control in Distributed Database Systems," *Proceedings of the 6th International Conference on Very Large Databases*, Montreal, Canada, October 1980, pp. 285–300.

[BHG87] Bernstein, P., V. Hadzilacos, and N. Goodman, *Concurrency Control and Recovery in Database Systems*, Reading, MA: Addison-Wesley, 1987.

[BeMa93] Bertino, E., and L. Martino, *Object-Oriented Database Systems: Concepts and Architecture*, Reading, MA: Addison-Wesley, 1993.

[Boo94] Booch, G., *Object Oriented Design with Applications*, 2nd ed., Reading, MA: Addison-Wesley, 1994.

[BJR98] Booch, G., I. Jacobson, and J. Rumbaugh, *The Unified Modeling Language User Guide*, Reading, MA: Addison-Wesley, 1998.

[Budd00] Budd, T., *Understanding Object-Oriented Programming with Java*, updated edition, Reading, MA: Addison-Wesley, 2000.

[Cal99] Callaway, D. R., *Inside Servlets: Server-side Programming for the Java Platform*, Reading, MA: Addison-Wesley, 1999.

[CaWa98] Campione, M., and K. Walrath, *The Java Tutorial*, 2nd ed., Reading, MA: Addison-Wesley, 1998. Also available online at http://java.sun.com/docs/books/tutorial/.

[CaOt93] Cannan, S., and G. Otten, *SQL—The Standard Handbook*, Maidenhead, UK: McGraw-Hill International, 1993.

[CBB97] Cattell, R. G. G., D. K. Barry, and D. Bartels (eds.), *The Object Database Standard ODMG 2.0*, San Francisco, CA: Morgan-Kaufmann, 1997.

[CePe84], Ceri, S., and G. Pelagatti, *Distributed Databases: Principles and Systems*, New York, NY: North-Holland, 1984.

[Cha76] Chamberlin, D. D., M. M. Astrahan, K. P. Eswaran, P. P. Griffiths, R. A. Lorie, J. W. Mehl, P. Reisner, and B. W. Wade, "Sequel-2: A Unified Approach to Data Definitions, Manipulation, and Control," *IBM Journal of Research and Development*, **20**:6, November 1976, pp. 560–575.

[Chen76] Chen, P. P., "The Entity–Relationship Model: Toward a Unified View of Data," *ACM Transactions on Database Systems*, **1**:1, January 1976, pp. 9–36.

[ClMi99] Cluet, S., and T. Milo (eds.), *Informal Proceedings of the ACM International Workshop on the Web and Databases (WebDB'99)*, Philadelphia, PA, June 1999. Also available online at http://www.rocq.inria.fr/~cluet/WEBDB/procwebdb99.html.

[Codd70] Codd, E. F., "A Relational Model of Data for Large Shared Data Banks," *Communications of the ACM*, **13**:6, June 1990, pp. 377–387. Republished in *Milestones of Research—Selected Papers 1958–1982, CACM 25th Anniversary Issue*, **26**:1, January 1983.

[Codd71] Codd, E. F., "A Data Base Sublanguage Founded on the Relational Calculus," *Proceedings of the ACM SIGFIDET Workshop on Data Description, Access and Control*, November 1971, pp. 1–17.

[Codd82] Codd, E. F., "The 1981 ACM Turing Award Lecture: Relational Database, a Practical Foundation for Productivity," *Communications of the ACM*, **25**:2, February 1982, pp. 109–117.

[Codd90] Codd, E. F., *The Relational Model for Database Management Version 2*, Reading, MA: Addison-Wesley, 1990.

[Com79] Comer, D., "The Ubiquitous B-Tree," *ACM Computing Surveys*, **11**:2, June 1979, pp. 121–137.

[Date75] Date, C. J., *An Introduction to Database Systems*, Reading, MA: Addison-Wesley, 1975.

[Date90] Date, C. J., "What Is a Distributed Database System," in C. J. Date, *Relational Database Writings 1985–1989*, Reading, MA: Addison-Wesley, 1990, pp. 267–298.

[Date99] Date, C. J., *An Introduction to Database Systems*, 7th ed., Reading, MA: Addison-Wesley, 1999.

[DaDa93] Date, C. J., and G. Darwen, *A Guide to the SQL Standard*, 3rd ed., Reading, MA: Addison-Wesley, 1993.

[DeDe97] Deitel, H. M., and P. J. Deitel, *Java: How to Program*, 2nd ed., Englewood Cliffs, NJ: Prentice-Hall, 1997.

[Den83] Denning, D. E., *Cryptography and Data Security*, Reading, MA: Addison-Wesley, 1983.

[DeDe79] Denning, D. E., and P. J. Denning, "Data Security," ACM Computing Surveys, **11**:3, September 1979, pp. 227–250.

[ElNa99] Elmasri, R., and S. B. Navathe, *Fundamentals of Database Systems*, 3rd ed., Reading, MA: Addison-Wesley, 1999.

[EnDu88] Enbody, R. J., and H. C. Du, "Dynamic Hashing Schemes," *ACM Computing Surveys*, **20**:2, June 1988, pp. 85–113.

[EGLT76] Eswaran, K. P., J. N. Gray, R. A. Lorie, and I. L. Traiger, "The Notions of Consistency and Predicate Locks in a Data Base System," *Communications of the ACM*, **19**:11, November 1976, pp. 624–633.

[FNPS79] Fagin, R., J. Nievergelt, N. Pippenger, and H. R. Strong, "Extendible Hashing—a Fast Access Method for Dynamic Files," *ACM Transactions on Database Systems*, **4**:3, September 1979, pp. 315–344.

[FHSS98] Fedorov, A., R. Harrison, D. Sussman, R. Smith, and S. Wood, *Professional Active Server Pages 2.0*, Chicago, IL: Wrox Press, 1998.

[FePr97] Feuerstein, S., with B. Pribyl, *Oracle PL/SQL Programming*, Cambridge, MA: O'Reilly & Associates, 1997.

[FiKo00] Fields, D., and M. Kolb, *Web Development with JavaServer Pages*, Greenwich, CN: Manning Publications, 2000.

[Fla97a] Flanagan, D., *Java in a Nutshell: A Desktop Quick Reference*, 2nd ed., Cambridge, MA: O'Reilly & Associates, 1997.

[Fla97b] Flanagan, D., *Java Examples in a Nutshell: A Tutorial Companion to Java in a Nutshell*, Cambridge, MA: O'Reilly & Associates, 1997.

[Fla99] Flanagan, D., *Java in a Nutshell: A Desktop Quick Reference*, 3rd ed., Cambridge, MA: O'Reilly & Associates, 1999.

[FZR98] Folk, M. J., B. Zoellick, and G. Riccardi, *File Structures: An Object-Oriented Approach Using C++*, Reading, MA: Addison-Wesley, 1998.

[For98] Forta, B., *The Coldfusion 4.0 Web Application Construction Kit*, Indianapolis, IN: Que Publishing, 1998.

[Fra92] Franklin, M. J., M. J. Zwilling, C. K. Tan, M. J. Carey, and D. J. DeWitt, "Crash Recovery in Client-Server Exodus," *Proceedings of the ACM SIGMOD International Conference on the Management of Data*, June 1992, pp. 165–174.

[FrSi76] Fry, J., and E. Sibley, "Evolution of Data-Base Management Systems," *ACM Computing Surveys*, **8**:1, March 1976, pp. 7–42.

[Gra93] Graefe, G., "Query Evaluation Techniques for Large Databases," *ACM Computing Surveys*, **25**:2, June 1993, pp. 73–170.

[Gray78] Gray, J. N., "Notes on Data Base Operating Systems," in R. Bayer, R. M. Graham, and G. Seegmuller (eds.), *Operating Systems: An Advanced Course*, New York, NY: Springer-Verlag, 1978, pp. 393–481.

[GLP75] Gray, J. N., R. A. Lorie, and G. R. Putzolu, "Granularity of Locks in a Large Shared Data Base," *Proceedings of the 1st International Conference on Very Large Data Bases*, September 1975, pp. 428–451.

[GLPT76] Gray, J. N., R. A. Lorie, G. R. Putzolu, and I. L. Traiger, "Granularity of Locks and Degrees of Consistency in a Shared Data Base," *Proceedings of IFIP Working Conference on Modelling of Data Base Management Systems*, 1976, pp. 365–394.

[GMB81] Gray, J. N., P. R. McJones, and M. Blasgen, "The Recovery Manager of the System R Database Manager," *ACM Computing Surveys*, **13**:2, June 1981, pp. 232–242.

[GrRe93] Gray, J. N., and A. Reuter, *Transaction Processing: Concepts and Techniques*, San Mateo, CA: Morgan Kaufmann, 1993.

[GrWa76] Griffiths, P. P., and B. W. Wade, "An Authorization Mechanism for a Relational Data Base System," *ACM Transactions on Database Systems*, **1**:3, September 1976, pp. 242–255.

[Gri97] Grimes, R., *Professional DCOM Programming*, Chicago, IL: Wrox Press, 1997.

[GGB00] Guelich, S., S. Gundavaram, and G. Birznieks, *CGI Programming with Perl*, 2nd ed., Sebastopol, CA: O'Reilly & Associates, 2000.

[Gut84] Guttman, A., "R-Trees: A Dynamic Index Structure for Spatial Searching," *Proceedings of the ACM SIGMOD International Conference on the Management of Data*, June 1984, pp. 47–57.

[HCF97] Hamilton, G., R. Cattell, and M. Fisher, *JDBC Database Access with Java: A Tutorial and Annotated Reference*, Reading, MA: Addison-Wesley, 1997.

[HCF99] Hamilton, G., R. Cattell, and M. Fisher, *JDBC API Tutorial and Reference, Second Edition: Universal Data Access for the Java 2 Platform*, Reading, MA: Addison-Wesley, 1999.

[Har97] Harold, E. R., *Java Network Programming*, Sebastopol, CA: O'Reilly & Associates, 1997.

[Hart97] Hart, J. M., *Win32 Systems Programming*, Reading, MA: Addison-Wesley, 1997.

[HeLo97] Heinckiens, P., and M. Loomis, *Building Scalable Database Applications: Object-Oriented Design, Architectures, and Implementations*, Reading, MA: Addison-Wesley, 1997.

[Her97] Herbst, H., *Business Rule-Oriented Conceptual Modeling*, Berlin, Germany: Springer Verlag, 1997.

[Howe89] Howe, D., *Data Analysis for Data Base Design*, 2nd ed., London, UK: Edward Arnold, 1989.

[HuCr98] Hunter, J., with W. Crawford, *Java Servlet Programming*, Sebastopol, CA: O'Reilly & Associates, 1998.

[Irv96] Irvine, K. R., *C++ and Object-oriented Programming*, Englewood Cliffs, NJ: Prentice-Hall, 1996.

[JavaCode] *Code Conventions for the Java Programming Language*, Sun Microsystems, http://java.sun.com/docs/codeconv/index.html.

[Jor97] Jordan, D., *C++ Object Databases: Programming with the ODMG Standard*, Reading, MA: Addison-Wesley, 1997.

[KaFa92] Kamel, I., and C. Faloutsos, "Parallel R-Trees," *Proceedings of the ACM SIGMOD International Conference on the Management of Data*, June 1992, pp. 195–204.

[KeRi88] Kernighan, B., and D. Ritchie, *The C Programming Language*, 2nd ed., Englewood Cliffs, NJ: Prentice-Hall, 1988.

[Kim95] Kim, W. (ed.), *Modern Database Systems*, New York, NY: ACM Press/Addison-Wesley, 1995.

[Knu98] Knuth, D., *The Art of Computer Programming*, vol. 3, *Searching and Sorting*, 3rd ed., Reading, MA: Addison-Wesley, 1998.

[KuRo81] Kung, H. T., and J. T. Robinson, "Optimistic Concurrency Control," *ACM Transactions on Database Systems*, **6**:2, June 1981, pp. 312–326.

[Lon98] Loney, K., *Oracle8 DBA Handbook*, Berkeley, CA: Osborne/McGraw-Hill, 1998.

[McDa89] McCarthy, D., and U. Dayal, "The Architecture of an Active Database System," *Proceedings of the ACM SIGMOD International Conference on the Management of Data*, June 1989, pp. 215–224.

[MJLF84] McKusick, M. K., W. M. Joy, S. J. Leffler, and R. S. Fabry, "A Fast File System for UNIX," *ACM Transactions on Computer Systems*, **2**:3, August 1984, pp. 181–197.

[Mel96] Melton, J., "An SQL-3 Update," *Proceedings of the International Conference on Data Engineering*, February 1996, pp. 666–672.

[Moh92] Mohan, C., D. Haderle, B. Lindsay, H. Pirahesh, and P. Schwarz, "ARIES: A Transaction Recovery Method Supporting Fine-Granularity Locking and Partial Rollbacks Using Write-Ahead Logging," *ACM Transactions on Database Systems*, **17**:1, March 1992, pp. 94–162.

[MoNa94] Mohan, C., and I. Narang, "ARIES/CSA: A Method for Database Recovery in Client-Server Architectures," *Proceedings of the ACM SIGMOD International Conference on the Management of Data*, May 1994, pp. 55–66.

[Mon99] Monson-Haefel, R., *Enterprise JavaBeans*, Sebastopol, CA: O'Reilly & Associates, 1999.

[MuKe98] Musciano, C., and B. Kennedy, *HTML: The Definitive Guide*, 3rd ed., Sebastopol, CA: O'Reilly & Associates, 1998.

[Ng98] Ng, S., "Advances in Disk Technology: Performance Issues," *Computer*, May 1998, pp. 75–81.

[O'Ne86] O'Neil, P. E., "The Escrow Transactional Method," *ACM Transactions on Database Systems*, **11**:4, December 1986, pp. 405–430.

[OrHa98] Orfali, R., and D. Harkey, *Client/Server Programming with Java and CORBA*, 2nd ed., New York, NY: John Wiley & Sons, 1998.

[ÖsVa91] Özsu, M. T., and P. Valduriez, *Principles of Distributed Database Systems*, Englewood Cliffs, NJ: Prentice-Hall, 1991.

[OuSc81] Ouskel, M., and P. Scheuermann, "Multidimensional B-Trees: Analysis of Dynamic Behavior," *Bit* **21**, 1981, pp. 401–418.

[Pap86] Papadimitriou, C., *The Theory of Database Concurrency Control*, Rockville, MD: Computer Science Press, 1986.

[Pat99] Patzer, A., S. Li, P. Houle, M. Wilcox, R. Phillips, D. Ayers, H. Bergsten, J. Diamond, M. Bogovich, M. Ferris, M. Fleury, A. Halberstadt, P. M. Mohseni, K. Vedati, and S. Zeiger, *Professional Java Server Programming: with Servlets, JavaServer Pages (JSP), XML, Enterprise JavaBeans (EJB), JNDI, CORBA, Jini and Javaspaces*, Chicago, IL: Wrox Press, 1999.

[Pin98] Pinnock, J., *Professional DCOM Applications Development*, Chicago, IL: Wrox Press, 1998.

[RaGe99] Ramakrishnan, R., and J. Gehrke, *Database Management Systems*, 2nd ed., Boston, MA: McGraw-Hill, 1999.

[Reed83] Reed, D., "Implementing Atomic Actions on Decentralized Data," *ACM Transactions on Computer Systems*, **1**:1, February 1983, pp. 3–23.

[Ree97] Reese, G., *Database Programming with JDBC and Java*, Sebastopol, CA: O'Reilly & Associates, 1997.

[RiTh74] Ritchie, B., and K. Thompson, "The UNIX Time-sharing System," *Communications of the ACM*, **17**:7, July 1974, pp. 365–375.

[Rob81] Robinson, J. T., "The K-d B-Tree: A Search Structure for Large Multidimensional Dynamic Indexes," *Proceedings of the 1981 ACM SIGMOD Conference on the Management of Data*, April 1981, pp. 10–18.

[Sha97] Shaffer, C. A., *Practical Introduction to Data Structures and Algorithm Analysis*, Upper Saddle River, NJ: Prentice-Hall, 1997.

[SiGa98] Silberschatz, A., and P. B. Galvin, *Operating System Concepts*, 5th ed., Reading, MA: Addison-Wesley, 1998.

[SKS97] Silberschatz, A., H. F. Korth, and S. Sudarshan, *Database System Concepts*, 3rd ed., New York, NY: McGraw-Hill, 1997.

[SGR99] Slama, D., J. Garbis, and P. Russel, *Enterprise CORBA*, Englewood Cliffs, NJ: Prentice-Hall, 1999.

[Sta95] Standish, T., *Data Structures, Algorithms and Software Principles in C*, Reading, MA: Addison-Wesley, 1995.

[StRo86] Stonebreaker, M., and L. Rowe, "The Design and Implementation of INGRES," *Proceedings of the ACM SIGMOD International Conference on the Management of Data*, May 1986, pp. 340–355.

[TaWo97] Tanenbaum, A. S., and A. S. Woodhull, *Operating Systems: Design and Implementation*, 2nd ed., Englewood Cliffs, NJ: Prentice-Hall, 1997.

[Tay99] Taylor, A., *JDBC Developer's Resource: Database Programming on the Internet*, 2nd ed., Englewood Cliffs, NJ: Prentice-Hall, 1999.

[Teo94] Teorey, T. J., *Database Modeling and Design: The Fundamental Principles*, San Francisco, CA: Morgan Kaufmann, 1994.

[Ull88] Ullman, J., *Principles of Database and Knowledge-Base Systems*, vol. 1, Rockville, MD: Computer Science Press, 1988.

[Val99] Valesky, T. C., *Enterprise JavaBeans: Developing Component-Based Distributed Applications*, Reading, MA: Addison-Wesley, 1999.

[VLDB99] Proceedings of the 25th International Conference on Very Large Data Bases, September 1999.

[Wal99] Walther, S., *Active Server Pages 2.0 Unleashed*, Indianapolis, IN: Sams Publishing, 1999.

[Wei99] Weissinger, A. K., *ASP in a Nutshell*, Sebastopol, CA: O'Reilly & Associates, 1999.

[WCL91] Widom, J., R. Cochrane, and B. Lindsey, "Implementing Set-Oriented Production Rules as an Extension to Starburst," *Proceedings of the International Conference on Very Large Databases*, September 1991, pp. 275–285.

[Wie81] Wiederhold, G., *Database Design*, 2nd ed., New York: McGraw-Hill, 1983.

[YoAr96] Yourdon, E., and C. Argila, *Case Studies in Object-oriented Design and Analysis*, Upper Saddle River, NJ: Prentice-Hall, 1996.

[Zlo77] Zloof, M. M., "Query-by-Example: A Data Base Language," *IBM System Journal*, **16**:4, 1977, pp. 324–343.

Index